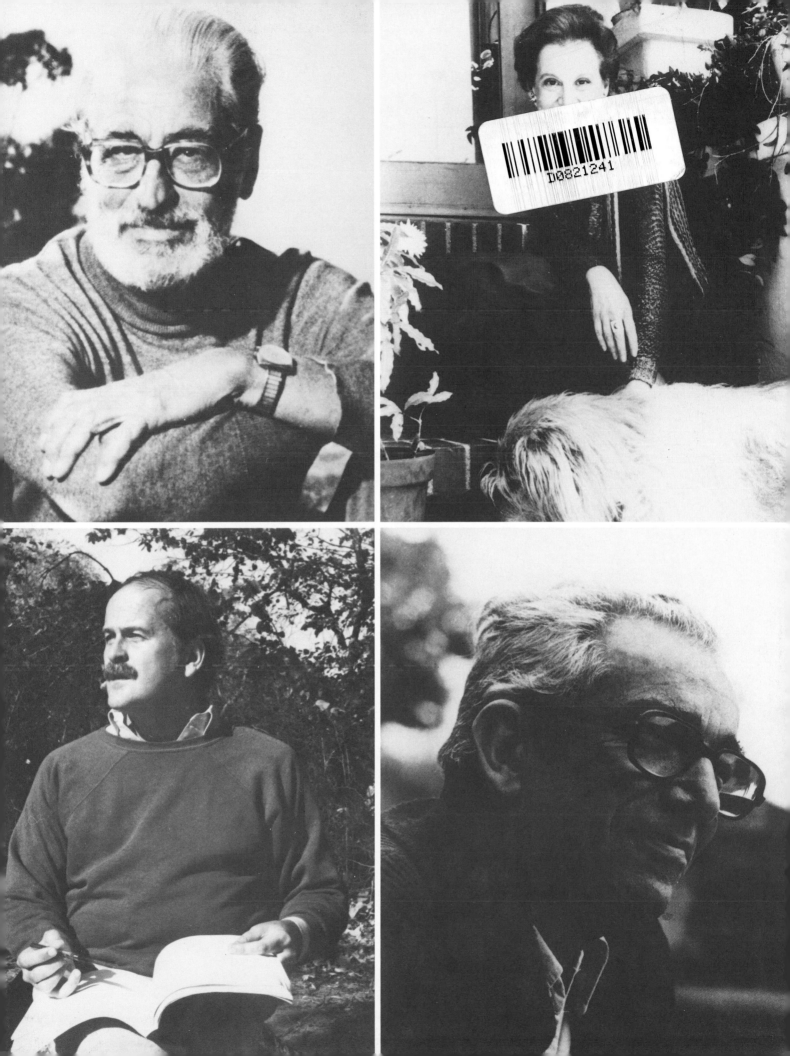

American Writers for Children Since 1960: Poets, Illustrators, and Nonfiction Authors

Dictionary of Literary Biography

American Writers for Children Since 1960: Poets, Illustrators, and Nonfiction Authors

Edited by
Glenn E. Estes
Graduate School of Library and Information Science
University of Tennessee

A Bruccoli Clark Layman Book
Gale Research Company • Book Tower • Detroit, Michigan 48226

Manufactured by Edwards Brothers, Inc.
Ann Arbor, Michigan
Printed in the United States of America

Library of Congress Cataloging-in-Publication Data

American writers for children since 1960. Poets,
    illustrators, and nonfiction authors.

    (Dictionary of literary biography; v. 61)
    "A Bruccoli Clark Layman book."
    Includes index.
    1. Children's literature, American—History and criti-
cism. 2. American literature—20th century—History and
criticism. 3. Children's literature, American—Bio-
bibliography. 4. American literature —20th century—Bio-
bibliography. 5. Authors, American—20th century—
Biography—Dictionaries. 6. Illustration of books—United
States—20th century. 7. Illustrators—United States—
Biography—Dictionaries. I. Estes, Glenn E. II. Series.
PS490.A45   1987   810'.9'9282   87-14352
ISBN 0-8103-1739-7

To
my parents
John Wess and Rita Mae Roeger Estes
with love and gratitude

Contents

Plan of the Series

The advisory board, the editors, and the publisher of the *Dictionary of Literary Biography* are joined in endorsing Mark Twain's declaration. The literature of a nation provides an inexhaustible resource of permanent worth. It is our expectation that this endeavor will make literature and its creators better understood and more accessible to students and the literate public, while satisfying the standards of teachers and scholars.

To meet these requirements, *literary biography* has been construed in terms of the author's achievement. The most important thing about a writer is his writing. Accordingly, the entries in *DLB* are career biographies, tracing the development of the author's canon and the evolution of his reputation.

The publication plan for *DLB* resulted from two years of preparation. The project was proposed to Bruccoli Clark by Frederick G. Ruffner, president of the Gale Research Company, in November 1975. After specimen entries were prepared and typeset, an advisory board was formed to refine the entry format and develop the series rationale. In meetings held during 1976, the publisher, series editors, and advisory board approved the scheme for a comprehensive biographical dictionary of persons who contributed to North American literature. Editorial work on the first volume began in January 1977, and it was published in 1978.

In order to make *DLB* more than a reference tool and to compile volumes that individually have claim to status as literary history, it was decided to organize volumes by topic or period or genre. Each of these freestanding volumes provides a biographical-bibliographical guide and overview for a particular area of literature. We are convinced that this organization—as opposed to a single alphabet method—constitutes a valuable innovation in the presentation of reference material. The volume plan necessarily requires many decisions for the placement and treatment of authors who might properly be included in two or three volumes. In some instances a major figure will be included in separate volumes, but with different entries emphasizing the aspect of his career appropriate to each volume. Ernest Hemingway, for example, is represented in *American Writers in Paris, 1920-1939* by an entry focusing on his expatriate apprenticeship; he is also in *American Novelists, 1910-1945* with an entry surveying his entire career. Each volume includes a cumulative index of subject authors and articles. The final *DLB* volume will be a comprehensive index to the entire series.

With volume ten in 1982 it was decided to enlarge the scope of *DLB*. By the end of 1986 twenty-one volumes treating British literature had been published, and volumes for Commonwealth and Modern European literature were in progress. The series has been further augmented by the *DLB Yearbooks* (since 1981) which update published entries and add new entries to keep the *DLB* current with contemporary activity. There have also been occasional *DLB Documentary Series* volumes which provide biographical and critical background source materials for figures whose work is judged to have particular interest for students. One of these companion volumes is entirely devoted to Tennessee Williams.

The purpose of *DLB* is not only to provide reliable information in a convenient format but also to place the figures in the larger perspective of literary history and to offer appraisals of their accomplishments by qualified scholars.

We define literature as the *intellectual commerce of a nation:* not merely as belles lettres but as that ample and complex process by which ideas are generated, shaped, and transmitted. *DLB* entries are not limited to "creative writers" but extend to other figures who in this time and in this way influenced the mind of a people. Thus the series encompasses historians, journalists, publishers, and screenwriters. By this means readers of *DLB* may be aided to perceive literature not as cult scripture in the keeping of cultural high priests but as at the center of a nation's life.

DLB includes the major writers appropriate to each volume and those standing in the ranks immediately behind them. Scholarly and critical counsel has been sought in deciding which minor figures to include and how full their entries should be. Wherever possible, useful references are made to figures who do not warrant separate entries.

Each *DLB* volume has a volume editor responsible for planning the volume, selecting the figures for inclusion, and assigning the entries. Volume editors are also responsible for preparing, where appropriate, appendices surveying the major periodicals and literary and intellectual movements for their volumes, as well as lists of further readings. Work on the series as a whole is coordinated at the Bruccoli Clark Layman editorial center in Columbia, South Carolina, where the editorial staff is responsible for the accuracy of the published volumes.

One feature that distinguishes *DLB* is the illustration policy—its concern with the iconography of literature. Just as an author is influenced by his surroundings, so is the reader's understanding of the author enhanced by a knowledge of his environment. Therefore *DLB* volumes include not only drawings, paintings, and photographs of authors, often depicting them at various stages in their careers, but also illustrations of their families and places where they lived. Title pages are regularly reproduced in facsimile along with dust jackets for modern authors. The dust jackets are a special feature of *DLB* because they often document better than anything else the way in which an author's work was launched in its own time. Specimens of the writers' manuscripts are included when feasible.

A supplement to *DLB*—tentatively titled *A Guide, Chronology, and Glossary for American Literature*—will outline the history of literature in North America and trace the influences that shaped it. This volume will provide a framework for the study of American literature by means of chronological tables, literary affiliation charts, glossarial entries, and concise surveys of the major movements. It has been planned to stand on its own as a vade mecum, providing a ready-reference guide to the study of American literature as well as a companion to the *DLB* volumes for American literature.

Samuel Johnson rightly decreed that "The chief glory of every people arises from its authors." The purpose of the *Dictionary of Literary Biography* is to compile literary history in the surest way available to us—by accurate and comprehensive treatment of the lives and work of those who contributed to it.

The *DLB* Advisory Board

Foreword

American writing for children from 1960 to the present, especially poetry, picture books, and nonfiction, reflects the healthy respect for the mind of the child expressed by noted children's poet Harry Behn. In his provocative study *Chrysalis: Concerning Children and Poetry* (1968), Behn states: "Knowing children better than I do most adults, at least finding their behavior more understandable, I believe them to be a distinct, wise, world-wide dominion worthy of celebration for their courage, dignity, and vision."

The clear-eyed vision of the poets who wrote for children during the twenty-six-year period covered in this volume underscores Behn's requirements for poetry: "to waken wonder and delight, to make magic or music, or to call up something beautiful or wise out of a true dream." These poets employed diverse approaches to the everyday world of the child through their original writing as well as their carefully designed anthologies of poetry.

The poetry of Harry Behn, David McCord, and Norma Farber provides a child's-eye view of life, laced with humor, in language that pleases and stretches the youthful participant. Eve Merriam, one of the most prolific and much anthologized poets of the period, joined her peers in addressing the serious as well as the fun aspects of life. Her poetry provides springboards for discussion of the social upheaval of the 1960s and 1970s.

Nancy Larrick's anthologies of poetry, including one coedited with Merriam, offer thematic approaches to poetry, both retrospective and current. In addition, Jack Prelutsky's *The Random House Book of Poetry for Children* (1983), illustrated by Arnold Lobel, and the Oxford University Press publications cited in the poetry section of "Checklist of Further Readings" at the end of this volume demonstrate the broad scope of poetry, both old and new, available to enrich the mind of the contemporary child.

Convinced that the contemporary child would only come to an appreciation of the poet's craft through an informed adult—parent or educator—Eve Merriam, Nancy Larrick, and noted children's poet Myra Cohn Livingston wrote extensively concerning the use and abuse of poetry. Their sharply focused professional writing underscores the importance of quality programs of poetry appreciation in language arts education.

Anne Devereaux Jordan's afterword to this volume, "Children's Book Illustration in the Twentieth Century," provides a succinct chronology of the development of picture books and carefully delineates art styles and criteria applicable to this important genre of children's literature. The user of this volume is encouraged to read Jordan's contribution and to consult the numerous works cited in the picture-book section of "Checklist of Further Readings." Especially noteworthy are Lyn Ellen Lacy's *Art and Design in Children's Picture Books: An Analysis of Caldecott Award-Winning Books* (1986) and Perry Nodelman's chapter, "How Picture Books Work," in *Image and Maker* (1984), edited by Harold Darling and Peter Neumeyer.

Educational reforms and increased federal funding for education programs through the National Defense Education Act of 1958 and the Elementary and Secondary Education Act of 1965 spurred publishers to increase their output of nonfiction books for children. In turn, the increased interest in the genre as a viable tool for classroom and self-education activities produced specific criteria for evaluating the output. Margery Fisher's *Matters of Fact* (1972) and a special issue of *Library Trends* (April 1974), focusing on science materials for children, were two early efforts to establish criteria. Numerous articles appeared in professional journals in the 1970s and early 1980s, and many of these plus excerpts from Fisher's book are reproduced in Jo Carr's *Beyond Fact: Nonfiction for Children and Young People* (1982).

Pioneer writers of the genre include Genevieve Foster and author / illustrator Leonard Fisher, whose books set standards for nonfiction. Milton Meltzer's carefully documented studies of social issues and the people involved in these issues provide readers with viewpoints that encourage discussion. David Macaulay's rich blend of text and illustration in his award-winning books such as *Cathedral: The Story of Its Construction* (1973) and *Castle* (1977) invites readers to investigate a host of related topics.

The writers in this volume are pioneers, trendsetters, and award winners. They represent the many American writers who take seriously the task of communicating with children and who do so artfully, and they join those included in volumes 22, 42, and 52 of this series to complete a panoramic view of American writing for children that celebrates their "courage, dignity, and vision."

—Glenn E. Estes

Acknowledgments

This book was produced by Bruccoli Clark Layman, Inc. Karen L. Rood is senior editor for the *Dictionary of Literary Biography* series. J. M. Brook was the in-house editor.

Copyediting supervisor is Patricia Coate. Production coordinator is Kimberly Casey. Typesetting supervisor is Laura Ingram. Lucia Tarbox and Michael Senecal are editorial associates. The production staff includes Kimberly Amerson, Rowena Betts, Mary S. Dye, Charles Egleston, Gabrielle Elliott, Sarah A. Estes, Kathleen M. Flanagan, Joyce Fowler, Cynthia Hallman, Judith K. Ingle, Judith E. McCray, Warren McInnis, Sheri Neal, Joycelyn R. Smith, Debra Straw, and Elizabeth York. Jean W. Ross is permissions editor. Joseph Caldwell, photography editor, and Joseph Matthew Bruccoli did photographic copy work for the volume.

Walter W. Ross and Rhonda Marshall did the library research with the assistance of the staff at the Thomas Cooper Library of the University of South Carolina: Lynn Barron, Daniel Boice, Donna Breese, Kathy Eckman, Gary Geer, Cathie Gottlieb, David L. Haggard, Jens Holley, Dennis Isbell, Marcia Martin, Jean Rhyne, Beverley Steele, Ellen Tillett, and Virginia Weathers.

The editor expresses his thanks to John Cech, Professor, University of Florida, for his initial outline of the contents of this volume and his assignments to many of the contributors; to Ann E. Prentice, Director, Graduate School of Library and Information Science, for her willingness to adjust teaching schedules to provide time to complete this volume; and to Anita Trout, his graduate assistant, and Lisa Pass, secretary, for their careful attention to every detail that supported the preparation of the copy for this volume.

American Writers for Children Since 1960: Poets, Illustrators, and Nonfiction Authors

Dictionary of Literary Biography

Harry Behn

(24 September 1898-6 September 1973)

Jon C. Stott
University of Alberta

BOOKS: *Siesta* (Phoenix: Golden Bough, 1931);
The Grand Canyon, as Giles Behn (Los Angeles: Privately printed, 1935);
The Little Hill (New York: Harcourt, Brace, 1949);
All Kinds of Time (New York: Harcourt, Brace, 1950);
Windy Morning (New York: Harcourt, Brace, 1953);
The House Beyond the Meadow (New York: Pantheon, 1955);
The Wizard in the Well (New York: Harcourt, Brace, 1956);
The Painted Cave (New York: Harcourt, Brace, 1957);
Timmy's Search, illustrated by Barbara Cooney (Greenwich, Conn.: Seabury, 1958);
The Two Uncles of Pablo, illustrated by Mel Silverman (New York: Harcourt, Brace, & World, 1959; London: Macmillan, 1960);
Sombra (Copenhagen: Christtreu, 1961);
Roderick, illustrated by Silverman (New York: Harcourt, Brace & World, 1961);
The Faraway Lurs (Cleveland: World, 1963); republished as *The Distant Lurs* (London: Gollancz, 1965);
Omen of the Birds (Cleveland: World, 1964; London: Gollancz, 1965);
The Golden Hive (New York: Harcourt, Brace & World, 1966);
Chrysalis; Concerning Children and Poetry (New York: Harcourt, Brace & World, 1968);
What a Beautiful Noise, illustrated by Harold Berson (New York: World, 1970).

Harry Behn (Gale International Portrait Gallery)

TRANSLATIONS: Rainer Maria Rilke, *The Duino Elegies*, translated and illustrated by Behn (Mount Vernon, N.Y.: Peter Pauper, 1957);

Cricket Songs (New York: Harcourt, Brace & World, 1964);

More Cricket Songs (New York: Harcourt Brace Jovanovich, 1971).

MOTION PICTURES: *The Big Parade,* scenario by Behn, M-G-M, 1925;

Proud Flesh, scenario by Behn and Agnes Christine Johnson, M-G-M, 1925;

La Bohème, continuity by Behn and Ray Doyle, M-G-M, 1926;

The Crowd, scenario by Behn, King Vidor, and John V. A. Weaver, M-G-M, 1928;

The Racket, scenario by Behn and Del Andrews, Caddo, 1928;

Frozen River, adaptation by Behn, Warner Bros., 1929;

The Sin Sister, scenario by Behn and Andrew Bennison, Fox, 1929;

Hell's Angels, scenario by Behn and Howard Estabrook, Caddo, 1930.

Although Harry Behn wrote children's novels, adult poetry, a critical book, and two translations of Japanese haiku, he is best remembered for his seven volumes of poems for children. All but one illustrated by the author, they capture the experiences of the growing child as he confronts the inner world of his imagination and the outer world of his senses. In the tradition of the major romantic poets, Behn focuses on a specific incident or moment of time and portrays sensitively not only the perceptions but the responses of the perceiver.

Born in Yavapai County, Arizona, to Henry K. and Maren Christensen Behn, Harry Behn grew up in the desert and mountain country of the Southwest. As a boy he was an avid reader; Hans Christian Andersen, William Blake, and George MacDonald were his favorite writers. In *Chrysalis; Concerning Children and Poetry* (1968), Behn said of these writers, "Their search was for a wholeness of vision eternally renewed by children, a healthy wonder that helps to cohere an unstable society fractured by causes and divided by reason." As a child in Arizona, Behn spent much of his time with the native Indians, playing with many of the boys and listening to the old tales of the elders. From these people he learned "a ceremonial response to the earth, to the dancing sun and singing winds; how to live in a world as magical as a dream; to speak with a soft voice as whitewing doves do on evenings in summer." After

graduation from high school he lived for a summer with the Blackfoot people of Montana. Behn later paid tribute to one of his Indian friends in his poem "Discovery."

Behn moved away from Arizona in 1918. He studied briefly at Stanford University, then earned an S.B. degree from Harvard in 1922. He spent a year studying in Sweden, married Alice Lawrence, helped raise a daughter and two sons, worked as a scenarist in Hollywood, and published *Siesta* (1931) and *The Grand Canyon* (1935), two books of poetry for adults. In 1938 Behn returned to Arizona, but not to rest. For nine years he taught creative writing at the University of Arizona. He was active in founding the University Radio Bureau and was the founding editor of the *Arizona Quarterly.* From 1940 to 1947 he was vice-president of the Tucson Regional Plan. As his children were growing, he wrote many stories and poems for them. In 1947 Behn moved to Greenwich, Connecticut, an area which, he said, reminded him of the Arizona mountains of his youth. Two years later he began his distinguished career as a writer of poems and stories for children with the publication of *The Little Hill* (1949). Behn illustrated and designed many of his fifteen children's books. In 1967 he received the George G. Stone Center for Children's Books Recognition of Merit Award. He died 6 September 1973.

Behn's six novels reflect his knowledge and love of nature and his respect for the integrity of the young child. *The Two Uncles of Pablo* (1959), the story of a Mexican child who is torn between loyalty to two uncles of vastly differing character; *Roderick* (1961), the tale of a crow who wishes to become a meadowlark; and *The Faraway Lurs* (1963), an adventure set in Bronze Age Denmark, are Behn's best-known novels, though these stories are not widely read today.

In his poems Behn "tried to capture those early years of primitive awareness." The arousing of wonder and delight based on the earliest, deepest, and nonrational responses to the world were, to him, the goals of poetry. "All we have to do . . . to find the source of poetry," he wrote, "is to track back within ourselves, back to the beginnings of the ancient energies that have come to us in myth. . . . Poetry is such experience fractured and reformed into shapes that the mind . . . can assimilate. Poetry is a pursuit (in words) of all beautiful mysteries." He particularly hoped that his poems would be read by children in cities, for he felt that they had been most cut off

Title-page spread for Behn's 1959 novel about a Mexican child torn between loyalty to two uncles of vastly differing character (Harcourt, Brace)

from the natural rhythms and energies of life. In the Indians, who lived close to the earth, he found people who had maintained a direct contact with nature.

Not surprisingly, therefore, Behn's poems deal with rural subjects; many are set in New England, the majority in the Southwest. Often they are about the simple ordinary aspects of a child's life. In "Far Away in the Morning" a small child wishes he were with the older children playing in the school yard. In "Teddy Bear" the speaker spanks his toy for staying awake too late. "Halloween," "A Christmas Carol," and "Fourth of July" celebrate annual festivals. "Miss Jones," "Mr. Potts," and "Gardeners" are about adults in the child's life.

Behn's best poems are about the mysteries of nature and of time as perceived and experienced by the child. Like William Blake, Behn believed that the child possessed visionary powers.

"Children see a world in every least thing," and they have a "willingness to wonder" in the senses of both questioning and feeling awe. They are, as well, "perfectly at ease with opposites." Often their deepest responses to nature are accompanied by a feeling of loneliness. Thus, in Behn's poems there is seldom more than one persona, the observer of nature.

There are three types of time in Behn's poetry: that measured by clocks, that experienced by a child, and that by which nature ceaselessly moves. In *All Kinds of Time* (1950) a five-year-old ponders the mysteries of time. At first he personifies clocks and takes one apart to try to find answers, only to discover that "even their ticking is just talk. Tick-talk." Then he tries to compare time to the known elements of his life: "Seconds are bugs . . . seasons are wild flowers tame flowers golden flowers and snow. . . . Centuries are George Washington." He comes to understand that the rhythms of the seasons are a kind of time. The poem concludes with the clock the boy dismantled running crazily and then stopping. He explains that the only part he left out was a "tiny wheel with a spring / like a butterfly's tongue . . ." which, he suggests, may be "now or perhaps, forever." The image is important: the spring looks like something from nature; time is not mechanical, it is a part of nature. The poem is simple, yet profound. The language and imagery are a child's, as is the vision. The poem is what Behn often called a "ceremony of innocence." Many of the nature poems celebrate the continuity of time and rhythms of the seasons. In "Waiting" dormant plants and hibernating bears await spring; "September" (*The Golden Hive*, 1966) is a time "When summer is almost gone / And autumn almost begun."

The most intense experiences in the poems generally take place when the individual is alone, in the quiet, still times of dawn or dusk. In "Early" (*The Little Hill*, 1949) Behn writes:

> Before the sun was quite awake
> I saw the darkness like a lake
> Float away in a little stream
> As swift and misty as a dream.

"Now" (*The Wizard in the Well*, 1956) describes twilight as "forever between / Music and silence, the invisible and the seen." One of Behn's most meaningful poems about a solitary experience in nature is "The Errand," from *The Golden Hive*, which the author has called "a book of poems about stillness." Riding alone across the desert, a boy delivers a book to the empty farmhouse of his father's friend, and, as the day ends, he returns home:

> Nothing happened. The sun set,
> The moon came slowly up, and yet
> When I was home at last, I knew
> I'd been on an errand I'd never forget.

Beneath its descriptive surface lies the profound experience of a boy's growing up.

Behn has been highly praised for two volumes of translated Japanese haiku, *Cricket Songs*

Dust jacket for Behn's 1964 volume of translated Japanese haiku. A second volume, More Cricket Songs, *was published in 1971 (Harcourt, Brace & World).*

(1964) and *More Cricket Songs* (1971). Each haiku is, Behn says in *Chrysalis*, "an experience of illumination," and each fulfills his criteria for a good poem: "Anything or any experience, to become a poem, must be presented with a careful incompleteness of information."

Behn achieves these qualities in his own works, as well as in his haiku translations. His descriptions are not overwhelming and his statements are simple, suggesting rather than forcing an impression. In reading his best poems, one is not (with the notable and highly successful exception of "Halloween") aware of the techniques of poetry. Rhyme, rhythm, and stanza patterns are used with a subtlety that is unusual in children's poetry.

Marcia Brown
(13 July 1918-   )

Mary Ann Heffernan
University of Tennessee

BOOKS: *The Little Carousel* (New York: Scribners, 1946);

Stone Soup, An Old Tale (New York: Scribners, 1947);

Henry-Fisherman: A Story of the Virgin Islands (New York: Scribners, 1949);

Dick Whittington and His Cat (New York: Scribners, 1950);

Skipper John's Cook (New York: Scribners, 1951);

The Flying Carpet (New York: Scribners, 1956);

Felice (New York: Scribners, 1958);

Peter Piper's Alphabet: Peter Piper's Practical Principles of Plain and Perfect Pronunciation (New York: Scribners, 1959);

Tamarindo! (New York: Scribners, 1960);

Once A Mouse . . . (New York: Scribners, 1961);

Backbone of the King: The Story of Paka'a and His Son Ku (New York: Scribners, 1966);

The Neighbors (New York: Scribners, 1967; London: Longmans & Young, 1968);

How, Hippo! (New York: Scribners, 1969; London: Longmans & Young, 1970);

The Bun: A Tale from Russia (New York: Harcourt Brace Jovanovich, 1972);

All Butterflies: An ABC (New York: Scribners, 1974);

The Blue Jackal (New York: Scribners, 1977);

Listen to a Shape (New York: Watts, 1979);

Touch Will Tell (New York: Watts, 1979);

Walk With Your Eyes (New York: Watts, 1979);

Lotus Seeds: Children, Pictures and Books (New York: Scribners, 1986).

BOOKS ILLUSTRATED: Virginia Cruse Watson, *The Trail of Courage: A Story of New Amsterdam* (New York: Coward-McCann, 1948);

Hans Christian Andersen, *The Steadfast Tin Soldier*, translated by M. R. James (New York: Scribners, 1953);

Philip M. Sherlock, *Anansi, the Spider Man* (New York: Crowell, 1954; London: Macmillan, 1984);

Peter Christen Asbjornsen and J. E. Moe, *The Three Billy Goats Gruff*, translated by G. W. Dasent (New York: Harcourt, Brace, 1957);

Marcia Brown (photo by Ann Atwood)

Hans Christian Andersen, *The Wild Swans*, translated by M. R. James (New York: Scribners, 1963; London: Longmans & Young, 1969);

Violette Verdy, *Giselle, or The Wilis*, adapted from Théophile Gautier (New York: McGraw-Hill, 1970); republished as *Giselle: A Role for a Lifetime* (New York: Dekker, 1977);

Hans Christian Andersen, *The Snow Queen*, translated by R. P. Keigwin (New York: Scribners, 1972).

TRANSLATIONS: Charles Perrault, *Puss in Boots*, translated and illustrated by Brown (New York: Scribners, 1952);

Perrault, *Cinderella, or The Little Glass Slipper*, translated and illustrated by Brown (New York: Scribners, 1954);

Blaise Cendrars, *Shadow*, translated and illustrated by Brown (New York: Scribners, 1982).

A lifetime of travel, reading, and art is the source of inspiration for author-illustrator Marcia Brown, resulting in dozens of picture books for children that are refreshingly unique. Her career in the field of children's literature is one of great distinction; she is the only three-time winner of the Caldecott Medal and has received the Caldecott Honor Award for six of her books. Brown was the American nominee for the Hans Christian Andersen Award for illustration in 1966 and again in 1975 and has received many awards, such as the University of Southern Mississippi Medallion and the Regina Medal. Both awards are given for the body of an author's work. Her artwork has been exhibited widely, including presentations at the Brooklyn Museum, Library of Congress, and Carnegie Institute.

Born 13 July 1918 in Rochester, New York, to Clarance Edward and Adelaide Zimber Brown, Marcia Brown was encouraged at a young age to use her eyes for more than just looking. One of her earliest studios was a kitchen wall that her father, a minister, had painted for her to use, and by the time she was a teenager Brown had determined she wanted to be an artist. However, for practical purposes, Brown enrolled at the New York College for Teachers (now the State University of New York at Albany) and received her B.A. in 1940. During the summers while she was in college she took instruction in painting from Judson Smith at the Woodstock School of Painting in New York. After graduation she taught high-school English and drama for several years in Cornwall, New York, before moving to New York City to study art with Yasuo Kuniyoshi and Stuart Davis at the New York School for Social Research. Also, she worked in the Central Children's Room of the New York Public Library from 1943 to 1948, where she was exposed to the library's international collection as well as the clientele. She gained invaluable experience in the world of children's literature.

Brown's concern for the quality of a book goes far beyond her individual contribution as illustrator and writer. She regards the connection between author and publisher, and the printing process itself, as one of great importance. Equally important is her belief that the author should have consideration for his audience, both the adult who buys the books being published and the child for whom the books are written.

Brown regards books as one of the building blocks of a child's personality. Although it may be difficult to specify the exact effect books have on children, in *Lotus Seeds: Children, Pictures and Books* (1986), Brown sees the importance of their influence "in images that will not be erased, in peo-

ple as real as those we know, in conversations heard as echoes." And if children's books can indeed be responsible for shaping attitudes and beliefs, Marcia Brown believes that the building of the self requires heroes whose lives reflect true goodness in act and spirit. This theme is a constant thread throughout her work. The beauty of her illustrations and the elegance of her prose imbue the humane spirit of her characters with benevolence.

Another distinctive quality of Marcia Brown's stories is a sense of timelessness. One may recognize as contemporary the city or the country setting of a story although the story itself retains an ageless quality. Brown's first book, *The Little Carousel* (1946), portrays the adventure of a particularly lonely boy who hears the sound of a merry-go-round nearby and is built around Brown's vivid description of a bustling neighborhood in Greenwich Village, where the author herself moved upon first arriving in New York City.

Clever French soldiers and a rustic French village filled with skeptical peasants are featured in Brown's next book, *Stone Soup* (1947). To Brown, folklore is an important and vital possession for one generation to pass along to the next, and *Stone Soup* is the first of many folktales she would retell and illustrate in her career. This well-paced, circular story begins and ends with an illustration of three soldiers walking down a dusty road–hungry in the first scene and well fed in the last. Much gaiety arises from the illustrations of healthy peasants feigning starvation and cunning soldiers preparing a soup from stones. *Stone Soup* was a Caldecott Honor Book, has been translated into French (*Une Drole de Soupe*, 1960) and has been produced as a short film in English and Spanish.

Along with her interest in folklore, Marcia Brown is also fascinated by different cultures. She has traveled extensively to islands and coastal areas around the world. Her first book that reflects this lifelong attraction is *Henry-Fisherman: A Story of the Virgin Islands* (1949), a Caldecott Honor Book. The illustrations are striking and realistic, stemming from the summers that Brown spent on St. Thomas. Brown uses predominantly bright colors of blue and orange and an unusual typeface to suggest the strong, exotic flavor of island life. In addition her use of alternating color schemes gives the book movement reminiscent of water and island breezes. This simple story is of Henry, a young island boy who fulfills his greatest wish: to go fishing with his father. Henry emerges as a true hero as he outswims a great shark while working on the fishing nets. He becomes a romantic figure not by his actions alone but through the language of the story, the unfamiliar expressions and dialect that set him apart from the reader.

While her stories may follow common themes, each of Marcia Brown's books is unique. What makes each distinct is often a result of her continual exploration into different mediums. One of her favorite techniques has been to create woodcuts by sketching onto pine blocks with charcoal and making corrections before cutting the image into the block. Her often spare designs provide a simple yet dramatic effect.

Simplicity and accuracy of detail are important aspects of *Dick Whittington and His Cat* (1950). The historical setting is portrayed in linoleum cuts, and only two colors, gold and black, are used in the stark illustrations that set the tone for this story of a boy's rise from rags to riches. Dick Whittington becomes a symbol of virtue which, despite hardship and because of steadfast spirit and unselfishness, is ultimately rewarded. In *Lotus Seeds* Brown asserts, "the most honest books we can give our children do not tarnish the dazzle by obliterating the gloom." *Dick Whittington and His Cat* was a Caldecott Honor Book, as was her next work, *Skipper John's Cook* (1951). Similar in style, this story is of a young boy's adventure on a fishing boat. Set in Colonial Provincetown, an ambitious boy named Si, along with his dog, takes a job on a ship as cook. The tone is lighthearted as Si remains happily unaware of the crew's growing dissatisfaction with his cooking. This amusing story is based upon a true story of an eight-year-old once told to Marcia Brown.

A swaggering spirit is apparent in yet another of Brown's books, *Puss in Boots* (1952). The spirit is central to the success of this rendition of Charles Perrault's tale of a famous cat who quite handily creates his master's future. The rise of the Marquis of Carabas from third son of a penniless miller to son-in-law of the king—and all in a day's time—is engineered solely by Master Slyboots. Marcia Brown brings these characters to life—the truly extravagant Puss, the simple but good-hearted miller's son, peasants who shudder under the cat's threats, and the robust, kind king. The crayon-and-ink illustrations add a strong French flavor to the tale.

Similar in character to the sly Puss are three goats looking for greener pastures in *The Three Billy Goats Gruff* (1957). Brown completed the formatting of an artist's dummy for the book in five days, a significant feat for one so conscious of detail. Yet the facility with which she set the design indicates the conception was quite clear before she began. The narrative is sparse but conveys the confidence of the three goats who will outwit the troll underneath the bridge. The yellow-and-blue crayon backgrounds perfectly control the tempo by both adding to and alleviating the tension throughout the story. The "great ugly troll with eyes as big as saucers and a nose as long as a poker" ends up kicked to pieces and tossed into the river.

The inspiration for illustrating the folktales of *Anansi, the Spider Man* (1954) developed while Brown lived in Jamaica. In 1953 she was invited by the author of this edition, Philip M. Sherlock, to teach puppetry at the University College of the West Indies in Jamaica. A cycle of folktales from West Africa, the book features Anansi, who is a favorite character in many of the island stories. Anansi appears sometimes as a man and sometimes as a spider. Simple line drawings capture the humor of this trickster and his friends in the forest.

The qualities that have endeared many fairy tales to generations of readers include the heroic element and realms of often unlimited possibilities. The manner in which Marcia Brown illustrates the fairy tale reflects the romantic ideal, a theme common to most of the stories she has chosen. She finds that working with the tales of Hans Christian Andersen presents rare challenges and often rare satisfactions. Brown has said, "Andersen is one of the most demanding authors for an illustrator. While some illustrators picture the facts of his stories delightfully, the deeper meanings elude them, glossed over in favor of a pretty charm. The child gets no hint that here is something more than a barnyard fable or an average fairy tale. It is easy to be beguiled by the trappings of a period, to become enmeshed in researches and lose the poetic significance of these distillates from several folk origins through the mind and heart of a most unusual man. But what a child remembers is more apt to be the poetic truth of the story than the factual truth of the pictures, if the artist has approached his task with understanding of that truth."

The soft red and blue colors predominant in the illustrations of *The Steadfast Tin Soldier* (1953) match the tone of this account of a love and a quest, lending an intensity to the Caldecott Honor Book which suggests much more than a children's story. Brown employs dark areas of color to portray M. R. James's translation of a tale riddled with pathos. Using four colors for the illustrations, the artist creates the mystifying and romantic presence of the Dancer, whose character remains distinct and elusive.

This story focuses on the Tin Soldier, who, like heroes throughout literature, endures repeated trials in order to fulfill his dreams. In *Lotus Seeds* Brown suggests that "a child can measure himself against the heroes in the stories of Hans Christian Andersen and find, many years later, that they are still with him. These stories, which often synthesize several folktales with simpler plots into one, are ageless. The stakes of the heroism are high; the moral choices are serious; the conflicts and the rueful humor that makes the conflicts bearable are those of life." Brown's subtle handling of the sense of adventure and true heroic action enlivens this classic tale.

All of the romance and suspense of the best-known fairy tale in literature is to be found in Marcia Brown's translation and illustrations for *Cinderella, or The Little Glass Slipper* (1954). This book presents another tale by Perrault, but whereas *Puss in Boots* was a tale of whimsy, *Cinderella, or The Little Glass Slipper* is characterized by the beauty of a young girl's dreams. The delicate use of line against pastels mirrors the character of the soft and kind-hearted Cinderella. She is the personification of goodness in the physical and spiritual worlds. Both outwardly and inwardly beautiful, the girl is untainted by the ugliness and unkindness of the family surrounding her.

The format of the illustrations further emphasizes the conflict between good and evil. A full-page illustration of the glamour and wealth of the step-family is juxtaposed against a much smaller corner illustration of the modest Cinderella by the open hearth. *Cinderella* was the Caldecott Medal winner for 1955.

The image of the hero surfaces again in *The Flying Carpet* (1956). The romantic sense of the Arabian nights is strengthened by Brown's vivid oriental-blue illustrations. Eastern motifs lend a mystical and exotic quality to the drawings of this condensed version taken from the *Tales of the Arabian Nights*. All of the central characters in this story are heroes, and all are equally important in saving the life of the beautiful and highly desired Princess Nur-Al Nihar. Brown's concern is not the heroism of fanfare; on the contrary, she explores the kind of heroism which is based on integrity and the will to do what may seem quite impossible. There is no loser or runner-up in this world where all who act in good spirit and heart are rewarded.

The next stage of Marcia Brown's career was a great departure from her work with folktales and fairy tales; she became enchanted with Italy and spent nearly four years traveling there and throughout Europe. A great deal of drama belies the simple story of *Felice* (1958), about a cat who is given a home and name. This story is set in Venice, a city that holds a sense of ageless mystery for Marcia Brown.

Felice is illustrated in a rotating color scheme; a page of blue-and-yellow washed illustrations is followed by illustrations of black-and-pink, thus establishing a current of feeling. The illustrations of Venice at night during the *festa*, complete with fireworks and lighted lanterns, enhance the story; it becomes apparent that this is a city that is like no other. And although this story tells of Marco, a kind hero who saves a nameless cat from a precarious existence, it is much more than it seems on the surface. *Felice* was included in the show of the New York Society of Illustrators.

A different Italy is the scene for another story filled with the same sense of love and admiration of things Italian. Four boys who offer to help Uncle Neddu in his unsuccessful search for his lost donkey find their actions rewarded in *Tamarindo!* (1960). The illustrations add a great sense of adventure to the journey of the boys as they traverse the countryside of Sicily. Here Italy, with its sleepy villages and rambling orchards, is rendered in crayon and ink. Marcia Brown spent the spring of 1956 in Sicily and, recalling a story told to her years before, brought together the beauty of Italy with a childhood recollection of a search for a lost donkey.

Peter Piper's Alphabet (1959) illustrates the alphabet with infinite possibilities for merriment and learning. Here are historical renderings of nonsense verse, each appropriately illustrated with delightful depictions of the text. First published in England in 1813, this edition of "Practical Principles of Plain and Perfect Pronunciation" retains much of the flavor of the older editions while adding a more current setting. "Neddy Noodle nipped his neighbor's nutmegs. Did Neddy Noodle nip his neighbor's nutmegs? If Neddy Noodle nipped his neighbor's nutmegs/Where

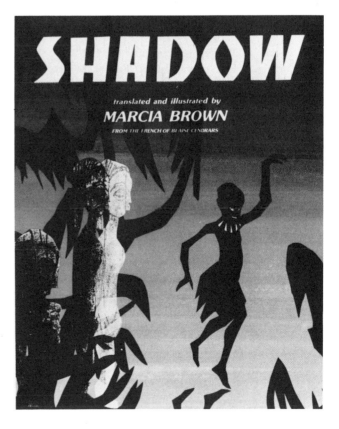

Dust jackets for Brown's three Caldecott Medal-winning books. Brown is the only person who has won the award more than twice (Scribners).

are the neighbor's nutmegs that Neddy Noodle nipped?" The illustrations of the verses offer much amusement for small children with each letter providing a riddle. The American Institute of Graphic Arts included *Peter Piper's Alphabet* along with *Felice* and *Tamarindo!* in the Children's Book Show for 1958-1960.

Two-color pink-and-black illustrations provide a soft detail which gives a dramatic quality to James's translation of Hans Christian Andersen's *The Wild Swans* (1963), which, according to Brown, "is a story from Andersen's maturity—a story of longing, terror, and steadfastness of spirit. The images of nature make bearable that longing. It is a story of contrasts of light and shade, and so I tried to picture it—in dragged pen line and ink and rubbed color."

In the early 1960s Brown became interested in working with a brief text whose theme could be depicted using colored wood-block prints. She used this method to illustrate *Once A Mouse . . .* (1961), a fable from the ancient *Hitopadesa* (a collection of stories written for an Indian rajah to impart the indispensable moral lessons of life to his sons). The colored woodblocks create the jungle in detail, an expressive habitat for both the hermit and the animals. In working on *Once A Mouse . . .* Brown felt she was involved with her best book at that point in her career. The book did indeed receive the Caldecott Medal in 1962, was a *New York Times* Best Illustrated Children's Book of the Year, and was included in a show of the New York Society of Illustrators.

The story of *Once A Mouse . . .* is circular and follows a hermit from peaceful meditation through action and back to his meditative state again. The colors used are those of sunlight through the jungle trees. More forceful aspects of the story are illustrated with red on alternating pages. Through woodcuts of few colors and a text of few words, the moral lesson of this tale emerges strongly in the transformations of a mouse who is shown kindness and then betrays the spirit in which it was offered him. The pictorial economy and the sparse text are a satisfying combination in this didactic tale.

Another book bearing strong resemblance to both the illustrations and the brief text of *Once A Mouse . . .* is *The Blue Jackal* (1977), a retelling of a story based on another tale of India found in the *Panchatantra*. The downfall of the jackal is similar to the victim of conceit in *Once A Mouse . . . .* This story also has a strong philosophical lesson which can be interpreted on many lev-

els. The four-color woodcuts lend an excitement and a sense of mystery to the story of a jackal who turns blue from hiding in a dye vat when he spies the approach of angry dogs. When he emerges and recognizes that the other animals are frightened of him, he begins to play on their fear—only to give himself away in the end.

Following a trip to Hawaii and the success of the woodcuts used to illustrate *Once A Mouse . . . ,* Marcia Brown chose to illustrate *Backbone of the King* (1966) in a similar fashion, using linoleum blocks. The Hawaiian legends comprising the book are distinctive in portraying Hawaii and its rich historical heritage. She chose to print the illustrations in a deep green, a color that best represented Hawaii for her.

The strong Hawaiian oral tradition has been passed along from generation to generation in the form of chants; they are central to the essence and atmosphere in *Backbone of the King.* These chants bring to this book a distinctive literary style through their repetitive nature. Paka'a teaches the chants to his son, Ku, enabling Ku to save his father's honor.

Backbone of the King is a departure from the picture-book format upon which Marcia Brown has focused much of her work. The more rigid form of the illustrated book became a challenge requiring a different approach for a different kind of reader. She thought these stories of a young boy coming of age into an adult world filled with unresolved anger from the previous generation might speak to children today. The struggles that Ku endured in finding himself are the same as those of children everywhere who must find their own unique place in the world.

Growing up is also the subject of *How, Hippo!* (1969). Double-page spreads of a jungle and river waters expressively present the story of a young hippo learning some of the necessary knowledge of living. The simply told story of the meeting of a baby hippo and a crocodile has great suspense engineered by illustrations that foreshadow the text. The enormous bulk and eyes of the hippos as they emerge from water create a playful atmosphere for the story. The illustrations of the hippos underwater create a sense of mystery in which the story can unfold. This book was chosen as an Honor Book for the Book World Spring Book Festival and was an American Library Association Notable Book for 1969.

Similar in the choice of colors and technique is a book published in 1974, *All Butterflies: An ABC.* The alphabet is never staid to Marcia

Dust jacket for Brown's alphabet book done in wood-block prints (Scribners)

Brown, who chose the butterfly as the unifying element in the illustrations of a creative and active approach to the continuity of the letters. The double-page spreads are filled with brilliant colors from woodcuts that add great texture to the illustrations of images created by the alphabet's progression. "All Butterflies, Cat Dance, Elephants Fly!, Giraffes High"—each illustration is a self-contained image within its pages. *All Butterflies: An ABC* was a *Boston Globe-Horn Book* Honor Book for illustration and an American Library Association Notable Book for 1974.

Marcia Brown has chosen two different Russian folktales to illustrate; they are similar in the starkness of story and illustration that shows little of the texture and detail of her other books. *The Neighbors* (1967) is the story of a small, pathetic hare who befriends a sly fox only to his disadvantage. *The Bun: A Tale From Russia* (1972) is a more robust story, a form of the familiar story of the gingerbread man. Crayons are used to illustrate this story in flat colors similar to those used in *The Neighbors*, where the use of red establishes tension in both of these folktales.

Three books published in 1979, *Listen to a Shape, Touch Will Tell,* and *Walk With Your Eyes,* represent the greatest departure in the artistic development of Brown's work. Based on a photo-

graphic essay style, these publications are far removed from her storybooks and center more on the experiential quality of nature as viewed through her photographs and text. Brown's love of nature and her unique ways of seeing it are prominent in all of her books, but the diversity of ways of looking and thinking are most fully explored in these three photographic works.

Brown's style of seeing is apparent in the bittersweet story of love and death from the ballet, *Giselle, or The Wilis* (1970). Illustrating a rendition which combines the works of Violette Verdy, Heinrich Heine, and Théophile Gautier, Brown evokes the love of both man and dance. This haunting story tells of the doomed love of a peasant girl, Giselle, and a count disguised as a commoner. The first illustration of the book, filled with pathos and a deep, dark sense of loneliness, beautifully foreshadows the story's unhappy ending.

Reminiscent of Giselle, Cinderella, and Elisa is the heroine of R. P. Keigwin's translation of Hans Christian Andersen's *The Snow Queen* (1972). Gerda is portrayed with the same qualities that made the others so becoming—goodness of heart and a lively spirit. The fine-line drawings interspersed throughout the text strongly reflect the story's emphasis of a multilayered story of love.

The most unique of all of Marcia Brown's illustrative effects proved to be her most controversial as well–*Shadow* (1982), the book for which she received her third Caldecott Medal. The complexity of the text, a poem by Blaise Cendrars, is mirrored by collages and silhouettes in this powerful depiction of the story of Shadow. At the beginning of the project Brown had fashioned the story using woodcuts but arthritis prevented her continuing in this medium. Instead of using only woodcuts, she used a variety of techniques, including paper cutouts and blotted papers.

Brown's travels in East Africa in 1975 initiated her desire to tell this story strongly depicted with mystery and brilliance of color. Her most sophisticated rendering, the bold effects of the printing and washes combine to create a vibrant work. In *Lotus Seeds* Brown states that "although the poem comes from an African inspiration, I believe it is a poem for anyone. It deals with the mystery behind our birth, stretching far into the past, the handing down of wisdom from older to younger; it deals with all children's fear of the dark and their pleasure at playing with their shadows. It deals with loss, with past ideals that can guide us but can also lead us into old, habitual responses such as war. These experiences are common to all. It was in that spirit that I made the book."

The controversy surrounding this book stemmed from what some considered to be negative stereotyping of the silhouetted Africans. Many critics believed the book had potentially damaging effects on children who might transfer these images toward real African and black American children.

The only book that Marcia Brown has written specifically for an adult audience is *Lotus Seeds*, a selection of speeches and articles she has delivered over the past thirty-five years, including her three Caldecott Medal acceptance speeches. In the short preface she reflects on the importance and need for high standards in regard to children's books. For Brown, "the ideas and images gathered by children from their books are like lotus seeds, endlessly reborn to bloom in successive seasons of their lives. All one's life one learns from the lotus."

As a highly distinguished author and illustrator, Marcia Brown has faced the challenges of success and is often unhappy at new trends appearing in the world of publishing. She feels that projects to document for children what prize-winning authors or illustrators have to say about the force behind the works they have accomplished is contrary to the primary purpose of the book, which is something that should be enjoyed for its own value. Books represent the message that authors and illustrators are trying to present; therefore, she sees little need for dissecting the book further. In *Lotus Seeds* Brown states, "There can sometimes be too much attention paid to the persons of the authors and illustrators of children's books, as if some of that individual energy and concentration on an ideal can be transmitted if one listens to words about it. The eternal curiosity about technique can never tell why, where, or even when."

Brown defines her ambitions as a children's writer and illustrator thus: "I would like to think of some of my books as not ending with themselves but setting up resonances, echoes and re-echoes, changes on the theme." Marcia Brown's books present a veritable wave of reverberation–for throughout her career she has never repeated herself. The direct appeal of her prose and her illustrations is consistent, and the unique quality of her work unmistakable.

References:

Norman Kent, "Marcia Brown–Author and Illustrator," *American Artist*, 27 (January 1963): 26-31;

Janet Loranger, "Marcia Brown," *Horn Book*, 59 (August 1983): 423-424;

Helen Masten, "From Caldecott to Caldecott," *Horn Book*, 38 (August 1962): 347-352.

Tomie dePaola
(15 September 1934-   )

Anne Sherrill
East Tennessee State University

BOOKS: *The Wonderful Dragon of Timlin* (Indianapolis: Bobbs-Merrill, 1966);

Fight the Night (Philadelphia: Lippincott, 1968);

Joe and the Snow (New York: Hawthorn, 1968);

Parker Pig, Esquire (New York: Hawthorn, 1969);

The Journey of the Kiss (New York: Hawthorn, 1970);

The Monsters' Ball (New York: Hawthorn, 1970);

The Wind and the Sun (Lexington, Mass.: Ginn, 1972);

Andy, That's My Name (Englewood Cliffs, N.J.: Prentice-Hall, 1973);

Charlie Needs a Cloak (Englewood Cliffs, N.J.: Prentice-Hall, 1973; London: Collins, 1975);

Nana Upstairs & Nana Downstairs (New York: Putnam's, 1973);

The Unicorn and the Moon (Lexington, Mass.: Ginn, 1973);

Watch Out for the Chicken Feet in Your Soup (Englewood Cliffs, N.J.: Prentice-Hall, 1974);

The Cloud Book: Words and Pictures (New York: Holiday House, 1975);

Michael Bird-Boy (Englewood Cliffs, N.J.: Prentice-Hall, 1975);

Strega Nona: An Old Tale (Englewood Cliffs, N.J.: Prentice-Hall, 1975); republished as *The Magic Pasta Pot* (London: Hutchinson, 1979);

Things to Make and Do for Valentine's Day (New York: Watts, 1976);

When Everyone Was Fast Asleep (New York: Holiday House, 1976);

Four Stories for Four Seasons (Englewood Cliffs, N.J.: Prentice-Hall, 1977);

Helga's Dowry: A Troll Love Story (New York: Harcourt Brace Jovanovich, 1977);

The Quicksand Book (New York: Holiday House, 1977);

Bill and Pete (New York: Putnam's, 1978; Oxford: University Press, 1982);

The Christmas Pageant (Minneapolis: Winston, 1978; London: Collins, 1981);

The Clown of God: An Old Story (New York: Harcourt Brace Jovanovich, 1978; London: Methuen, 1979);

Pancakes for Breakfast (New York: Harcourt Brace Jovanovich, 1978);

Tomie dePaola (photo by Dan O'Connor)

The Popcorn Book (New York: Holiday House, 1978);

Criss-Cross Applesauce, by dePaola and B. A. King (Danbury, N.H.: Addison House, 1979);

Big Anthony and the Magic Ring (New York: Harcourt Brace Jovanovich, 1979);

Flicks (New York: Harcourt Brace Jovanovich, 1979);

The Kids' Cat Book (New York: Holiday House, 1979);

Oliver Button Is a Sissy (New York: Harcourt Brace Jovanovich, 1979; London: Methuen, 1981);

Songs of the Fog Maiden (New York: Holiday House, 1979);

The Family Christmas Tree Book (New York: Holiday House, 1980);

The Knight and the Dragon (New York: Putnam's, 1980; London: Methuen, 1980);

The Lady of Guadalupe (New York: Holiday House, 1980);

The Legend of Old Befana: An Italian Christmas Story (New York: Harcourt Brace Jovanovich, 1980);

The Prince of the Dolomites (New York: Harcourt Brace Jovanovich, 1980; London: Methuen, 1981);

The Comic Adventures of Old Mother Hubbard and Her Dog (New York: Harcourt Brace Jovanovich, 1981; London: Methuen, 1981);

Fin M'Coul the Giant of Knockmany Hill (New York: Holiday House, 1981);

The Friendly Beasts: An Old English Christmas Carol (New York: Putnam's, 1981; London: Methuen, 1982);

The Hunter and the Animals: A Wordless Picture Book (New York: Holiday House, 1981; London: Andersen Press, 1982);

Now One Foot, Now the Other (New York: Putnam's, 1981; London: Methuen, 1982);

Francis: the Poor Man of Assisi (New York: Holiday House, 1982);

Giorgio's Village (New York: Putnam's, 1982);

Strega Nona's Magic Lessons (New York: Harcourt Brace Jovanovich, 1982);

Legend of the Bluebonnet: An Old Tale of Texas (New York: Putnam's, 1983);

Marianna May and Nursey (New York: Holiday House, 1983);

Noah and the Ark (Minneapolis: Winston, 1983);

Sing, Pierrot, Sing: A Picture Book in Mime (San Diego: Harcourt Brace Jovanovich, 1983);

The Story of the Three Wise Kings (New York: Putnam's, 1983);

Country Farm (New York: Putnam's, 1984);

David and Goliath (Minneapolis: Winston, 1984);

The First Christmas, a Pop-up Book (New York: Putnam's, 1984);

Mother Goose Story Streamers (New York: Putnam's, 1984);

The Mysterious Giant of Barletta (New York: Harcourt Brace Jovanovich, 1984);

Tomie dePaola's Mother Goose (New York: Putnam's, 1985);

Merry Christmas, Strega Nona (New York: Harcourt Brace Jovanovich, 1986);

Tomie dePaola's Favorite Nursery Tales (New York: Putnam's, 1986);

Bill and Pete Go Down the Nile (New York: Putnam's, 1987).

SELECTED BOOKS ILLUSTRATED: Pura Belpre, *The Tiger and the Rabbit and Other Tales* (Philadelphia: Lippincott, 1965);

Lisa Miller, *Sound* (New York: Coward-McCann, 1965);

Miller, *Wheels* (New York: Coward-McCann, 1965);

Jeanne B. Hardendorff, *Tricky Peik and Other Tales* (Philadelphia: Lippincott, 1967);

Joan M. Lexau, *Finders Keepers, Losers Weepers* (Philadelphia: Lippincott, 1967);

Melvin Alexenberg, *Sound Science* (Englewood Cliffs, N.J.: Prentice-Hall, 1968);

James A. Eichner, *The Cabinet of the President of the United States* (New York: Watts, 1968);

Leland Blair Jacobs, *Poetry for Chuckles and Grins* (Champaign, Ill.: Garrard, 1968);

Alexenberg, *Light and Sight* (Englewood Cliffs, N.J.: Prentice-Hall, 1969);

Robert Bly, *The Morning Glory* (San Francisco: Kayak Books, 1969);

Samuel Epstein and Beryl Epstein, *Take This Hammer* (New York: Hawthorn, 1969);

Mary C. Jane, *The Rocking-Chair Ghost* (Philadelphia: Lippincott, 1969);

Nina Schneider, *Hercules, the Gentle Giant* (New York: Hawthorn, 1969);

Eleanor Boylan, *How to be a Puppeteer* (New York: Dutton, 1970);

Samuel and Beryl Epstein, *Who Needs Holes?* (New York: Hawthorn, 1970);

Barbara Rinkoff, *Rutherford T. Finds 21B* (New York: Putnam's, 1970);

Philip Balestrino, *Hot as an Ice Cube* (New York: Crowell, 1971);

Samuel and Beryl Epstein, *Pick It Up* (New York: Holiday House, 1971);

John Fisher, *John Fisher's Magic Book* (Englewood Cliffs, N.J.: Prentice-Hall, 1971);

William Wise, *Monsters of the Middle Ages* (New York: Putnam's, 1971);

Peter Zachary Cohen, *Authorized Autumn Charts of the Upper Red Canoe River Country* (New York: Atheneum, 1972);

Sibyl Hancock, *Mario's Mystery Machine* (New York: Putnam's, 1972);

Jean Rosenbaum and Lutie McAuliffe, *What is Fear?* (Englewood Cliffs, N.J.: Prentice-Hall, 1972);

Rubie Saunders, *The Franklin Watts Concise Guide to Babysitting* (New York: Watts, 1972);

Samuel and Beryl Epstein, *Hold Everything* (New York: Holiday House, 1973);

Kathryn F. Ernst, *Danny and His Thumb* (Englewood Cliffs, N.J.: Prentice-Hall, 1973);

Samuel and Beryl Epstein, *Look in the Mirror* (New York: Holiday House, 1973);

Valerie Pitt, *Let's Find Out About Communications* (New York: Watts, 1973);

Charles Keller and Richard Baker, eds., *The Star-*

Spangled Banana and Other Revolutionary Riddles (Englewood Cliffs, N.J.: Prentice-Hall, 1974);

Alice Low, *David's Windows* (New York: Putnam's, 1974);

Mary Calhoun, *Old Man Whickutt's Donkey* (New York: Parents' Magazine Press, 1975);

Norma Farber, *This is the Ambulance Leaving the Zoo* (New York: Dutton, 1975);

Martha and Charles Shapp, *Let's Find Out About Houses* (New York: Watts, 1975);

Eleanor Coerr, *The Mixed-Up Mystery Smell* (New York: Putnam's, 1976);

John Graham, *I Love You, Mouse* (New York: Harcourt Brace Jovanovich, 1976);

Lee Bennett Hopkins, ed., *Good Morning to You, Valentine* (New York: Harcourt Brace Jovanovich, 1976);

Bernice Kohn Hunt, *The Whatchamacallit Book* (New York: Putnam's, 1976);

Stephen Kroll, *The Tyrannosaurus Game* (New York: Holiday House, 1976);

Martha Shapp, *Let's Find Out About Summer* (New York: Watts, 1976);

Barbara Williams, *If He's My Brother* (New York: Harvey House, 1976);

Farber, *Six Impossible Things Before Breakfast* (Reading, Mass.: Addison-Wesley, 1977);

Jean Fritz, *Can't You Make Them Behave, King George?* (New York: Coward-McCann & Geoghegan, 1977);

Patricia Lee Gauch, *Once Upon a Dinkelsbühl* (New York: Putnam's, 1977);

Hopkins, ed., *Beat the Drum, Independence Day Has Come* (New York: Harcourt Brace Jovanovich, 1977);

Tony Johnston, *Odd Jobs* (New York: Putnam's, 1977);

Stephen Mooser, *Ghost with the Halloween Hiccups* (New York: Watts, 1977);

Annabelle Prager, *The Surprise Party* (New York: Pantheon, 1977);

Malcolm E. Weiss, *Solomon Grundy, Born on Oneday: a Finite Arithmetic Puzzle* (New York: Crowell, 1977);

Nancy Willard, *Simple Pictures are Best* (New York: Harcourt Brace Jovanovich, 1977);

Jane Yolen, *The Giants' Farm* (New York: Seabury, 1977);

Sue Alexander, *Marc, the Magnificent* (New York: Pantheon, 1977);

William Cole, ed., *Oh Such Foolishness!* (Philadelphia: Lippincott, 1978; London: Methuen, 1980);

Johnston, *Four Scary Stories* (New York: Putnam's, 1978);

Steven Kroll, *Fat Magic* (New York: Holiday House, 1978);

Kroll, *Santa's Crash-Bang Christmas* (New York: Holiday House, 1978);

Jan Wahl, *Jamie's Tiger* (New York: Harcourt Brace Jovanovich, 1978);

The Cat on the Dovrefell: A Christmas Tale, translated from the Norse by Sir George Webbe Dasent (New York: Putnam's, 1979; London: Methuen, 1980);

Hopkins, ed., *Easter Buds are Springing* (New York: Harcourt Brace Jovanovich, 1979);

Anne Rose, *The Triumphs of Fuzzy Fogtop* (New York: Dial Press, 1979);

Naomi Panush Salus, *My Daddy's Moustache* (Garden City: Doubleday, 1979);

Daisy Wallace, *Ghost Poems* (New York: Holiday House, 1979; London: Pepper Press, 1981);

Yolen, *The Giants Go Camping* (New York: Seabury, 1979);

Gauch, *The Little Friar Who Flew* (New York: Putnam's, 1980);

Patricia MacLachlan, *Moon, Stars, Frogs, and Friends* (New York: Pantheon, 1980);

Clement C. Moore, *The Night Before Christmas* (New York: Holiday House, 1980; Oxford: Oxford University Press, 1982);

Daniel M. Pinkwater, *The Wuggie Norple Story* (New York: Four Winds Press, 1980);

Pauline Watson, *The Walking Coat* (New York: Walker, 1980);

Malcolm Hall, *Edward, Benjamin and Butter* (New York: Coward-McCann & Geoghegan, 1981);

Michael Jennings, *Robin Goodfellow and the Giant Dwarf* (New York: McGraw-Hill, 1981);

Mooser, *Funnyman's First Case* (New York: Watts, 1981);

Prager, *The Spooky Halloween Party* (New York: Pantheon, 1981);

Fritz, *The Good Giants and the Bad Pukwudgies* (New York: Putnam's, 1982);

Johnston, *Odd Jobs and Friends* (New York: Putnam's, 1982);

David Adler, *The Carsick Zebra and Other Animal Riddles* (New York: Holiday House, 1982);

Shirley Rousseau Murphy, *Tattie's River Journey* (New York: Dial Press, 1983);

Johnston, *The Vanishing Pumpkin* (New York: Putnam's, 1983);

Sara Josepha Hale, *Mary Had a Little Lamb* (New York: Holiday House, 1984);

Valentine Davies, *Miracle on 34th Street* (New York: Harcourt Brace Jovanovich, 1984);

Johnston, *The Quilt Story* (New York: Putnam's, 1984);

Jill Bennett, *Teeny Tiny* (New York: Putnam's, 1986);

Thomas Yeomans, *For Every Child a Star: A Christmas Story* (New York: Holiday House, 1986);

Carolyn Craven, *What the Mailman Brought* (New York: Putnam's, 1987);

Jean Fritz, *Shh! We're Writing the Constitution* (New York: Putnam's, 1987).

Over the past twenty-two years Tomie dePaola has illustrated over eighty children's books by various authors and written and illustrated sixty books of his own. His books, which have been published in over a dozen countries, have sold close to two million copies. He began his career as a book illustrator with Lisa Miller's *Sound* in 1965, and since then his career as an artist and writer has grown steadily. He has received recognition from professional publications and organizations including *School Library Journal, Horn Book, Kirkus,* American Library Association, American Institute of Graphic Arts, and the International Reading Association. In 1976 *Strega Nona* (1975) was selected as a Caldecott Honor Book, and in 1978, it received the Nakamore Prize. In 1981 dePaola received the Kerlan Award from the University of Minnesota, and in 1983 he was awarded the Regina Medal in recognition for outstanding accomplishments in the field of children's literature. He has firmly established himself as one of the century's leading picture-book artists and has become popular both as an artist and as an author for children.

The son of Irish and Italian Catholic parents, Thomas Anthony dePaola was born in Meriden, Connecticut, to Joseph N. and Florence Downey dePaola on 15 September 1934. There he grew up with an older brother and two younger sisters. He has said on several occasions that he knew he wanted to be an artist from about age four. Growing up during World War II in a home where books were scarce but treasured, he developed a love for literature early on, and he has fond recollections of his mother reading aloud to him.

After getting his B.F.A. from Pratt Institute in 1956, he free-lanced, doing Christmas cards, theater designs, and liturgical art. He taught art at Newton College of the Sacred Heart in Newton, Massachusetts, first as an instructor (1962-1963) and then as an assistant professor (1963-1966). He received an M.F.A. degree from the California College of Arts and Crafts in 1969 and a doctoral equivalency in 1970 from Lone Mountain College in San Francisco. It was during this period in California that he underwent therapy, which he credits with releasing the child in him, freeing him to create a more honest art than he had before. After teaching at Lone Mountain College for three years, dePaola returned to New England. He taught art at Chamberlayne Junior College in Boston from 1972 to 1973 and then took a teaching position at Colby-Sawyer College in New London, New Hampshire, from 1973 to 1976. There he was an associate professor, designer, and technical director in speech and theater. He also started the children's theater funded by the New Hampshire Commission on the Arts. From 1976 to 1979 he was associate professor of art and artist in residence at New England College in Henniker, New Hampshire. He now resides in New London, New Hampshire, in a remodeled farmhouse.

An artist and writer of seemingly boundless energy, dePaola has worked in several areas of children's literature. For instance, he has been highly successful in retelling traditional folktales and in writing stories in the folktale tradition. In an interview with Phyllis Boyson, he speaks of the origin of *Strega Nona*. In doing research for writing a porridge pot story, he found among other variations the rice pot in India but no Italian variant for the well-known tale, so he created one. Porridge became pasta and the magic character became Strega Nona, his own creation. "That was when I became aware of the folktale variant," dePaola said.

Strega Nona (Grandmother Witch) hires Big Anthony to help with chores. He soon tries his touch with her magic pasta pot, not realizing that he has missed the secret of blowing three kisses to make it stop. Pasta comes out of windows and doors and invades the entire town. Strega Nona returns and sets things right. Anthony's just punishment for touching the forbidden pot is having to eat all the pasta. DePaola's illustrations, inspired by Fra Angelico, include Big Anthony riding the pasta which is portrayed like waves in the ocean. The pasta takes up more and more of the picture as it engulfs the Italian Mediterranean village of Calabria.

In *Big Anthony and the Magic Ring* (1979), *Strega Nona's Magic Lessons* (1982), and *Merry*

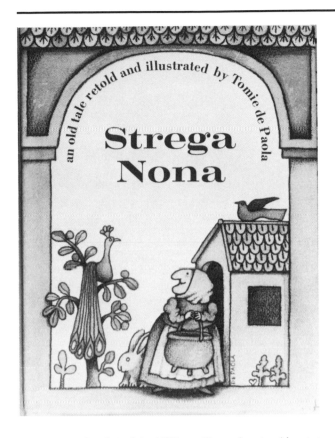

Dust jacket for dePaola's 1975 retelling of a porridge pot story which was named a Caldecott Honor Book in 1976 (Prentice-Hall)

Christmas, Strega Nona (1986), dePaola creates three new stories using the same characters and rural Italian setting of *Strega Nona*. Bambolina, the baker's daughter, is a new character in these books. In *Big Anthony and the Magic Ring* it is spring in Calabria, and Big Anthony is somewhat listless. This time the misuse of magic involves Strega Nona's magic ring, which Big Anthony sees her use to transform herself into a beautiful lady who dances the night away. When he uses the ring to transform himself into a handsome man, he is so successful that he must run to escape the village women as they pursue him throughout the countryside.

In *Strega Nona's Magic Lessons* Bambolina (the baker's daughter Anthony should have taken dancing originally and so avoided all the mischief in the previous book) decides to take magic lessons from Strega Nona to solve the impossible work load her father expects of her. Bungling Big Anthony tries his hand at working for the baker only to put too much yeast in the bread and have the dough go all over the bakery, reminiscent of his antics with pasta. When he disguises himself as a girl Strega Nona consents to

give him magic lessons too, but as usual he attempts to misuse magic, and she and Bambolina get the best of him. In *Merry Christmas, Strega Nona* Big Anthony returns to Strega Nona's house without the ingredients needed for her annual Christmas feast. Instead the townfolk bring the feast to her. These extensions of *Strega Nona* were well received by reviewers. The antics of fat, long-nosed Strega Nona and Big Anthony the buffoon make for a hilarious series.

DePaola presents an old Italian tale retold in *The Prince of the Dolomites* (1980). Instead of the Mediterranean, the setting is a village in the Italian Alps where Zio Narratore, the storyteller, tells children how the Dolomites were changed from dreary mountains to bright ones by an act of love in this romantic fantasy of sacrifice and reward. A prince falls in love with the moon princess, and though he goes to the moon he must return to earth or face blindness. The princess accompanies him to earth but grows sad at the dreariness of the Dolomites. The Salvani climb to the peaks and gather moonbeams, weaving them into nets to brighten the dark peaks.

The Legend of Old Befana (1980) is a retold Italian Christmas story. The familiar red-tiled village roofs from the Strega Nona books reappear. The three wise kings on their way to see the Christ child bid grumpy Befana to follow. She does and takes baked goodies for the child and a broom to save the mother from sweeping. As she runs to catch up with the wise men, angels help her go faster until she runs across the sky. From this time on, every year, on the sixth of January (the Feast of the Kings), she runs across the sky, delivers baked gifts to children, and sweeps their rooms clean. A majority of reviewers welcomed this familiar Italian counterpart to Santa Claus. DePaola has written several other books with a Christmas theme, including *The Christmas Pageant* (1978), *The Family Christmas Tree Book* (1980), *The Friendly Beasts: An Old English Christmas Carol* (1981), *The Story of the Three Wise Kings* (1983), and *The First Christmas, a Pop-up Book* (1984).

In honor of the 800th anniversary of the birth of Saint Francis of Assisi, dePaola wrote and illustrated *Francis: the Poor Man of Assisi* (1982). Paintings of Francis and his friend and companion, Saint Clare Scifi, were inspired by the frescoes of Cimabue and Simone Martini in the Basilica of San Francesco in Assisi. In his preface dePaola tells of his trip to Assisi in 1956 and a return in 1978 to do photographic research and read accounts of the saints' lives. As he told

Ann Rodgers, "I think I would like the book to introduce people to Francis who have never known him. I think Francis has gotten sugar-coated too much." He said seeing where Francis lived and worked brought home "how really simple his existence was. . . ." The book continues to be popular.

In the same interview dePaola related *Francis* to another book, *The Lady of Guadalupe* (1980), based on the story of how the Virgin Mary became the patron of Mexico. DePaola says that he and his editor tried to make the text of both books read as legend rather than religious indoctrination. The success of *Francis* lies both in the art, which is faithful to the thirteenth century, and in the dramatic episodes from the saint's life which dePaola selected: Francis as a wild rich kid; Francis saving lambs from slaughter; Francis enjoying his one luxury–the delicious cakes Brother Jacopa bakes. The success of *The Lady of Guadalupe*, also translated into Spanish, lies both in its highly acclaimed art, faithful to Mexican architecture, history, and folklore, and in its narrative enjoyable by children of any religion as a folktale.

DePaola says in an author's note to *The Clown of God: An Old Story* (1978) that he was inspired by Anatole France's version of the legend about a juggler who offers his talent as a gift to the Christ child. DePaola retells it with an Italian Renaissance setting. A young clown and juggler, Giovanni, joins a traveling troop of performers and delights his audiences by juggling sticks, plates, torches, balls, and other items. One particular ball he calls Sun in the Sky. At the end of the story, elderly and rejected, Giovanni joins a procession at a monastery to bring gifts to the statue of the Madonna and Child. He notices a sad expression on the Christ child's face and juggles to make him happy. The result is a miracle. On the child's face is a smile and in his hand the yellow ball Giovanni had been juggling. DePaola's familiar use of architectural elements, reminiscent of those seen in the works of Fra Angelico and others of the period, is an effective unifying motif. Skillfully rendered figures such as traveling players, monks, and gondoliers all contribute to the Italian Renaissance setting. Most reviewers wrote favorably of the book, particularly praising authenticity of time and place.

Sing, Pierrot, Sing (1983) is dePaola's original story of a French pantomimist incorporating elements of the Italian commedia dell'arte, namely the characters of Pierrot and Pierrette, an archetypal couple in the commedia and in puppetry

Dust jacket for dePaola's 1980 story, which describes the Virgin Mary's appearance to a Mexican peasant (Holiday House)

and mime in general. They are frequently referred to in continental literature, particularly Pierrot, who, in the nineteenth century, was made into a weeping clown figure and glorified by writers such as Jules Laforgue. In dePaola's version Pierrot sets out for Columbine's red-tile-roofed house with a rose and a mandolin. As she steps out on her balcony he tosses her a rose, but Harlequin catches it. The despondent Pierrot decides to climb to the moon, but the children of the town bid him climb down first and retrieve his mandolin. He does so, joining them in song and dance, and then they climb to the moon together.

Helga's Dowry: A Troll Love Story (1977), structured in the folktale tradition, is dePaola's own invention based on his research about trolls. He told Susan Hepler that he discovered troll women could not marry without dowries because troll men were more interested in amassing fortunes than in marriage. If the women didn't marry, they were bound to wander the world forever–unless they came down from the mountains and tricked humans into marrying them. Helga is the most beautiful of troll maidens but also the poorest. She has no dowry to marry the

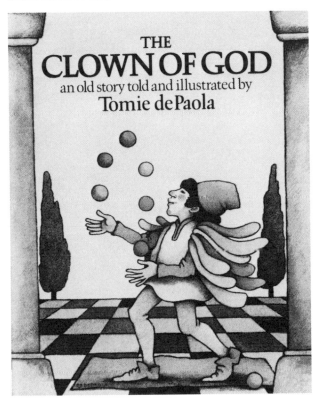

Dust jacket for dePaola's 1978 book based on the medieval legend about a juggler who offers his talents as a gift to the Christ child (Harcourt Brace Jovanovich)

handsomest troll, Lars, but, performing some troll magic, the spunky Helga acquires cows, gold, and land and forsakes Lars in the end. DePaola has said many times that he consciously tries to avoid presenting sexual stereotypes, and certainly the independent Helga underscores that. His comic dramatic scenes, such as when Helga becomes a boulder and fights Inge, her rival for Lars, keep the story lively throughout. Reviewers praised the comic illustrations and Helga's humor and determination.

A popular Irish giant is the source for dePaola's retold tale *Fin M'Coul the Giant of Knockmany Hill* (1981). In this story of trickery engineered by his wife, Oonagh, Fin wards off confrontation with rival giant Cucullin, who won't rest until he has assaulted Fin. Comic illustrations show Cucullin losing his teeth as he bites into bread loaves that contain frying pans. Red-haired, freckled Fin, dressed as a baby in a pink ruffled outfit, adds to the hilarity. Cucullin decides that if the baby is any indication of Fin's strength, he'd best not take on the father. Reviewers mentioned the feeling of another culture dePaola successfully conveys through the green hills and whitewashed cottages and household

utensils as well as the use of designs of early Irish jewelry found in the picture frames.

Bold, bright colors in designs appropriate to the spirit of much American Indian art enhance the retold Commanche tale, *Legend of the Bluebonnet* (1983). The shaman announces to the people that they must burn their most treasured possessions as a sacrifice to the Great Spirit to bring an end to drought and famine. She-Who-Is-Alone, a young girl, offers her warrior doll. Rain comes and so do the bluebonnets, filling the fields with their beautiful blossoms. The *Booklist* (1 June 1983) reviewer praised the artwork, noting dePaola's successful rendering of electric blues, star-studded skies, and the fire where the young girl prepares her sacrifice.

An Italian legend is the basis for *The Mysterious Giant of Barletta* (1984), a humorous story of trickery similar in that respect to *Fin M'Coul the Giant of Knockmany Hill*. When a medieval Italian village is about to be attacked, Zia Concetta's faith brings the giant statue of a Roman boy to life, and the enemy is convinced he is the typical village boy.

DePaola has illustrated two notable folktales written by other authors. Patricia Lee Gauch's *Once Upon a Dinkelsbühl* (1977) is based on the German legend of Lore. Lore is the gatekeeper's daughter who leads the town children in saving their city when invaders attack. Instead of opposition the children offer food as a peace offering. DePaola's rendering of the colonel as he listens to Lore's pleas is particularly effective. DePaola also provided memorable illustrations for Sir George Webbe Dasent's translation from the Norse of *The Cat on the Dovrefell* (1979). In this Scandinavian folktale a man on his way to deliver a bear to the king of Denmark stops at Halvor's cottage on Christmas Eve and is told that trolls invade each year. DePaola uses rich colors in the paintings of Halvor's feast for the trolls to depict food spilling out of bowls and fat, hairy, mirthful monsters frolicking about the house. Other effective details include the big white bear set against the snowy landscape and Scandinavian furnishings such as the big blue-and-white stove under which the bear rests until a troll pokes him with a sausage.

Besides folktales, dePaola has also produced books based upon well-known rhymes. In *The Comic Adventures of Old Mother Hubbard and Her Dog* (1981) he presents each verse of the Mother Hubbard rhyme in a stage setting with an arch and purple curtain. In the first couple of pages are scenes of balcony seats where Humpty Dumpty, the King and Queen of Hearts, and Little Bo-Peep look on. As Mother Hubbard makes trips to meet the dog's progressively more humanlike needs, the dog's expression gets more humanlike until he is completely believable as a gentleman in full dress with a powdered wig.

With *Mary Had a Little Lamb* (1984) dePaola created new interest in Sara Josepha Hale, who is usually credited with authorship of this well-loved poem. He includes all five verses and sets them against a New England backdrop as pig-tailed Mary goes about her various activities with the ever-present lamb at her side. Donnarae MacCann and Olga Richard (*Wilson Library Bulletin*, April 1984) praised dePaola's authenticity to the old-fashioned setting and his inventiveness, for example, in wallpaper patterns and a cross section of a house containing triple images of Mary and the lamb. Four nursery rhymes are featured in *Mother Goose Story Streamers* (1984): "Baa, Baa, Black Sheep," "Hey Diddle Diddle," "Jack & Jill," and "Little Miss Muffet." Four folded pages open out to present large illustrations of these well-known rhymes.

DePaola's works visit the world of knights, unicorns, and other fantastic elements. In his first published book, *The Wonderful Dragon of Timlin* (1966), a gentle, pink dragon with memorable eyelashes creates fireworks displays, plays croquet, and sips strawberry ice cream sodas. In *The Knight and the Dragon* (1980), produced fourteen years later, dePaola offers a humorous commentary about rituals being carried out long after their purpose is forgotten. In this story a knight and a dragon decide it is time to do battle, but neither knows how, so they read books on the subject. The encounter is a fiasco, but all ends well as the castle librarian arrives with a book on cooking that puts their talents to use: the dragon offering the fire and the knight the equipment for a barbecue. One particularly good scene has the knight and the dragon in aprons as the townsfolk dine on their barbecue. Interesting too is the disappearance of boundaries from around the pictures—from the no-win battle onward—as the knight and the dragon learn to work together rather than being enemies.

In *The Unicorn and the Moon* (1973) a unicorn must rescue the moon trapped between two hills which want to look as beautiful by moonlight as does the unicorn. After several unsuccessful attempts, the unicorn, with the aid of an alchemist, scatters mirrors in the sky. When the hills eagerly reach for them, the moon is freed. The effective use of color tones gives the story a dreamlike quality which also pervades *When Everyone Was Fast Asleep* (1976) and its sequel *Songs of the Fog Maiden* (1979).

The Fog Maiden lives between the Sun and the Cold in a castle. Outside are two gardens: the Day Garden and the Night Garden. In *When Everyone Was Fast Asleep*, a sumptuous adventure in pastels, the Fog Maiden's mysterious blue cat, Token, awakens two children and leads them first to the land of trolls and then to a ball at the palace of the king and queen where crocodiles, doves, peacocks, and lions sing and dance. The Fog Maiden's arrival signals the coming of day, and her dress and train predominate, spilling off the picture plane in double-page spreads. *Songs of the Fog Maiden*, a sequel which presents the statues, birds, and fountains that are part of the Fog Maiden's glorious Day Garden, was generally considered by reviewers to be inferior. John Cech (*Children's Book Review Service*, April 1979) mentions the contrast between the highly successful art and the often wooden, predictive quality of the text. Particularly disappointing was the cat Token, whose mysterious haunting quality in the first book lost much of its effectiveness in the sequel.

Several of dePaola's fantasies feature animals. In *The Hunter and the Animals: A Wordless Picture Book* (1981) a bluebird warns the forest animals that a hunter is coming. While the hunter is asleep, they steal his equipment. Then they bring him food and lead him home. As in *The Knight and the Dragon*, there is here the questioning of senseless ritual, for the young hunter in traditional dress and accoutrements sets out to hunt a false enemy. There is also the suggestion of rebirth or renewal as the animals change the forest from oak to pine, the first tree to appear after the destruction of a forest by fire.

Another book involving an animal and hunting is *Bill and Pete* (1978). A human trapper captures Bill, a crocodile who has a bird friend, and plans to make him into a suitcase. The bird is able to free Bill. In *Parker Pig, Esquire* (1969) a fox, sheep, cat, and dog visit their friend Parker and decide to change his messy housekeeping. The animals, all dressed as humans, take on memorable personalities. The sheep is a snooty woman, the fox is sophisticated and impeccably dressed, and the dog, who never wanted to change Parker, looks like an old man with a beard. In *Joe and the Snow* (1968) a boy has a per-

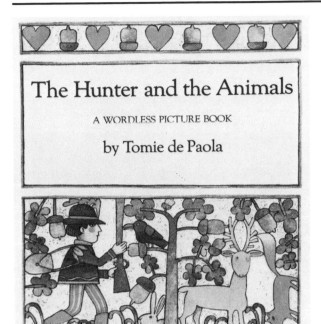

Dust jacket for dePaola's 1981 fantasy about a group of forest animals that foil a hunter's outing (Holiday House)

fectly believable animal family. Among them is Martin, a dog who wears glasses and reads constantly, and who resembles Tom, the wise dog visitor in *Parker Pig, Esquire. Four Stories for Four Seasons* (1977) features all animal characters: a dog, cat, pig, and frog. Each story begins with a picture of the same house set in a particular season, and in each story seasonal foliage frames the pages. The episodic stories portray the animal friends as they go for a boat ride, visit gardens, dine, and finally celebrate Christmas with their sleepy friend, the frog.

Besides works dealing with various shades of fantasy, dePaola has produced stories grounded in real life. The little rich girl in *Marianna May and Nursey* (1983) could be any child whose fun is spoiled by having to worry about keeping her clothes clean. Her solution is to have different colored clothing to match such activities as rolling in the grass and making mudpies. The book offers luscious colors and is an example of dePaola's frequent tendency to use doorways, windows, and other frames in his art. The clothesline where the child's clothing hangs resembles a frame for a stage curtain, and in the first picture Marianna and her family are framed in gold–rather like a family portrait– establishing their social class and aloofness. There is a hint of red-tiled roofs from the Italian

settings on the doghouse, and a big white dog pictured in other stories romps through this one also.

Oliver Button Is a Sissy (1979) has been said by dePaola to be autobiographical. The young boy in the story would rather walk in the woods, draw, and read than play sports. Yet, after he shows talent as a tap dancer, his schoolmates no longer call him sissy but admire him. Despite the seriousness of a child being teased for being different, as usual with dePaola, the overall tone is playful and the drawing and coloration ingenuous.

DePaola's work is particularly strong when it builds upon his Irish and Italian family background. In *Watch Out for the Chicken Feet in Your Soup* (1974) Joey takes his friend Eugene to visit Joey's old-fashioned grandmother who puts chicken feet in soup and uses the boys' coats to keep her bread dough warm. Joey is embarrassed, but Eugene is completely enchanted as he gobbles down the soup, dons an apron, and helps Joey's grandmother make bread dolls. Besides showing a boy in a nonstereotypical role, the story provides a good sprinkling of Italian words that make the Italian grandmother memorable and authentic.

Both of dePaola's grandmothers were the inspiration for *Nana Upstairs & Nana Downstairs* (1973). In the story a boy's great-grandmother, who is bedridden, lives upstairs and must be tied when she sits in a chair to avoid falling. His grandmother lives downstairs. When the four-year-old great-grandson comes to visit Nana Upstairs, he asks to be tied, too. They eat candy together and become good friends. After she has died, the boy sees a shooting star and his parents explain she may be sending him a kiss and that, though she is gone, he can always call her back in memory. Years later when the grandmother dies, he thinks of them both as Nana Upstairs. Though the book deals with the death of loved ones, the focus is on affection and fond memories.

DePaola told an interviewer for *Books to Grow On* about *Nana Upstairs & Nana Downstairs* that people said, "Oh, that's such a wonderful book about death. Why did you decide to write a book about death?" DePaola answered that "For me it wasn't a book about death. All I was trying to do was tell the story of what happened between my great grandmother and me. She was 94 years old and I was only four, and she died."

Another fine autobiographical story about youth and old age is *Now One Foot, Now the Other* (1981). The protagonist, Bobby, whose grandfather once taught him to walk, teaches the grandfa-

Dust jacket for dePaola's 1973 book about a four-year-old boy's relationship with his grandmother and great-grandmother (Putnam's)

ther to walk after a stroke. Bobby at first has the natural reaction of fear when his grandfather appears not to recognize him. However, the two used to build a tower of blocks, and when the elephant block was in place the grandfather would sneeze, and they would topple as the young boy laughed. The grandfather sneezes one day when the grandson builds the block tower, and the slow recovery begins. As in *Watch Out for the Chicken Feet in Your Soup* and *Nana Upstairs & Nana Downstairs*, the focus is not on the illness but on the affection between the boy and a grandparent, and it is partially shown by memory of something special associated with the loved one: finding chicken feet in soup, tying oneself to a chair to be like the grandmother, building block towers that topple at a sneeze.

Information books represent a major category of dePaola's work, and of the numerous books he has illustrated for other writers, a good number have been information books on a broad range of subjects. Two of these books center around holidays. In *The Family Christmas Tree Book* (1980) he presents a family going through all the

steps from cutting a tree and bringing it home to decorating it. He includes historical information through dialogue about the origin of Christmas trees and the use of lights. At the end of the book are directions for making an angel ornament. Although the historical insertions are at times awkward, the approach overall is a good one for presenting information within the natural setting of a family preparing for Christmas. *Things to Make and Do for Valentine's Day* (1976) not only gives directions for making valentines and envelopes, it also includes a game, tongue twisters, a recipe for cake, and instructions for making painted dough valentines.

In the highly acclaimed *Charlie Needs a Cloak* (1973) a youngster learns about the steps in producing a wool cloak–from shearing the sheep to sewing the material. One playful sheep becomes Charlie's companion throughout the process. He holds on to the strands as Charlie attempts to put them in the loom, models the cloth, and stands on the table as Charlie cuts it into pieces. At the end he seems as proud as Charlie of the new coat. Another humorous slant to the book in-

Dust jacket for dePaola's first wordless picture book, published in 1978 (Harcourt Brace Jovanovich)

volves a mouse who steals scissors, yarn, and other items and takes them to his tree stump.

Cats are companions of many of the children in dePaola's books, and he has two of his own, Satie and Rosalie, so it is not surprising that he would do an information book on them. In *The Kids' Cat Book* (1979) he gives the history of attitudes toward cats starting in Egyptian times and continuing through other periods. This story is told by Granny Twinkle as a young boy selects one of the cats she is giving away. The reader comes away from the book with a knowledge of cats in history and famous cats in children's literature, as well as some knowledge about caring for cats.

A number of dePaola's books feature food in some way; Big Anthony and his problems with pasta in *Strega Nona* is but one example. Two of his information books are about food. In *Pancakes for Breakfast* (1978), dePaola's first wordless picture book, a plump, black-haired grandmotherly lady awakens on a cold, snowy morning dreaming of making pancakes. She goes through all the steps such as gathering eggs, mixing the in-

gredients, and milking the cow only to find upon her return from buying syrup that her cat and dog have devoured the mix. In *The Popcorn Book* (1978) tousle-haired male twins with look-alike cats learn some history of popcorn as one reads aloud and the other pops corn. The book includes two ways to pop corn. Although it does not include information about cultivation, and as one reviewer, Lazar Goldberg (*Appraisal: Science Books for Children*, 1979), noted, some of the numbers in connection with facts may be beyond the child's scope, the book does give general information about popcorn and presents boys in nonstereotypical roles.

Two books give information about natural phenomena: clouds and quicksand. In *The Cloud Book* (1975) the reader learns about myths associated with clouds, types of clouds, and how clouds predict weather. Illustrations are comic in making explanations memorable; for example, since cumulus clouds resemble cauliflower, dePaola includes a booth where it is being sold. *The Quicksand Book* (1977) offers another humorous approach to information. In it a young girl is caught in quicksand. While she waits, a boy accompanied by a monkey proceeds to tell her how quicksand is formed, how to avoid it, and how some animals can rescue themselves from it. After telling her step by step how to rescue herself, he falls in. She has sweet revenge as she and the monkey then leisurely have tea at an elegant table setting the monkey has prepared. Humorous illustrations of the distraught girl, the bookish boy, and the assortment of animals who arrive on the scene make this one of dePaola's best information books. He even includes a recipe for quicksand.

Although colored inks and watercolors on handmade watercolor paper are used most frequently as a base for dePaola's books, he also uses pencil drawings, etchings, charcoal drawings, and other techniques. He has mentioned on several occasions the importance of line in his art and the numerous techniques necessary to create the desired effect. His work draws upon a number of sources. In *The Story of the Three Wise Kings* (1983) he painted the Mother and Child in the traditional pose used in romanesque paintings. In *Francis: the Poor Man of Assisi* he was inspired by the frescoes of Cimabue and Simone Martini in the Basilica of San Francesco. He adhered to sixteenth-century Mexican dress in *The Lady of Guadalupe* and used designs from early Irish jewelry in *Fin M'Coul the Giant of Knockmany Hill*. In *The Hunter and the Animals* he explains in a note how he tried to capture the quality of Hungarian folk art by use of negative space. By using a combination of dry brush and colored inks, the result is traces of dots and smudges on blank spaces of the pictures. His aim, he told Susan Hepler, is "absolute simplicity": "I really care about the two dimensional design. I do what the Sienese painters do but not in the same way. I almost reduce features to a symbol. And yet I think of my faces as good and warm. I try to show expression in very few lines. If you look at Fra Angelico and Giotto, they're able to do that."

Paintings in dePaola's work range from the action and frenzy of costumed townfolk dancing in *Big Anthony and the Magic Ring* or rollicking trolls feasting in *The Cat on the Dovrefell* to the quiet in *The Unicorn and the Moon* and dreamlike quality in *When Everyone Was Fast Asleep*. Designs from clothing are frequently picked up in borders or other objects within the pictures. Both children and adults wear a variety of fascinating hats. The action and characters are often framed by arches or seen through windows, as in *Strega Nona*. DePaola's interest in theater is evident from pictures that frequently resemble stage sets. Cats, hearts, and birds are found in most of his works. Characters in the stories are made distinctive through dePaola's treatment of eyes, facial expressions, noses, hair, and mouths. Tousle-haired children have become an identifying characteristic of his work.

Highest critical acclaim to date has gone to the folktales, some of the information books, and the autobiographical selections. Perhaps the two qualities that consistently emerge from the work of this popular and talented author-illustrator are his keen sense of humor and his love of childhood and children. When asked by Dennis Andersen if he would ever give up his writing for children, dePaola's reply reflects well his love for his work:

> Never. It's my calling. There's a marvelous southwestern Indian image–Pueblo, I think. It's a clay figure sitting with its mouth open surrounded by little figures–and it's called the storyteller. The storyteller has always been an extremely important person in our culture. A good children's author/illustrator is the storyteller of a new era. Of today. And that's what I want to be more than anything else in the world.

References:

Richard Abrahamson and Marilyn Colvin, "Tomie dePaola–Children's Choice," *Reading Teacher* (December 1979): 264-268;

Dennis Andersen, "Tomie dePaola: Tough and Tender Storyteller," *Instructor* (March 1980): 32-38;

Phyllis Boyson, "Tomie dePaola: Story Teller of a New Era," *New Era* (May-June 1981): 76-29;

Susan Hepler, "Profile: Tomie dePaola, A Gift of Children," *Language Arts* (March 1979): 296-301;

"Interview with Tomie dePaola," in *Books to Grow On: A Parent's Guide to Encouraging Readers*, volume 1 (Washington, D.C.: Reading is Fundamental, 1983), pp. 4-6;

Ann Rodgers, "He's a Local Author Who Traded Monasticism for Children's Books," *Concord Monitor*, 13 November 1982, p. 13.

Papers:
The bulk of dePaola's artwork and manuscripts is housed in the Kerlan Collection of the University of Minnesota, Minneapolis.

William Pène du Bois
(9 May 1916-   )

Susan Garness
University of Minnesota

BOOKS: *Elisabeth, the Cow Ghost* (New York: Nelson, 1936; London: Museum Press, 1944); republished with new illustrations (New York: Viking, 1964);

Giant Otto (New York: Viking, 1936; London: Harrap, 1937); revised, with new illustrations, as *Otto in Africa* (New York: Viking, 1961; Leicester: Brockhampton, 1962);

Otto at Sea (New York: Viking, 1936; London: Harrap, 1937); republished with new illustrations (New York: Viking, 1958; Leicester: Brockhampton, 1962);

The Three Policemen; or Young Bottsford of Farbe Island (New York: Viking, 1938); republished with new illustrations (New York: Viking, 1960);

The Great Geppy (New York: Viking, 1940; London: Hale, 1942);

The Flying Locomotive (New York: Viking, 1941; London: Museum Press, 1946);

The Twenty-One Balloons (New York: Viking, 1947; London: Hale, 1949);

Peter Graves (New York: Viking, 1950);

Bear Party (New York: Viking, 1951);

Squirrel Hotel (New York: Viking, 1952);

The Giant (New York: Viking, 1954);

Lion (New York: Viking, 1956);

Otto in Texas (New York: Viking, 1959; Leicester: Brockhampton, 1961);

The Alligator Case (New York: Harper & Row, 1965);

Lazy Tommy Pumpkinhead (New York: Harper & Row, 1966);

The Horse in the Camel Suit (New York: Harper & Row, 1967);

Pretty Pretty Peggy Moffitt (New York: Harper & Row, 1968);

Porko Von Popbutton (New York: Harper & Row, 1969);

Call Me Bandicoot (New York: Harper & Row, 1970);

Otto and the Magic Potatoes (New York: Viking, 1970);

Bear Circus (New York: Viking, 1971);

The Hare and the Tortoise & the Tortoise and the

William Pène du Bois

Hare: La Liebre y la Tortuga & La Tortuga y la Liebre, with Lee Po (Garden City: Doubleday, 1972);

Mother Goose for Christmas (New York: Viking, 1973);

The Forbidden Forest (New York: Harper & Row, 1978; London: Chatto & Windus, 1978);

Gentleman Bear (New York: Farrar, 1985).

SELECTED BOOKS ILLUSTRATED: Richard Plant and Oskar Seidlin, *S.O.S. Geneva* (New York: Viking, 1939);

Charles McKinley, *Harriet* (New York: Viking, 1946);

Patricia Gordon, *The Witch of Scrapfaggot Green* (New York: Viking, 1948);

Daisy Ashford, *The Young Visiters; or Mr. Salteena's Plan* (Garden City: Doubleday, 1951);

Leslie Greener, *Moon Ahead* (New York: Viking, 1951);

Rumer Godden, *The Mousewife* (New York: Viking, 1951);

Claire Huchet Bishop, *Twenty and Ten* (New York: Viking, 1952);

Evelyn Ames, *My Brother Bird* (New York: Dodd, Mead, 1954);

George Plimpton, *The Rabbit's Umbrella* (New York: Viking, 1955);

Marguerite Clement, *In France* (New York: Viking, 1956);

Madeleine Grattan, *Jexium Island*, translated by Peter Grattan (New York: Viking, 1957);

Edward Fenton, *Fierce John, a Story* (Garden City: Doubleday, 1959);

Dorothy Kunhardt, *Billy the Barber* (New York: Harper, 1961);

Edward Lear, *The Owl and the Pussycat* (Garden City: Doubleday, 1961);

George MacDonald, *The Light Princess* (New York: Crowell, 1962);

The Three Little Pigs in Verse; Author Unknown (New York: Viking, 1962);

Jules Verne, *Dr. Ox's Experiment* (New York: Macmillan, 1963);

Rebecca Caudill, *A Certain Small Shepherd* (New York: Holt, Rinehart & Winston, 1965);

Roald Dahl, *The Magic Finger* (New York: Harper & Row, 1966);

Betty Yurdin, *The Tiger in the Teapot* (New York: Holt, Rinehart & Winston, 1968);

Richard Wilbur, *Digging for China: A Poem* (Garden City: Doubleday, 1970);

Isaac Bashevis Singer, *The Topsy-Turvy Emperor of China* (New York: Harper & Row, 1971);

Charlotte Zolotow, *William's Doll* (New York: Harper & Row, 1972);

Peter Matthiessen, *Seal Pool* (Garden City: Doubleday, 1972);

Norma Farber, *Where's Gomer?* (New York: Dutton, 1974);

Zolotow, *My Grandson Lew* (New York: Harper & Row, 1974);

Zolotow, *The Unfriendly Book* (New York: Harper & Row, 1975);

Paul Jacques Bonzon, *The Runaway Flying Horse* (New York: Parents' Magazine Press, 1976);

Zolotow, *It's Not Fair* (New York: Harper & Row, 1976);

Tobi Tobias, *Moving Day* (New York: Knopf, 1976);

Mildred Hobzek, *We Came A-Marching . . . One,* *Two, Three* (New York: Parents' Magazine Press, 1978);

Patricia MacLachlan, *The Sick Day* (New York: Pantheon, 1979);

Madeleine Edmondson, *Anna Witch* (Garden City: Doubleday, 1982);

Mark Strand, *The Planet of Lost Things* (New York: Crown, 1982);

Strand, *The Night Book* (New York: Crown, 1985).

OTHER: "Animal History Will Bear This Out," in *The Contents of the Basket and Other Papers On Children's Books and Reading*, edited by Frances Lander Spain (New York: New York Public Library, 1960), pp. 35-40.

PERIODICAL PUBLICATION: "Newbery Acceptance Paper–1947," *Horn Book*, 24 (July-August 1948): 235-244.

William Pène du Bois was born in Nutley, New Jersey, on 9 May 1916. The son of American painter and art critic Guy Pène du Bois and Florence Sherman Pène du Bois, he seemed destined by family influence to become an artist. His ancestry includes painters, architects, and designers in every generation since 1738. His first wife, Jane Bouché, was also the daughter of an artist; his second wife, Willa Kim, a theatrical designer. Pène du Bois began school in the United States but received most of his education in France at the Lycée Hoche in Versailles. The rigorous discipline of the French school gave him the sense of order and careful planning evident in the precision of his writing and illustration.

Home from the boarding school every weekend, he and his sister Yvonne begged to go to the circus or some other form of live entertainment in Paris. Here he observed the atmosphere of amazing and astounding feats which permeate' most of his stories. The family returned to the United States when Pène du Bois was fourteen, and he went on to prepare himself to enter Carnegie Technical School of Architecture in 1933. When his parents informed him that there was not going to be enough money to send him to school, he declared that he was going to write and illustrate children's books. He published his first three works before his twenty-first birthday and has continued writing and illustrating with only sporadic interruptions since.

Pène du Bois has stated that "In writing and illustrating children's books, I keep but one audience in mind, and that audience is myself as a child and the children I used to play with. That is my system. I have never dared to test a book of mine on children before publication for fear that they would be completely bored, a situation which could only prove to be most distressing and perplexing. As a child I hardly read at all, although I loved to look at books. I was the sort of fellow who just looks at the pictures. I try to keep such impatient children in mind in making by books."

This method has worked well, for Pène du Bois has received several distinguished children's book awards. *The Twenty-One Balloons* (1947) won the 1948 Newbery Medal; *Bear Party* (1951) and *Lion* (1956) were Caldecott Honor Books in 1952 and 1957 respectively; *Bear Circus* (1971) won the Lewis Carroll Shelf Award, was placed on the *New York Times* Best Illustrated Children's Book of the Year list, and was included in the 1972 Children's Book Showcase sponsored by the Children's Book Council. His illustrations have apeared in several award-winning picture books, notably Norma Farber's *Where's Gomer?* (1974), which was included in 1975 Children's Book Showcase, and *Moving Day* (1976) by Tobi Tobias, which was featured at the 1977 American Institute of Graphic Artists Book Show.

Pène du Bois's first book, *Elisabeth, the Cow Ghost*, was not noted by reviewers when it appeared in 1936. Barbara Bader, in her commentary *American Picture Books from Noah's Ark to the Beast Within* (1976), calls it "a neat tight little book" and notes the clever use of the second color to function along with the drawings to tell the story. Elisabeth is a gentle cream-colored cow who desires to be "fierce"; after she dies she returns as a ghost, with the intention of frightening her owner. However, she has to go through several disguises before this is accomplished (for even when she appears as a ghost she is remembered as "the most gentle cow that ever lived"), and when she does succeed she vows to "never do it again, never, never again."

Giant Otto and *Otto at Sea*, the adventures of a giant otter hound and his master Duke, appeared in 1936 as a boxed set of picture books. Otto is so big that when he wags his tail the wind created knocks trees to the ground. In *Giant Otto* Duke decides that Otto is too big to live in a small town in France. They join the French Foreign Legion and single-handedly save the fort from an invasion by Arabs. Duke receives a medal for bravery, and Otto is decorated with a medal for "extraordinary courage in the face of ex-

Pène du Bois as the goalie for his school's ice hockey team

treme danger." *Otto at Sea* continues the pair's adventures as Otto and Duke make a goodwill trip to America after winning their medals in Africa. Their ship is caught in a storm at sea and although Otto tries valiantly to save it, it is lost; however, he does save the lives of everyone on board, and the captain's garden table, and so is given a hero's welcome and another medal when he and Duke arrive in New York City.

Both stories are well done, delightfully told, and deservedly popular. In *Giant Otto* repetition of events brings humor into the simple plot: Otto defeats the Arabs by running around them to create a sandstorm, and at the awards ceremony where he receives his medal he again, by wagging his tremendous tail, creates a sandstorm which sends the soldiers and flags, drums and bugles floating up in the air. *Otto at Sea* contains more humorous elements: the captain of the ship signals to his deaf first mate by wearing enormous gloves, because the mate is also nearsighted. The illustrations are very much like cartoons, a style which Pène du Bois had changed by 1958 when he reillustrated *Otto at Sea* for republication. *Giant Otto* was extensively rewritten and republished in 1961 as *Otto in Africa*. The original picture books received very favorable reviews; typical is the comment in the *New York Times* (15 November 1936): "They have that solemn and perfectly reasonable absurdity which little children adore, and which, when it is as well carried out as is the case in the Otto books, delights grown-ups as well."

In 1938 *The Three Policemen; or Young Bottsford of Farbe Island* was published, a comic and imaginative story containing many elements of Pène du Bois's best work. The humor is of a tongue-in-cheek style which depicts people as foolish or pompous but always good-natured and never truly evil. The plot is filled with impossible events told in such a straightforward manner and with such attention to detail that they seem quite reasonable: the elaborate "fish suits" which the three policemen design and construct in one day are so carefully described and illustrated with schematic drawings that one is confident they will be able to function as splendid one-man submarines.

The story is carefully unified, and elements which seem extraneous when introduced are eventually wound back into the resolution. The illustrations mirror Pène du Bois's writing style in that they are precise and filled with humorous detail; moreover they supplement the text and tell part of the story (young Bottsford is shown to be black in the drawings although this fact is never mentioned in the text).

The Three Policemen is set on the idyllic island of Farbe where all of the inhabitants are prosperous fishermen descended from French sailors. There has never been any crime, and so the three policemen of Farbe Island never have any work to do. They spend their time designing and making elaborate uniforms which they wear to the café every morning. Then one day all of the fishing nets disappear, and the three policemen must solve the mystery. It is young Bottsford who provides the elaborate scheme to capture

the robbers, and who eventually reveals that the "Boss" of the robbers is none other than the good mayor of Farbe Island, who was simply testing the three policemen by pretending to steal the nets. In the happy resolution medals are presented and great honors bestowed upon the hero, as in the Otto books. And, like the Otto books, *The Three Policemen* was a popular book well received by reviewers.

In 1940 *The Great Geppy* appeared, inspired by Pène du Bois's love of the French circus. Dedicated to his parents, the book was written in Pène du Bois's tongue-in-cheek style in which outrageous events are reported in a straight-faced manner. The famous detective agency of Armstrong and Trilby is asked to send out a sleuth to investigate the theft of ticket money from the safe of the Bott Brothers' Three Ring Circus. This detective must be able to walk a tightrope, train lions, be shot from a cannon, and also be a circus freak. Attempting to uphold the company slogan of "A Suitable Sleuth for All Solvable Crimes," Armstrong and Trilby commission Geppy, the red-and-white-striped horse of Sergeant Murphy, to capture the thief.

Assuming the roles of the various circus performers, Geppy investigates the members of the circus troupe and solves the mystery. As in *The Three Policemen*, there is no crime: the circus had been doing so badly that one of the Bott Brothers was actually breaking into the safe to put in money rather than to take it out. Like Pène du Bois's previous works, there is a grand resolution in which the hero is greatly honored and everyone is satisfied: the mystery is solved, so the company slogan of Armstrong and Trilby is upheld; Geppy proves to be such an outstanding performer when shot from the cannon that he becomes the circus's new star, "The Great Geppy"; with the addition of the new act, the future looks bright for the circus; and even old Dobbin, Geppy's stablemate at Sergeant Murphy's, is to be given Geppy's ration of oats while Geppy is traveling with the circus.

The Flying Locomotive (1941), presented in picture-book format, is hampered by a lengthy text and a writing style too sophisticated for prereaders. It also has an obvious moral, a device which was absent from Pène du Bois's earlier work; the proud and boastful steam engine, Toto No. 2, learns humility and the value of friendship after a fantasy experience in which he is given the ability to fly through the air. During the course of the flight he loses his navigator, Ma-

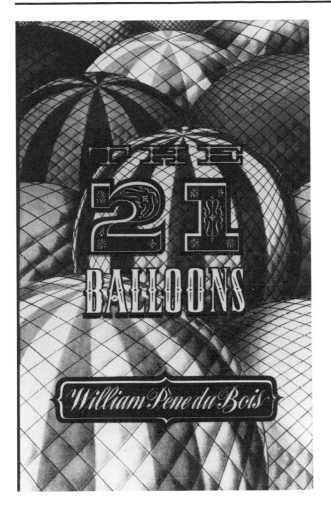

*Dust jacket for Pène du Bois's 1947 novel. His best-known
work, the book was awarded the Newbery Medal in
1948 (Viking).*

dame Suzie, a prize-winning dairy cow who
shares the shed in which he is housed and who is
the only one who will listen to his endless
boasting.

When Madame Suzie returns safely to their
shed, Toto No. 2 vows never again to talk about
himself, and they spend the rest of their lives in
pleasant conversation and companionship. The
story is not as cleverly imaginative as *The Three Policemen* or *The Great Geppy*; although it is typical
of Pène du Bois's work in the French flavor of
the characters and in their actions, the climax of
the plot depends on the introduction of a fairy
godmother who misinterprets Toto No. 2's wish
to be a Swiss flyer locomotive and grants him the
ability to fly. Pène du Bois did not use such a magical device again in his stories.

From 1941 to 1946 Pène du Bois served in
the armed forces but did not entirely suspend his
literary or artistic career. While in the coast artillery in Bermuda he edited the camp newspaper
and illustrated maps of strategic locations while
he continued to paint portraits. Apparently he
was also working on his next children's project, because *The Twenty-One Balloons*, a novel, was delivered to the publisher in 1947. By far his
best-known work, it contains many elements of
classic fantasies, mainly the desire to escape from
the humdrum of life to a simple self-sufficient life-
style with plenty of time for reflection. In the
book this is to be contrasted with a life of complete luxury where every need or whim is gratified, presented with an abundance of tantalizing
material evidence.

Professor William Waterman Sherman plans
to escape his dull life as a teacher of arithmetic
by sailing off in a huge hot-air balloon to remain
aloft for a year. Unfortunately his balloon is punc-
tured and he crashes on Krakatoa Island, where
he discovers a colony of Americans living a life
of luxury made possible by the existence of a fabulous diamond mine on the island. The diamonds
must be kept secret in order to preserve their
value on the world market, so Professor Sherman
prepares to spend the rest of his life on the island. Only days after his arrival, the very active volcano on the island erupts, a disaster for which
the Krakatoans had prepared by inventing an escape vehicle in the form of a large platform to
be carried aloft by twenty hot-air balloons. All
manage to escape safely, but because Professor
Sherman is the only one who does not have a parachute, he must crash-land the platform in the
ocean after all of the others have jumped off. He
is picked up by a passing freighter, is given a
hero's welcome, and tells his story to the world.

The humor of *The Twenty-One Balloons* is sa-
tirical rather than absurd, a new development in
Pène du Bois's style. The people who are anxious
to welcome Professor Sherman back after his adventures show themselves to be foolish and pompous in their attempts to vie for his attention and
the honor of being seen with him in public. Pène
du Bois also makes a comment on the irony that
human greed enslaves the wealthy so that the cov-
etous Americans must live on top of an active volcano in order to be near their diamonds. But
though they are foolish or greedy, Pène du Bois's
characters are not evil; even the Krakatoans, anxious to guard the secret of their fabulous wealth,
do not kill Professor Sherman or make him their
prisoner, but rather allow him to live with them
as their equal, participating in their "gourmet government" and helping in the invention of many

Cover for Pène du Bois's 1951 picture book. The story of a costume ball put on by koala bears, it was a 1952 Caldecott Honor Book (Viking).

wonderful mechanical devices to make their lives more comfortable.

The reasonableness and compassion of the Krakatoans is just the opposite of F. Scott Fitzgerald's short story "The Diamond as Big as the Ritz," with which *The Twenty-One Balloons* shares many similar elements of plot. Pène du Bois points out in an author's note dated 19 January 1947 and printed in the first edition of the book that he had no knowledge of Fitzgerald's story and the resemblance of the two is an "embarrassing and, to me, maddening coincidence." The resemblance is only superficial, because in Fitzgerald's story the secret of the fabulous diamond mine is preserved by murder and enslavement, and in the end the entire mountain is blown up by its owner so that none of the wealth will ever be shared. In Pène du Bois's story, the diamond mine is also lost, but all of the citizens of Krakatoa are still alive and Professor Sherman plans to take off in another balloon, perhaps to discover other islands and adventures.

In his Newbery Medal acceptance speech for *The Twenty-One Balloons*, Pène du Bois talked about some of the imaginative sources from which the story sprang. The setting of Krakatoa Island came from one of the geography books he was supposed to be reading as a student in the French lycée, but in which he used to conceal the "ferocious and forbidden magazines" called *Les Aventures de Nick Carter* and *Les Aventures de Buffalo Bill*, which were the only reading he remembers having done as a child. Apparently a magazine had for several days been squeezed between two pages which discussed the event of the explosion of Krakatoa Island on 26 August 1883, for the book fell open to that page repeatedly, and the picture of the island remained vivid in his memory. The island's "gourmet government" is based on the expositions and fairs Pène du Bois attended in Paris as a boy, where he became quite ill from sampling the food of many nations. And finally the balloons and mechanical inventions were inspired by the books of Jules Verne, which he loved from before the time he was able to read them himself.

Pène du Bois's next book, *Peter Graves* (1950), was a less than satisfying follow-up to its Newbery Medal-winning predecessor. For all its humor and cleverness, the plot tends to ramble and contains many extraneous scenes, notably the long game of "Follow the Leader" which is the means of introducing the two main characters. Peter Graves is a fifteen-year-old boy with great curiosity and a vivid imagination who helps a retired inventor named Houghton Furlong to demonstrate the capabilities of his wonderful inventions. During a number of astounding and record-breaking exploits, all of Houghton's anti-gravitational alloy is lost; but again Pène du Bois provides the happy resolution in which all that was lost may be regained, and Peter's wild imagination goes on to dream up new schemes.

The theme of the loss of a wonderful invention carries into Pène du Bois's story *Squirrel Hotel* (1952), which originally appeared in *Mademoiselle* magazine. The book presents an odd tale about the encounter of the writer and an old man who tells him about an elaborate model hotel he has built for squirrels in a secret place, though, unfortunately, the old man dies before he reveals the location of the hotel. *Squirrel Hotel* received mixed reviews: *Horn Book*'s reviewer called it an "ingenious new yarn" while the *New York Herald Tribune* critic called it "all very slight." Nevertheless, *Squirrel Hotel* was chosen for inclusion in the Gregg Press Children's Literature Series in 1979, though it is not the best example of Pène du Bois's work. *The Giant* (1954), the tale of El Muchacho, a seven-story-tall boy, is typical of Pène du Bois's style in its continental atmosphere and humorous detail, but it too lacks the imaginative quality of *The Three Policemen* or *The Twenty-One Balloons*.

Pène du Bois had been illustrating for other authors since 1939, when he produced twenty-nine drawings for *S.O.S. Geneva* by Richard Plant and Oskar Seidlin. In 1946 Charles McKinley's *Harriet* appeared, the story of a horse who likes hats and who looks very much like a Geppy without the stripes. In 1948 Viking published a modern fantasy by Patricia Gordon called *The Witch of Scrapfaggot Green* which Pène du Bois illustrated, and which probably appealed to him because it is the kind of fantasy he might have written himself. In 1951 Pène du Bois's illustrations appeared in three diverse books: his precise drawings of mechanical inventions highlighted a juvenile science fiction book called *Moon Ahead* by Leslie Greener; the fussy and proper Victorian people of *The Twenty-One Balloons* were shown in a curious love story in Daisy Ashford's *The Young Visiters; or Mr. Salteena's Plan*; and he provided wonderfully realistic pen-and-ink drawings for Rumer Godden's animal fantasy *The Mousewife*.

Pène du Bois's whimsical sense of humor shows in *The Mousewife*, adding a little detail to the text which makes the illustrations worthy of such a fine story. In the series of portraits of several generations of mice, he shows the changes in styles of portraiture, as well as manners and dress, through the ages, a motif not suggested in the text. During the 1950s he illustrated for many other authors, working carefully to capture and portray their stories in pictures that are in themselves interesting to study. He experimented with new mediums and techniques as the technology of picture-book illustration grew and changed.

In the 1950s Pène du Bois wrote and illustrated two Caldecott Honor Books of his own, *Bear Party* (1951) and *Lion* (1956). The plot of *Bear Party* is very simply the story of the costume ball put on by the "real teddy bears" in Koala Park, but it affords the author-artist great fun in drawing the many elaborate costumes of the bears and the gay whirling scenes of the party. *Bear Party* is in the tradition of the finest picture books with its simple text, repetition of phrases,

Dust jacket for Pène du Bois's second Caldecott Honor Book, a 1956 fable about a group of angels in charge of creating animals to populate the universe (Viking)

and delightful illustrations which make it worth looking at again and again.

Pène du Bois's original fable *Lion* is also an outstanding picture book. In it, Foreman Angel, the artist in charge of creating animals to populate the universe, thinks of a new name for an animal and after several unsuccessful attempts designs a creature worthy of being called a "Lion." The clever story line is supplemented by detailed illustrations produced by the exacting technique of color preseparation on Dinobase. In a lecture delivered at the New York Public Library, Pène du Bois spoke about the Christmas card which was the inspiration for *Lion* and some of the ideas he wanted to include in the tale. He concluded with a comment about the creation of children's books: "I have the feeling that when I'm asked 'How did you ever think of such a crazy idea?' the person who asked the question felt that the book was thought of in a moment, illustrated in a week, and printed in a day. There is a widespread feeling that doing children's books is a divertissement or a hobby, never a full-time job, and that it's quick and easy. I don't want to discourage people who want to dash off a children's book, but I would like to slow them down a bit."

Pène du Bois, the perfectionist who does not simply dash off a children's book, began in 1958 to revise several of his earlier books. First he did new illustrations for *Otto at Sea,* changing Otto from a cartoon character into a more realistic shaggy otter hound by adding more detail and more color. *Giant Otto* was completely rewritten as *Otto in Africa* (1961), in which Otto loses his ability to speak with his master in dialogue but remains the same courageous savior of the foreign legion outpost. New adventures were added to the series as well. *Otto in Texas* (1959) is less successful as a picture book than the previous installments because the text is quite lengthy. However, it is very popular with children who have met Otto before. This time Otto and Duke are the guests of a wealthy Texas oil baron, Sam Hill. During their visit, Otto reveals that someone is tapping Sam's best well, and he leads the posse in chasing down and unmasking the bad guys, for which he receives another medal.

Otto and the Magic Potatoes (1970) is written and illustrated in the style of Pène du Bois's early fantasies for children in the middle grades. While trying to hide away from his many admirers and fans, Otto is kidnapped by Baron von Backgammon, who wishes to use him as a subject for his experiments with giant roses and potatoes. Although they are prisoners, Duke and Otto find that their captor treats them as honored guests and provides for every comfort. Once again Pène du Bois has a villain who is not really evil: the baron is thought by the villagers to be a mad scientist when he is really a misunderstood philanthropist. Through a terribly complicated chain of events involving Otto's bravery in a dangerous situation, the baron is at last revealed to the villagers as one who wishes to create roses big enough to hide the ugliness of the world and potatoes big enough to feed the world's hungry. Though *Otto and the Magic Potatoes* is completely misrepresented as a picture book (it is an illustrated storybook which is not accessible to prereaders) it does have an appeal to older children who are acquainted with the Otto series.

In 1960 Viking Press republished *The Three Policemen* with new and better illustrations. The text of the story remained the same and the composition of most of the scenes was not changed; Pène du Bois added more detail, reflecting his ma-

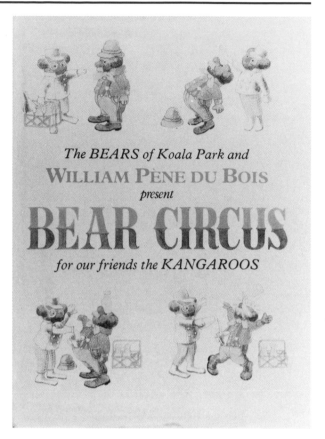

Dust jacket for Pène du Bois's 1971 sequel to Bear Party, *which was chosen as one of the Best Illustrated Children's Books of the Year by the* New York Times, *included in the Children's Book Showcase, and honored with the Lewis Carroll Shelf Award (Viking)*

ture style of illustration, and the new book is a brilliant reissue. In 1964 *Elisabeth, the Cow Ghost* was republished, radically changed from the first version. The plot remains the same; but the new illustrations are not an improvement over the earlier book, and though there is a familiar French flavor to the characters, Pène du Bois's attempt at humor (with the repeated line "Come as you are, with false noses") seems strained.

By 1965 Pène du Bois had returned to writing nonsense stories for older children and came up with a mystery called *The Alligator Case.* The young hero is a small-town boy who fancies himself as a great detective, and in his desire to solve a baffling mystery he begins to work on the case even before the crime is committed. The complicated story is told solemnly with a sophisticated air which satirizes the *Dragnet* television series. The book received mixed reviews, from the *Book Week* (3 October 1965) critic's assessment that it was "one of the finest children's books of the season" to the *Library Journal* (15 September 1965) reviewer's comment that it was "a great disappointment from this author-artist." In 1967 a sequel was published, *The Horse in the Camel Suit*, which is so complicated in plot that it only confuses the reader and leaves one grateful that the series has not been continued.

In the mid 1960s Pène du Bois began a series of stories which were to have as their themes the seven deadly sins. *Lazy Tommy Pumpkinhead* (1966) deals with the sin of sloth and is the story of a boy so lazy that his every physical need is taken care of by machines. One day the machines go awry, and he is dumped into an ice-cold bath, combed and dressed upside down, and stuffed with seven days' worth of food. It would be a mistake to take the story as a denunciation of the modern machine age for there is no resolution. Lazy Tommy simply says that he must "turn over a new leaf before it is The End." The tale is imaginative and clever, and the illustrations feature Pène du Bois's favorite mechanical inventions drawn in minute detail.

Pretty Pretty Peggy Moffitt (1968) deals with the sin of vanity. Peggy Moffitt spends so much time looking at herself in any reflective surface available that she is always tripping and falling. Because of her many bruises she loses a chance to try-out before a movie scout, and so she goes home and smashes all of her mirrors. Pène du Bois's illustrations place the book firmly in the era of miniskirts and Rudi Gernreich designs and show his frequent preoccupation with costume and dress as evidenced in *The Three Policemen*, *Bear Party*, and Betty Yurdin's *The Tiger in the Teapot*, which he illustrated in 1968.

The hilarious and quite successful *Porko Von Popbutton* (1969) treats the sin of gluttony. Pat O'Sullivan Pinkerton is a 274-pound thirteen-year-old boy whose only interest is food until it is discovered that he is absolutely unbeatable as a goalie for his prep school's hockey team. Although gluttony is an interesting element in the story, the real theme is the adoration of sports in the prep school world which Pène du Bois satirizes well. The chapter describing the biggest game of the season appeared in *Sports Illustrated* magazine in December 1968, thus bringing children's literature to the world of professional sports.

Call Me Bandicoot (1970) is a tale supposedly about covetousness but really dealing with "That oldest of professions, storytelling." Herman Vanden Kroote, Jr., is a creepy young kid who haunts the Staten Island ferryboat and manages to charm his fellow passengers into feeding him and handing him money by telling them outrageously tall tales. This beggar's mode of making a living is really the result of avarice, for Herman is the son of an extremely wealthy cigarette magnate.

After *Call Me Bandicoot* Pène du Bois appears to have abandoned the Seven Deadly Sins series. In 1971 he returned to an earlier success, *Bear Party*, producing a sequel, *Bear Circus*, which is dedicated to the great French clowns Paul, Albert, and François Fratellini and which recalls the author's love of the circuses of his childhood. The real teddy bears of Koala Park are saved from starvation by their friends the kangaroos, and in gratitude they decide to put on a circus to entertain them. It takes the teddy bears seven years to learn how to put up the tent and practice their acts (real teddy bears are slow), but the show is well worth the wait. As in many of Pène du Bois's picture books, the text is very long, but the illustrations are adequately geared to the preschooler.

In 1973 Pène du Bois entered the fantasy world of Mother Goose with *Mother Goose for Christmas*. When Mother Goose is apparently kidnapped by two strangers all of her friends must think of a way to save her. The kidnappers turn out to be Simple Simon and the Pieman who have come to the village at Mother Goose's invitation to reopen the bakery which has been closed since the Knave of Hearts stole the tarts. *Mother Goose for Christmas* recalls several elements of Pène du Bois's earlier tales: the foolishness of the villagers, the villain who is not really evil but merely misunderstood, and the grand resolution in which everyone is satisfied. The illustrations, examples of his best mature work, contain details which are not mentioned in the text but which add to the story.

Pène du Bois's most ambitious book, *The Hare and the Tortoise & the Tortoise and the Hare: La Liebre y la Tortuga & La Tortuga y la Liebre* (1972), is a bilingual picture book of two fables on which Pène du Bois collaborated with Lee Po. Pène du Bois adapted and illustrated the traditional Aesop's fable and also did the illustrations for Lee Po's rendition of a classical Oriental tale in which the tortoise tries to trick the hare into sacrificing her liver for the Queen of All Fish. In his illustrations, Pène du Bois gives unique personalities to the characters, as he did in his earlier adaptations of traditional tales, *The Three Little Pigs in Verse; Author Unknown* (1962), Edward Lear's *The Owl and the Pussycat* (1961), and

It was a beautiful sight: soldiers, flags, drums, and bugles flying high in the African sky.

34

As the sun set Otto slowed down his tail, and the soldiers landed comfortably in the sand.

35

(Viking, 1961)

(Harper & Row, 1978)

Illustrations from Pène du Bois's Otto in Africa *and* The Forbidden Forest

Norma Farber's *Where's Gomer?* (1974); and his re-writing of the fable is humorous; however, the book received mixed reviews because of the gruesomeness of the Oriental tale and the many grammatical errors in the Spanish text.

Pène du Bois's book *The Forbidden Forest* (1978) shows a dark side of the fantasy world not present in his other work. It is the story of how Lady Adelaide, a boxing kangaroo, together with her trainer Spider Max and a bulldog named Buckingham brought an end to World War I by sabotaging the great German cannon used to bombard Paris from Aachen. The ironic and almost tragic tone of the story is established with a prologue about the stupidity of war (the book is dedicated to Jane Fonda). *The Forbidden Forest* features beautifully detailed drawings of balloons, dirigibles, and airplanes; however, these are not the wonderful inventions that characterize his work but machines of destruction and war. A scene which portrays the explosion of the ammunition dump is reminiscent of the scene in *Otto in Africa* which depicts soldiers and equipment floating up in the air; however, in *The Forbidden Forest* the soldiers are dying. Lady Adelaide receives four medals for her distinguished service and many kisses on both cheeks in true French style, but the adulation of the crowds is not the same cheerful hero worship that Otto received.

Pène du Bois's latest book to date is *Gentleman Bear*, published in 1985. It follows very much in the style of *The Forbidden Forest*, the life story of a teddy bear named Bayard, "a gentleman of courage and honor." The text is very long and the pace of the story is quite slow; it spans the years of World War I and the peace between the wars, and it climaxes at the Olympic Games of 1936. There is quite a bit of a mystery when Bayard is kidnapped, and the eccentricity of the characters is very much in the Pène du Bois style. The most interesting element of the book is the beautifully detailed illustrations.

Pène du Bois's career as an author and illustrator has been long and productive. He has illustrated a wide variety of works, including fantasies, fairy tales, books about France or French characters, and many realistic picture books which deal honestly with the emotions and experiences of young children. He often adds elements in his illustrations which are not a part of the text, which make his drawings an integral element of the book. For example, in Pène du Bois's version of *The Owl and the Pussycat*, the turkey is really a Turkish bird, complete with a fez. Roald

Dahl's *The Magic Finger* (1966) contains some inside jokes for art history buffs: one drawing captioned "after Honoré Daumier" parodies the great French caricaturist's drawing "The Too-Hot Bath," and on the facing page the young heroine is depicted a la James Montgomery Flagg's famous World War I recruiting poster of Uncle Sam. *Where's Gomer?*, an imaginative retelling of the story of Noah's Ark, is made all the more humorous by Pène du Bois's depiction of Noah spiffily dressed in a yachting costume. And only Pène du Bois's illustrations reveal that the couple who are turned out into the cold night by the neighbors in Rebecca Caudill's *A Certain Small Shepherd* (1965) are black. In Richard Wilbur's *Digging for China: A Poem* (1970), Pène du Bois shows two pictures of what is taking place in the action, one a realistic illustration of a boy digging a large and not very deep hole and on the facing page a fantastic representation of his imaginings about what he is doing.

William Pène du Bois is best known for the humorous fantasies of his early career in which good characters have all kinds of marvelous adventures with their own fantastic inventions. He occupies a rather unique place in American children's literature as an artist who has created his own brand of fantasy, though his greatest contribution may be as an illustrator who combines freshness of imagination and great technical skill to produce clear and detailed pictures which not only complement, but expand upon the texts they illustrate.

References:

Barbara Bader, *American Picture Books from Noah's Ark to the Beast Within* (New York: Macmillan, 1976);

Nancy Ekholm Burkert, "A Second Look: Lion," *Horn Book*, 61 (December 1980): 671-676;

Rochelle Girson, "Juvenile Authors: Some Bows & Encores," *Saturday Review of Literature*, 33 (11 November 1950): 34;

Diana Klemin, *Art of Art for Children's Books* (New York: Potter, 1966);

May Massee, "Du Bois Gets Newbery Medal," *Library Journal*, 73 (15 June 1948): 914-915, 923;

Yvonne Pène du Bois, "William Pène du Bois, Boy and Artist," *Horn Book*, 24 (July-August 1948): 245-250.

Papers:

William Pène du Bois's manuscripts are housed in the May Massee Collection at Emporia State University, Kansas.

Roger Duvoisin
(28 August 1904-30 June 1980)

Agnes D. Stahlschmidt

BOOKS: *A Little Boy Was Drawing* (New York: Scribners, 1932);

Donkey-Donkey, The Troubles of a Silly Little Donkey (Racine, Wis.: Whitman, 1933; London: Chatto, Boyd & Oliver, 1969);

All Aboard! (New York: Grosset & Dunlap, 1935);

And There Was America (New York: Knopf, 1938);

The Christmas Cake in Search of Its Owner (New York: American Artists Group, 1941);

The Three Sneezes and Other Swiss Tales (New York: Knopf, 1941); republished as *Fairy Tales from Switzerland: the Three Sneezes and Other Fairy Tales* (London: F. Muller, 1958);

They Put Out to Sea, The Story of the Map (New York: Knopf, 1943; London: University of London Press, 1947);

The Christmas Whale (New York: Knopf, 1945);

Chanticleer: The Real Story of this Famous Rooster (New York: Grosset & Dunlap, 1947);

The Four Corners of the World (New York: Knopf, 1948);

Petunia (New York: Knopf, 1950; London: Lane, 1958);

Petunia and the Song (New York: Knopf, 1951);

A For The Ark (New York: Lothrop, Lee & Shepard, 1952; London: Bodley Head, 1961);

Petunia's Christmas (New York: Knopf, 1952; London: Bodley Head, 1960);

Petunia Takes a Trip (New York: Knopf, 1953; London: Bodley Head, 1959);

Easter Treat (New York: Knopf, 1954);

One Thousand Christmas Beards (New York: Knopf, 1955; Kingswood, Surrey: World's Work, 1975);

Two Lonely Ducks, A Counting Book (New York: Knopf, 1955; London: Bodley Head, 1966);

The House of Four Seasons (New York: Lothrop, Lee & Shepard, 1956; Leicester: Brockhampton Press, 1960);

Petunia, Beware! (New York: Knopf, 1958; London: Bodley Head, 1962);

Day and Night (New York: Knopf, 1960);

The Happy Hunter (New York: Lothrop, Lee & Shepard, 1961; Edinburgh: Oliver & Boyd, 1962);

Veronica (New York: Knopf, 1961; London: Bodley Head, 1962);

Our Veronica Goes to Petunia's Farm (New York: Knopf, 1962); republished as *Veronica Goes to Petunia's Farm* (London: Bodley Head, 1963);

Lonely Veronica (New York: Knopf, 1963; London: Bodley Head, 1964);

Spring Snow (New York: Knopf, 1963; Kingswood, Surrey: World's Work, 1966);

Veronica's Smile (New York: Knopf, 1964; London: Bodley Head, 1965);

Petunia, I Love You (New York: Knopf, 1965; London: Bodley Head, 1966);

The Missing Milkman (New York: Knopf, 1967; Kingswood, Surrey: World's Work, 1968);

What is Right for Tulip (New York: Knopf, 1969);

Veronica and the Birthday Present (New York: Knopf, 1971; London: Bodley Head, 1972);

The Crocodile in the Tree (London: Bodley Head, 1972; New York: Knopf, 1973);

Jasmine (New York: Knopf, 1973; London: Bodley Head, 1974);

See What I Am (New York: Lothrop, Lee & Shepard, 1974);

Petunia's Treasure (New York: Knopf, 1975; London: Bodley Head, 1977);

Periwinkle (New York: Knopf, 1976);

Crocus (New York: Knopf, 1977; London: Bodley Head, 1977);

Snowy and Woody (New York: Knopf, 1979);

The Importance of Crocus (London: Bodley Head, 1980; New York: Knopf, 1981).

SELECTED BOOKS ILLUSTRATED: Robert Browning, *The Pied Piper of Hamlin* (New York: Grosset & Dunlap, 1936);

William Rose Benét, comp., *Mother Goose: A Comprehensive Collection of the Rhymes* (New York: Heritage, 1936);

Kathleen M. Elliott, *Riema, Little Brown Girl of Java* (New York: Knopf, 1937);

Elliott, *Soomoon, Boy of Bali* (New York: Knopf, 1938);

Roger Duvoisin

Charlet Root, *The Feast of Lamps, A Story of India* (Chicago: Whitman, 1938);

Elliott, *Jo-Yo's Idea* (New York: Knopf, 1939);

William Henry Hudson, *W. H. Hudson's Tales of the Pampas* (New York: Knopf, 1939);

Heluiz Washburne, *Rhamon, a Boy of Kashmir* (Chicago: Whitman, 1939);

Marjorie Fischer, *The Dog Cantbark* (New York: Random House, 1910);

Mary Riley and Andre Humbert, *Petits Contes Vrais* (New York & Chicago: Merrill, 1940);

John G. McCullough, *At Our House* (New York: Scott, 1943);

Harold Ettlinger, *Fair, Fantastic Paris* (Indianapolis & New York: Bobb-Merrill, 1944);

Janet Howard, *Jumpy, The Kangaroo* (New York: Lothrop, Lee & Shepard, 1944);

Robert Louis Stevenson, *A Child's Garden of Verses* (New York: Limited Editions Club, 1944);

Robert Fontaine, *The Happy Time* (New York: Simon & Schuster, 1945);

Mildred A. Jordan, *"I Won't," Said the King; or, The Purple Flannel Underwear* (New York: Knopf, 1945);

Tom Powers, *Virgin with Butterflies* (New York: Bobbs-Merrill, 1945);

Christine Weston, *Bhimsa, the Dancing Bear* (New York: Scribners, 1945);

Daniel Defoe, *The Life and Adventures of Robinson Crusoe* (Cleveland & New York: World, 1946);

Robert Jay Misch, *At Daddy's Office* (New York: Knopf, 1946);

Margaret Pratt, *The Successful Secretary* (New York: Lothrop, Lee & Shepard, 1946);

Helen Walker Puner, *Daddies, What They Do All Day* (New York: Lothrop, Lee & Shepard, 1946);

Douglas Rigby, *Moustachio* (New York: Harper, 1947);

Alvin R. Tresselt, *White Snow, Bright Snow* (New York: Lothrop, Lee & Shepard, 1947);

William Norman Hall, *Christmas Pony* (New York: Knopf, 1948);

Walter Retan, as George Walters, *The Steam Shovel That Wouldn't Eat Dirt* (New York: Aladdin, 1948);

Tresselt, *Johnny Maple-Leaf* (New York: Lothrop, Lee & Shepard, 1948);

William Attwood, *The Man Who Could Grow Hair: or, Inside Andorra* (New York: Knopf, 1949);

Frances Mary Frost, *The Little Whistler* (New York: Whittlesey House, 1949);

Puner, *The Sitter Who Didn't Sit* (New York: Lothrop, Lee & Shepard, 1949);

Tresselt, *Sun Up* (New York: Lothrop, Lee & Shepard, 1949);

Frederic Attwood, *Vavache, the Cow Who Painted Pictures* (New York: Aladdin, 1950);

Niccolò De Quattrociocchi, *Love and Dishes* (Indianapolis: Bobbs-Merrill, 1950);

Louise Fatio, *The Christmas Forest* (New York: Aladdin, 1950);

Mabel Watts, *Dozens of Cousins* (New York: Whittlesey House, 1950);

Tresselt, *Follow The Wind* (New York: Lothrop, Lee & Shepard, 1950);

Tresselt, *"Hi, Mister Robin!"* (New York: Lothrop, Lee & Shepard, 1950);

Fatio, *Anna the Horse* (New York: Aladdin, 1951);

Helen Hilles, *Farm Wanted* (New York: Messner, 1951);

Tresselt, *Autumn Harvest* (New York: Lothrop, Lee & Shepard, 1951);

Jack Tworkov, *The Camel Who Took a Walk* (New York: Aladdin, 1951);

Natalie Savage Carlson, *The Talking Cat, and Other Stories of French Canada* (New York: Harper, 1952);

Herbert Leonard Coggins, *Busby & Co.* (New York: Whittlesey House, 1952);

Idwal Jones, *Chef's Holiday* (New York: Longmans, Green, 1952);

Gian Carlo Menotti, *Amahl and the Night Visitors,* adapted by Frances Frost (New York: Whittlesey House, 1952);

Doris Van Liew Foster, *Tell Me, Little Boy* (New York: Lothrop, Lee & Shepard, 1953);

Tresselt, *Follow The Road* (New York: Lothrop, Lee & Shepard, 1953);

Fatio, *The Happy Lion* (New York: Whittlesey House, 1954);

Clement Clarke Moore, *The Night Before Christmas* (Garden City: Garden City Books, 1954);

Jim Moran, *Sophocles, the Hyena; a Fable* (New York: Whittlesey House, 1954);

Margaret Pratt, *Flash of Washington Square* (New York: Lothrop, Lee & Shepard, 1954);

Tresselt, *I Saw the Sea Come In* (New York: Lothrop, Lee & Shepard, 1954);

Harold Courlander, ed., *Ride With the Sun; An Anthology of Folk Tales and Stories from the United Nations* (New York: Whittlesey House, 1955);

Fatio, *The Happy Lion in Africa* (New York: Whittlesey House, 1955);

Edith L. Marsh, *Trillium Hill*, jacket and endpapers by Duvoisin (New York: Lothrop, Lee & Shepard, 1955);

Miriam Schlein, *Little Red Nose* (New York: Lothrop, Lee & Shepard, 1955);

Tresselt, *Wake Up, Farm!* (New York: Lothrop, Lee & Shepard, 1955);

Charlotte Zolotow, *One Step, Two . . .* (New York: Lothrop, Lee & Shepard, 1955);

Beatrice and Ferrin Frasher, *Bennie, the Bear Who Grew Too Fast* (New York: Lothrop, Lee & Shepard, 1956);

Wilma Pitchford Hays, *Christmas on the Mayflower* (New York: Coward-McCann, 1956);

Tworkov, *Tigers Don't Bite* (New York: Dutton, 1956);

Mary Calhoun, *The Sweet Patootie Doll* (New York: Morrow, 1957);

Susan Dorritt, *Wait Till Sunday* (London & New York: Abelard-Schuman, 1957);

Fatio, *A Doll for Marie* (New York: Whittlesey House, 1957);

Fatio, *The Happy Lion Roars* (New York: Whittlesey House, 1957);

Arthur S. Gregor, *Does Poppy Live Here?* (New York: Lothrop, Lee & Shepard, 1957);

Stevenson, *Travels With a Donkey* (New York: Limited Editions Club, 1957);

Tresselt, *Wake Up, City!* (New York: Lothrop, Lee & Shepard, 1957);

Zolotow, *Not a Little Monkey* (New York: Lothrop, Lee & Shepard, 1957);

Calhoun, *Wobble, the Witch Cat* (New York: Morrow, 1958);

Hall, *Winkie's World* (Garden City: Doubleday, 1958);

Hazel Effie Hershberger, *The Little Church on the Big Rock* (New York: Scribners, 1958);

Tresselt, *The Frog in the Well* (New York: Lothrop, Lee & Shepard, 1958);

Pedro Antonio de Alarcón, *The Three-Cornered Hat* (Los Angeles: Limited Editions Club, 1959);

Calhoun, *Houn' Dog* (New York: Morrow, 1959);

Fatio, *The Three Happy Lions* (New York: Whittlesey House, 1959);

Virginia Haviland, ed., *Favorite Fairy Tales Told in France* (Boston: Little, Brown, 1959);

Patricia Miles Martin, *The Pointed Brush* (New York: Lothrop, Lee & Shepard, 1959);

Mary Natalie Tabak, *A Fish Is Not a Pet* (New York: Whittlesey House, 1959);

Leone Adelson, *Please Pass the Grass!* (New York: McKay, 1960);

Janice Brustlein, as Janice, *Angelique* (New York: Whittlesey House, 1960); republished as *A Duck Called Angelique* (London: Bodley Head, 1962);

Elizabeth Coatsworth, *The Children Come Running* (New York: Golden Press, 1960);

Tresselt, *Timothy Robbins Climbs the Mountain* (New York: Lothrop, Lee & Shepard, 1960);

Zolotow, *In My Garden* (New York: Lothrop, Lee & Shepard, 1960);

Calhoun, *The Nine Lives of Homer C. Cat* (New York: Morrow, 1961);

Fatio, *The Happy Lion's Quest* (New York: Whittlesey House, 1961);

Priscilla and Otto Friedrich, *The Wishing Well in the Wood* (New York: Lothrop, Lee & Shepard, 1961);

Aesopus, *The Miller, His Son, and Their Donkey* (New York: Whittlesey House, 1962; London: Bodley Head, 1963);

Calhoun, *The Hungry Leprechaun* (New York: Morrow, 1962);

Adelaide Holl, *Lisette* (New York: Lothrop, Lee & Shepard, 1962);

Tresselt, *Under the Trees and Through the Grass* (New York: Lothrop, Lee & Shepard, 1962);

Fatio, *Red Bantam* (New York: Whittlesey House, 1963);

Priscilla and Otto Friedrich, *The April Umbrella* (New York: Lothrop, Lee & Shepard, 1963);

Dean Frye, *The Lamb and the Child* (New York: McGraw-Hill, 1963);

Fatio, *The Happy Lion and the Bear* (New York: Whittlesey House, 1964);

Grete Janus Hertz, *Teddy* (New York: Lothrop, Lee & Shepard, 1964);

Zolotow, *The Poodle Who Barked at the Wind* (New York: Lothrop, Lee & Shepard, 1964);

Frye, *Days of Sunshine, Days of Rain* (New York: McGraw-Hill, 1965);

Holl, *The Rain Puddle* (New York: Lothrop, Lee & Shepard, 1965; London & Toronto: Bodley Head, 1965);

Tresselt, *Hide and Seek Fog* (New York: Lothrop, Lee & Shepard, 1965);

William Lipkind, *Nubber Bear* (New York: Harcourt, Brace & World, 1966; London: Faber, 1968);

Jean B. Showalter, *Around the Corner* (Garden City: Doubleday, 1966);

Fatio, *The Happy Lion's Vacation* (New York: McGraw-Hill, 1967); republished as *The Happy Lion's Holiday* (London: Bodley Head, 1968);

William Jay Smith, comp., *Poems From France* (New York: Lothrop, Lee & Shepard, 1967);

Tresselt, *The World in the Candy Egg* (New York: Lothrop, Lee & Shepard, 1967);

Berniece Freschet, *The Old Bullfrog* (New York: Scribners, 1968; London: Hamilton, 1968);

Holl, *The Remarkable Egg* (New York: Lothrop, Lee & Shepard, 1968);

Mona Dayton, *Earth and Sky* (New York: Harper & Row, 1969);

Tresselt, *It's Time Now!* (New York: Lothrop, Lee & Shepard, 1969);

Richard Shaw, comp., *The Owl Book* (New York: Warner, 1970);

Tresselt, *The Beaver Pond* (New York: Lothrop, Lee & Shepard, 1970);

Fatio, *The Happy Lion's Treasure* (New York: McGraw-Hill, 1971);

Freschet, *The Web in the Grass* (New York: Scribners, 1972);

Fatio, *Hector Penguin* (New York: McGraw-Hill, 1973);

Fatio, *The Happy Lion's Rabbits* (New York: McGraw-Hill, 1974);

Fatio, *Marc And Pixie, and the Walls in Mrs. Jones's Garden* (New York: McGraw-Hill, 1975);

Anne Duvoisin, *Heinz Hobnail And The Great Shoe Hunt* (New York: Abelard, 1976);

Mirra Ginsburg, *Which Is The Best Place?* (New York: Macmillan, 1976);

Pat Ross, *What Ever Happened to the Baxter Place?* (New York: Pantheon, 1976);

Fatio, *Hector And Christina* (New York: McGraw-Hill, 1977);

Brustein, as Janice, *Mr. And Mrs. Button's Wonderful Watchdogs* (New York: Lothrop, Lee & Shepard, 1978);

Tresselt, *What Did You Leave Behind?* (New York: Lothrop, Lee & Shepard, 1978);

Fatio, *The Happy Lioness* (New York: McGraw-Hill, 1980).

TRANSLATION: Aesopus, *Le Meunier, sons fils, et l'âne,* translated and illustrated by Duvoisin (New York: Whittlesey, 1962).

PERIODICAL PUBLICATIONS: "Caldecott Acceptance Paper–1947," *Horn Book,* 24 (July 1948): 392-303;

"Design in Children's Books," *Horn Book,* 37 (August 1961): 367-372;

"Children's Book Illustration: The Pleasures and Problems," *Top Of The News,* 22 (November 1965): 22-33.

For nearly half a century Roger Duvoisin has entertained children all over the world with his amusing stories and endearing animal personalities such as Petunia the silly goose, Veronica the friendly hippopotamus, Jasmine the independent cow, and Crocus the not-so-sure-of-himself crocodile. The Happy Lion, one of his more popular characters, resulted from a collaboration with his wife, Louise Fatio. Duvoisin illustrated the entire Happy Lion series, which contains ten titles beginning with *The Happy Lion,* published in 1954, and ending with *The Happy Lioness,* published in September 1980, soon after Duvoisin's death. Duvoisin also illustrated his wife's Red-Bantam series.

Between 1936 and 1980 Duvoisin wrote and illustrated more than forty children's books and illustrated over one hundred classics, textbooks, and children's books by scores of authors, receiving numerous honors and awards for his work. In 1948 his illustrations for Alvin R. Tresselt's *White Snow, Bright Snow* (1947), won the Caldecott Medal, and in 1966 another of their joint efforts, *Hide and Seek Fog* (1965), was named a Caldecott Honor Book. Duvoisin's books have frequently been selected for their excellence in design and manufacture and exhibited at the

Covers for four of Duvoisin's enduring animal stories (Knopf)

annual American Institute of Graphic Arts Book Show. His works have been included on the *New York Times* Best Illustrated Children's Book of the Year and the American Library Association's Notable Books listings.

Duvoisin has also received international recognition for his work. In 1956 he shared with his wife the first West German children's book award for *The Happy Lion* (translated into German in 1955), and in 1968 he was nominated for the Hans Christian Andersen Award. In addition, Duvoisin has been the recipient of the Rutgers Award for distinguished contribution to literature for children and young people, the University of Southern Mississippi Medallion for distinction in the children's book field, and the University of Minnesota's Irwin Kerlan Award in recognition of achievement in children's literature and in appreciation of generous donation of resources to the Kerlan Collection.

Roger Duvoisin was born of French-Swiss ancestry on 28 August 1904 in Geneva, Switzerland, to Jacques J. Duvoisin (an architect) and Judith More Duvoisin. As a young child, Duvoisin showed a keen interest in drawing and delighted in visiting the city zoo and the traveling circus where he could practice drawing animals. Duvoisin's early interest in reading also served as a wellspring from which he would later draw during his career as author and illustrator of children's books. As a child, Duvoisin read everything from classics to cheap comics, immersing himself in tales of the jungles and of the great wilderness of the American West. He recalls that it was one of his parents' worries that he spent so much time with his nose in books. They would frequently force him out of the house so he could go bicycling with his brother and sister in the Swiss countryside.

The books he read as a child were in French, his native tongue. He read many translated English and American classics, as well as the fables of La Fontaine, the fairy tales of the Grimm brothers, and Hans Christian Andersen. Duvoisin later reread many of the same works in English. When he came to America, Duvoisin would return home each evening to his Brooklyn apartment where he would improve his schoolboy English by reading Jack London's *Call of the Wild* with the help of a French-English dictionary.

Duvoisin received his art training in Geneva at the Ecole des Arts et Metiers and the Ecole des Beaux Arts, graduating in 1923 with a teaching diploma. After receiving his basic training in drawing and design, he pursued a variety of experiences that contributed to making him a well-rounded artist and designer, initiating his artistic career by painting murals and designing stage scenery for the Geneva Opera. He also free-lanced as an illustrator and poster designer. He became interested in ceramics and, in 1924, accepted a position as manager of a century-old pottery plant which Voltaire had founded in the little French town of Ferney-Voltaire. After managing the pottery plant for one year, Duvoisin moved on to Lyons and Paris where he worked as a designer of textiles. In Paris the art director for Mallison's Silk Company saw some of Duvoisin's designs and offered him a contract to go to New York, with all travel expenses paid, if he would consent to stay for four years. Duvoisin signed the contract and in 1927 sailed to America with his wife, Louise Fatio, whom he had married on 25 July 1925. In 1931, during the Depression, the silk firm failed; however, Duvoisin and his wife remained in New York, where he had already begun to free-lance advertising art and magazine illustration. He stayed well beyond his initial four-year commitment and became a naturalized citizen in 1938.

Like many of his colleagues Duvoisin did not plan to be a children's writer and illustrator. He discovered the pleasures of working with children's literature accidentally, when his four-year-old son, Roger, drew himself into a story of a little boy whose drawings came to life. When he had difficulty resolving the story, the elder Duvoisin came to his rescue and made what was to become his first book, *A Little Boy Was Drawing*. This book, published by Scribners in 1932, started Duvoisin in a field that was just becoming big business.

The following year Duvoisin's second book, *Donkey-Donkey, The Troubles of a Silly Little Donkey*, appeared in the original Whitman edition and sold at Woolworth for ten cents. The book sold well and was republished by Grosset and Dunlap in 1940 and again in 1967 by Parents' Press. With sly humor, Duvoisin tells of a donkey's desire to be what he is not. Discontented with the look of his ears, Donkey, donkey tries to hold them down like Hector the dog, straight out like Fuzzy-fuzzy the lamb and Fanny the cow, and in front like Rosa the pig. The donkey, of course, faces ridicule with each permutation and eventually comes to realize that being himself is best. What makes the story convincing is Duvoisin's ability to convey Donkey, donkey's frustration as he tries in vain to imitate his barnyard friends, and the book's success stems from Duvoisin's ability to create a vulnerable character with genuine feelings.

Donkey-Donkey was the first of many animal fables that Duvoisin created as a means of passing on to children his ideas and various bits of wisdom. Duvoisin chose the animal fable not only because he liked to draw animals but because animal fables have traditionally been used to symbolize man's quest to understand himself. On the Duvoisins' fifteen-acre New Jersey farm, which they purchased in 1939, they surrounded themselves with many of the wild and domestic animals that eventually turned up in their books. As is the case with many authors and illustrators, the Duvoisins' books became extensions of their lives. To them, animal fables seemed a natural way to express in stories and illustrations their philosophy of life. To Roger Duvoisin, every animal had its particular name and characteristics so it was easy to breathe life into the character. Creating such a vital character was not, however, without its problems. Duvoisin commented that when the animal becomes alive in the mind of its creator, it becomes a familiar pet, and it then becomes very tempting to make the animals live on in other tales. It was difficult for Duvoisin to let his animal characters "die."

In his 1948 Caldecott acceptance speech, Duvoisin talked about other concerns when creating books for children. He felt that one of the more difficult challenges of children's authors and illustrators is to present children with books that portray the world through a child's eyes rather than to create a child's world as seen through adult eyes. He felt that there were two ways of understanding and appreciating the child's viewpoint. One is through memory, the other through observations. You can either put yourself back into your childhood memories and attempt to recreate them, or you can obtain the child's point of view through observing children, telling them stories, or reading to them. He used both methods, since he felt that being in touch with children provided the necessary balance between what he wanted to give out of his own memories and what he knew children wanted and were interested in.

Besides maintaining a child's point of view, Duvoisin stressed the importance of combining quality illustrations with imaginative texts. He felt that unless a story is imaginative it will not compete in a child's estimation with comics. He cited an example from his own boyhood reading

experiences and the effect they had on him. He recalled that the classic struggle which takes place in many homes between children who try to smuggle in comic books and parents who try to focus their children's energy on more appropriate reading material was going on in his home between his father and his brother and himself. The literature that his father was trying unsuccessfully to weed out was the inexpensive, illustrated comic books that were available for two cents. He and his brother spent hours reading the Wild West tales of Texas Jack, not because they were well written or well illustrated but because they were imaginative.

Duvoisin received his first impression of the American West from these fanciful, over-romanticized stories. The impressions were lasting, and none of the lessons of history about America which he had in school ever completely stamped out his Texas Jack conception of America. This he attributed to the fact that most history is presented to children as a moribund thing, and Texas Jack, however poorly written, was alive. When he came to America a few years later, "it was not the land of Washington, Jefferson, and Lincoln" that he landed upon, but it was "the land of Texas Jack."

From this experience, Duvoisin surmised that if authors and illustrators are to compete successfully with comic books, they must create books that are imaginative and have a strong story line. This, he believed, was the strength of the comics. Good illustrations are secondary to a strong story line. He also believed that stories should be accurate, both in text and in illustrations. He formed his image of the Adirondacks when reading James Fenimore Cooper's works and was vaguely disappointed on his first visit to the Adirondacks when they did not measure up to the illustrations from the books. Duvoisin felt that the author or illustrator should guide the child while giving him what he liked and wanted and should fully satisfy the child's imagination without distorting his conception of the world about him.

Duvoisin's belief that even history could be presented in an imaginative way like fiction, while keeping an eye on the accuracy of the statements, led him to write and illustrate several story histories. *And There Was America*, published in 1938 (the same year he became a U.S. citizen), contains brief stories of the voyages and discoveries of the early explorers who touched America.

It is written in a lively, conversational style and is illustrated with several full-page color illustrations. Another book along the same line, *They Put Out to Sea, The Story of the Map*, was published in 1943. It tells the story of early men, showing who they were and why and how they added to the map of the world. The book, which contains numerous black-and-white line drawings as well as several double-page color illustrations, makes history come alive as full-blooded living characters strut through the pages. Both books attest to Duvoisin's belief that history can be exciting.

Throughout the 1930s and the 1940s Duvoisin wrote and illustrated several books, but he spent most of his time illustrating the works of other authors. His versatility as an artist gave him tremendous freedom in illustrating a variety of texts, and his talent in being able to unify text and illustrations is evident in much of his work. The works that he illustrated captured the spirit of the particular piece of literature while at the same time bearing his characteristic stamp as illustrator.

Many of the books Duvoisin illustrated were traditional literature based on folklore or classic literary works. The nature of this material allowed him the opportunity to lend his own interpretation to the material. Duvoisin illustrated his first literary classic, Robert Browning's *The Pied Piper of Hamlin*, in 1936. The illustrations and design of the book from the book jacket to the endpapers to the bordered double-paged spreads represent one of Duvoisin's better efforts. He effectively alternates stark black-and-white line drawings with pastel watercolor illustrations. His use of perspective in the line drawings creates a three-dimensional effect that draws the viewer into the picture. The overall result is striking.

In the same year Duvoisin created quite a stir with his nontraditional interpretation of the very traditional Mother Goose rhymes. The illustrations he created for William Rose Benét's compilation, *Mother Goose: A Comprehensive Collection of the Rhymes*, bore a distinctly Gallic flavor that virtually exploded with color. Printers and production people heralded the book, which contained 274 rhymes written in bold script, many having their own illustrations. Although criticized for being crowded and chaotic, the book sold well and was reissued in a new, more subdued edition in 1943. It still retained much of the spirit of the earlier edition even though it contained fewer rhymes, less color, and an entirely new set of drawings.

Duvoisin illustrated three books for the Limited Editions Club, two of them by Robert Louis Stevenson. In 1944 he illustrated *A Child's Garden of Verses* with black-and-white line drawings. The full-page illustration that Duvoisin drew to accompany "The Land of Nod" provides a glimpse of some of the characters who later made their appearance in Duvoisin's animal fables.

In April 1955 Duvoisin was commissioned to illustrate Stevenson's *Travels With a Donkey* (1957). Duvoisin had a special affection for that story since it was the first book he read in English while he was still in school. He used his dilapidated text as a guidebook when he reenacted Stevenson's journey through the Cevennes, using pencil sketches and color slides from that journey to draw the lithographs for the illustrations. Color was added to the lithographs by hand, and the result truly reflects Duvoisin's artistic talent.

During this time Duvoisin continued to do advertising and editorial illustration, magazine covers, display design, and murals. His commercial work bore the same indelible mark of his personality that was evident in the books he created. The covers he drew for the *New Yorker*, beginning in 1935, represented a departure from the usual stylized cartoon which had become rather commonplace. His posterlike covers made powerful visual statements. Of the serious covers done during this time, most were by Duvoisin.

One of his more famous ads that he produced during the mid 1940s was a spoof of perfume names that he created for the Lord & Taylor department store. The ad, which appeared in the 23 December 1945 Sunday edition of the *New York Herald Tribune*, successfully combined his droll sense of humor with his favorite animal characters.

By the late 1940s Duvoisin gradually gave up other work and began to concentrate on illustrating picture books. His most important works during this time are the nature books he did in collaboration with Alvin R. Tresselt for Lothrop. The first, *White Snow, Bright Snow*, won him the Caldecott Medal in 1948. In rhythmic prose, Tresselt describes the activities surrounding an unexpected snowfall. The children greet it with feelings quite different from those of the postman, the farmer, the policeman, and the policeman's wife. But just as quietly as the snow comes, it departs, leaving behind the first signs of Spring. Duvoisin, using a limited red, yellow, black, and white color scheme, skillfully recreated these reac-

Dust jacket for Alvin R. Tresselt's 1947 story about the various activities surrounding an unexpected snowfall (Lothrop, Lee & Shepard). Illustrated by Duvoisin, the book was awarded the 1948 Caldecott Medal.

tions and events. As the snow gradually accumulates, the visual images darken, until only the red and yellow light from the windows of the house glow at nightfall. When the snowstorm ends and morning dawns, the viewer is presented with a full-page spread of bright, blinding snow. Duvoisin's expressionistic style captured the excitement of the season.

Duvoisin and Tresselt shared a mutual love of nature. This led them to collaborate on eighteen nature and science books over a thirty-one-year period. One of their best efforts, *Hide and Seek Fog* (1965), was named a Caldecott Honor Book in 1966. Using a combination of poetry and prose, Tresselt describes a fog which rolls in from the sea to veil an Atlantic seacoast village for three days. Duvoisin's pastel watercolor paintings done in expressionistic style beautifully portray the mysterious feel of this natural phenomena. The illustrations for *Hide and Seek Fog* represent a departure from Duvoisin's usual style and are a tribute to his versatility as an artist.

Holiday stories, especially Christmas stories, were another favorite of Duvoisin's. Whether creating his own stories or illustrating the stories of other authors, Duvoisin's approach was fresh and playful. In his illustrations for Clement Clarke

Moore's famous poem, *The Night Before Christmas*, published in 1954 (the same year as *The Happy Lion*), Duvoisin drew the Happy Lion peering out of a Christmas stocking hung on the mantel.

The Christmas Whale, published in 1945, offers a delightful twist to Moore's familiar poem. With Christmas only one week away, all of Santa's reindeer come down with the flu. All of the other animals want to help, but they just aren't big or strong enough. At last a codfish suggests the Kindly Whale, who graciously agrees to carry the presents on his back. In record time the Kindly Whale and Santa Claus deliver all the gifts to New York, South America, Africa, Europe, and Australia. Working in black, white, and red, Duvoisin illustrated a charming story that has lasting appeal and is still in print over forty years later. In *One Thousand Christmas Beards*, published in 1955, Duvoisin explained why there are so many Santas around at Christmas. A clue to revealing the impostors appears on the wraparound jacket design.

In the early 1950s Duvoisin began to concentrate more on his own picture books, bringing to them a strong sense of design. He believed that a book that is done with taste and good craftsmanship is more pleasant to look at and can educate a child visually. He liked to plan his books from cover to cover, specifying the type, the margins, the binding, and the placement of the illustrations. He would make a complete dummy for each book with the type pasted in place and the pictures sketched in.

A For The Ark (1952), an alphabet book woven around the Old Testament story of the Flood, is considered one of his most outstanding picture books in terms of graphic design. In the book, when God commands Noah to take two of every kind of animal into the Ark, Noah goes straight through the alphabet to be sure to include them all. Every other double-page spread of this picture alphabet book is in full color, the lower half of each page being a continuous picture frieze while the upper part carries the bold, simple text and elegant capital letters in alternate shades of blue and coral red. Each page is well designed with a sense of balance that comfortably carries the eye and readily invites the turning of the page. The drama of the story builds simultaneously in the witty text and in the illustrations, as the gathering clouds grow bigger and blacker on every page, and Noah's perplexity increases as he nears the end of the alphabet.

Duvoisin's work in textile design no doubt

Dust jacket for Duvoisin's 1952 alphabet book based on the Old Testament story of the Flood (Lothrop, Lee & Shepard)

contributed to his highly developed sense of color. His ability to work with limited colors was exceptional. In the 1940s, when Duvoisin began writing and illustrating picture books, production costs were high, and illustrators were obliged to become more skilled in the utilization of small amounts of color. Duvoisin became an expert in the planning of limited color pictures and the execution of the necessary color separations. The process involved the selection of two, three, or more colors which were lively and harmonious in themselves and which would produce interesting intermediate colors by overprinting. Working entirely in black-and-white values, the illustrator had to visualize the final printed result in color. Even the experienced illustrator could never be completely sure of the final results since the slightest aberration on the part of the engraver or printer could sabotage the most carefully planned combination.

Duvoisin's fascination with color led him to create two children's books about color. In *The House of Four Seasons* (1956), two children help their parents paint their house, a task which gives Duvoisin the opportunity to present a creative lesson on how to mix colors. Duvoisin actually demonstrated the color separation process in *See What I Am* (1974). Using a story format and bright, collage pictures, Duvoisin tells how Max

the kitten learns about the primary and secondary colors and their relationships, using examples from the world around him. For this book Duvoisin won the New York Academy of Science Children's Science Book Award in 1974.

In addition to having a well-developed sense of color and design, Duvoisin had a special talent for drawing humor into his illustrations. Not a forced, exaggerated, or superficial humor, but humor that is gained through the slightest touches: the delineation of an eye or eyebrow, the tilt of the head, or the stance of the body. His humor appears in people as well as in animals, expressing the way they feel. The most memorable of his humorous stories center on the animals from the Pumpkin and Sweetpeas' farms. *Petunia*, published in 1950, began a series of seven adventures of the very silly goose. The story begins when Petunia finds a book and carries it around believing that it alone will make her wise, though her own foolishness soon proves her wrong.

The theme of *Petunia Takes a Trip* (1953) is a variation of the age-old fable of the country mouse and the city mouse. Duvoisin illustrates the contrast between the simple life in the small family farm community of the country and the inhumanity of the overcrowded city. In *Petunia's Treasure* (1975), Petunia finds a treasure chest and thinks she is rich and important. Her barn-yard friends are eager to share her fortune, but she soon learns about all the worries wealth can bring and what it can do to friendships.

Not all of the Petunia books have a message; some merely entertain. *Petunia's Christmas* (1952) features a series of thrilling adventures wherein Petunia rescues Charlie, a handsome gander, just before he becomes someone's Christmas dinner. All ends happily as Petunia and Charles are wed. Duvoisin uses bold line drawings and a minimum of color to create the humorous illustrations for this series of stories. Even though the seven Petunia books span a twenty-five-year period, Duvoisin remains faithful to the original style of illustrations.

Veronica, the friendly hippopotamus, began her literary life in 1961 and continued to entertain readers until 1971, when she made her last appearance. Veronica, a rugged individualist, longs to be different. She leaves the herd when no one is looking and walks until she reaches the city. There she is not just different but gloriously conspicuous, so conspicuous that she ends up in jail. After her misadventures in the city, Veronica returns to the herd with a newly established sense of her identity. The simple, humorous illustrations of the five Veronica books are similar in style to those Duvoisin created for the Petunia series.

By the time he began what was to become his last series of animal fables, Duvoisin had begun working with a new medium. The first book in that series, *The Crocodile in the Tree*, was published in 1972. Duvoisin used collage pictures in jewel-like colors to show that it is often the discovery of mutual tastes and desires between people which destroys suspicion and fear and replaces them with confidence and friendship. Each page is well designed and makes full use of the double-page spreads. The friendly crocodile appears again in 1977 in a book simply titled *Crocus*. This book is especially well designed from the wraparound book jacket to the double-page spread of Crocus stretched out full length under a tree. The lesson that everyone needs some attribute in order to feel important is a bit tarnished as Crocus's prized possession is his set of intimidating teeth. Duvoisin's last book, *The Importance of Crocus*, was published just prior to his death in June of 1980. The message that everyone has a quality that is unique and the bright, colorful collage illustrations are vintage Duvoisin.

Dust jacket for the first installment in the Happy Lion series (Whittlesey House, 1954). Illustrated by Duvoisin and written by his wife, Louise Fatio, the series eventually included ten titles.

When Duvoisin first made the transition from his characteristic bold, line drawings to collage pictures in the late 1960s, his illustrations were attractive, but lifeless. He tried working solely with collages, using no line. Gradually he added line to the collages, and, after several tries, he succeeded in achieving a good balance between his bold, expressive line drawings and his more static, collage pictures. By the time he illustrated the Crocus books, he had achieved that balance.

The longest series that Duvoisin illustrated was done in collaboration with his wife, Louise Fatio. The husband-wife team produced ten Happy Lion titles over a twenty-six-year period. The first book in that series, *The Happy Lion*, was published in 1954. It was inspired by a true story that Fatio had read in a French newspaper. A friendly, well-fed lion had escaped from a circus which had set up its tent in a small French town. People screamed and ran off in all directions when they saw the good lion stroll through their streets. The lion was saved when the circus owner brought him back to the circus. Duvoisin, working in his characteristic style, created an unforgettable character. With the utmost simplicity, Duvoisin showed the bewilderment of the poor lion as he walked peacefully through the streets of the town.

Duvoisin used the same style throughout the first eight books. Then in 1974 he illustrated *The Happy Lion's Rabbits* with colorful, collage pictures. He used line sparingly, and the effect was less satisfying than his earlier style. The illustrations are more static and lack the warmth and humor that can be achieved with line. However, by the time he illustrated the last book in that series, *The Happy Lioness*, he had achieved a better balance between line and collage. Unfortunately, Duvoisin did not live to see the publication of that book. He died of a heart attack on 30 June 1980, three months before the book was published.

The success of Duvoisin's books can be attributed to more than his technical expertise in drawing and design. The qualities that give his stories their lasting appeal are the warm, human spirit and droll sense of humor that permeate his books and give them an old-fashioned charm that is timeless. His books bear the imprint of his personality.

References:

Barbara Bader, *American Picturebooks From Noah's Ark To The Beast Within* (New York: Macmillan, 1976), pp. 128-139;

Ruth E. Kane, "Roger Duvoisin–Distinguished Contributor to the World of Children's Literature," *Elementary English*, 33 (November 1956): 411-419;

Henry C. Pitz, "Roger Duvoisin," *American Artist*, 13 (December 1949): 44-47, 76;

Nora S. Unwin, "Artist's Choice," *Horn Book*, 35 (April 1959): 110-111;

Dorothy Waugh, "Roger Duvoisin as Illustrator for Children," *Horn Book*, 24 (January-February 1948): 11-22.

Papers:

Manuscripts and illustrations for many of Duvoisin's books are in the Kerlan Collection, University of Minnesota, Minneapolis; the Rutgers University Library, New Brunswick, New Jersey; and the de Grummond Collection, University of Southern Mississippi, Hattiesburg.

Norma Farber

(6 August 1909-21 March 1984)

Norma Bagnall
Missouri Western State College

BOOKS: *The Hatch,* in *Poets of Today II,* edited by John Hall Wheelock (New York: Scribners, 1955);

Look to the Rose (Boston: Fandel, 1958);

Did You Know It Was the Narwhale?, illustrated by Carole Vizbara (New York: Atheneum, 1967);

A Desperate Thing: Marriage Is a Desperate Thing (Boston: Plowshare Press, 1973);

I Found Them in the Yellow Pages, illustrated by Marc Brown (Boston: Little, Brown, 1973);

Where's Gomer?, illustrated by William Pène du Bois (New York: Dutton, 1974);

As I Was Crossing Boston Common, illustrated by Arnold Lobel (New York: Dutton, 1975);

Household Poems (Jamaica Plain, Mass.: Hellric, 1975);

This Is the Ambulance Leaving the Zoo, illustrated by Tomie dePaola (New York: Dutton, 1975);

A Ship in a Storm on the Way to Tarshish, illustrated by Victoria Chess (New York: Greenwillow, 1977);

Six Impossible Things Before Breakfast, illustrated by dePaola, Charles Mikolaycak, Friso Hentra, Trina Schart Hyman, Lydia Dabcovich, and Hilary Knight (Reading, Mass.: Addison-Wesley, 1977);

How the Left-Behind Beasts Built Ararat, illustrated by Antonio Frasconi (New York: Walker, 1978);

There Once Was a Woman Who Married a Man, illustrated by Dabcovich (Reading, Mass.: Addison-Wesley, 1978);

Three Wanderers from Wapping, illustrated by Mikolaycak (Reading, Mass.: Addison-Wesley, 1978);

How Does It Feel to be Old?, illustrated by Hyman (New York: Dutton, 1979);

Never Say Ugh to a Bug, illustrated by José Aruego (New York: Greenwillow, 1979);

Small Wonders, illustrated by Kazue Mizumura (New York: Coward-McCann & Geoghegan, 1979);

Something Further . . . (Ann Arbor, Mich.: Kylix, 1979);

Norma Farber (photo by Jamie Cope)

There Goes Feathertop!, illustrated by Brown (New York: Dutton, 1979);

Up the Down Elevator, illustrated by Annie Gusman (N.p., 1979);

How the Hibernators Came to Bethlehem, illustrated by Barbara Cooney (New York: Walker, 1980);

A Night on Gars Mountain, illustrated by Allen Atkinson (Boston: Houghton Mifflin, 1981);

Mercy Short: A Winter Journal, North Boston, 1692-93 (New York: Dutton, 1982);

How to Ride a Tiger, illustrated by Claire Schumacher (Boston: Houghton Mifflin, 1983);

All Those Mothers at the Manger, illustrated by Megan Lloyd (New York: Harper, 1985).

PLAY PRODUCTION: *Mary Chesnut's Diary*, Cambridge, Mass., M.I.T. Little Theater, 21 November 1961.

TRANSLATION: Pedro Salinas, *To Live in Pronouns: Selected Love Poems*, translated by Farber with Edith Helman (New York: Norton, 1974).

Norma Farber was a poet steeped in both New England and Old World tradition. Born in Boston, Massachusetts, on 6 August 1909 to G. Augustus and Augusta Schon Holzman, Farber began writing poetry in grammar school. She was educated at the Girls' Latin School in Boston where she was the class poet and matriculated at Wellesley College. On 3 July 1928, at age eighteen, she married recent Harvard Medical School graduate Sidney Farber. She finished her undergraduate work at Wellesley in 1931 and took a master's degree in comparative literature at Radcliffe in 1932; she also studied with poet Robert Hillyer of Harvard. She had four children: Ellen, Stephen, Thomas, and Miriam.

As a child, Farber was encouraged to develop her natural talents, and as an adult she continually strove to increase her artistic awareness and range. Trained as a concert singer, she performed in the United States and abroad, receiving a "premier prix" in singing from Jury Central des Etudes Musicales in Belgium in 1936. Though best known as a poet, Farber was also an actress, a playwright, and a novelist.

Early in their marriage, the Farbers lived in Europe, where Dr. Farber was working and doing research in pathology. Norma continued her studies and her writing as the two of them lived in Belgium, Germany, and Switzerland. She began publishing her poetry in periodicals in the 1950s and was encouraged by noted poets John Holmes and John Hall Wheelock, among others. Her first published book, *The Hatch* (1955), is part of the Scribners Poets of Today series. *Poets of Today II*, edited by Wheelock, presents fifty-six of Farber's poems (*The Hatch*) with those of two other poets, Robert Pack and Louis Simpson, in one volume. *The Hatch* anticipates Farber's subsequent poetry in that it covers a vast range of experiences and explores the topics—children, the creation, the nativity, the crucifixion—that she would treat repeatedly in future writings though she always managed to present them in a fresh way.

"The Night Before America," which appeared in the *Christian Science Monitor* (12 October 1956), is a long narrative poem about Columbus's voyage which was praised by John Holmes and further honored by being placed in the Congressional Record in August 1957. This was followed by Farber's second book, *Look to the Rose* (1958), another collection of adult poetry, published in chapbook form.

Did You Know It Was the Narwhale? (1967) was Farber's first book for children; it treats two of her favorite themes, the Great Flood and the survival of the outcast. In this poetry book Farber gives credit to the unicorn for rounding up the creatures which were to be saved from the Flood. In a tragic moment the unicorn realizes he cannot come aboard, for he has no mate. He is saved, however, through a grand transformation.

Farber's next published book was for an adult audience. *A Desperate Thing: Marriage Is a Desperate Thing*, published in 1973 after the death of Farber's husband, is a gathering together of her marriage poems, which had appeared in over twenty magazines. The poems celebrate life generally and marriage in particular—its joys, its importance, its small and large tragedies, providing a chronicle of Farber's marriage from the time she was a very young bride, through the tumultuous years of child rearing, to the mature woman she had become, faced with the death of her beloved partner. Alicia Ostriker, writing for *Parnassus: Poetry in Review* (Fall-Winter 1974), said about Farber's writing in *A Desperate Thing*, "Since Yeats, I cannot recall any poet who has dealt quite so directly with old age and the prospect of death."

Household Poems (1975), also for an adult audience, is a chapbook that praises domesticity. Norma took very seriously her role as wife and mother; she felt that by putting all her careers into perspective she elevated what others might see as mundane into its rightful importance.

I Found Them in the Yellow Pages (1973), Farber's second children's book, is a lighthearted yet close look at the occupations found in the telephone directory of a large city. An alphabet book in verse, it emphasizes Farber's fascination with the unusual found in very ordinary places. *Where's Gomer?* (1974) is another telling of Noah and the Flood. The Ark is ready to sail, but Noah's young grandson is not to be found, and

Dust jacket for Farber's 1974 story in which Noah's grandson, Gomer, misses the Ark and must survive the Flood through his own ingenuity and perseverance (Dutton)

the Ark must set off without him. Like the narwhale in Farber's earlier book, Gomer can survive only through his own ingenuity and perseverance.

An unusual bestiary, *As I Was Crossing Boston Common* (1975), earned the Children's Book Showcase Award and was nominated for the prestigious National Book Award in children's books. The book's narrator, a turtle, leads readers through the famous Boston park, encountering rare animals in a parade through the alphabet. Farber includes a pronunciation guide and definitions in the book, necessary for the unusual creatures like *"Quirquincho* (kir-keén-choh), a small, hairy armadillo of South America"–but even this careful guide and list of definitions did not prevent artist Arnold Lobel (who illustrated the volume) from calling Farber (they had never met) and saying, "Norma, this is Arnold, and I don't know what a galliwasp looks like."

This Is the Ambulance Leaving the Zoo (1975) is another of Farber's unique alphabet books; it tells a logical story in alphabetical sequence, and

then it takes the reader back through the alphabet to repeat the story in reverse in a charming closing. Farber explained part of her penchant for alphabet stories this way: "Some while ago I fell in love with the English language. Making alphabet stories is my way of writing love letters."

The story of Noah is only one of the biblical themes Farber used as inspiration for poetry and children's stories. *A Ship in a Storm on the Way to Tarshish* (1977) is a rich and unusual retelling of the Old Testament tale of Jonah and the whale. Farber learned through her extensive reading that an infant whale keeps in contact with its mother by nudging her, and she envisions Jonah's whale as being but a calf looking for its mother as it nudges poor Jonah's ship.

Farber's first prose work .for children was "Flyaway Dough," one of the six offerings included in *Six Impossible Things Before Breakfast* (1977). The title of the book alludes to Lewis Carroll's queen, who "sometimes believed as many as six impossible things before breakfast." Her next children's book, *How the Left-Behind Beasts Built Ararat* (1978; first published in the

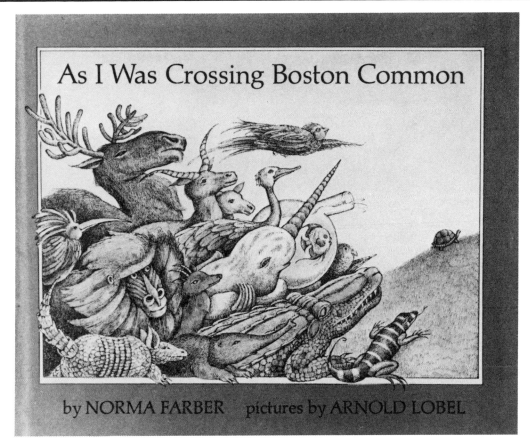

Dust jacket for Farber's 1975 bestiary which earned the Children's Book Showcase Award and was nominated for a National Book Award (Dutton)

Christian Science Monitor, 1966), is a newly created legend that tells how a cow led the dampened animals left by Noah into action, action that saved their lives and made for a welcoming committee for Noah at Ararat.

Farber's humor and her sense of rollicking verse is nowhere more apparent than in *There Once Was a Woman Who Married a Man* (1978). Her idea sprang from an article she had read about a man cured of muteness following a ride on a Coney Island roller coaster. In Farber's story her heroine pleads, threatens, wheedles, and connives to get her husband to talk to her, and she gets results in an astonishing way. As in the story Farber had read, the man recovered his speech following a roller coaster ride, but she has added an impish twist that makes the telling hilarious.

Farber's seriousness as an artist is evident in *Three Wanderers from Wapping*, also published in 1978. A prose narrative of the plague year in London, *Three Wanderers from Wapping* is an elaboration of an idea of Daniel Defoe's in his *Journal of the Plague Year*. It is a somber topic for children,

treated with the respect and sobriety it deserves in Farber's tale. The story is of three young men who leave the suburb of Wapping and take to the countryside where the air, they believe, will be purer and give them a better chance of surviving the dreaded plague. The terror and the restrictions they encounter are faithfully set down so that the reader feels drawn back to the seventeenth century and its time of despair.

How Does It Feel to be Old? (1979), a beautifully moving response in verse to a beloved granddaughter's question, is at once lighthearted, warm, and serious. Its fresh perspective is welcome and different from other recent children's books about the elderly in that it is told from the point of view of the grandmother–a grandmother who is vibrant and appreciative of all life's experiences, one who can respond with humor, empathy, and love without ever regressing to the trite and sentimental. By seriously exploring her own feelings Farber adds dignity and depth to this experience–a remembering of the past with clarity and comprehension, a look at the present with concern and compassion, and a facing of the future with confidence and capability. It is Farber at her best because she invested so much of herself into it.

Never Say Ugh to a Bug (1979) is a collection of twenty poems, several of which appeared in earlier periodical publications. Each is about a bug–bugs that are rarely celebrated. The grub, the snail, and Farber's own special left-winged cricket are all honored here. *Small Wonders* (1979) is also a celebration of small things. Twenty-six poems, each praising a tiny thing–a walnut, ants, the noise of nothing–constitute this collection.

Something Further . . . (1979) is a collection of poems for an adult audience; the title comes from the last line in Herman Melville's *The Confidence Man*–"Something further may follow of this masquerade." About this collection Melvin Maddocks (columnist for the *Christian Science Monitor* and *Time*) said, "Norma Farber takes an extraordinary variety of subjects . . . to their outer limits, and then a little beyond . . . making us look until it hurts." Like *How Does It Feel to be Old?*, this again is Norma Farber at her very best; this time her best is at a different level and in a different direction from the other work.

From Herman Melville, Norma went to Nathaniel Hawthorne for her next story–this one for children. *There Goes Feathertop!* (1979) is taken from a story by Hawthorne and is set in rhyme and rhythm. Feathertop, a scarecrow, is transformed by Mother Rigby into a fine and handsome fellow with clothing and a wig she provides, and he charms the ladies until he glimpses himself as he really is. Heartbroken because he is a sham, he asks to be made back into a scarecrow where he can take joy in being himself.

With *Up the Down Elevator* (1979), Farber published her first counting rhymes. The book portrays a motley assortment of characters who get into an elevator in a modern apartment building and ride together–more crowded at each stop–to the tenth floor.

How the Hibernators Came to Bethlehem (1980) is about the holy birth–a subject Norma wrote of repeatedly in poetry for both adults and children–and of animals never included in the Nativity scene. Her explanation of how the sleeping animals got the word and made the journey is both believable and charming. Writing of the birth, Farber said, permitted her to replay the incidents–the birth of her own children–most important in her own life.

Dust jacket for Farber's 1979 adaptation of a story by Nathaniel Hawthorne (Dutton)

A Night on Gars Mountain (1981), for children, is a prose narrative set in Switzerland. Children, going to visit their grandparents over the mountain on Christmas Eve, are trapped when a sudden snowstorm causes them to become confused and lose their way. The story has the charm and feeling of a folktale, and it is a moving account of courage and self-reliance.

In addition to the books discussed Farber published her poetry in a wide assortment of prestigious journals. More than a thousand of her poems have been published since they first began appearing in the 1950s. The *Christian Science Monitor* published her work frequently and regularly; her poetry also appeared in *Cricket, Horn Book*, the *New Yorker, Poetry Northwest, Saturday Review*, and *Yankee*, among others. The reason for her prolific outpouring is summed up in an essay, "How do you *not* write poetry?," in the *Christian Science Monitor* (23 July 1976). Farber insisted that a poet cannot *not* make poems, and in taking the reader through a mythical morning in her life, she shows that the poem will *out* no matter how much she procrastinates. Her essays, which have

Dust jacket for Farber's 1980 story about a group of animals who travel to Bethlehem to celebrate the holy birth (Walker)

appeared in *Horn Book*, the *Christian Science Monitor*, and *Word Guide*, are not so numerous as her poems and concern themselves with the poet as musician, with poetry as second language for children, and with the joy of putting poetry into works for children.

Shortly before her death, some of Farber's poetry was set to music by two Boston composers, Daniel Pinkham and Leo Snyder, with several of her poems in solo and choral settings. *Love Can Be Still: Music on Verses of Norma Farber (Song Cycles by Daniel Pinkham and Leo Snyder)* was produced in 1981 by Northeastern Records of Boston's Northeastern University. Pinkham had worked with Farber's material earlier; "Tell Me About the Mother of Judas" is part of his *The Passion of Judas* presented at King's Chapel, Boston, 20 June 1976, and two of her poems–"Tree of Blame" and "While Eve"–are prominent in his *Garden Party*, which had its world premiere for the Handel and Haydn Society on 25 March 1977 in Jordan Hall in Boston.

The early 1980s appeared to be the beginning of another exciting career for Farber, who had been engrossed with the writing of her first adult novel for a good part of 1980 and well into 1981. *Mercy Short: A Winter Journal, North Boston, 1692-93* (1982) is set in Boston and Salem and involves, among other things, the Salem witch trials. It is the fictional journal of an actual young woman, Mercy Short. Prominently featured is Cotton Mather, who claimed to have cured Mercy of bedevilment by means of fasting and prayer; the tension Farber created between this man of religion and the innocent Mercy is strong evidence of her skill as a writer and of her clear observance of human nature. Farber researched her subject well. She became so involved with the characters she had created that she had firm ideas about a sequel while she was in the throes of typing her final version of the novel.

The sequel, however, never appeared. Farber suffered a stroke in late 1983 and never recovered. Her *How to Ride a Tiger* (1983) was published soon after she became ill. Illustrated by Claire Schumacher, the book is about an intrepid young backpacking heroine who follows the advice of the narrator in order to help a tiger down from his high perch in a tree. The heroine is rewarded for her courage and perseverance by getting to ride the tiger through the jungle.

The most recent book by Norma Farber is *All Those Mothers at the Manger* (1985), a picture-book retelling of the birth of Christ illustrated in full color by Megan Lloyd. The poem which is the basis for this work was published in the December 1979 issue of *Cricket*. How many more of Farber's poems that may eventually become books for children remain to be seen. There is a wealth of her poetry amenable to such transformation. Some of it has been published in *Cricket*, the *Christian Science Monitor, Horn Book*, and other places; some is unpublished. Poetry commanded her attention at all times so that whatever she did, wherever she went, Farber was viewing the world as a poet.

Her later years, spent in a high rise overlooking the Charles River and much of Cambridge, were highly prolific. Although writing was her major work, she interacted with the literary community of Boston and gave support to the Center for the Study of Children's Literature at Simmons College. She was a frequent lecturer and reader at the center's programs, and she chaired their development committee from 1982 until her death. Her view from high above Cambridge gave her new visions of the world; a mottled leaf, sun and mist on the river, or the way shadows took on a life of their own in highway traffic intrigued her. Through her careful observance and skillful writing, she provided a new way of looking at these things through her poetry.

Papers:

Manuscript materials for *Mercy Short: A Winter Journal, North Boston, 1692-93*, as well as for a number of Farber's other titles, are part of the Kerlan Collection, Children's Literature Research Collection, University of Minnesota, Minneapolis.

Leonard Everett Fisher

(24 June 1924-   )

O. Mell Busbin

Appalachian State University

BOOKS: *Pumpers, Boilers, Hooks and Ladders; a Book of Fire Engines* (New York: Dial, 1961);

Pushers, Spads, Jennies, and Jets; a Book of Airplanes (New York: Dial, 1961);

A Head Full of Hats (New York: Dial, 1962);

But Not Our Daddy, by Fisher and Margery M. Fisher (New York: Dial, 1962);

One and One, by Fisher and Margery M. Fisher (New York: Dial, 1963);

The Glassmakers (New York: Watts, 1964);

The Silversmiths (New York: Watts, 1964);

The Hatters (New York: Watts, 1965);

The Papermakers (New York: Watts, 1965);

The Printers (New York: Watts, 1965);

The Wigmakers (New York: Watts, 1965);

The Cabinetmakers (New York: Watts, 1966);

The Tanners (New York: Watts, 1966);

The Weavers (New York: Watts, 1966);

The Schoolmasters (New York: Watts, 1967);

The Shoemakers (New York: Watts, 1967);

The Doctors (New York: Watts, 1968);

The Peddlers (New York: Watts, 1968);

The Limners: America's Earliest Portrait Painters (New York: Watts, 1969);

The Potters (New York: Watts, 1969);

The Architects (New York: Watts, 1970);

Picture Book of Revolutionary War Heroes (Harrisburg, Pa.: Stackpole Books, 1970);

Two if by Sea (New York: Random House, 1970);

The Shipbuilders (New York: Watts, 1971);

The Death of Evening Star; the Diary of a Young New England Whaler (Garden City: Doubleday, 1972);

The Art Experience: Oil Painting 15th-19th Centuries (New York: Watts, 1973);

The Homemakers (New York: Watts, 1973);

The Warlock of Westfall (Garden City: Doubleday, 1974);

Across the Sea from Galway (New York: Scholastic, 1975);

Sweeney's Ghost (Garden City: Doubleday, 1975);

The Blacksmiths (New York: Watts, 1976);

Leonard Everett Fisher's Liberty Book (Garden City: Doubleday, 1976);

Letters from Italy (New York: Four Winds Press, 1977);

Alphabet Art: Thirteen ABCs from Around the World (New York: Four Winds Press, 1978);

Noonan: A Novel about Baseball, ESP, and Time Warps (Garden City: Doubleday, 1978);

The Factories (New York: Holiday House, 1979);

The Railroads (New York: Holiday House, 1979);

The Hospitals (New York: Holiday House, 1980);

A Russian Farewell (New York: Four Winds Press, 1980);

The Sports (New York: Holiday House, 1980);

The Newspapers (New York: Holiday House, 1981);

The Seven Days of Creation; Adapted from the Bible (New York: Holiday House, 1981);

Storm at the Jetty (New York: Viking, 1981);

Number Art: Thirteen 1 2 3s from Around the World (New York: Four Winds Press, 1982);

The Unions (New York: Holiday House, 1982);

The Schools (New York: Holiday House, 1983);

Star Signs (New York: Holiday House, 1983);

Boxes! Boxes! (New York: Viking, 1984);

The Olympians: Great Gods and Goddesses of Ancient Greece (New York: Holiday House, 1984);

The Statue of Liberty (New York: Holiday House, 1985);

Symbol Art: Thirteen Squares, Circles & Triangles from Around the World (New York: Four Winds Press, 1985);

Ellis Island: Gateway to the New World (New York: Holiday House, 1986);

Great Wall of China (New York: Macmillan, 1986);

Calendar Art: Thirteen Days, Weeks, Months, Years from Around the World (New York: Four Winds Press, 1987).

SELECTED BOOKS ILLUSTRATED: Trevor Nevitt Dupuy, *The Military History of Civil War Land Battles* (New York: Watts, 1960);

James Playsted Wood, *The Queen's Most Honorable Pirate* (New York: Harper, 1961);

Jean Lee Latham, *Man of the Monitor* (New York: Harper, 1962);

Henry Wadsworth Longfellow, *The First Book Edition of Paul Revere's Ride* (New York: Watts, 1963);

Anico Surany, *The Golden Frog* (New York: Putnam's, 1963);

Ernest Lawrence Thayer, *The First Book Edition of Casey at Bat* (New York: Watts, 1964);

E. Brooks Smith, *The Coming of Pilgrims* (Boston: Little, Brown, 1964);

Lois Perry Jones, *The First Book of the White House* (New York: Watts, 1965);

Martha Shapp, *Let's Find Out About John Fitzgerald Kennedy* (New York: Watts, 1965);

Florence Stevenson, *The Story of Aida* (New York: Putnam's, 1965);

Surany, *The Burning Mountain* (New York: Holiday House, 1965);

Washington Irving, *The Legend of Sleepy Hollow* (New York: Watts, 1966);

Clifford Lindsey Alderman, *The Story of Thirteen Colonies* (New York: Random House, 1966);

Irving, *Rip Van Winkle* (New York: Watts, 1966);

Robert Carl Suggs, *The Archaeology of New York* (New York: Crowell, 1966);

Surany, *Kati and Kormos* (New York: Holiday House, 1966);

Madeleine L'Engle, *The Journey with Jonah* (New York: Farrar, Straus & Giroux, 1967);

L. Sprague DeCamp, *The Story of Science in America* (New York: Scribners, 1967);

Surany, *Monsieur Jolicoeur's Umbrella* (New York: Putnam's, 1967);

Surany, *The Covered Bridge* (New York: Holiday House, 1967);

Bernard Shaw, *The Devil's Disciple* (New York: Watts, 1967);

Nathaniel Hawthorne, *The Great Stone Face & Two Other Stories* (New York: Watts, 1967);

Bret Harte, *The Luck of Roaring Camp* (New York: Watts, 1968);

Richard Brandon Morris, *The First Book of the Founding of the Republic* (New York: Watts, 1968);

Surany, *Malachy's Gold* (New York: Holiday House, 1968);

Gerald White Johnson, *The British Empire* (New York: Morrow, 1969);

Julian May, *Why the Earth Quakes* (New York: Holiday House, 1969);

Robert Meredith, *Exploring the Great River* (Boston: Little, Brown, 1969);

Surany, *Lora, Lorita* (New York: Putnam's, 1969);

Bernice Robinson Morris, *American Popular Music: The Beginning Years* (New York: Watts, 1970);

May, *The Land Beneath the Sea* (New York: Holiday House, 1971);

Isaac Bashevis Singer, *The Wicked City* (New York: Farrar, Straus & Giroux, 1972);

Milton Meltzer, *All Times, All Peoples* (New York: Harper & Row, 1980);

Myra Cohn Livingston, *A Circle of Seasons* (New York: Holiday House, 1982);

Livingston, *Sky Songs* (New York: Holiday House, 1984);

Livingston, *Celebrations* (New York: Holiday House, 1985);

Richard B. Morris, *The American Revolution* (Minneapolis: Lerner, 1985);

Morris, *The Constitution* (Minneapolis: Lerner, 1985);

Morris, *The War of 1812* (Minneapolis: Lerner, 1985);

Morris, *The Indian Wars* (Minneapolis: Lerner, 1985);

Livingston, *Sea Songs* (New York: Holiday House, 1986).

Leonard Everett Fisher is a painter, an illustrator, an author, a designer, and an educator. Born in New York City on 24 June 1924, Fisher spent his childhood in the Sea Gate community in Brooklyn, New York. As a third grader he attended drawing classes in a professional school for gifted children. It was his father, Benjamin M. Fisher, marine engineer and amateur artist, who inspired him at his drafting table and created for him a loose-leaf "how to draw this and that" book. He attributes his broad range of interests to his mother, Ray Shapiro Fisher, who read aloud to him from *Compton's Encyclopedia* when he was a child. He won his first art award at age seven in the Wanamaker Art Competition for New York City School Children for a picture of a Pilgrim shooting a turkey. His formal art lessons began when he was eight at the Heckscher School of Art in Manhattan. He studied art with Moses Soyer and Reginald Marsh and was graduated from Brooklyn's Abraham Lincoln High School, a school with an extraordinary arts program. At age sixteen he entered Brooklyn College where he studied art with Serge Chermayeff. A short time later, in 1943, Fisher left his college studies to begin active duty with the U.S. Army Corps of Engineers. Serving as a topographer with the army he participated in the cartographic planning of major campaigns in European and Pacific areas. His first professional writing experience involved describing some of his unit's involvement in these operations for the army.

Following his stint in the army, Fisher enrolled at Yale University, from which he earned a B.F.A. in 1949 and an M.F.A. in 1950. While a graduate student at Yale, Fisher served as an assistant instructor, teaching design theory. As recipient of the Joseph Pulitzer Scholarship in Art and the William Wirt Winchester Traveling Fellowship, he sailed to Europe in 1950 for extensive travel throughout Europe. Upon his return from Europe he accepted a job with Auriel Bessemer as assistant muralist, but gave it up one week later to become the dean, at the young age of twenty-seven, of the Whitney School of Art in New Haven, Connecticut. Following his marriage to Margery Meskin on 21 December 1952, Fisher resigned from the deanship to devote more time to illustrating and painting. Over the years he

has served as a frequent lecturer at schools, colleges, universities, and professional associations throughout the United States.

Since 1954 Fisher has contributed graphics to over 200 children's works for all ages, both fiction and nonfiction. Since 1960 he has written and illustrated more than fifty books of his own. Additionally, he has designed several postage stamps, coins, cachets, and posters. His first stamp creation was the block of four U.S. postage stamps commemorating the bicentennial and issued at Williamsburg, Virginia, on the Fourth of July 1972. These stamps depicted colonial American craftsmen. Another stamp creation, Ichabod Crane and the Legend of Sleepy Hollow, was part of the American Folklore Series.

Fisher is known primarily for his dramatic black-and-white scratchboard illustrations. In the 1980s Fisher began adding rich full-color paintings to his book art. For the most part his writing has been confined to history, his illustrating to historical themes.

His career as an artist/author began with the publication in 1961 of two books by the then newly created children's department of Dial Press. *Pumpers, Boilers, Hooks and Ladders; a Book of Fire Engines* is a picture book which presents a succinct historical approach to fire engines from bucket brigade to the modern fire truck. The simple text is attractively arranged on the pages in large print with handsome first initials which have a touch of the Victorian in their design. His vigorous drawings occupy double-page spreads in fire-engine red, showing each engine, from the earliest pumpers on, being put to appropriate use. *Pushers, Spads, Jennies, and Jets; a Book of Airplanes*, also in picture-book format, is a history of flight featuring two-color separation illustrations.

Fisher's Colonial Americans series, published between 1964 and 1976 by Franklin Watts, has received wide use in classrooms throughout the United States, especially in the arts and social sciences. It includes nineteen titles (beginning with *The Glassmakers*) which focus on the crafts, trades, and extraordinary products that colonial Americans created with the tools and techniques of their times. The first third of each volume in the series is devoted to history, the last two-thirds to technique. The books reflect much specialized research and deliberate writing for the intended child audience. Fisher used engraving-like cut illustrations for this series, done on British scrapeboard. In this process a soft clay-covered board is coated with India ink and etched or

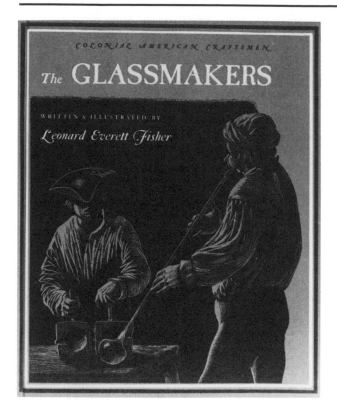 

Covers for two volumes in Fisher's Colonial Americans series (Watts)

scratched away so that only the ink remains revealing the picture. Fisher's scrapeboards depict costume details and customs, and show the delicate shading and depth of a medium he has mastered well. Over 500,000 copies of his books from the Colonial Americans series have been sold. Fisher reports that the series, once out of print, is being reissued by David Godine of Boston.

Picture Book of Revolutionary War Heroes (1970) devotes, from the thousands who paved the way for American Independence, one page each to Fisher's chosen fifty representatives. Each of the pages consists of a descriptive paragraph along with one heroic-size scratchboard drawing and a lively photograph that tells of the individual's part in the struggle. Fifteen people were chosen from each of the three clusters of colonies, and five from America's foreign allies, among them Henri Christophe of Haiti. Both type and drawings are in blue. The subjects are arranged alphabetically within four sections: New England, Middle Colonies, Southern Colonies, and Foreign Allies.

Two if by Sea (1970) is a dramatic description of the actions of Paul Revere and his three colleagues during two hours of the eventful evening of 18 April 1775. This book is also divided into

four sections, each giving a historically based account with background information of the actions of four men: Joseph Warren, who sent Revere the famous message ("one if by land, two if by sea"); Paul Revere; Robert Newman, who lit the signal lanterns; and Thomas Gage, the commanding general of the British forces. Fisher uses a shift of viewpoint to provide suspense and dialogue to bring history to life. His use of strong lines and dramatic contrast of dark blue and white illustrations are an attractive complement to the narratively produced tension of the events which took place.

The Art Experience: Oil Painting 15th-19th Centuries (1973) is a historical-technical explanation of the various ways in which oil paint has been applied to different surfaces, beginning with a clear explanation of the characteristics of oil as a medium. An interesting account of the Flemish artists of the Middle Ages who first used the new technique is included. From the historical viewpoint, the book unfolds the evolution of oil painting: how painters moved from a water-based egg tempera to the more atmospheric oil medium; and how the changing application of oil paint created dynamic possibilities. Details about periods of art, methods of painting, and techniques of painting are included and a glossary and index are appended. Diagrammetrical illustrations by the author and full-color reproductions complement the text in an appealing format.

Alphabet Art: Thirteen ABCs from Around the World (1978) is the first in a four-volume series. It is a brief, well-written history of the development of written language. Each of the thirteen alphabets—Arabic, Cherokee, Chinese, Cyrillic, Eskimo, Gaelic, German, Greek, Hebrew, Japanese, Sanskrit, Thai, and Tibetan—is individually and vibrantly explored. The introduction traces the beginnings of human language, including Egyptian hieroglyphs, Semitic pictographs, and the Sumerian system of cuneiform. Following a basic explanation of the development of written language, each alphabet is given a one-page description of its historical and cultural context accompanied by Fisher's beautiful full-page scratchboard drawings. Letters of each alphabet are used to form decorative captions for these illustrations. Standard English equivalents, the name of the letter, and the letter transliterated into English are given where possible.

Number Art: Thirteen 1 2 3s from Around the World (1982) is the second in the art series. In a format similar to his *Alphabet Art* Fisher traces the development of number systems from their inception to their variety of forms throughout the world. Each system (Arabic, Armenian, Brahmi, Chinese, Egyptian, Gothic, Greek, Mayan, Roman, Runes, Sanskrit, Thai, Tibetan) is preceded by a succinct one-page commentary setting it in the context of the culture from which it came and indicating, where appropriate, significant individual contributors to its development. An alphabetical arrangement of cultures obscures any sense of historical development of number systems. Text pages are faced with glorious royal blue and white scratchboard drawings depicting scenes from the ancient cultures. Subsequently, there are two-page spreads that reproduce the numbers in bold blue and the name of the number and its Arabic sign. Fisher has achieved diversity by exploring the possibilities of line, perspective, and composition to evoke a variety of effects such as pyramids dwarfed by a night sky and flame-lit arches framing invading Goths. In an interdisciplinary approach, he has treated numerical notation as both symbol and as art, thereby investing a familiar subject with new vigor. The last two books in this series, *Symbol Art* and *Calendar Art,* have recently been published.

Leonard Everett Fisher's Liberty Book (1976), a

Dust jacket for Fisher's history of the development of written language (Four Winds)

bicentennial extravagance, is a compilation of songs, slogans, and quotations from America's revolutionary period, all containing the word "Liberty." Among the selections are Patrick Henry's volatile remarks before the Virginia Provincial Assembly, an excerpt from John Adams's diary describing colonists' actions against the Stamp Act, and facsimiles of colonial works of art and design that honor liberty. Too many of the scant forty-seven pages, however, contain only bold type print or filler designs. There are appended notes which identify the contents, but they provide only partial explanations. In the preface Fisher maintains that though American freedom is for many an unfilled promise, the essential integrity of purpose remains. His bold and exquisite red, white, and blue scratchboard illustrations powerfully reflect the bicentennial spirit.

In 1979 Fisher began his distinguished Nineteenth Century America series, aimed at presenting an overall view of the American nation in the nineteenth century. Seven volumes have been completed, beginning with *The Factories,* a well-researched discussion of how New England became the manufacturing center of the country

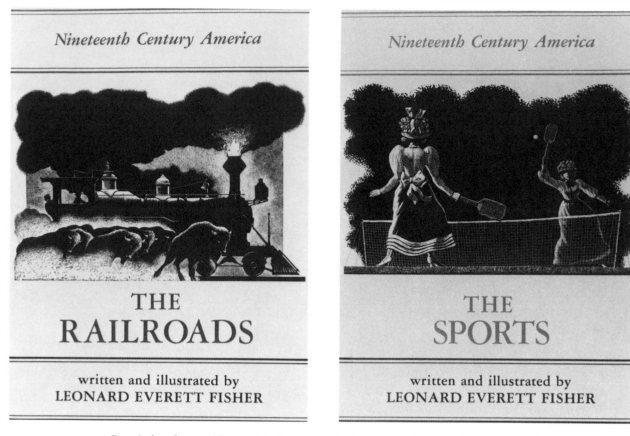

Dust jackets for two titles in Fisher's Nineteenth Century America series (Holiday House)

and what influences led to the spread of these industries across the nation, beginning in 1789 with Sam Slater, who set up the first mechanized textile mill. Other titles in the series include *The Railroads* (1979), in which Fisher traces the westward development of the "iron horse"; *The Hospitals* (1980), a social history of nineteenth-century America which focuses on the paucity of medical help available in many parts of the country; *The Sports* (1980), which describes the inception of American sports, the ways they were organized or played, and the people who were prominent in their development; *The Newspapers* (1981), which traces the burgeoning of newspapers in the United States from the beginning of the 1800s to the end of the century; *The Unions* (1982), which describes the development of unions from their beginnings in the United States up to the turn of the century; and *The Schools* (1983), a broad overview of the beginning of public education, a nineteenth-century development, in the United States.

One of Leonard Fisher's long-cherished ambitions was to adapt the first chapter of Genesis and illustrate it with paintings, rather than with his usual scratchboard illustrations. He felt the need to "deal with monumental abstractions that involve the human reach for the unknown." For him the idea of the Creation was so vast he had to think about it for years before finally coming to grips with it artistically. His *The Seven Days of Creation; Adapted from the Bible* (1981), an American Library Association notable book, fulfilled this ambition. In it he remained true to the Genesis account, although he simplified the language for young children. Breathtaking, impressionistic full-color paintings celebrating the majestic beauty of God's handiwork accompany the text. Amorphous shapes show the separation of heaven and earth, the inert land and oceans, until living things are made. Fisher creates a balance between heavily textured but simply composed pictures and a careful but minimal text, resulting in an amplification of an awesome story.

Star Signs (1983) is a cautious and open-ended historical introduction to astrological interpretations of the zodiac in which Fisher points out that not everyone believes in astrological signs, leaving readers the option of independent decision on the topic. For each sign of the zodiac, he includes a full-color, full-page painting facing the text. Opposite each painting he gives the dates for the sign, the part of the human body it affects, its controlling planet, the myth on which its constellation is based, traits supposedly pertinent to those born under the sign, and a line drawing of the constellation. The complex, vibrant colored illustrations on the recto pages are quite realistic. Foreground designs are lavishly pleasing.

Boxes! Boxes! (1984) is a story in rhyme with an illustration for each line. Each of the robust acrylic paintings is a box housing some everyday or unexpected object. The eighty boxes come in different sizes, shapes, and colors and serve as containers for toys, paints, puppies, ants, plants, and candy, as well as toys themselves, providing children with an opportunity to infer concepts of size, shape, and color. Strong shapes and a wide range of acrylic paints give the pictures a sturdy, full-blown look, and most of the spreads stretch across two pages of clean composition. Bright, clean colors and the deft use of shadows add to the effectiveness of the compositions. Each of Fisher's boxes is realistic and clear in this concept book for very young children.

The Olympians: Great Gods and Goddesses of Ancient Greece (1984) briefly profiles the twelve deities (seven gods and five goddesses) who dwelt on Mount Olympus. Although some profiles are unduly brief, users are likely to delve deeper on their own. Portraits rendered in Fisher's signature layered acrylics accompany the paragraphs characterizing each god's or goddess's traits and attributes, with occasional references to important myths. Included, also, is a concise description of ancient beliefs about the gods and their battle with the Titans for control of the world. The stylized paintings are trenchant summaries of the deities' personalities; however, they lack vitality and are unrepresentative of the timeless, vital characters who move through the myths, mirroring humankind's strengths and failings. Included are a bibliography, a chart juxtaposing Greek and Roman names for the gods and goddesses, and a family tree depicting the relationships between those most eminent Olympians.

The Statue of Liberty (1985) dramatically relates how the idea of the Statue of Liberty began in 1865. Fisher describes the various stages of thought that the French people, and especially the young artist, Frédéric-Auguste Bartholdi, went through before deciding upon an appropriate present for the American people as a memorial to their independence. Described also are the construction techniques, the materials used, and the help provided by many generous people. Historical perspective is provided by tying the statue into world events and the social climate of the time. Photographs and scratchboard illustrations by the author are an integral part of the book.

Great Wall of China (1986) is a carefully designed and outstanding history of the building of the Great Wall of China. Fisher describes how 2,200 years ago King Cheng of Ch'in conquered surrounding provinces and became the first Supreme Emperor of China. The building of the long wall across the north of China resulted from the necessity to do something about the fierce Mongol tribes that threatened to invade. More than a million people—peasants, artisans, prisoners, and soldiers—were forced to work on the wall, many losing their lives. That the Ming emperors made improvements is mentioned on the last page. Each page is captioned in Chinese characters that are translated at the end of the book. Fictionalized dialogue results in a personalized narrative, and impressive black-and-white acrylic illustrations by the author set the tone for the book.

Nine of Fisher's books have been works of fiction. His first, *A Head Full of Hats* (1962), is a picture book for young children. The protagonist, Alfie, decides that important people wear important hats, so he tries on those of Sultans, Indians, generals, admirals, hunters, explorers, and presidents, before he learns that the man makes the hat.

The Death of Evening Star; the Diary of a Young New England Whaler (1972) was chosen by the American Library Association as a notable book. The tale of whaling is a slight atmospheric documentary set aboard an ill-fated whaling ship, *Evening Star,* sailing out of early New England in the 1840s. Readers learn of the ship's having been lost at sea from the diary of cabin boy Jeremiah Poole, whose illness caused him to be left in the Canaries while the ship sailed on the fatal voyage. The journal reflects a catalog of evils—death, murder, whippings, blackmail, and shipwreck—along with some descriptions of whaling procedures. The diary is prefaced by an account of how it came into the storyteller's possession, having been delivered to him by a ghostly figure one stormy night. The atmosphere of the supernatural gives the book an added appeal for young readers, though Fisher's achievement in incorporating period material and authentic details of shipping and whaling is hampered somewhat by

Page 5

THE GREAT WALL

lef

More than 2300 years ago, Prince Cheng, a boy of 13, became
~~the ruler of the~~ Kingdom of Chin, in eastern Asia. He ~~then~~
~~waged war against~~ rival kingdoms and conquered them all~~,~~ one
by one. ~~Prince Cheng united the Kingdom of Chin and all of~~
The ~~defeated~~ kingdoms into one ~~huge~~ country. The new nation
was called "China". Prince Cheng made himself Ch'in Shih
Huang Ti — The First Supreme Emperor of China.

The ~~powerful~~ Emperor demanded that everyone ~~do things his~~
~~way and obey~~ new laws. ~~But~~ There were those -- followers
of Confucius, an ancient scholar -- who refused. They said
that the old ~~ways were better and too special to be changed.~~
The Emperor burned their books and buried them alive.

Next, Ch'in Shih Huang Ti turned his attention to China's
~~long northern~~ frontier. There, wild Mongolian tribesmen had
been raiding border villages ~~for years.~~ They had become
so bold that they threatened to attack all of China. Neither
the Emperor nor his people were safe ~~unless~~ Something
done. ~~Quickly, The Emperor decided to built a great wall~~

Page from the revised typescript and a preliminary sketch for The Great Wall of China *(courtesy of the author)*

the relentless aura of doom and abundance of violence.

The Warlock of Westfall (1974) is a convincing tale of witch hunting set in a small village in colonial America, where Samuel Swift, a lonely, eccentric bachelor in his late seventies, is accused by a group of boys of being a warlock and is tried and hanged by the villagers. A concluding segment chronicles the settlement's desertion and destruction when its numbers flee at the sight of Samuel's long lost brother Nathan inside dead Samuel's cabin, which is aflame from an untended fire. Both the physical atmosphere and the moods of the times are skillfully evoked by Fisher, whose stark black-and-white illustrations, somber yet dramatic, are particularly well suited to the taut and brooding atmosphere evoked.

Three of Fisher's novels are of the ethnic-historical type, stories about victims and survivors among American immigrants. The first, *Across the Sea from Galway* (1975), tells of 145 Irish refugees who are lost when the ship carrying them to the New World slams against a rock at Cohasset, Massachusetts, in 1849. Patrick Donovan, one of the few survivors, was being sent with his brother and sister to America ahead of his parents. After the shipwreck, the setting switches to Ireland and in a flashback the Donovan family is introduced. Because famine is sweeping their country and they are faced with British oppression, the Donovan family is determined to seek a better life. The depiction of Irish life during the great famine is accurate, and forceful intensity is given to the moving tale by Fisher's stark, haunting black-and-white scratchboard drawings which realistically capture the mood and effectively reveal the feelings of the people whose story is being told.

Letters from Italy (1977) is a novella based upon the reminiscences of aging Angelo Cappelo, retired Italian-American restaurant owner. The sober and slow-moving, third person, four-part narrative shifts back and forth in time between Angelo's meditations about his son Vinny, who is fighting in Italy during World War II; the effect Angelo's solidly nationalistic grandfather Piero, who fought with Garibaldi, had on his youth; his family's 1883 emigration from Italy; and his bereavement over Vinny's death.

A Russian Farewell (1980), winner of the 1981 National Jewish Book Award for Juvenile Literature, deals with a thirteen-member Jewish family living in Krolevets, in the Russian Ukraine, in the early 1900s. The country is on the verge of in-

surrection and chaos following the defeat of Czarist forces by the Japanese. Krolevets' 3,000 Jews are in danger from unhappy peasants who have been incited by the local government to harass and intimidate them. After such local acts as the vandalizing of the Shapiro delicatessen and the wrecking of the village synagogue, the Shapiros, urged by Hannah's sister-in-law in Brooklyn, say goodbye to everything they and their ancestors have labored for and immigrate to America.

Sweeney's Ghost (1975) is a sociological tract on suburbia. Though the Framer family of five from Aspetuck, Connecticut, hopes to spend a quiet week at a villa in Jamaica, they end up having to deal with the mischief of the ghost of the pirate Thomas Sweeney. The story line is heavily padded and interrupted by long monologues by Sweeney, much of which is used to provide information about himself and other pirates.

Noonan: A Novel about Baseball, ESP, and Time Warps (1978) is a time-shift fantasy which unfolds like an old postgame yarn told to a bunch of cronies. The unsuccessful Brooklyn Dutchmen Baseball Club of 1896 is pinning its hopes on the pitching of fifteen-year-old Johnny Noonan. Johnny, after being hit by a foul ball while awaiting his turn to bat, is transported in time to the year 1996, where he discovers he has psychokinetic powers, including the power to think a baseball to a place of his choice. After winning a perfect game by pitching eighty-one strikes, Johnny causes a national sensation, resulting in his being hospitalized for protection. A fantasy, the story lacks credibility, but as a baseball spoof and tall tale, sports style, it is humorously chock-full of baseball action and team shenanigans. Its strongest feature is the baseball world as pictured in 1996, a time when baseball is only on television and Wrigley Field has been declared a national monument. Fisher's rather comical illustrations, black-line-on-white for the present reality and white-line-on-black for the future, spruce up the format.

Storm at the Jetty (1981) is an effective mood piece. The text, rather than tell a story, describes the moods and sensory details of the jetty where Levi Farber witnesses the change of a bright August day from calm and clear sea through wild sea and violent thunderstorm and back to quiet summer day. Fisher's masterful use of shades of white, blue-gray, and blue-black paintings, strong in line and composition, conveys the drama of the summer story, moving beyond reality into symbols of the magnificent power of the natural world. The initially well-lit scenes grow progressively darker as the storm intensifies and then light again as the calm returns.

Leonard Everett Fisher's pride in craftsmanship has not changed over the years; however, his style has. The figurative drawings done between 1949 and 1968 gave way to hard-edge acrylic geometric done studies between 1968 and 1979 and to softer, more romantic paintings done from 1980 to the present. The more recent work has a sharper focus than his earlier art. He applies the medium to the concept in the illustrating process. It is his belief that clear visual communication is the result of an artist's fundamental discipline and knowledge of craft. His painting and illustrating are characterized by a sharp focus which reflects this belief.

Between 1966 and 1987 Leonard Fisher served as a faculty member at the Paier College of Art in Connecticut where he conducted courses in painting, life drawing, book illustration, and art history. Four of those years (1978-1982) he served the school as its academic dean.

Fisher has been involved in numerous art shows and exhibitions, and his illustrations for children's books by other authors have earned him several awards, most notably the Christopher Medal in 1981 for *All Times, All Peoples,* by Milton Meltzer. In 1979 he received the Medallion of the University of Southern Mississippi for "distinguished contribution to children's literature," and he also served as a delegate to the White House Conference on Library and Information Services. Leonard and Margery Fisher, a school librarian, have for a number of years made their home in Westport, Connecticut, and their three children, Julie Anne, Susan Abby, and James Albert, reside in New York City.

References:
"Artist of the Month: Leonard Everett Fisher, Pulitzer Prize-Winner," *Design,* 53 (June 1952): 213;

Monica M. Carroll, "Leonard Everett Fisher: 'My Life Is Art . . . ,' " *Biography News,* 2 (May-June 1975): 527;

Jean F. Mercier, "PW Interviews Leonard Everett Fisher," *Publishers Weekly,* 221 (26 February 1982): 62-63.

Papers:
The three major collections of Leonard Everett Fisher's original illustrations, manuscripts, and related papers are located in the Kerlan Collection of the University of Minnesota, at the University of Southern Mississippi, and at the University of Oregon. The largest of the three collections is at Oregon.

Genevieve Foster

(13 April 1893-30 August 1979)

O. Mell Busbin
Appalachian State University

BOOKS: *George Washington's World* (New York: Scribners, 1941);

Abraham Lincoln's World (New York: Scribners, 1944);

Augustus Caesar's World, a Story of Ideas and Events from B.C. 44 to 14 A.D. (New York: Scribners, 1947);

George Washington; an Initial Biography (New York: Scribners, 1949);

Abraham Lincoln; an Initial Biography (New York: Scribners, 1950);

Andrew Jackson; an Initial Biography (New York: Scribners, 1951);

Birthdays of Freedom, 2 volumes (New York: Scribners, 1952, 1957); republished as *Birthdays of Freedom; From Early Man to July 4, 1776*, 1 volume (New York: Scribners, 1973);

Theodore Roosevelt; an Initial Biography (New York: Scribners, 1954);

When and Where in Italy: a Passport to Yesterday for Readers and Travelers of Today (Chicago: Rand McNally, 1955);

The World of Captain John Smith, 1580-1631 (New York: Scribners, 1959);

The World of Columbus and Sons (New York: Scribners, 1965);

Year of the Pilgrims, 1620 (New York: Scribners, 1969);

Year of Columbus, 1492 (New York: Scribners, 1969);

Year of Lincoln, 1861 (New York: Scribners, 1970);

Year of Independence, 1776 (New York: Scribners, 1970);

The World of William Penn (New York: Scribners, 1973);

The Year of the Horseless Carriage, 1801 (New York: Scribners, 1975);

The Year of the Flying Machine, 1903 (New York: Scribners, 1977).

BOOKS ILLUSTRATED: Frances Cavanah, *Children of the White House* (New York & Chicago: Rand McNally, 1936);

Genevieve Foster (Gale International Portrait Gallery)

Cavanah, *Boyhood Adventures of Our Presidents* (New York & Chicago: Rand McNally, 1938).

Genevieve Stump Foster was born in Oswego, New York, on 13 April 1893. After the death of her father, John William Stump, in 1894, she moved with her mother, Jessie Starrin Stump, to the Starrin home in Whitewater, Wisconsin. Three years later her grandfather died, leaving Genevieve, her mother, grandmother, and an aunt to fill a twenty-odd-room house. Both her grandmother and this home, according to Foster, had a great influence on her. Growing up among the memories of the four generations who had inhabited the house gave her a sense of stability, of deep roots, and of a feeling for the continuity of past and present.

Foster would go on to establish her reputation as a creative craftswoman from the materials of history and her youth. That reputation has since afforded her international recognition in the fields of biography and history, especially the interpretation of American history in its relation to world history. Her highly developed but well-controlled imagination enabled her to project herself into the past in the role of a reporter who could see, feel, hear, taste, and smell the goings-on in the world and retell them in vivid words and pictures.

Although an only child, Foster never experienced loneliness. This was due to the liveliness of her grandmother, whom she remembered as being full of fun and always ready to play games. It was she who taught Genevieve to sew and embroider, and above all, the importance of finishing one task before beginning another. Drawing was another activity Foster enjoyed as a young child. Since there had always been someone painting, drawing, or modeling in the family, this kind of activity was taken as a matter of course by her mother. After Foster had begun school at age six, she and two classmates, who also liked to draw, established a studio one summer in the top floor of her grandmother's house. It was in this same studio that Foster, at age ten, began to write her one and only novel, with the same chapter serving as both the end and the beginning.

Being interested in almost everything, Foster liked grade school. The only thing she found difficult to learn and to remember was history, which confused her. While attending the University of Wisconsin, she found herself with little time to pursue her interest in drawing. After she had earned a B.A. degree in 1915, she eagerly enrolled in the Chicago Academy of Fine Arts for a year of study during the 1916-1917 term.

Encouraged by the director of the academy, who seemed pleased with her artwork, she ventured to start a career as a free-lance commercial artist. For several years she did various kinds of drawings, copywriting, and layouts for newspapers, booklets, and magazines. Although she found the commercial art field to be interesting, she was never entirely satisfied with it. Upon her marriage to Orrington Foster in 1922, she gave it up.

Upon the arrival of their two children, a boy, named for his father but called by the nickname Tony, and a girl, Joanna, four years younger, Foster centered her interest at home for the next few years. During this time she began doing illustrations for children's stories, beginning with drawings for *Child Life* magazine and eventually moving on to children's books. Finding her role as an illustrator not entirely satisfying, she one day hit upon the idea of combining all the things she best liked to do: finding out what she had always wanted to know about history, writing history books that children and perhaps their parents might like to read, and designing and illustrating books. Her children later served as sounding boards for her writing, giving her the feel of the audience she hoped to reach, while her husband provided a more critical response.

While she was in grade school Foster had viewed history as being dreadful. She loathed it, feeling that what teachers said was simply to be memorized and given back to them. If right one received a good grade and then forgot the whole terrible experience. Convinced she could remedy such a situation, Foster wanted to write history that showed not only what was going on in the United States but all over the world, and how events in the various nations were related. This kind of history could help readers acquire an understanding of the historical process, a complicated concept. Such a broad view of what happened in the past could also help readers form value judgments.

Each book in her resulting World series presents a time slice of history, a total picture of the world–historical, religious, scientific, cultural, social, and economic–in relationship to the span of one man's life. In each of the five volumes in this series, Foster takes a horizontal look across and around the world to tell what of importance was happening when the hero was born, during his childhood, in his youth and early manhood, and throughout his life. By beginning each of the World books with the childhood of the protagonist Foster has been able to pique the interest of youngsters to realize that history makers were once just boys and girls like themselves. This world's-eye view of countries, periods, and people permits young readers to see movements rise and culminate or disappear, men who turn the tide of history in one direction or another leaving the world markedly better or worse for their presence. The rounded sense of history presented through these five volumes is one textbooks rarely suggest. The illustrations, maps, and charts, also done by Foster, provide much information and graphically portray her theme of parallel events.

It was important for Foster to plan and sketch illustrations, maps, and charts at the time she wrote the text, rather than subsequently. Foster was an author-artist with a remarkable sense of design which permitted her to integrate text and illustrations successfully. Two indexes are included in each book, one for characters and another general one of nations, places, and events. Each book is richly documented, and the lively style of each lends itself to an excellent reading-aloud experience.

The first book in the World series, *George Washington's World* (1941), a Newbery Honor Book for 1942, was a three-year painstaking creation for Foster. Covering the period from 1732 to 1799, it is a six-part comparative, streamlined history divided into sections on Washington's life as a boy, a soldier, a farmer, the commander of the Continental Army, a private citizen, and the first president of the United States. Each part begins with a double spread of line drawings which serves as a sort of curtain-raising presentation of the cast of characters before each act of the play begins. The illustrations are clever and descriptive, the style of writing and vocabulary clear.

Abraham Lincoln's World (1944), a 1945 Newbery Honor Book, portrays the history of the early to mid nineteenth century in relation to the lives of two of America's top heroes. Lincoln's life, divided by time periods, is used as an outline for the telling of events happening in each of those time periods. The Charge of the Light Brigade, the Black Hole of Calcutta, Beethoven, Tecumseh, and Old Ironsides all take their places around the president in this well-integrated picture of the changing world between the years 1809 and 1865.

In terms of action the first two volumes in the World series kept close to history and biography. Foster consciously widened the scope of the next World book, *Augustus Caesar's World* (1947), a clever presentation of world civilization during the lifetime of the first Roman emperor. Reforms instilled by Augustus and great buildings he inspired constitute fascinating reading for any age. The personalities, however, stand out for young readers. The text is divided into five periods which include the history of Rome and contemporaneous events in every part of the world. In animated style, people, ideas, and events are shown in relation to each other. Foster illustrated the book with many graphic illustrations in the form of charts, diagrams, and pictures, and her

line drawings are used both symbolically and historically.

Her publishers eventually persuaded Foster to fill one of the gaps in children's literature, the well-written, simple biography. She used her research and skill to create the Initial Biographies series for a younger audience than that targeted by the World books. Each brief biography in this series has been distilled to the essential facts. Text, style, and illustrations are the facets of each presentation which have been used effectively in adding something to the conception of the character and his life story. Style of writing, dialogue, vocabulary, and sentence length have been used as tools in the telling of the lives of the characters.

Illustrations in the Initial Biographies always supplement the textual descriptions. Foster's aim was to give an idea of the life of the subject to a child looking at the book, regardless of whether he could read it. Being an artist as well as a writer, Foster saw each page in its completeness of text, illustration, and design. In each case the illustrations and page layout were conceived by Foster as she produced the text, and she produced the entire design for each of her volumes, including the color separations for the illustrations.

George Washington; an Initial Biography (1949), a Newbery Honor Book for 1950, is a stirring story of the subject's entire life told simply and briefly but in a dignified way for young readers with a minimum of fictionalization. There is an emphasis on small, homely details which appeal to young children. Cleverly woven into the story are customs and historical background further illuminating the colonial period of United States history; and short summaries of the French and Indian Wars and the Revolution contribute toward a feeling of the times. Overall, the book's authoritativeness is derived from good, unobtrusive documentation.

Abraham Lincoln; an Initial Biography (1950) is an interesting, though somewhat fictionalized account of the childhood and manhood of its subject. Many exceptionally fine episodes in the life of the man and president are portrayed with deep feeling and skill, including the legends that have been associated with Lincoln, such as the Ann Rutledge affair. Because of its interesting text and lively pictures the book appeals to older children too. In both text and drawings Foster shows respect for the intelligence of her audience as well as the stature of the character she has chosen to portray.

Dust jackets for the first and third volumes in Foster's Initial Biographies series (Scribners)

Andrew Jackson; an Initial Biography (1951) is written in a rather animated style. It succeeds at conveying Jackson's intensity of feeling and informality of manner. Foster provides the reader with a factual, yet lively portrait (via stirring anecdotes) which provides a sense of nearness to the times. Both the strengths and weaknesses of Jackson's personality emerge, as Foster presents in good taste and without bias such delicate phases of his stormy life as his marriage and dueling. Especially well done are the chapters concerning the difficult topics of the Nullification law and the bank question. Foster demonstrates her ability to write biography as a storyteller rather than a historian, though the omission of any mention of Jean Lafitte in the account of the Battle of New Orleans is questionable.

Theodore Roosevelt; an Initial Biography (1954), the last installment in the series, is a realistic interpretation and remarkably well-rounded picture of this dynamic, many-faceted American patriot which examines personal details of his private life and significant events of his public career. The adventurousness and ebullience of Theodore Roosevelt make a lively, enjoyable story.

The first volume of *Birthdays of Freedom* (1952) was a 1953 Newbery Honor Book. Writ-

ten to celebrate the seventy-fifth anniversary of the American Library Association and with a later second volume in mind, it opens with a moving account of the Declaration of Independence and the proclamation of freedom. Foster then goes to the first birthdays of freedom–early man's learning to make use of fire, to talk, and to write–and traces the forward steps and the setbacks in the growth of freedom from early Egypt to the fall of Rome. Elaboration on single events, however, was precluded by space limitations. The result is that the reader needs a good background in world history to be able to follow the text and relate the individual events to the overall ideas of man's growth toward freedom. Although striking illustrations on every page accompany the well-written and interesting text, the page layouts are overly elaborate and confusing. Three different type sizes, ranging from extra large caption size to extremely small, are used. On some pages the large type captions are an integral part of the text and must be read in proper sequence for the text to make sense; on other pages the captions bear little relation to the accompanying text.

The second volume of *Birthdays of Freedom*

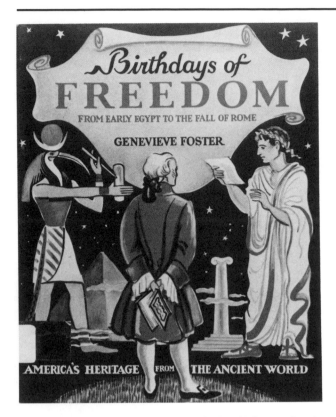

Dust jacket for the first of Foster's two books which trace the advances of freedom (Scribners)

(1957) takes up where the first left off and highlights great events in the course of man's struggle for freedom from the fall of Rome to America's War of Independence. Volume two, however, can stand alone as a separate unit since it begins with the Declaration of Independence and then goes back to present the great historical events between the fall of Rome and 1776. Such events as Europe being overrun by the barbarians, the beginnings of law and order, the Magna Charta, printing, the Renaissance, and the founding of the New World are included. Foster has selected and synthesized her material with skill and has presented it dramatically. Included are charts, maps, and illuminating drawings by the author in this fitting sequel to the first *Birthdays of Freedom* volume.

When and Where in Italy: a Passport to Yesterday for Readers and Travelers of Today (1955) is a guidebook and travel history designed to serve both tourists and students of ancient history. Foster divides Italian history into three periods: the Roman, Middle Ages, and Renaissance. Included for each period are monuments and treasures the author felt to be representative of the Italian history surveyed. The author-illustrator describes

the sights of modern Italy in terms of the men and times that produced them. As she moves from city to city, each is shown in its golden age and linked to the highlights of its past with tangible evidence in buildings, paintings, and statues. The book serves as a brief but illuminating chronological tour for both those who read and those who can travel. Foster's drawings with their accompanying brief text are informative and packed with little-known sidelights into the romantic past of Italy.

The era in which John Smith lived is reflected in *The World of Captain John Smith, 1580-1631* (1959), a segmented-type presentation of his life as a boy, soldier, explorer, and writer. In another of her horizontal approaches to history Foster has created a graphic and vigorous interpretation of events and international relationships and brought to life Capt. John Smith and his contemporaries. The spirited account contains a fund of information of historical, religious, cultural, social, and economic nature related to the span of Smith's life. Pointed up are Smith's outstanding qualities of courage and determination. Details are ample and colorful, yet without any sense of a mere dull recounting of the "facts." The book is eminently readable, well illustrated by the author, and well indexed according to people, places, events, and general topics.

A richly creative book characterized by its graceful, straightforward style is Foster's *The World of Columbus and Sons* (1965). In it she traces Columbus's life from age nine through his days of triumph and disaster. A panorama of the world in the time of Columbus is a result of Foster's interweaving of significant people (artists, scientists, writers, rulers) and political and cultural events. The publication has an attractive open format and imaginative line drawings created by the author. Its extensive index is an added value.

Year of the Pilgrims, 1620 (1969) is a horizontal approach to the history of the *Mayflower* pilgrims, providing perspective and touching on cultures and accomplishments elsewhere in the world at the time. The book briefly portrays William Bradford, William Brewster, and the Indians Massasoit and Squanto, and also explains and summarizes the beliefs of the Puritans. Rulers and happenings in Africa, India, China, and Japan are also included. The text is simply written and has maps, diagrams, and pictures by the author to accompany it.

In *Year of Columbus, 1492* (1969) Foster presents the discovery of America as the result of many interacting people, ideas, and influences, but especially as an outgrowth of the impetus to travel and explore. Conveyed is the view that 1492 was notable not for Columbus's achievement alone but for being part of a period in which considerable progress was made by countries undergoing, or being influenced by, the Renaissance. Linked to the summary of the Christopher Columbus story is the work of Copernicus, Leonardo da Vinci, and Michelangelo, with a bird's-eye view of contemporaneous China, Japan, and the Incan and Aztec empires. Included among the multitude of illustrations are maps and charts which have been carefully researched by the author.

Foster's *Year of Independence, 1776* (1970) is a three-part book of short, focused segments. The people and events surrounding this date in history are explored in fact-filled, quick, and vivid sketches. Part one describes political events in the United States from 1776 to 1783. Parts two and three present some of the artistic and scientific developments in other parts of the world during the same period.

Year of Lincoln, 1861 (1970) portrays numerous people and events all loosely tied together through an examination of the year 1861. Major events preceding and during the Civil War and Lincoln's role in them make up the first part of the book. Brief introductions to Darwin, Dickens, Twain, and Frederick Douglass follow. The reigns of Queen Victoria, Empress Tzu Hsi of China, and Emperor Matsuhito of Japan are included. Coverage is broad, however superficial, due to its intended young audience.

Foster's final World book was *The World of William Penn* (1973), though in the 1960s she published simplified versions of the earlier books supplemented with two-color illustrations. *The World of William Penn* is a smooth interweaving of the William Penn story with other events of his time, resulting in an enlightened approach to the study of world history. Penn's story is told briefly in parts one, six, and nine of the book. Other parts focus on such vivid subjects as the French explorers Marquette, Jolliet, and La Salle; the court of Louis XIV; two Mongul emperors; the scientists Halley and Newton; a Manchu emperor; and Peter the Great of Russia. Backgrounds and activities of the second half of the seventeenth and the first quarter of the eighteenth century—in the arts and sciences, and in war and peace—are brought to life in a clear textual treatment.

Cover for Foster's 1965 book which provides a panorama of the world during Christopher Columbus's lifetime (Scribners)

Additionally, the text is clarified and enlivened by portraits, scenes, diagrams, and pictorial maps created by the author.

In *The Year of the Horseless Carriage, 1801* (1975) Robert Trevithick, maker of the first run in a steam-propelled horseless carriage in 1801, serves as the pivotal point around which history takes place during the years 1801-1821. The title, therefore, is a misnomer. Preceding the text events of importance in chosen years, such as Napoleon Bonaparte's rule of France, Thomas Jefferson's election as president, Toussaint L'Ouverture's rise to power in Haiti, and Beethoven's writing of a symphony dedicated to Bonaparte, are charted. The text, then, covers such events, following them in subsequent years but returning repeatedly to the world of Trevithick, Fulton, and Stephenson in building and operating steam-driven vehicles. Trevithick's "horseless carriage," however, receives little attention. The simple writing style is direct and brisk. Although many of the illustrations by the author stress and amplify major points, they are not always informative. The index is excellent.

Foster's last book before her death in Westport, Connecticut, in 1979 was *The Year of the Flying Machine, 1903* (1977). Orville and Wilbur Wright serve as major interest points in the text which reveals happenings around the world from 1900 to 1909, when the Wrights made their first flights. In each of the three sections, the exploits of the brothers serve as frames of reference upon which other events and personages are hinged, such as Theodore Roosevelt becoming "the youngest man to assume the Presidency of the United States"; Marconi and his perfection of his wireless telegraph; Marie and Pierre Curie and their experiments with radium; Ford and his motor car; Lenin and the Russian revolution of 1905; Einstein and his theory of relativity; Freud and *The Interpretation of Dreams;* Admiral Peary and his expedition to the North Pole; and, as climax, the United States War Department's acceptance of the Wright brothers' plane for army use. This is a well-written text supplemented by bold black-and-white illustrations.

As a writer of nineteen children's books Fos-ter was best known for her technique of choosing historical figures and creating a story around their perception of events around them. Her favorite pastime, that of recreating history and biography out of words and drawings, has touched thousands of children. Her books have been translated into at least fifteen languages, including Urdu, Hindi, Bengali, Chinese, Korean, and Vietnamese.

References:

Mitchell Dawson, "Genevieve Foster's Worlds," *Horn Book*, 28 (June 1952): 190-195;

Sara Innis Fenwick, "Exploring History with Genevieve Foster," *Elementary English*, 31 (October 1954): 315-321;

Joanna Foster, "Genevieve Foster," *Horn Book*, 28 (June 1952): 196-198.

Papers:

Genevieve Foster's miscellaneous papers are located at the University of Oregon and at the Uni-

Theodor Seuss Geisel
(Dr. Seuss, Theo. LeSieg)
(2 March 1904-)

Myra Kibler
Belmont College

BOOKS: *And to Think That I Saw It on Mulberry Street*, as Dr. Seuss (New York: Vanguard Press, 1937; London: Country Life, 1939);

The 500 Hats of Bartholomew Cubbins, as Dr. Seuss (New York: Vanguard Press, 1938; London: Oxford University Press, 1940);

The Seven Lady Godivas, as Dr. Seuss (New York: Random House, 1939);

The King's Stilts, as Dr. Seuss (New York: Random House, 1939; London: Hamish Hamilton, 1942);

Horton Hatches the Egg, as Dr. Seuss (New York: Random House, 1940; London: Hamish Hamilton, 1942);

McElligot's Pool, as Dr. Seuss (New York: Random House, 1947; London: Collins, 1975);

Thidwick, The Big-Hearted Moose, as Dr. Seuss (New York: Random House, 1948; London: Collins, 1968);

Bartholomew and the Oobleck, as Dr. Seuss (New York: Random House, 1949);

If I Ran the Zoo, as Dr. Seuss (New York: Random House, 1950);

Scrambled Eggs Super!, as Dr. Seuss (New York: Random House, 1953);

The Sneetches, and Other Stories, as Dr. Seuss (New York: Random House, 1953);

Horton Hears a Who!, as Dr. Seuss (New York: Random House, 1954);

On Beyond Zebra, as Dr. Seuss (New York: Random House, 1955);

Signs of Civilization!, as Dr. Seuss (La Jolla, Cal.: La Jolla Town Council, 1956);

If I Ran the Circus, as Dr. Seuss (New York: Random House, 1956; London: Collins, 1969);

The Cat in the Hat, as Dr. Seuss (New York: Random House, 1957; London: Hutchinson, 1958);

How the Grinch Stole Christmas, as Dr. Seuss (New York: Random House, 1957);

The Cat in the Hat Comes Back!, as Dr. Seuss (New York: Beginner Books, 1958; London: Collins, 1961);

Photo by Antony DiGesu

Yertle the Turtle, and Other Stories, as Dr. Seuss (New York: Random House, 1958; London: Collins, 1963);

Happy Birthday to You!, as Dr. Seuss (New York: Random House, 1959);

One Fish Two Fish Red Fish Blue Fish, as Dr. Seuss (New York: Random House, 1960; London: Collins, 1962);

Green Eggs and Ham, as Dr. Seuss (New York: Beginner Books, 1960; London: Collins, 1962);

Ten Apples Up on Top!, as Theo. LeSieg, illustrated

by Roy McKie (New York: Beginner Books, 1961; London: Collins, 1963);

Dr. Seuss' Sleep Book, as Dr. Seuss (New York: Random House, 1962; London: Collins, 1964);

Hop on Pop, as Dr. Seuss (New York: Beginner Books, 1963; London: Collins, 1964);

Dr. Seuss' ABC, as Dr. Seuss (New York: Beginner Books, 1963; London: Collins, 1964);

The Cat in the Hat Dictionary, by the Cat Himself, as Dr. Seuss, with Philip D. Eastman (New York: Beginner Books, 1964);

I Wish That I Had Duck Feet, as Theo. LeSieg, illustrated by B. Tokey (New York: Beginner Books, 1965; London: Collins, 1967);

Fox in Socks, as Dr. Seuss (New York: Beginner Books, 1965; London: Collins, 1966);

I Had Trouble in Getting to Solla Sollew, as Dr. Seuss (New York: Random House, 1965; London: Collins, 1967);

Come Over to My House, as Theo. LeSieg, illustrated by Richard Erdoes (New York: Beginner Books, 1966; London: Collins, 1967);

Dr. Seuss' Lost World Revisited: A Forward Looking Backward Glance, as Dr. Seuss (New York: Award Books, 1967);

The Cat in the Hat Songbook, as Dr. Seuss (New York: Random House, 1967);

The Foot Book, as Dr. Seuss (New York: Random House, 1968; London: Collins, 1969);

The Eye Book, as Theo. LeSieg (New York: Random House, 1968; London: Collins, 1969);

I Can Lick 30 Tigers Today, and Other Stories, as Dr. Seuss (New York: Random House, 1969; London: Collins, 1970);

My Book About Me, By Me, Myself. I Wrote It! I Drew It!, as Dr. Seuss, illustrated by McKie (New York: Random House, 1969);

Mr. Brown Can Moo! Can You?, as Dr. Seuss (New York: Random House, 1970; London: Collins, 1971);

I Can Draw It Myself, as Dr. Seuss (New York: Random House, 1970);

I Can Write—By Me, Myself, as Theo. LeSieg (New York: Random House, 1971);

The Lorax, as Dr. Seuss (New York: Random House, 1971; London: Collins, 1972);

In a People House, as Theo. LeSieg, illustrated by McKie (New York: Random House, 1972; London: Collins, 1973);

Marvin K. Mooney, Will You Please Go Now?, as Dr. Seuss (New York: Random House, 1972; London: Collins, 1973);

The Many Mice of Mr. Brice, as Theo. LeSieg, illustrated by McKie (New York: Random House, 1973; London: Collins, 1974);

Did I Ever Tell You How Lucky You Are?, as Dr. Seuss (New York: Random House, 1973; London: Collins, 1974);

The Shape of Me and Other Stuff, as Dr. Seuss (New York: Random House, 1973; London: Collins, 1974);

Wacky Wednesday, as Theo. LeSieg, illustrated by George Booth (New York: Beginner Books, 1974; London: Collins, 1975);

There's a Wocket in My Pocket!, as Dr. Seuss (New York: Random House, 1974; London: Collins, 1975);

Great Day for Up!, as Dr. Seuss, illustrated by Quentin Blake (New York: Random House, 1974; London: Collins, 1975);

Because a Little Bug Went Ka-Choo!, by Geisel and Michael Frith, as Rosetta Stone (New York: Beginner Books, 1975);

Would You Rather Be a Bullfrog?, as Theo. LeSieg, illustrated by McKie (New York: Random House, 1975);

Oh, The Thinks You Can Think!, as Dr. Seuss (New York: Random House, 1975; London: Collins, 1976);

The Cat's Quizzer, as Dr. Seuss (New York: Random House, 1976; London: Collins, 1977);

Hooper Humperdink . . . ? Not Him!, as Theo. LeSieg (New York: Random House, 1976; London: Collins, 1977);

Please Try to Remember the First of Octember!, as Theo. LeSieg, illustrated by Arthur Cumings (New York: Beginner Books, 1977);

I Can Read With My Eyes Shut, as Dr. Seuss (New York: Random House, 1978);

Oh Say Can You Say?, as Dr. Seuss (New York: Beginner Books, 1979);

Maybe You Should Fly a Jet! Maybe You Should Be a Vet, as Theo. LeSieg, illustrated by Michael J. Smullin (New York: Beginner Books, 1980);

The Tooth Book (New York: Random House, 1981);

Hunches in Bunches, as Dr. Seuss (New York: Random House, 1982);

The Butter Battle Book, as Dr. Seuss (New York: Random House, 1984);

You're Only Old Once, as Dr. Seuss (New York: Random House, 1986);

The Tough Coughs As He Ploughs the Dough (New York: Morrow, 1986).

BOOKS ILLUSTRATED: *Boners* (New York: Viking, 1931);

More Boners (New York: Viking, 1931).

MOTION PICTURES: *Your Job in Germany,* U.S.
   Army, 1946; released as *Hitler Lives,* Warner
   Bros., 1946;
Design for Death, by Geisel and Helen Palmer Gei-
   sel, RKO Pictures, 1947;
Gerald McBoing-Boing, Columbia, 1951;
The 5,000 Fingers of Dr. T, by Geisel and Allen
   Scott, Columbia, 1953.

TELEVISION SCRIPTS: *How the Grinch Stole
   Christmas,* CBS, 18 December 1966;
Horton Hears a Who, CBS, 19 March 1970;
The Cat in the Hat, CBS, 10 March 1971;
Dr. Seuss on the Loose, CBS, 15 October 1973;
Hoober Bloob Highway, CBS, 19 February 1975;
Halloween is Grinch Night, ABC, 28 October 1977;
Pontoffel Pock, Where Are You?, ABC, 2 March 1980;
The Grinch Grinches the Cat in the Hat, ABC, 20
   May 1982.

Once referred to by Robert Wilson of the
New York Times Book Review as "probably the best-
loved and certainly the best-selling children's
book writer of all time," Theodor Geisel, better
known as Dr. Seuss, initiated the Random House
division Beginner Books and gave new life to juvenile literature. From his first children's book in
1937, *And to Think That I Saw It on Mulberry Street,*
to his recent *The Butter Battle Book* (1984), Dr.
Seuss has provided his audience with entertainment as well as an occasional moral lesson.

Born on 2 March 1904 to parents of German origin, Theodor Seuss Geisel grew up in
Springfield, Massachusetts. His mother, Henri-
etta Seuss Geisel, was the daughter of a baker in
Springfield and his father, Theodor Robert Geisel, worked in the family-run Springfield brew-
ery, Kuhlmbach & Geisel, which locals
pronounced "come back and guzzle." It was later–
after Geisel was grown–that his father became su-
perintendent of the public park system in
Springfield. Because the park system included a
zoo, overactive imaginations, stimulated by Dr.
Seuss's characters, have pictured the young Geisel frequenting the zoo during his formative
years. How perfectly appropriate that would be
if it were true.

Geisel went to high school in Springfield
where an art teacher told him he would never
learn to draw realistically, and, whether due to inability or refusal, he never has. All of his illustrations are distinctively fantastic. From high school
he went to Dartmouth where he became editor

of the college humor magazine, *Jack-o-Lantern.*
He contributed reams of cartoons in the now famous style with bizarre animals. A happy relationship with Dartmouth continued beyond his 1925
graduation, and in 1955 Dartmouth legitimized
his self-proclaimed title of "Dr." by awarding him
an honorary Doctorate of Humane Letters. Following his undergraduate years, Geisel went to Oxford for graduate work in English. He intended
to become an English professor but became frustrated when he was shunted into a particularly insignificant field of research. A fellow student,
Helen Palmer, advised him to follow his real talent which she observed as he doodled in a Milton class. Geisel took her advice, made her his
chief advisor and manager, and married her on
29 November 1927. Their marriage lasted until
Helen's death in 1967. A year later he married
Audrey Stone Dimond on 6 August 1968.

In the early days after leaving Oxford, Geisel successfully marketed his cartoons and prose
for *Judge, College Humor, Liberty, Vanity Fair,* and
Life. One of his cartoons attracted the interest of
the Flit division of Standard Oil Company, and
he was contracted to do cartoon ads. His "Quick
Henry the Flit" ads became famous. Geisel also
did billboard advertising, and he created some
monsters for Standard Oil–the Moto-Raspus, the
Zerodoccus, the Moto-Munchus, the Karbo-
Nockus, and the Oilio-Gobelus–that are distant
kin to characters in the Circus McGerkus and
Zoosky McGrewsky. In 1931 Viking Press asked
him to illustrate a book of humor which was published as *Boners.* It did well, as did the sequel,
More Boners, and gave Geisel the idea of doing a
book of his own. He wrote and illustrated an
ABC book which contained all sorts of fantastic animals, but he could not find a publisher for it.
Not until four years later did he try another
children's book. As the often-recounted story
goes, inspiration came on a transatlantic voyage.
Geisel translated the monotonous rhythm of the
ship's engines–"da da *da* da da *dum* dum de *da de*
de da"–into "And to think that I saw it on Mulberry Street." Later he developed that line into a
book and tried to sell it. It seemed to be a rerun
of the ABC book experience. Even though he sub-
mitted it widely, no one wanted it.

One day by fortunate accident, he ran into
an old Dartmouth friend who had just become juvenile editor of Vanguard Press. In the typical
what-are-you-doing-now exchange, it quickly developed that one had a book and was looking for
a publisher, and the other had an editorship and

was looking for a book. Such a fortunate meeting is the stuff of fantasy, an appropriate beginning for the career of Dr. Seuss. Geisel used his middle name, his mother's maiden name, for his children's books, saving his last name for greater, more serious writing. To that he added the Dr. in a flippant gesture to the doctorate he never finished. As he explained to Cynthia Lindsay of *Good Housekeeping* (December 1960), "my father had always wanted to see a Dr. in front of my name, so I attached it. I figured by doing that, I saved him about ten thousand dollars."

In 1937 when *And to Think That I Saw It on Mulberry Street* was published, it was very different from the traditional books for children, but it contained elements that became standard in Seuss books. The story line is extremely simple, beginning and ending in the ordinary world. Marco is on his way home from school and knows he will be asked to tell what he saw. But Marco has a creative mind and begins to improve upon reality. Most of the book develops Marco's fantasy by simple accumulation. The actual horse and wagon on Mulberry Street become a zebra and cart, then the cart becomes a chariot, the zebra is superseded by a reindeer and so on until Marco's imagination has created a marvelous, joyous parade of people and animals all in bright primary colors and motion. Marco feels "GREAT" about his story. In the presence of his father, who disapproves of his creative vision ("Your eyesight's much too keen"), Marco abandons his story and gives only facts. But the reader knows that what Marco saw with his imagination was far superior to reality, and the story is a celebration of the creative spirit. As such it is counter to the adult message that one must always tell the truth. The conflict between fantasy and reality is recurrent in Seuss's work, having been started perhaps by that high school art teacher who wanted his animals to look like real animals.

The 500 Hats of Bartholomew Cubbins (1938), Geisel's second book, is one of his best. Certainly the illustrations are more sophisticated than in subsequent books, and the story of the magical hats is superbly realized in the use of color. The red hats seem to have a life of their own in the black and white and gray pictures. The text and the pictures complement one another, as when Seuss expresses the distance between King Derwin and Bartholomew, the distance between king and commoner. The text reads,

Dust jacket for Geisel's first book, about a boy's imaginative interpretation of an ordinary walk home from school (Vanguard)

his palace stood high on the top of the mountain. From his balcony, he looked down over the houses of all his subjects– first, over the spires of the nobleman's castles, across the broad roofs of the rich men's mansions, then over the little houses of the townsfolk, to the huts of the farmers far off in the fields.

In synchrony with the text, the illustration shows King Derwin looking down on his kingdom, which recedes to pinpoint perspective. For the king "it was a mighty view and it made King Derwin feel mighty important." For Bartholomew the view is from low to high, emphasizing his smallness.

The story is based on a conflict between a literal-minded king and the forces of magic which are subject to no one's control. The king determines to enforce the letter of the law requiring hats to be doffed in his presence. As Bartholomew takes off a hat, one with a feather pointed straight up in the air, another appears, and red hats accumulate–500 in all–throughout the book. The literal letter of the law which got Bartholomew in trouble also saves him. The executioner cannot behead him with his hat on; the law requires that it be removed. Since Bartholomew cannot remove his hat, the executioner cannot execute him. The plot climaxes with the 500th hat, which the reader anticipates, but there is no lesson to be learned. The hat which would not be humbled has only grown more splendid until it winds up on the king's head. Instead of being killed, Bartholomew goes home rich, but not for any reason. No one "could ever explain how the strange thing had happened. They only could say it just 'happened to happen' and was not very likely to happen again."

In *The King's Stilts* (1939), Seuss again effectively uses a brilliant red in otherwise gray pictures. This book does have a thesis that a kingdom works better when the king takes time to play, for when his stilts are stolen the king is depressed and neglects his job. The whole kingdom suffers and is threatened with extinction before the stilts are returned.

As *Mulberry Street* was inspired by an auditory stimulus, Seuss making words to go with a rhythm, *Horton Hatches the Egg* (1940) had a visual stimulus. By accident again–Geisel certainly has had his share of fortunate ones, or perhaps he is good at capitalizing on chance–two transparent sheets on his drafting table landed together, one on top of the other. There he had a sketch of an elephant superimposed on a sketch of a tree. For weeks he wondered why an elephant would be sitting in a tree. Finally, he realized, "Of course! He's hatching an egg!"

The illustrations and the text depart from the style of the previous two books and introduce the style that characterizes his work for the next thirty years. That style includes a playfulness with language and rhythm, humor based on incongruity, and outlandish creatures. In *Horton Hatches the Egg*, which earned a Lewis Carroll Shelf Award in 1958, Seuss begins playing with language for the effect of the sound. He uses sound repetitions, as in *Horton Hatches* and *Lazy Mayzie*, as well as strong rhyme patterns. And the refrain that Horton recites over and over is so strong that even a child who does not read will quickly pick it up:

> I meant what I said
> And I said what I meant. . . .
> An elephant's faithful
> One hundred per cent!

He is not yet inventing words–that comes later. But his work has acquired that distinctive

Cover for Geisel's 1940 book in which his mature style–characterized by a playfulness with language and rhythm, humor based on incongruities, and outlandish characters–fully emerged (Random House)

Seuss sound. Similarly, animals in the drawings are still recognizable as lion, moose, giraffe, or hippopotamus. The elephant-bird that hatches as a result of Horton's faithful labor is the first "brand new" creature. But just the situation of the immense elephant sitting in the tree on the small egg opens a whole new world of incongruities.

While Geisel worked on *Horton* in 1940, Paris fell to the Nazis, and Geisel thought the United States was being too complacent. He turned to drawing political cartoons that attacked American isolationism and became editorial cartoonist for a newspaper, *PM*. The cartoons he did were quite serious, devoid of humor. He also did drawings for the Treasury Department, the War Production Board, and the Committee on Inter-American Affairs. In 1942 he joined the armed forces and was stationed in California with a documentary filmmaking unit. Out of the service in 1946, Geisel continued to work on documentary films and returned to doing children's books. His documentary short *Hitler Lives* won an

Oscar in 1946, and the following year, he and his wife wrote a documentary film, *Design for Death,* which also won an Academy Award. Geisel also created a movie cartoon character, *Gerald McBoing-Boing,* another Oscar winner (1951), and wrote and designed costumes and sets for *The 5,000 Fingers of Dr. T* (1953), a musical satire on piano lessons. During this period, he also received the Legion of Merit for his educational and informational films.

While the Geisels were not busy with films, Dr. Seuss went back to writing for children. He constructed *McElligot's Pool* (1947), a Caldecott Honor book, on the same basic pattern as *Mulberry Street.* A discouraging adult voice tells a hopeful young fisherman that he'll never catch fish in McElligot's pool. The boy remains open to possibility and lets his imagination propose an underground connection to the sea from whence all sorts of fish might come. Then he dreams up the fantastic kinds of creatures for which Seuss has become famous. *McElligot's Pool* is the first book in which Seuss freely invents new life forms; it was the obvious next step after Horton's elephantbird. He has not yet begun to invent names for them, except for the climactic THING-A-MA-JIGGER, but we see rudiments of word invention with the creation of *CLURK* to rhyme with *murk.* In this text, however, he describes the new fish forms with standard words and unleashes his inventiveness in the bizarre drawings, using an explosion of color on every other page, alternating with black, white, and gray.

Thidwick, The Big-Hearted Moose (1948) recalls *Horton* not only in his character but also in the two-color drawings. As Horton's loyalty is exploited by lazy Mayzie, so is Thidwick's hospitality abused. One guest after another piles on to Thidwick's antlers until Thidwick is overburdened and unable to protect himself. He is their victim because of his allegiance to the principle that "a host, above all, must be nice to his guests." Thidwick is delivered of his guests not a moment too soon, when his antlers come off, and he escapes the hunters. All of his ill-mannered guests meet a just end, becoming stuffed trophies on the Harvard Club wall.

Bartholomew and the Oobleck (1949), another recipient of the Caldecott Honor Award, turns Seuss morality upside down. For once the voice of conservatism is the child's, and the wish for something new and extraordinary is bad. When King Derwin tires of snow, fog, sunshine, and rain and wants something new to come down

Dust jacket for the 1954 sequel to Horton Hatches the Egg, *in which Geisel presents a fable about minority rights (Random House)*

from the sky, he gets not marvelous things, but oobleck. When the whole kingdom is gummed up with oobleck, Bartholomew Cubbins, in finger-pointing accusation, tells the king that he should say some "simple words, 'I'm sorry.'" Those simple words have power to melt oobleck, and the kingdom is restored to "old-fashioned things" like rain, sunshine, fog, and snow. The text is appropriately prosaic, with the onomatapoeic oobleck being the only example of inventive language. The green oobleck in the otherwise colorless illustrations has a similar effect as the red hats in the earlier Bartholomew Cubbins book.

Gerald McGrew, in *If I Ran the Zoo* (1950), is not unlike King Derwin when he wants "something new" because ordinary lions and tigers are "not quite good enough." Preceded by the subjunctive, *if* I ran the zoo, Gerald dreams up ever more fantastic creatures from farther away. The bizarre animals also have bizarre names, as do the places they come from. The language and the pictures are outlandish, ridiculous, and fun. Vocal expression is built in, and the language-conservative adult will find reading this book aloud a liberating experience. It is a favorite among children and was named Seuss's third Caldecott Honor Book.

Scrambled Eggs Super! (1953) is a repetition of *If I Ran the Zoo* but is even better. Peter T. Hooper, in search of the ultimate omelet, goes looking for egg-layers as Gerald McGrew looked for zoo tenants. Repetitious in plot though it is, it still works, and the playfulness with language and the quality of the illustrations surpass Seuss's previous performance. He forces his rhymes harder than ever and comes up with sounds funnier than ever. For instance, there is Ali who climbed "Mt. Strookoo / To fetch me the egg of a Mt. Strookoo Cuckoo," an egg destined "For my Scrambled Eggs Super-dee-Dooper-dee-Booper / Special de luxe à-la-Peter T. Hooper!" The illustrations keep pace with the text; in fact they provide pace. To lead the reader into the story, Seuss uses a diagonal line sloping toward the bottom right side of the page, leaving the corner of the page unprinted. The effect is that the page is turning of its own accord, not even waiting for the will of the reader. He does it again at the end of the story to lead the reader to the conclusion. Finally the reader sees Peter in his kitchen, which is piled high with eggs in precarious balance (one cannot help but wonder where he was putting them all). Only two eggs have broken, as far as the reader can see, in a scene with eggs balanced on ends of handles, in potted plants, between the spout and neck of a bottle, in the tines of a fork, on top of each other—in an impossible tension. The reader will be like Liz who, as she listens to his story, is firmly seated in her chair on the first page and by the last page is perched on the edge of her stool in amazement as Peter T. Hooper describes his culinary extravaganza.

The Sneetches, and Other Stories (1953) is a collection of three stories that attack the practice of stereotyping. The title story illustrates the superficiality of stereotyping, when the prejudice of the Sneetches makes them vulnerable to exploitation by Sylvester McMonkey McBean, who is an opportunist. Only after their money is gone do they realize that physical appearance is unimportant. In "Too Many Daves" Mrs. McCave does not bother to acknowledge the individual differences of each of her twenty-three sons by giving them different names, much to her eventual regret. And "What Was I Scared Of?" tells a story about a marvelous pair of green pants that frightens the speaker, but as it turns out, the pants are as frightened as

he. When the two overcame their fright, they become friends.

Horton Hears a Who! (1954) is a fable about minority rights. Geisel had the Japanese people in mind who, after the war, were "trying to find a voice and make it known." Children will miss that level of the story but will likely feel that "a person's a person no matter how small" applies to themselves. The general principles in the story are universal ones about the responsibility of the strong to protect the weak and the importance of every individual, even the smallest, participating in the effort to preserve the society. The microcosm that Horton discovers on a clover introduces the concept of relativity that intrigues most children. The plot of the story and the flow of the verse build to a dramatic peak when a very small shirker adds his voice to the general cry and saves the Whos. The cartoon adaptation of this work won a Peabody Award in 1971.

On Beyond Zebra (1955) is for the graduate of the ABC's. Here Seuss invents new letters and names them. The letters are quite fanciful, but the names are not funny or memorable, and Seuss's creatures are beginning to look familiar.

Seuss uses the pattern of *Mulberry Street, If I Ran the Zoo,* and *Scrambled Eggs Super!* once more in *If I Ran the Circus* (1956). Again a child creates a marvelous world with his imagination, a world that vastly improves on the real one. Morris McGurk thinks the vacant lot behind Sneelock's store would make a good place for a circus, and old Sneelock won't mind because Morris includes him in his imaginary circus. Always, no matter how daring the trick Morris imagines him doing, Sneelock has the same complacent look on his face that he had on the first page as he leaned against the door of his store smoking his pipe. Only at the end as Morris proclaims him Hero, does Sneelock's eye open in surprise.

In 1957 Seuss published a book that more than any other influenced the market in children's primers. John Hersey had published an article in *Life* in 1954 titled "Why Johnny Can't Read." He complained about the dull, repetitious primers used to teach reading and stated the need for livelier books. Seuss responded with *The Cat in the Hat.* Using a limited vocabulary, he told a story that was exciting—even anxiety-producing—with one of the most engaging characters in children's literature: a talking cat in a striped hat.

The structure of the book is typical of Seuss's work. It opens in the ordinary world as

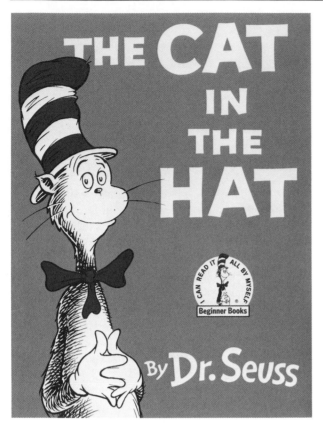

Cover for a paperback edition of Geisel's 1957 book which was the Beginner Books prototype (Random House). Geisel initiated the Beginner Books division at Random House with the intention of providing preschoolers with books that help them learn to read by following the pictures.

two children sit staring out the window on a rainy day. Their mother is gone, and they have nothing to do. The Cat in the Hat enters, unsummoned, and proposes to entertain them. Over the admonitions of the fish, the Cat takes over, and his games make a horrible mess. To make matters worse, he releases Thing One and Thing Two, who compound the chaos. At the height of the "fun," which the children watch from the sidelines (and therefore incur no guilt), Mother returns. Only her foot is visible through the window, but the prospect of Mother finding the house in such a wreck is terrifying. In the time that it takes Mother to cover the few steps to the door, Thing One and Thing Two must be captured and contained, and the mess must be cleaned up. The pessimistic voice of the fish seems justified:

> this mess is so big
> And so deep and so tall,
> We cannot pick it up.
> There is no way at all.

But the cat reassures them: "Have no fear of this mess / I always pick up all my playthings," which he proceeds to do with a many-handed machine that even tosses the fish back into his bowl. Miraculously, all is back to normal, and the children return to the window before Mother enters. A long way from "Run Jane Run," *The Cat in the Hat* was the prototype for the Beginner Books that came later.

How the Grinch Stole Christmas (1957), winner of another Peabody Award, has become a contemporary Christmas classic, with the Grinch as a modern replacement for Scrooge. The Grinch hates Christmas and sets out to ruin it for the Whos down in Whoville. He thinks he can steal Christmas by stealing material things. When Christmas comes anyway, the Grinch learns a lesson about the intangible meaning of Christmas (but without any mention of the religious meaning). The story is frankly moralistic, but it is so without being trite or sentimental. The language is fun, with *Grinch* being as good a word for a Christmas villain as *oobleck* is for green goo. The pictures capture the contrasts between the mean red-eyed Grinch and the innocent round-bellied Whos, between the noisy chaos of a Christmas day celebration and the cold, barren room in the stripped Who-house. The red-and-white treatment makes the illustrations lively and seasonal.

The Cat in the Hat Comes Back! (1958) is another limited vocabulary book based on the antics of the infamous Cat. This time the children try to prevent the Cat's mischief but are powerless to stop him. He leaves a pink ring on the bathtub that resists destruction. He calls on little cats under his hat, one for each letter of the alphabet, to try various ways to clean away the pink spots. The last uses Voom ("Now, don't ask me what Voom is / I never will know") which does the job and sets things right again.

Yertle the Turtle, and Other Stories (1958) is a collection which presents creatures who attempt to outdo others. In the title story Yertle disrupts his happy pond-kingdom when he decides to be king of a greater territory. Since he is king of all he sees, he becomes greater the higher he goes. Unfortunately he must raise himself by climbing on the backs of other turtles, who then suffer pain, hunger, and loss of freedom. A burp from the bottom turtle corrects the situation.

In "Gertrude McFuzz," the title character is jealous of Lolla-Lee-Lou's fancy tail and wishes to have one as pretty. When she discovers a bit-

Cover for Geisel's 1957 story which has become
a Christmas classic (Random House)

ter berry bush that makes her tail grow beautiful plumes, she eats all the berries, and her tail becomes enormously intricate, large, and beautiful. But then she cannot fly and has to be helped home where she must pluck out all the burdensome feathers.

"The Big Brag," in the tradition of the tall tale, shows a rabbit and a bear arguing over whose senses are keenest. The rabbit claims he can hear a fly cough on a mountain ninety miles away. The bear then brags that he can smell a stale hummingbird egg over six hundred miles away. Finally a worm pops up and has the last word; he says he can see so far that he can look all the way around the world back to the hill where they are, and he can see the two biggest fools who have nothing better to do than to argue "who's better than who." As in *Bartholomew and the Oobleck*, the message seems to be in favor of accepting things the way they are. Appropriately the stories are told simply, and the drawings are uncomplicated.

Happy Birthday to You! (1959) is an exuberant birthday wish that the speaker could say happy birthday the way they do in Katroo. Then the story is an accumulation of extravagances done for a birthday in Katroo. The book ends with a reminder that all has been fantasy: "So that's / What the Birthday Bird / Does in Katroo. / And I wish / I could do / All these great things for you!" It's one of the most colorful of the Seuss books and does a bang-up job of celebrating.

With *One Fish Two Fish Red Fish Blue Fish* (1960), Geisel began doing even simpler primers than *The Cat in the Hat*. Random House started a separate division for Beginner Books and appointed Geisel to head the imprint. The books used limited vocabulary and keyed description to pictures, one picture to a page. The other rule Geisel insisted on was that no book could be "cute" or what he derogatorily called a "bunny-bunny book." Some of the Beginner Books were done by Seuss; others were written by Seuss but illustrated by others. In the latter he used the pseudonym Theo. LeSieg (Geisel spelled backwards).

Some of the Beginner Books were done entirely by others but under Seuss's close scrutiny. The early ones that Seuss did, like *One Fish Two Fish Red Fish Blue Fish*, *Green Eggs and Ham* (1960), and *Hop on Pop* (1963), are fresh in approach and provide nonsense stories that are fun to read. By reading the pictures a young child can quickly learn the words, but the formula books eventually become mechanical. The ones that Seuss wrote and illustrated are generally better than the Theo. LeSieg books that he did with other illustrators.

Despite the sameness of many of the Beginner Books, the accomplishment is considerable. Geisel created the materials that Hersey had asked for. They are easy to read but bright, boisterous, and engaging. They most certainly changed the nature of early learning materials. The immensely popular television program for children, *Sesame Street*, was developed as perhaps the farthest extension yet of what Geisel began. Whether these high stimulus materials prepare a child to move on to more subdued materials or whether they leave him deaf and blind to subtle shades and suggested meanings will be for others to determine, but as Geisel explains to Miles Corwin of the *Los Angeles Times*, "Nonsense wakes up the brain cells. And it helps develop a sense of humor, which is awfully important in this day and age."

During the 1960s and 1970s Geisel concentrated largely on Beginner Books, but he did occasionally do other books. *Dr. Seuss' Sleep Book*

Cover for Geisel's popular 1963 nonsense rhyme volume written and illustrated in Beginner Books format (Random House)

(1962) successfully attempts to lull the reader-listener into a quiet, sleepy state, a task quite opposite the usual Seuss approach. Here he catalogs the falling asleep of creatures all over the Seuss world—all draped, tucked, or hung here and there with happy smiles, closed eyes, and limp bodies. The light blue background in the early pages darkens as the book progresses. A count is kept as creatures everywhere go to sleep until finally there is only the little one draped over the book. "So how about you? / When you put out *your* light, / Then the number will be Ninety-nine zillion / Nine trillion and three." The change in tone and the novelty of seeing Seuss characters inactive make this book distinctive. But it also amuses with language and pictures as well as the more lively ones.

I Had Trouble in Getting to Solla Sollew (1965) chronicles the many troubles of an escapist who is trying to find a place where no troubles exist. The plot progresses by the familiar process of accumulation until the escapist decides to deal with his troubles. The book is typical of Seuss, but there is nothing new in it, and some of the energy is missing.

I Can Lick 30 Tigers Today, and Other Stories (1969) is a collection of three stories not thematically connected. The title story is a very simple one built on the modifications the little cat makes to his boast. King Looie Katz in the second story is very like Yertle the Turtle. By insisting on royal treatment, he enslaves everyone else. He finally learns that he, like all the others, must be responsible for himself. The most interesting of the three stories is "The Glunk That Got Thunk," about a little girl who amuses herself with her imagination. One time, however, she "thunk up a Glunk," who is as uncontrollable in his mischief as the earlier Cat in the Hat. Only with help from her brother (a little cat in the hat) can the Glunk be unthunk. Her brother chastizes her for her creativity, and she controls her thinking. The message seems all wrong for Dr. Seuss and is very much out of character.

The Lorax (1971) came out during the height of ecology consciousness. The criticism of the Once-ler who exploited natural resources and polluted the air and the water so he could go on "biggering" his factory probably appealed more to adults than children. The business practices of the Once-ler who puts all his relatives to work have adult humor, but the message is simplified and clear: the Once-ler has taken his gain and left a mess, and the responsibility for rejuvenation is passed to the young. The language is inventive and onomatopoeic. Seuss captures the opportunism of the Once-ler in the pace of his speech:

> I called all my brothers and uncles and aunts
> and I said, "Listen here! Here's a wonderful chance
> for the whole Once-ler family to get mighty rich!
> Get over here fast! Take the road to North Nitch.
> Turn left at Weehawken. Sharp right at South Stitch."

With contrast between colorful Truffula Trees and the grey, devastated landscape at the end, Seuss supports his thesis visually. Although some people object to the didacticism, the craftsmanship with both language and drawings is top quality.

After a three-year silence from the Dr. Seuss part of Theodor Geisel, *Hunches in Bunches* (1982) appeared. It is still the familiar artwork and language of the previous books, but there is no joy, and the character's world as represented by the unadorned walls of the house he lives in and the view out the window is the sterile landscape we saw at the end of *The Lorax*. But according to the text, the boy still has plenty to do, and his problem is to decide what to do. This boy seems to be afflicted with a stereotypically modern mind, so introspective and self-doubting that to settle on a single option seems inconceivable. His options appear to him as animated creatures called Hunches. The difficulty of making decisions is visually supported in a series of doorways beyond which other doorways can be seen. As usual every part of the drawings tilt, lean, or balance impossibly. The Hunches wearing gloves with pointing fingers for hats are typical Seuss creations, but the exuberance and fun are missing.

The Butter Battle Book (1984), a satire on war, is not at all funny. A grandfather Yook takes his grandson to the wall that divides Yooks from Zooks. Their chief difference and source of enmity is that Yooks butter the top side of their bread, and Zooks butter the bottom side. The grandfather has spent his life in a war that began with his "tough-tufted prickely Snick-Berry Switch" but has escalated each time the Zooks invented an equal or bigger weapon. Finally the boys in the Top-est Secret-est Brain Nest, who design the weapons, came up with The Bitsy Big-Boy Boomeroo. All Yooks were sent underground, and the grandfather tells the child he should be there too, but instead he can watch him make history. As he leaps to the top of the wall to drop the Boomeroo on the Zook side, his counterpart from the Zooks does the same. They each have a Boomeroo and pause in a posture of imminent destruction of each other's worlds. The frightened child, now up a tree, shouts, "Grandpa! Be careful! Oh gee!" and asks who will drop it, "Will you . . . ? Or will he . . . ?" The only answer is, "We will see." And so the child is left powerless in a world poised for annihilation. There is not even the glimmer of hope that was left in the last truffula seed in *The Lorax.* And Dr. Seuss, who in so many other books showed children how to escape reality by the power of the creative imagination, seems to see no creative antidote for the modern threat of nuclear war.

Dr. Seuss has always been a moralist taking stands against prejudice, tyranny, ecological abuse, and other flaws of human beings individually and collectively. In *The Butter Battle Book* he takes a tough moral stand in showing children that their elders have been foolish, and their foolishness has become dangerous to the survival of the world.

Critics have debated whether Seuss is primarily a writer and only a cartoonist in his drawings

Cover for the 2 March 1984 issue of Publishers Weekly

or whether his real creativity is in the drawings, and the verse is only doggerel. Seuss does draw cartoons and write doggerel, but in a highly integrated way. That skill at integration along with his natural wit and humor and his high standards of quality help to explain why he is so successful. His books have sold millions of copies, and he has won dozens of awards for his work, including an Emmy Award in 1977 for *Halloween is Grinch Night,* the Laura Ingalls Wilder Award in 1980, the Regina Medal in 1982, and a Pulitzer Prize in 1984.

Dr. Seuss knows what children find humorous and just what limits of fantasy a child will permit. And when he finds something that is successful, he uses it again. He has written a few works for adults–*The Seven Lady Godivas* (1939) and *Signs of Civilization!* (1956), for example–but he prefers to create for children. As he explains, "I'd rather write for kids. They are more appreciative. Adults are obsolete children and the hell with them."

References:

Barbara Bader, *American Picturebooks from Noah's*

Ark to the Beast Within (New York: Macmillan, 1976);

John P. Bailey, Jr., "Three Decades of Dr. Seuss," *Elementary English*, 42 (January 1956): 7-11;

Robert Cahn, "The Wonderful World of Dr. Seuss," *Saturday Evening Post*, 46 (6 July 1957): 18-19, 42, 46;

Clifton Fadiman, "Professionals and Confessionals: Dr. Seuss and Kenneth Graham," in *Only Connect: Readings on Children's Literature*, edited by Shelia Egoff, G. T. Stubbs, and L. F. Ashley (New York: Oxford University Press, 1969), pp. 316-332;

M. Kasindorf, "Happy Accident; Work of T. Seuss Geisel," *Newsweek*, 79 (21 February 1972): 100;

Selma G. Lanes, "Seuss for the Goose is Seuss for the Gander," in *Down the Rabbit Hole: Adventures and Misadventures in the Realm of Children's Literature* (New York: Atheneum, 1971), pp. 79-89;

Mary Lystad, *From Dr. Mather to Dr. Seuss; 200 Years of American Books for Children* (Boston: G. K. Hall, 1980);

Donnaroe MacCann and Olga Richard, *The Child's First Books* (New York: Wilson, 1973);

Roger Sale, *Fairy Tales and After; From Snow White to E. B. White* (Cambridge, Mass.: Harvard University Press, 1978);

James Steel Smith, *A Critical Approach to Children's Literature* (New York: McGraw-Hill, 1967);

Zena Sutherland and May Hill Arbuthnot, *Children and Books* (Glenview, Ill.: Scott Foresman, 1977);

Mary Lou White, *Children's Literature: Criticism and Response* (Columbus, Ohio: Merrill, 1976).

Papers:

The manuscript of *The 500 Hats of Bartholomew Cubbins* is located at Dartmouth College, Hanover, New Hampshire. Geisel also has manuscripts located in the Special Collections department of the University of California Library, Los Angeles, California.

M. B. Goffstein

(20 December 1940-)

Janice Alberghene
Bowling Green State University

BOOKS: *The Gats!* (New York: Pantheon, 1966);

Sleepy People (New York: Farrar, Straus & Giroux, 1966);

Brookie and Her Lamb (New York: Farrar, Straus & Giroux, 1967);

Across the Sea (New York: Farrar, Straus & Giroux, 1968);

Goldie the Dollmaker (New York: Farrar, Straus & Giroux, 1969),

Two Piano Tuners (New York: Farrar, Straus & Giroux, 1970);

The Underside of the Leaf (New York: Farrar, Straus & Giroux, 1972);

A Little Schubert (New York: Harper & Row, 1972);

Me and My Captain (New York: Farrar, Straus & Giroux, 1974);

Daisy Summerfield's Style (New York: Delacorte, 1975);

Fish for Supper (New York: Dial, 1976);

My Crazy Sister (New York: Dial, 1976);

Family Scrapbook (New York: Farrar, Straus & Giroux, 1978);

My Noah's Ark (New York: Harper & Row, 1978);

Natural History (New York: Farrar, Straus & Giroux, 1979);

Neighbors (New York: Harper & Row, 1979);

The First Books, includes *The Gats!, Sleepy People, Brookie and Her Lamb, Across the Sea, Goldie the Dollmaker, Two Piano Tuners, Me and My Captain* (New York: Avon, 1979);

An Artist (New York: Harper & Row, 1980);

Laughing Latkes (New York: Farrar, Straus & Giroux, 1980);

Lives of the Artists (New York: Farrar, Straus & Giroux, 1981);

A Writer (New York: Harper & Row, 1984);

An Artist's Album (New York: Harper & Row, 1985);

My Editor (New York: Farrar, Straus & Giroux, 1985);

School of Names (New York: Harper & Row, 1986);

Our Snowman (New York: Harper & Row, 1986);

Your Lone Journey (New York: Harper & Row, 1986);

Artist's Helpers Enjoy the Evening (New York: Harper & Row, 1987).

M. B. Goffstein (photo by Peter Schaaf)

For over twenty years, M. B. Goffstein has demonstrated in her books for children and young adults that both good things and big issues can come in small packages. Of her twenty-six published books to date, twenty-three are picture books with illustrations that are often no bigger than 2 ¾ by 3 ¼ inches, and some of the texts which accompany the illustrations tell their respective stories in as few as seven or eight sentences.

This brevity results from Goffstein's focus on essential elements—choosing the right words and drawing the right lines to tell her stories about friendship, family, the rituals of holidays and every day, natural history, and the importance of finding and following one's vocation. In a number of her latest books, Goffstein approaches the subject of vocation by exploring what it means to be an artist. The tiny figures she presents write or paint, but most of all they wonder about the universe and all that it contains.

Born 20 December 1940 to Albert A. and Esther Rose Goffstein, Goffstein's attention to the significance of vocation began in childhood, and her own choice of art as a profession dates from that time as well. As she herself has explained, both Goffstein and her little brother "grew up in St. Paul, Minnesota, feeling that work was the only real dignity, the only real happiness, and that people were nothing if their lives were not dedicated. My choice was art–a talent which shows up early." Goffstein pursued this interest at Bennington College, where, by the time she graduated with a B.A. in 1962, she had composed "short stories, which became more and more condensed," studied poetry, and had a one-woman show of her drawings and watercolors. In addition to the Bennington show, she had one-woman shows at the Wakefield Gallery in New York City, at the Suzanne Kohn Gallery in St. Paul, and at the St. Paul Institute of Art. Rounding off what Goffstein has called her "apprenticeship" were two college winter-work terms spent at printers in New York.

If Goffstein's college years represent her apprenticeship as a writer and artist, her earliest volumes can be seen as a rite of passage to the status of author-illustrator. Moving to New York in 1962, she looked for work as an illustrator. None appeared, but Goffstein sold children's books in two stores and soon decided that she was ready to write her own book. Like many of her fellow author-illustrators, Goffstein first turned for inspiration to nursery literature and several of its subgenres. Her nonsense tale, *The Gats!* (1966), a go-to-sleep story, *Sleepy People* (1966), and an idiosyncratic version of a Mother Goose tale, *Brookie and Her Lamb* (1967), all demonstrate an original sensibility at work on subjects often associated with young children.

Although definitely a picture book, Goffstein's *The Gats!* reads like the notation for a comic ballet, which is only fitting, since the story comes from a person who sees the picture book form as a "sparkling little theatre in black and white, where I am the author, stage manager, actor." Such an analysis emphasizes Goffstein's control of materials, nowhere more evident than in a mastery of line which lends wonderful agility to the essentially lump-shaped gats. While they occasionally trip over tree roots, they also prance,

dance the "gamba," and stir a vat of soup with a baseball bat. Internal rhyme and occasional end rhyme appropriately syncopate the narrative of these events, for the gats are nothing if not off-beat. They treat looking for a home as a lark, and when their treetop abode snaps from too much dancing, they leave with no regrets. The nonsense in this book does not depend on disquieting incongruities, as in Edward Lear's work, or on frenetic buildup and repetition, as in the books of Dr. Seuss. Goffstein relies instead on celebrating the gats' nonchalance and joie de vivre.

Nonsense gives way to drowsiness in *Sleepy People*, a virtually quintessential bedtime story. Critic Selma G. Lanes, in *Down the Rabbit Hole: Adventures and Misadventures in the Realm of Children's Literature* (1972), credits the book's effectiveness to "the artist-author's unique conception. The notion of a minuscule, droopy-lidded race, some of whose members may be 'living in one of your old bedroom slippers,' is inspired, helping to make her small work a rival to the sandman in summoning slumber." Equally important, however, is the *sound* of the text of *Sleepy People*–a murmur of soft *l* and *s* sounds that end with a lullaby sung by a sleepy mother to her sleepy children. The book is visually quiet as well with its dusky gray washes and comforting details. Sweet dreams await the reader of this book where "Every evening the sleepy father goes to find cocoa and cookies for a little bedtime snack."

Goffstein's third volume, *Brookie and Her Lamb*, features a heroine whose name is a diminutive of Goffstein's middle name, Brooke, but naming is just one of the ways Goffstein refashions the Mother Goose prototype of child and pet lamb into a story that is her own. Brookie is considerate of her lamb, much more so than the Mary of the nursery rhyme who does nothing more for her lamb regarding its education than allowing it to follow her to school. In contrast, Brookie teaches the lamb to read and to sing, and is not discouraged when all he can sing and read is "baa." She provides him with songs and books to match his ability–they too say only "baa."

Writing about the story in 1980, in *Children's Literature in Education*, Barbara Ann Porte commented: "Children need to know that love is unconditional. Goffstein's books help provide that reassurance. In *Brookie and Her Lamb*, for example, never mind that the beloved lamb can't learn to read or even sing–'she loved him anyhow.'" This story is just the first of many in which Goffstein celebrates the joy of expressing

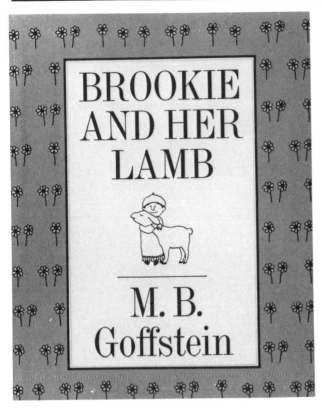

Dust jacket for Goffstein's 1967 book about a young girl who teaches her pet lamb to read and sing (Farrar, Straus & Giroux)

love, a concern so fundamental to many of her stories that it is less a theme than an essential characteristic of her vision as an author and illustrator.

The nursery world of Goffstein's first books opens up in her fourth, *Across the Sea* (1968), a collection of five short pieces dedicated to Goffstein's "Grandma Rosie and the memory of Grandpa Nathan." The book departs from Goffstein's previous use of black and white by including several shades of red and blue along with gray and white. The old man of the title story brings to mind grandfathers and the stories that they tell the young. In this case, the narrator of the piece expresses a wish to hear a story while sitting at the knee of an old man who would whittle a "good friend" for the listener. The old man described is the first of many artist figures to appear in Goffstein's work and is also the kind of person who might have told the last story in the book, "The Mill," a tale adapted from a Jewish folk song.

Across the Sea is a transitional book in its title story's depiction of a carver who makes "small figures that come to life." In *Horn Book*, critic George Shannon has noted several ways the story prefigures much of Goffstein's later work: "She ex-

plores feelings about an artist's bringing life to wood and his way of working; about the longing for a friend, the friendship of art, and the connection of story to art and friends."

The idea of making small figures that come to life is expanded into a fully realized exploration of art, understanding, and vocation in *Goldie the Dollmaker* (1969). Here Goffstein not only builds upon her previous book's glimpse of an old man whittling a friend for a little girl, but also reaches back to her own work during college: "I had even carved some small wooden figures and a large cherry log in preparation for writing *Goldie the Dollmaker*, one day." Goldie Rosenzweig is an orphan who lives alone in her parents' house and carries on their work of making dolls. She works four times as fast as they did; in four years she makes as many dolls as her two parents made in eight, but she does not mass-produce—every doll is crafted individually. Her speed is a sign of her devotion to the meaning and experience of her work. To Goldie, a doll is a "little wooden person," and she cannot rest until she has completed its arms and legs as well as its face and body. Goldie's dedication to her work mirrors Goffstein's: as the author told Joann Giusto-Davis in *Publishers Weekly*, "When I'm doing the text, I think about it 24 hours a day and sometimes get so drained that I forget I'm physical."

Goldie's efforts result in dolls that "no little girl, no parent, aunt, or uncle of a little girl anywhere in the world" can resist. They attract because of the smiles that Goldie paints on them while smiling herself at each doll. Her friend the carpenter, however, who ought to smile back at Goldie's work because he too works with wood fails to understand why Goldie does not take short cuts in making the dolls. Neither does he understand why she buys a beautiful Chinese lamp that she cannot afford:

> "You know, Goldie," Omus said slowly,
> "I think you must be a real artist."
> Goldie flushed with pleasure. "Why?"
> she asked him. "Why do you think so?"
> "Because you're crazy."
> "Oh." Goldie tried to smile.

After talking with Omus, Goldie returns home lonely and scared, but *Goldie the Dollmaker* is not a story about the alienation of an artist. When Goldie falls asleep that night, she dreams that she speaks with the artist who made the lamp. He tells her that she understands him, and

Dust jacket for Goffstein's 1969 book about an orphaned girl and the dolls she creates
(Farrar, Straus & Giroux)

when she replies that he does not know her, he says, "Yes I do. I made the lamp for you—whoever you are." Later that night Goldie wakes and looks at the lamp and at the house around her filled with the lamp's light. This moves her to think for the first time: "My own little house, with my knife and lamp and tea, my bed and worktable and wood, where I make little wooden dolls for friends."

The dream has redefined for Goldie what it means to be an artist. Contrary to what Omus thinks, it does not have anything to do with being crazy. It means being alive to beauty, faithful to one's vision, and diligent in its communication. Reassured by this knowledge, Goldie can affirm that her parents' house is now hers, and that the life she leads has purpose and satisfaction.

Goldie the Dollmaker is a sophisticated story, but its sophistication is matched by the clarity of its prose and by the intimacy of its illustrations. Although some adult readers have expressed their concern that *Goldie the Dollmaker* and the book which followed it (*Two Piano Tuners*, 1970) are too sophisticated for children, librarian Porte disagrees: "I have not found their reservations confirmed at all in the reactions of the children with whom I've shared these books."

Two Piano Tuners looks at art and at finding one's vocation from yet another perspective. Reuben Weinstock, a piano tuner, wants his granddaughter Debbie to be a concert pianist, but Debbie wants to be a piano tuner just like her grandfather with whom she has lived since her parents' death two years earlier. It is not until the great Isaac Lipman comes to town to give a concert that Debbie's grandfather is reconciled to her ambition. After listening to Debbie play a piano which she decided to tune on her own, Mr. Lipman cannot praise her playing, saying instead that "Everybody should take the responsibility for finding out what it is he really wants to do." Debbie already knows what she wants to do—the advice is actually for Reuben Weinstock's ears. He accedes to this advice and to Debbie's wanting to help him.

The respect for the vocation of the artist shown in *Goldie the Dollmaker* is here extended to Debbie's choice as well. Despite her special interest in artists, Goffstein does not propose that an artistic vocation is necessarily the worthiest choice of career. When Reuben Weinstock tells Isaac Lipman that he wanted "something better" than piano tuning for Debbie, Lipman replies, "What could be better than doing what you love?" Lipman's response pays Debbie, and by extension

Goffstein's child readers, the compliment of taking them seriously.

This is not to say that the tone of *Two Piano Tuners* is predominantly somber. Throughout the book Goffstein hints at the wry or bittersweet comedy of ignoring perception in favor of expectation or desire. This is nowhere more apparent than in the illustration of Reuben Weinstock listening to Debbie play the piano. The slight tilt forward of his profiled body, the intent set of his mouth, and the slightly anxious look of his one eye visible to the viewer all testify to the excruciating sound of Debbie's playing. The drawing itself testifies to Goffstein's affection for her characters, an affection her readers cannot help but share.

The composer that Goffstein introduces in *A Little Schubert* (1972) also inspires affection. Goffstein contrasts the physical person of Franz Schubert with the bleakness of his surroundings so that even the youngest reader can appreciate the composer's situation: "In a cold and snowy town called Vienna, a short fat young man with a small round nose, round eyeglasses and curly hair, lived in a bare little room without a fire." The above sentence is spread out over four pages, the breaks coming at the commas. There is plenty of time to take in all that the words suggest.

The illustrations for these and for succeeding pages are each framed within a neatly outlined rectangle centered on its respective page. This is a device that Goffstein employs in many of her picture books, but nowhere to better effect than in *A Little Schubert*. The viewer is drawn into each illustration with all the intimacy that looking at a miniature implies, and sees moments when Franz Schubert "heard music that no one had ever heard before." The most engaging illustrations of Schubert, however, are on the last two pages as he dances to keep warm. On the four previous pages he prepares to dance, and the reader sees him launch into some dance steps. To signal Schubert's feelings and to hint at the nature of his music, Goffstein omits the framing device once Schubert actually begins to waltz. His joyous and unfettered figure whirls across the pages. These two pictures require no text for accompaniment, although a record on which Goffstein's ex-husband, concert pianist Peter Schaaf, plays five of Schubert's "Noble Waltzes" is included.

In 1972, the same year Goffstein published *A Little Schubert*, she also published her first adolescent novel, *The Underside of the Leaf*. Like the three books before it, the novel deals with art and with finding a vocation, but these concerns are subordinate to Goffstein's account of her heroine's coming of age. It is an account which occasionally recalls Maureen Daly's *Seventeenth Summer* (1942). Both novels evoke the sights, smells, and sounds of a midwestern summer at the lake, and both portray the sexual and romantic (with the emphasis on the romantic) awakenings of their protagonists.

The similarities between the two novels end there. Daly's heroine is seventeen, while Paula Nathanson, the heroine of Goffstein's book, is twelve when the reader first meets her. Paula spends her summer vacation with her grandparents at their lake cottage. While they fish, Paula paints with her watercolors and daydreams about Tom Kadrie, jazz musician, artist, and the boyfriend of the girl next door. On his return to New York he sends Paula one of his paintings.

Five and a half years later, although now an art student at a small women's college in Vermont, Paula still thinks about him. On her way home for Christmas vacation, she stops in New York to see an exhibit of Maurice Prendergast's work, but not before seeing Tom Kadrie, who unsuccessfully attempts to seduce her. Enough of a romantic to ignore his boorishness, Paula retains her idealized image of him until she boards a plane for home and notices a handsome boy wearing a Princeton scarf.

Goffstein's portrait of Paula is both funny and tender. This young lady is not one of the sophisticated, wise-cracking protagonists fashionable in adolescent novels published in the 1970s. Neither are her grandparents examples of the superhip elders usually found in these books. Paula's personality and the incidents in which the reader sees her are fictional, but Goffstein drew on her knowledge of Bennington College and New York City for such details as locating Paula's school and guiding her through a New York art gallery.

The Underside of the Leaf introduces characters, material, and thematic concerns that reappear in other guises or to different ends in later books. Details of *Fish for Supper* (1976) dovetail with passages from *The Underside of the Leaf*, while "Daisy Summerfield," the name of the heroine in *Daisy Summerfield's Style* (1975), is also the name of Paula Nathanson's college roommate. The salient fact here is the craft Goffstein shows when she reworks material. Rather than repeat

Page from Goffstein's 1970 book, Two Piano Tuners *(Farrar, Straus & Giroux)*

herself, she discovers new meanings or new uses for the material.

Me and My Captain (1974) can be seen as a case in point. The central situation in the story is similar to that of *The Underside of the Leaf*. Like

Paula, the "me" of the story has a crush on a man she sees as somewhat experienced and knowledgeable. The man in the second story is, however, very different from Kadrie. The difference is so great that the situation takes on an entirely

Dust jacket for Goffstein's 1974 book about a wooden doll's affection for a carved sea captain (Farrar, Straus & Giroux)

new aspect: *Me and My Captain*'s male lead is none other than a wooden carving of a sea captain who stands with his boat on a shelf beneath the shelf of the wooden woman who admires him. She owns some shells and a ship in a bottle which she thinks are a link between them and which she would like to show him. She is, in short, looking for a soulmate, but as critics John L. Ward and Marion Nitt Fox note, her contentment with simply dreaming of the captain helps make the book "a model of understatement and of poignant innocence and charm."

Goffstein turned her attention from wooden figures to a wide range of sculpture in *Daisy Summerfield's Style*, Goffstein's second book for young adults. Daisy Summerfield has just failed her first year of college and is on her way back to New York in September of 1959 to enroll in the Minnie Peabody School of Fashion Design. Instead of enrolling in the school, Daisy surreptitiously switches luggage with an artsy-looking girl named Daphne Stephen and decides to study art and become a sculptor. Her naiveté (she does not know enough to see the difficulty of her plan), enthusiasm, dedication, and real talent enable her

to fulfill her dream.

Goffstein presents Daisy's adventures in a realist mode, but *Daisy Summerfield's Style* is also a Cinderella story of the transformation of an ordinary person into an artist, complete with the costume change motif which here, as in the fairy tale, triggers recognition of (but does not in itself change) the heroine's true identity. Moreover, even though Daisy has no fairy godmother to help her, she is encouraged and inspired by the sculpture she sees in a museum and in the art books which she buys. She enjoys the volume *Artists in Their Studios* so much that she buys a second volume in the series.

Cinderella is not the only heroine that Daisy's story brings to mind. Daisy is like Goldie in *Goldie the Dollmaker* in that she too finds comfort in the light shed by a beautiful lamp. In this case, the light is diffused through a shade which has yellow cellophane-covered cutouts for the windows in the buildings in the background of its scene of Central Park. Daisy's rationale for buying the lamp is that she ought to be able to see the lamp's version of Central Park since she cannot see any of New York City from her hotel window. The rationale is comic, yet it is emblematic of the way in which Daisy spends her first nine months imagining community and creating it through sculpting figures, each of which she can take by its hand so as to look into its face. By the end of the book, Daisy's love of art and her own art help her to find human companionship as well. Through its portrait of the artist as a young woman, *Daisy Summerfield's Style* shows its young adult audience the pleasures of work well done.

In *Fish for Supper* the reader is never told outright what the book's central character, the narrator's grandmother, is thinking. Yet the important fact, her satisfaction with the ritual order and accomplishment of her day, is clear. Goffstein's grandmother Rosie was the model for the fisherwoman whom the reader sees wearing the little heeled shoes and big round sun hat like those Paula's grandmother wore in *The Underside of the Leaf*. That book's yellow boathouse is here too, but this time the story is the grandmother's, not the child's.

Even so, the book engages its child readers in several important ways. The first, in terms of encountering the text, is the narrator's voice. It is both humorous and confiding: "When my grandmother went fishing, she would get up at five o'clock in the morning and make herself breakfast, then clean up the dishes fast, fast, and go

Dust jacket for Goffstein's 1977 Caldecott Honor Book about a grandmother and the way she organizes her day (Dial)

down to the water wearing her big sun hat." The sentence's playful doubling of the words "fast, fast" is matched by an equally playful and pleasing repetition in the text's conclusion. Here the reader sees that the whole story repeats, not just certain parts of sentences. After fishing all day, the grandmother eats her supper and cleans up the dishes "fast, fast" so that she can get up early and go fishing again. The circularity of this conclusion is perfectly in tune with young readers' tentative sense of closure and their pleasure in successive retellings of favorite narratives.

Goffstein's illustrations for *Fish for Supper* show quite literally, yet subtly, that the grandmother is a many-sided person despite the sameness of her days. The reader never sees her from the same angle twice in a row. Her right profile gives way in the next illustration to her left, then she is shown full-face, from her right, full-face again, followed by her left profile, then from the rear, and so on. Her facial expressions range from purposeful to gratified. She never smiles outright, which is in keeping with the text but which prompted one reviewer's complaint that children would therefore be unable to tell if she were happy or not. Whatever its young readers surmise about the grandmother's state of mind, *Fish for Supper* is a favorite among both children and adults. It was named a Caldecott Honor Book in 1977.

My Crazy Sister (1976) portrays a woman with imagination, one who takes an idea and elaborates it into a wonderful play fantasy that she and her sister (the book's narrator) can share. The crazy sister is, however, the sort of person who needs a little introduction. Goffstein provides it in a way which ingeniously exploits the picture book form. Three pictures sequenced on the title page, copyright page, and dedication page act as a silent preface which show: 1) a woman receiving a letter; 2) the same woman reading a letter; 3) a second woman driving a car. A little head sticks up in the back seat behind the driver's. The stage is set for the arrival of the sister and her baby in the first of the book's three stories.

The sister does not travel light. The car is packed with all of her possessions, yet when transferred to the house they "fit in without crowding," even the baby whom the newcomer has absent-mindedly misplaced on a high shelf. Temporarily losing the baby is an example of the sister's craziness (especially for those readers who earlier noticed the little head popping up from the back seat of the sister's car), but at the same time it allows the sisters to see and greet each other first. Then together they search for the baby and find the child a special place in the home. More than the crazy sister's possessions "fit in without crowding"; the phrase also describes Goffstein's sense of community, for it is really the two sisters plus newcomer—the baby—who fit in without crowding.

Goffstein continues her exploration of family relationships in *Family Scrapbook* (1978), which shows the warmth and closeness of the Frankel family as seen through the eyes of the older of its two children. The stories also deftly mark key moments of recognition where the narrator sees her parents in new ways, learns about her own aspirations, and perceives the transcendent beauty of a work of art.

The book includes seven short narratives, all about the Frankel family. The first, "The Night We Got a Pickup Truck," establishes the Frankels as a family whose comfort and security is in loving each other. Referring to the new truck, Mrs. Frankel says, "It seems safer than a car," but the real safety in this story is the narrator's having a mother and a father who hear her singing a camp song in the back of the truck and add their voices to hers. The harmony is so sweet that it never disturbs the little brother discovered asleep when the truck's ceiling light comes on.

Although the incidents in the following six stories vary widely, they each indicate a like moment of harmony or grace, right through to "Alberto Giacometti," the last story in the book. While sitting on the porch, the narrator reads a magazine with an article about the artist. She sees that he and everything in his studio are gray, and that both he and his sculpture seem to ask, "What is man but dust?" The answer is one word: "Glory!" The narrator's recognition of this testifies not only to the power of the work of art and of the photographs which record it, but also to the breadth of her own mental snapshots or stories. They reflect an imagination which seeks to share experience and find community and family feeling.

It is not surprising, then, that four of Goffstein's next five books also explore the ties which link person to person and generation to generation. Memory is one such link; imaginative projection is another. In *My Noah's Ark* (1978), the toy ark of the title prompts stories about past events—in this case, in the mind of an elderly narrator—and makes them live again. Although Goffstein herself has never owned a toy ark, the importance of the object lies in the fact that she could imagine having one. As she told Sylvia and Kenneth Marantz in an interview for *Horn Book*, "The fun of writing is that you can take a persona. Once I told *My Noah's Ark* to a group of chil-

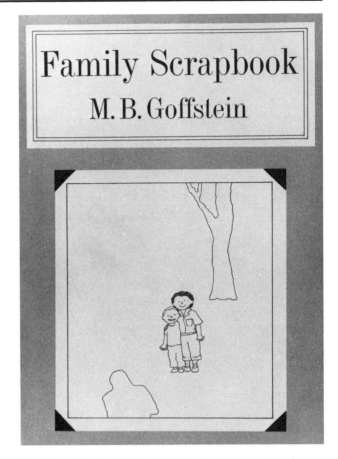

Dust jacket for Goffstein's 1978 book which consists of seven short narratives about one family (Farrar, Straus & Giroux)

dren, and a little girl asked, 'Do you still have it?' I wondered: Do I look like I'm ninety-four? But it's true in its way."

The truth of the book lies in its capturing of emotions. The narrator speaks simply but movingly of her father's carving her an ark, her husband's carrying it to their new home, and her children's listening to stories of their grandfather's playful shouting out as he built the boat. As George Shannon has noted in "All Times in One," each detail the old woman recounts widens the ark's circle of associations; this boat has room to hold a hundred years and more of joys and sorrows. Kathy Piehl extends this insight with her observation that "No one . . . expresses the Noah theme of life's continuity more clearly and movingly than M. B. Goffstein."

The ark's implicit reminder of the interdependence of all living things becomes explicit in *Natural History* (1979). The book's cover shows a little girl opening the door to the night sky and to a tree which in the next illustration reaches up toward the stars and moon. The reader's eye penetrates still further into space in the following picture of the earth as one "lively ball in the universe." This sweep out curves back in again as succeeding pictures show the ocean, its individual creatures, grains of sand, a tree. All these are wondrous, made more so by both the watercolors Goffstein uses here for the first time and by one last view of earth from far away.

Wonder is, however, only one of the emotions with which the book is concerned. Compassion and hope are equally important. After surveying the earth's harmony and rhythm, *Natural History* bears witness to its disruptions. Men fight and break mountains, dogs and cats are homeless, old people look through garbage for their food. Few children's books reveal painful truths so clearly. Of those that do, still fewer offer truthful cause for hope and consolation: "we have riches we are born to share. . . . Every living creature is our brother and our sister, dearer than the jewels at the center of the earth. So let us be like tiny grains of sand, and protect all life from fear and suffering!" The final pages of *Natural History* show a protected cat and dog asleep on the beds of their respective child owners. Barla, Goffstein's dog to whom the book was dedicated, would approve.

The pictures of the pets remind the reader that fellow feeling starts close to home. So too does *Neighbors*, also published in 1979, the same year as *Natural History*. The book's four brief chapters (one for each of the seasons) involve the attempts of two women in adjacent houses to reach out to one another. Their gestures of kindness finally lead to a conversation which establishes them as friends.

Goffstein turns to tradition and ritual in the last book in this informal "sequence" of books which explore the nature of community. *Laughing Latkes* (1980) asks why the latkes laugh; answering that question becomes an occasion for relating events and traditions associated with Hanukkah. Affection between parent and child, food shared in quiet celebration, and good humor are highlighted here as in *Family Scrapbook*'s "Yom Kippur." *Laughing Latkes* brought the total of Goffstein's books to eighteen, a number which holds special significance for her: "In the Hebrew system . . . 18 is the luckiest number. I guess I never thought I'd make it."

It could be argued that Goffstein's luck actually picked up with her seventeenth book, *An Artist* (1980). This volume and four which follow it show Goffstein's interest in artists shift from de-

picting apprenticeships such as Daisy's and Paula's to examining the impulses of genius. *An Artist* begins with an epigraph from Pissaro, "Only painting counts," but the vision in *An Artist* is clearly Goffstein's. She pictures both the artist and the world in which he moves and breathes. Within this world, "An artist is like God, but small." Both this simile and the further definition, "An artist is like God as God created him," subordinate the artist's ego to a transcendence much larger than himself. Only one small part of all creation, the artist struggles to create that part he sees: "Choosing and brushing his colors, he tries to make paint sing." True to her explanation, Goffstein's own watercolors sing throughout this subtle book.

Lives of the Artists (1981) and *An Artist's Album* (1985) show Goffstein taking a break from her own illustrating to look at the work other artists have produced. Taken together, the two volumes present brief biographies of Rembrandt, Guardi, van Gogh, Bonnard, Nevelson, Vermeer, Boudin, the Woodland Indians, Cezanne, and Monet. The taut energy of these books recalls the passion Daisy Summerfield felt for her three volumes of *Artists in Their Studios* and fulfills Goffstein's "hope that my passions [nature, art, and literature] are clear in my books." Here, as in her fiction, Goffstein's prose is spare yet evocative; as she told the Marantzes, it reflects her desire to communicate that art is "beautiful and exciting and worth growing up for."

Given that ambition, Goffstein begins the series of biographies with Rembrandt, "the greatest artist of them all." The details she selects bring Rembrandt to life while at the same time mirroring Goffstein's own concerns. When she describes Rembrandt's artistry she outlines her own minimalist aesthetic as well: "Every outside has an inside, and every inside has an outside. Just one stroke of Rembrandt's chalk, needle, brush, or pen could tell both tales."

And although one reviewer found Goffstein's inclusion of the Woodland Indians in *An Artist's Album* "incongruous," the selection is problematic only in that both illustrations chosen to represent them are black and white (rather than having one in full color, as is the case for the other artists). Goffstein's own photograph of a Woodland Indian doll shows the beads Goffstein wore when she photographed it "reflected at the upper left; and that white line's my camera chain mirrored on her friendly face. For many years this portrait has hung alone above

Woodland Indian Woman, *Doll*, circa 1890
Buckskin and cloth, approximately 12 inches tall (30.5 cm)
Photograph by M. B. Goffstein

Page from Goffstein's 1985 book An Artist's Album, *featuring her photograph of a Woodland Indian doll*
(Harper & Row)

my desk, and I often wonder: what is that distortion in the bottom right-hand corner?" The photograph also shows the doll's turquoise-color seed beads. The doubling of beads (both object and observer wear them) and the reference to the camera's reflection signal Goffstein's sympathetic identification, yet she also shows that no act of identification is without some version of "distortion in the bottom right-hand corner." The photograph could not be more fitting as an emblem of the artist's attempt to reach beyond the self to the mystery of the other.

When the mystery is that of communication the writer must turn to metaphor to shape abstractions into shared perceptions. *A Writer* (1984) and *My Editor* (1985, Goffstein's first book for adults) employ contrasting sets of metaphor (both visual and verbal) to evoke different aspects of the effort to communicate. The first set, in *A Writer*, is organic: a writer "is a gardener, never sure of her ground, or of which seeds are rooting there."

She works "hoping her books will spread the seeds of ideas." The illustrations for this book are watercolors like those in *Natural History* and *An Artist*, but they abandon outlining, a technique in which Goffstein "lost interest." Such enclosure would be antithetical to the book's central metaphor of growth and to its exploration of the writer's impulse to reach out. Goffstein elaborated on this impulse in her interview with Sylvia and Kenneth Marantz: "A book is a communication. You have to want to touch someone on the arm and say, 'Could I please tell you this?' "

My Editor tells the other half of the story of trying to write; it shows the author struggling to find out what she has to say. The controlling metaphor is that of the writer as an "archaeologist" who "rebuild[s] a little temple." When her editor "pokes here and pushes there, to see where it caves in" she "can't find the buried words" until she "remove[s] one big block." More than just the pun on writer's block suggests an adult audience. The book's abstract illustrations (line drawings of geometric shapes; a circle represents the author, while the editor is a triangle) and focus on the writer's inner struggle are both sophisticated and self-conscious; they let the reader eavesdrop, but they do not reach out to touch her arm.

In contrast, *School of Names* (1986) reaches to embrace the whole of creation. The illustrations expand to one-and-a-half times their usual size, colors deepen, and edges blur. This is Goffstein's first book illustrated with pastels instead of watercolors, and its energy passes beyond celebration to incantation. The narrator wants to know all names–of continents, seas, rivers, grasses, winds, clouds: "I would like to recognize and greet everyone by name." Although the Library of Congress cataloging data classifies *School of Names* under science and ecology, the book is really about the highest art of all: the art of naming and of true speech and understanding.

At first glance, *Our Snowman* (1986) may seem far removed from any such concern with art. A little girl and her brother go outside after the first big snowfall of the year and make a snowman. Later, the girl and her father make a wife to keep him company. It is a simple story, yet it is one of creation. The snowman and his wife are fashioned from winter's dust–snow–and though they will melt, "Year after year, these things work!"

Like *School of Names*, this book is also illustrated in pastels. The girl and her brother are engaging figures (the reader first sees them from behind as they stand looking out at the falling snow) whose faces are no less expressive for being little smudges of color with no features. The tilt of the girl's head as she zips her jacket and her brother's upturned face as he watches her pat a snowball show concentration and affection.

No wonder then that Goffstein's books have been called "rubies" by Ted Morgan in the *Saturday Review* (24 November 1979) and that she has been referred to as a "mistress of understatement" by Ethel L. Heins in a 1976 *Horn Book* review. The American Library Association, the *New York Times*, and the American Institute of Graphic Arts have all cited one or more of her books for special honor. In 1979 seven of Goffstein's earliest books were reprinted in one volume, and new editions or reissues of *Sleepy People, Brookie and Her Lamb, Goldie the Dollmaker, Two Piano Tuners,* and *A Little Schubert* have recently appeared.

Most of the attention Goffstein has received has been from reviewers of individual books, but her steadily growing reputation ensures that more sustained studies of her work will be forthcoming, particularly from critics interested in children's books as occasions for literary or aesthetic experience. The small number of reviewers who have expressed reservations have usually done so for pedagogical reasons.

It is not surprising that Goffstein's work sometimes frustrates child-centered criticism. Her books elude systematic definition. Timeless, yet particular, they speak to needs and wishes shared by people of all ages. Like C. S. Lewis, who explained that he wrote children's books because they were the best art form for saying what he wanted to say, Goffstein believes that "You have to be thinking of the work, and not about yourself at all. It's the books I give everything to.... My books are for whoever reads them."

Interview:

Sylvia and Kenneth Marantz, "M. B. Goffstein: An Interview," *Horn Book*, 62 (November/ December 1986): 688-694.

References:

Joann Giusto-Davis, "The Art of M. B. Goffstein," *Publishers Weekly*, 218 (24 October 1980): 22-23;

Dust jacket for the first book in which Goffstein used pastel illustrations (Harper & Row)

Selma G. Lanes, *Down the Rabbit Hole: Adventures and Misadventures in the Realm of Children's Literature* (New York: Atheneum, 1972), p. 185;

Kathy Piehl, "Noah As Survivor: A Study of Picture Books," *Children's Literature in Education*, 13 (Summer 1982): 80-86;

Barbara Ann Porte, "The Picture Books of M. B. Goffstein," *Children's Literature in Education*, 11 (Spring 1980): 3-9;

George Shannon, "All Times in One," *Children's Literature Association Quarterly*, 10 (Winter 1986): 178-181;

Shannon, "Goffstein and Friends," *Horn Book*, 59 (February 1983): 88-95;

John L. Ward and Marion Nitt Fox, "A Look at Some Outstanding Illustrated Books for Children," *Children's Literature Association Quarterly*, 9 (Spring 1984): 19-21.

Edward Gorey
(22 February 1925-   )

Douglas Street

Bibliographical Note: Because Edward Gorey has produced several privately printed works and limited editions, this list includes only those books which have been commercially available.

SELECTED BOOKS: *The Unstrung Harp; or, Mr. Earbrass Writes a Novel* (New York: Duell, Sloan & Pearce, 1953);

The Listing Attic (New York: Duell, Sloan & Pearce, 1954);

The Doubtful Guest (Garden City: Doubleday, 1957);

The Object-Lesson (Garden City: Doubleday, 1958; London: Blond, 1958);

The Bug Book (New York: Looking Glass Library, 1959);

The Fatal Lozenge: An Alphabet (New York: Obolensky, 1960); republished as *The Gorey Alphabet* (London: Constable, 1960);

The Curious Sofa, as Ogdred Weary (New York: Obolensky, 1961);

The Hapless Child (New York: Obolensky, 1961);

The Beastly Baby, as Ogdred Weary (New York: Fantod, 1962);

The Willowdale Handcar: or, The Return of the Black Doll (New York: Bobbs-Merrill, 1962);

The Wuggly Ump (Philadelphia: Lippincott, 1963);

The Insect God (New York: Simon & Schuster, 1963);

The West Wing (New York: Simon & Schuster, 1963);

The Gashlycrumb Tinies; or, After the Outing (New York: Simon & Schuster, 1963);

The Remembered Visit: A Story Taken from Life (New York: Simon & Schuster, 1965);

The Sinking Spell (New York: Obolensky, 1965);

The Evil Garden, as Eduard Bluting (New York: Fantod, 1966);

The Gilded Bat (New York: Simon & Schuster, 1966; London: Cape, 1967);

The Inanimate Tragedy (New York: Fantod, 1966);

The Pious Infant, as Mrs. Regera Dowdy (New York: Fantod, 1966);

Fletcher and Zenobia, with Victoria Chess (New York: Meredith, 1967);

The Utter Zoo (New York: Meredith, 1967);

The Other Statue (New York: Simon & Schuster, 1968);

The Blue Aspic (New York: Meredith, 1969);

The Epiplectic Bicycle (New York: Dodd, Mead, 1969);

The Chinese Obelisks, Fourth Alphabet (New York: Fantod, 1970);

Donald Has a Difficulty, with Peter F. Neumeyer (New York: Fantod, 1970);

The Osbick Bird (New York: Fantod, 1970);

Why We Have Day and Night, with Neumeyer (New York: Young Scott, 1970);

The Deranged Cousins; or Whatever (New York: Fantod, 1971);

The Disrespectful Summons (New York: Fantod, 1971);

The Eleventh Episode, illustrated by Gorey as Om (New York: Fantod, 1971);

Fletcher and Zenobia Save the Circus, illustrated by Chess (New York: Dodd, Mead, 1971);

The Sopping Thursday (Santa Barbara: Capricorn, 1971);

The Untitled Book, as Edward Pig (New York: Fantod, 1971);

The Abandoned Sock (New York: Fantod, 1972);

The Audrey-Gore Legacy (New York: Dodd, Mead, 1972);

The Lavender Leotard; or, Going a Lot to the New York City Ballet (New York: Gotham, 1973);

The Glorious Nosebleed: Fifth Alphabet (New York: Dodd, Mead, 1975);

L'Heure bleue (New York: Fantod, 1975);

The Broken Spoke (New York: Dodd, Mead, 1976);

The Loathsome Couple (New York: Dodd, Mead, 1977);

Dracula: A Toy Theatre for All Ages: The Sets and Costumes of the Broadway Production of the Play (New York: Scribners, 1979);

Dancing Cats and Neglected Murderesses (New York: Workman, 1980);

Le Mélange (New York: Gotham, 1981);

Mélange Funeste (New York: Gotham, 1981);

The Dwindling Party (New York: Random House, 1982);

The Waterflowers (New York: Congdon & Weed, 1982);

Edward Gorey

A Mercurial Bear (New York: Gotham Book Mart, 1983);

The Prune People (New York: Albondocani, 1983);

The Tunnel Calamity (New York: Putnam's, 1984);

Les Echanges Malendreaux (New York: Metacom, 1985);

The Eclectic Abecedarium (New York: Adama Books, 1985).

Collections: *Amphigorey* (New York: Putnam's, 1972);

Amphigorey Too (New York: Putnam's, 1975);

Amphigorey Also (New York: Congdon & Weed, 1984).

SELECTED BOOKS ILLUSTRATED: Merrill Moore, *Case Record from a Sonnetorium* (New York: Twayne, 1951);

Rex Warner, *Men and Gods* (New York: Farrar, Straus & Giroux, 1959);

John Ciardi, *The Man Who Sang the Sillies* (Philadelphia: Lippincott, 1961);

Ciardi, *You Read to Me, I'll Read to You* (Philadelphia: Lippincott, 1962);

Rhoda Levine, *Three Ladies Beside the Sea* (New York: Atheneum, 1963);

Ciardi, *You Know Who* (Philadelphia: Lippincott, 1964);

Frank Jacobs, *Alvin Steadfast on Vernacular Island* (New York: Dial, 1965);

Ciardi, *The King Who Saved Himself from Being Saved* (Philadelphia: Lippincott, 1965);

Eric Potter, ed., *Monster Festival* (New York: Vanguard, 1965);

Polly Redford, *Christmas Bower* (New York: Dutton, 1966);

Felicia Lamport, *Cultural Slog* (Boston: Houghton Mifflin, 1966; London: Gollancz, 1967);

Ciardi, *Monster Den; or, Look What Happened at My House and to It* (Philadelphia: Lippincott, 1966);

Ennis Rees, *Brer Rabbit and His Tricks* (New York: Young Scott, 1967);

Jane Trahey, *Son of the Martini Cookbook* (New York: Clovis, 1967);

Edward Lear, *The Jumblies* (New York: Young Scott, 1968; London: Chatto & Windus, 1969);

Henry Mazzeo, ed., *Hauntings: Tales of the Supernatural* (Garden City: Doubleday, 1968);

Rees, *More of Brer Rabbit's Tricks* (New York: Young Scott, 1968);

Muriel Spark, *The Very Fine Clock* (London: Macmillan, 1968; New York: Knopf, 1968);

Jan Wahl, *Cobweb Castle* (New York: Holt, Rinehart & Winston, 1968);

Lear, *The Dong with a Luminous Nose* (London: Chatto & Windus, 1969; New York: Young Scott, 1969);

Levine, *He Was There from the Day We Moved In* (New York: Quist, 1969);

Doris Orgel, *Merry, Rose, and Christmas Tree June* (New York: Knopf, 1969);

Peter F. Neumeyer, *Donald and the . . .* (Reading, Mass.: Addison-Wesley, 1969);

Ciardi, *Someone Could Win a Polar Bear* (Philadelphia: Lippincott, 1970);

Edward Fenton, *Penny Candy* (New York: Holt, Rinehart & Winston, 1970);

Felice Holmein, *At the Top of My Voice and Other Poems* (New York: Norton, 1970);

Florence P. Heide, *The Shrinking of Treehorn* (New York: Holiday House, 1971; Harmondsworth, U.K.: Puffin, 1975);

Donald Nelson, *Sam and Emma* (New York: Parents' Magazine Press, 1971);

Rees, *Lions and Lobsters and Foxes and Frogs: Fables From Aesop* (Reading, Mass.: Young Scott, 1971);

Jacob David Townsend, *Miss Clafooty and the Demon* (New York: Lothrop, Lee & Shepard, 1971);

Beatrice de Regniers, *Red Riding Hood; Retold in Verse for Boys and Girls to Read Themselves* (New York: Atheneum, 1972; London: Collins, 1973);

John Bellairs, *The House with a Clock in Its Walls* (New York: Dial, 1973);

De Regniers, *The Enchanted Forest* (New York: Atheneum, 1974);

Brothers Grimm, *Rumpelstiltskin*, retold by Edith H. Tarcor (New York: Four Winds, 1974);

Howard Moss, *Instant Lives* (New York: Saturday Review Press, 1974);

Edmund Wilson, *The Rats of Rutland Grange* (New York: Gotham, 1974);

Terence Winch, *Nuns: Poems* (Warwick, N.Y.: Wyrd Press, 1976);

Heide, *Treehorn's Treasure* (New York: Holiday House, 1981);

T. S. Eliot, *Old Possum's Book of Practical Cats* (New York: Harcourt Brace Jovanovich, 1982);

Lamport, *Light Metres* (New York: Everest House, 1982);

Heide, *Treehorn's Wish* (New York: Holiday House, 1984);

Bellairs, *The Eyes of the Killer Robot* (New York: Dial, 1986).

PLAY PRODUCTION: *Tinned Lettuce; or, The New Musical*, with David Aldrich, New York University, Tisch School of the Arts Undergraduate Theatre, 30 April 1985.

OTHER: *The Haunted Looking Glass*, edited and illustrated by Gorey (New York: Looking Glass Library, 1959);

Alphonse Allais, *Story for Sara: What Happened to a Little Girl*, translated and illustrated by Gorey (New York: Albondocani, 1971).

Edward Gorey, the craftsman of numerous little books for the child and childlike, is a unique figure in contemporary literature. It could be safely argued that his eminent domain within the world of children's fiction lies in particular in the realm of illustration, his stories pondered and sidestepped by the squeamish or the uninitiated. Yet, though his drawings have enhanced the work of John Ciardi, Edward Lear, and Edmund Wilson, among others, it is his own written works (many rather macabre little picture books) that sustain his uncanny fascination with the child and the adult. Though his drawings easily rank him with the most respected children's illustrators, these little books show that he also deserves recognition as this century's heir-apparent to the great tradition of Heinrich Hoffmann and Edward Lear—two of the nineteenth century's most esteemed practitioners of nonsense literature for children. And as with the best of Hoffmann—*Struwwelpeter* (1845) and *King Nutcracker* (1851)—it is often hard to discern between the children's tale and the adult's. The most whimsical of Gorey's children's tales seem quite adult; while many of his adult pieces exude the devilish merriment only allowable in the fantastical confines of childhood.

The man who writes graphically of "the Beastly Baby" and "the Hapless Child" was born in Chicago on 22 February 1925, the son of Edward Leo Gorey, a Catholic newspaperman, and Helen Garvey Gorey, his Episcopal wife. Gorey was christened Edward St. John Gorey and was initially instructed as a Catholic—it lasted but a short time. The young Gorey began to draw early on, such talent being encouraged by his parents (who divorced when he was eleven, only to remarry sixteen years later). After Gorey graduated from high school, a near three-year tenure in the army (June 1944-February 1946) preceded matriculation at Harvard and a B.A. in French in 1950: this last feat has prompted the author to remark on occasion, "God knows, I didn't get much out of college." Three years out of college, after several undistinguished art and writing projects, Gorey found himself in New York, writing and working in design for Doubleday's art department. In 1953 Gorey also published his first novel, *The Unstrung Harp*. This unorthodox tale for adults, coupled with Gorey's 1954 piece, *The Listing Attic*, awoke a curious yet receptive readership, particularly in the small, vociferous bohemian community of the New York literati. Doubleday's publication of *The Doubtful Guest* three years later carried his work out of New York to curious children and adults across the country. *The Doubtful Guest* appears to be Gorey's first concerted effort for the child audience. The style and content of these three offerings and Gorey's other 1950s publications for children—*The Object-Lesson* (1958) and *The Bug Book* (1959)—solidify the technique and concept which still dog this eccentric, rather mystical creator.

Gorey's creations for children are at times hard to delineate, but it does seem appropriate to so label *The Doubtful Guest*. The rather Edwardian creations peopling Gorey's seemingly British upper-crust household, resplendent in high collars and smoking jackets, floor-length frocks, and Fauntleroy sailor suits, receive an unlikely houseguest one night who, despite all manner of cajoling, never leaves: "It came seventeen years ago—and to this day/It has shown no intention of going away." The creature, a sort of penguin / anteater mix adorned with a flowing scarf and high-top sneakers, is not dangerous, merely frustrating; not stopped, merely sidestepped; not condoned, merely tolerated. Gorey seems to have created both a child metaphor—for the character is quite childlike—and a symbolic representation of himself, the young author garbed in fur coat and sneakers, who like his creation has entered into households, caused consternation and outrage, and yet remained unmoved through all, "the Doubtful Guest."

If consternation abounds in the trials and tribulations surrounding Gorey's besneakered misfit, then the starker contrivances of *The Object Lesson*, with its pseudo-Gothic veneer covering a parody of many an Edwardian child's concept of the dime novel romance and intrigue, confound yet tantalize on a subtler level. This tale, loosely constructed melodramatic escapades about "his lordship," along with the man in the fur coat and long, flowing scarf, "Madame O," and others, seems to be about nothing in particular; yet such is told in the most serious of tones. The events are ludicrous, the characters clichéd; the entire piece sophisticated nonsense. For example:

> It was already Thursday, but his lordship's artificial limb could not be found; therefore, having directed the servants to fill the baths, he seized the tongs and set out at once for the edge of the lake, where the Throbblefoot Spectre still loitered in a distraught manner. He presented it with a length of string. . . .

Children would have little trouble understanding and enjoying the mock seriousness here as Gorey presents an adult romance perceived from the child's point of view. *The Object Lesson* utilizes the same sort of illustrations as his previous offerings. By this time in his career Gorey's drawings had become distinctive—always in the Victorian pen-and-ink style depicting properly dressed, turn-of-the-century fashion-conscious characters, one most likely attired in fur coat and scarf.

A departure from this stark style came in 1959 when the Looking Glass Library (who also that year published *The Haunted Looking Glass*, a collection of ghost stories edited by Gorey) released *The Bug Book*—a red, blue, yellow, black, and white extravaganza. *The Bug Book* is a parable of sorts which details three sets of bugs and their traumas and eventual triumphs over "a black bug, who was related to nobody," and who one day "appeared in the neighborhood" and proceeded to terrorize the others. The bugs band together and drop a large boulder on the black bug which squashes him flat, and slipping the flat remains into an envelope, they leave it "propped against the fatal stone to be mailed." *The Bug Book*'s drawings, more suggestive than those in earlier works (the black bug being drawn as a silhouette and like the other bugs without features), show a freedom from restrictions imposed in earlier works; however, the now-typical Gorey hand-lettered text is here too a mainstay.

By 1959 only one major critic had written of Gorey's off-beat creations, yet when Edmund Wilson, in the 26 December *New Yorker*, compared Gorey's expertise to that of Max Beerbohm and Aubrey Beardsley, readers nationwide began to seek out and explore the surreal twists and curves of the world according to Gorey. With his illustrations for publications of the Looking Glass Library as a start, he began to illustrate the work of other writers. His most lengthy engagement in this new position was as chief artist for John Ciardi's children's poetry books pub-

Dust jacket for Gorey's first book aimed primarily at the child audience (Doubleday)

lished by Lippincott. His drawings, nearly all of which are two-color sketches with the usual array of Gorey characters, enhance six Ciardi collections, from the 1961 *The Man Who Sang the Sillies* through the 1970 *Someone Could Win a Polar Bear.*

Gorey's output of original stories for children continued. In 1961 and 1963 he published two quite grotesque (each in its own way) yet appealing pieces: *The Hapless Child*, a black-and-white mock-Victorian cautionary tale about a demure waif, Charlotte Sophia, and *The Wuggly Ump* (which could be subtitled "the hapless children"). Each is a tale about innocent children powerless to stop or even impede the dangers of the adult society rapidly descending upon them.

The macabre scenes of *The Hapless Child* are so intentionally overdone that both child and adult relish the eerie humor with its heightened sense of adult reality. Sophia is picked on, abused, shuffled from low-life, and sold to a "drunken brute" who puts her to work "making artificial flowers." In the end she escapes and runs into the snowy streets only to be run down by an auto, driven by her father, "who was not dead after all." Gorey has given today's children a wonderful parody of that type of tale so much a part of the last century in Europe and Britain–indeed, if one knew not it would be easy to mistake this piece for one of its middle-nineteenth-century predecessors, so skillful is this author-illustrator at capturing the mode.

The Wuggly Ump tells the story of three playmates who are eaten by a strange creature (the Wuggly Ump) who comes nearer and nearer with each turn of the page. The book, like *The Doubtful Guest*, arrayed in rhymed couplets, uses naiveté in the shadow of disaster to counterpoint the worldliness and tawdriness experienced in *The Hapless Child*. While the three children spend their "happy childhood hours, / In weaving endless chains of flowers / Across the hills the Wuggly Ump / Is hurtling on, kerbash, kerblump!" The danger is upon them, and these ineffective children are left only to "Sing glugalimp, sing glugalump / From deep inside the Wuggly Ump." Edward Gorey has been quoted as saying he portrays children so frequently, even in his works for adults, because he sees their vulnerability. Certainly *The Hapless Child* and *The Wuggly Ump* do nothing to contradict this rationale.

Gorey was quite prolific during the 1960s. Between the publications of *The Wuggly Ump* in 1963 and his next children's story, *The Osbick Bird* (1970), for example, he produced sixteen other titles. The 1960s allowed him a time for further experimentation, and hence during this period Gorey displayed a refinement of artistic technique through variations of style, as in *The Evil Garden* (1966) and *The Gilded Bat* (1966), both of a softer stroke than the pseudo-Edwardian attempts. Also, his stories began to appear first in

Dust jacket for John Ciardi's 1961 children's poem illustrated by Gorey (Lippincott)

periodicals before final book release (*Evergreen Review*, *Holiday*, and *Ballet Review*), allowing an even wider exposure to the book-buying public. During this period Gorey at times took to using (in a playful manner) pseudonyms, usually anagrams of his own name–his most frequent alter-egos are "Ogdred Weary" and "Mrs. Regera Dowdy." In the late 1960s and early 1970s Gorey's most distinctive work was his illustrations for Peter F. Neumeyer's *Donald and the . . .* (1969), his collaboration with Neumeyer on *Donald Has a Difficulty* (1970), and his drawings for new editions of two of Edward Lear's story poems, *The Jumblies* (1968) and *The Dong with a Luminous Nose* (1969). While Gorey prefers to think of himself as a writer first and an artist second, the drawings for these four works exhibit all the detail, composition, and technique afforded a great illustrator. Most particularly with Lear, Gorey shows an intimate understanding of each poem: its mood, characters, and rhythm; the seeming collaboration is almost uncanny.

Perhaps inspired by the recently close acquaintance with the work of Lear, Gorey created *The Osbick Bird*, another offering in rhyming couplets reminiscent of *The Doubtful Guest* and *The Wuggly Ump* in style, yet quite superior to both in illustrations. Not only does the rhyme remind one of *The Doubtful Guest*, that strange birdlike creature that shows up one day and never leaves, here too is a similar occurrence: "An osbick bird flew down and sat / On Emblus Fingby's bowler hat / It had not done so for a whim, / But meant to come and live with him." The bird does so, and in the course of the adventure shares tea with Emblus, beats him at cards, accompanies him on a lute, attends his sickbed until Emblus dies, and stands sentinel at his grave, until, in typical Gorey style, the bird, after several months of perching on Emblus's headstone, "one day / . . . changed its mind and flew away." The drawings are crisp and precise without losing any of the characteristic whimsy. One might say it is as if the artist, after ten years, finally decided to sharpen his drawing pencil, the detail and clarity of stroke in *The Osbick Bird* being the result.

Nineteen seventy was also the year for *The Chinese Obelisks*, a rhyming alphabet in the tradition of the famous "A was an Archer and shot at a frog." Gorey's piece begins, "A was an Author who went for a walk." The "Author" in this scenario encounters several people and situations on his walk before he is trapped in a thunderstorm with the improbable misfortune that:

U was the Urn it dislodged from the sky
V was the Victim who cried out 'But why?'
W was the Wagon in which his life ended
X was the Exequies sparsely attended
Y was the Yew beneath which he was laid
Z was the Zither he left to the maid.

The "Author" wears the unmistakable fur coat and sneakers (or are those ballet slippers?) linked with Gorey himself (he is fanatic about both fur coats with sneakers and the ballet), and the faces and clothing of the other characters portrayed betray equally unmistakable members of the long-established Gorey "clan."

The beginning of the 1970s witnessed several Gorey-illustrated children's works for the popular market augmenting his continued output of the little books for his rather limited adult market. Two of Gorey's most successful collaborations for children appeared in 1970 and 1971–*Why We Have Day and Night* (with Peter Neumeyer) and *Fletcher and Zenobia Save the Cir-*

Cover for the 1969 edition of Edward Lear's nonsense rhyme which Gorey illustrated (Young Scott)

cus (illustrated by Victoria Chess) respectively. In each instance Gorey is renewing a collaboration; he previously coauthored one book with Neumeyer and illustrated another (the two "Donald" stories) and is listed as joint author with Chess on *Fletcher and Zenobia* (1967). *Fletcher and Zenobia Save the Circus* reunites the cat and dog of the original story for an adventure involving a wrecked circus train and its scattered performers. Gorey restrains his wry, macabre humor to create possibly his most conventional children's tale. The plot is straightforward, the characters agreeable. Gorey is a cat fancier, and here as in other novels of his doing the cats are the preferred ones–such creatures saunter through a majority of the author's works, including *Why We Have Day and Night*. One of his cats appears on nearly every page therein.

Why We Have Day and Night is a wonderfully imaginative explanation of the title concept that is taken to the usual absurd extremes by Gorey and Neumeyer, his willing and able cohort. In explaining the concept of day and night the authors use the traditional "bug on the orange" demonstration, with an absurd twist. The story closes with the following adult reply to a child's question: "But why is it dark all over now?"

> Because this little bug on the spinning orange got hungrier and hungrier. The hun-

grier he got, the more he would spin. And the more he would spin, the hungrier he got. And finally he got SO hungry that he ate right through the outside, and into the middle; and he crawled down deep inside and it was all, all, all. . . .

The adult cannot think of a proper reason and so the reader, like the child, awaits an explanation that will not come.

Gorey's international following picked up in 1972 when several of his earlier works were published in German by Diogenes Press in Zürich. Further adult writing and illustration for other authors continued. *Amphigorey*, a collection of fifteen of his previously published small books, appeared in 1972; the volume, which sold well in the United States, became a best-seller across Europe. Amid this flurry of activity there Gorey produced that year a rather intriguing yet unpretentious little book entitled *The Abandoned Sock*: "One summer morning a sock on the line decided that life with its mate was tedious and unpleasant. It persuaded the clothespin to relinquish its hold, and blew away on the next breeze." The story then develops the adventures of this sock with dogs, boys, fish, and the elements until at last it is caught fast in a thorn bush. "Rain fell frequently, then snow. With spring birds came and took bits of it for their

Cover for the paperback edition of Gorey's 1983 collection of seventeen previously published books
(Congdon & Weed)

nests. By the end of summer nothing was left of the sock to speak of." Gorey's simple yet effective text and black-and-white renderings combine to signal the reader that, it is presumed, one needs to be satisfied with a bad situation since in attempting to better it, it will (according to Gorey) only become worse.

Edward Gorey's next children's book, *The Lavender Leotard; or, Going a Lot to the New York City Ballet* (1973), is a homage to his fanatical admiration for the ballet (he has attended nearly every performance of the New York City Ballet since 1957). In *The Lavender Leotard* "The author introduces two small, distant, ageless, and wholly imaginary relatives to fifty seasons of the New York City Ballet," who ramble through various dances and ballet repartee developing both awareness and appreciation (along with the reader) of this special art form. Gorey has captured, through his youthful characters, the charm and the difficulty of execution that have been drawing fans like Gorey for decades. He has given the child reader an accessible yet lighthearted introduction to a normally remote (for many youths) area of the dance.

With the exception of the titles mentioned above, during the 1970s Gorey occupied himself primarily with adult pieces, a second collection of his small books (*Amphigorey Too*, 1975), the costume and set designs for the 1977 revival of *Dracula*, which became a Broadway hit (and for which Gorey was awarded a Tony), and numerous illustration assignments for other children's authors. Among his most respected illustrations for other children's works during this time are those for *Red Riding Hood; Retold in Verse for Boys and Girls to Read Themselves*, by Beatrice de Regniers (1972), *Lions and Lobsters and Foxes and Frogs: Fables From Aesop*, retold by Ennis Rees (1971), Edith H. Tarcor's retelling of *Rumpelstiltskin* (1974), and the well-received *The Shrinking of Treehorn*, Florence P. Heide's brilliant satire of the ignored child (1971).

This diversity of projects has continued into the 1980s. *Dancing Cats and Neglected Murderesses*, another small book, not really for children, not exclusively the domain of adults, was published in 1980. Nineteen eighty-one saw the ten-year reunion in print of Heide and Gorey; *Treehorn's Treasure*, text by Heide, drawings by Gorey, shows what happens to our hapless child when the maple tree begins producing dollar bills. The reunion was amiable enough for the duo to collaborate in 1984 on *Treehorn's Wish*. In each case, the same sardonic humor and the incredibly alienated family are punctuated by Gorey's black-and-white drawings. While Gorey seems to collaborate well with several writers, his relationship with Heide has produced the best results.

Exploring other avenues of drawing-to-text composition, Gorey returned to the children's market with the 1982 Random House "pop-up" story of *The Dwindling Party*. While the story is vintage Gorey, the approach and execution are a departure from his normally stark, black-on-white renderings. The entire offering is lavishly detailed in full color. Even the rear views of the pop-up figures and scenes are meticulously drawn and colored. While sacrificing none of the Gorey humor, this storybook is by far the most appealing and best conceived "children's book" yet produced by the author. The "dwindling party" is the MacFizzet family, who while staying at Hickyacket Hall—"hic jacit"—dwindle one by one until only young Neville remains. The macabre tale allows the family to be eaten by demons and carried away by a giant bat, while remaining family members carry out business in their remarkably matter-of-fact Victorian manner. This cautionary tale in verse closes with the unperturbed Neville presuming such happenings were "all for the best."

This venture into lavishness attracted Gorey to similar projects, such as the wordless "Magic Window"–styled *The Tunnel Calamity* (1984), a nine-page accordian book (the cover and interior pages fold out into a long, seemingly three-dimensional storyboard sans text). The time as usual is Victorian, "St. Frumble's Day, 1892" to be exact, and the players are typically Gorey. Through an actual window in the book's cover, the reader views the children, ladies, and gentlemen through the tunnel connecting East Shoetree with West Radish. Unfortunately for these folks, they and the reader also view the menacing ULUUS, a long, primeval creature. Without text, it is left up to the artistry, and the unknown-beyond-the-next-page gimmickry, that only Edward Gorey can muster. The book is enjoyable and the art work is close in quality to the still more complex *The Dwindling Party. The Tunnel Calamity* is a diversion, more for the childlike than for the child. The appeal of the story is dissipated after the first "reading," with the charm remaining only for those for whom the drawings hold fascination.

As can be seen, Edward Gorey has explored several new creative avenues utilizing the same tried-and-true thematic consciousness through the first half of this decade, though his earlier work remains popular. In 1984 Congdon and Weed published *Amphigorey Also*, a companion volume to *Amphigorey* and *Amphigorey Too*. Finally, as if his writing outlets are not sufficient to consume Gorey's waking hours, the writer/artist has gone back to the theater as a designer and collaborator.

Obviously the success of his designs for the revival of *Dracula* whetted his theatrical appetite, though his close involvement with the actual production was minimal. The following year, Stephen Currens and David Aldrich took *Gorey Stories*, a musical entertainment based on eigh-

teen of the writer's vignettes, to a successful Broadway run. Again, while assisting minimally with the actual production, Gorey designed both sets and costumes. However, on *Tinned Lettuce; or, The New Musical*, the 1985 musical by Gorey and musician Aldrich, the writer collaborated closely, selecting material, editing text to fit music, watching rehearsals, and designing and costuming the show. If Gorey has established a particular place for himself within children's literary history, it is as this century's unclassifiable, most unorthodox children's writer and illustrator. The times have caught up with his eccentricities, a fact which may tend to hamper originality in future offerings. Yet Gorey remains philosophic as he looks toward the 1990s—"When I began, I went too far with my books occasionally. I've given that up. It gets harder and harder to outrage the world. I sometimes think, what more can anybody possibly do?" If this question has a visual answer, one may rest assured that Gorey will find it.

References:

David Ansen and Phyllis Malamud, "Gothics by Gorey," *Newsweek*, 90 (31 October 1977): 81;

Barbara Bader, *American Picturebooks from Noah's Ark to the Beast Within* (New York: Macmillan, 1976), pp. 552-559;

Darlene Geis, "The Doubtful Interview," in *Gorey Posters* (New York: Abrams, 1979);

John Hollander, "Modern Victorian," *Commentary*, 55 (January 1973): 96-99;

Lee Kingman, et al., eds., *Illustrators of Children's Books, 1957-1966* (Boston: Horn Book, 1968), p. 115;

Thomas M. McDade, "Edward Gorey: An American Gothic," *American Book Collector*, 21 (May 1971): 12-17;

Alexander Theroux, "The Incredible Revenge of Edward Gorey," *Esquire*, 81 (June 1974): 110-111, 144-148;

Edmund Wilson, "The Albums of Edward Gorey," *New Yorker*, 35 (26 December 1959): 60-66.

Trina Schart Hyman
(8 April 1939-)

Hugh Crago

BOOKS: *How Six Found Christmas* (Boston: Little, Brown, 1969);

A Little Alphabet Book (Boston: Little, Brown, 1980);

Self-Portrait: Trina Schart Hyman (Reading, Mass.: Addison-Wesley, 1981).

SELECTED BOOKS ILLUSTRATED: Edna Butler Trickey, *Billy Finds Out* (Boston: United Church Press, 1964);

Sandol Stoddard Warburg, *Curl Up Small* (Boston: Houghton Mifflin, 1964);

Virginia Haviland, *Favorite Fairy Tales Told in Czechoslovakia* (Boston: Little, Brown, 1966);

Ruth Sawyer, *Joy to the World: Christmas Legends* (Boston: Little, Brown, 1966);

Elizabeth Johnson, *Stuck with Luck* (Boston: Little, Brown, 1966);

John Travers Moore, *Cinnamon Seed* (Boston: Houghton Mifflin, 1967);

Josephine Poole, *Moon Eyes* (Boston: Little, Brown, 1967);

Jacob David Townsend, *The Five Trials of the Pansy Bed* (Boston: Houghton Mifflin, 1967);

Eve Merriam, *Epaminondas* (Chicago: Follett, 1968);

Susan Meyers, *The Cabin on the Fjord* (Garden City: Doubleday, 1968);

Paul Tripp, *The Little Red Flower* (Garden City: Doubleday, 1968);

Joyce Varney, *The Half-Time Gypsy* (Indianapolis: Bobbs-Merrill, 1968);

Johnson, *All In Free but Janey* (Boston: Little, Brown, 1968);

Peter Hunter Blair, *The Coming of Pout* (Boston: Little, Brown, 1969);

Clyde Robert Bulla, *The Moon Singer* (New York: Crowell, 1969);

Tom McGowen, *Dragon Stew* (Chicago: Follett, 1969);

Ruth Nichols, *A Walk Out of the World* (New York: Harcourt, Brace & World, 1969);

Claudia Paley, *Benjamin the True* (Boston: Little, Brown, 1969);

Ellin Greene, *The Pumpkin Giant* (New York: Lothrop, Lee & Shepard, 1970);

Phyllis Krasilovsky, *The Shy Little Girl* (Boston: Houghton Mifflin, 1970);

Maureen Mollie Hunter McIlwraith, *The Walking Stones: A Story of Suspense* (New York: Harper & Row, 1970);

Blanche Luria Serwer, *Let's Steal the Moon: Jewish Tales* (Boston: Little, Brown, 1970);

McGowen, *Sir MacHinery* (Chicago: Follett, 1970);

Donald J. Sobol, *Greta the Strong* (Chicago: Follett, 1970);

Tripp, *The Vi-Daylin Book of Minnie the Mump* (Columbus: Ross Laboratories, 1970);

Eleanor Cameron, *A Room Made of Windows* (Boston: Little, Brown, 1971);

Greene, *Princess Rosetta and the Popcorn Man* (New York: Lothrop, Lee & Shepard, 1971);

Johnson, *Break a Magic Circle* (Boston: Little, Brown, 1971);

Carolyn Meyer, *The Bread Book . . .* (New York: Harcourt Brace Jovanovich, 1971);

Osmond Molarsky, *The Bigger They Come* (New York: Walck, 1971);

Molarsky, *Take It or Leave It* (New York: Walck, 1971);

Willy Folk St. John, *The Ghost Next Door* (New York: Harper & Row, 1971);

Gladys Baker Bond, *Boy in the Middle* (Lexington, Mass.: Ginn, 1972);

Carol Brink, *The Bad Times of Irma Baumlein* (New York: Macmillan, 1972);

Eleanor Clymer, *How I Went Shopping and What I Got* (New York: Holt, Rinehart & Winston, 1972);

Krasilovsky, *The Popular Girls Club* (New York: Simon & Schuster, 1972);

Paula Hendrick, *Who Says So?* (New York: Lothrop, Lee & Shepard, 1972);

Dori White, *Sarah and Katie* (New York: Harper & Row, 1972);

Jan Wahl, *Magic Heart* (New York: Seabury Press, 1972);

Elizabeth Jane Coatsworth, *The Wanderers* (New York: Four Winds Press, 1972);

Myra Cohn Livingston, ed., *Listen, Chil-*

Photo by Nancy Wasserman

dren, Listen . . . (New York: Harcourt Brace Jovanovich, 1972);

Nichols, *The Marrow of the World* (New York: Atheneum, 1972);

Brink, *Caddie Woodlawn* (New York: Macmillan, 1973);

Charles Causley, *Figgie Hobbin* (New York: Walker, 1973);

Greene, ed., *Clever Cooks . . .* (New York: Lothrop, Lee & Shepard, 1973);

Phyllis La Farge, *Joanna Runs Away* (New York: Holt, Rinehart & Winston, 1973);

Howard Pyle, *King Stork* (Boston: Little, Brown, 1973);

Dorothy Sharp Carter, ed., *Greedy Mariani and Other Folktales of the Antilles* (New York: Atheneum, 1974);

Jean Fritz, *Why Don't You Get a Horse, Sam Adams?* (New York: Coward-McCann & Geoghegan, 1974);

Doris Gates, *Two Queens of Heaven: Aphrodite, Demeter* (New York: Viking, 1974);

Brothers Grimm, *Snow White*, adapted by Paul Heins (Boston: Little, Brown, 1974);

Charlotte Herman, *You've Come a Long Way, Sybil MacIntosh: A Book of Manners and Grooming for Girls* (Chicago: J. P. O'Hara, 1974);

Eleanor Graham Vance, *The Everything Book* (New York: Golden Press, 1974);

Marcia Wiesbauer, *The Big Green Bean* (Lexington, Mass.: Ginn, 1974);

Margaret Mary Kimmel, *Magic in the Mist* (New York: Atheneum, 1975);

William Sleator, *Among the Dolls* (New York: Dutton, 1975);

Tobi Tobias, *The Quitting Deal* (New York: Viking, 1975);

Louise Moeri, *Star Mother's Youngest Child* (Boston: Houghton Mifflin, 1975);

Fritz, *Will You Sign Here, John Hancock?* (New York: Coward-McCann & Geoghegan, 1976);

Daisy Wallace, ed., *Witch Poems* (New York: Holiday House, 1976);

Betsy Gould Hearne, *South Star* (New York: Atheneum, 1977);

Aileen Lucia Fisher, *And a Sunflower Grew* (Los Angeles: Bowmar, 1977);

Tobias, *Jane, Wishing* (New York: Viking, 1977);

Spiridon Vangeli, *Meet Guguze* (Reading, Mass.: Addison-Wesley, 1977);

Patricia Lee Gauch, *On to Widecombe Fair* (New York: Putnam's, 1978);

Hearne, *Home* (New York: Atheneum, 1979);

Pamela Stearnes, *The Mechanical Doll* (Boston: Houghton Mifflin, 1979);

Norma Farber, *How Does It Feel To Be Old?* (New York: Dutton, 1979);

Barbara Shook Hazen, *Tight Times* (New York: Viking, 1979);

Wallace, ed., *Fairy Poems* (New York: Holiday House, 1980);

James Matthew Barrie, *Peter Pan* (New York: Scribners, 1980);

Fritz, *The Man Who Loved Books* (New York: Putnam's, 1981);

Kathryn Lasky, *The Night Journey* (New York: Warne, 1981);

Brothers Grimm, *Rapunzel*, retold by Barbara Rogasky (New York: Holiday House, 1982);

Mary Calhoun, *Big Sixteen* (New York: Morrow, 1983);

Charles Dickens, *A Christmas Carol* (New York: Holiday House, 1983);

Pamela Espeland, *The Cat Walked Through the Casserole and Other Poems for Children* (Minneapolis: Carolrhoda Books, 1984);

Livingston, ed., *Christmas Poems* (New York: Holiday House, 1984);

Saint George and the Dragon, adapted by Margaret Hodges (Boston: Little, Brown, 1984);

Elizabeth Winthrop, *The Castle in the Attic* (New York: Holiday House, 1985);

Dylan Thomas, *A Child's Christmas in Wales* (New York: Holiday House, 1985);

Vivian Vande Velde, *A Hidden Magic* (New York: Crown, 1985);

Brothers Grimm, *The Water of Life*, retold by Rogasky (New York: Holiday House, 1986);

Livingston, *Cat Poems* (New York: Holiday House, 1987).

OTHER: Brothers Grimm, *The Sleeping Beauty*, retold and illustrated by Hyman (Boston: Little, Brown, 1977);

Brothers Grimm, *Little Red Riding Hood*, retold and illustrated by Hyman (New York: Holiday House, 1983).

Trina Schart Hyman is an illustrator whose work began to be noticed in the 1960s and came to full flowering in the 1970s. Her work grapples with an unusually wide range of emotions, and it openly celebrates sexuality and physical beauty, while also conveying a compassionate acceptance of physical deformity and old age. She encompasses realism and fantasy, humor and seriousness. To date, these qualities have been most richly demonstrated in her powerful full-color sequences for the folktales *Snow White* (1974), *The Sleeping Beauty* (1977), and *Rapunzel* (1982) and in her line and sepia work for Norma Farber's *How Does It Feel To Be Old?* (1979). She has been honored several times by the *New York Times* in its Best Illustrated Books of the Year lists. She has also won the *Boston Globe-Horn Book* Award for illustration twice, and her work has been displayed in the American Institute of Graphic Arts Book Show and the Children's Book Showcase. In 1985 Hyman won the Caldecott Medal for her illustrations for Margaret Hodges's adaptation of *Saint George and the Dragon* (1984).

Trina Schart was born in Philadelphia on 8 April 1939 to Albert H. and Margaret Bruck Schart and describes in vivid words and pictures the formative experiences of her childhood (*Self-Portrait: Trina Schart Hyman*, 1981): "I was a really strange little kid. I was born terrified of anything and everything that moved or spoke. I was afraid of people, especially. . . . who knows why? My mother is a beautiful woman with red hair and the piercing blue gaze of a hawk. She never seemed afraid of anyone. It was she who gave me the courage to draw and a love of books. . . . *Little Red Riding Hood* . . . was so much a part of me that I actually became Little Red Riding Hood. . . . I was Red Riding Hood for a year or more. I think it's a great tribute to my mother that she never gave up and took me to a psychiatrist, and if she ever worried, she has never let me know."

Visiting a huge old farmhouse nearby and playing elaborate fantasy games with her sister Karleen, Hyman drew constantly and endured school until she could escape to the Philadelphia Museum College of Art, which she attended from 1956 to 1959. In *Self-Portrait* she says, "Suddenly I was not only *allowed* to draw all day long, I was *expected* to! . . . It was as though I had been living, all my life, in a strange country where I could never quite fit in–and now I had come home." In 1959 she married Harris Hyman, a mechanical engineer, and they moved to Boston where Hyman spent a year at the Boston Museum School of Fine Arts before she and her husband went to Sweden where she studied at the Swedish State Art School. There author-editor Astrid Lindgren gave Hyman her first commission for illustrations, but it was not until after her return to the United States that she got a firm foothold as an artist, with Little, Brown in Boston. Her daughter, Katrin (model for many of her heroines), was born in 1963. Hyman and her husband divorced in 1968, and she moved

Dust jacket for Hyman's 1977 retelling of the Brothers Grimm fairy tale (Little, Brown)

with her daughter to New Hampshire, where she has lived ever since.

Since 1972 Trina Schart Hyman has worked as art director (and later staff artist) for *Cricket* magazine, for which she created the characters Cricket, Ladybug, Ugly Bird (the only bird in the world with fangs and dandruff) and Everybuggy Else. Like many artists, she has been fairly reticent about her private life, and the self-therapy of writing *Self-Portrait* clearly cost her a good deal of anguish ("It was awful. I *hated* writing that book," she told David White in an interview published in 1983); in fact, though the information it contains is both honest and interesting, the emotional themes of Hyman's life are evident in her pictures, especially those illustrating the folktales that call out deep resonances in her own personality. *They* are her true autobiography.

Trina Schart Hyman's early illustrative style is well exemplified in *Joy to the World: Christmas Legends* (1966), a collection of Christmas tales by Ruth Sawyer, where a medieval background contrasts with human figures that are more fully-developed and realistic. This allows a nice balance between drama (as when Brother Froilan confronts the wolf and the dead burro in the forest) and pure decoration (as in the title piece). The technique of combining forceful, naturalistic close-ups with stylized, surrealistic landscapes is developed further in Hyman's line work for Ruth Nichols's youthful fantasy, *A Walk Out of the*

World (1969), which matches the perfunctory text in some places, while extending its range and richness in others. More consistent is the somewhat similar style adopted for Blanche Luria Serwer's collection of Jewish tales, *Let's Steal the Moon* (1970), which compares interestingly with Maurice Sendak's and Margot Zemach's illustrations for Isaac Bashevis Singer's collections.

All In Free but Janey (1968), which received a *Boston Globe–Horn Book* citation for its illustrations, is a hide-and-seek story written by Elizabeth Johnson which displays Hyman's ability to produce a fully realized, emotionally convincing narrative sequence around a brief picture-book text. Here the recurring motif of sturdily realistic children against abstract foliage evokes the childhood experience of "invisibility" in an environment geared to adult-sized people. The children's feelings, and their physical comfort or discomfort, are real—but the rest of the world is sometimes only dimly present to them. Janey's daydreams of life as a princess are sketchy-heraldic, with the obsessively personal quality of a latency-age child's stiff, detail-packed drawings. Much of the book's impact comes from Hyman's contrasting of empty, lonely spaces (reminiscent of Andrew Wyeth) with spaces that are filled to overflowing with figures: the result is a statement about security and anxiety, freedom and restriction, that loads the emotional dice for neither side and allows all possibilities to coexist.

How Six Found Christmas (1969), a small-format volume in paper covers, is the artist's first original fiction, and its mannered style indicates some uneasiness at this early venture into the verbal medium. But its archness is redeemed by some robust dialogue. In the course of her quest, the heroine asks a fox what "a Christmas" is, and he replies: "A *Christmas* you say? Now let me see.... Perhaps I know it by another name. Would you describe the thing for me? What does it taste like? Is there lots of juicy blood? Is it sweet, or salty, or sour, or peppery? Is it crisp? Does it go crunch when one bites it, or does it slip between one's teeth and slide down one's throat?" The pictures, in red and green on black and white, create snowy forests based (as so often) on the New Hampshire woods the artist knows at such close range.

Hyman's pictures for Osmond Molarsky's *Take It or Leave It* (1971) show an easy mastery of inner-city landscape, with children–fat, thin, ascetic, gross, black, white–lounging and strutting against backdrop glimpses of characterful adults. Here again, the artist celebrates the unfettered freedom of childhood, while reminding the reader of grown-up realities.

In Jan Wahl's *Magic Heart* (1972) and Howard Pyle's *King Stork* (1973) Hyman developed a much more free-flowing style, in line and watercolor, for two lighthearted pastiche folktale texts. *King Stork*'s illustration convinces by its magnificent rendering of character and by its enthusiastic, appreciative eroticism: the cocksure young soldier hero; the mature handsomeness of his magic benefactor, King Stork; the beautiful, scantily-clad and unmistakably untrustworthy princess. Only the two minor characters, the King and the Witch, are stereotypes rather than fully-developed personalities. *King Stork*, a Caldecott Honor Book in 1974, also won the *Boston Globe-Horn Book* Award for illustration in 1973, and predictably this prompted a letter to the artist from the Dallas Library System requiring a justification of the princess's see-through dress. Hyman replied that the princess was "amoral, cruel, tricksy, and not a 'nice' young lady at all" and that such a woman would deliberately use her allure to gain her own ends. Here the artist's habit of thinking "a lot about the characters that I am drawing, . . . what motivates them . . . and what they are like in their everyday lives" seems to have stood her in good stead, since the librarians withdrew their protest. However, from the other side of the Atlantic, this same tendency

to go beyond the literal sense of the text drew criticism (this time on aesthetic grounds) from Brian Alderson, writing in *Children's Book Review* (1975): "The sheerness of the technique itself runs counter to the primitive essence of the story. Miss Hyman's rich details have taken over from Howard Pyle's straightforward accents, and his standard fairy tale hero and heroine have been replaced by a butch drummer boy and a princess closely resembling Elizabeth Taylor in her svelte younger years." Whether Pyle's story is really as "primitive" as Alderson suggests is arguable, but the artist concedes, "I have been accused of it many times and I think it is a just accusation: that I say too much in my pictures, that I don't leave the story well enough alone. All I can answer is that I'm a compulsive filler-in of space, and also I'm basically a storyteller myself."

Nowhere is this last comment more clearly demonstrated, and the artist's practice better vindicated, than in her 1974 acrylics for *Snow White*. This is in every sense a pictorial narrative, the number of full-color paintings being well over the minimum necessary to illustrate Paul Heins's version of the Grimm text, leisurely though it is. The artist has scope to display her feel for the symbolic potential of natural imagery, her emotional range, her realism, and her romanticism, and the result is perhaps the finest *Snow White* of the century. Unlike Nancy Eckholm Burkert's more widely acclaimed interpretation, Trina Schart Hyman refuses to retreat from feelings into decoration: her Witch-Queen is both stately and passionately jealous; her minor characters (the King, the serving women, the Hunter) come vividly alive as individuals; her Prince is a real man, not a handsome dummy; the moment of Snow White's awakening from living death is both touching and clumsy-tender. In this series of rich, sombre paintings, where careful and often significant background detail never overwhelms the drama of foreground events, the longing, devotion, hatred, suspicion, and fear that are explicit in the Grimm tale are given full rein as never before in a version for young viewers. Above all, the artist presents *Snow White* as a statement about human closeness and human loneliness–the same theme that appears in *All In Free but Janey*, and one which is presumably central to Trina Schart Hyman's own life.

Snow White remains Hyman's masterpiece: its direct successor, *The Sleeping Beauty* (1977), has not the same concentrated power, perhaps because its text (retold by Hyman herself with some

In this disguise she went over the seven mountains to the house of the seven dwarfs, knocked at the door, and called out: "Pretty things for sale, for sale."

Snow White looked out of the window and said: "Good day, dear woman. What are you selling?"

"Good things, pretty things," she answered. "Lacings of all colors," and she took one out that was made of bright silk.

"I can let this honest woman in," thought Snow White, who unbolted the door and bought the handsome lacings.

"Child," said the old woman, "what a sight you are! Come, I will lace you up properly—for once."

Snow White was not worried. She stood before the woman, and permitted herself to be laced up with the new ribbons; but the old woman tightened them so swiftly and so firmly that Snow White gasped and fell down as if dead.

"Now you are no longer the most beautiful," the Queen said, and hurried away.

Not long after, toward evening, the seven dwarfs came home, but how frightened they were when they saw their beloved Snow White lying on the ground. She neither stirred nor moved. It was as if she were dead. They lifted her up, and when they saw that she was too tightly laced, they cut the ribbons in two. Then she began to breathe a bit and after a while became more and more lively.

When the dwarfs heard what had happened, they said, "The old pedlar was none other than the evil Queen. Take care and let nobody in if we are not with you."

Hyman's preliminary sketches for her book dummy of Snow White *(courtesy of the artist)*

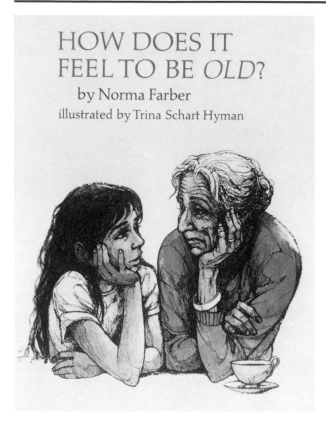

HOW DOES IT
FEEL TO BE *OLD*?

by Norma Farber

illustrated by Trina Schart Hyman

Dust jacket for Norma Farber's 1979 book illustrated by Hyman (Dutton)

nice turns of phrase) is both more diffuse and more optimistic. As in *Snow White,* the narrative proper is preceded by preliminary scenes that convey the passing of time, as the changing seasons are observed from within the palace walls. Indeed, *Sleeping Beauty* celebrates the man-made interior, as its predecessor celebrated the forest. The arches and colonnades of the palace are an important presence throughout, with carved faces on the column capitals dispassionately watching the human action. The princess Briar Rose is Spring to Snow White's Fall: robust, impish, copper-haired; and again there is a gallery of superbly realized cooks, servants, and courtiers. The fairies break with convention in being of all ages, though the artist follows tradition in giving large butterfly wings to the twelfth good fairy, a touch that seems somehow out of keeping with the spirit of the interpretation, and is perhaps explicable as a survival of a childhood fantasy of the artist's own (see *Self-Portrait*). So, too, the double-page spread of the thorn hedge, crowded with the bones and corpses of those who have tried to break through to rescue Briar Rose, is rather overstated. But the magnificent scenes of

the sleeping palace, with flies "like a crust all over the walls," more than redeem such falterings.

The illustrations for Norma Farber's metrical text, *How Does It Feel To Be Old?* (1979), demonstrate the maturity of Hyman's work in line and wash. Beginning with the dust jacket, with its striking juxtaposition of an old woman's and a young girl's face, this volume compels attention and emotional involvement, and there is a nicely calculated use of sepia to represent the old lady's memories, flooding over into the present as she recalls her life to her youthful listener. Hyman's visual statement lifts this book well above the merely didactic level at which another artist might have left it, so that it becomes a moving evocation of human life and death. Similarly, the line drawings and color plates for *Peter Pan* (1980) go well beyond mere prettiness. Both the cozy romanticism and the melodrama of James Matthew Barrie's story are present, but there is more: a hint (especially in the elongated, almost-naked Peter) of the way that Barrie, for all his tiresome whimsy, can at times connect in an uncanny way with the powers of the unconscious.

Rapunzel (1982), the third of Hyman's trio of folktales in full color, is a rich and accomplished work, but in some senses seems a retreat from the positions reached in *Snow White.* The retelling, by editor Barbara Rogasky, is less satisfactory than either Heins's or Hyman's (for *Sleeping Beauty*), overstating the emotion of this stark tale. The pictures themselves have all of Hyman's usual ability to convey fear, despair, and self-doubt in the protagonists, against landscapes and interiors painted in subtle, dusky colors. But her decision to surround them all, not only with solid-color margins but with decorative borders that vary from page to page, is ultimately counterproductive. The sense of restriction which the technique imparts is appropriate to the greater portion of the narrative, since it deals with confinement and longing for freedom, but when the eventual catharsis comes, the relentless borders remain, and offer no release. While some reviewers such as Linnea D. Lilja, in *Language Arts* (April 1984), have praised the technique for its enhancement of the "folk quality of the story," there is an emerging consensus among others that the borders detract from the impact of the paintings themselves, both in *Rapunzel* and in the somewhat similarly handled *Little Red Riding Hood* (1983), a Caldecott Honor Book in 1984. A February 1983 *Horn Book* reviewer commented on *Rapunzel* that "the excessive use of ever-

Dust jacket for Margaret Hodges's retelling of the legend of Saint George and the Dragon. Hyman received the Caldecott Medal in 1985 for her illustrations for this book (Little, Brown).

changing ornamental borders becomes a graphic cliché, . . . they unnecessarily break up the pages, distracting the eye and almost trivialising the artwork," and in the April 1983 issue, a reviewer of *Red Riding Hood* stated, "The visual impact of the full page paintings are hampered, however, by the elaborate borders rigidly framing the text on opposite pages." The text of the latter volume is retold by the artist herself, but like Rogasky's for *Rapunzel*, it is open to criticism on the grounds that it softens or weakens the "original," but then, what exactly constitutes the original text in the case of a folktale?

The autobiographical material in both *Self-Portrait* and the 1983 *Language Arts* interview with David White makes clear what has been happening to Hyman's work as she enters midlife. The folktale texts that she has increasingly illustrated over the past ten years have an intensely personal significance for her, and her courageous grappling with the feelings they embody has resulted in impressive interpretations, which restore basic ambiguities in the structure of the tales (thus Mother Gothel, the witch in *Rapunzel*, is compassionate and kind to the child Rapunzel, while being cruel to Rapunzel's parents and to the prince, both of whom she sees as threatening her "property"). However, alongside powerful emotions, the artist's delvings into childhood feelings have brought up equally powerful wishes for protection from those feelings. This is where the

decorative borders in *Rapunzel* and *Little Red Riding Hood* begin to make sense. There is no doubt that in themselves, the borders, and the whole apparatus of decoration of which they form a part, are intensely gratifying: like the fox's notion of "a Christmas," *Rapunzel* looks good enough to eat.

Hyman's illustrations for Margaret Hodges's *Saint George and the Dragon* (an adaptation of Edmund Spenser's version of the legend in *The Faerie Queene*) earned her the coveted Caldecott Medal in 1985. *Saint George,* though a consistent and engaging piece of work, represents no new departure for the artist, and the award is therefore best considered as a retrospective honoring of Hyman's oeuvre as a whole.

References:

Hugh Crago, "Who does Snow White look at?," *Signal*, 45 (September 1984): 129-145;

Jill P. May, "Illustration as Interpretation: Trina Hyman's Folktales," *Children's Literature Association Quarterly,* 10 (Fall 1985): 127-130;

David E. White, "Profile: Trina Schart Hyman," *Language Arts,* 60 (September 1983): 782-792.

Papers:

Trina Schart Hyman has papers located in the Kerlan Collection at the University of Minnesota, Minneapolis, and in Baker Library, Dartmouth College.

Ezra Jack Keats

(11 March 1916-6 May 1983)

Richard Seiter
Central Michigan University

BOOKS: *My Dog is Lost,* with Pat Cherr (New York: Crowell, 1960);

The Snowy Day (New York: Viking, 1962; London: Bodley Head, 1967);

Whistle for Willie (New York: Viking, 1964);

John Henry, an American Legend (New York: Pantheon, 1965);

Jennie's Hat (New York: Harper & Row, 1966);

Peter's Chair (New York: Harper & Row, 1967);

A Letter to Amy (New York: Harper & Row, 1968);

Goggles! (New York: Macmillan, 1969);

Hi, Cat! (New York: Macmillan, 1970);

Apt. 3 (New York: Macmillan, 1971);

Over in the Meadow, adapted and illustrated by Keats (New York: Four Winds, 1971);

Pet Show! (New York: Macmillan, 1972);

Psst! Doggie– (New York: Watts, 1973);

Skates! (New York: Watts, 1973);

Dreams (New York: Macmillan, 1974);

Kitten For a Day (New York: Watts, 1974);

Louie (New York: Greenwillow, 1975);

The Trip (New York: Greenwillow, 1978);

Maggie and the Pirate (New York: Four Winds, 1979);

Louie's Search (New York: Four Winds, 1980);

Regards to the Man in the Moon (New York: Viking, 1981);

Clementina's Cactus (New York: Viking, 1982).

BOOKS ILLUSTRATED: Elizabeth C. Lansing, *Jubilant for Sure* (New York: Crowell, 1954);

Frances Carpenter, *Wonder Tales of Dogs and Cats* (Garden City: Doubleday, 1955);

Phyllis A. Whitney, *Mystery on the Isle of Skye* (Philadelphia: Westminster, 1955);

Lansing, *Sure Think for Shep* (New York: Crowell, 1956);

George S. Albee, *Three Young Kings* (New York: Watts, 1956);

Jay Williams and Raymond Abrashkin, *Danny Dunn and the Anti-Gravity Paint* (New York: Whittlesey House, 1956);

William McKellar, *Wee Joseph* (New York: McGraw-Hill, 1957);

Tillie S. Pine, *The Indians Knew* (New York: McGraw-Hill, 1957);

Pine and Joseph Levine, *The Pilgrims Knew* (New York: McGraw-Hill, 1957);

Williams and Abrashkin, *Danny Dunn on a Desert Island* (New York: Whittlesey House, 1957);

Williams and Abrashkin, *Danny Dunn and the Weather Machine* (New York: Whittlesey House, 1957);

Pine and Levine, *The Chinese Knew* (New York: McGraw-Hill, 1958);

Williams and Abrashkin, *Danny Dunn and the Homework Machine* (New York: Whittlesey House, 1958);

Dorothea F. Fisher, *And Long Remember* (New York: McGraw-Hill, 1959);

Irmengarde Eberle, *Grasses* (New York: Walck, 1960);

Eleanor A. Murphey, *Nihal of Ceylon* (New York: Crowell, 1960);

Williams, *The Tournament of the Lions* (New York: Walck, 1960);

Paul Showers, *In the Night* (New York: Crowell, 1961; London: Adam & Charles Black, 1971);

Patricia M. Martin, *The Rice Bowl Pet* (New York: Crowell, 1962);

Pine and Levine, *The Eskimos Knew* (New York: Whittlesey House, 1962);

Solveig P. Russell, *What Good Is a Tale?* (Indianapolis: Bobbs-Merrill, 1962);

Ruth P. Collins, *The Flying Cow* (New York: Walck, 1963);

Lucretia P. Hale, *The Peterkin Papers* (Garden City: Doubleday, 1963);

Ann Nolan Clark, *Tia Maria's Garden* (New York: Viking, 1963);

Millicent Selsam, *How to Be a Nature Detective* (New York: Harper & Row, 1963);

Maxine Kumin, *Speedy Digs Downside Up* (New York: Putnam's, 1964);

Ann McGovern, *Zoo, Where Are You?* (New York: Harper & Row, 1964);

Pine and Levine, *The Egyptians Knew* (New York: McGraw-Hill, 1964);

John Keats, *The Naughty Boy, a Poem* (New York: Viking, 1965);

Richard Lewis, ed., *In a Spring Garden* (New York: Dial, 1965);

Ester R. Hautzig, *In the Park: An Excursion in Four Languages* (New York: Macmillan, 1968);

Katerine Davis, *The Little Drummer Boy* (New York: Macmillan, 1968);

Lloyd Alexander, *The King's Fountain* (New York: Dutton, 1971);

Florence B. Freedman, *Two Tickets to Freedom: The True Story of Ellen & William Craft, Fugitive Slaves* (New York: Simon & Schuster, 1971);

Myron Levoy, *Penny Tunes and Princesses* (New York: Harper & Row, 1972).

OTHER: *God is in the Mountain*, selected and illustrated by Keats (New York: Holt, Rinehart & Winston, 1966);

Night, compiled by Keats, photographs by Beverly Hall (New York: Atheneum, 1969).

PERIODICAL PUBLICATIONS: "Caldecott Award Acceptance," *Horn Book*, 39 (August 1963): 361-363;

"The Artist at Work: Collage," *Horn Book*, 40 (June 1964): 269-272.

Ezra Jack Keats, prominent children's picture-book author and illustrator, was born 11 March 1916, in Brooklyn, New York, the son of Benjamin and Augusta Podgainy Keats. He is best known for his bold, beautiful, and honest interpretations of minority children living and growing in a mid-twentieth-century inner-city landscape. He attended public schools and graduated from Thomas Jefferson High School in Brooklyn, but received no formal training in art.

Keats began to paint pictures at the age of four with encouragement from his mother. After he painted a village mural on the top of the white enameled kitchen table, his mother praised his work. Instead of destroying the mural by washing it off the table, Ester Hautzig records in a biographical sketch of Keats for *Horn Book* magazine (August 1963) that his mother took her best tablecloth, "covered the whole little mural and every time a neighbor would come in, she'd unveil it to show what [he] had done."

Benjamin Keats worried about his son's artistic ambitions but had his own way of encouraging the boy's talent. Mr. Keats would come home with a pack of cheap brushes or a tube of paint saying that a starving artist had traded them for a bowl of soup at the Greenwich Village beanery where he worked as a waiter. "It dawned on me that my father was buying this stuff for me and had a terrible conflict. He was proud of my painting and he wanted to supply me with paint, but at the same time he lived in real dread of my living a life like that of the artists he had seen."

Although Ezra Keats was offered three scholarships to study art after he graduated from high school, he could not take advantage of them because of the Depression. For a while he drifted away from art and helped to support his family by loading produce on trucks for one dollar a day. Eventually, he became a muralist for the Works Progress Administration (WPA) and later began to illustrate in magazines such as *Esquire*, *Colliers*, *Reader's Digest*, and *House Beautiful*. An editor from Doubleday asked him to do some book cover illustrations, the most notable being the cover for Irving Stone's *The Agony and the Ecstasy* (1961). After seeing this book jacket, another editor asked Keats to illustrate some children's books, thereby launching his career as a children's illustrator.

As he was working as an illustrator for other writers' books in the 1950s, Keats was troubled by two concerns: "one was that in many of the manuscripts I was given there was a peculiar quality of contrivance and rigid structure; the other was that I never got a story about Black people, Black children. I decided that if I ever did a book on my own it would be more of a happening—certainly not a structured thing, but an experience. My hero would be a Black child." Keats began to address these concerns in the 1960s, when he started to write and illustrate children's picture books about his home, Brooklyn.

Except for the years he served as a camouflage expert in the United States Air Corps during World War II, Ezra Jack Keats lived in Brooklyn, New York. His love for Brooklyn blooms in his fictional inner-city neighborhood where his books portray the lives of several minority children, seen in an environment of stoplights, mailboxes, garbage cans, and layers of advertisements on fences and walls—the landmarks for Keats's inner-city setting. By using collage and later a rich impasto of creamy acrylic paints, Keats created exciting textures and shapes. Frequently walls are decorated with children's artwork and sidewalks are chalked with hopscotch or tic-tac-toe games, revealing the

Ezra Jack Keats (photo by Weston Woods)

streets as playgrounds for inner-city children. In Keats's later books toys such as puppets created by "his" children give more dramatic insight into their private lives and emotional needs.

Keats first received recognition as a major picture-book illustrator and writer when he was awarded the Caldecott Medal for *The Snowy Day* (1962). This book became the first in a series of picture books with Peter, a black child, as the central character. *Whistle for Willie* (1964), *Peter's Chair* (1967), *A Letter to Amy* (1968), and the Caldecott Honor Book *Goggles!* (1969) trace Peter's physical and emotional growth in the inner-city setting. He is a minority child, but he is also a universal child who copes with the typical problems of growing up: acquiring motor skills such as whistling; accepting a new sibling; discovering girls, and taking care of himself outside the security of the home–important steps in Peter's maturation as they are for all children. As Keats stated in the 28 March *Milwaukee Journal*, "The important thing is that kids in the book have to be real–regardless of color. . . . What's really important is the honesty." This honesty is apparent in the universal childhood pleasures and concerns which permeate Keats's books. Caring for a pet, making and playing with puppets, celebrating spe-

cial occasions such as a birthday, or participating in a pet show fill his characters' days and spill over into Keats's illustrations with a spontaneous enthusiasm.

Keats understood that his neighborhood children grew up and changed so he consistently introduced a younger generation of children who became the central characters in his later picture books. As Peter grows older in *Goggles!*, he becomes friends with a younger black child named Archie, who becomes the central character in *Hi, Cat!* (1970) and *Pet Show!* (1972). Other characters, including Peter's sister Susy, introduced as a newborn in *Peter's Chair*, and her friend Roberto, briefly seen in *Pet Show!*, emerge as major characters in *Dreams* (1974) and *Louie* (1975). Their mutual interest in puppetry forms the basis for their friendship as well as providing the narrative link with other children in the neighborhood. Peter and Archie are present in three later books but function primarily as older chaperons for Susy. This sense of character continuity is a rare quality in children's picture books.

The Snowy Day is an excellent example of what Keats calls a "happening." Through the informal plot Peter discovers the delight of playing in the snowdrifts on a peaceful neighborhood

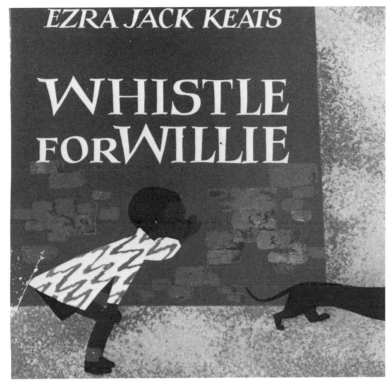

(Viking)

(Macmillan)

Covers for two of Keats's books which trace the development of an inner-city black child named Peter

street. There are few details in this book's setting; apartment buildings are suggested by different colored rectangular pieces of construction paper while gently undulating pieces of construction paper in the foreground suggest snowdrifts. The narrative flows naturally as young Peter makes discoveries in the snow with his boots—toes pointing in, toes pointing out, feet dragging through the snow. Peter builds a snowman, makes angel shapes in the snow, and pretends he is a mountain climber on a huge snowdrift. When he comes home in the late afternoon, he tucks a snowball in his pocket for tomorrow. He forgets about this snow treasure and eventually learns that snow melts.

These scenes demonstrate Keats's expertise in selecting materials to build his collage illustrations. When Peter comes indoors at the end of his day in the snow he sits on a stool on an oval braided rug, made from concentric pieces of construction paper, as his mother helps him undress for his bath. She wears a yellow gingham dress which Keats cut from oilcloth used for lining cupboards. Keats's exceptional control in graphic design is shown in the creation of Peter's underwear from the white paper which forms the background of the illustration. The underwear area is surrounded with pieces of brown construction paper that represent Peter's legs and torso and the stool on which Peter sits is fashioned from black construction paper. The effect of steamy water in Keats's illustrations of Peter's bath was created by overlapping circles of transparent paper.

This secure, peaceful mood changes when Peter discovers the darkening wet stain on his snowsuit pocket from the melting snowball. Peter's sadness is accentuated by a gray background which Keats made by splattering India ink on the paper with a toothbrush through a screen. That night Peter dreams the snow has melted, but the morning light reveals a fresh snowfall for him and his friend from across the hall to explore. In the last pages of text the snowflake pattern increases until only the gentle snowfall is present once again in the endpapers.

Peter is still a preschooler in *Whistle for Willie*, only now he is longing for enough muscle control to pucker his lips and whistle. He wants to whistle in order to call his dachshund, Willie. In this book the dog becomes Peter's close friend and appears in the remaining Peter books and others set in Keats's inner-city neighborhood. Peter is again on the street, only this time it is summer

and he is wearing shorts. The setting of the inner-city street is previewed effectively in the endpapers, where Keats used rectangular cut, textured paper to resemble a gray sidewalk. Summer is evident in the early pages filled with an orange sun-drenched sky.

When Peter discovers he cannot whistle, he becomes distracted in a game of spinning himself around and around until he becomes dizzy. Keats illustrates Peter's dizziness effectively by floating the green, yellow, and red circles of a nearby stoplight outside their regular positions in this familiar city landmark. After a second unsuccessful attempt to whistle, Peter begins another sidewalk activity, drawing a chalk line to his apartment building entrance. These games, along with walking on cracks in the sidewalks and playing with his shadow, reveal Peter's limited social interaction with peers and his ability to entertain himself. When he manages to whistle, both parents praise him. The book concludes with another sign of his growth as Peter goes on an errand for his mother to the grocery store; Peter's head is held high, and Willie proudly follows his whistling master.

Whistle for Willie includes more details and textures than *The Snowy Day*. The buildings contain brush strokes resembling bricks; fences and walls along the sidewalk where Peter plays exhibit children's chalk art sandwiched between layers of old advertisements. These fences along with garbage cans, in particular, become visual motifs for Keats's inner-city neighborhood.

Peter's joy is partially eclipsed when a baby sister, Susy, is introduced and limitations are placed upon him in *Peter's Chair*. When Susy is brought home, Peter discovers his blue bassinet has fallen victim to pink paint. Peter continues to enjoy games until he and Willie smash a building block tower and are hushed by his mother. When his blue youth chair becomes his father's next painting project, Peter decides to run away from home taking the chair, his baby picture, a few toys, and Willie. On the sidewalk in front of his apartment building Peter discovers he is too big for his youth chair. With understanding and loving from his parents, Peter decides to help his father paint the chair pink. Keats pasted pieces of newspaper under the work area where Peter is busily painting the chair as well as himself while Willie walks off the newspaper leaving a trail of pink paw prints as a humorous visual conclusion to this narrative which focuses on sibling acceptance.

He told his mother all about his adventures
while she took off his wet socks.

25

Page from The Snowy Day *featuring one of Keats's collage illustrations (Viking)*

An interest in girls blooms in *A Letter to Amy*. When Peter begins to appreciate girls romantically, he decides to invite Amy, a girl who lives in the neighborhood, to his birthday party. This invitation is special because it is handwritten; the other invitations to his boyfriends are made by telephone. Peter's mother gently tells him he needs more information in Amy's invitation since it simply says "Will you please come to my birthday party. Peter." Because he has sealed the envelope, he writes on the outside, "It is Saturday at 2." This small detail is humorous, yet realistic, because it reveals Peter is struggling to use written language as a communication tool. As Peter hurries to post his letter before a gathering rainstorm breaks, he wonders, "What will the boys say when they see a girl at my party?" Concern for peer acceptance becomes another trait in Peter's developing personality.

Keats's details in the sidewalk setting function more dramatically in *A Letter to Amy* than in previous books. The wind in the storm that stalks Peter suddenly snatches Amy's invitation from his hand. The letter "skips" across a hopscotch game chalked on the sidewalk while a pair of eyes made from two letter D's in an old and torn sign on a nearby wall watch with wide-eyed excitement as Peter chases the envelope. In his haste to catch the envelope Peter collides with Amy who happens to be rushing down the street too. Amy runs off crying, and Peter assumes she will not come to his party, but to Peter's surprise, Amy comes to his birthday celebration and brings her pet parrot, Pepe, which squawks birthday greetings to Peter.

The more sophisticated conclusion of *A Letter to Amy* encourages children to guess Peter's birthday wish as he blows out the candles on his cake. While the boys chant for "a truckload of candy with no stomach ache," Amy shyly looks at Peter, who may be considering a wish for a kiss from her. Continuity with the earlier Peter books is maintained in the closing illustrations with sister Susy wearing a party hat and sitting in her pink high chair as the ever-present Willie is stationed close to the birthday cake. This book celebrates another year of life and growth for Peter.

In the Caldecott Honor Book *Goggles!* the joy of growing older is replaced by the practical experience of fending for oneself on inner-city streets when Peter finds himself threatened by older kids. Peter, along with his dog, Willie, and a younger friend, Archie, flee from a group of older boys who are chasing them in order to get a pair of old goggles Peter and Archie found on a vacant, rubble-filled lot. The endpapers (which Keats generally utilized to great advantage) foreshadow the story's tension with burnt orange construction paper resembling a city wall where kids have daubed various drawings. Intense, dark acrylic paints project the decay and rust in this inner-city setting; abandoned bed headboards, doors, and drainpipes are scattered on the lot, which Peter and Archie claim as their playground and hideout. The drainpipe eventually becomes a refuge where the boys hide as the older gang searches for them. Willie helps Archie and Peter by picking up the goggles and running with them when Peter is knocked down by one of the older boys. By eluding this gang Peter and Archie become streetwise kids, capable of taking care of themselves in dangerous situations.

The new character to emerge from *Goggles!* is Archie. He is younger than Peter and more aware of his black identity, sporting a moderate Afro in contrast to Peter's closecropped hair. At first Archie is frightened when Peter stands up to the older boys, but when he is safely back on his apartment building steps with Peter, Willie, and the goggles, Archie begins to show his sense of humor as he puts on the goggles and brags with satisfaction, "We sure fooled 'em, didn't we?" After being reassured by Peter, Archie continues, "Things look real fine, now." With the conclusion

of this book, Keats directed his narrative energies toward the spunky, less inhibited character Archie.

Hi Cat! and *Pet Show!* focus on Archie's acquiring a pet and becoming involved in a pet show involving the whole neighborhood. *Hi Cat!* is another one of those light, narrative, "happenings" that Keats was fond of spinning. Archie is casually walking down a street, licking an ice cream cone when he happens to peer into a storefront window and sees his ice cream beard reflection. This reflection and an umbrella from a nearby garbage can inspires Archie to go into a slapstick routine, impersonating an old man, for the group of neighborhood kids which includes Peter and Susy.

Other "characters" become more interested in the ice cream than in Archie's antics; a cat looks at the cone and follows Archie. Willie, Peter's dachshund, springs from the audience, jumps up to Archie's face, and begins to lick Archie's ice cream beard. Wry-faced Archie croaks, "No respect for old age!" to the delight of the audience. A more visually sophisticated routine follows when Archie creates a character named Mr. Big Face, improvised from a large shopping bag with Archie's tongue protruding from one of the eyes and his hand projecting from Big Face's ear. Curiosity draws the children and the cat nearer to Mr. Big Face until the cat jumps up into the disguise, causing a wild dance that ends abruptly when the bag splits.

The street show must go on and Archie, with help from Peter, continues to improvise until twilight when Archie returns home with the cat following at a safe distance. This is the same cat Archie is trying to find at the beginning of *Pet Show!*, in which Keats's neighborhood children gather their menagerie of pets, including turtles, mice, frogs, and goldfish. Although Peter is visibly taller and older in this book, he is caught up in the excitement of the contest and predictably brings Willie, while his little sister Suzy is old enough to bring her goldfish.

The special touch in this happy picture book is that everyone gets a blue ribbon award. "There was the noisiest parrot, the handsomest frog, the busiest ants, the brightest goldfish, the longest dog, the fastest mouse, the softest puppy, the slowest turtle—and many more." The only shadow on this bright day is Archie's inability to locate his cat, but, true to his resourceful character, Archie brings a germ in a glass jar and receives a blue ribbon for "the quietest pet." Eventually

Dust jacket for Keats's 1972 book in which a group of neighborhood children put on a pet show (Macmillan)

Archie's cat appears beside an older neighbor lady who receives a ribbon for the cat with the "longest whiskers." She offers the ribbon to Archie because she knows the cat belongs to him (apparently the cat is an alley pet appearing for daily nourishment near Archie's doorstep), but Archie tells her to keep the ribbon, "It looks good on you." Shared joy between old and young is the gratifying "happening" in this text.

Keats previews his next inner-city narrative through one of the children in *Pet Show!* A small boy named Roberto and his pet mouse are among the contestants. In *Dreams* (1974) Roberto has made a paper puppet mouse at school which he brings home and places on the window sill of his apartment. Ultimately Keats turns the narrative so that the puppet mouse saves Archie's cat by frightening a large dog threatening the cat.

Roberto witnesses this late night drama because he cannot fall asleep. The other children in the apartment building are sleeping and dreaming, which Keats creatively interprets by placing colorfully patterned papers in the apartment building windows of the sleeping occupants. The book does succeed in maintaining continuity within Keats's neighborhood since Roberto's interest in making this mouse puppet is an important narrative thread leading to *Louie*, which focuses

on a lonely child who attends a puppet show staged in the street by Roberto and Susy. Keats continues to explore a more somber view of inner-city life and loneliness in childhood in this picture book where puppetry and dreams sustain and help Louie to feel more accepted.

As *Louie* opens, Roberto and Susy are preparing to stage a puppet show in their neighborhood. The endpapers show the puppets, Roberto's mouse and Susy's puppet Gussie, and the work involved in making these creations. Gussie, a finger puppet, resembles a green-faced baby replete with bonnet, frock, and rattle. It is Gussie who evokes an enthusiastic "Hello! Hello!" from Louie, a lonely, fatherless, ostracized child who has never spoken a word to anyone until this moment.

When the show concludes, Susy invites Louie to hold Gussie until Peter comes to take her home. Yearning for the puppet Gussie, Louie walks home alone with his face down, shoulders slumped. As he falls asleep at home, he dreams of sharing a huge ice cream cone with Gussie. Keats has quietly included the ice cream cone as a visual motif in earlier illustrations—one where a little girl is licking a yellow cone while watching the puppet show, and the other as part of an ice cream advertisement placed on an aging board fence. When Louie awakens, his mother tells him a note has been left for him, which begins with a significant word for Louie, "Hello! Hello! Hello! Go outside and follow the green string!" The remainder of the book is without text as Keats traces Louie's journey along the green string leading to Gussie and the knowledge there are children who like him, who realize his needs, and who are willing to share part of themselves with him. The visual ice-cream-cone motif and the textless conclusion show Keats placing more thematic emphasis in the illustrations as generosity and concern are shown rather than stated.

Just as Louie secures friendships in his neighborhood, he and his mother move to another New York neighborhood in *The Trip* (1978). Again, homemade toys, dreams, and costumes become the focus in this book. The endpapers show Louie has taken Gussie with him and that this puppet inspires more creativity since Louie is constructing a diorama of a city landscape from a shoe box and sheets of various colored papers and plastic.

This project seems to fill a lonely void Louie feels intensely in his new home, "No kids, no dogs, no cats. And there weren't even any steps in the front of the door to sit on." Louie suspends a toy airplane from a string in his diorama shoe box and pretends he is flying among skyscrapers in his old neighborhood. In this dream sequence Louie lands the plane in his old neighborhood. There he meets costumed creatures, the first clue that Halloween must be near. Louie runs from the creatures until he recognizes that the mouse costume is similar to the mouse puppet which performed with Gussie. As Louie concludes Roberto is wearing the mouse costume, Susy and Archie remove their masks and chant, "Trick or Treat." In his dream Louie takes his old friends, including Archie's cat, for an airplane ride until Louie awakens to the chants of "Trick or Treat" from the children in his neighborhood. Wearing an ice cream cone costume, the object in an earlier dream which he had shared with Gussie, Louie joins other children for the annual late-October ritual.

This repeated visual motif of the ice cream cone provides added continuity between *Louie* and *The Trip*, as well as the assurance that Louie is adjusting to his new neighborhood as he goes with his new friends on Halloween. *The Trip* is significant because Keats leaves the old neighborhood where Peter, Archie, Susy, Amy, and Roberto have grown up to follow Louie on his quest to find stability in his life. Keats challenged himself as a writer in exploring Louie's character and emotional needs.

In *Louie's Search* (1980) Keats follows Louie on a new journey to complete his family by finding a father. Before he sets out on his search, Louie, who is still fascinated with costumes, dresses up in a paper bag hat, a colorful necktie, and a red nose. Although he hopes to draw attention to himself, Louie is not successful since most of the adults pay no attention to him.

In *Louie's Search* Keats examines more closely the lives in the inner city (as he did in *Apt. 3*, 1971, which explores a developing friendship between two boys and a blind man in a run-down tenement). Louie notices two dozing, derelict men on a bench who are leaning against each other; other adults on the street are arguing or working, seemingly too preoccupied to notice Louie. Several workmen, including a street worker wearing a yellow hardhat and a baker wearing a pastry hat, visually repeat the idea of the importance of hats to Louie. When Louie picks up a music box that has fallen from a second-hand furniture truck, the costumed child finally draws the attention of a fierce-looking, red-bearded truck driver, named Barney, who assumes Louie has stolen the "music maker." After catching Louie, Barney takes him home and "rants and raves" at Peg, Louie's mother, for having a thief for a son.

When this misunderstanding is corrected, a summer romance blooms between Peg and Barney; their relationship is highlighted by a glorious sun-drenched, water-sprayed tugboat ride in New York Harbor which Keats illustrates with great painterly enthusiasm. The summer romance culminates in a late summer wedding with Louie on Barney's shoulders, wearing Barney's hat, the visual sign that Louie has found his father. The hat as visual motif is more subtly stated than the earlier ice cream cone in *Louie* and *The Trip*.

The need for a father's affection so prominent in *Louie's Search* is remembered poignantly by Keats in an interview for *American Artist* (September 1971), when he describes having to identity his father's body after he died from a sudden heart attack. "As part of the procedure, the police asked me to look through his wallet. I found myself staring deep into his secret feelings. There in his wallet were worn and tattered newspaper clippings of the notices and awards I had won. My secret admirer and supplier [of painting

Cover for Keats's 1975 book in which a lonely boy secures the friendship of neighborhood children after watching them put on a puppet show (Greenwillow)

brushes and tubes of paint], had been torn between the dread of my leading a life of hardship and his real pride in my work."

Ezra Jack Keats and his books are loved by children throughout the world; several of his books have been translated into many languages including Spanish, Italian, Portuguese, and Turkish. In turn, Keats promoted interest in other languages for American children when he illustrated *In the Park: An Excursion in Four Languages* (1968), written by Ester Hautzig. Because of this international interest Keats was invited to design UNICEF cards on four separate occasions. Such books as *In a Spring Garden* (1965), a collection of twenty-three classic Japanese haiku edited by Richard Lewis, show Keats's understanding, sensitivity, and reverence for life through his striking interpretations of beauty in nature.

In his later career Keats used less collage, preferring painting for sheer sensual pleasure and intensity apparent in the joyful colors of *Pet Show!* and the more somber hues of *Apt. 3*. Because of this need to explore his range, critic Selma Lanes called Keats the Jackson Pollack and William de Kooning of American children's books in her *Horn Book* tribute (September-October 1984). Keats's continuous search for artistic expression through more dramatic painterly media resembles the search for expression his later characters undertake. Keats's ability to communicate beauty and creative potential in the ordinary is the legacy he leaves to children. He died of a heart attack in New York City on 6 May 1983.

References:

Ester Hautzig, "Ezra Jack Keats," *Horn Book*, 39 (August 1963): 364-368;

Margo Huston, "Honesty is the Author's Best Policy for Children's Books," *Milwaukee Journal*, 28 March 1974; republished in *Biography News*, volume 1 (Detroit: Gale Research, 1974), p. 553;

Selma Lanes, "Ezra Jack Keats: In Memoriam," *Horn Book*, 60 (September-October 1984): 551-558;

Erma Perry, "The Gentle World of Ezra Jack Keats," *American Artist*, 35 (September 1971): 49-52, 71-73.

Steven Kellogg
(26 October 1941-   )

Millicent Lenz
State University of New York at Albany

BOOKS: *The Wicked Kings of Bloon* (Englewood Cliffs, N.J.: Prentice-Hall, 1970);
Can I Keep Him? (New York: Dial, 1971);
The Mystery Beast of Ostergeest (New York: Dial, 1971);
The Orchard Cat (New York: Dial, 1972);
Won't Somebody Play with Me? (New York: Dial, 1972);
The Island of the Skog (New York: Dial, 1973);
The Mystery of the Missing Red Mitten (New York: Dial, 1974);
There Was an Old Woman, adapted by Kellogg (New York: Parents' Magazine Press, 1974);
Much Bigger than Martin (New York: Dial, 1976);
The Mysterious Tadpole (New York: Dial, 1977);
The Mystery of the Magic Green Ball (New York: Dial, 1979);
Pinkerton, Behave! (New York: Dial, 1979);
The Mystery of the Flying Orange Pumpkin (New York: Dial, 1980);
A Rose for Pinkerton (New York: Dial, 1981);
The Mystery of the Stolen Blue Paint (New York: Dial, 1982);
Tallyho, Pinkerton (New York: Dial, 1982);
Ralph's Secret Weapon (New York: Dial, 1983);
Paul Bunyan: A Tall Tale (New York: Morrow, 1984);
Chicken Little (New York: Morrow, 1985);
Best Friends (New York: Dial, 1986);
Pecos Bill (New York: Morrow, 1986);
Aster Aardvark's Alphabet Adventures (New York: Morrow, 1987).

BOOKS ILLUSTRATED: George Mendoza, *Gwot! Horribly Funny Hairticklers* (New York: Harper & Row, 1967);
James Copp, *Martha Matilda O'Toole* (Englewood Cliffs, N.J.: Bradbury, 1969);
Eleanor B. Heady, *Brave Johnny O'Hare* (New York: Parents' Magazine Press, 1969);
Mary Rodgers, *The Rotten Book* (New York: Harper & Row, 1969);
Hilaire Belloc, *Matilda Who Told Lies and Was Burned to Death* (New York: Dial, 1970);

Steven Kellogg

Ruth Loomis, *Mrs. Purdy's Children* (New York: Dial, 1970);
Perry Parish, *Granny and the Desperadoes* (New York: Macmillan, 1970);
Fred Rogers, *Mr. Rogers' Songbook* (New York: Random House, 1970);
Miriam Young, *Can't You Pretend?* (New York: Putnam's, 1970);
Anne Mallett, *Here Comes Tagalong* (New York: Parents' Magazine Press, 1971);
Jan Wahl, *Crabapple Night* (New York: Holt, Rinehart & Winston, 1971);
Aileen Friedman, *The Castles of the Two Brothers* (New York: Holt, Rinehart & Winston, 1972);
Wahl, *The Very Peculiar Tunnel* (New York: Putnam's, 1972);
Jeanette Franklin Caines, *Abby* (New York: Harper & Row, 1973);
Joan M. Lexau, *Come Here, Cat* (New York: Harper & Row, 1973);

Doris Herold Lund, *You Ought to See Herbert's House* (New York: Watts, 1973);

Leisel Moak Skorpen, *Kisses and Fishes* (New York: Harper & Row, 1974);

Cora Annett, *How the Witch Got Alf* (New York: Watts, 1975);

Alice Bach, *The Smartest Bear and His Brother Oliver* (New York: Harper & Row, 1975);

Belloc, *Hilaire Belloc's "The Yak, the Python, the Frog"* (New York: Parents' Magazine Press, 1975);

Margaret Mahy, *The Boy Who Was Followed Home* (New York: Watts, 1975);

Jean Van Leeuwen, *The Great Christmas Kidnaping Caper* (New York: Dial, 1975);

Bach, *The Most Delicious Camping Trip Ever* (New York: Harper & Row, 1976);

Edward Bangs, *Steven Kellogg's Yankee Doodle* (New York: Parents' Magazine Press, 1976);

Judith Choate, *Awful Alexander* (Garden City: Doubleday, 1976);

Lou Ann Bigge Gaeddert, *Gustav the Gourmet Giant* (New York: Dial, 1976);

Bach, *Grouchy Uncle Otto* (New York: Harper & Row, 1977);

Carol Chapman, *Barney Bipple's Magic Dandelions* (New York: Dutton, 1977);

Bach, *Millicent the Magnificent* (New York: Harper & Row, 1978);

Mercer Mayer, *Appelard and Liverwurst* (New York: Four Winds, 1978);

Marilyn Singer, *Pickle Pan* (New York: Dutton, 1978);

Julia Castiglia, *Jill the Pill* (New York: Atheneum, 1979);

Douglas Davis, *There's an Elephant in the Garage* (New York: Dutton, 1979);

Susan Pearson, *Molly Moves Out* (New York: Dial, 1979);

William Sleator, *Once, Said Darlene* (New York: Dutton, 1979);

Jean Marzollo, *Uproar on Hollercat Hill* (New York: Dial, 1980);

Trinka H. Noble, *The Day Jimmy's Boa Ate the Wash* (New York: Dial, 1980);

Amy Ehrlich, *Leo, Zack, and Emmie* (New York: Dial, 1981);

Mayer, *Liverwurst is Missing* (New York: Four Winds, 1981);

Alan Benjamin, *A Change of Plans* (New York: Four Winds, 1982);

Cathy Warren, *The Ten-Alarm Camp-Out* (New York: Lothrop, Lee & Shepard, 1983);

Jane Bayer, *A My Name is Alice* (New York: Dial, 1984);

Noble, *Jimmy's Boa Bounces Back* (New York: Dial, 1984);

Carol Purdy, *Iva Dunnit and the Big Wind* (New York: Dial, 1985);

David M. Schwartz, *How Much is a Million?* (New York: Lothrop, Lee & Shepard, 1985).

PERIODICAL PUBLICATION: "The Christmas Witch," *Family Circle* (December 1974): 117-121.

Steven Kellogg grew up in Norwalk, Connecticut, with a crayon in his hand drawing and telling stories to his younger sister. He loved animals and he loved drawing, two interests that led to his desire to become a "naturalist-illustrator"; a combination he called "the best of all possible worlds." As a child, he wallpapered his room with drawings and fantasized about being invited to join a *National Geographic* expedition to sketch animals in Africa. He remembers his room as "a crayoned aviary-bestiary." Some of his stories portray animal characters modeled on his sisters' stuffed animals and the ceramic animal figurines that graced a shelf in his family's living room.

His best friend in his early years and the most important influence upon his decision to become an artist was his grandmother, whom he recalls as "much more at ease with children than adults." She spent hours with him, relating stories of her childhood in the late nineteenth century. She taught him to know the flora and fauna of the New England woods and instilled in him an appreciation for the wonderful variety of trivial "treasures" to be found in the "Victorian clutter" of her room. Kellogg recognizes with surprise and pleasure how often the images in his writing and illustration reflect experiences he shared with her.

He continued to draw and paint throughout his high school years, and when he graduated he was given a Pitney-Bowes scholarship to the Rhode Island School of Design, where he majored in illustration. During the second semester of his senior year he studied in Florence on a European honors grant from the Carnegie Foundation. It was in Florence that he discovered his love for the opera. Following his graduation from the Rhode Island School of Design in 1963, Kellogg undertook graduate study at the American University in Washington, D.C. There he taught etching and exhibited his artwork. His interest in children's books grew, and he began submitting manuscripts to New York publishers.

His career as an illustrator of children's books began in 1966 when Harper and Row commissioned him to illustrate *Gwot! Horribly Funny Hairticklers.* When, in 1967, he married his wife, Helen, who had six children, they moved back to Connecticut, and he began writing full-time. Helen, the children, and family pets have all appeared in Kellogg's startlingly prolific illustrations.

Pinkerton, Kellogg's 180-pound spotted Great Dane, is the subject of *Pinkerton, Behave!* (1979). Kellogg's comments on the theme of *Pinkerton, Behave!* give insight into many of his books. The high-spirited and mischievous Great Dane's salient characteristic is his individuality. Kellogg has quoted a passage in Thoreau's *Walden* to illuminate the meaning of Pinkerton's nonconformity: "If a man does not keep pace with his companions, perhaps it is because he hears a different drummer. Let him step to the music which he hears, however measured or far away." Pinkerton has, like a human being, his own distinct personality, described by Kellogg as that of an antihero, who does things in his own way, giving his own interpretation to commands issued by humans. This autonomy turns out to be an asset, not a liability. The book, Kellogg observes, says to children in a lighthearted way that it is very important to be yourself. A respect for individuality can be seen also in the sensuously illustrated *The Mysterious Tadpole* (1977), where the eccentric tadpole turns out to be not a tadpole at all (no "ordinary frog") but one-of-a-kind—the unique Loch Ness monster—and the intriguing ending of the book introduces an "unusual stone" which hatches to produce an exotic bird, another rarity.

The importance of the bond between humans and animals is a constant theme in Kellogg's work. He praises the infinite variety found in the world, and that celebration is reflected in the rich detail and variegation in his drawings, which radiate an exuberant delight in "God's plenty" and an almost Rabelaisian pleasure in the wonders of creation. Harking back, perhaps, to the wondrous trivia of his grandmother's room, his illustrations at their richest are visual equivalents of the "Pied Beauty" celebrated by Gerard Manley Hopkins. His portrayals of animals are noteworthy for exuding joy (as for example in *Paul Bunyan: A Tall Tale,* 1984), as though the illustrator had envisioned them in an Eden-like garden, where they live in unalloyed harmony with humans.

The reviews of Kellogg's books chronicle his journey from his beginnings as an illustrator for others to the creator of his own texts. His illustrations for George Mendoza's *Gwot!* were welcomed by the reviewer for the *New York Times Book Review* (22 October 1967) as "superbly grotesque" and "quite literally horrible" in a way appropriate to the text. Kellogg's first single-handed creation, *The Wicked Kings of Bloon* (1970), was thought by Euple Wilson in a *Library Journal* (15 April 1971) review to be "garish" and "overdone" in its art, yet its child appeal can be inferred from its selection as a Junior Literary Guild offering.

Can I Keep Him? (1971) aroused some controversy over its portrayal of a mother in a ruffled apron; perhaps in reaction to this implication of sexist stereotyping, Kellogg, in *The Island of the Skog* (1973) portrayed a notably strong female leader and (at the behest of his editors) for *Steven Kellogg's Yankee Doodle* (1976) altered one line of the chorus of Edward Bangs's famous song, changing "Mind the music and the step / And with the girls be handy" to "And with the folks be handy"—an attempt to please feminists which unfortunately pleased no one and offended some purists.

Kellogg's own *The Orchard Cat* (1972) is an exceptional little parable, the text in rhyming lines of red ink providing a fine contrast to the intricate black-and-white illustrations. Mama Cat's misanthropic deathbed advice ("You gets what you takes and you takes what you gets") to her son proves unworkable as a philosophy of life. The young cat discovers he does not after all want to become "King": he learns from a houseful of children how to play and how to "care"—and is converted from a power-hungry tyrant to a lovable, loving cat. The 1 April 1973 issue of *Booklist* featured a review which praised the "honest emotions" and "bizarre humor" of Kellogg's 1972 book *Won't Somebody Play with Me?* The same year Paul Heins, in the June issue of *Horn Book,* commented favorably on Kellogg's drawings for Joan Lexau's *Come Here Cat,* stating that Kellogg "squanders his inventive ingenuity in occasional corners only and sets up a happy contrast between the single-minded little girl and the bustling, exuberant community in which she lives."

Olga Richard and Donnarae MacCann, in a detailed review of Mercer Mayer's *Appelard and Liverwurst* (1978) in *Wilson Library Bulletin,* succinctly describe the qualities of Kellogg's art: his "cartoon illustrations make fun of farmers as well as small-town hoi polloi. The pages contain dozens of tiny, visual sub-plots: slapstick, pie-throwing feuds, dog-cat wars, some excessive crowding

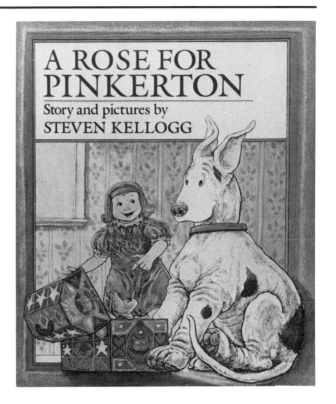

Dust jackets for Kellogg's three books about the antics of a free-spirited Great Dane (Dial)

(five beasts) in Appelard's bed. On some pages
Kellogg allows color to overpower his elaborate animated line. Yet the color is used to heighten the
comical dimension. . . . Most of the time the compositions are well organized in layers." This book
may be a benchmark in Kellogg's development of
a simplified background for his wealth of detail.
Pinkerton, Behave! in 1979 received an even more
enthusiastic review from Barbara Elleman in *Booklist:* "Kellogg wittily captures expressions and
movements of animal and human, wisely allowing the focal humor to emanate through the
faces and action and foregoing the background detail usually found in his work, . . . bright lively colors and spare use of narrative blend to help
make this a splendid comedic success. Kellogg at
his best."

Several of Kellogg's most recent creations
have met with strong appreciation, especially
Chicken Little (1985), a "fantasy within a fantasy"
story wherein Foxy Loxy's dreams of his "poultry
feasts" are shown in balloons which multiply the
comic effect, and *Paul Bunyan: A Tall Tale* (1984),
for which Kellogg's outrageous illustrations are
splendidly fitting.

Kellogg has used a variety of materials and
variations in style. Some of his illustrations are
soft and gentle, an effect produced by pastels
and watercolors; he has also shown himself to be
the master of the black-and-white line drawing enhanced with meaningful touches of color, as in
The Mystery of the Missing Red Mitten (1974). To prepare illustrations to be reproduced by the color
separation process on the four-color offset press,
he works on four sheets of clear acetate, shading
it gray or black according to the intensity of color
desired. As he has commented, "I must think in
color but work in black and white. It was a challenge, but I've gotten used to it." This method provides more accurate color printing at less cost
than photographic processes.

Kellogg is eloquent in expressing his belief
in the importance of picture books in the development of a child's love for reading. He believes
first that books should be "deliberately enjoyable," since pleasure is uppermost and crucial in
creating lifelong readers and because children
open their hearts to books they enjoy; second, he
gives unstintingly of his time to visit schools
across the nation, introducing children to books
and storytelling and lecturing to college students,
parents, and librarians. He has been particularly
vocal about the contrasting effects of viewing television and reading books upon the development

*Dust jacket for Kellogg's 1985 retelling of the Chicken Little
nursery rhyme (Morrow)*

and growth of children's minds. Television, he observes, captivates children, seducing them away
from books, depriving them of the special intimacy that is a part of sharing books and reading
aloud in the evenings. "Reading is a much more
supportive activity than television," he notes.
Books have far more potential for nourishing the
emotions and imagination than do the images on
the television screen. Kellogg has also written co-
gently of his philosophy of art: "Art is the language of feeling." He wants his books to have
the "emotional intensity," the approachability, of
opera. Kellogg believes that emotion as expressed in opera and as experienced by children
is "unbridled"; hence the parallel.

He recognizes the musical qualities of language and visual images, which "can be orches-
trated by the artist as he moves them across the
pages of the book. Rhythms and harmonies can
be established on some spreads, and atonal effects or dissonances can be introduced on others." Further, he believes a meaningful analogy
can be drawn between the sense of "movement"
possible through the art of the picture book and
the movement of film images. He begins with a
definition of the picture book as "a synthesis of lit-

Preliminary sketch for Kellogg's forthcoming alphabet book (courtesy of the artist)

erature and the visual arts," the essence of which is "the relationship of the written word and the picture." Words and pictures do not exist in a static relationship, for, in Kellogg's words, "children's books are the forerunner of film. As you turn the pages, you 'move' the pictures. This relates, in turn, to the momentum and sense of timing that is so important.... The turning page ... gives the illustrator the chance to utilize the element of surprise to advance the movement of the story and deepen the involvement of the viewer in much the same way that the theatrical director uses the revolving stage or the rising curtain between the scenes and acts of a play."

The illustrators he admires are able to "animate" their characters and to design pages "so that they crackle with graphic vitality. The characters seem to speak, cavort and leap from the page so energetically that their life and movement are totally convincing." The moving qualities of individual pictures are enhanced by the artistic use of the turning pages. Picture book design and filmmaking are both arts that "deal with the phenomenon of 'moving pictures.'" The most imaginative picture books achieve the "uncanny fusion" between picture and text, with relationships and tensions between the two "allowing magical discoveries and subtle revelations to emerge" in a "dynamic new expression" which can enchant young readers and invite them to enjoy a lifetime association with art.

Picture books are universal in their appeal, belonging to people of all ages and to a rich tradition that harks back "to the pictorial narration of the cave paintings, and to the sequences and tales that were illustrated on the walls of ancient temples and tombs." Kellogg has achieved a secure place among leading contemporary illustrators for children. His works frequently appear on best books of the year lists, and he has garnered several distinguished awards. *Pinkerton, Behave!*, *Can I Keep Him?*, and *The Orchard Cat* were placed in the American Institute of Graphic Arts Book Show; *Can I Keep Him?* won the Dutch Zilveren Griffel Award; and *The Mysterious Tadpole* received the Irma Simonton Black Award. He has devised a style unmistakably his own, its hallmarks being the qualities of the artist himself— whom Joel C. Thompson has described as "a man full of sunshine, bubbling over with enthusiasm, laughter and thought." Judith Elkin has noted how "his simple caricatures of people and animals combine ingenuity and wit with a feeling for the ridiculous that appeals to the imagination of many young children."

Kellogg is now in control of the prodigious energy of his art, and the "busyness" criticized by some early reviewers has been replaced by an artistic balance of rich detail against a simplified background. His progressively more distinguished style and his boundless creative energies promise ever more delightful books in the years ahead.

References:

Judith Elkin, Review of *The Mystery of the Missing Red Mitten* and *The Mystery of the Magic Green Ball*, *Times Literary Supplement*, 18 July 1980, p. 809;

Olga Richard and Donnarae MacCann, Review of *Appelard and Liverwurst* by Mercer Mayer, *Wilson Library Bulletin* (October 1978): 178-179;

Joel C. Thompson, "Kellogg's Great Dane Listens to the Beat of a Different Drummer," *Bridgeport, Connecticut, Sunday Post*, 2 December 1979, p. B1.

Nancy Larrick

(28 December 1910-)

Laura M. Zaidman
University of South Carolina

BOOKS: *Printing and Promotion Handbook; How to Plan, Produce, and Use Printing, Advertising, and Direct Mail*, with Daniel Melcher (New York: McGraw-Hill, 1949);

See For Yourself: A First Book of Science Experiments, illustrated by Frank Jupo (New York: Aladdin, 1952);

A Parent's Guide to Children's Reading (Garden City: Doubleday, 1958; revised, 1964; revised again, 1969 and 1975; revised again, Philadelphia: Westminster, 1983);

Color ABC, illustrated by Rene Martin (New York: Platt & Munk, 1959); republished as *First ABC* (New York: Platt & Munk, 1965);

Rockets Into Space, with Alexander L. Crosby (New York: Random House, 1959);

A Teacher's Guide to Children's Books (Columbus, Ohio: Merrill, 1960);

Rivers, What They Do, with Crosby (Racine, Wis.: Whitman, 1961);

Junior Science Book of Rain, Hail, Sleet, & Snow, illustrated by Weda Yap (Champaign, Ill.: Garrard, 1961);

A Parent's Guide to Children's Education (New York: Trident, 1963);

Children's Reading Begins at Home: How Parents Can Help Their Young Children (Winston-Salem: Starstream, 1980);

Encourage Your Children to Read (New York: Dell, 1981).

RECORDING: *Books for the Preschool Child*, Children's Book Council, 1977.

OTHER: *Reading in Action*, edited by Larrick (New York: Scholastic Magazines, 1957);

Piper, Pipe that Song Again! Poems for Boys and Girls, edited by Larrick, illustrations by Kelly Oechsli (New York: Random House, 1965);

Poetry for Holidays, edited by Larrick, illustrated by Oechsli (Champaign, Ill.: Garrard, 1966);

What Is Reading Doing to the Child?, edited by Larrick (Danville, Ill.: Interstate Printers & Publishers, 1967);

Green is Like a Meadow of Grass: An Anthology of Children's Pleasure in Poetry, edited by Larrick, illustrated by Oechsli (Champaign, Ill.: Garrard, 1968);

Piping Down the Valleys Wild: Poetry for the Young of All Ages, edited by Larrick, illustrated by Ellen Raskin (New York: Delacorte, 1968);

Reading: Isn't It Really the Teacher?, edited by Larrick and Charles J. Versacci (Danville, Ill.: Interstate Printers & Publishers, 1968);

On City Streets: An Anthology of Poetry, edited by Larrick, illustrated with photographs by David Sagarin (New York: Evans, 1968);

I Heard a Scream in the Street: Poems by Young People in the City, edited by Larrick, illustrated with photographs by students (New York: Evans, 1970);

Somebody Turned On a Tap in These Kids: Poetry and Young People Today, edited by Larrick (New York: Delacorte, 1971);

The Wheels of the Bus Go Round and Round: School Bus Songs and Chants, edited by Larrick, illustrated by Gene Holtan (San Carlos, Cal.: Golden Gate Junior Books, 1972);

More Poetry for Holidays, edited by Larrick, illustrated by Harold Berson (Champaign, Ill.: Garrard, 1973);

Male and Female Under 18: Frank Comments from Young People about Their Sex Roles Today, edited by Larrick and Eve Merriam (New York: Avon, 1973);

Room for Me and a Mountain Lion: Poetry of Open Space, edited by Larrick (New York: Evans, 1974);

Crazy to Be Alive in Such a Strange World: Poems about People, edited by Larrick, illustrated with photographs by Alexander L. Crosby (New York: Evans, 1977);

Bring Me All of Your Dreams: Poems, edited by Larrick, illustrated with photographs by Larry Mulvehill (New York: Evans, 1980);

Tambourines! Tambourines to Glory!: Prayers and Poems, edited by Larrick, illustrated by Geri Grienke (Philadelphia: Westminster, 1982);

When the Dark Comes Dancing: A Bedtime Poetry

Nancy Larrick (photo by Alexander Crosby)

Book, edited by Larrick, illustrated by John Wallner (New York: Philomel, 1983).

PERIODICAL PUBLICATIONS: "The All-White World of Children's Books," *Saturday Review*, 48 (11 September 1965): 63-65;
"Poetry Becomes a Way of Life," *Top of the News* (January 1971): 148-155;
"Divorce, Drugs, Desertion, the Draft: Facing Up to Realities in Children's Literature," *Publishers Weekly*, 201 (21 February 1972): 90-91;
"Will Children Still Read Children's Books?," *Publishers Weekly* (10 April 1972): 122-123;
"Minority Books for White Children? Some Teachers Say No," *Bulletin of the Council for Interracial Books for Children*, 6, nos. 3-4 (1975): 4-7;
"Poetry in the Story Hour," *Top of the News*, 32 (January 1976): 151-161;
"The Changing Picture of Poetry Books for Children," *Wilson Library Bulletin*, 55 (October 1980): 113-117;
"From Tennyson to Silverstein: Poetry for Children 1910-1985," *Language Arts*, 63 (October 1986): 594-600.

Nancy Larrick has exerted a significant influence on contemporary children's poetry as the editor of numerous poetry anthologies and also as a teacher and critic. Through her work as a university professor of education and her many periodical articles she has shared her innovative approaches to poetry with her colleagues, and as an editor for language arts journals she has inspired teachers for over three decades. She has published twenty-eight books for or about children since 1952, perhaps her most significant contribution to the field of children's literature. With her extensive work in various aspects of language arts, particularly reading and poetry, Larrick has earned her reputation as a foremost critic and anthologist.

Larrick, daughter of Herbert S. and Nancy Nulton Larrick, was born on 28 December 1910 in Winchester, Virginia. She received her A.B. from Goucher College in 1930, an M.A. from Columbia University in 1937, and her Ed.D. from New York University in 1955. Her thesis, "Your Child and His Reading: How Parents Can Help," is based on a survey of parents' comments and questions about their children's reading. She followed this study with the very successful *A Parent's Guide to Children's Reading* (1958), now in its fifth edition, which has given practical advice to parents and teachers for encouraging children to read.

After completing her undergraduate education, Larrick taught in Winchester public schools from 1930 to 1942. For the next three years, during World War II, she served as education director for the U.S. Treasury Department's War Bond Division in Washington, D.C. Moving to New York City after the war, she edited *Young America Readers* weekly news magazines for children until 1951; she also edited *The Reading Teacher* in the early 1950s and served as educational director of children's books at Random House from 1952 to 1959. She edited "Poetry Parade" recordings for Weston Woods in 1967 and was the poetry editor for *English Journal*, a publication of the National Council of Teachers of English, for two years in the mid 1970s. Her contributions to periodicals, such as *Saturday Review*, *Parents' Magazine*, the *New York Times Book Review*, and the *Christian Science Monitor*, have further established Larrick as a leading authority on teaching language skills to children.

In 1958 Larrick married Alexander L. Crosby, a writer with whom she coauthored *Rockets Into Space* in 1959. For her many books and work with reading and literature, Larrick has received many honors: New York University Founder's Day Achievement Award (1955); the presidency of the International Reading Association (1956-1957); Edison Foundation Award (1959); Carey-Thomas Award (1959); an LL.D. degree from Goucher College (1975); IRA's Certificate of Merit (1977); membership in the Reading Hall of Fame (1977); and various other awards from universities and educational foundations. She had a productive teaching career as adjunct professor of education at Lehigh University from 1964 to 1979; she has held teaching posts at New York University's Graduate School of Education, Indiana University, and Bank Street College of Education; and she has been a lecturer at several distinguished universities.

In her influential article "The All-White World of Children's Books" (*Saturday Review*, 1965), Larrick criticized the racial biases of children's literature, pointing to the omission of black characters in children's books. A study analyzing trade books over a three-year period showed that only four-fifths of one percent included contemporary black Americans. When blacks outside the United States or blacks before World War II were portrayed, they were depicted as slaves, sharecroppers, or menial workers.

Consequently, Larrick argues forcefully against racial stereotypes. Larrick called the lack of racial equality in children's books one of the most critical issues in American education of the time. "Integration may be the law of the land," she wrote in 1965, "but most of the books children see are all white." The impact she described was destructive to black children, but whites suffer even worse, she explained. White children learn from these "gentle doses of racism" that they are in the majority, when in fact, they are a minority in the world. Her words sound even more prophetic today. "There seems little chance of developing the humility so urgently needed for world cooperation," she concluded, if Americans continue to assume such a superior attitude. Her article had considerable impact on children's books, but even to the present there has been only a slight increase in books displaying the racial, regional, and religious diversity of America's cultures with their various life-styles.

The same year Larrick's article appeared in *Saturday Review*, she produced *Piper, Pipe that Song Again! Poems for Boys and Girls*, an anthology of seventy-eight poems about nature, the seasons, animals, and children's playfulness. Some of children's lovely, most-wished-for things in the world are represented here, along with such classics as William Wordsworth's "My Heart Leaps Up," Robert Louis Stevenson's "My Shadow," and Robert Frost's "Stopping by Woods on a Snowy Evening." However, the *New York Times Book Review* critic who stated that "verbal magic," "maverick vision," and the ability to "stretch the imagination" are lacking in this anthology failed to read these traditional poems from a child's perspective and, furthermore, ignored such clever poems as Alfred Noyes's "Daddy Fell into the Pond," Ogden Nash's "Adventures of Isabel," and John Ciardi's "Some Cook!"–all gems included to provoke a child's giggles and imaginative response. In her introduction Larrick reminds readers that poems are meant to be read aloud to appreciate the rhythm, just as songs are meant to be sung aloud for the melody and lyrics to come alive.

The following year *Poetry for Holidays* (1966) was published. It contains fifty-eight poems for popular celebrations, beginning with Halloween (perhaps because it is the most magical, imaginative, and nonreligious holiday) and including Thanksgiving, Christmas, New Year's Day, Saint Valentine's Day, Saint Patrick's Day, Easter, May Day, the Fourth of July, and birthdays. Of course, Christmas is represented by the most poems, with twenty-one selections. Had the poems been compiled today, one might find a more representative sampling of holidays celebrated by religious and ethnic minorities: Hanukkah, Passover, the Chinese New Year, and the Feast of Our Lady of Guadalupe. To Larrick's credit, this anthology does include two poems by black poets (Langston Hughes's "Carol of the Brown King" and Gwendolyn Brooks's "Otto"); furthermore, three black children are pictured (one each with the above two poems and one dancing with five whites around the maypole for Eleanor Farjeon's "For a Dance"). Undoubtedly, even for Larrick, breaking into the "all-white world" of children's literature was not easy. A sequel, *More Poetry for Holidays*, a collection for various holidays, was published in 1973.

The title of Larrick's 1968 anthology *Piping Down the Valleys Wild: Poetry for the Young of All Ages* comes from the first line of William Blake's "The Piper." Aimed at adults, Larrick's introduction explains how children react to poetry and how parents and teachers can nurture that intuitive interest. The connection with Blake's work stresses the importance of children's pleasurable response to musical language, allowing them to observe the world more clearly and sensitively. Having studied a variety of poetry which appeals to a wide range of children, preschool to twelve, Larrick finds that youngsters are "particularly responsive to the simple, almost conversational language" of modern poets such as Robert Frost, Carl Sandburg, and T. S. Eliot; of earlier poets, Robert Louis Stevenson is the favorite.

Larrick presents young readers with a large sampling of imaginative poems, yet they are rather traditional in content. Larrick states in her introduction that children "in the realm of fantasy, . . . are ready to suspend their disbelief more readily. Witches–even elves and fairies–have appeal. Talking animals win almost every child, particularly if they are funny. The humor of 'The Owl and the Pussy-Cat' seems to be as popular today as when it was created almost a hundred years ago." To help children enjoy poetry, Larrick suggests that they hear its rhythm; consequently, adults who like poetry themselves can help young children by selecting the right poems and by reading aloud effectively. The sixteen sections, organized loosely by quoted lines that reflect various themes of the nearly 250 poems, cover humor and nonsense, nature and seasons, evening sights, fantasy, people, animals and insects, travel, the city, dreams, and poetry. The

final poem (written by Chinese poet Yuan Mei) sums up Larrick's vision of poetry's transcending the explainable, the commonplace:

> Only be willing to search for poetry, and
>   there will be poetry.
> My soul, a tiny speck, is my tutor.
> Evening sun and fragrant grass are
>   common things,
> But, with understanding, they can become
>   glorious verse.

Another 1968 anthology, *Green is Like a Meadow of Grass: An Anthology of Children's Pleasure in Poetry*, presents seventy-four poems written by children; these original verses are rather simple, some two and three lines, and are arranged thematically for a kaleidoscopic array of children's interests: spring, fog, grass, sea shells, animals, fairies, the moon, the city, and their feelings.

On City Streets: An Anthology of Poetry was also published in 1968. Here poems for readers ages ten and up mirror both the exciting and the bleak aspects of city dwellers' lives. The poetry is complemented by black-and-white photographs to heighten the stark reality of various facets of urban experiences. In her introduction Larrick explains how at fifteen she moved from an easygoing country town to Baltimore, with its excitement, clutter, and noise; later, attending Columbia University for graduate study, she was even more impressed by a great city's rhythms. Consequently, Larrick offers readers poems "sometimes nonsensical, more often tinged with tragedy, but always vibrant with the drama of city life." Familiar selections include Langston Hughes's "Dream Deferred," Carl Sandburg's "Jazz Fantasia" and "Prayers of Steel," Gwendolyn Brooks's "We Real Cool," and Robert Frost's "Acquainted with the Night." The less familiar are even more fascinating: for example, Eve Merriam's fantasy "Alligator on the Escalator," about an alligator in a department store, and Gregory Corso's tragic "Italian Extravaganze," an elaborate funeral for an infant. Larrick's selections, based on the choices of over one hundred young inner-city children, reflect what life is like on city streets, as well as what it might be like when the imagination runs wild.

Larrick followed this theme of urban experience with *I Heard a Scream in the Street: Poems by Young People in the City* (1970), in which racial minorities and other inner-city groups are represented. Poems by youths range from those with

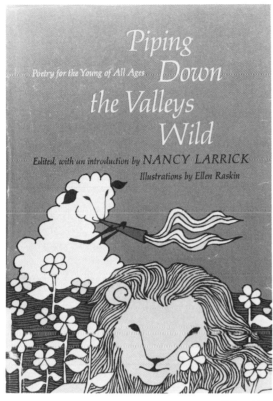

(Delacorte)

(Evans)

Dust jackets for two of Larrick's three 1968 anthologies

musing, introspective tones to those with stronger, more muscular language and challenging spirit. These poems by and for adolescents from inner-city ghettoes mirror their sensitivity and courage as well as their anger and misery. An example of their awareness of the world's insanity at the height of the Vietnam War is "A War Game," which calls war "uniformed murder" and mourns all those killed in war–especially innocent children.

It is obvious that Larrick speaks out for an awareness of social realities and for justice and equality in an unjust, unequal society. With Eve Merriam, a popular poet with similar views of social consciousness, Larrick coedited *Male and Female Under 18* (1973), an anthology of poems and comments by young people, eight to eighteen, expressing their social roles and their awareness of sociological realities. In a 1972 *Publishers Weekly* article Larrick speaks out on ways books can help young people cope with the reality of their confusing world. She defends realistic children's books as aids in dealing with concerns such as divorce, drugs, and the draft. Consequently, those studying children's literature must be taught to face controversial issues in the books they will be teaching and offering young readers.

Larrick continued to edit poetry anthologies for children in the following decade: *Room for Me and a Mountain Lion: Poetry of Open Space* (1974), *Crazy to Be Alive in Such a Strange World: Poems about People* (1977), *Bring Me All of Your Dreams: Poems* (1980), *Tambourines! Tambourines to Glory!: Prayers and Poems* (1982), and *When the Dark Comes Dancing: A Bedtime Poetry Book* (1983). In addition to these collections, she published books to guide parents in their children's readings: *Children's Reading Begins at Home: How Parents Can Help Their Young Children* (1980) and *Encourage Your Children to Read* (1981).

To encourage teachers and parents to turn children into enthusiastic readers, Larrick has published many articles in magazines and journals designed to help teachers of children's literature provide the best possible experiences for their students. One article demonstrating Larrick's tremendous influence on the teaching of children's literature is "Poetry in the Story Hour," which appeared in *Top of the News* in 1976. Her innovative

approaches in both the elementary school classroom and the university classes are based on the conviction that "a child's appreciation of poetry depends upon involvement–immediate involvement." Consequently, she structured her poetry workshop class to enhance that individual participation. Citing Eve Merriam's advice in "How to Eat a Poem" ("Bite in. /Pick it up . . . It is ready and ripe now, whenever you are"), Larrick stresses that poetry should be experienced in all its delights without verbal preliminaries to get between the reader and the poem. The possibilities for creative involvement in poetry are endless, and for children are "ready and ripe now."

Also, Larrick has written an excellent concise history of the illustration of children's poetry, "The Changing Picture of Poetry Books for Children," which appeared in the *Wilson Library Bulletin* in 1980. Beginning with the didactic, condescending verses of the early chapbooks, she traces milestones of children's poetry from the beautifully "written, designed, illustrated, engraved, hand-colored, and bound" volumes of William Blake's *Songs of Innocence* (1789) through illustrators Walter Crane, Kate Greenaway, and Randolph Caldecott and the giants of the nineteenth century's golden age of children's literature–Edward Lear, Lewis Carroll, and Robert Louis Stevenson. After discussing several twentieth-century poets, such as A. A. Milne, and illustrators such as Ernest H. Shepard and Alice and Martin Provensen, she cites her own poetry anthologies (*On City Streets* and *I Heard a Scream in the Street*) and four other works as examples of books illustrated with photographs. Also Larrick gives examples of modern printing and exciting new concepts in children's poetry–certainly a long journey from the poor quality of eighteenth-century chapbooks.

Nancy Larrick's contributions to children's poetry warrant her reputation as an authoritative voice offering advice about teaching and enjoying literature. She has exerted tremendous influence as an editor of language arts journals, author of many professional journal and popular magazine articles, and anthologist of more than a dozen poetry books. Her work has enlightened two generations of children and adults about the pleasures of poetry.

Leo Lionni

(5 May 1910-   )

Lesley S. Potts
University of Tennessee

BOOKS: *Little Blue and Little Yellow* (New York: Mc-Dowell, Obolensky, 1959; Leicester: Brockhampton Press, 1962);

Inch by Inch (New York: Obolensky, 1960; London: Dobson, 1967);

On My Beach There Are Many Pebbles (New York: Obolensky, 1961; London: Abelard Schuman, 1977);

Swimmy (New York: Pantheon, 1963);

Tico and the Golden Wings (New York: Pantheon, 1964);

Frederick (New York: Pantheon, 1967; London: Abelard Schuman, 1971);

The Alphabet Tree (New York: Pantheon, 1968);

The Biggest House in the World (New York: Pantheon, 1968; London: Andersen Press, 1978);

Alexander and the Wind-Up Mouse (New York: Pantheon, 1969; London: Abelard Schuman, 1971);

Fish Is Fish (New York: Pantheon, 1970; London: Abelard Schuman, 1972);

Theodore and the Talking Mushroom (New York: Pantheon, 1971; London: Abelard Schuman, 1972);

The Greentail Mouse (New York: Pantheon, 1973);

In the Rabbitgarden (New York: Pantheon, 1975; London: Abelard Schuman, 1976);

A Colour of His Own (London: Abelard Schuman, 1975; New York: Pantheon, 1976);

Pezzettino (New York: Pantheon, 1975; London: Andersen Press, 1977);

La Botanica Parallela (Milan: Adelphi, 1976); translated by Patrick Creagh as *Parallel Botany* (New York: Knopf, 1977);

I Want to Stay Here! I Want to Go There! A Flea Story (New York: Pantheon, 1977; London: Andersen Press, 1978);

Geraldine, the Music Mouse (New York: Pantheon, 1979; London: Andersen Press, 1979);

Let's Make Rabbits (New York: Pantheon, 1982; London: Andersen Press, 1982);

Cornelius (New York: Pantheon, 1983);

Who? (New York: Pantheon, 1983);

What? (New York: Pantheon, 1983);

Where? (New York: Pantheon, 1983);

Leo Lionni

When? (New York: Pantheon, 1983),

Frederick's Fables: A Leo Lionni Treasury of Favorite Stories (New York: Pantheon, 1985);

Colors to Talk About (New York: Pantheon, 1985);

Letters to Talk About (New York: Pantheon, 1985);

Numbers to Talk About (New York: Pantheon, 1985);

Words to Talk About (New York: Pantheon, 1985);

It's Mine! (New York: Pantheon, 1986);

Nicholas, Where Have You Been? (New York: Pantheon, 1987).

BOOKS ILLUSTRATED: Hannah Solomon, *Mouse Days: A Book of Seasons* (New York: Pantheon, 1981);

Naomi Lewis, *Come With Us* (London: Andersen Press, 1982).

PERIODICAL PUBLICATIONS: "Resurgent India: Photographs," *Fortune,* 55 (May 1957): 139-147;

"My Books for Children," *Wilson Library Bulletin*, 39 (October 1964): 142-145;

"Before Images," *Horn Book*, 60 (November/ December 1984): 727-734.

Although he has become an author and illustrator of children's books late in life, following a successful career as a commercial designer and painter, Leo Lionni has nevertheless made an enormous and invaluable contribution to picture books for young children over the past three decades. He has combined his skill as a designer and as a graphic artist continually seeking to wed form with content in each of his books, and his integrity as an author-illustrator in conveying a sense of great care and craftsmanship in the making of picture books, to produce a series of illustrated fables and parables for children that stress the importance of aesthetic values, individuality, and self-worth.

In contrast to illustrators who have evolved a consistent personal style, Lionni has sought to match his style and choice of medium to the content of each individual story, and in so doing has brought a freshness and originality of technique to his work that has seldom been surpassed. His influence on the development of present-day children's book illustration has been pervasive, and particularly important in the areas of page design and the use of collage.

Leo (Leonard) Lionni was born in Amsterdam, Holland, on 5 May 1910, the son of Louis and Elizabeth Grossouw Lionni. Born into an artistic and creative family—his mother was a concert soprano, his uncle an architect—Lionni spent the first twelve years of his life in Amsterdam and much of his time in the art museums there, studying the works of the great masters and forming an early resolve to become an artist. The Amsterdam school system placed great emphasis on nature studies, and Lionni was continually collecting and drawing plants, shells, stones, leaves, and small animals, a habit which was to remain with him and which would strongly influence his later career as a designer and illustrator. Lionni spent the remainder of his childhood traveling with his family in Belgium, France, Switzerland, and Italy, and he received some schooling in each of these countries.

He attended the University of Zurich from 1928 to 1930, and in December 1931 he married Nora Maffi. In the next few years Lionni began to establish himself as a painter, opening his own advertising agency, exhibiting his oil paintings and contributing articles on art and the cinema to European art journals while working to obtain his doctorate in economics from the University of Genoa in 1935. In 1939 Lionni emigrated to the United States, becoming a naturalized citizen in 1945. Almost immediately he established himself as a dynamic talent in commercial design. Working variously as art director for N. W. Ayer and Sons, a Philadelphia advertising agency, design director for the Olivetti Corporation, art director for *Fortune* magazine, coeditor of *Print*, and head of the graphics design department for the Parsons School of Design, Lionni received numerous honors and awards and served at one time as president of the American Institute of Graphic Arts.

In 1947 he began to exhibit his paintings and sculpture in one-man shows throughout Europe and the United States. Reviewers of his work described Lionni as a phenomenon, genuinely versatile, and one of the world's most original designers. He did not consider making a career of children's book illustration until 1958 when, while traveling by train with his grandchildren between New York and Greenwich, Connecticut, he created the story of *Little Blue and Little Yellow* (1959) for their amusement. From that time, Lionni's considerable talents were devoted to writing and illustrating books for young children.

Lionni is the father of two sons, Louis and Paolo, one an architect and the other a poet and painter. He and his wife presently divide their time between a New York apartment and a seventeenth-century farm house in the Tuscan hills of Italy. His homes are plentifully furnished with art and folk objects acquired in his travels, as well as with the works of artists who have influenced his work, such as Jean Arp and Paul Klee.

In describing how *Little Blue and Little Yellow* came about, Lionni remarked: "This first book just happened. I told a story to my grandchildren, made it into a dummy, and showed it to an editor friend. The book was successful." *Little Blue and Little Yellow*, now an established classic, is the story of two blobs of color who are the best of friends, so much so that they hug each other until they become a single blob of green. This creates problems with their parents, who fail to recognize their children, but Little Blue and Little Yellow manage to separate into their original colors, and all ends happily.

Illustrated entirely with torn-paper collage, a dramatically innovative technique for its day,

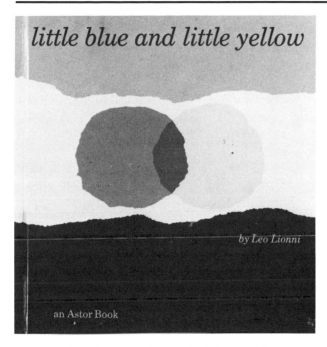

little blue and little yellow

by Leo Lionni

an Astor Book

Cover for Lionni's 1959 allegorical tale in which he uses two colored shapes as his protagonists (McDowell, Obolensky)

the theme of the book is the unfairness of judging by appearances. Some critics have also interpreted *Little Blue and Little Yellow* as social commentary, specifically as a plea for racial integration, although Lionni has denied that this was his intention. Deceptively simple, with its brief, economical narrative and torn-paper characters, *Little Blue and Little Yellow* is a profound parable displaying both humor and pathos; it is also a very neat little lesson in color theory.

The characters, as they jump about on the page against backgrounds of various shapes and colors, are vivid personalities with which children consistently identify. Lionni once said in an interview with Rose H. Agree for the *Wilson Library Bulletin*: "Wherever you go, when you ask, 'Who is the mother and who is the father,' you always get the same answer–it's fantastic. Overwhelmingly, the round one is the mother and the long one is the father. I always ask that of every group of children." Critical reception of *Little Blue and Little Yellow* was uniformly enthusiastic; it was the first picture book to tell an allegorical tale about human problems and human situations using neither humans nor animals as its protagonists, but merely bits of torn paper distributed across the picture space in such a way as to denote specific actions, purposes, and emotions.

Lionni finds the inspiration for his stories in his own childhood. In "Before Images," an essay

that appeared in the November/December 1984 issue of *Horn Book*, Lionni states: "When I was a child, I was a passionate collector of small animals. . . . I kept them within the glass walls of terrariums where . . . I arranged sand and stones, mosses and ferns, to simulate a natural habitat. . . . I suddenly recognized them, after half a century, in the fables I had written and illustrated, . . . now I knew how much they had conditioned the choices of theme, the formal preferences, the whole intricate game of symbols which characterize my work as an artist."

Inch by Inch (1960), Lionni's second book for children, is a fable about an inchworm who saves himself from being eaten by birds by agreeing to measure the tails, legs, and necks of his predators. While it is easy enough to measure the tail of the robin, the neck of the flamingo, and the legs of the heron, the inchworm must resort to strategy when the nightingale demands that the worm measure his song. In creating this tongue-in-cheek tale, Lionni drew upon the nature studies of his childhood, creating a microcosmic world peopled by small animals. In this hostile environment the inchworm survives by using his talents and intelligence.

Illustrated in richly textured collage and crayon against a white background, *Inch by Inch* combines lavish surface texture with careful page layout and dramatic design; the story's protagonist and focal point, the bright-green inchworm, is carried along page by page through his vividly colored and textured world until at last he "inches out of sight." The simple text, which seems to nestle unobtrusively in the upper and lower corners of each page, also paces the tale with poetic economy.

Lionni, whose personal opinion is that "a good children's book is, inevitably, autobiography," has noted that *Inch by Inch* reflected his life in advertising. "When I had to make a living, I had to survive and I really made a living telling people things that they didn't need to know. That's what the inchworm did and he managed, very cleverly, to survive."

At a time when full-color reproduction in children's picture books was becoming more feasible, *Inch by Inch* strongly influenced other artists to employ collage as an illustrative medium. However, *Inch by Inch*, a Caldecott Honor Book in 1961 and winner of the Lewis Carroll Shelf Award in 1962, has seldom been equaled in the areas of collage design and technique.

Following *Inch by Inch*, Lionni produced a

Dust jacket for Lionni's 1963 story of a small black fish who must learn to survive on his own after his family is eaten (Pantheon)

book which focuses on another aspect of nature. *On My Beach There Are Many Pebbles* (1961) reflects Lionni's lifelong habits of collecting pebbles and making careful drawings of natural objects. Once again matching style to content, Lionni used black-and-white pencil drawings to illustrate the book; the absence of color focuses attention on the forms of the pebbles themselves. The presence of pebbles is a recurring motif in Lionni's nature fables: "Perhaps the pebble is a sort of symbol to me. . . . We have endless objects but nature has only a few and I try to keep things as close as possible to a very elementary situation."

If *Inch by Inch* reflects Lionni's pragmatic period of survival in the world of advertising, his fourth book, *Swimmy* (1963), mirrors his increasing involvement in politics. *Swimmy* is the story of a small black fish whose brothers and sisters are devoured by a hungry tuna. Alone in his undersea world, Swimmy moves on until he finds another school of fish and concocts a clever plan to safeguard himself and his new family from predators by teaching them to swim in a formation resembling one giant fish, proclaiming, "I'll be the eye" as he leads his family out into the world.

Again the theme has to do with the ingenu-

ity and resourcefulness of a small animal hero, but in *Swimmy* Lionni draws upon a personal conviction. As he told Agree: "I didn't think it was enough to be an artist—I had to be a protest painter. . . . The artist is a man like other men . . . with the same responsibilities. But when the time comes, the artist must realize that he has a specific function to perform—he is the eye—not the body."

Unlike the clean-edged, sharply realistic cut-paper world of *Inch by Inch*, Swimmy's undersea world is composed of highly textured watercolor washes and prints that create an impressionistic underwater locale. In *Swimmy* Lionni has been criticized for displaying too much preoccupation with the surface qualities of forms for their own sake, but the illustrations are undeniably beautiful, creating moods and impressions through the alternate use of greyed tones and vibrant colors. Moreover, the simple and economical text is both extended and embellished by the illustrations, which reflect Lionni's philosophy of suiting the style to the content of the story. In "My Books for Children," an essay published in the October 1964 *Wilson Library Bulletin*, Lionni states: "I find greater joy and satisfaction in developing a form for each idea, . . . style is more than a technical mannerism. . . . It is a method of going directly to the heart of each situation and . . . finding the proper technique for expressing it."

Though *Swimmy*'s pages come close to being overwhelmed by the abundance of experimental textures and special effects, the book aptly demonstrates Lionni's versatility as an illustrator. Winner of the German Children's Book Prize in 1963 and a Caldecott Honor Book in 1964, *Swimmy* was also chosen to receive the Golden Apple Award at the Bratislava First Biennial in Czechoslovakia in 1967, the first picture book by an American illustrator to be so honored.

In 1956, while working as art director for *Fortune* magazine, Lionni visited India. The immediate result was a photographic portfolio for *Fortune* entitled "Resurgent India"; however, the visit made a lasting impression on Lionni, reflected in *Tico and the Golden Wings* (1964). A picture book invented in the style of an old Hindu folktale, *Tico and the Golden Wings* is the story of a bird born without wings. One night a magic "wishingbird" grants Tico's wish for a pair of golden wings. But his friends find Tico's wings strange and different, and they forsake him. One by one Tico gives away his golden feathers to help the needy, growing plain black feathers in their place. At last Tico is like the other birds. But even after he has become one of them he tells himself, "and yet I am not like my old friends. We are *all* different. Each for his own memories, and his own invisible golden dreams."

In *Tico and the Golden Wings* Lionni deals with the familiar themes of the search for identity and appreciation of one's own uniqueness. The illustrations are stylized after the manner of Far Eastern art. The figures are one dimensional, frequently painted in profile against a background of stylized leaves in a variety of rich dark-green and golden hues. The overall color scheme creates a somber and dignified effect, and the pictures, when carefully arranged against the white background, have a static quality that contributes to the universality of the theme.

As ever, Lionni suits the artistic style to the content of his fable. In "My Books for Children" he wrote: "When a story takes shape in my imagination, it does so in sentences and images. Sometimes the words trail the pictures and often it is the other way around, but the give and take between the two happens almost simultaneously in the privacy of my own mind. And so the form expresses the content in a direct, convincing manner." Though *Tico and the Golden Wings* is a departure from the brightly colored collages of his earlier fables, it is still firmly grounded in the natural world Lionni knows so well, the world of plants and small animals: birds, fish, and, in his next picture book, mice.

With *Frederick* (1967), considered by critics to be among his best work, Lionni began to employ mice as his heroes and antiheroes; indeed the mouse has become a Lionni trademark. *Frederick* is the story of a "chatty family of field mice" who spend the summer storing up food for the coming winter months–all except Frederick. He works instead at gathering sun rays, colors, and words to ward off the cold, silent bleakness of winter. When winter arrives and all the food is eaten, the other mice turn to Frederick, who shares with them his stored memories of sunshine and flowers and the mysteries of nature in rhyme.

Frederick's theme is a variation on the grasshopper and the ant; it stresses the value of the artist in society and his spiritual contribution to the community. Lionni has placed *Frederick* at that period in his life during which he began to reexamine the function of the artist in society: "I became more introspective and began to feel that, after all, as an artist, you're really justified

Dust jacket for Lionni's 1967 book which stresses the value of the artist in society and his spiritual contribution to the community (Pantheon)

enough; maybe you should, for awhile, concentrate on that. You perform a function in society even if it does not actually involve running about in the streets with a flag in your hand."

The collage illustrations, done in a range of soft browns and grays, convey the introspective mood of the story. The torn-paper mice stand out against the clean edges and textures of the background, and the double-page spreads, with their assortment of shapes–rocks, mice, trees–fill the picture plane without overwhelming it. The subdued palette and carefully arranged designs well support the sensitive, spare text.

In a sense, *Frederick* is one of the most autobiographical of Lionni's fables, going back to his early childhood development as an artist. In "Before Images," which discusses the origins of literacy in children, Lionni wrote: "Since the picture book seems to be the door that leads into the complexities of literacy, it is surprising that it has been given so little attention. . . . The study of literacy is all too often a matter of spinning words about words without looking back to the images that precede words and to the feelings that precede both." Frederick's story is one of the progression from feelings to images and finally to words—an emergence into literacy—as he experiences the warmth of the sunlight and the colors of nature, then the poetic expression of all that he has felt and seen. *Frederick* was a Caldecott Honor Book in 1968.

From the outset, Lionni sought to create stories that have a beginning, a middle, and an end and that convey a moral. In "My Books for Children" he wrote: "In some of my stories the moral is quite simple and obvious; in others it may be more difficult to articulate, . . . my stories are meant to stimulate the mind, to create an awareness, to destroy a prejudice." While his early fables succeeded in conveying this moral intent with subtlety and charm, his handling of a moral message was less sure in *The Alphabet Tree* (1968), a fable about letters of the alphabet living on the leaves of a tree. When a strong wind blows some of the letters away, the rest form themselves into words for greater safety at the suggestion of a friendly insect. It is a purple caterpillar, however, who suggests to the words that they should form themselves into sentences that "mean something." The words take his advice, spelling out "peace on earth good will toward men," a message which the caterpillar determines to carry to the president.

While the idea of letters living in a tree has charm, and the collage and watercolor illustrations are gracefully executed, the story line is overwhelmed by a heavy-handed pacifism that detracts from the whimsical appeal of a parable about the origin of words and meanings. For this reason critics have found *The Alphabet Tree* far less satisfying in conveying its political moral than *Swimmy*, and it is considered the least successful of Lionni's books. According to Elva Harmon of *School Library Journal* (February 1969), "The acid political overtones of the topical punch line are more likely to hold attraction and meaning for political hip-to-yip adults rather than for . . . young children."

Far more successful in presenting its simpler message of living in harmony with nature is *The Biggest House in the World* (1968). Illustrated with colorfully realistic, at times surrealistic, crayon technique, *The Biggest House in the World* is a nature parable reminiscent of the stories in medieval bestiaries. When a little snail living on a cabbage leaf tells his father he wants to have the biggest house in the world, his father recites a cautionary tale about another little snail who learned to make his shell grow to a great size, so large

that its owner perished because he could no longer move. "That was the end of the story. The little snail was almost in tears. But then he remembered his own house. 'I shall keep it small,' he thought, 'and when I grow up I shall go wherever I please.'" On the last pages the little snail, with his tiny house, is shown against a beautiful forest floor filled with flowers, ferns, and multicolored stones.

Perhaps more than any of his preceding books, the illustrations for *The Biggest House in the World* extend the story line as the foolish snail's house grows bigger and bigger, more brightly colored and more oddly shaped from page to page, until it is mistaken by a swarm of butterflies for a circus and a cathedral. Lionni's use of bright translucent colors and unusual aerial perspective demonstrate a perfect blending of style with story content. *The Biggest House in the World* has been placed on a par with *Inch by Inch* and *Frederick* for its neat, tightly constructed nature plot and its adroit wedding of pictures and text.

Lionni continued his use of mice as protagonists in *Alexander and the Wind-Up Mouse* (1969), "about the conflict between traditional values, rooted in the human condition, and the gradual mechanization of Man." At this period in his life, he remarked: "*Alexander* found me tremendously involved. . . . I intended to do a group of books with mice as characters around the same theme." *Alexander and the Wind-Up Mouse* also marked a gradual turning point in Lionni's style of illustration, a style depending heavily on bold, bright colors, lavishly textured collages, and a flat, posterlike effect. Though continuing to produce picture books illustrated with a variety of media, Lionni began to employ these techniques more frequently.

Alexander and the Wind-Up Mouse is the story of a lonely mouse who finds a friend in Willy, a mechanical mouse who is the favorite toy of the children in the house where Alexander lives. Alexander envies Willy, who is loved, while Alexander is chased and persecuted every time he appears. Determined to become a mechanical mouse like Willy, Alexander seeks the help of a magical lizard who can grant wishes. But in the meantime Willy, his mainspring broken, has been tossed onto a scrap heap. Alexander, instead of wishing himself to be like Willy, wishes Willy to become a real mouse, and the two friends are happily reunited.

Alexander's story illustrates the importance of remaining human, of thinking for oneself,

Alexander and the Wind-Up Mouse

by Leo Lionni

Pantheon

Cover for Lionni's 1969 story of a lonely mouse who befriends a mechanical mouse (Pantheon)

and of the transforming power of love. Illustrated with lavishly textured and marbleized collages, *Alexander and the Wind-Up Mouse* shows evidence of the artist's preoccupation with textures and special effects for their own sake. Nevertheless the brightly colored, bold designs set against black and white backgrounds are spectacular. Alexander and Willy are mirror images of Frederick and his family, and, while the story lacks the depth of *Frederick*, the surprise twist of plot at the end makes it a satisfying tale. *Alexander and the Wind-Up Mouse* was a Caldecott Honor Book in 1970 and also won the first Christopher Award in the Children's Book Category the same year.

The simple plot of Lionni's next book, *Fish Is Fish* (1970), like *The Biggest House in the World*, is reminiscent of the cautionary tales in medieval bestiaries. In an underwater world rendered in soft crayon pastels, a minnow and a tadpole are the best of friends, until the tadpole turns into a frog and goes out into the world. One day the frog returns and tells his friend about the wonders he has seen in the world outside the pond. The minnow, in a series of colorful pen-and-ink images, tries to picture such oddities as birds, cows, and people. His curiosity getting the better

of him, the minnow tries to leave the pond to see the world for himself but quickly learns the impossibility of living on land like his friend the frog. With the frog's help he returns to the pond, happy to be a fish. The moral of the tale is spelled out by the frog when he says, "Frogs are frogs and fish is fish and that's that!"

In *Fish Is Fish* Lionni shows that there are restrictions which inhibit self-reliance and individuality, namely, the limitations imposed on all creatures by nature. However, the vivid contrast between the minnow's imagination and his softly crayoned aquatic world points up the quiet beauties of his simple life. As in all of Lionni's fables, in which his heroes come to realize an underlying truth about the beauties of nature, friendship, freedom, or life itself, the minnow learns to recognize and appreciate the peculiar value and beauty of his pond existence. Lionni also makes an interesting humorous observation about the nature of imagination when he depicts the minnow imagining brightly colored flying fish, fishlike cows, and walking fish-people.

In his next few books Lionni's usually deft and humorous moral messages became more complex and less suited to a picture-book format than his earlier, simpler themes. In still another mouse fable, *Theodore and the Talking Mushroom* (1971), Lionni deals with a problem that, like the pacifism message in *The Alphabet Tree*, is more comprehensible to adults than to young children, namely, people who set themselves up as false messiahs. Theodore, who has a low opinion of himself and his ability to run, finds a blue mushroom that says "Quirp!" He "translates" this message to his friends as "the mouse should be revered above all other animals." The trick works, and the animals begin to pay homage to Theodore and his mushroom until one day when they come upon a whole valley filled with blue mushrooms saying "Quirp!" The angry animals turn on Theodore, who runs away and is never seen again.

The earth-tone collages contrast sharply with the bright-blue mushroom and crisp-edged flower garlands, creating a more restrained mood than that in *Alexander and the Wind-Up Mouse*; Lionni's use of collage with mixed media here is designed to convey a more subtle message. Although the illustrations are visually effective, the story itself is uncomfortably moralistic. Here, as in *The Alphabet Tree*, Lionni places too burdensome a moral in a picture book. While *Theodore and the Talking Mushroom* shows Lionni the illustrator at his best, his greatest successes, such as *Frederick, Inch by Inch,* and *Swimmy,* have more to do thematically with aesthetic truths than with political or social commentary.

Much the same holds true of *The Greentail Mouse* (1973). Illustrated with double-page paintings resembling his collages and rendered in subdued oranges, browns, and blues, *The Greentail Mouse* is the story of a group of happy field mice who are visited one day by a mouse from the city. He tells them about the festivities of Mardi Gras, particularly about the wearing of masks. The field mice decide to hold their own Mardi Gras, complete with their own ferocious disguises. They soon forget, however, that they are merely pretending, and their happy community becomes filled with suspicion and hatred. It takes another visiting mouse to point out to them that it is the masks that are the cause of their troubles. When the masks are removed and destroyed, the mice are happy and peaceful again.

The fable deals with the problems of appearance versus reality and the dangers of pretending to be what one is not. Appropriately, the illustrations are at first cheerful and pleasantly colored in rich complementary blues, oranges, and soft grays, darkening to menacing shades of gray, green, and black as the mice fall under the evil spell of their masks. At the story's end the bright, cheerful colors return.

However, the psychology involved in the tale is too complex for young children. The aftereffects of the mice's ordeal are glossed over; the whole problem of dealing with fears and bad memories is never really addressed. The mouse called Greentail chooses to hide her fears behind cheerful evasiveness. The story depends too much upon telescoping and manipulation of events to convey its message. In *The Greentail Mouse* Lionni undertakes too great a task in too short a space, though the illustrations are finely rendered and well match the tone and mood of the story.

The quality of the illustrations is more questionable in Lionni's next fable, *In the Rabbitgarden* (1975). This tongue-in-cheek story concerns two happy rabbits who live and play in a beautiful garden. One day they are warned by their mentor, the Old Rabbit, not to eat the apples from the apple tree "or the fox will get you." When the Old Rabbit leaves, however, the carrot supply runs out and the hungry rabbits are befriended by a serpent who gives them apples from the tree. The three friends play happily together until one day when the fox appears. By means of

Cover for Lionni's 1971 fable about a mouse who sets himself up as a false messiah (Pantheon)

a trick the serpent saves the rabbits, and when the Old Rabbit returns he soon relents and eats an apple himself.

The point of the fable is that appearances are often deceiving, but one is never too old to learn. The opaque mixed-media illustrations, consisting of collage, crayon, and pastel, create a flat, lusterless effect of thick color. They lack the richness and clarity of Lionni's usual designs, and the story itself is thin and often confusing, for at times it appears to be allegory and at other times simply a statement that adults are not always right. Lionni's usual meticulous care in rendering and wedding pictures and plot is lacking in this fable, though the illustrations do retain a characteristic boldness of style.

In *A Colour of His Own* (1975) Lionni employed watercolor printmaking to do a study in color somewhat reminiscent of *Little Blue and Little Yellow.* The theme also is similar: love and friendship as the solution to problems of identity. In this small picture book, with a text pared down to the bare essentials, Lionni tells the story of an unhappy chameleon who longs for a color of his own. He tries living on a leaf so that he will always be green, but autumn comes and the chameleon turns yellow, then red, and finally black in the long winter night. In the spring, however, he meets an older and wiser chameleon who suggests that they stay together so that they will always be the same color.

The setting of *A Colour of His Own* returns to the terrariums of Lionni's childhood. The softly textured watercolor prints against white backgrounds suggest nature with a simplicity and directness reminiscent of *Inch by Inch* and *Swimmy*. Lionni uses pure color and the quizzical expressions in his chameleon's eyes to express mood and message in a satisfying blend of pictures and text. In *A Colour of His Own* Lionni also returns to the picture book in its earlier, purer form, as a work capable of conveying a story largely on the strength of pictures alone. As in his first books, his pictures speak for themselves; the text is greatly simplified and unobtrusive, as in *Little Blue and Little Yellow*. At this point Lionni had turned away from heavily moralistic themes and allegory and back to a more satisfying picture/story combination: appreciation of the beauties of nature and of life itself.

In *Pezzettino* (1975) Lionni once more used shapes as his characters, with a little orange shape called Pezzettino, or "little piece," as his hero. In this simple search-for-identity story, Pezzettino feels insignificant compared to his bigger friends, who can run, fly, swim, and climb mountains. He feels he must be a little piece of someone else bigger and more important, but cannot discover whose little piece he is. Finally he seeks the help of the wise-one who sends him to the island of Wham. There, while searching up and down, Pezzettino falls and breaks into many little pieces, making the immense discovery "I am myself!"

The brilliantly colored illustrations of primitive checkered creatures suggest the work of contemporary British illustrator Brian Wildsmith, while the collage backgrounds of land and sea, done in textured and beautifully marbleized papers, are pure Lionni. The two media wed very well, and the theme of the story—that each person is an individual in his own right, no matter how small—is a perceptive lesson to offer young children. The cheerful colors, which seem to glow against the white background, and the simplicity of line and form aptly complement the simple, straightforward text.

Even though his most frequently used medium remains collage, Lionni continually uses new techniques to enliven his cut-paper illustrations. In *I Want to Stay Here! I Want to Go There! A Flea Story* (1977) Lionni uses the humorous device of two "invisible" heroes whose whereabouts are made known by their dialogue, which is enclosed in red and blue balloons. An adventurous flea, followed reluctantly by his more nervous, stay-at-home companion, hops joyously from animal to animal in his eagerness to see something of the world. Finally he hops aboard a bird to discover the wonders of flight, while his friend returns home reflecting that, after all, a little travel can be interesting.

Lionni uses an assortment of marbleized, textured, and patterned papers to depict the fur on a dog, the feathers on a chicken, as well as flowers, water, and trees. Though the style lacks originality, it is the humor of the story situation, the novelty of unseen characters and the naturalness of their dialogue as they talk, bicker, and protest that lift the story out of the ordinary. The theme is, simply, "be yourself," and Lionni adroitly creates empathy both for the adventurous flea and his more practical friend through their character-delineating dialogue. Lionni takes his readers on a nature tour, encouraging them to look closely, as a flea might do, at the familiar and commonplace things we take for granted: birds, animals, earth, water, and sky.

Lionni's fifth mouse fable, *Geraldine, the Music Mouse* (1979), is illustrated entirely in crayon, a style well suited to the soft, imaginative mood of the story. Geraldine finds a large block of parmesan cheese and, with the help of her friends, carries it back to her home. After nibbling off a few chunks as payment for her friends' help, she is surprised to see the head of a mouse-sculpture emerging. She soon nibbles out the form of a mouse blowing upon its tail like a flute, and that night listens in rapture as magical music pours from the sculpture. Night after night Geraldine listens to the music, and one day her friends, unable to find food, demand that she share the cheese with them. Geraldine protests, "But that is not possible! . . . Because . . . it is MUSIC!" After a few unsuccessful attempts to demonstrate, Geraldine plays a tune for her friends, who agree that such a magical cheese cannot be eaten. Now, however, the cheese can be eaten, says Geraldine, "Because . . . now the music is in me."

Geraldine, like Frederick, is a defender of the arts. Though the soft, meditative illustrations are not as enterprising as much of Lionni's preceding work, they express perfectly the tone of this

Geraldine, the Music Mouse

Leo Lionni

Dust jacket for Lionni's 1979 mouse fable illustrated entirely in crayon (Pantheon)

imaginative story about the importance of beauty in life and of the artist as a spiritual guide in the community. *Geraldine, the Music Mouse*, along with *Frederick* and *Alexander and the Wind-Up Mouse*, ranks as one of Lionni's most successful mouse fables.

Just as he offered a simple lesson in color theory in *Little Blue and Little Yellow*, Lionni presented a lesson in art appreciation and creativity in *Let's Make Rabbits* (1982). In this tale, illustrated in pencil, crayon, and collage, a scissors and pencil consult together and decide to "make rabbits." The pencil quickly sketches a rabbit while the scissors creates a rabbit from scraps of colored paper. The two rabbits become hungry, and the pencil and scissors supply carrots. When the rabbits awake hungry from a nap, however, the pencil and scissors have gone. After a brief search for their creators, the rabbits discover a carrot that one of them proclaims is real because "it has a shadow!" After gobbling up the carrot, the rabbits grow shadows of their own, exclaiming, "We are *real*!" as they hop happily away.

The artwork of the story is attractively varied with its combinations of crisp shapes, lines, and patterns, and the book neatly portrays the nature of creativity and the imagination. The story

is less a story, however, than a presentation on creating the appearance of reality, known in the art world as "trompe l'oeil," and *Let's Make Rabbits*, while a pleasant artistic exercise, lacks the substance of *Little Blue and Little Yellow*.

Lionni's next book, *Cornelius* (1983), is a comical view of human nature. Cornelius is an unusual crocodile who walks upright and takes pleasure in learning new things. To all his observations, however, his unimaginative friends reply, "So what!" Frustrated, Cornelius leaves his riverbank home and goes into the jungle where he meets a monkey who can stand on his head and hang by his tail. The excited Cornelius urges the monkey to teach him these tricks, and when he has learned them he returns home and demonstrates his new accomplishments. Still his friends reply, "So what!," and the discouraged Cornelius decides to leave. But, glancing back, he sees his friends eagerly practicing standing on their heads and hanging by their tails. Cornelius smilingly observes that "life on the riverbeach would never be the same again."

This tale about the trials and triumphs of leadership, illustrated in textured and torn-paper collage, conveys no deep message, only a wry and gently humorous comment about the difference between leaders and followers. Nothing new is introduced in the way of technique; Lionni's handling of collage is as distinctive and visually effective as ever, but the story, like *Let's Make Rabbits*, is basically light and whimsical. The direct and simple text is well complemented by the posterlike pictures.

Recently Lionni has used his familiar collage mice characters to illustrate such preschool wordless board books as the Pictures to Talk About series. In a style highly reminiscent of Italian artist Bruno Munari, whose style is characterized by simplicity of design and masterful use of color against white space, these books offer pictures of two appealing mice examining objects, places, and animals in a manner that raises, for very young children, the questions who? what? where? and when? The stated purpose of the books is "to engage the eye and mind of the young child." His Colors, Letters, Numbers and Words to Talk About series accomplishes the same purpose; hence Lionni's work has come largely full circle, returning to the simplicity of pictorial statements that stand, with or without texts, on the strength of their own careful design and skillful artistry.

Because of his desire to achieve coherence between form and content in his books, Lionni has seldom collaborated with other authors. His position, as stated in "My Books for Children," is that "For an artist, to work for others means compromises which, however reasonable they may be, often leave the initial idea marred, transformed, devitalized." In *Mouse Days: A Book of Seasons* (1981), with text by Hannah Solomon, he offers a series of twelve crayon paintings depicting the months of the year. The simple narrative, combined with the colorful antics of Lionni's mice, produces a pleasant picture book for very young children. The paintings are highly detailed and humorous, rendered in soft, glowing colors.

There is little genuine collaboration between author and artist, however; the text is merely a light-weight commentary upon the pictures. *Mouse Days* could succeed equally well or better as a wordless book of seasons. In spite of its failure as a collaborative effort, however, *Mouse Days* is visually beautiful, restating Lionni's considerable talents for telling a tale or creating a mood with pictures.

Artistically and thematically, Lionni's books have developed in ways that reflect his own childhood and its influences, as well as his life as a designer, artist, and thinker. Several concerns and themes consistently manifest themselves in his books. The majority of his fables convey themes rooted and grounded in nature: the ethereal beauty of Swimmy's undersea world, the meadow setting of *Frederick*, and the varied beauties of the forest floor in *The Biggest House in the World* are the essential stage settings for the themes of joy in life and inner strength and courage derived from the wonders of the natural world. As Lionni remarked: "The world in which we move is an ever-changing spectacle, revealing around each corner new adventures, new beauty and, of course, new problems."

This preoccupation with nature has characterized his books throughout his career, beginning as it did with the nature studies, drawings, and terrariums of his childhood. In his observations on the beginnings of literacy in his article "Before Images," Lionni makes a strong case for the autobiographical nature of children's books: "For the author of children's books the act of recapturing and expressing the feelings of his earliest encounters with things and events is essential." Art, to his mind, always expresses the feelings of childhood, and it is these feelings that emerge in the simple, direct designs and techniques that characterize his books and appeal so strongly to children for whom collage, crayon, and pressed prints are familiar forms of picture making.

Lionni's work is further characterized by a deep concern for quality. He believes that children must grow up with a sense of excellence and pride in workmanship: "To have little respect for our materials and for the things we make means to have little respect for the people for whom these things are meant. Shoddy workmanship makes for a shoddy environment for Man." The precision with which Lionni matches his medium of expression to the content of each fable exemplifies the care he feels is so essential for the creation of a superior picture book: "I have the feeling that if you are very thorough and put love and care into a thing it will come out well somehow." Critics have agreed that, even though his stories themselves are usually above average, it is his illustrations that lift his books into the realm of excellence.

Lionni's books are moral in nature, occasionally moralistic, but always seeking to convey a sense of awareness of the world, of the importance of personal choice and of thinking for oneself. His protagonists generally emerge as victors because they display the virtues of patience, goodness, intelligence, or the willingness to learn through suffering, as do Little Blue, Swimmy, and Tico. As Lionni has said concerning the typical hero in his books: "It is always his own vitality, his discovery that life is a positive, exciting fact, that makes him come out on top." While he denies that his books have hidden meanings—such as racial messages in *Little Blue and Little Yellow* or Marxist overtones in *Swimmy*—Lionni believes that "all works of art, no matter how simple in scope, must have more than one level of meaning. Children's books are no exception."

While Lionni is noted for his innovative use of collage, a strong sense of design underlies each medium or combination of media which illustrates his stories. A technique of filling the picture area with large, simple shapes without overwhelming or cluttering it is a Lionni trademark, as is his use of white backgrounds, cropping, and carefully informal arrangement of objects within the picture plane. Lionni uses color as carefully as shape and form, employing a balance of vivid and grayed hues to convey mood and setting. In the use of textured and patterned papers for his collages he is unsurpassed. The overall effect is one of both pictorial richness and great economy of shape, line, and form,

Lionni's "first idea-scribbles" for Cornelius. *According to Lionni, "I have no sketches—I go directly from the scribbles into the finished stage" (courtesy of Leo Lionni)*

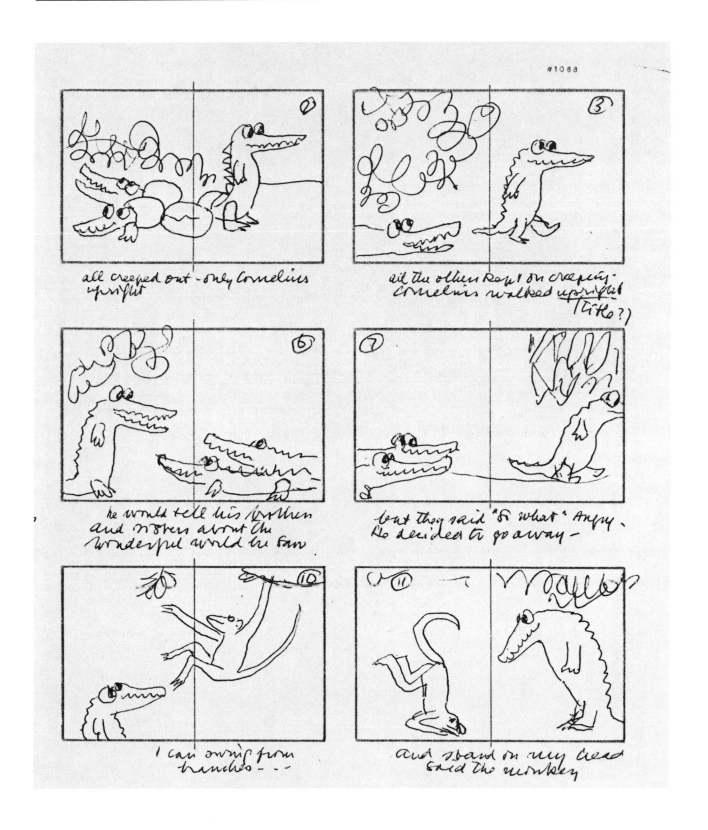

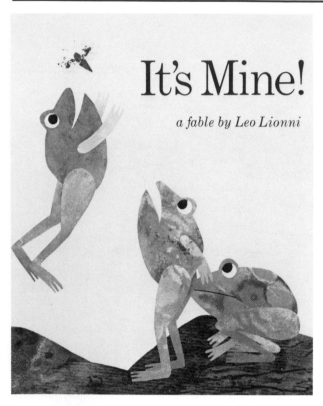

Dust jacket for Lionni's most recent book (Pantheon)

an impression which is further enhanced by his lean, spare texts, which occasionally sparkle with gentle humor.

Lionni's books have frequently reflected his own changing ideas and attitudes about art and the place of the artist in society. *Little Blue and Little Yellow* bears out Lionni's belief that images totally lacking in detail can be decoded by young children as long as their shapes, positionings, and spatial relationships on the page express the meaning of the text and thereby evoke recognizable emotions. *Inch by Inch* reflected his attitudes toward his early career in advertising, *Swimmy* his political sentiments of the artist-as-activist, and *Frederick* his later attitude of the artist as social contributor apart from political or other considerations. Following *Frederick* his work turned toward the theme that had by then assumed the greatest importance for him: personal choice in an increasingly impersonal world. *Alexander and the Wind-Up Mouse* exemplified this new theme, which remains Lionni's prime area of concern in his books: "It's no accident that exactly those books which pose basic problems of choice are my favorite books—*Inch by Inch*; *Swimmy*; *Frederick* and *Alexander*. They are the ones which, I find, say the most to me."

Lionni has succeeded in creating picture books which critics praise for their variety and excellence of technique in depicting the natural world and for the subtlety of his messages. He has also succeeded in producing stories to which children relate because of their bold, colorful pictures reminiscent of kindergarten art. Though a Lionni theme may occasionally have more meaning for an adult than for a child reader, in general his stories are suitable for young children. In his interview with Ruth Agree he stated: "It has always been important that grownups like my books—I have always said that I do not write for children specifically but for the child in myself as well as in other adults." In his article "My Books for Children" Lionni wrote that he is never conscious of the average age of his readers because a children's book "should appeal to all people who have not completely lost their original joy and wonder in life."

Though Lionni's later work appears to be more formulated in style and his fables more whimsical and lacking in depth, he remains a consummate artist whose greatest strength lies in creating images that tell a story with charm, elegance, and grace. His source of inspiration, nature, is a vast and varied one and has proven to be an apt teacher of his lessons for children. As he stated in "My Books for Children," "This infinite stream of experiences will never run dry. It is in the realities around me, in fact, that I find the assurance that my work will continue, for it is there that I will always find the stuff for my stories."

Interviews:

Rose H. Agree, "We Meet Leo Lionni," *Top of the News*, 19 (October 1962): 65-67;

Agree, "Lionni's Artichokes: An Interview," *Wilson Library Bulletin*, 44 (May 1970): 947-950.

References:

"Art in Many Forms," *Time*, 72 (22 December 1958): 53;

Barbara Bader, *American Picture Books from Noah's Ark to the Beast Within* (New York: Macmillan, 1976), pp. 525-543;

Fabio Coen, "Leo Lionni," *Library Journal*, 89 (15 March 1964): 100;

Eugene M. Ettenberg, "Leo Lionni," *American Artist*, 17 (April 1953): 30;

Donnarae McCann and Olga Richard, *The Child's First Books: A Critical Study of Pictures and Texts* (New York: Wilson, 1973), pp. 58-59.

Myra Cohn Livingston
(17 August 1926-)

Hazel Rochman

BOOKS: *Whispers, and Other Poems*, illustrated by Jacqueline Chwast (New York: Harcourt, Brace, 1958);

Wide Awake and Other Poems, illustrated by Chwast (New York: Harcourt, Brace, 1959);

I'm Hiding, illustrated by Erik Blegvad (New York: Harcourt, Brace, 1961);

See What I Found, illustrated by Blegvad (New York: Harcourt, Brace & World, 1962);

I Talk to Elephants, photographs by Isabel Gordon (New York: Harcourt, Brace & World, 1962);

I'm Not Me, illustrated by Blegvad (New York: Harcourt, Brace & World, 1963);

Happy Birthday!, illustrated by Blegvad (New York: Harcourt, Brace & World, 1964);

The Moon and a Star, and Other Poems, illustrated by Judith Shahn (New York: Harcourt, Brace & World, 1965);

I'm Waiting, illustrated by Blegvad (New York: Harcourt, Brace & World, 1966);

Old Mrs. Twindlytart and Other Rhymes, illustrated by Enrico Arno (New York: Harcourt, Brace & World, 1967);

A Crazy Flight, and Other Poems, illustrated by James J. Spanfeller (New York: Harcourt, Brace & World, 1969);

The Malibu and Other Poems, illustrated by Spanfeller (New York: Atheneum, 1972);

When You Are Alone / It Keeps You Capone: An Approach to Creative Writing with Children (New York: Atheneum, 1973);

Come Away, illustrated by Irene Haas (New York: Atheneum, 1974);

The Way Things Are, and Other Poems, illustrated by Jenni Oliver (New York: Atheneum, 1974);

4-Way Stop, and Other Poems, illustrated by Spanfeller (New York: Atheneum, 1976);

A Lollygag of Limericks, illustrated by Joseph Low (New York: Atheneum, 1978);

O Sliver of Liver: Together with Other Triolets, Cinquains, Haiku, Verses, and a Dash of Poems, illustrated by Iris Van Rynbach (New York: Atheneum, 1979);

No Way of Knowing: Dallas Poems (New York: Atheneum, 1980);

A Circle of Seasons, illustrated by Leonard Everett

Fisher (New York: Holiday House, 1982);

Sky Songs, illustrated by Fisher (New York: Holiday House, 1984);

Monkey Puzzle and Other Poems, illustrated by Antonio Frasconi (New York: Atheneum, 1984);

153

A Song I Sang to You: A Selection of Poems, illustrated by Margot Tomes (New York: Harcourt Brace Jovanovich, 1984);

The Child as Poet: Myth or Reality? (Boston: Horn Book, 1984);

Celebrations, illustrated by Fisher (New York: Holiday House, 1985);

Worlds I Know and Other Poems, illustrated by Tim Arnold (New York: Atheneum, 1985);

Sea Songs, illustrated by Fisher (New York: Holiday House, 1986);

Earth Songs, illustrated by Fisher (New York: Holiday House, 1986);

Higgledy-Piggledy, Verses and Pictures (New York: Atheneum, 1986).

RECORDINGS: *Myra Cohn Livingston: The Beautiful Poet Who Writes Beautiful Poems for Children*, Center for Cassette Studies, 1973;

Reading Poetry Aloud, by Livingston and Sam Sebasta, Children's Book Council, 1975;

First Choice: Poets and Poetry, Pied Piper Productions, 1979;

Selecting Poetry for Young Children, Children's Book Council, 1980;

The Writing of Poetry, Harcourt Brace Jovanovich, 1981.

OTHER: *A Tune Beyond Us: A Collection of Poetry*, edited by Livingston, illustrated by James J. Spanfeller (New York: Harcourt, Brace & World, 1968);

Speak Roughly to Your Little Boy; a Collection of Parodies and Burlesques, Together with the Original Poems, Chosen and Annotated for Young People, edited by Livingston, illustrated by Joseph Low (New York: Harcourt Brace Jovanovich, 1971);

"What the Heart Knows Today," in *Somebody Turned on the Tap in These Kids*, edited by Nancy Larrick (New York: Delacorte, 1971), pp. 6-26;

Listen, Children, Listen: An Anthology of Poems for the Very Young, edited by Livingston, illustrated by Trina Schart Hyman (New York: Harcourt Brace Jovanovich, 1972);

"The Rest is Silence," in *A Forum for Focus*, edited by Martha L. King, Robert Emans, and Patricia J. Cianciolo (Urbana, Ill.: National Council of Teachers of English, 1972), pp. 354-372;

What a Wonderful Bird the Frog Are: An Assortment of Humorous Poetry and Verse, edited by Livingston (New York: Harcourt Brace Jovanovich, 1973);

Poems of Lewis Carroll, edited by Livingston, illustrated by John Tenniel and others (New York: Crowell, 1973);

One Little Room, An Everywhere: Poems of Love, edited by Livingston, illustrated by Frasconi (New York: Atheneum, 1975);

O Frabjous Day! Poetry for Holidays and Special Occasions, edited by Livingston (New York: Atheneum, 1977);

Callooh! Callay!: Holiday Poems for Young Readers, edited by Livingston, illustrated by Janet Stevens (New York: Atheneum, 1978);

Poems of Christmas, edited by Livingston (New York: Atheneum, 1980);

"Nonsense Verse: The Complete Escape," in *Celebrating Children's Books*, edited by Betsy Hearne and Marilyn Kaye (New York: Lothrop, Lee & Shepard, 1981), pp. 122-139;

How Pleasant to Know Mr. Lear!, edited by Livingston (New York: Holiday House, 1982);

Why Am I Grown So Cold: Poems of the Unknowable, edited by Livingston (New York: Atheneum, 1982);

"Some Afterthoughts on Poetry, Verse and Criticism," in *Signposts to Criticism of Children's Literature*, edited by Robert Bator (Chicago: American Library Association, 1983), pp. 211-218;

The Scott, Foresman Anthology of Children's Literature, edited by Livingston and Zena Sutherland (Glenview, Ill.: Scott, Foresman, 1984);

Christmas Poems, edited by Livingston, illustrated by Hyman (New York: Holiday House, 1984);

Easter Poems, edited by Livingston, illustrated by John Wallner (New York: Holiday House, 1985);

Thanksgiving Poems, edited by Livingston, illustrated by Stephen Gammell (New York: Holiday House, 1985);

A Learical Lexicon: A Magnificent Feast of Boshblobberbosh and Fun from the Works of Edward Lear, edited by Livingston, illustrated by Joseph Low (New York: Atheneum, 1985);

Poems For Jewish Holidays, edited by Livingston, illustrated by Lloyd Bloom (New York: Holiday House, 1986);

I Like You, If You Like Me, edited by Livingston (New York: Atheneum, 1987);

Cat Poems, edited by Livingston (New York: Holiday House, 1987);

Valentine Poems, edited by Livingston, illustrated by Patricia Brewster (New York: Holiday House, 1987).

PERIODICAL PUBLICATIONS: "Not the Rose
. . . ," *Horn Book*, 40 (August 1964): 355-360;

"The Poem on Page 81," *Top of the News*, 24 (November 1967): 28-41;

"A Tune Beyond Us: The Bases for Choice," *Wilson Library Bulletin*, 44 (December 1969): 448-455;

"I Still Would Plant My Little Apple Tree," *Horn Book*, 47 (February 1971): 75-84;

"Poetry–Stepchild of Children's Literature: Searching CSD's Notable Book Lists 1940-1955: Part I," *School Library Journal*, 20 (15 May 1974): 28-31;

"Poetry–Stepchild of Children's Literature: Searching CSD's Notable Book Lists 1956-1970: Part II," *School Library Journal*, 21 (15 September 1974): 36-41;

"But Is It Poetry? Part I," *Horn Book*, 51 (December 1975): 571-579;

"But Is It Poetry? Part II," *Horn Book*, 52 (February 1976): 24-31;

"Beginnings," *Language Arts*, 55 (March 1978): 346-354;

"David McCord: The Singer, the Song and the Sung," *Horn Book*, 55 (February 1979): 25-39;

"Imagination: The Form of Things Unknown," *Horn Book*, 58 (June 1982): 257-268;

"The Light in His Attic," *New York Times Book Review*, 9 March 1986, p. 36.

Myra Cohn Livingston's poetry for the small child has earned her both popularity and critical acclaim. Widely anthologized, her early work evokes a simple, cheery, protected world of play and dreamy innocence, much in the tradition of Robert Louis Stevenson. Some of her more recent poetry, which has been highly recommended for middle grades and up, shows an increasing complexity in form, mood, and theme, even while it retains the immediacy of the contemporary child's voice and experience, and a continuing delight in play. Since her first book, *Whispers, and Other Poems*, was published in 1958, twenty books of her poetry have appeared, many of which have received awards; and in 1980 she received the National Council of Teachers of English Excellence in Poetry Award for the body of her work. She is also a discriminating and lively anthologist, who draws on a wide range of times and cultures. Her books and articles on sharing poetry and teaching creative writing to children continue to have an important influence.

"The trouble with you," the poet Horace Gregory told the young Myra Cohn when she was his college student in New York in the 1940s, "is that there's no devil in your world." She attributes this quality in her early books to her quiet, idyllic childhood. Born in Omaha, Nebraska, to Mayer Louis and Gertrude Marks Cohn on 17 August 1926, she started to write poems and stories at an early age. She has kept a journal since she was ten years old. Her mother read to her from a wide range of literature and encouraged her writing, and she remembers her father as a visionary with a great sense of humor. When she was eleven the family moved to California, and the next year she became a professional musician, studying counterpoint with Darius Milhaud in 1944 and playing the French horn in orchestras until she was eighteen. But by the time she entered Sarah Lawrence College in 1945 (where she studied under poets Horace Gregory and Robert Fitzgerald) writing had won out over music.

She wrote *Whispers, and Other Poems* as a college freshman. It was not published until twelve years later, but the title poem appeared in 1946 in *Story Parade*, a magazine for children. "Whispers" is still probably her most popular and anthologized poem, capturing the sensuous experience of the very young child and the delighted sibilant opposition of "secrets" and "others":

> Whispers
>   tickle through your ear . . .

Another poem included in the volume, "Discovery" ("Round and round and round I spin/ Making a circle so I can fall in"), rhythmically expresses immediate experience and then makes a leap that is both physical and imaginative. Poems like "The Merry-Go-Round" and "In the Sand" use the form of so many of her poems of childhood experience: starting directly with an everyday object or situation, slowly expanding to a wider world of imagination, and then returning abruptly down to earth. Many themes, like the celebration of play and of being alone, are central to Livingston's work; so also is the tension between fact and mystery as it is expressed in "October Magic," with its movement from the vehement "I know / I saw" to the tentative "I think / perhaps I saw."

After graduating from Sarah Lawrence with a B.A. in 1948, Livingston returned to California, where she wrote book reviews for the *Los Angeles Mirror* and the *Los Angeles Daily News* and was an assistant editor for *Campus Magazine*. She worked in public relations with movie and musical personalities and as personal secretary to singer Dinah Shore and later to violinist Jascha Heifetz, with whom she has remained close friends. She married Richard Livingston, a Certified Public Accountant, in 1952 and moved to Dallas, where their three children, Joshua, Jonas, and Jennie, were born. The Livingstons lived in Dallas for thirteen years, and many years later Myra Cohn Livingston was to draw directly on her experience there for her book *No Way of Knowing: Dallas Poems* (1980).

Whispers, and Other Poems, which won a *New York Herald* Spring Children's Book Festival award, began Livingston's long association with Margaret K. McElderry, who was at the time an editor at Harcourt, Brace. McElderry has served as Livingston's editor for most of the poet's career. Since 1974 many of her books have appeared under McElderry's imprint at Atheneum.

In 1959 Livingston published *Wide Awake and Other Poems*, still drawing on her own happy childhood as well as her experience with her young children. These are poems for the small child, for whom, as the poem "Reflection" shows, the world is "mostly—me." In the tradition of Robert Louis Stevenson the child's experience is warm and sheltered: a rock is "a place to keep a lizard warm / or a frog asleep." The emphasis on play includes "Lamplighter Barn" (with its onomatopoeic "prickly" hay) and also the wild movement of "Ocean Call," where, as in William Blake's poetry, the child at play is in harmony with nature, unafraid of the waves "rushing to swallow me." There are several poems about the ocean included in the volume which are characterized by a striking immediacy, reinforced in "Seaweed" by the onomatopoeia ("slippery") and the funny rhyme ("gummy" / "tummy"), and in "Beach" by the close-up details which alternate with the sense of repeatedly looking far into the distance ("so few sandpipers / ever so few").

The imagery in "A Time for Building" is concrete, physical, noisy, with alliterative pumps pushing, graders groaning, mixers moving; and then suddenly, as in "Discovery," there is that imaginative leap: "moving the road / to another place in town." "The House at the Corner" expresses an isolated fearful moment within the stable, comfy world; but only in "Moon" is there a sense of the fierce, with the menacing repetition, "And the sky turns gray / And the sky turns pale."

As she watched her children grow, Living-

ston wrote several books of rhythmic prose for the small child, from *I'm Hiding* (1961), winner of the Texas Institute of Letters Award, to *Happy Birthday!* (1964); they were published as picturebooks, most of them illustrated by Erik Blegvad. In the Dallas Public Library she started the sharing of poetry with young people and the teaching of creative writing that she has continued in lectures, classes, and workshops throughout the United States for over twenty years.

In 1964 Livingston moved with her family back to Los Angeles, and she has lived in California ever since, in the mountains overlooking the Pacific Ocean. Besides being a passionate beach bum she enjoys raising camellias, bookbinding, bookmark collecting, bridge, and working double crostics. An avid book collector, she has a poetry library of over ten thousand volumes. She has collected rare books since she was fifteen and owns special editions of Yeats, Joyce, and Crane, as well as an extensive collection of illustrations by Randolph Caldecott.

As an instructor and teacher of creative writing in public libraries and schools throughout the country since 1966 and as poet in residence for the Beverly Hills Unified School District since 1972, she works with kindergarten through high-school students. She is also a senior instructor to teachers and librarians at the University of California Los Angeles Extension, offering courses on creative writing in the classroom and the background of poetry children enjoy. Her tape *Selecting Poetry for Young Children* (1980) is part of the Children's Book Council's *Prelude* series; and her set of eight sound filmstrips for classroom use *The Writing of Poetry* (Harcourt Brace Jovanovich, 1981) has won several awards. In her early book on teaching creative writing, *When You Are Alone / It Keeps You Capone: An Approach to Creative Writing with Children* (1973), in her eloquently argued *The Child as Poet: Myth or Reality?* (1984), and in numerous articles, she draws on her wide classroom experience to attack the "ridiculous posture" of those who say that children are born poets and that the spilling out of raw emotion is poetry. She is equally scathing of those who mistake the tools of poetry for poetry, and she condemns what she calls the "Truth Wisdom Beauty" approach that limits poetry to special subjects and diction. Her article "Beginnings" (*Language Arts*, March 1978) summarizes her approach: "No one can teach creative writing. . . . One can only make children aware of their sensitivities, and help children learn of the forms, the basic tools of poetry, into which they can put their own voices. During these [twenty] years I have touched the lives of thousands of children and I have given praise when it is due, and criticism when it is warranted. But I have never told a child that he is a *poet*, for I know only too well the years and work it takes to be considered a poet."

Soon after moving to California, Livingston published more books of poems for the young child: *The Moon and a Star, and Other Poems* (1965), *Old Mrs. Twindlytart* (1967), and *A Crazy Flight, and Other Poems* (1969). *The Moon and a Star* celebrates the quiet growing moments of childhood. Nature is unthreatening; if it is raining, the child thinks of indoor games to play. In the beautiful poem "Empty Lot" the rhythm strengthens the sense of meandering, dreaming, messing about; and with wonderful unity and economy, the poem shows that the title is a perfect pun: all the negatives ("forgot," "left," "empty"), the very lightness of "featherweed," fulfill a valuable need.

That "empty lot" is threatened by pollution and encroachment in *The Malibu and Other Poems* (1972); yet, at the same time, the play of knowledge and creativity is exciting, as the child explores a wider world, a contemporary California landscape. More complex than her earlier books, this outstanding collection for the middle grades and up won the 1972 award of the Southern California Council on Literature for Children and Young People.

As in all her books, the simple child's world is portrayed in *The Malibu and Other Poems*. "Father" is a moving view of the protective parent, an Atlas figure of moral and physical strength. The witty "74th Street" is an affectionate, funny (and popular) poem about a child's learning to roller skate, falling down and getting up again and again. The experience is wonderfully evoked in the colloquial diction, the onomatopoeia, and the jerky rhythm of the free verse with its careful placing of words:

> She brushes off the dirt and the
> blood and puts some
> spit on it and then
> sticks out the other foot
>
> *again.*

The poem "Driving" evokes a special play experience of modern life is the freedom of the open road, not concerned with destination, but "over and over and ever and along," with the self

Dust jacket for Livingston's 1969 volume of poetry for the young child (Harcourt, Brace & World)

given up to a larger continuous rhythm. The same sense of freedom, vitality, rhythm, and connection is expressed in "The Way It's Going," where play has become creativity both the making of art, music, and literature and the active response to them. The "fast-beating" rhythm expresses the sense of the process, the "picture-frame" controlling the pulsating energy, as the child can look

> and can think
> and can wander
>   alone
>   in my
>   book

"Math Class" portrays confinement; the child would rather be "buzzing free" like the fly. But the poem "German Shepherd" is not as simple: it celebrates both the joy of instinctive pleasure and also the widening excitement of

157

knowledge. The rhythm reinforces the sense of the dog's darting back and forth in the waves; "the joy of a wetness" is like the earlier poems of the small child at play on the beach. But this child's pleasure also includes what the dog "has never heard of" and "can never name": knowledge about the moon and the tides, awe about the mysterious powers of a whole universe.

Also more complicated is the use of the colloquial voice. In the title poem, "The Malibu," the casual, tentative tone beautifully expresses the sense of a half-deserted beach where vague things seem to change their nature and merge, and man, dogs, and plants are not able to make much imprint. In tension with this is the down-to-earth voice that is anything but vague "(ha)" and knows "you" can "yank" the weeds. In "Only a Little Litter," a poem that is a funny, half-rueful apostrophe to the moon ("Hey moonface / man-in-the-moonface,"), the colloquial expresses a range of moods. The puns on the vernacular ("thanks a heap") express the irony, especially of man's false perception ("can you stand the view?"), and the reversal and half rhyme strengthen the sense of increasing encroachment: "did you notice ours / with the stripes and stars?"

"On a Bike" also explores how the devil of pollution affects the way man views his experience. In a scene reminiscent of Wordsworth's "Composed Upon Westminster Bridge," the cyclist, alone in the quiet hills, can see "just where the city makes / its pattern in the earth below," a view of man and nature in harmony. She can observe small things around her, "A dusty toad / Bulged gray / and bulbous in the road," where Livingston's use of assonance, alliteration, and rhyme strengthen the meaning of connection. When the quiet is broken by an angry man in a car, the view becomes brown and lifeless, and the cyclist hurries down after the car, toward town. Livingston dedicated *The Malibu* to Jascha Heifetz.

Simple experiences continue to be the subjects of several poems in *The Way Things Are, and Other Poems* (1974), which won the 1975 award of the Society of Children's Book Writers. The rhythmic onomatopoeic "Street Song" ("me and potato chips / munching along") and the poem "Ocean Dancing" evoke the child's physical bliss. Trouble is distant in "Poor," which depicts the middle-class child's view, "I heard of poor." But there is a sense of yearning in the childhood poems like "Lonesome," "For Laura," and "We Could Be Friends."

The devil is closer, though understated, in

"To a Squirrel," where those in cars are involved in pollution, even death: "I spot you as I ride" the child persona says, foreseeing that the animal will be hit by a speeding car. In the poem "Earthquake" there is a threat to all coziness as windows, books, and lamp shade are caught up in a primary chaos. The invented transitive verb in "It . . . / trembles the lampshade" emphasizes the child's state as well as the physical happening. The poem is controlled, partly through alliteration and assonance (her bed is a "kayak," a wonderful echo of "earthquake"); this is just a jarred moment, but

> It makes me wonder
> where I can go
> and be unafraid.

Several poems in this book deal with growing up. In the deceptively simple "The Way Things Are," the use of the most basic diction, much of it monosyllabic, such as "But still, you've got to go," and the pushing, insistent rhythm and assonance emphasize that this is the everlasting pattern of growing up, even while the conversational voice keeps the universal immediate. The colloquial tone and vernacular idiom in "It's Neat" express the sense of the child's identification, almost making the moon a role model for growing up ("How do you do it? . . . All by yourself"). In the poems "Mummy," "Natural History Museum," and "Dinosaurs," the child's emotional identification makes her reach out to imagine the people and creatures of other times; this is opposed to the sterile kind of learning of the school history lesson with its "stuffy room" and "big blackboards." But it is through the imagery of her beloved music that Livingston best expresses the creative learning experience. In "Record" she describes the physical sensation of listening to music, the way a haunting melody "Will whirl within my head for days and days." This "play" is active and rigorous; it is also tentative and mysterious. The individual must search independently, "Asking what it is that Mozart knew / That I must find myself," and such knowledge, connecting "knew" and "new," transforms her, becoming "a part of all I know."

Her *4-Way Stop, and Other Poems* (1976) continues with many of the same themes, but in general it is more diffuse and polemical, stated rather than shown. Verse about national holidays and famous historical figures is entertaining, but the best poems in the book recreate the child's ex-

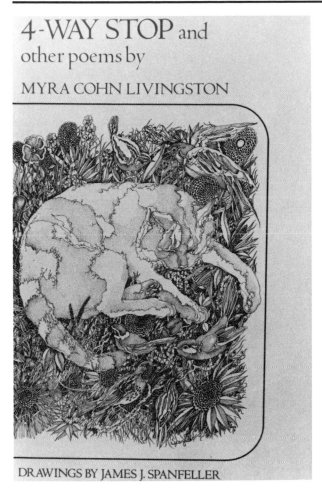

4-WAY STOP and
other poems by

MYRA COHN LIVINGSTON

DRAWINGS BY JAMES J. SPANFELLER

Dust jacket for Livingston's 1976 volume of poetry (Atheneum)

Said an old man from Needles-on-Stoor,
"I eat all of my meals on the floor;
    Though I'm perfectly able
    To sit at the table,
I find it a terrible bore."

Livingston has always written and collected humorous verse, and the nineteen highly successful anthologies she has edited show that levity is not alien to good poetry. In *Speak Roughly to Your Little Boy; a Collection of Parodies and Burlesques, Together with the Original Poems, Chosen and Annotated for Young People* (1971) her notes comment on how parody can be spoof, satire, ridicule, or serious social comment. *What a Wonderful Bird the Frog Are: An Assortment of Humorous Poetry and Verse* (1973) is a collection of verse from the fifth century A.D. to modern times. Livingston has edited collections of Lewis Carroll and Edward Lear, but most of her anthologies combine the humorous with more serious moods. *Listen, Children, Listen: An Anthology of Poems for the Very Young* (1972) includes nonsense and lyrics. In her introduction to *O Frabjous Day! Poetry for Holidays and Special Occasions* (1977) she says: "whereas holidays can be joyous, they can also be fraught with unhappiness, sad memories, or worry." Mary M. Burns praised *Callooh! Callay!: Holiday Poems for Young Readers* (1978) for offering "new perspectives on familiar events or personalities through fresh material or by juxtaposing contrasting views" (*Horn Book*, April 1979).

While insisting that all poetry is not for children, whose experience is necessarily limited, Livingston chooses poems for her anthologies from many times and places, including translations, lesser-known writers, and the less familiar works of the famous. In an important article, "A Tune Beyond Us: The Bases for Choice" (1969), she says she is committed to "the idea of humane literacy," to finding poems "relevant to today's young person in subject, emotion and rhythm, that will broaden his view of the human condition, and present him with as many possibilities for self-identification and identification with the experiences of others as is possible." Zena Sutherland in *Children and Books* (1981) points out that many of Livingston's selections "may please both the read-aloud audience and adults." She comments particularly on Livingston's "excellent" anthology for adolescents, *A Tune Beyond Us: A Collection of Poetry* (1968). For grades six and up *Poems of Christmas* (1980) includes poems and carols about the Nativity–the animals, the wonder, and the celebra-

perience, both physically (as in "Bubble Gum," "starting with a tiny blob upon your tongue" and moving without a break, almost without punctuation, to the climax) and emotionally (as in "Bedtime," with the fear of what lies behind the closet door). "The Trouble Is–" captures the irritated rhythm of the nagging adult: "Have you practised?" There is no abuse, no fear; this is a cared-for child; and even the "Haiku for Halloween" ("Feel the / Pale eyeballs of a dead cat–") has a delicious horror. Included are poems which deal with nature: peaceful and mysterious in "Ocean At Night"; the child in connection with grass, trees, and sun in "Summer Morning," and the symbolic meaning of circles within circles, which is rooted in the child's physical experience in "Moving Clouds."

A Lollygag of Limericks (1978) is a relishing of delightful nonsense, inspired by the unusual place-names Livingston encountered on a trip to England. The situations are immediate and dramatic. with a crazy logic:

tion, from fifteenth-century France to contemporary America. The 1984 anthology *Christmas Poems*, illustrated in red, green, and white by Trina Schart Hyman, has eighteen poems for young children, some specially commissioned for this collection (by John Ciardi, Valerie Worth, David McCord, and others), some published before, some traditional. In the same holiday series are *Easter Poems* (1985) and *Thanksgiving Poems* (1985): the latter, beautifully illustrated by Stephen Gammell, includes two traditional Indian poems and Psalm 100, as well as commissioned poems from contemporary poets.

Livingston continues to write her own light, irreverent verse, as in *O Sliver of Liver: Together with Other Triolets, Cinquains, Haiku, Verses, and a Dash of Poems* (1979), but the book is dedicated to the memory of her recently deceased father, and some poems express a darker reality. "Somewhere between Utah and Nevada: Airborne," written in five tercets, opposes the limited view ("no tears, no grief") of the first and last stanzas, with the stark vision of death and abandonment ("Nameless, naked and alone") of the three middle stanzas. In the pun, "Airborne," and in the grim perception of an elemental landscape, this poem looks forward to Livingston's major 1984 book, *Sky Songs*, which won the Parents Choice Award. The ghost, in the eerily dramatic poem "A Ghostly Conversation" (reminiscent of Harold Munro's "Overhead on a Saltmarsh"), is defined by negatives, yearning but horrifying, coming closer and closer ("Be with me . . .") to the rising denial of the listener. The poem "Never" is a nastier "Whispers," with "gobs of guile" and sibilant onomatopoeia, "surreptitious telephones."

There are also deeply celebratory poems in *O Sliver of Liver*. In "Sea Level Drive" the separation between earth, sky, and ocean "loosens" and "melts," so that waves fly and clouds sail. "Lights: Cambridge, Massachusetts," with its wonderful evocation of driving along the river at night, the lights flashing past, their reflections "undulating" in the water, proclaims the power of the poem to give form to all that energy and movement. The intensity of imaginative experience is recreated in "Storyteller," where mermaids and waves come right up to the storyteller's chair: like the Mozart theme in "Record," stories change us and become part of us; "They dive/among us . . . They swim / into our lives." The poem "Parched Earth" looks forward to *A Circle of Seasons* (1982) in its imagery and its acceptance of the dark: the "jigsaw-puzzle ground" allows you to go down

Dust jacket for Livingston's 1979 volume which contains both light, irreverent verse and poems that express a darker reality (Atheneum)

into the mystery; and the shape of the lines reinforces the idea of rebirth—

In time
      the grass
                                  too.
                      these
           will cover

Drawing on her Dallas experience of many years before, Livingston wrote *No Way of Knowing: Dallas Poems* (1980), a series of individual vignettes which, in their speech patterns, rhythms, and language, lovingly evoke her friends in Dallas's black community. The book won the 1981 Texas Institute of Letters Award and was praised by Mary M. Burns as "fresh and haunting . . . particularly effective in suggesting the personae of the speakers" (*Horn Book*, February 1981).

Livingston's books of individual poems have

Dust jackets for two of Livingston's book-length poems illustrated by Leonard Everett Fisher (Holiday House)

been illustrated by Jacqueline Chwast, James J. Spanfeller, Jenni Oliver, Tim Arnold, and others with quiet drawings that express the child's world. Some of her most recent books show a great change in form and format, as well as considerable development in theme. *A Circle of Seasons*, *Sky Songs*, and *Sea Songs* (1986) each consist of one long unified poem, though each section (particularly in *Sky Songs*) has its own unity and can be read individually. All these are large-size books and are illustrated by Leonard Everett Fisher's full-page acrylic impressionist paintings: in *A Circle of Seasons* a framed painting appears next to each section; in *Sky Songs* and *Sea Songs* each poem is printed within a double-page painting. *Celebrations* (1985), also illustrated by Fisher in bold acrylics and with the same large-size format, includes poems for sixteen holidays from Martin Luther King Day to Passover and April Fools' Day.

A Circle of Seasons was praised by Paul Heins (*Horn Book*, October 1982) for the way in which "words and pictures taken together create a surprising combination of exaltation and serenity." Named a Notable Book by ALSC, the children's division of the American Library Association, the poem combines the nature themes of Keats and Shelley and the play of Blake with the imagery and voice of a contemporary child.

Each of the poem's thirteen sections consists of a descriptive quatrain (three rhymed lines and one unrhymed) and an invocation (a couplet printed in three lines). There are three sections for each season, and the last section repeats the first except for a change in the invocation. The seasons are personified, each section expressing a sustained mood and metaphor.

Play unifies the seasons. Spring "pokes," "sticks," and "skips" in the first section; then baseball is the metaphor, with vigorous verbs expressing the sense of energy released:

> Spring brings out her baseball bat, swings
>   it through the air,
> Pitches bulbs and apple blossoms, throws
>   them where it's bare,
> Catches dogtooth violets, slides to mea-
>   dowsweet,
> Bunts a breeze and tags the trees with
>   green buds everywhere.

Summer's first metaphor is of fireworks; in the next section dreamy, easily flowing Summer "Fishes for a frog prince" in story and imagination. Autumn "makes a last long play" in a football metaphor of fighting and losing. Nature is

an artist at play, fingerpainting and sculpting, in the strange, still, frozen depths of Winter.

There is drama in the contrasts and connections between the seasons and within each season, and suspense in the overall movement from awakening to growth to dying and rebirth. Spring pokes down "far below" in the "cracked earth" searching for "sleeping seeds." In a wonderful onomatopoeic section that focuses on sound, Spring bubbles with stream waters, splatters with warm rain, and listens to what a "wakening" breeze has stirred. Summer's powerful fireworks join earth, sun, and sky, even while Summer, like Spring, "dives deep." The final summer metaphor, reminiscent of Keats's "Ode to Autumn," is filled with bursting growth expressed in sensuous imagery, especially of taste. Autumn is the bleakest season, jarring half-rhymes emphasizing the dying fall which is also growth; movement is fast and "across," the world is "grown gray and old" and must "Rest well." In Winter furious attack on the earth from above slowly "Quiets down," and after the "strange" delicate creativity of ice and snow, nature wakes with a birth "cry" as the wind rises, the crust on earth thins, "and above–a blue patch in the sky." The repetition of the first Spring quatrain emphasizes that the seasons' cycle is forever. The change in the invocation from the plant imagery of the first section to

> O life,
> O birth,
> You start again in earth!

both generalizes the cycle to all life and applies it to the growth of each individual. In earth, the ground far below, is where life starts and ends.

No living things are the subjects of *Sky Songs*. These are poems about the basic elements: air, water, dust; their light, color, and movement; and the sun, moon, stars, and weather. In a starred review in *Booklist* (15 May 1984) Betsy Hearne praised Livingston's imagery and her use of the "swelling rhythm" of the cinquain. Within a traditional form of fifteen lines in three cinquain stanzas the fourteen poems show extraordinary diversity, moving from the sky at night with the moon, stars, and planets through daybreak and burning noon to a rising storm, the plague of smog, then snow, rain, and sunset. Each poem can stand alone, but each is also part of a whole and gains resonance from the way its images, moods, and rhythms are developed and varied.

Gone is the cheeky, affectionate "Hey, moonface." These apostrophes to the sky are often informal and immediate, but they are more distant than the child's easy identification in the earlier books. In the first poem, "Moon," the "always" of the first question, "Why is / The moon always / changing?" is echoed in the "away" of the last question with its falling rhythm, "What is it they see when they look / away?"

But the "you" invoked is not only the sky, or God; it is also the individual. "Suns live in you"; each person must "journey" as the planets do. The personifications and the domestic, often contemporary, imagery (of clothing, houses, cooking, and play) reinforce that it is the individual vision that gives meaning to the physical universe. Every poem is about perception; the suns are "eyes"; "you are . . . floodlit by waking sun" to transform and connect with the power of the creative imagination.

"Clouds" is about those "strange animals" that come out, and in their play they creep, stalk, fly, tumble, die, and vanish in the rising wind—as the species have evolved and as each person grows and dies. The fierce wind shows the dynamic tension between protection and destruction: it tears the enveloping storm clouds, and it tears the blankets of the sky into pieces that fall to make a "sleeping bag" on earth. The dark must be accepted: in "Noon" the attempt to chase away all shadows has turned the sun into a Cyclops, energy out of control. In the last poem, with the exquisite, tenuous beauty of sunset yielding to the gray and the dark, alliteration, assonance, and repetition strengthen the widening meanings of "sun set," the energy that must die and is always renewed within an everlasting form. From that melancholy, wondering first question about "always changing," *Sky Songs* shows in form, tone, and theme that the change happens in all ways, and that it is forever, and that the mystery remains.

Monkey Puzzle and Other Poems (1984), illustrated with woodcuts by Antonio Frasconi, contains poems for grades five through nine, combining detailed description of particularized trees with wider associations of dreams and the natural cycle. The beautiful, mysterious "Irish Yew":

You are the once upon a time of green,
of mist. Of turrets, towers and of
    spiraled stair.
A ring of bugles in the quiet air,

is full of literary echoes, especially of Tennyson. Its focus on

            all shapes unseen
    and known,

with the startling "and known" instead of the expected "unknown," emphasizes the power of imaginative truth. Livingston continues to use the cinquain with concentration, and several shaped poems are witty and rhythmic, including "Monterey Cypress: PT. LOBOS," which begins dramatically,

    at whim of winds
            my limbs are bent.

"Trees: the seeds" is reminiscent of *Circle of Seasons* with the seeds hoping an animal "will bury us in earth." "Forest: an invitation" celebrates not only "the foxglove / in the spring" but also "the tangling / claw and root" and "Ferns and fungus / nursed in dark." But this natural cycle that includes the fierce and the dark is shattered in the last poem, "Rain Forest: Papua, New Guinea," when the Binandere tribespeople tell of how the lumbering operations have destroyed their way of life: "The forest was like the bones in our body. / Now they have our forest."

In her introduction to the poems she selected for *The Scott, Foresman Anthology of Children's Literature* (1984), coedited with Zena Sutherland (designed mainly for adults working with children and for students in children's literature classes), Livingston says that she has organized the poems to "suggest the growth patterns of children. This pattern begins with concepts of self and family and moves out into the world of school, the realities of the universe as well as the realm of the imagination and spirit." Her own work has shown a similar development as she has continued to grow and change. Her poems for the very young still speak to today's children: *A Song I Sang to You* (1984) is a selection from her early books published between 1958 and 1969; and *Worlds I Know and Other Poems* (1985), new poems for grades three through six, focuses on the young child, especially in relation to the extended family. But the poet praised by Rebecca Lukens in the 1978 edition of *Twentieth Century Children's Writers* for "An unusual capacity to relate to the small child" is now also being highly recommended "for all ages" in starred reviews.

"I am writing entirely differently now," Liv-

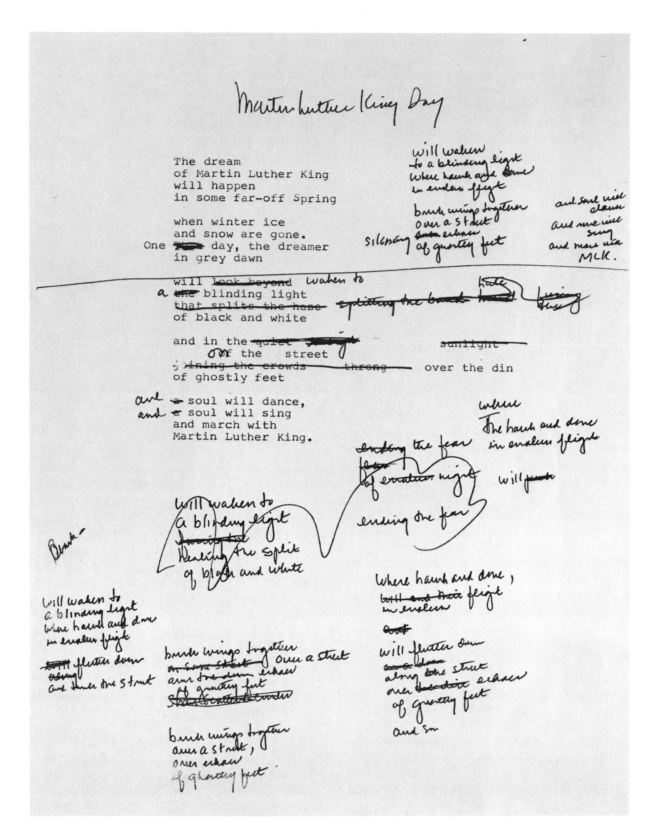

Page from a revised typescript for a poem by Livingston that appeared in her 1985 volume Celebrations *(courtesy of the author)*

ingston says, "and I see the devil's pitfalls. But I still see with the eyes of a child. Each of us must live life anew and discover the simple things of childhood. It is not the thing encountered that matters so much as the humanness with which we meet, apprehend, and possibly comprehend it."

The circles of "Discovery" have widened. In the tradition of the nineteenth-century romantic poets, Livingston believes in nature as model, and her view of nature includes an acceptance of

the dark; individual growth is part of the universal cycle of life and decay. Her devil is the threat of man's interference with the natural process, in the physical universe and in the individual imagination.

Papers:

Some of Myra Cohn Livingston's manuscripts and papers are located in the Kerlan Collection at the University of Minnesota, Minneapolis.

Arnold Lobel
(22 May 1933-)

Jacqueline Gmuca
University of North Carolina at Charlotte

BOOKS: *A Zoo for Mister Muster* (New York: Harper & Row, 1962);

A Holiday for Mister Muster (New York: Harper & Row, 1963; London: Harper & Row, 1963);

Prince Bertram the Bad (New York: Harper & Row, 1963; Tadworth, U.K.: World's Work, 1970);

Lucille (New York: Harper & Row, 1964; Kingswood, U.K.: World's Work, 1964);

Giant John (New York: Harper & Row, 1964; Kingswood, U.K.: World's Work, 1965);

The Bears of the Air (New York: Harper & Row, 1965; Kingswood, U.K.: World's Work, 1966);

Martha, the Movie Mouse (New York: Harper & Row, 1966; Kingswood, U.K.: World's Work, 1967);

The Great Blueness and Other Predicaments (New York: Harper & Row, 1968; Tadworth, U.K.: World's Work, 1970);

Small Pig (New York: Harper & Row, 1969; Tadworth, U.K.: World's Work, 1970);

Frog and Toad are Friends (New York: Harper & Row, 1970; Tadworth, U.K.: World's Work, 1971);

The Ice-Cream Cone Coot and Other Rare Birds (New York: Parents' Magazine Press, 1971);

On the Day Peter Stuyvesant Sailed into Town (New York: Harper & Row, 1971);

Frog and Toad Together (New York: Harper & Row, 1972; Tadworth, U.K.: World's Work, 1973);

Mouse Tales (New York: Harper & Row, 1972; Tadworth, U.K.: World's Work, 1973);

The Man Who Took the Indoors Out (New York: Harper & Row, 1974; Tadworth, U.K.: World's Work, 1976);

Owl at Home (New York: Harper & Row, 1975; Tadworth, U.K.: World's Work, 1976);

Frog and Toad All Year (New York: Harper & Row, 1976; Tadworth, U.K.: World's Work, 1977);

How the Rooster Saved the Day, illustrated by Anita Lobel (New York: Greenwillow, 1977; London: Hamilton, 1977);

Mouse Soup (New York: Harper & Row, 1977; Tadworth, U.K.: World's Work, 1978);

Grasshopper on the Road (New York: Harper & Row, 1978; Kingswood, U.K.: World's Work, 1979);

A Treeful of Pigs, illustrated by Anita Lobel (New York: Greenwillow, 1979; London: Julia MacRae Books, 1980);

Days with Frog and Toad (New York: Harper & Row, 1979);

Fables (New York: Harper & Row, 1980; London: Cape, 1980);

On Market Street, illustrated by Anita Lobel (New York: Greenwillow, 1981);

Uncle Elephant (New York: Harper & Row, 1981);

Ming Lo Moves the Mountain (New York: Greenwillow, 1982);

The Book of Pigericks (New York: Harper & Row, 1983);

The Rose in My Garden, illustrated by Anita Lobel (New York: Greenwillow, 1984);

Whiskers and Rhymes (New York: Greenwillow, 1985);

The Frog and Toad Pop-Up Book (New York: Harper & Row, 1986);

Frog and Toad Coloring Book (New York: Harper & Row, 1986).

SELECTED BOOKS ILLUSTRATED: Sol Scharfstein, *Bibletime* (New York: Ktav, 1958);

Scharfstein, *Hebrew Dictionary; Activity Funbook* (New York: Ktav, 1958);

Scharfstein, *Holiday Dictionary* (New York: Ktav, 1958);

Fred Phleger, *Red Tag Comes Back* (New York: Harper & Row, 1961);

Susan Oneacre Rhinehart, *Something Old, Something New* (New York: Harper & Row, 1961);

Peggy Parish, *Let's Be Indians* (New York: Harper & Row, 1962);

Millicent E. Selsam, *Terry and the Caterpillars* (New York: Harper & Row, 1962);

Betty Baker, *The Little Runner of the Longhouse* (New York: Harper & Row, 1962);

Selsam, *Greg's Microscope* (New York: Harper & Row, 1963);

Charlotte Zolotow, *The Quarreling Book* (New York: Harper & Row, 1963);

Mildred Myrick, *The Secret Three* (New York: Harper & Row, 1963);

Nathaniel Benchley, *Red Fox and His Canoe* (New York: Harper & Row, 1964);

Miriam Young, *Miss Suzy* (New York: Parents' Magazine Press, 1964);

Phil Ressner, *Dudley Pippin* (New York: Harper & Row, 1965);

Selsam, *Let's Get Turtles* (New York: Harper & Row, 1965);

Zolotow, *Someday* (New York: Harper & Row, 1965);

Lilian Moore, *The Magic Spectacles and Other Stories* (New York: Parents' Magazine Press, 1966);

Felice Holman, *The Witch on the Corner* (New York: Norton, 1966);

Benchley, *Oscar Otter* (New York: Harper & Row, 1966);

Selsam, *Benny's Animals and How He Put Them in Order* (New York: Harper & Row, 1966);

Andrea DiNoto, *The Star Thief* (New York: Macmillan, 1967);

Parish, *Let's Be Early Settlers with Daniel Boone*

Arnold Lobel (photo by Ian Anderson)

(New York: Harper & Row, 1967);

Benchley, *The Strange Disappearance of Arthur Cluck* (New York: Harper & Row, 1967);

Myrick, *Ants are Fun* (New York: Harper & Row, 1968);

Edward Lear, *The Four Little Children Who Went Around the World* (New York: Macmillan, 1968);

Sarah Catherine Martin, *The Comic Adventures of Old Mother Hubbard* (Englewood Cliffs, N.J.: Bradbury, 1968);

Maxine Kumin, *The Microscope* (New York: Harper & Row, 1968);

Moore, *Junk Day on Juniper Street* (New York: Parents' Magazine Press, 1969);

Judith Viorst, *I'll Fix Anthony* (New York: Harper & Row, 1969);

Benchley, *Sam, the Minuteman* (New York: Harper & Row, 1969);

Jack Prelutsky, *The Terrible Tiger* (New York: Macmillan, 1969);

Lear, *The New Vestments* (Englewood Cliffs, N.J.: Bradbury, 1970);

Laura Cathon, *Tot Botot and His Flute* (New York: Macmillan, 1970);

Cheli Durán Ryan, *Hildilid's Night* (New York: Macmillan, 1971);

Sulamith Ish-Kishor, *The Master of Miracles* (New York: Harper & Row, 1971);

Jacob and Wilhelm Grimm, *Hansel and Gretel* (New York: Delacorte, 1971);

Young, *Miss Suzy's Easter Surprise* (New York: Parents' Magazine Press, 1972);

Robert A. Morris, *Seahorse* (New York: Harper & Row, 1972);

Paula Fox, *Good Ethan* (Scarsdale, N.Y.: Bradbury, 1973);

Cynthia Jameson, *The Clay Pot Boy* (New York: Coward-McCann & Geoghegan, 1973);

Norma Farber, *As I Was Crossing Boston Common* (New York: Dutton, 1973);

Parish, *Dinosaur Time* (New York: Harper & Row, 1974);

Prelutsky, *Circus* (New York: Macmillan, 1974);

Young, *Miss Suzy's Birthday* (New York: Parents' Magazine Press, 1974);

Anne K. Rose, *As Right As Right Can Be* (New York: Dial, 1976);

Prelutsky, *Nightmares: Poems to Trouble Your Sleep* (New York: Greenwillow, 1976);

Doris Orgel, *Merry Merry FIBruary* (New York: Parents' Magazine Press, 1977);

Prelutsky, *The Mean Old Mean Hyena* (New York: Greenwillow, 1978);

Jean Van Leeuwen, *Tales of Oliver Pig* (New York: Dial, 1979);

Carol Chapman, *The Tale of Meshka the Kvetch* (New York: Dutton, 1980);

Prelutsky, *The Headless Horseman Rides Tonight: More Poems to Trouble Your Sleep* (New York: Greenwillow, 1980);

The Random House Book of Poetry for Children (New York: Random House, 1983);

Laura Geringer, *A Three Hat Day* (New York: Harper & Row, 1985).

OTHER: *Gregory Griggs and Other Nursery Rhyme People*, selected and illustrated by Lobel (New York: Greenwillow, 1978).

PERIODICAL PUBLICATION: "Frog and Toad: a Short History," *Claremont College Reading Conference Yearbook*, 42 (1978): 147-154.

As both author and illustrator, Arnold Lobel's importance is undeniable. The various awards that his books have received underscore this evaluation, but even more importantly, the prominent qualities of his works–their warmth and humor, social commentary, and basic truth–make Arnold Lobel an important figure in contemporary children's literature.

Although he was born in Los Angeles, Lobel spent almost all of his childhood in Schenectady, New York. His parents, Joseph and Lucille Stark Lobel, discouraged over not having found a western "pot of gold," had moved back east when he was six months old. Shortly after, they decided to get a divorce and arranged for Lobel to be brought up by his grandparents. Despite his parents' breakup, these very early years of childhood were happy ones for Lobel; he especially admired his grandmother's calm ability to handle any crisis. However, from kindergarten to the second grade, he was often sick with a number of illnesses and was frequently hospitalized for extended periods of time. Absent from school for so long, Lobel found himself isolated from most of his third grade classmates when he did return, and in an effort to make friends, he told stories to the class, drawing pictures on the blackboard to accompany his words.

This early fascination with text and illustration continued for Lobel. As a teenager he avidly read and looked at a number of children's books, and when he entered Pratt Institute in Brooklyn, he chose the field of illustration as his special interest. While pursuing this field, Lobel also became involved in drama and met Anita Kempler when they performed in the same play. After he graduated from Pratt in 1955, Lobel and Kempler married and settled in Brooklyn (Anita Lobel is also a well-known children's artist). Three years later, after some unsuccessful jobs with advertising agencies, Arnold Lobel's illustrations to three activity fun books by Sol Scharfstein were published. However, it was not until 1961 that his first drawings to a picture book, *Red Tag Comes Back*, were published.

During the 1960s Lobel illustrated over twenty books for other writers. These works, many of them in Harper and Row's I Can Read series, ranged from picture-book narratives concerned with science and history to poetry, fantasy, and realistic fiction. Among this variety of texts, several key elements of Lobel's style emerge: facial expressions are simply, yet effectively drawn; backgrounds are well detailed; and the color scheme is fairly limited. At times Lobel uses pen and ink or pencil alone. In other books he adds two or three colors, and only rarely, as in Miriam Young's *Miss Suzy* (1964), does a full range of colors appear. Representative of the majority of evaluations of Lobel's ability to integrate his illustrations into someone else's text is a comment made in the 12 May 1963 *New York Times Book Review* on Mildred Myrick's *The Secret Three* (1963): "Everything–text, pictures, format–add up to near perfection."

Very soon after Lobel began illustrating the stories of other authors, he wrote his first picture book for children, *A Zoo for Mister Muster*, in 1962, and the following year its sequel–*A Holiday for Mister Muster*–appeared. Lobel considers Muster, the main character of these books, as a "child substitute" since "he has all the attributes of a child but moves through the story with the independence of an adult." Muster's most prominent quality, his love of animals, permeates both books. In the first, the animals return his love when they escape from their cages and appear at his apartment to live. In the second book, Muster lovingly takes the animals that have been sick with colds to the seashore.

A zookeeper and several policemen provide the complication of plot in *A Zoo for Mister Muster* as they, understandably enough, want the unwilling animals to come back to the zoo. But in the end Mister Muster is deputized as an assistant zookeeper, and the animals happily return. While *A Zoo for Mister Muster* is simply plotted, its sequel contains more complications. The animals love the seashore but, even more than that, are enthralled by the amusement park nearby and its rides; needless to say, they are reluctant to leave the roller coaster, Ferris wheel, and parachute jump. But finally Muster paints the van that they rode to the seashore in, disguises himself, and tricks the animals into thinking they will take the most exciting ride of all, and they do, as they travel all the way back to the zoo.

A Holiday for Mister Muster is clearly the more interesting, imaginative story of the two and was recognized by the *New York Times* as one of the best illustrated books of the year for 1963. Lobel's style of illustration is very similar for each story: pen and ink combined with orange in the first book and yellow in the second along with the cartoonlike animals and humans visually link the two books together.

The comic tone established in Lobel's first two books continues in his third, *Prince Bertram the Bad*. Published in 1963, this story revolves around a very naughty prince who first finds out that badness will be punished: he is turned into a dragon when he hits a witch with a slingshot. Conversely, he learns by the end of the story that goodness is rewarded, for the witch reverses her spell when he thaws her out of a snowdrift with his fiery breath. Eloise Rue, writing for *Library Journal* (15 March 1963), praised *Prince Bertram the Bad* as "one of the best of recent 'mean' stories," and Elizabeth Graves, reviewing this book for *Commonweal* (24 May 1963), noted the "crisp, humorous text and the equally sure and witty three-color illustrations." Certainly, comic details such as the gingersnaps the departing dragon takes with him and cartoonish characters are responsible for the book's humorous nature, but its typical folktale theme has been treated elsewhere in ways which are likewise perceptive and comical.

Although he had illustrated several I Can Read books from 1961 to 1963, it was not until *Lucille* (1964) that Lobel wrote his own. The pages tell, very disjointedly at first and then much more smoothly, of a horse who yearns to be what she is not–a lady. A farmer's wife helps to make her dream come true as she buys her a fine hat, shoes, and dress and then invites Lucille inside the farmhouse to sip tea and listen to the radio. But when Lucille becomes nervous over the large number of ladies who have come to call on her and awkward as she bumps into the farm wives and spills the tea, she herself declares that she is a horse, not a lady. Lucille then runs into the fields and back into her stable, happy in having discovered her own identity. Lobel's theme is clear–accept who you are–and the story which expresses it is both interesting and humorous. The humorous quality is highlighted by Lobel's illustrations, which rely on cartoon art and so enhance the comic nature of the plot.

In *Prince Bertram the Bad* Lobel used folktale characters and a folktale theme to tell how a bad prince was transformed into a good one, and in *Giant John* (1964) characters from fairy tales appear once more. Portrayed are fairies who play magic music, Giant John who must dance to their melodies, and a princess, queen, and king who hire John for a week so that the money he earns will keep himself and his mother from starving. No strong theme emerges from this book; at the climax, the fairies make Giant John dance, he knocks down the castle, the princess and her family cry, and the fairies, saddened over what they have done, help John rebuild what was destroyed. In the resolution, Giant John brings home a bag of gold to his mother, and they all, including the fairies, sit down to dinner. While not one of Lobel's most humorous and imaginative texts, the strength of the book rests in his illustrations of the gentle giant, his loving mother, and the carefree fairies.

With his next two books, *The Bears of the Air* (1965) and *Martha, the Movie Mouse* (1966), Lobel again turns to animals as his main characters. The major conflict in *The Bears of the Air* is set up at the beginning of the story: four young bears want to do things that are fun instead of the more "useful" activities their grandfather insists they do. They want to juggle and somersault, perform rope tricks and play a violin; not take naps, climb trees, go for walks, or catch fish. A second conflict joins this first as the grandfather begins to show them the correct way to climb trees and a bird, whose nest has been disturbed by his climbing, angrily grabs the glasses off his nose. However, one of the four young bears, Harold, quickly lassos the bird; another, Ronald, juggles a third bear, Donald, over his head so that he can somersault and catch the falling glasses while the fourth bear, Sam, plays his violin so sweetly that the bird, no longer angry, says, "What beautiful music. . . . My little eggs will hear it and they will soon hatch happily!" Thus, the grandfather comes to appreciate the bears of the air and the "fine and useful things" they do. This story, with its well-defined and humorous plot, is also enhanced by Lobel's depiction of the bears' facial expressions and reactions to each unfolding event in the book.

Lobel's next work, *Martha, the Movie Mouse* (1966), is a "rags to riches" story of a homeless mouse who finds both a place to stay–a movie theater–and a friend–the man who runs the projector. But even more importantly, she discovers her own creative potential to sing movingly of her past: "of mousetraps / Tightly set / And city streets / All dark and wet." As a blues singer and a dancer, Martha wins acclaim and admiration, yet, for her, nothing can quite compare to the pleasure of watching movies with popcorn and a lemon Coke at hand. Inspired by Lobel's love of movies and the remembrance of pet mice he had raised, this story is significant in two ways: it is told in verse, a genre that Lobel returns to a few years later, and its illustrations are a mixture of bordered and unbordered pictures. Until 1963 Lobel had not used any type of bordering device, but in Myrick's *The Secret Three* and Young's *Miss Suzy* he began to establish undefined borders around several illustrations in each book. Lobel roughly sketched formal borders around all of his pictures for Millicent E. Selsam's *Let's Get Turtles,* published in 1965. Then, in 1966, *Martha, the Movie Mouse* and *Oscar Otter,* an I Can Read book

Cover for Lobel's 1965 book about four young bears who want to have fun instead of engaging in the useful activities that their grandfather wants (Harper & Row)

by Nathaniel Benchley, were published with distinct line borders, an artistic pattern which Lobel continues to follow in the 1980s.

His last two books to be published in the 1960s, *The Great Blueness and Other Predicaments* (1968) and *Small Pig* (1969) reflect a surer hand in many ways. In *The Great Blueness and Other Predicaments,* an overall unity results from a circular border surrounding the opening and closing illustrations and two separately bordered pictures each time the wizard portrayed walks down to his cellar and concocts a different color. Lobel's tale of how colors came to be is both cumulative and climactic. For a world without color, the wizard first creates blue, but when that makes everyone sad, he mixes up yellow. Yellow, however, hurts everyone's eyes, so the wizard finally mixes up red. Unfortunately, that color makes everyone cross. Nonetheless, the book ends happily as the wizard, unable to concoct any new colors, accidentally upsets the old ones, creating all the hues that anyone could wish for. This resolution is ably complemented by a climax in Lobel's color scheme. Throughout the book the colors shift from black and white to blue, then to yellow, and finally to red until the last two illustrations conclude the story with a profusion of color and detail as the townspeople paint the world around them and then show their gratitude to the wizard for a world "too beautiful ever to be changed again."

In *Small Pig,* however, a world *is* changed. A farmer's wife, intent on cleaning the entire farm, sucks up the small pig's lovely mud hole, washes him, and then places a blue ribbon around his neck. From that point, according to the August 1969 *Horn Book* reviewer, "Small Pig's saga grows funnier by the episode" as he runs away, searching for a new mud hole, gets chased from a pond, fails to find mud in a junkyard, and then settles into soft cement in the city. Rescued by firemen, the small pig returns with the farmer and his wife, who have been looking for him, and when it rains harmony is restored by the water which forms new mud for the small pig. Interwoven with his humorous plot and well-drawn characters, Lobel's theme is quietly evident. The farmer's wife learns that the basic nature of others must be respected. This perception clearly ties the second of Lobel's I Can Read books to the first, *Lucille,* for in that text the horse comes to accept her own nature.

In the nine books that Lobel wrote and illustrated during the 1960s, two elements continually appear. First of all, the tone of almost every work is decidedly humorous, and both the text and illustrations add to this comic quality. Second, the works abound with main characters who are, as Lobel designates them, "child substitutes." From Mister Muster eating a chocolate soda to console himself to Harold, Ronald, Donald, and Sam, who enjoy being bears of the air, to the small pig who angrily runs away from the problem of no mud, Lobel comically reflects the children that he is illustrating and writing for.

Early in his career Lobel realized that "A good illustrator . . . should have a repertory of styles at his command–like an actor switching from role to role." This assessment of diversity and its significance becomes even more important and evident in the books that Lobel illustrated in the 1970s. These works, although they contain nearly the same range as those done earlier, show a definite shift in concentration. Lobel illustrated only two I Can Read books during this period, but he provided illustrations for several books of poems, including Edward Lear's *The New Vestments* (1970), Jack Prelutsky's *Nightmares: Poems to Trouble Your Sleep* (1976), and a collection of Mother Goose rhymes, *Gregory Griggs and Other Nursery Rhyme People* (1978). In addition,

Cover for Lobel's 1968 imaginary tale about the creation of color (Harper & Row)

Lobel drew the scenes for three folktales while he continued to illustrate animal fantasies and realistic fiction.

Such a diversity of texts requires a variety of styles, and illustrations such as those for Jean Van Leeuwen's *Tales of Oliver Pig* (1979), Prelutsky's *Circus* (1974), and Sulamith Ish-Kishor's *The Master of Miracles* (1971) reflect Lobel's differing techniques. For Van Leeuwen's five stories Lobel chose soft pastel colors, outlined details in pen and ink, and bordered every illustration to reflect the warm, secure world of Oliver Pig. In *Circus,* bright colors and a great deal of movement and detail visually capture Prelutsky's poem on circus performers, and in *The Master of Miracles* dark lines embody the sadness, mystery, and awe surrounding this tale of the man who lets the fabled Golem live when it should have been returned to clay.

The response of librarians and teachers, reviewers and readers to Lobel's work during the 1970s was very complimentary as evidenced by the many awards and honors that he received. In 1972 Cheli Durán Ryan's *Hildilid's Night*

(1971)–one of Lobel's own favorite stories–was named a Caldecott Honor Book. That story, along with two others illustrated by Lobel, Robert A. Morris's *Seahorse* (1972) and Norma Farber's *As I Was Crossing Boston Common* (1973), was also included in the Children's Book Showcase for 1972 and 1973. Later in the 1970s two more works illustrated by Lobel, Anne K. Rose's *As Right As Right Can Be* (1976) and *Merry Merry FIBruary* by Doris Orgel (1977), were chosen by the *New York Times* to be among the best illustrated children's books of the year. These honors and others reflect Lobel's constant growth as an artist.

Critical recognition was extended to Lobel's own stories as well. *Frog and Toad are Friends* (1970), for instance, was named a Caldecott Honor Book in 1971. This third I Can Read book by Lobel includes five stories about its two main characters and their deep friendship. Although Toad is easily fooled, fretful, or overly shy at times, he cares deeply for his friend Frog, who in turn is supportive and loving. Lobel's simple theme–the value of friendship–is ably expressed through the warmth and humor of each story. In "The Letter," for example, Frog finds out that Toad sadly waits for the mailman every day, hoping for a letter which never comes, and so Frog writes him a note, thanking Toad for being his best friend. The friendship between the two is evident, and the humor of the story appears when Frog rushes back to Toad and they wait four days for a snail to deliver the letter. The book's illustrations, done in shades of brown, green, and gray with details outlined in pen and ink, nicely suit the earthbound world of Frog and Toad, while the animals' expressive faces truly reflect Lobel's stories of friendship.

With his next two books, both published in 1971, Lobel returned to poetry, a genre that he had first used in *Martha, the Movie Mouse*. While his verse is rather strained in that poem, those included in *The Ice-Cream Cone Coot and Other Rare Birds* (1971) and the narrative verse of *On the Day Peter Stuyvesant Sailed into Town* (1971) flow smoothly. The comical verses of *The Ice-Cream Cone Coot* are especially imaginative as Lobel tells of various inanimate objects transformed into birds. There are the Buttonbeaks which button up the front of a shirt, the Milkbottle Midge which contains milk, the Key Cranes which fly overhead looking for locked doors, and other birds that animate salt shakers, brooms, gloves, and pencils. Helping to suspend disbelief, Lobel's

drawings of these strange creatures contain just enough detail to make their imaginary natures real.

Included in the Children's Book Showcase for 1971 and given the Christopher Award for that year, Lobel's poem on Peter Stuyvesant has a slightly different tone. While still humorous, it relates the historically documented transformation of New Amsterdam from a dirty, garbage-filled, unkempt village to a clean, well-planned town through the leadership of Governor Stuyvesant. Both literary and visual devices emphasize the before and after state of this Dutch village and the strength of the man who changed it. The repetition of key lines, for instance, underscores Stuyvesant's disgust and dismay as well as the force of his proclamation:

> All you men and you maids, get your brooms and
> your spades.
> We must work now without hesitation!
> Yes, Let's work now without hesitation!.

Visually, Lobel's bordering of almost every page of text and illustration also conveys the order that Stuyvesant brings with him, and the book's three double-spread illustrations dramatically present New Amsterdam as it is when he arrives, the village after its changes, and in a dream that Stuyvesant has, its growth into New York City.

Praised by Evelyn Stewart in the 15 May 1972 *Library Journal* as "a masterpiece of child-styled humor and sensitivity" and named a Newbery Honor Book for 1973, Lobel's next work, *Frog and Toad Together* (1972), continues the story of the two friends. The five stories of this text, however, are even more perceptive than those in the first Frog and Toad book. Human tendencies to follow lists and the schedules they define, to give in to temptation, to feel brave and afraid at the same time, and to elevate oneself at the expense of diminishing another are the focus of four of the stories. In the third tale Frog and Toad test their will power on a freshly made batch of delicious cookies. While Frog overcomes his desire to eat every single one, the more realistic Toad exclaims that Frog can keep his will power as he goes home to bake a cake. Actually, even Frog's character is not strong enough to resist temptation since he has to remove it by throwing the cookies to the birds.

The last story in the collection, "The Dream," is equally insightful. By dreaming of surpassing Frog in his newfound role as the great

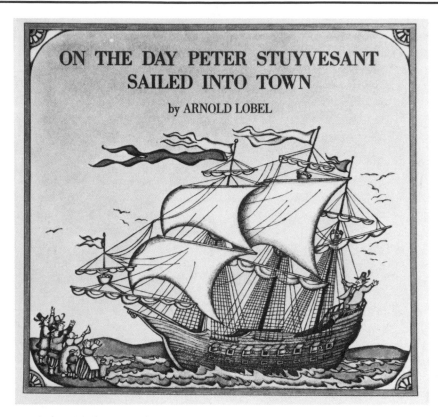

Dust jacket for Lobel's 1971 book. Though humorous in tone, the book provides a historically documented account of New Amsterdam's progress under the leadership of Peter Stuyvesant (Harper & Row).

Toad, Toad reveals how inferior he feels. Yet every time the dream elevates Toad, Frog decreases in size until he can hardly be seen. When Toad realizes that Frog might be lost, he rejects his wish to be the best and so regains Frog's friendship. For Toad a best friend, not achievement or fame, comprises the enduring quality of life. Lobel's second Frog and Toad book, then, affirms the central concern of the first one—friendship.

Unlike *Frog and Toad are Friends* or *Frog and Toad Together*, the stories in Lobel's fifth I Can Read book, *Mouse Tales* (1972), contain neither a common theme nor characters. Instead, each of the separate tales is told by a father mouse to his seven sons as bedtime stories. Appropriately enough, the book concludes with the father saying good night to his sleeping children and then joining his wife for a cup of tea. Within this unifying frame, the stories range from a little girl mouse being granted wishes by a magic well and a little boy mouse whose imagination sees a fierce cat in the clouds to a very dirty mouse who lets the whole town flood as he takes a bath.

Lobel visually separates these seven bedtime stories from the unifying tale of the father

mouse and his children by bordering each page of the stories but leaving unbordered the pages of narrative frame. Thus, the borders distinguish one fiction from another. Contemporary reactions to these stories-within-a-story were very favorable. Carol Chatfield, in the 15 December 1972 *Library Journal*, praised the work's "good humor and sense of the ridiculous," and the December 1972 *Horn Book* reviewer concluded with a very positive evaluation of the illustrations: "Scattered through most of the cream-colored pages are small drawings in pastel tones of gray, brown, yellow, and magenta; and the joy of looking at the mice and their adventures equals the joy of reading about them." In 1973 the book received the Irma Simonton Black Award given by the Bank Street College of Education.

Told in rhyming verse, Lobel's third narrative poem, *The Man Who Took the Indoors Out* (1974), is another highly imaginative story of a man who invites all of his indoor things outside but finds them behaving uncontrollably as they head toward the village and then out to sea. Bellwood Bouse searches for his furniture, his kitchen utensils, and appliances in vain and spends the next year without his "Indoors."

Then one winter morning all of his possessions return, and in celebration he dances with his white wicker rocker, the only piece of outside furniture.

Although described by Judith S. Kronick in *Library Journal* (15 October 1974) as "an amusing though pointless fantasy," Lobel's tale has a very strong point, for Bellwood Bouse, by resolving, "I will not let my Indoors / Run loose anymore," has learned that there is a sense of order which must be followed. Certainly, the illustrations themselves are structured through Lobel's use of borders around each picture. Included in the Children's Book Showcase and selected as one of the best illustrated books of 1974 by the *New York Times*, this work continues to show the more absurd side of Lobel's humor.

A gentler humor pervades Lobel's next two picture books, both in the I Can Read series. *Owl at Home* (1975) follows the precedent set in *Frog and Toad are Friends* as five stories are told about a central character, an owl. Much of the humor in this book springs from his personality. The owl is anything but wise as he invites Winter inside his house as a guest, is scared of the bumps his own feet make in bed, tries to be both upstairs and downstairs at the same time, and believes the inanimate moon to be his friend, but for all this, he is ultimately appealing.

Perhaps the strangest story in the collection, "Tear-Water Tea," suggests that a periodic catharsis of the soul is needed as Owl, determined to make some tear-water tea, thinks of life's sad things—broken-legged chairs, unsung songs because of forgotten words, unfound spoons behind stoves—and cries into his kettle. When the kettle is full he stops crying, heats the water, and drinks his tear-water tea as if to say that sadness nourishes as well as depletes.

In *Frog and Toad All Year* (1976), winner of the Christopher Award, humor also predominates as the two friends sled together, wait out a spring rain by Frog telling a story, eat ice cream cones under a tree, rake autumn leaves, and share Christmas Eve together. The winter-to-winter progression of the stories emphasizes the permanence of the two characters' friendship while the contents of the last three tales especially show its depth. In "Christmas Eve," for example, Toad worries that something has happened to Frog when he does not come to dinner on time. His imagination envisions his friend at the bottom of a deep hole, lost in the woods, or chased by a huge animal, and so Toad rushes out the door with a rope, lantern, and frying pan

to handle each danger. Much to his surprise, he meets Frog, late because of wrapping Toad's present, and the two sit down to eat and to enjoy Toad's new gift, a clock to keep proper time so that Toad will not have to worry so much.

Both *Owl at Home* and this third book of Lobel's Frog and Toad series reflect a similarity of visual techniques. Lobel uses very expressive faces; limited, highly appropriate colors with details and outlines done in pen and ink; and a mixture of bordered and unbordered illustrations to ably complement and embody his stories.

Lobel once explained that he and his wife hesitated to collaborate because their styles were "very dissimilar." However, Lobel was only thinking of their visual styles, and as his written work became stronger, it was perhaps inevitable that he would one day create a story in words for Anita Lobel to illustrate. Reminiscent of a folktale in its use of a trickster character and cumulative plot, their first collaboration, *How the Rooster Saved the Day*, was published in 1977.

Lobel's story tells of a thief who plans to cause eternal night by killing the rooster who crows up the sun each day. Under the cover of this lasting night the robber intends to rob and plunder. However, the wise rooster, in the tradition of Chanticleer, pretends to be deaf and unable to hear the robber's plans. The thief laughs when the rooster explains that his deafness was caused by quacking, barking, oinking, and mooing, and then he tries to show the rooster the noise that really should be made. But, as the robber loudly crows cock-a-doodle-doo, he calls forth the day himself and ruins his own plans. *How the Rooster Saved the Day* was lauded by Dana Pinizzotto, writing for *School Library Journal* (April 1977), as "a first-rate, first-time collaboration from the Lobels" while the reviewer for *Horn Book* (June 1977) complimented its "enchanting blend of two individual yet compatible talents in a handsome entity."

In two works which follow this collaboration—*Mouse Soup* (1977) and *Grasshopper on the Road* (1978)—Lobel returns to a now-familiar format for his I Can Read books: a number of stories revolving around one or two animal characters. *Mouse Soup* also shares a similar structure and visual technique with one of Lobel's earlier books, *Mouse Tales*. In each work one story is used to unify several unrelated ones; in *Mouse Soup* that relationship is especially tightly woven. Following the tradition of the Arabian Nights and Scheherazade's dire need to weave stories, Lobel

Arnold and Anita Lobel (photo by Ian Anderson)

Dust jacket for Arnold and Anita Lobel's 1981 alphabet book (Greenwillow)

depicts the protagonist of *Mouse Soup* caught by a weasel. The mouse, knowing that he will be the main ingredient in the weasel's soup, stalls for time by telling four stories which he claims will make the soup taste even better. Characterized by humor, these four tales are visually set off from the main story through the use of borders, the same technique that Lobel had used in *Mouse Tales*.

After the stories are told (of a mouse who tricks the bees who are nesting on his head, of two rocks who yearn to see the other side of the hill, of a girl mouse who needs quiet instead of cricket songs, and of an old lady mouse who is grieving over the dying thornbush that had been growing from her sofa), the next part of the mouse's plan unfolds. He tells the weasel that the soup now needs animals and objects that represent each of the stories, and so the weasel is finally tricked. While he goes off to find bees, mud, rocks, crickets, and a thornbush, the mouse follows only long enough to see the weasel stung, dirtied, tired, and pricked and then runs home to eat supper and read before bedtime. Clearly this conflict between a small mouse and a large weasel not only results in an interesting story but strongly emphasizes the importance of the four tales that are told.

Evaluated by David Winder in the *Christian Science Monitor* (23 October 1978) as "a worthy successor to the popular 'Frog and Toad' volume," *Grasshopper on the Road* is a criticism of contempo-

rary society. The reader readily identifies with the main character–the grasshopper–who enjoys the world around him and its many changes. Through his eyes the reader sees the various animals that he meets and perceives in most of them an obsessive allegiance to statistics. There are the beetles who only love the morning, the housefly who wants to sweep up every speck of dust, the mosquito who has to obey the rules concerning his ferry, and the three butterflies who do the same thing the same way every day. The last insects that Grasshopper encounters on his journey down the road, the dragonflies, are an emblem of those who are too busy to really appreciate life, for the dipping, diving, and zooming that the dragonflies do preclude the "time to look at sunsets and mountains." Lobel's book, then, satirizes those who live in too narrow a world.

In an interview conducted for *Publishers' Weekly* in 1971, Lobel distinguished between the roles of an author and an illustrator in the creation of a picture book: "A good writer of picture books will not overstep his area, he will know how to underwrite. Bad writers will start doing the artist's work for him–they will describe visually what should not be described at all." Certainly, Lobel followed this conviction in the first work that he and his wife collaborated on, and in their second one, *A Treeful of Pigs* (1979), his mode of underwriting is even more evident.

In the tradition of a droll, cumulative folktale, Lobel's text focuses on a lazy farmer and his hardworking wife. The farmer agrees to help her raise pigs when the animals are still unbought, but when the piglets are actually on the farm, he makes up a number of impossible conditions under which he will help her one day. He promises to help her plant corn, for example, when the "pigs bloom in the garden like flowers," to dig a mud hole when the "pigs grow in the trees like apples," to carry buckets of water when the "pigs fall out of the sky like rain," and to harvest the corn when "those pigs would disappear like the snow in the spring." Much to his amazement, each of these events happens, but he still refuses to help until all the pigs disappear. Then he wants his wife's help, but she wisely refuses, saying that she will help when he promises "never to be lazy again." Under this condition he promises, she releases the penned-in pigs, and they all rejoice with a corn-on-the-cob supper. While Lobel's story presents the main events of the plot, Anita Lobel's illustrations further endow it with humor as she reveals that the one responsible for the pigs blooming in the garden, growing on the apple tree, falling from the sky, and disappearing like the snow is the farmer's wife. Thus, the illustrations truly integrate, as well as depict, the plot.

Lobel had begun the 1970s with the publication of the first Frog and Toad book and appropriately ended the decade with another work in this highly popular series. Published in 1979, *Days with Frog and Toad* continues the excellent blend of humor and warmth, companionship and friendship that permeated the earlier stories of the series. In the first four stories of this work, Toad promptly cleans his house early so that he can rest later, the two friends successfully fly a kite, Frog tells a scary story causing both himself and Toad to shiver, and Toad's birthday gift–a hat–is reduced in size so that he can wear it. The fifth story concludes the book with another strong affirmation of friendship as Toad, thinking that Frog's sudden absence means that he does not want him as a best friend anymore, is reassured when Frog exclaims that he just wanted to be alone "to think about how fine everything is," especially his friendship with Toad.

In the 1980s Lobel continues to illustrate,

Dust jacket for Lobel's 1983 book of limericks and nursery rhymes (Harper & Row)

write, and collaborate on children's books. As an artist, his illustrations for Jack Prelutsky's *The Headless Horseman Rides Tonight: More Poems to Trouble Your Sleep* (1980) and Carol Chapman's *The Tale of Meshka the Kvetch* (1980) are ably suited to each text. The combination of both his dark drawings and Prelutsky's macabre poems "elicit feelings of exquisite terror" according to an August 1980 *Horn Book* review, while the simpler drawings of Meshka, her difficulties, and her character change reflect Chapman's droll story of a woman who is really afflicted by all she complains of. His illustrations for *The Random House Book of Poetry for Children* (1983) capture in full-color illustrations the essence of Jack Prelutsky's selection of poetry from poets representing many periods. A January-February 1985 *Horn Book* reviewer noted the special quality of Lobel's illustrations for Maxine Kumin's *The Microscope* (1968), which includes "humorous parodies of the Dutch painters of Leeuwenhoek's era. But only Arnold Lobel would deflate the brooding passion of the stormy sea by including a sign-bearing fish."

Lobel's inventiveness as author-illustrator is evident in *Fables* (1980), a collection of wholly modern fables with animal characters and morals.

Lobel had been encouraged to do an adaptation of Aesop's tales by Harper and Row but, finding them too "didactic and dry," turned to his favorite animals instead, letting their characteristics suggest new stories. These fables, like Aesop's, show both the virtues and faults of society in their accounts of a camel who keeps on dancing not because she is good but because she enjoys ballet; of a mouse who undergoes many hardships to reach his goal–the sight of the sea; and of a hippopotamus who eats so much that he cannot physically leave the table. For these fables and seventeen others, Lobel chose a double-line border around each page of text and illustration and a third border around each individual picture as well. The drawings, done in a full range of colors, were praised in *Newsweek* (18 August 1980) by Annalyn Swan "as witty and homey as the tales themselves," and the book was honored with the Caldecott Medal in 1981. Lobel's humorous animals and his joy of rhyme combined in two books that provide an exciting approach to poetry for children. *The Book of Pigericks* (1983) and *Whiskers and Rhymes* (1985) include original limericks and nursery rhymes on well-designed pages that capture the visual and aural attention of young readers.

On Market Street (1981), illustrated by Anita Lobel, is an alphabet book. Its poetic text, describing the various presents that a little boy buys on Market Street for a good friend, his cat, embodies all of the elements of warmth, caring, and love that make so many of Lobel's books appealing. While Lobel's text quietly presents the story, his wife's illustrations vividly focus on the apples, books, clocks, and doughnuts that each respective merchant is selling. Furthermore, one of the book's closing pictures depicts the boy's cat surrounded by presents, a highly unifying illustration, for Lobel's verse had not named the friend for whom the gifts were intended. *The Rose in My Garden* (1984) represents an equally successful collaboration with his wife that results in a stunning horticultural excursion.

In Lobel's creation of either a story or an illustration, he constantly revises and deletes so that only those words or lines that truly fit are retained. As an illustrator, this means placing layers of tracing paper over various sketches and only redrawing those lines that he really likes–an enjoyable process that comes easily. But in the "unwriting" that Lobel does with his stories, the decisions over which word to choose or cross out weigh heavily.

Despite this difficulty, however, Lobel's works testify to his excellence as both a writer and artist. Undoubtedly, their qualities of warmth and humor, affirmation and truth greatly contribute to this excellence, but one more element adds to this spirit–a capacity and necessity for growth reflected most clearly in Lobel's attitude toward future books. For him, the work that is not yet conceived or visualized offers the most challenge and excitement, for his "favorite is always the next one, the one I haven't done yet. I like to think that's because I'm still growing."

Interviews:

"Arnold Lobel . . . the natural illustrator . . . the entertainer," *Early Years*, 11 (November 1980): 34-35, 103;

"Authors and Editors," *Publishers' Weekly*, 199 (17 May 1971): 11-13.

David Macaulay

(2 December 1945-   )

Nellvena Duncan Eutsler

BOOKS: *Cathedral: The Story of Its Construction* (Boston: Houghton Mifflin, 1973);
City: A Story of Roman Planning and Construction (Boston: Houghton Mifflin, 1974);
Pyramid (Boston: Houghton Mifflin, 1975);
Underground (Boston: Houghton Mifflin, 1976);
Castle (Boston: Houghton Mifflin, 1977);
Great Moments in Architecture (Boston: Houghton Mifflin, 1978);
Motel of the Mysteries (Boston: Houghton Mifflin, 1979);
Unbuilding (Boston: Houghton Mifflin, 1980);
Electricity, edited by Bill Sims (Knoxville, Tenn.: Tennessee Valley Authority, 1983);
Mill (Boston: Houghton Mifflin, 1983);
Baaa (Boston: Houghton Mifflin, 1985).

BOOKS ILLUSTRATED: David Lord Porter, *Help! Let Me Out!* (Boston: Houghton Mifflin, 1982);
Robert Ornstein and Richard F. Thompson, *The Amazing Brain* (Boston: Houghton Mifflin, 1984).

David Macaulay was born in Burton-on-Trent, Lancashire, England, on 2 December 1945, son of James and Joan Lowe Macaulay. His books provide an excellent example of the fact that childhood experiences, interests, memories, and associations come to the surface in adult years and have a significant impact upon creative performance. His father, an industrial engineer, introduced him at an early age to simple technology–how to construct and make things work. When Macaulay was eleven he moved to the United States with his parents but did not leave his love for England behind. He still retains his British citizenship and collects memorabilia of his life there, such as a miniature coronation set complete with golden carriage and royal band on horseback. His cherished memories and experiences surface by way of the imagination in his books.

Macaulay's academic background includes a

David Macaulay (photo by Jim Kalett)

bachelor's degree in architecture from the Rhode Island School of Design and a year of study in the European Honors Programs in Rome, Herculaneum, and Pompeii. He acknowledges a respect for the works of Giambattista Piranisi, Milton Glaser, and Maurice Sendak. He thoroughly researches all of his projects, travels to the site, takes numerous photographs, and literally walks the land; thereby lending authenticity to the finished product. Marc Treib in *Print* magazine calls Macaulay's process the "archeological method."

The recognition and list of awards he has received are impressive. His first book, *Cathedral: The Story of Its Construction* (1973), received a Caldecott Honor Medal and the German Jugend-

177

buchpreis and the Dutch Silver Slate Pencil Award. It appeared on the ALA, the *New York Times*, and the *School Library Journal* best books of the year lists, and on the *New York Times* Best Illustrated Children's Books of the Year list. It was a runner-up for the *Boston Globe-Horn Book* Award and was a *Horn Book* "Fanfare" book. *City: A Story of Roman Planning and Construction* (1974) was included on the ALA, the *New York Times*, and the *School Library Journal* lists for best books of the year, and was also a *Horn Book* "Fanfare" book. *Pyramid* (1975) received the Christopher Award and the New York Academy of Sciences Children's Science Book Award. It was also listed by the ALA, the *New York Times*, and the *School Library Journal* on their best books of the year lists. *Underground* (1976) was also an ALA Notable Book and was listed by both the *New York Times* and the *School Library Journal* on their best books of the year lists and was a *Horn Book* "Fanfare" book. *Castle* (1977) was a Caldecott Honor Book, and ALA and *School Library Journal* listed it on their best books of the year lists. It was a *Horn Book* "Fanfare" book. The New York Academy of Sciences gave it Honorable Mention. *Unbuilding* (1980) was included on both best illustrated and best books of the year lists by the *New York Times*. The *School Library Journal* listed it as one of the best books of the year, and *Horn Book* cited it as a "Fanfare" book. David Macaulay has been awarded the Washington Children's Book Guild Nonfiction Award, and in 1977 the American Institute of Architects presented him with their medal for his contribution as "an outstanding illustrator and recorder of architectural accomplishment."

Macaulay's output during the past thirteen years certainly represents unremitting activity. Though research and layout take the most time, Richard Ammon has reported that Macaulay executes "the final drawings with lightning speed." Geoffrey House explains that for Macaulay "writing is laborious" and the "drawing of each line of detail is the most tedious part of composing a book" because each strand of hair, each brick, and each stone must be carefully drawn. Whether Macaulay finds the drawing process tedious or sketches with felicity, he accomplishes a great deal. In drawing, Macaulay has a definite purpose in mind: "to illustrate the way these large structures came to be built and to give some insight into actual problems of early technology, materials and tools."

Cathedral (1973), Macaulay's first book, developed from his interest in gargoyles. Macaulay's concerns in this book, as evidenced in the text, are numerous–the culture of thirteenth-century France, the process of governing, the geography and landscape, religion, architecture, death, burial, and the process of building. The reason for the building of the cathedral reflects one aspect of man's nature, his pride, his drive "not to be outdone!" Giving thanks to God, the people of Chutreaux, Macaulay's imaginary city, wish to build the "longest, widest, highest, and most beautiful cathedral in all of France." Although this temple of worship is built for the glory of God, man, as is typical, is building the edifice for his own honor and glory.

The monumental task begins in 1252, and the reader sees the passage of time not only in the construction of the cathedral but in the change of roofing material on the houses which surround the building site. At one point Macaulay calls attention to the cathedral roof which is begun in 1275. Therefore, it is natural to look at the roofs of surrounding houses. In the year 1270 all houses are thatched. By 1275, it is vaguely suggested, there is the beginning of change in a few houses, which by 1280 is made apparent by the growing number of slate roofs. By the year 1302, many more houses have the slate roofs and by 1306 they nearly predominate. By 1338, when the cathedral is completed, the houses visible both within and without the city wall have been reroofed.

The information in *Cathedral,* as in all of Macaulay's books, is given with clarity and directness. The professionals in charge are introduced. The money is in the hands of the clergy; the Flemish architect, with his knowledge of architecture and engineering, is in charge of design and supervision, and he directs the master craftsmen. Each craftsman is introduced and pictured, and the tools of each trade are pictured and explained. The floor plan is given and a wall elevation illustrates the elaborate design.

The first double spread of the book introduces a whimsical scene with two ducks swimming in a stream and a fox jumping a riverlet. In *Cathedral* the people and the workers have very little identity; the focus is on the building, and the workers are dwarfed by all of the activity. The only names given are for those figures which are drawn larger than life: the bishop, the clergymen, and the architect.

However, Macaulay does portray village life, depicting a sleeping cat, oblivious of the nearby mouse, and children at play with their dogs while

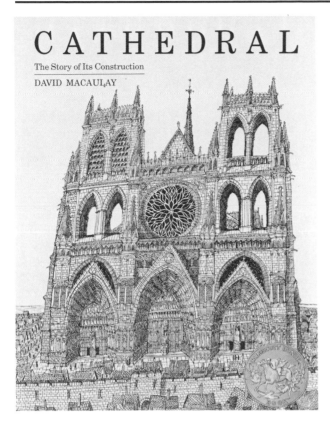

Dust jacket for Macaulay's first book, which describes the building of a medieval French cathedral (Houghton Mifflin)

others are swimming nearby. The workers are shown in a relaxed moment drinking their mead while watching a few performers. There is little indication, because of the length of the project, that seasons are passing, but one spring birds hatch their eggs. In the year 1302 May Day is celebrated with a fair and the traditional dancing around the Maypole.

Each activity of preparation for building the cathedral is carefully delineated. The trees are felled, the stones quarried, the site cleared. Foundations are dug; materials are assembled; mortar is mixed; foundations are completed; stone is set on stone for the walls. The architect grows old and is replaced; the bishop dies, is buried. Roofers, stonecutters, and sculptors are introduced. Devices such as the great wheel and the windlass are employed and explained. Carpenters begin the finishing; glassmakers make the stained glass for the windows. The bells are cast and the lost wax process is explained. Decorations and sculpture are added, and finally, after eighty-six years have passed, "the people of Chutreaux have built their cathedral and offer it to God." The presentation of the text is simple and straightforward; the

book's outstanding feature is the stunning perspective and imaginative views of the building.

City (1974) follows the format of *Cathedral;* however, the text is more elaborate. The time frame for *City* is between 300 B.C. and A.D. 150. Cities were then "designed and built to serve the needs of all the people," for "the Romans knew that well planned cities did more to maintain peace and security than twice the number of military camps." They also knew that a city had to be "a place where people wanted to live." Planners were well aware of the importance of water supply, sewage, traffic systems, and the dangers of overpopulation. But all of their motives were not entirely pure. During the building of the city, certain wealthy "Verbonians" insured their own niches "in some prominent place."

Plans for this imaginary Roman city, Verbonia, were started in 26 B.C. The specialists involved are military engineers, including planners, and the city is planned to provide for both the sacred and secular aspects of its citizens' lives. The environment is then explored; customs are explained; rites are observed. Terms unfamiliar to most readers are always carefully explained and pictures detail specific information.

The tools used are all enumerated, described, and pictured, and their functions are explained. Materials (stone, clay, mortar, wood) are listed and their sources identified. Shops are built, laborers are enlisted. Roads and bridges are built. Walls rise and an aqueduct is built. The city takes shape.

The reader is told that "to maintain as high a level of work as possible the laborers were treated almost as well as the soldiers." To prove this point Macaulay even provides a picture of these laborers showing them all in a pleasant mood, with smiles carefully drawn on every face. Not only are the workers happy, the Roman soldiers observing their period of relaxation are happy too. Macaulay's figures do not leap, soar, or bound about the page. They have little animation but suit the purpose for which they are used.

Process is important in building this city, but people are important, too, because the city is "designed and built to serve the needs of all the people who lived within." After three years of construction families move to the city, and Macaulay portrays the activities of daily life. Apartments and homes have been built; businesses have been established. Daily life is reflected as citizens meet by the neighborhood well. Children play; water is drawn for the laundry. An intimate picture of their life is revealed as the citizens recline for their meals and relax in the atrium. Their most personal requirements are met as well. Toilets are pictured and the operation of the sewage disposal is explained.

The baker, the olive oil merchant, and the goldsmith are introduced. The barber's role is defined as the purveyor of news. For the spreading of the news "barbers were almost as important as the government decrees read in the forum, and they were definitely faster." By A.D. 14 the city is thriving. Grocery shops, pastry shops, furniture shops, clothing shops, drugstores, wine shops, snack bars all cater to the needs of the people.

Next, the forum is built and the temples to Jupiter, Juno, and Minerva rise. Government is formed; senators are elected. The Court of Justice is established and offices and schools are provided. A large triumphal arch is constructed to the glory of the emperor. Public baths, complete with steam rooms, swimming pool, and an exercise room serve the people, and an amphitheater is built for entertainment activities. All of life's needs are satisfied, and by A.D. 100 Verbonia has reached its optimal size. Everything is still in working order, having been maintained through the years.

Those who have assumed that technology is a modern phenomenon need only to read *City* to explore a lesson in efficiency in city planning in Roma at the dawn of the Christian era. Roger Downey declares that *City* is "not just a tribute to the efficiency and common-sense of Roman planning but also an appeal to modern city planners to relearn the forgotten lessons of the past."

For *Pyramid* (1975) Macaulay traveled to Egypt. He rode on a camel, scaled the Great Pyramid, and shot eighteen rolls of film. The book opens in the year 2470 B.C. as the new pharaoh begins his reign, and, as is the custom, he prepares for the end of his life and his burial. Here the preoccupation is with death. Some workers look as if they are barely animated mummies while others look as if they have just stepped off a decorated tomb wall.

In *Pyramid* the reader becomes familiar with the geography of Egypt as it relates to the pyramid, acquires some concept of the culture of the times, and is given an introduction to the concept of the pyramid as the book explains the Egyptian religious belief of life after death. Little of the aspect of government is explored. The major focus is on the architecture of the pyramid as a tomb. The text explains the plans of the funerary complex, gives an overview of the process of building, explains where the laborers come from, and identifies them with their specialized tasks. Macaulay also pictures and labels the tools used.

Land is cleared and the project begun. Several thousand men are assembled: stonecutters, masons, surveyors, mortar makers, carpenters, and general laborers. During flood time over 50,000 workers, mostly farmers, are drafted. Over two million blocks of stone are used to create a man-made mountain to protect the "sacred" body of the pharaoh. Perhaps the greatest understatement in the book is that "each year the villages lost several of their men" during the construction process.

The pharaoh dies in 2439 B.C., thirty-one years after the pyramid was begun. His body is prepared for burial; the tomb is blessed, and he is finally laid to rest, unless his *ka* (spirit) decides to make a nightly journey into another world. The pyramids, as Macaulay notes, "continue to serve as a tribute to those who so skillfully organized the efforts of thousands of people in an attempt to deny the finality of death and the limitations of time by leaving behind something that would last forever." In this story the workers are expendable, but the pharaoh is immortalized.

With *Underground* (1976) Macaulay moves into the twentieth century, where the reader views, at a typical intersection, building foundations and also the constructions that exist underneath streets and sidewalks. Macaulay explores subways, sewers, telephone and power systems, columns, cables, pipes, tunnels, and other underground elements of a large city. His information is accurate, but the method of presentation is idealistic.

A guide for the reader is conveniently supplied early in the book on a double-page spread, and Macaulay next explains and pictures the various types of foundations: the floating foundation, friction piles, bearing piles, and piers. He diagrams a site plan and the soil profile which determines the type of foundation needed. He explains that "the best foundation for a particular building is determined by the weight of the building, the area over which the weight is to be distributed, and the soil conditions." He notes that for most small buildings a spread foundation is used. This process he explains and illustrates, showing the entire process of building a spread foundation.

Then Macaulay tackles the greater job. Through thirty pages he pictures and explains the process for making a floating foundation for

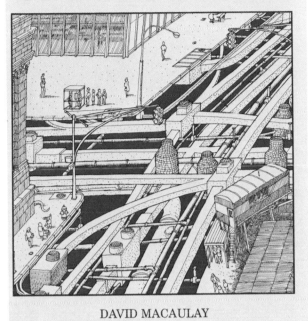

Dust jacket for Macaulay's 1976 book, which details the sub-structure of a modern city block (Houghton Mifflin)

one building, friction piles for a second, bearing piles for a third, and for a fourth, piers. A double spread directs attention to the area beneath the surface of the streets and sidewalks, which is filled with the basic utility systems: water, sewage removal and drainage, electricity, steam, gas, and telephone communications.

Macaulay shows an ideal utility layout, noting that each utility is given a specific location. Again he excavates and exposes and explains the water supply system and pictures a typical water system layout. He follows the flow of water from the pumping station, explains the matter of pressure, the materials of the pipes, the testing, the valves, and the route of water flow.

He next introduces a typical sewer system layout, the sewer profile, and describes how the sewer pipe is laid. The storm drain system is depicted, as are the electrical system, the steam distribution system, the gas distribution system, and the telephone system. Also the matter of repairing each system is clearly explained. The last section of the book is allotted to the subway transportation system. Macaulay's subway system uses both the "cut and cover" tunnel and the deep bored tunnel. He shows both types, with

tracks, elevators, escalators, and pedestrian cross-over ramps. He also shows the air ventilation systems.

As usual, Macaulay has presented a clear and detailed picture of his material. But the curious and attentive reader will find much humor in details Macaulay has hidden in this maze of pipes and tunnels, and indeed on the open city streets. Dogs and fire hydrants abound, and the reader meets expected critters as well as exotic ones. An archaeologist following these workers around would have a field day.

In writing *Castle* (1977) Macaulay was able to return to his childhood haunts. The setting is Wales, where Macaulay often vacationed with his family when he was a child. The building of this castle and the town which surrounds it is part of a "military program [which] displays both superior strategical skill and the farsightedness required for truly successful conquest." It was built as a "tool of conquest" and as a "defensive structure." The offensive use is evidenced by its "placement along important supply and communication routes and to some extent from [its] intimidating appearance." The town which surrounds the castle, once it is established and prospers "provide[s] a variety of previously unavailable social and economic opportunities." Therefore, the town contributes "to both conquest and peace."

The setting for this project is determined by the monarch of England to fulfill his ambitions for conquering the Welsh. He chooses Kevin le Strange to be Lord of Aberwyvern. Macaulay's imaginary district is a "rich but rebellious area of northwest Wales." The construction of the castle and town must be paid for by Lord Kevin, who collects rent and taxes from his tenant farmers, earns income from his own livestock and produce, or donates personal funds.

James Babbington, the master engineer, designs the project and supervises the work. The specific setting chosen is a high limestone outcrop along the coast. Master James brings with him diggers, carpenters, laborers, and many supplies: timber, tools, and hardware. The castle is designed first and the castle defenses are outlined and explained. A plan for Aberwyvern, the town, is given. Living quarters for the men are built and workshops erected. A birds-eye view of the area is shown and a plan for the castle is laid out. The workers: quarrymen, blacksmiths, mortar makers and carriers, masons, carpenters, diggers, and even Master James's dog are pictured. Also, the full complement of tools is shown.

On 8 June 1283 Master James and the surveyors mark off the location of all the main walls and towers. The masons build the castle and town walls as Macaulay carefully pictures and describes each step. Seasons change, winter comes, and work is temporarily halted. In the spring work is resumed. The reader understands the reasons for the minutest details of merlins, battlements, arrow loops, each strategy of defense provided for the castle.

By spring 1284 several towers and much wall have been built. By October 1285 the outer curtain is almost finished and much of the inner curtain. This castle is complete with basements for food storage, dungeons, garderobes, cesspits, and a magnificent chapel and gatehouses.

By 1286 the town wall is finished. The town grows and boasts a master shoemaker and master tailor. Workroom and workshops teem with activity. After the town becomes a parish and has a priest assigned, a church is built. In 1287 the gatehouses are complete, and Macaulay provides a double-spread view of an almost finished castle complete with battlements.

Permanent quarters to house the garrison are then built, and the reader is provided with illustrations of their defensive weapons: the lance, sword, dagger, crossbow, longbow and arrow, mace, shield, and battle ax. Last, the great hall and kitchen are completed. Attention is turned to the "finer" aspects of life. The arrival of Lady Catherine and her attendants is anticipated. The staff consists of Walter, the bailiff, Robert, the chaplain, and Lionel, the barber and doctor. Quarters are provided for the servants, laborers, and general storage. Kennels are built for the dogs and a mew for the hunting birds. A lawn and garden for flowers and herbs are also prepared. In April 1288 Lady Catherine arrives with her ladies-in-waiting, children, and servants.

In 1290 Aberwyvern is given a charter. It is not until 1294 that King Edward visits, and a banquet and entertainment are prepared. He has come to give warning of the unrest that prevails. It is at this point that preparations are made for defense of the stronghold. However, it is not until 1295 that the defenses are put to the test. As the battle is mounted, the reader is shown the offensive weapons used by the assailants: catapults, battering rams, siege towers, and a sapper's tent used as a protective cover while attempting to undermine the wall.

The castle and its battlements prove worthy of defense against the onslaught. But the "conquest" of Wales is effected only after 200 years when the town built in conjunction with the castle integrates the intruders with the local inhabitants. *Castle* is filled with lore of the period, which is deftly integrated through Macaulay's words and illustrations.

During 1978 and 1979 Macaulay was involved with the publication of *Great Moments in Architecture* (1978) and *Motel of the Mysteries* (1979). *Great Moments in Architecture*, as K. Greenland Barry writes in an amusing preface, is "the generally misunderstood and frequently misrepresented drawings of the distinguished twentieth-century draftsman and amateur historian David Macaulay. Although the works of this hitherto neglected artist crystallize the formal and intellectual preoccupations of generations of quintessentially disillusioned visionaries, many of the plates have lain untouched for years. Those that surfaced periodically were more often than not the victims of a misguided aestheticism." *Motel of the Mysteries* is set 3,000 years in the future. According to Marc Treib it is a "minor parable of our 'modern' society and built environment." He says, "This book is no doubt Macaulay's tongue-in-cheek nose-thumbing at all [the] archeological noise surrounding the 'King Tut madness.' " Junior high school students find the book very appealing and entertaining. It fits in well with their comic book preoccupation.

Unbuilding (1980), Macaulay's eighth book, is one of demolition rather than of construction. The scene shifts to the United States, specifically New York City, in 1989, significantly on April first. Macaulay interviewed demolition firms, asking questions about the "unbuilding" process. For this book he also took many photographs and researched exhaustively.

To set the scene Macaulay provides a brief history of the reasons for building the Empire State Building, the building which is to be dismantled. This building was built between 1929 and 1931. Its great height is accounted for "because [of] the high cost of land and the desire to build as much rentable space as possible," in other words—greed. However, the Empire State Building, Macaulay asserts, is a "masterpiece of organization." It was finished in less than eighteen months.

Macaulay, in a flight of fantasy, decides to symbolically dismantle the building. The book was no doubt influenced by the attention directed in the late 1970s to the problems the United States was having with Arab oil

Dust jacket for Macaulay's 1980 satire about the dismantling of the Empire State Building (Houghton Mifflin)

outlined the rationale for the original construction. Krunchit estimates it will take three years to dismantle, more time than it originally took to build. One hundred twenty workers are hired, such as house wreckers, iron workers, and operating engineers, a scaffolding contractor, electricians and plumbers, as well as teamsters. Derricks and cranes are used, as well as pneumatic demolition hammers, oxypropane torches, bulldozers, air compressors, propane bottles, temporary piping, wrecking bars, and assorted hand tools. These tools are listed and pictured.

A sidewalk shed is built, scaffolding is secured to the buildings, a chute is built to carry off debris. As each piece to be saved is removed, it is carefully numbered to record its position for rebuilding. The television tower is removed first, next the mooring mast. Two derricks are secured to the structural skeleton and material to be salvaged is lowered below. Next two climbing cranes are installed. One is lowered to the roof by helicopter.

Floor by floor the reader is led through the process both through words and graphic illustrations. Every ten days a floor is reduced to rubble and steel. The rubble is taken to a New Jersey landfill and the steel is recycled.

Finally, the pieces to be shipped to the Middle East are loaded aboard the *Desert Queen* which has been docked near 34th Street at a Hudson River pier. At the end of 1992 the site is cleared, and the mooring mast which had already been designated as an historic landmark is rebuilt from the original materials. A basement and subbasement of the building are converted into a midtown gallery for the Metropolitan Museum of Art; trees and shrubs are planted and a new park is created.

In the meantime, the *Desert Queen* sinks and the cargo is lost. Prince Ali resigns himself to his loss. The dismantling of the Empire State Building has been much to do about nothing, but Prince Ali will have an office building—he returns home, planning to submit plans for buying the Chrysler Building. In a closing scene, the reader sees that apparently no one has learned a lesson. The World Trade Center buildings have cranes in place, and the Statue of Liberty is encased in scaffolding.

Macaulay's use of perspective is always stunning. If the page does not have sufficient length for an idea, Macaulay simply turns the book sideways and provides the view on two pages. This is a fascinating book if one has any imagination

consortiums. Macaulay creates the character of Prince Ali Smith of Arabia, buyer of this structure, which he has determined to transport to the Arabian desert to reconstruct for an office building there. The picture Macaulay paints of the Arab is not an attractive one, picturing him as a perpetual student and implying that the Arabs are unable to do anything for themselves but must rely on others, that money is the solution to all problems, that they can never agree among themselves.

This story is also a satire, evident in many ways, the most obvious being the play on words as Macaulay selects names: The Greater Riyadh Institution of Petroleum (GRIP), the conglomerate which purchases the building, and Krunchit and Sons, the demolition concern hired to supervise and carry out the unbuilding. This story, too, could be a reaction to the purchase of London Bridge, which was imported and rebuilt in an American desert.

Carefully Macaulay details not only the demolition process but also gives various reasons for choosing certain procedures. In so doing he has

and wishes to understand that Macaulay is saying more than can be said in words. Roger Downey suggests that it is "not hard to read a serious message between the lines of Macaulay's fantasy: a message about the value of the past to the present, about waste, about the danger of becoming the world's first entirely disposable society."

Electricity (1983) was undertaken at the request of the Tennessee Valley Authority. It tells the story of the production of electricity from "dams to coal plants to nuclear facilities to solar energy." Macaulay has said, "At first I thought I was being asked to do a piece of propaganda, but I was finally persuaded that they really wanted a clear, accurate account of how and why they do what they do." Macaulay is certainly aware of the dangers of this nuclear age: "The technology for producing nuclear energy is fascinating, they really have no idea what to do with the rapidly accumulating amounts of spent fuel. The five hundred thousand years required before the plutonium byproduct of the fission process becomes safe is mindboggling."

Mill (1983), Macaulay's latest architectural book, is his most ambitious book in terms of story line. In it Macaulay explores the cotton mill industry from its inception in the United States in the late eighteenth century through modern times. *Mill* contains not only the plans and construction methods for four textile mills built at twenty-year intervals in Rhode Island, it also explains that "unprecedented period of technological invention known as the Industrial Revolution," particularly that part which involves the mechanization of spinning and weaving represented by the textile industry.

As Macaulay explains in the preface, the Wicksbridge mills are imaginary, but "their planning, construction, and operation are typical of those developed throughout New England during the nineteenth century." He further explains that "each New England mill is an architectural statement of the financial resources and ambitions of its owners. The permanence and often remarkable state of preservation of these mills are a tribute to the ingenuity and hard work of their builders. The number and density of communities that grew up around these mills still recall the lure of financial independence and personal prosperity that these structures once symbolized. In their physical domination of the surrounding landscape, however, many mills continue to remind us that no opportunity comes without a price."

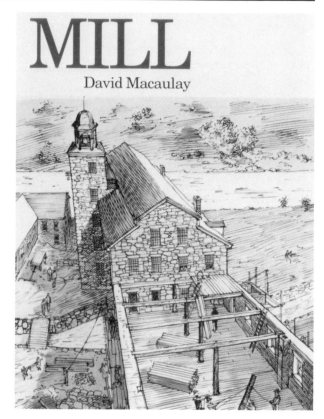

Dust jacket for Macaulay's 1983 book about the building and maintenance of a succession of New England mills (Houghton Mifflin)

In the introduction Macaulay gives historical background for the need for developing cotton mills independent of Europe and especially Great Britain following the American Revolution, and through his story Macaulay shows the growth of this important industry. Before 1790 there were other mills in colonial America, all water powered: saw mills, fulling mills, and grist mills. A few water-powered mills spinning cotton existed after 1790. It was not until 1810 that the first cotton mill was built. The incentive for building cotton mills in America was provided by the embargo prohibiting the importation of any foreign goods, which was in effect in 1807.

As usual, Macaulay selects the site for his building project; an overview of this site is shown on the double-spread title page. The new kind of building designed to accommodate great numbers of new machines is the subject of this book. From the illustrations, the reader has a good sense of place and an intimate look into the lives of real people. This book involves more than the construction process. It becomes an exercise in engineering, with explanations for using river power efficiently.

Since the water wheel is a most important element of a mill, Macaulay first introduces various types of wheels: the flutter wheel, the tub wheel, the undershot wheel, and the overshot wheel. Each wheel uses a wheel pit which is linked to the river by a raceway; the upper portion is the headrace, the lower portion, the tailrace. The saw mill uses both the flutter wheel and a tub wheel. A fulling mill uses an undershot wheel, and the grist mill uses an overshot wheel.

On 27 February 1810 four men form a partnership for building the Yellow Mill. Three of the men provide the backing. Two of the partners provide money for the machinery and the initial supply of cotton. The third partner furnishes materials, workers, and money to build the mill. The fourth member, twenty-seven-year-old Zachariah Plimpton, provides the experience and the expertise. As a fourteen-year-old boy he had been apprenticed for eight years in a mill in England. He was familiar with every area of cotton spinning, weaving, and factory management. He came to America at age twenty-two and for five years had managed a small mill, gaining knowledge and firsthand experience.

On 19 March Plimpton begins the process to select a site, taking into consideration access to a river for power and to a road or canal for transportation. He estimates the river's flow and selects the "highest available head." Next Plimpton designs a wheel which will operate efficiently. He selects the breast wheel and explains the difference between the breast wheel and the overshot wheel, also explaining the variations by which he modifies the breast wheel to a mid-breast wheel. In order to plan the mill and determine the dimensions of the building, he designs the power train, that system of gears, shafts, pulleys, and belts needed to transmit power from the water wheel to the machines. Of major concern is the "placing [of] walls as close as possible [to the machinery] in order to let the most daylight into the work space."

Wood is chosen as the most practical building material. Benjamin Quigg, a millwright, is hired to design the timber frame for the building and supervise the construction. Macaulay provides plans for the power train and a layout of the machinery. Front, side, and rear views of the mill are included. The building is sixty-four feet long and thirty-four feet wide, with two full floors and a usable attic. Plans for the mill are accepted and construction begins.

Nearby saw mills supply the well-seasoned timber for siding, roofing, and flooring. Window frames, glass, nails, tools, and various cast-iron pieces are ordered from Providence, Rhode Island. Additional timber is cut from local trees. A local farmer quarries stone for the foundations and wheel pit from his property. Itinerant laborers help with the project.

The site is cleared and excavation begun for the tailrace. The wheel pit is dug as Macaulay explains and pictures the process. Next, when the river is lowest, a dam is built. The process involves the use of a coffer dam, all clearly pictured and explained. While the dam is being built the headrace is dug and a spillway created.

Posts and beams have been cut and fitted together by a system of tenons and mortices and secured by treenails (wooden dowels). The foundation for the building is capped with sills; floor beams are installed; joists connect the beams and support floor planks. Frames for the building are assembled, and on 31 August all partners assemble. On 1 September the frames are raised and the skeleton for the building is ready for completion. The neighboring farmers have assembled en masse for the "raising" as they recognize that a new market for their agricultural products and various skills has been created. The process for framing the building is delineated, explained, and illustrated.

Plimpton next concentrates on completing the wheel, and the reader learns of the gudgeon, journal bearing, felloe, and spoke, soaling, and bucket falls and understands how the wheel provides the power. Finally the headrace is excavated and lined. Next the power train is constructed and the gears installed.

During the winter months window glass is inserted, cast-iron stoves are installed, and the interior is whitewashed; the building is finished. In March cotton is delivered to nearby farmers who clean it for processing. By April the machinery is installed; the first cotton is carded, and after the fiber is drawn, roved, and spun, it is wound on a bobbin ready for another machine where it is further spun on a throstle before the yarn is tied in bundles ready for the manufacture of cloth. Each process of spinning is illustrated and explained.

The Yellow Mill in full operation, Macaulay turns his attention to a more intimate view in terms of family life and living conditions of the Plimptons and factory workers. Originally Plimpton and his partner Quigg had rented beds from local families during the construction of the mill until Quigg supervises the building of a storage shed, a privy, two wooden houses for mill workers, and a stone cottage for Plimpton. The widow Lucy Tripp arrives with her children. She will take in boarders, and her children will work in the mill. The reader, by way of illustrations, visits both the bedroom and the kitchen of a house. The Sparrows and their three teenaged daughters arrive; they will also take in boarders. Sparrow will run the company store. Next Macaulay explains the wage scale for the workers, including that for child labor.

On 25 June 1811, one year and four months from the beginning of construction, the first sacks of yarn are ready for delivery. As the section for the Yellow Mill closes, the reader is invited to a very intimate picture of Zachariah Plimpton in the form of selected excerpts from his diary. Entries between 4 July 1811 and 6 June 1829 reveal routine problems at the mill, Zach's marriage, the War of 1812, the birth of his five children, the death of one, the building of a meeting house, a new bridge, completion of a new canal, and his purchase of shares in the mill with his father-in-law so together they can own the entire mill complex.

The Plimptons weather the depression of 1829, see opportunity in the market for "Negro cloth," created by the increase of the slave population, and decide to build the Stone Mill which will both spin and weave cloth. Macaulay goes through the same construction process with choosing a new site, and plans are drawn for a larger, more efficient modern plant.

The Stone Mill is added to the complex already begun by the Yellow Mill. The site selected is directly across the river from Yellow Mill. Plimpton also purchases a nearby fulling mill and its water rights. Again the reader sees the planning, design, and construction of a cotton mill, with explanations for changes and refinements, the changes necessitated by the larger project and the rationale for each change, and additionally the reader is introduced to the process of weaving. The use of a power loom introduces new terms: warp and weft, shed, quill, and shuttle.

By October 1832 the community has grown and prospered. Plimpton has started a Sunday school, and we see a young girl and her brother buying "a spelling book, a writing book, and some quills" for schooling. Macaulay again indicates the passage of time as he concludes the Stone Mill section with excerpts from the diaries of Zachariah Plimpton and Ephraim Dodge, the

new manager. The saw mill upstream is purchased by Plimpton and his father-in-law. Ephraim Dodge becomes Plimpton's son-in-law.

In 1837 the market declines, Yellow Mill burns, and new equipment is purchased for Stone Mill. In 1838 son Samuel Plimpton goes west. Zach and his wife move to Providence in their old age. William Plimpton and Dodge become partners, though Dodge dies in a tragic accident in 1842. William, now the sole owner of Stone Mill and other mills in Rhode Island, by this time shares his new wife's abolitionist views and decides to abandon the production of "Negro cloth." He is ready to widen the variety of his product. As he increases the size of Stone Mill, the reader is led through the process of updating the machinery and enlarging the plant with a larger addition.

This time an engineer is hired, and the reader sees the study of a new site and the proposed changes; because of the convenience of the railroad, brick is chosen as the new building material. A new heating system using steam for power replaces the cast-iron stoves. A boiler house is built. The water power system is rebuilt to increase the "head," and the breast wheels are replaced by the more efficient water-powered turbine. The turbine is pictured and its operation explained.

A stone foundation is prepared for the brick walls. A new dam is built. Step by step again the reader sees the new mill built, a power train installed, and the turbine set in place. By mid-September 1853 Plimpton Mill starts producing fine checks, stripes, and plaids. This mill employs twenty-five men, forty-five women, and thirty-five children. The Plimpton Mill has grown with the nation and has changed with the times.

The story of Plimpton Mill ends with personal letters and diary excerpts by Alonzo Humphrey, the new agent. By September 1860 there are rumbles of the Civil War, but the Plimptons, anticipating a shortage, stock up on white cotton (buying four times the usual quantity). Little is recorded during the period of the war, but the years following it are years racked with problems at the mill. In 1870 there is news that Harwood Company will build a new cotton mill. Business is not good for the Plimptons as local competition enters the scene.

The Harwood mill is to be "an absolutely modern cotton mill." This mill, in contrast to the Plimpton Mill with its 1,300 spindles, will have 30,000 spindles and 700 looms and will be run by an enormous steam engine. The site chosen for the new mill is across the river from the Plimpton Mill, with a spur from the main rail providing transportation for coal which will run the engine, transportation for receiving raw cotton and delivering finished fabrics.

Foundation for this mill is granite; the building is brick, with windows of the building spanned by brick arches. Construction was geared so the building would withstand the tremendous vibration of the machinery. Building requirements are altered because of past experiences with construction problems. Insurance companies insist on certain requirements in construction to reduce fire hazard and insist on the installation of a sprinkler system.

Aesthetics are considered when installing a mansard roof and the dormer windows. The reader sees this huge new mill and surrounding complex as they near completion on a double spread. By 1872 the great steam engine is installed; the shafting is put in place and aligned and, due to its self-aligning device, operates quite smoothly. This mill employs one hundred men, two hundred women, and one hundred fifty children over the age of twelve. Most of the workers are emigrants from Canada, and a new Catholic church is built to minister to their spiritual needs.

In *Mill* the reader has scanned through seventy years–from the water wheel to the steam turbine. He has witnessed the hazards of small children working around the machinery and has seen some concern for the welfare of the worker. In addition, he has learned of many changes other than methods of building a mill. Gradually, attracted by low taxes and poor people willing to work for low wages without union protection, the textile industry moved south.

In 1893 the Plimpton Mill burns to the ground, but Harwood survives to the twentieth century. However, the life of it finally "ebbs away." In 1950 Wicksbridge becomes a residential suburb. Between the years 1956 and 1968 the Harwood Mill building becomes a mini-mall. By 1974 the owners have converted it to apartments and condominiums. While laying a sewer line under a parking lot, workmen discover a Roman coin, the one which had been placed there by Zachariah Plimpton in 1810 while he was finishing the wheel pit for the Yellow Mill. The story has come full circle. *Mill* is more than an explication of the design and building of four mills. Macaulay's ultimate purpose in the book is to provide the reader with a view of the life and times

Dust jacket for Macaulay's most recent work, a parable about the last people on earth (Houghton Mifflin)

of a people in a small New England community.

Macaulay has illustrated two works for other authors: David Lord Porter's *Help! Let Me Out!* (1982) and Robert Ornstein and Richard F. Thompson's *The Amazing Brain* (1984). The latter book "takes the reader on a visual and intellectual exploration into the history, evolution, construction, and chemical and electrical operation of the only object we know of that is able to contemplate, study, and describe itself," the brain. The "many drawings by David Macaulay provide both an actual and metaphorical picture of the brain that makes even its most hidden secrets not only comprehensible but filled with beauty as well."

Macaulay's latest work to date is *Baaa* (1985), a story of the last people on earth. Macaulay has said that he is not certain where this idea came from "–a little bit of gloom and doom from news here and there. Maybe it's a personal response to the neutron bomb; I don't know." This small volume is not, as has been reported by Larry McCarthy, "a parable about what happens after people disappear from society and sheep take over and begin acting like their human predecessors"; this story is really about how people have come more and more to act like sheep.

David Macaulay has also been involved in preparing television versions of *Castle, Cathedral,* and *Pyramid.* Both *Castle* and *Cathedral* have been presented on PBS in 1983 and 1986 respectively. Both have been very enthusiastically received. Videotapes of these books were produced by Unicorn, and distribution is handled by PBS video.

Roger Downey has suggested that neither the art nor the words of Macaulay's books have been adequately valued. Downey suggests that there are three reasons for Macaulay's comparative obscurity. First, he is a draftsman; second, his art is not "pure"; and third, since his "art is not merely beautiful but useful–educational, even–so naturally it is relegated to the children's rooms and young-adult sections of libraries and bookstores. . . ." These books, Downey suggests, could be "shelved with the 'how-to' books," and, in fact, Macaulay's books are used in many schools of architecture.

Macaulay's first books may be concerned simply with the process of building and construction, but in his later books he strives to develop meaning and theme. He is interested in more than construction; he is also interested in preservation and education.

References:

Richard Ammon, "Profile of David Macaulay," *Language Arts,* 59 (6 April 1982): 374-378;

Roger Downey, "Of Castles and Other Imaginings," *Northwest Orient* (May 1984): 47-54;

Geoffrey House, "The Work of David Macaulay," *Children's Literature in Education* (Spring 1977): 12-20;

Larry McCarthy, "Bright Lights, Big Season," *Saturday Review* (September-October 1985): 37;

Nancy Shute, "The Scientist's Favorite Cartoonist," *Smithsonian* (April 1984): 113-119;

Marc Treib, "Drawing a Narrative: Fact and Fancy," *Print* (February 1982): 8-18.

James Marshall
(10 October 1942-   )

Hugh T. Keenan
Georgia State University

BOOKS: *George and Martha* (Boston: Houghton Mifflin, 1972; London: Methuen, 1974);

What's the Matter with Carruthers? A Bedtime Story (Boston: Houghton Mifflin, 1972);

George and Martha Encore (Boston: Houghton Mifflin, 1973);

Miss Dog's Christmas Treat (Boston: Houghton Mifflin, 1973);

Yummers! (Boston: Houghton Mifflin, 1973; London: Methuen, 1974);

Willis (Boston: Houghton Mifflin, 1974);

Four Little Troubles—includes *Eugene, Sing Out Irene,* and *Snake* by Marshall and *Someone is Talking About Hortense,* by Laurette Murdock, illustrated by Marshall (Boston: Houghton Mifflin, 1975);

The Guest (Boston: Houghton Mifflin, 1975);

George and Martha Rise and Shine (Boston: Houghton Mifflin, 1976);

Speedboat (Boston: Houghton Mifflin, 1976);

A Frog and Her Dog (Boston: Houghton Mifflin, 1977);

Picnic (Boston: Houghton Mifflin, 1977);

Turkey O'Toole's New Neighbor (Boston: Houghton Mifflin, 1977);

A Summer in the South (Boston: Houghton Mifflin, 1977; London: Evans Brothers, 1978);

George and Martha: One Fine Day (Boston: Houghton Mifflin, 1978);

The Stupids Have a Ball, by Marshall and Harry Allard (Boston: Houghton Mifflin, 1978);

James Marshall's Mother Goose (New York: Farrar, Straus & Giroux, 1979);

Portly McSwine (Boston: Houghton Mifflin, 1979);

George and Martha: Tons of Fun (Boston: Houghton Mifflin, 1980);

Space Case, as Edward Marshall (New York: Dial, 1980);

Troll Country, as Edward Marshall (New York: Dial, 1980; London: Bodley Head, 1981);

Taking Care of Carruthers (Boston: Houghton Mifflin, 1981);

The Stupids Die, by Marshall and Allard (Boston: Houghton Mifflin, 1981);

Three by the Sea, as Edward Marshall (New York: Dial, 1981);

Miss Nelson is Back, by Marshall and Allard (Boston: Houghton Mifflin, 1982);

Fox and His Friends, as Edward Marshall (New York: Dial, 1982);

Fox in Love, as Edward Marshall (New York: Dial, 1982);

Fox at School, as Edward Marshall (New York: Dial, 1983);

Fox on Wheels, as Edward Marshall (New York: Dial, 1983);

Rapscallion Jones (New York: Viking, 1983; London: Bodley Head, 1984);

The Cut-Ups (New York: Viking, 1984);

Fox All Week, as Edward Marshall (New York: Dial, 1984);

George and Martha Back in Town (Boston: Houghton Mifflin, 1984);

Four on the Shore (New York: Dial, 1985);

Miss Nelson Has a Field Day, by Marshall and Allard (Boston: Houghton Mifflin, 1985);

Wings: A Tale of Two Chickens (New York: Viking Kestrel, 1986);

Merry Christmas, Space Case (New York: Dial, 1986);

Three Up a Tree (New York: Dial, 1986);

Yummers Too (Boston: Houghton Mifflin, 1986).

SELECTED BOOKS ILLUSTRATED: Byrd Baylor, *Plink Plink Plink* (Boston: Houghton Mifflin, 1971);

Lore Segal, *All the Way Home* (New York: Farrar, Straus & Giroux, 1973);

Harry Allard, *The Stupids Step Out* (Boston: Houghton Mifflin, 1974; London: Methuen, 1976);

Norma Klein, *Dinosaur's Housewarming Party* (New York: Crown, 1974);

E. H. Tarcov, *The Frog Prince* (New York: Four Winds, 1974);

Charlotte Pomerantz, *The Piggy in the Puddle* (New York: Macmillan, 1974; London: Methuen, 1977);

Russell Hoban, *Dinner at Alberta's* (New York: Crowell, 1975; London: Cape, 1977);

Allard, *The Tutti Frutti Case: Starring the Four Doc-*

tors of Goodge (Englewood Cliffs, N.J.: Prentice-Hall, 1975);

Jeffrey Allen, *Mary Alice, Operator Number 9* (Boston: Little, Brown, 1975);

Cynthia Jameson, *A Day With Whisker Wickles* (New York: Coward, McCann & Geoghegan, 1975);

Allen, *Bonzini: The Tattooed Man* (Boston: Little, Brown, 1976);

Freya Littledale, *The Boy Who Cried Wolf* (New York: Scholastic, 1976);

Diane Wolkstein, *Lazy Stories* (New York: Seabury, 1976);

Allard, *It's So Nice to Have a Wolf Around the House* (Garden City: Doubleday, 1977);

Allard, *Miss Nelson is Missing* (Boston: Houghton Mifflin, 1977);

Frank Asch, *MacGoose's Grocery* (New York: Dial, 1978; London: Kestrel, 1979);

Jan Wahl, *Carrot Nose* (New York: Farrar, Straus & Giroux, 1978);

Allard, *Bumps in the Night* (Garden City: Doubleday, 1979);

Allard, *I Will Not Go to Market Today* (New York: Dial, 1979);

Jane Yolen, *How Beastly! A Menagerie of Nonsense Poems* (New York: Collins, 1980);

Allard, *There's a Party at Mona's Tonight* (Garden City: Doubleday, 1981);

John McFarland, *The Exploding Frog and Other Fables from Aesop* (Boston: Little, Brown, 1981);

Daniel Manus Pinkwater, *Roger's Umbrella* (New York: Dutton, 1982);

Allen, *Nosey Mrs. Rat* (New York: Viking Kestrel, 1985);

Clement C. Moore, *The Night Before Christmas* (New York: Scholastic, 1985);

Allen, *Mary Alice Returns* (Boston: Little, Brown, 1986).

James Edward Marshall is best known for his series of George and Martha books and as the illustrator and occasionally the coauthor with Harry Allard of the Stupid Family books, a more sophisticated and satiric series. His work is unusual in the wit, humor, and sophistication employed in the treatment of themes especially suitable for very young children: respect, kindness, and friendship. He has said that when he creates a story he begins with the character or characters and then puts them into unlikely situations. As a result, he gives the reader "two diverse elements that shouldn't go together, but when they do it clicks." Often this means putting the familiar animal characters of children's stories into parodies of adult situations. Thus his books become attractive both to young children and to the adults who read to them.

Marshall was born 10 October 1942 in San Antonio, Texas, the son of George E. Marshall, an insurance salesman, and Cecille Harrison Marshall. James Marshall, who lived on a farm outside the city, was discouraged in his drawings by an unsympathetic first grade teacher, so he concentrated on studying English history and playing the violin and the viola. At seventeen he won a scholarship to the New England Conservatory of Music in Boston, which he attended in 1960-1961. However, he suffered an injury to his hand in 1961 which put an end to hopes for a professional music career. He then attended various schools, including Trinity College and Southern Connecticut State College, from which he was graduated with a B.A. in history in 1967. From 1968 to 1970 he taught French and Spanish at Cathedral High School in Boston's South End.

About this time he returned to the drawing that he had enjoyed as a child. Persuaded by a friend, he took a portfolio of drawings to Houghton Mifflin in Boston. A few weeks later the company commissioned him to illustrate Byrd Baylor's *Plink Plink Plink* (1971), and a year later Marshall produced his own book, which was listed among the *New York Times* Best Illustrated Books of the Year. The American Library Association named it a notable book, and the Children's Book Showcase included it in their 1973 list of awards.

For his style of illustrating, Marshall acknowledges a debt to both Maurice Sendak and Edward Gorey. His work is also similar to that of two popular earlier illustrators: Jean de Brunhoff (1899-1937), creator of the Babar books, and Roger Duvoisin (1904-1980), a prolific illustrator of books for children. Marshall's hippos, George and Martha, are reminiscent of Brunhoff's elephant Babar family in their simple, chunky outlines and in the use of a few bright colors. Though Marshall is less the draftsman than Brunhoff, Duvoisin, Sendak, and Gorey, he combines some of their qualities: the rounded figures of Sendak and Brunhoff, the wit of Gorey, and the freedom of space favored by Duvoisin.

In the illustrations for *Plink Plink Plink* Marshall displays almost all the techniques he would use in later books. The ink drawings are tinted with green, orange, red, brown, and black. Sometimes the entire page is colored; at other times

James Marshall

only details are colored. The drawings of the night scenes, in which the small boy in bed imagines what could be making the sounds he hears, are dark and elaborate, filling the page completely. The contrasting scenes which disclose the real causes of the noises are simple, linear, and light. The reader is also introduced to animal characters that will reappear in later books: a bear like Carruthers and a turtle like Eugene, introduced in *What's the Matter with Carruthers? A Bedtime Story* (1972), and a peg-legged pirate-alligator like those seen in Russell Hoban's *Dinner at Alberta's* (1973).

In *George and Martha* (1972), however, Marshall uses a simpler kind of illustration, large line drawings washed with gray, pink, yellow, and green. The title characters are hippos, George and Martha, named after the viciously battling academic couple in Edward Albee's *Who's Afraid of Virginia Woolf?* In five brief stories Marshall plays against picture and text the incongruity of these large ungainly hippo friends being considerate and kind to each other while respecting the limits of friendship (unlike Albee's characters). For example, Martha tosses the bathtub over George's

head when she catches him peeping in upon her in the bath, but later she consoles him when he breaks a tooth and has to have a gold replacement. Likewise, George eats Martha's split-pea soup although he hates it, and when she catches him pouring a bowlful into his slipper, she is not angry but says she does not like to eat it either. She just likes to make it. She offers him chocolate cookies instead.

In *What's the Matter with Carruthers? A Bedtime Story* (1972), Marshall cleverly suggests the analogy between the cross child at bedtime and the ill-mannered bear Carruthers, who should be hibernating. His friends Emily Pig and Eugene Turtle, who do not understand his disposition, try to amuse Carruthers until he suddenly falls asleep in the leaves they have raked up. The mystery solved, they put Carruthers to bed in his own house, expecting that he will awake with his own sweet nature. The illustrations are perhaps superior to the text, which occasionally is too literary in style or too loose in its episodic plot, but overall the book continues Marshall's success with *George and Martha*.

George and Martha Encore (1973) expands

Dust jacket for the first of Marshall's six George and Martha books (Houghton Mifflin), which feature two hippos named for characters in Edward Albee's play Who's Afraid of Virginia Woolf?

upon the theme of friendship between the two hippos, retaining the five-story format as Marshall again explores the incongruity between the bulky creatures and their delicate social graces. George reluctantly attends Martha's dance recital and enjoys it so much that he takes lessons as well. In "The French Lesson," Martha teaches George at his request how to say "Bonjour" and "Voulez-vous m'embrasser." In "The Beach" George resists the temptation to say "I told you so" when Martha gets burned while sunning. These adult sit-

uations are used to show the child how friendship helps one both to grow and to support and help others.

In 1973 Marshall also published *Miss Dog's Christmas Treat*, in which the reader is invited to help Miss Dog find the one box of candy that she did not eat before Christmas so she can treat her invited guests, and *Yummers!*, in which Marshall devilishly exposes the gluttony of a greedy, overweight pig named Emily in a story that attracts both child and adult. The overweight Emily stuffs herself with food while she and her friend Eugene, a prudent and taciturn turtle, take a stroll for exercise. After eating two sandwiches, corn on the cob, scones, jam, and tea, Eskimo pies, Girl Scout cookies, milk, free pizza slices, cherry pop, and a candied apple, Emily gets sick and blames it on the exercise, causing Eugene to blandly suggest, "Maybe you should stay in bed and eat plenty of good food." Emily replies, "Oh, yummers!" In 1973 Marshall also illustrated *All the Way Home* by Lore Segal. The book, which portrays a noisy procession of animals who follow the crying girl Juliet home from the park, was entered in the American Institute of Graphic Arts Book Show in 1973-1974 and was listed in the Children's Book Showcase of 1974.

In *Willis* (1974) Marshall treats the theme of friendship among a different set of animals, though they are again placed in an unlikely situation. Bird, Lobster, and Snake find their friend Willis the alligator squinting his eyes because he has no sunglasses to wear at the beach. They set out to earn nineteen cents to add to the ten cents they have so they can buy a pair of glasses for twenty-five cents (this is Bird's faulty arithmetic). They are inept or unqualified for the series of jobs they undertake until they capitalize on their talents and put on a show to make the money. The Snake charms the Lobster to sleep, and Bird plays the cello while Willis dances. The result is enough money for sunglasses for all four, with moral and instructional messages presented wittily and indirectly. In 1974 Marshall also illustrated Norma Klein's *Dinosaur's Housewarming Party,* wherein the various animals compete with their presents; E. H. Tarcov's *The Frog Prince,* an adroitly illustrated retelling of the fairy tale by the Grimm brothers; and Charlotte Pomerantz's *The Piggy in the Puddle,* which was placed in the American Institute of Graphic Arts Book Show in 1973-1974 and whose delicately drawn pig characters recall Marshall's character Emily.

In 1974 Marshall also illustrated the first of the better known Stupid Family books by Harry Allard. In *The Stupids Step Out* (1974), which was listed in the Children's Book Showcase in 1975, Marshall's heavy black line drawings and bold colors complement the antics of the obtuse family of father Stanley Q. Stupid, Mrs. Stupid, their children Buster and Petunia, their cat Xylophone, and their dog Kitty. The illustrations embellish this satire on the nuclear American family as presented in children's books and television shows of the 1950s. Everything is reversed. For example,

the family goes to sleep with dunce caps on their heads and their feet on the pillow. As the adult laughs at this parody of the stereotype of the ideal family, the children enjoy the simple pleasure of being superior to the characters and events in the story, where, for example, the children try to slide up a banister and the dog Kitty drives the car. The treat of the family outing—potato sundaes with butterscotch syrup for all—reflects the child reader's level of comedy.

By the mid 1970s Marshall had moved to Charleston, Massachusetts, with his English bulldog and a large family of cats. The bulldog shows up in several illustrations. In *Four Little Troubles* (1975) Marshall presents a collection of four picture books, cased together, like Sendak's *Nutshell Library* (1962). He was the author and illustrator of three: *Eugene,* the adventures of a turtle preparing for school with "two brand new pencils, a new box of Crayolas, and a brand new tablet"; *Sing Out Irene,* the triumph of the girl bulldog Irene in the unlikely role of a toadstool in the school's spring pageant; and *Snake,* in which being able to hear makes the snake first an outcast and then a hero. The fourth book, *Someone is Talking About Hortense,* was written by Laurette Murdock and features a paranoid white mouse who learns that the whispering of friends was only their plans for her birthday party. The collection effectively captures the anxieties about and the resolutions to problems common to small children.

In *The Guest* (1975), Marshall deals with friendship in the unlikely pair of Mona, a moose, and Maurice, a snail. The large amorphous drawings of the gray moose are framed by the cheerful pink, green, and yellow colors of the house and surroundings. Maurice disappears, Mona becomes disconsolate, but then Maurice reappears as a parent of twenty baby snails, all with French names. Mona makes French toast for all—an irony that along with several jokes about eating snails shows that the book is aimed for a sophisticated child audience.

In 1975 Marshall also illustrated four books by other writers using his familiar cartoon styles. In Cynthia Jameson's *A Day With Whisker Wickles,* about a comic mix-up in an animal day nursery, Marshall used colored black line drawings. For the award-winning *Dinner at Alberta's* by Russell Hoban he used black-and-white drawings to illustrate the story of how the crocodile Arthur improves in his social graces after becoming infatuated with Alberta Saurian. The first illustra-

Dust jacket for Marshall's 1973 book in which he exposes the gluttony of a greedy, overweight pig named Emily
(Houghton Mifflin)

tion, an overhead view of the crocodile family at a table, is reminiscent of the optical puzzles of M. C. Escher. In Jeffrey Allen's *Mary Alice, Operator Number 9*, Marshall's boldly colored drawings suit the small-town story of Mary Alice, the duck telephone operator who cannot be replaced satisfactorily by substitutes when she is ill. He also illustrated Harry Allard's *The Tutti Frutti Case: Starring the Four Doctor's of Goodge*, which was included on the *New York Times* Best Illustrated Children's Books of the Year list.

In 1976 Marshall produced *George and Mar-* *tha Rise and Shine*, another in his series using the five-story format and the familiar drawings of the hippos. Most of the stories turn on reversals of expectations. George gets caught in a lie; Martha studies fleas until they hop on her; George is frightened by the scary movie he takes Martha to; and Martha discovers that George's secret club from which she is excluded is her fan club. In *Speedboat* (1976) Marshall introduces two characters reminiscent of reckless Toad and his more prudent friends in Kenneth Grahame's classic *Wind in the Willows* (1908). The dog Jasper

Dust jacket for Marshall's 1975 story of the friendship between a moose and a snail (Houghton Mifflin)

Raisintoast has irresponsible adventures upriver with his speedboat while his friend Tweedy-Jones stays home but has an even more marvelous adventure. The bubble he blows with gum turns into a balloon and takes him high into the air. The story delicately explores the tolerance demanded in the friendship of these two personality types—one active and adventurous, and the other passive and a homebody.

Marshall illustrated three books by others in 1976: Jeffrey Allen's *Bonzini: The Tattooed Man*, which was listed in the Children's Book Showcase in 1977, Freya Littledale's *The Boy Who Cried Wolf*, and Diane Wolkstein's *Lazy Stories* (folktales from Japan, Mexico, and Laos retold). The illustrations of Allen's book are particularly well done; they capture the flat, dull landscape of Kazoo, Texas (a reflection surely of Marshall's childhood experience in that state), with its western space and isolation. Marshall dedicated the illustrations to Edward Gorey, and the Edwardian costumes show his influence, but unlike Gorey's characters, the children in *Bonzini* are cheerful and hopeful. The simple ink drawings in *Lazy Stories* differentiate nicely the nationalities of Mexico, Laos, and Japan.

In *A Summer in the South* (1977), Marshall was less successful with a longer story intended for grades four to six. An episodic parody of an Agatha Christie type of mystery novel, it features the sleuthing of detective Eleanor Owl and her assistant, the cat Mr. Paws, as they attempt to discover by whom and why the various and eccentric guests in the resort hotel are being disturbed. The characters are cleverly distinguished: Miss Marietta Chicken, a retired circus performer; Foster Pig, a querulous, wealthy, and family-proud landowner; Don Coyote, a hypochondriac and recluse; the Cootie family of Puddle Rapids who arrive via envelope; and a grotesque band of four bogus baboon musicians. The parody, the puns (Don Coyote), and the musical misinformation of the baboons may appeal more to adults than children, but the book sells well in England, no doubt because the English are mad about mysteries.

Marshall's illustrations for Harry Allard's *It's So Nice to Have a Wolf Around the House* (1977), a reversal of the ordinary wolf story, are better attuned to the modern child. Black line drawings washed with green, red, pink, and gold underscore the tongue-in-cheek story of Cuthbert Q. Devine, a wolf on the lam, who hides out by becoming a devoted companion and servant to an old man and his three equally aged pets—a dog, a cat, and a fish. Revealed to be a bank robber, Cuthbert reforms and the judge lets him off, and the five retire to the more healthful climate of Arizona.

In another Allard book, *Miss Nelson is Missing* (1977), Marshall was allowed the opportunity to illustrate situations more immediate to the young child's world. In this book, which won the Georgia Children's Book Award and was included in American Institute of Graphic Arts Book Show in 1980, Marshall's black line drawings washed with yellow, green, pink, and blue found a more compatible mystery story. Marshall portrays the innocence of the nice blond teacher, Miss Nelson, as she fails to cope with the worst behaved class in school, Room 207. He pictures vividly her "substitute," Miss Viola Swamp, in an ugly black dress and green horizontally striped stockings. The illustrations cleverly reveal to the reader why and how Miss Nelson disappears to be replaced by Miss Swamp and then reappears once the classroom is brought under control.

In 1978 Marshall wrote and illustrated *George and Martha: One Fine Day*, five moral tales about his hippo characters and their friendship. The incongruity of Martha happily walking a tightrope in the first story sets off the collection. "The Icky Story" has Martha capping one of

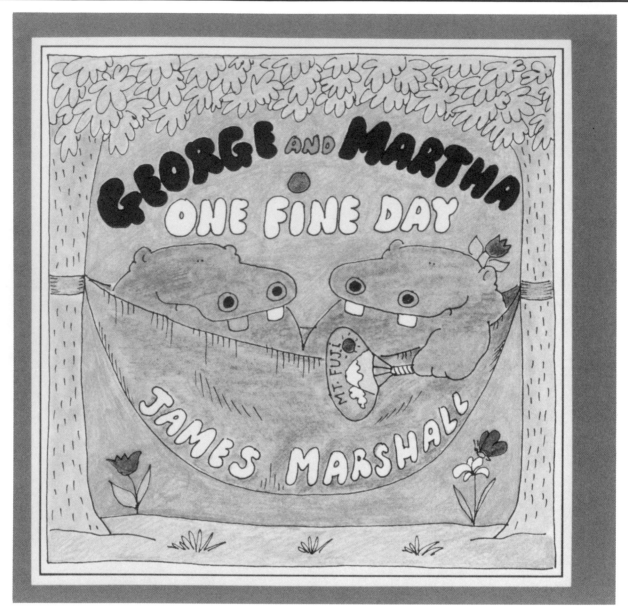

Dust jacket for Marshall's fourth George and Martha book which includes five moral tales focusing on their friendship
(Houghton Mifflin)

George's nauseating stories with one of her own that makes him queasy. The final two stories in the book are related: Martha lets George worry in anticipation after he frightens her in "The Big Scare" before she finally scares him in retaliation in the tunnel of love in "The Amusement Park."

In 1978 Marshall coauthored with Harry Allard *The Stupids Have a Ball*, a sequel to *The Stupids Step Out*, which features a reversed situation that many young school children can relate to and laugh at. To celebrate the failing report cards of their children, the Stupids invite their relatives to a costume ball. The dog Kitty writes the invitations, while the excited cat Xylophone gets his tail caught in his nose. Together the pets prepare an outrageous punch for the party. The illustrations in bold, primary colors are clever and consistent with the text. The simple plot and silly puns are also appropriate for the child audience.

Marshall also illustrated two books by other authors in 1978: Jan Wahl's *Carrot Nose* in black and white with orange accents and Frank Asch's *MacGoose's Grocery*. In the latter, sure line drawings and simple, cheerful colors of blue and orange and clever touches such as the grocery signs "Our Turnips are Tops" and "Cream of Junebug

Soup," show the affinity of the illustrator for the text.

In 1979 Marshall selected thirty-four rhymes and did the illustrations for *James Marshall's Mother Goose*, which includes both the familiar, such as "Little Boy Blue," and the lesser known, such as "I am Queen Anne." He also published *Portly McSwine*, in which he portrays a worrywart pig who agonizes over each imagined thing that may go wrong with his party on National Snout Day. At one point, Portly even takes the precaution of getting a swine-flu shot.

In his illustrations for Allard's *Bumps in the Night* (1979), Marshall pays tribute to Edward Gorey's 1977 stage designs for *Dracula* by imitating their stylization. Marshall's black-and-white drawings are washed with gray and black while selected details are accented in pink (Gorey had used a single red detail in each of his gray and black scenes). The story is a parody of the detective and ghost tale, consisting of six short chapters. The characters Trevor Hog, Dagmar Baboon, and the crocodile medium, Madam Kreepy—are familiar Marshall creations, but the story has a greater appeal for knowing adults than for children. A better book for the child reader is Allard's *I Will Not Go to Market Today* (1979), which was featured on the *New York Times* Ten Best Illustrated Books of the Year list. Marshall's illustrations greatly enhance the story, which concerns the repeated attempts by the rooster Fenimore B. Buttercrunch to get to market for strawberry jam. The bold drawings in red, pink, black, brown, and white capture the humorously exaggerated series of disasters—including a blizzard, hurricane, and earthquake—that prevent him from reaching his destination.

George and Martha: Tons of Fun (1980) is dedicated to Maurice Sendak. The five stories are slighter than in the previous George and Martha books, but the interweaving of them is more skillfully done. The familiar line drawings of the gray hippos are lightened by the pink, green, and yellow colors used effectively throughout. The friendship of the two withstands Martha's absurd vanity in a close-up picture showing mainly her nostrils, her criticism of George's eating sweets, and her interruption of his handstand practice. One clever illustration juxtaposes the bulk of George against the outlined bulk of the refrigerator he is raiding. In another Marshall pays subtle tribute to various children's authors by placing their names on the books on shelves in a shop.

Dust jacket for Marshall's 1981 sequel to his 1972 book What's the Matter with Carruthers? A Bedtime Story. *Both stories focus on the friendship between a bear, a pig, and a turtle (Houghton Mifflin).*

Marshall illustrated Jane Yolen's *How Beastly! A Menagerie of Nonsense Poems* in 1980 and wrote and illustrated two books, *Space Case* and *Troll Country*, published under the name Edward Marshall. Marshall illustrated Yolen's book in the tradition of Edward Lear, treating such fanciful animals as the "fanger," "slummings," "shirk," "octopie," and "canterpillar." In *Space Case* a flying saucer which arrives on Halloween is taken to be just another kid in costume. To the family of Buddy McGee, who takes it home, it is just another gadget. And at Buddy's school, it is seen as an electronic calculator. Thus the plot of the story cleverly reveals how the marvelous is reduced to the mundane.

The saucer leaves the dull schoolroom but promises to return for Christmas. The black ink drawings, colored by overlays in red, blue, and yellow, and the solid wash backgrounds in *Space Case* mark a new variant of Marshall's style. Both the story and illustrations of *Troll Country*, in which a little girl confronts and defeats the trolls that her mother believes in and that her father does not, recall works by Sendak in which children confront and defeat similar monsters as they mature.

The dominant themes and illustrative styles have continued in the work of James Marshall, who now divides his time between an apartment in New York and a house in Mansfield Hollow, Connecticut. He completed illustrations for John McFarland's retelling of some of Aesop's fables in *The Exploding Frog and Other Fables from Aesop* in 1981, using the vivid colors and black background of *Space Case*. Marshall's drawings are superior to McFarland's rather undistinguished retelling. The final picture of the exploding frog shows it swelling beyond the picture frame before it explodes into brightly colored bits scattered all over in and outside the frame.

The Stupid family reappears in *The Stupids Die* (1981), coauthored by Marshall and Allard, but the story is thinner than those of the previous books and directed more to the humor of adults. The Stupids wake up expecting a great day, but nothing out of the ordinary happens— that is, according to the Stupid mentality. When the lights go out, they conclude happily that they must be dead. And when the lights come on again, they think they are in heaven. But Grandfather, who happens by, tells them that they are still in Cleveland, an inside joke that adults will appreciate more than children. However, Marshall's humorous illustrations are still on the child's level, especially one of Mrs. Stupid's dresses made of live chickens.

Marshall has also published a sequel featuring Carruthers in *Taking Care of Carruthers* (1981). The format of this book is more elaborate, consisting of a prologue, twelve chapters, and an epilogue. In the prologue Carruthers is grumpy because he has a cold on a rainy winter Sunday. To entertain him, Eugene the turtle makes up a story about them and Emily the pig and their adventures as they row down the Chattahoola river. Many of their adventures are quite clever, especially the saving of a seasick swan and the fending off of an autograph hound who only wants signatures of famous persons. The fictional visit of Eugene, Emily, and Carruthers to the home of the famed cookbook author Ambrosia Suet and her secretary Miss Prune suggests a satire on Gertrude Stein and Alice B. Toklas in the illustrations. The story ends with Carruthers taking the role of the baby bear in a production of "Goldilocks," staged at the town of Stupendousberg.

Three by the Sea (1981), written under the name Edward Marshall, concerns three small children, Lolly, Spider, and Sam, in a storytelling competition after lunch on the beach. Through their stories, Marshall manages both to write a clever easy-to-read book and to make fun of poor examples of that genre. Lolly starts with an inane example from her reader about a cat, a dog, and a rat. Sam takes the same characters and develops them in a more imaginative manner but then resorts to a stereotyped trick ending. Spider's scary version is about a hungry sea monster who passes up eating cheese, the rat, or the cat for a lunch of two boys and a girl on toast. True to the nature of small children, the other two jump when Sam yells, "Look out!"

Between 1982 and 1984, Marshall wrote five other witty, easy-to-read books under the name Edward Marshall: *Fox and His Friends* (1982), *Fox in Love* (1982), *Fox at School* (1983), *Fox on Wheels* (1983), and *Fox All Week* (1984). In all the stories Fox tries for the upper hand, but more often than not, he is outfoxed by his younger sister Louise or by fate. These books have been recognized for their superiority by the Junior Literary Guild and the American Bookseller's Association. *Fox at School* was even chosen an alternate by the Book-of-the-Month Club.

The hero of *Rapscallion Jones* (1983) is a more grown-up fox, but he fumbles through life in similar fashion when he has to come up with some way to pay the rent demanded by the boarding house owner, the bulldog Mama Jo. He considers marrying a rich widow, and then tries being a writer, but he can not get beyond "Once upon a time." At last he is shown attempting to paint Mama Jo, with cigar in mouth, as the Statue of Liberty. The story does not have a line of illustration nor a word more than necessary.

In *The Cut-Ups* (1984), Marshall portrays two boys, Spud Jenkins and Joe Turner, who get into all sorts of trouble during their summer vacation to the dismay of their parents. They snorkel in a flooded bathroom; and they set up a magic-marker tattoo parlor for the neighborhood kids. But they meet more than their match in Mary Frances Hooley, who uses them in her plot against assistant principal Lamar J. Spurgle to recover his cache of her confiscated toys. The story is as vivid as its blue, orange, green, yellow, and purple-colored illustration. The story is every child's dream of summer license but also a nightmare of the final authority to be reckoned with when school starts in the fall.

George and Martha Back in Town (1984) presents the familiar hippos in five more stories in which each tests their friendship either by snooping, making rash boasts, playing practical jokes, or giving gratuitous advice. However, at the end they are still friends; George gives up trying to read a book alone and settles for telling stories to Martha until dark. Their acceptance or each other's foibles is more generous than that of two hens in *Wings: A Tale of Two Chickens* (1986). In this story the sensible Harriet has to rescue silly Winnie from the clutches of Mr. Johnson, whom she fails to recognize as a fox and her enemy. The plot depends on disguises in the episodic adventures including a balloon ride and a church revival. Nice touches in the illustrations include the sign on the water tower and the Fox's chicken costume that looks more like Little Red Riding Hood's cloak. The climax of the story is a real cliffhanger for the hens are perched on a sharp bluff with sharks in the water below and the fox racing towards them. Of course the message is that Winnie got into all this trouble because she failed to be a reader like Harriet and had never seen foxes in books.

During recent years, Marshall has continued to illustrate a variety of books by other authors. After doing Harry Allard's *There's a Party at Mona's Tonight* (1981), which features transparent disguises that Potter Pig adopts in his attempts to crash Mona's party, Allard and Marshall coauthored two more books about Miss Nelson and her alter-ego Miss Viola Swamp. In *Miss Nelson is Back* (1982) and *Miss Nelson Has a Field Day* (1985), they give a few new twists to her disguise as Viola Swamp. In *Miss Nelson is Back*, the teacher has to go to the hospital to have her tonsils out. The children dress up as her and fool the dotty principal, Mr. Blandsworth, into thinking she's back. That leaves them free to play hooky in town. However, from her hospital window, Miss Nelson sees them, and Miss Viola Swamp reappears to whip Room 207 of the worst school in Texas back into shape. In *Miss Nelson Has a Field Day*, Viola Swamp returns to the Horace B. Smedley School to substitute for Coach Armstrong, who has been driven to a nervous breakdown by his football team's antics and failure to score a single point, much less win a game. But she soon has the Smedley Tornadoes in shape to meet the Central Werewolves. Marshall's illustrations of the zany elementary kids and elementary school life are clever as always, especially the one of the dowdy and glum cafeteria ladies in the serving line.

Other books illustrated during this recent period include Daniel Manus Pinkwater's *Roger's Umbrella* (1982), in which the cat Roger finds himself whisked away by a bewitched, unruly umbrella; Jeffrey Allen's *Nosey Mrs. Rat* (1985), in which a nosy neighbor, Mrs. Shirley Rat, meets her comeuppance in little Brewster Blackstone; and a retelling of Clement C. Moore's famous story, *The Night Before Christmas* (1985). Marshall has written a sequel about Lolly, Spider, and Sam called *Three Up a Tree* (1986); a sequel to *Yummers!* called *Yummers Too* (1986); and he has illustrated Allen's forthcoming sequel to *Mary Alice, Operator Number 9*. Announcement of a sequel to *The Cut-Ups* has been made as well. Readers may look forward, therefore, to seeing many other books featuring Marshall's familiar casts of animals and small children.

Mercer Mayer

(30 December 1943-   )

P. Gila Reinstein

SELECTED BOOKS: *A Boy, a Dog, and a Frog* (New York: Dial, 1967);

If I Had (New York: Dial, 1968);

The Terrible Troll (New York: Dial, 1968);

There's a Nightmare in My Closet (New York: Dial, 1968);

Frog, Where Are You? (New York: Dial, 1969);

I Am a Hunter (New York: Dial, 1969);

A Special Trick (New York: Dial, 1970);

Mine, by Mayer and Marianna Mayer (New York: Simon & Schuster, 1970);

The Queen Always Wanted to Dance (New York: Simon & Schuster, 1971);

A Boy, a Dog, a Frog, and a Friend, by Mayer and Marianna Mayer (New York: Dial, 1971);

Me and My Flying Machine, by Mayer and Marianna Mayer (New York: Four Winds, 1971);

A Silly Story (New York: Parents' Magazine Press, 1972);

Bubble, Bubble (New York: Parents' Magazine Press, 1973);

Frog on His Own (New York: Dial, 1973);

Mrs. Beggs and the Wizard (New York: Parents' Magazine Press, 1973);

Frog Goes to Dinner (New York: Dial, 1974);

One Monster After Another (New York: Golden Press, 1974);

Two Moral Tales (New York: Four Winds, 1974);

Two More Moral Tales (New York: Four Winds, 1974)–includes *Bird's New Hat* and *Bear's New Clothes;*

What Do You Do With a Kangaroo? (New York: Four Winds, 1974);

You're the Scaredy-Cat (New York: Parents' Magazine Press, 1974);

The Great Cat Chase (New York: Four Winds, 1974);

Walk, Robot, Walk (Lexington Mass.: Ginn, 1974);

Just For You (New York: Golden Press, 1975);

One Frog Too Many, by Mayer and Marianna Mayer (New York: Dial, 1975);

Ah-Choo (New York: Dial, 1976);

Hiccup (New York: Dial, 1976);

Liza Lou and the Yeller Belly Swamp (New York: Par-

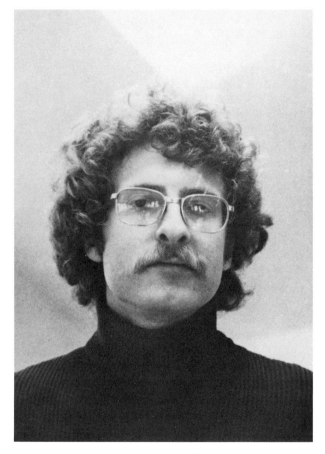

Mercer Mayer

ents' Magazine Press, 1976);

Just Me and My Dad (New York: Golden Press, 1977);

Little Monster's Word Book (New York: Golden Press, 1977);

Mercer's Monsters (New York: Golden Press, 1977);

Oops (New York: Dial, 1977);

Professor Wormbog in Search for the Zipperump-a-Zoo (New York: Golden Press, 1977);

Professor Wormbog's Gloomy Kerploppus: A Book of Great Smells (And A Heart-Warming Story, Besides) (New York: Golden Press, 1977);

Appelard and Liverwurst, illustrated by Steven Kellogg (New York: Four Winds, 1978);

Little Monster at Home (New York: Golden Press, 1978);

Little Monster at School (New York: Golden Press, 1978);

Little Monster at Work (New York: Golden Press, 1978);

Little Monster's Alphabet Book (New York: Golden Press, 1978);

Little Monster's Bedtime Book (New York: Golden Press, 1978);

Little Monster's Counting Book (New York: Golden Press, 1978);

Little Monster's Neighborhood (New York: Golden Press, 1978);

Little Monster's You-Can-Make-It Book (New York: Golden Press, 1978);

How the Trollusk Got His Hat (New York: Golden Press, 1979);

Little Monster's Mother Goose (New York: Golden Press, 1979);

East of the Sun & West of the Moon (New York: Four Winds, 1980);

Herbert, the Timid Dragon (New York: Golden Press, 1980);

Little Monster's Scratch and Sniff Mystery (New York: Golden Press, 1980);

Professor Wormbog's Crazy Cut-Ups (New York: Golden Press, 1980);

Liverwurst is Missing, illustrated by Kellogg (New York: Four Winds, 1981);

Merry Christmas, Mom and Dad (New York: Golden Press, 1982);

Play With Me (New York: Golden Press, 1982);

Just A Snowy Day (New York: Golden Press, 1983);

Malcom's Race (New York: Scholastic, 1983);

Gator Cleans House (New York: Scholastic, 1983);

Just Go to Bed (New York: Golden Press, 1983);

Too's Bracelet (New York: Scholastic, 1983);

Sweetmeat's Birthday (New York: Scholastic, 1983);

Possum Child Goes Shopping (New York: Scholastic, 1983);

When I Get Bigger (New York: Golden Press, 1983);

Bat Child's Haunted House (New York: Scholastic, 1983);

All By Myself (New York: Golden Press, 1983);

I Was So Mad (New York: Golden Press, 1983);

Just Grandma and Me (New York: Golden Press, 1983);

Me Too! (New York: Golden Press, 1983);

The New Baby (New York: Golden Press, 1983);

Tuk Takes a Trip (New York: Bantam, 1984);

Teep and Beep, Go to Sleep (New York: Bantam, 1984);

Tink Goes Fishing (New York: Bantam, 1984);

Tinka Bakes a Cake (New York: Bantam, 1984);

Little Critter's Day at the Farm (New York: Scholastic, 1984);

Little Critter's Holiday Fun (New York: Scholastic, 1984);

Little Monster's Moving Day (New York: Scholastic, 1984);

Little Monster's Sports Fun (New York: Scholastic, 1984);

Trouble in Tinktonk Land (New York: Bantam, 1985);

The Tinktonks Find a Home (New York: Bantam, 1985);

Just Me and My Puppy (New York: Golden Press, 1985);

Tonk Gives a Magic Show (New York: Bantam, 1985);

Zoomer Builds a Racing Car (New York: Bantam, 1985);

Just Grandpa and Me (New York: Golden Press, 1985);

Policeman Critter (New York: Simon & Schuster, 1986);

Fireman Critter (New York: Simon & Schuster, 1986);

Cowboy Critter (New York: Simon & Schuster, 1986);

Astronaut Critter (New York: Simon & Schuster, 1986);

Just Me and My Little Sister (New York: Golden Press, 1986);

Just Me and My Babysitter (New York: Golden Press, 1986);

Whinnie the Lovesick Dragon (New York: Macmillan / London: Collier Macmillan, 1986);

There's An Alligator Under My Bed (New York: Dial, 1987).

SELECTED BOOKS ILLUSTRATED: John D. Fitzgerald, *The Great Brain* (New York: Dial, 1967);

Sidney Offit, *The Boy Who Made a Million* (New York: St. Martin's, 1968);

George Mendoza, *The Crack in the Wall and Other Terribly Weird Tales* (New York: Dial, 1968);

Mendoza, *The Gillygoofang* (New York: Dial, 1968);

Liesel M. Skorpen, *Outside My Window* (New York: Harper & Row, 1968);

Kathryn Hitte, *Boy, Was I Mad!* (New York: Parents' Magazine Press, 1969);

Sheila La Farge, *Golden Butter* (New York: Dial, 1969);

Mildred Kantrowitz, *Good-Bye Kitchen* (New York: Parents' Magazine Press, 1969);

Fitzgerald, *More Adventures of the Great Brain* (New York: Dial, 1969);

Warren Fine, *The Mousechildren and the Famous Collector* (New York: Harper & Row, 1970);

Jean Russell Larson, *Jack Tar* (Philadelphia: Smith, 1970);

Marianna Mayer, *Me and My Flying Machine* (New York: Parents' Magazine Press, 1971);

Barbara Wersba, *Let Me Fall Before I Fly* (New York: Atheneum, 1971);

Jane H. Yolen, *The Bird of Time* (New York: Crowell, 1971);

Jan Wahl, *Margaret's Birthday* (New York: Four Winds, 1971);

Fitzgerald, *Me and My Little Brain* (New York: Dial, 1971);

Wahl, *Grandmother Told Me* (New York: Little, Brown, 1972);

Fitzgerald, *The Great Brain at the Academy* (New York: Dial, 1972);

Candida Palmer, *Kim Ann and the Yellow Machine* (Lexington, Mass.: Ginn, 1972);

Fitzgerald, *The Great Brain Reforms* (New York: Dial, 1973);

Mabel Watts, *While the Horses Galloped to London* (New York: Parents' Magazine Press, 1973);

Wersba, *Amanda Dreaming* (New York: Atheneum, 1973);

Fitzgerald, *Return of the Great Brain* (New York: Dial, 1974);

John Bellairs, *The Figure in the Shadows* (New York: Dial, 1975);

Fitzgerald, *The Great Brain Does It Again* (New York: Dial, 1975);

Jay Williams, *Everyone Knows What a Dragon Looks Like* (New York: Four Winds, 1976);

Williams, *The Reward Worth Having* (New York: Four Winds, 1977);

Marianna Mayer, *Beauty and the Beast* (New York: Four Winds, 1978).

OTHER: *The Poison Tree and Other Poems*, edited by Mayer (New York: Scribners, 1977);

The Sleeping Beauty, edited and retold by Mayer (New York: Macmillan / London: Collier Macmillan, 1984);

Charles Dickens, *A Christmas Carol*, abridged by Mayer (New York: Macmillan, 1986).

Mercer Mayer, artist and author, has written and illustrated more than eighty picture books since he became involved in children's literature in 1967. Among his works are fantasies, folktales, and realistic stories, both with and without text, and picture books with overtly educational content. The visual wit of his illustrations has won him wide popularity among small children, and his clear and unusual appreciation of the full range of human emotions has earned him the interest and respect of critics and educators.

Mercer Mayer was born in Little Rock, Arkansas, on 30 December 1943. His father served in the navy during World War II and was away from home for much of Mercer Mayer's first years. The Mayers lived on a navy base, and the young Mercer divided his free time between snake and lizard hunting in the nearby swamps and immersing himself in picture books and art. Among those artists who influenced him as a child were Arthur Rackham, John Tenniel, N. C. Wyeth, and Aubrey Beardsley.

His family traveled widely within the United States and settled in Hawaii when Mercer Mayer was thirteen years old. He was graduated from Theodore Roosevelt High School in Honolulu and attended the Honolulu Academy of Arts. One of his first professional assignments was as political cartoonist for the International Brotherhood of Teamsters in Hawaii. Another was painting a series of pictures with his mother, who is also an artist, to decorate the Kahala Hilton Hotel.

He later continued his art training at the Art Students League in New York City, where he met his first wife, Marianna, with whom he eventually collaborated on several children's books. They were married in 1963, moved to Sea Cliff, Long Island, and in 1973 moved again to a fifteen-acre farm in the Connecticut countryside. Mayer worked for a time in the art department of an advertising agency before he began illustrating and writing children's books. Although an art school instructor had discouraged him against book illustration on the grounds that it was unprofitable, Mayer nevertheless showed his portfolio to several editors and received a number of books to illustrate. Among these early commissions were John D. Fitzgerald's *The Great Brain* (1967) and its numerous sequels; George Mendoza's *The Gillygoofang* (1968) and *The Crack in the Wall and Other Terribly Weird Tales* (1968); Liesel M. Skorpen's *Outside My Window* (1968); and Sidney Offit's *The Boy Who Made a Million* (1968). Mercer continues to illustrate books written by other authors, several of which have received awards and critical acclaim.

In 1967 Mayer also began creating his own original children's books. The first to be pub-

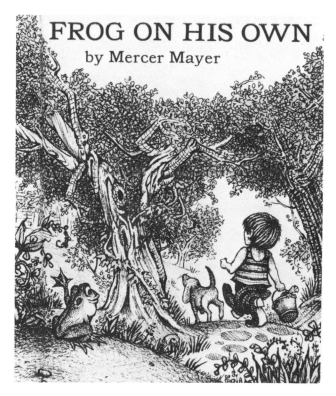

Covers for four volumes in Mayer's first wordless picture-book series (Dial)

lished was a wordless picture book, *A Boy, a Dog, and a Frog* (1967). This small volume presents a contest of wills between an adventuresome boy and the frog he tries to capture in his net. After several attempts, the boy and his dog go home disappointed. The frog, lonely, follows the boy and surprises him in the bathtub. The pleasure of friendship when it is given freely contrasts with the child's previous desire for dominance over the would-be friend. The success of this led Mayer to produce five more books, similar in format, characters, style, and wit: *Frog, Where Are You?* (1969); *A Boy, a Dog, a Frog, and a Friend,* with Marianna Mayer (1971); *Frog on His Own* (1973); *Frog Goes to Dinner* (1974); and *One Frog Too Many,* also with Marianna Mayer (1975).

In these books the boy is essentially isolated from other people and seeks to assert himself in the world of small animals. The frog often serves as the boy's alter ego, misbehaving in a park or restaurant, rejecting the arrival of a sibling and so on. Anger, frustration, resentment, anxiety, malicious glee, and embarrassment are displayed by the characters, along with joy, determination, loving concern, and loyalty. The breadth and subtlety of emotion presented in the six books of this series, a series suitable for a very young, prereading audience as well as for an older one, set Mayer apart from the writers / illustrators of more conventional and limited books.

The Boy and Frog books are visually subdued: the strong use of brown pencil line on the white page, the simplicity and directness of style, and the pictorial wit all contribute to their success. *A Boy, a Dog, and a Frog* won the 1970 Society of Illustrators Annual National Exhibit Citation and a Brooklyn Art Books Citation in 1973; *Frog Goes to Dinner* also won the Brooklyn award in 1976. In 1974 two of the books in the series received the International Books for Children Award from the Association for Childhood Education: *A Boy, a Dog, and a Frog* and *A Boy, a Dog, a Frog, and a Friend.*

The first storybook that Mayer began to work on, in 1967, was not *A Boy, a Dog, and a Frog* but *There's a Nightmare in My Closet* (1968), which features a cast of monsters, terrifyingly ugly but totally benign and, ultimately, childlike. Anthropomorphic monsters such as these, sometimes threatening but more often amiable, are a major component of Mayer's later work. These prototypical creatures hide in a small boy's closet: they are his night fears incarnate. When he forces himself to confront them, he finds them

Cover for Mayer's 1968 book about a small boy's fear of monsters and how he overcomes it (Dial)

easy to subdue and live with; he makes peace with his own private nightmares. The artwork in this book is reminiscent of the spare line drawings and simple backgrounds of *A Boy, a Dog, and a Frog,* but a wider range of colors is used.

The desire of a small child to master his fears and command power in his world are themes that appear in many of Mayer's books of the late 1960s and early 1970s. *If I Had* and *The Terrible Troll,* both published in 1968, are two examples. In the former book, a small boy fantasizes the revenge he could enjoy against those children who bully and bother him, if only he owned a gorilla, an alligator, a lion, or a snake, animals that would defend him against his perceived enemies. In the end he concedes to reality, but reality is not without its comfort: he has the loyal protection of a big brother. *The Terrible Troll* presents a threatening fantasy world, too. This time the setting is medieval, and the protagonist is a twentieth-century boy who wishes himself into the role of page to a brave knight. After several humorous adventures, the knight enters a troll's castle to fight. At the end of a long, anxious day, the troll emerges the victor; the boy quickly wishes himself back into the modern world. The threatening force here is too powerful to master or befriend; escape is the only solution.

I Am a Hunter (1969) combines the motifs of mastery and escape that have been observed in the previous books and adds a disturbingly open ending. A boy uses his imagination to turn mundane things around his house into mighty enemies to vanquish or props for adventures of which he is the all-powerful hero. Each transformation—for example, of the garden hose into a snake—angers his parents and neighbors. The adults here, as well as in other of Mayer's early books, are essentially the enemy, insensitive to the child's need for fantasy, escape, and control over his world. The adult authority figures in this book are conventional, literal, and restricting; the child is inventive, imaginative, and destructive of property. Adults are concerned with good behavior; children ignore decorum to pursue more interesting ends. The child in *I Am a Hunter* is allowed to have his way: at the end of the book, he sails off in his bathtub, rejecting the parents who angrily urge him to sit down and wash. Mayer neither reconciles the child with parental authority nor reintegrates him into the real world. He is allowed to reject frustrating reality in favor of imaginative fulfillment.

A Special Trick (1970), a variation on the sorcerer's apprentice story, provides a successful, well-integrated synthesis of the themes of the preceding books. A boy, working for a magician, accidentally lets loose some creatures, monstrous and otherwise, who make shambles of the magician's place. With the help of the sorcerer's book of spells, the boy restores order and also keeps one spell for himself: the ability to turn his bed into a flying horse. Though Mayer again presents an aggressive attack on order and authority, in *A Special Trick* the child successfully masters his antisocial feelings. He overcomes them, not only conforming to adult standards but also keeping some of their power for his own use, for later escape to freedom. This book, illustrated in warm, muted colors with dramatic, swirling black lines and forms, uses a style that is reminiscent of Arthur Rackham yet decidedly contemporary at the same time and subtly reflective of "Pop" art. *A Special Trick* won the AIGA Children's Book Award in 1970-1971.

Other picture books of the early 1970s also reflect Mayer's preoccupation with the child's need to fantasize that he has power and compe-

tence, despite the difficult and sometimes dangerous obstacles in his path. *Mrs. Beggs and the Wizard* (1973), *You're the Scaredy-Cat* (1974), and *What Do You Do With a Kangaroo?* (1974) are characteristic of this group of books.

The protagonist of *Me and My Flying Machine* (1971) sets out to build a fantastic airplane by himself from junk parts, but fails. "Tomorrow, I'll build a rowboat," he decides. He is disappointed but undaunted. *You're the Scaredy-Cat*, which was listed by the Child Study Association in 1974 as one of the Books of the Year, is another realistic tale. Two brothers camp in their backyard. The older one frightens himself with a monster story, then, to save face, accuses his brother of being a coward. Like *Me and My Flying Machine*, this book shows children coping with an unwelcome reality.

Mrs. Beggs and the Wizard uses a cast of adult characters to act out a child's hostile fantasies. *What Do You Do With a Kangaroo?* is a more playful treatment of the same theme. Both books create suspense and use improbable, surprise events for humor. The former ends with the suggestion of some untold, horrible revenge on Mrs. Beggs and her boarders by the wizard whom she had previously foiled. The fantasy is played out to its end rather than assimilated into the conventional, real world. The latter book closes with a young girl taking several obstreperous, demanding animals to bed with her, accepting them as parts of herself, rather like the monsters in *There's a Nightmare in My Closet*. *What Do You Do With a Kangaroo?* won the 1975 Brooklyn Arts Books for Children citation.

The illustrations in the books of this period contain strong, swirling lines, sometimes as outlines, sometimes for texture and detail. Colors tend to be tinted or muted and rarely, if ever, saturated. Crosshatching is widely used. Some of these books employ cartoon conventions, such as multiple picture boxes on a page.

Another group of books by Mercer Mayer which can be considered together are the wordless (or nearly wordless) fantasies: *Bubble, Bubble* (1973), *Two Moral Tales* (1974), *Two More Moral Tales* (1974), *Ah-Choo* (1976), *Hiccup* (1976), and *Oops* (1977). In small format, using a humorous, cartoonlike style and little if any text, Mayer presents imaginative stories in which people or anthropomorphic animals act out fears and wishes, aggressive and affectionate behavior, rivalry and cooperation. The circumstances are sometimes rather sophisticated in these books, dealing, for in-

(Parents' Magazine Press)

(Four Winds)

Covers for two of Mayer's early 1970s books that reflect his preoccupation with the child's need to fantasize that he has power and competence despite the difficult and sometimes dangerous obstacles in his path

stance, with chivalry and courtship, arrest and trial. Although wordless, like the Boy and Frog books, the mood here is very different, more exuberant and hyperbolic. The impossible happens; ideas are carried to their logical limit and beyond; wishes, for good and evil, are granted. The art in these later picture books is more flamboyant, more cartoonlike than in the earlier wordless series, in keeping with the comic exaggerations and slapstick humor.

In 1974 Mayer began writing and illustrating for Golden Press, a division of Western Publishing Company. This decision to produce books for mass marketing as well as for the more expensive and exclusive publishers was generated, according to Mayer, by a desire to reach a wider audience, one that visits the supermarket and drugstore but rarely, if ever, the bookstore.

The Golden books bear the clear stamp of Mayer's distinctive artistic style, sense of humor, and fascination with strange creatures of his imagination. These books, even more than his others, abound in visual jokes that reward the attentive picture reader. Despite the similarities, the Golden books, as a group, differ in texture and tone from those that Mayer has published with Dial and Four Winds. Visually, they are much busier; emotionally, they are simpler. The Golden story books project security and affection. Problems are easily resolved in the course of each story, and the conclusions are emotionally satisfying. These Golden books are designed to entertain, teach, and gratify the needs of small children more peaceable, trusting, and innocent than those for whom *You're the Scaredy-Cat* or *I Am a Hunter* were written. The Golden books are easier for adults to live with because they omit the strongly rebellious, vengeful, terrified feelings that are brought forward in many of Mayer's other books. Not that these books deny all negative emotions: frustration, loneliness, and embarrassment, for example, are included, but characters display these feelings to a rather mild degree and are brought to emotional comfort within each book.

Some of Mercer Mayer's Golden books are set in a fantasy land on the Edge of Nowhere and peopled with monsters, most of whom are loving, bumbling, and childlike. Human beings occasionally appear, but they are a minority of the population, outsiders. Language is used inventively, and Mayer freely makes up names and plays with the sounds of words.

One group within the Golden books deals with Little Monster, an upright, winged reptilian being with fangs, who dresses and acts like a little boy of about five. Some of the books in this grouping are educational, such as *Little Monster's Alphabet Book* (1978) and *Little Monster's Counting Book* (1978). Others provide a moral or social lesson through the medium of a story, such as *Little Monster at School* (1978), a book in which the protagonist helps a misbehaving schoolmate through honest praise and the offer of friendship. There are gimmick books, too: *Little Monster's You-Can-Make-It Book* (1978) and *Little Monster's Scratch and Sniff Mystery* (1980), for instance.

Related to these book are others that are set in the same imaginary land but do not feature Little Monster as their protagonist. This group includes stories essentially for entertainment, stories that accumulate improbable events, building to a sometimes frantic climax before coming to a calm conclusion. *One Monster After Another* (1974), *How the Trollusk Got His Hat* (1979), and the books about Professor Wormbog typify this category.

A third grouping within the Golden books are those which present a hairy little creature called Little Critter whose well-meaning intentions do not match his limited abilities and who, therefore, often falls into trouble. The adventures in *Just for You* (1975) and *Just Me and My Dad* (1977) are realistic and familiar: the little child tries to please and impress his parents by showing his competence, but in the end, the best–and only–way he can succeed is by giving them his love. These books reinforce the young child's need for acceptance, forgiveness, and love. *Merry Christmas, Mom and Dad* (1982) and *Just Grandma and Me* (1983) are other titles in this series.

While creating the Golden books, Mayer continued writing and illustrating for other publishers. His work in Jay Williams's *Everyone Knows What a Dragon Looks Like* (1976) was given the Irma Simonton Black Award, and the book was cited by the *New York Times* in its Best Illustrated Children's Books of the Year list.

In 1978 he illustrated *Beauty and the Beast,* a version retold by Marianna Mayer. His version of *East of the Sun & West of the Moon* followed in 1980. These folktale books are a departure in subject matter, mood, and, to some extent, style from his other work. The traditional material is handled seriously, with considerable emotional intensity. The illustrations are luminous, richly and subtly colored paintings with graceful, wiry lines. In some, such as *Beauty and the Beast,* he uses a bor-

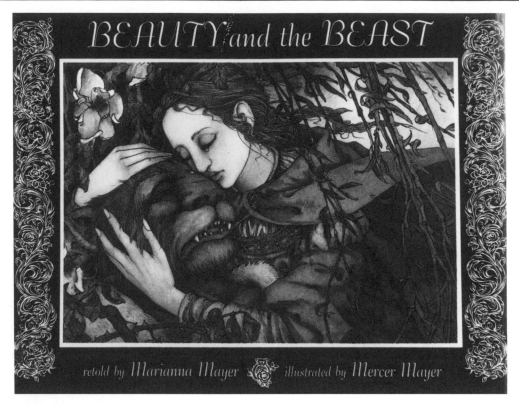

Dust jacket for Marianna Mayer's 1978 retelling of the well-known French fairy tale, with illustrations by Mercer Mayer (Four Winds)

der decoration to frame each illustration. Unexpected angles and dramatic variations in distance and point of view are utilized. Visual imagery is developed for symbolic effect: in *Beauty and the Beast* roses bloom and droop, paralleling events in the story. There is a wealth of detail in the pictures, which appear full and lavish without being busy. Exotic settings and foreign cultures are presented. These books lack the humorous cartoon quality of many of his earlier illustrations, focusing instead on grace and dignity. It is, perhaps, no wonder that Mercer Mayer's own favorite among his books is *East of the Sun & West of the Moon.*

In 1978 Marianna and Mercer Mayer were divorced. In 1979 he married his current wife, Jo. They are jointly bringing up Jo's son, Len, whom Mayer adopted in 1980, and a daughter, Jessie Browning, who was born to them in 1979. They live in Bridgewater, Connecticut, where Mayer enjoys fishing, composing music on a Kurzweil 250 sequencer synthesizer, and listening to opera.

Although Mercer Mayer sees himself primarily as an artist, his storytelling powers are considerable. In quiet, realistic tales like the Boy and

Frog series, as well as in wild flights of fancy, like *One Monster After Another,* he plots a story clearly, accumulating incidents, building to a strong climax and a clear conclusion. Sometimes the conclusions are unexpected, open-ended, and thought-provoking, even disturbing; sometimes they are traditional and restore sense and peace to the world. Either way, the stories he creates are eventful and original.

Mayer's work for Western Publishing Company has a built-in popularity because of the distribution techniques for Golden books. It is interesting that these books have received little critical attention, although they are for the most part clever, subtle, and attractive. It should also be noted that *Just For You* (1975), the first book in Mayer's Little Critter series, recently sold its one-millionth copy. His books for other publishers have been awarded numerous prizes and honorary citations and are important in the canon of children's literature for their visual beauty and wit, for their ingenious stories, and for their expression of human feeling.

From the outset of his career as a writer and illustrator, Mayer has developed a strong and unusual approach to children's literature, one that does not condescend to the child or romanticize childhood. On the contrary, he has empathetically explored the depths of children's passions and revealed their rich variety. He asserts, when speaking about his work, that he has never written *for* children, but has tried instead to capture his own childhood in his books. He also admits that having children of his own has changed his sense of childhood somewhat, softening the resentment against adult authority figures, who appear as the enemy in many of his early books. Reflecting the world, real and imaginary, from the child's point of view has been a hallmark of his work from the beginning of his career, and whatever changes come in his approach to children and their books, the honesty

and emotional intensity that are essential to his work will remain unchanged.

References:

Barbara Bader, *American Picture Books from Noah's Ark to the Beast Within* (New York: Macmillan, 1976), p. 540;

Lee Kingman, Grace Allen Hogarth, and Harriet Quimby, eds., *Illustrators of Children's Books* (Boston: Horn Book, 1978), pp. 144-145;

Zena Sutherland, ed., *The Best in Children's Books 1966-1972* (Chicago: University of Chicago Press, 1973);

Sutherland, ed., *The Best in Children's Books 1973-1978* (Chicago: University of Chicago Press, 1980).

David McCord
(15 November 1897-   )

Priscilla N. Grundy
North Central College

SELECTED BOOKS: *Oddly Enough* (Cambridge: Washburn & Thomas, 1926);

Floodgate (Cambridge: Washburn & Thomas, 1927);

Stirabout (Cambridge: Washburn & Thomas, 1928);

The Crows; Poems (New York & London: Scribners, 1934);

Bay Window Ballads, illustrated by John Lavalle (New York & London: Scribners, 1935);

And What's More (New York: Coward-McCann, 1941);

About Boston; Sight, Sound, Flavor & Inflection (Garden City: Doubleday, 1948);

A Star by Day (Garden City: Doubleday, 1950);

The Camp at Lockjaw, illustrated by Gluyas Williams (Garden City: Doubleday, 1952);

Far and Few, Rhymes of the Never Was and Always Is, illustrated by Henry B. Kane (Boston: Little, Brown, 1952);

The Old Bateau, and Other Poems (Boston: Little, Brown, 1953);

Odds Without Ends (Boston: Little, Brown, 1954);

Take Sky, More Rhymes of the Never Was and Always

Is, illustrated by Kane (Boston: Little, Brown, 1962);

All Day Long; Fifty Rhymes of the Never Was and Always Is, illustrated by Kane (Boston: Little, Brown, 1966);

Every Time I Climb a Tree, illustrated by Marc Simont (Boston: Little, Brown, 1967);

Notes from Four Cities, 1927-1953 (Worcester, Mass.: A. J. St. Onge, 1969);

For Me to Say; Rhymes of the Never Was and Always Is, illustrated by Kane (Boston: Little, Brown, 1970);

Pen, Paper and Poem (New York: Holt, Rinehart & Winston, 1971);

Mr. Bidery's Spidery Garden, illustrated by Kane (London: Harrap, 1972);

Away and Ago, Rhymes of the Never Was and Always Is, illustrated by Leslie Morrill (Boston: Little, Brown, 1974);

The Star in the Pail, illustrated by Simont (Boston: Little, Brown, 1975);

One at a Time: His Collected Poems for the Young, illustrated by Kane (Boston: Little, Brown, 1977);

Speak Up, More Rhymes of the Never Was and Always

Is, illustrated by Simont (Boston: Little, Brown, 1979);

All Small, illustrated by Madelaine Gill Linden (Boston: Little, Brown, 1986).

OTHER: *Once and For All*, edited by McCord (New York: Coward-McCann, 1929);

What Cheer: An Anthology of American and British Humorous and Witty Verse, edited by McCord (New York: Coward-McCann, 1945); republished as *The Pocket Book of Humorous Verse* (New York: Pocket Books, 1946); republished as *The Modern Treasury of Humorous Verse* (Garden City: Garden City Books, 1951).

David McCord ranks among the handful of top twentieth-century poets for children. Critics have said shining things about him, awards have showered down on him, and his poems are often anthologized. These poems embody a curiosity about the world which echoes with sounds to please and tickle the young and which shows a lightness in relation to a subject which plays games with and yet simultaneously keeps a distance from the reader. McCord conducted a crusade to reach children with poems and through that medium to wake them to the pleasures and satisfactions of observation, word play, and sound.

David Thompson Watson McCord was born in New York City on 15 November 1897 and spent his earliest years in the East: on Long Island and in Princeton, New Jersey, with summers in the Poconos. The only child of Joseph Alexander and Eleanore Baynton Reed McCord, when he was twelve financial reverses resulted in his family moving to Oregon. A small glimpse of his feelings about that move appear in his poem "A Fool and His Money": "In the observation car /Of our California train / I sat out back; and far / Behind me slid the plain. / And what would become of me / In the land where I was to be?"

Out west he stayed out of school for three years, during which he spent much time alone on his uncle's ranch. "I didn't see five kids my age once a year," he said of that time. After three years in Lincoln High School in Portland, Oregon, he worked a while in Des Moines, Iowa, and spent the rest of the year in Washington, Pennsylvania, preparing for entrance examinations for Harvard. McCord enjoyed recalling that, having had no science in high school, he barely passed his exam in physics but went on to major in physics at Harvard, from which he graduated in 1921. In between he had spent part of 1918 in the field artillery as a second lieutenant and was about to be shipped overseas when World War I ended.

McCord went back for a master's degree from Harvard in romance languages, which he earned in 1922, and remained at Harvard all his working life, primarily as executive director of the Harvard Fund Council from 1925-1963. He wrote drama reviews for the *Boston Evening Transcript* from 1923 to 1928; he was associate editor of the *Harvard Alumni Bulletin* from 1923 to 1925 and editor from 1940 to 1946. He wrote as an avocation: light essays, book reviews, poetry for adults, and poetry for children. When he gave his objectives for his retirement in 1962 ("Chinese, Debussy, tobacco, trout are the things I want to investigate, in that order"), poetry didn't even make the list. It is a tribute to his talent and to his extraordinary energy that he achieved his high rank among children's poets in this context.

Nonetheless, writing verse was part of McCord's life from early boyhood. He says he began writing when he was fifteen and tried his hand at verse for children right after leaving graduate school. Although his first book was a collection of light essays (*Oddly Enough*, 1926), his first book of verse, *Floodgate*, followed the next year. McCord's first volume of poetry for children, *Far and Few*, did not appear until 1952, twenty years after the manuscript was completed. A few poems which first appeared in books for adults, however, later showed up in children's collections: for instance, "The Starfish." After 1952 McCord produced new children's books regularly, highlighted by *One at a Time: His Collected Poems for the Young* in 1977, which contains 450 poems reprinted from five earlier volumes. Many of his poems appeared first in magazines, and many have been anthologized. McCord estimated that by 1983 his work had appeared in nearly 400 anthologies.

In retirement McCord carried his campaign vigorously to his audience. He visited schools, reading his poems, talking about poetry, and selling his books. At eighty-six he claimed to have talked to some 100,000 children. X. J. Kennedy, in a 1981 article for *Horn Book*, describes McCord speaking to third-graders, telling "a few blood-curdling yarns about snakes and man-eating fish he had known in his boyhood," reading his own poems, and commenting on poems written and read by children. He "exhibits tremendous respect for children's intelligence," wrote Kennedy,

David McCord (photo by Thomas Garland Tinsley)

and although he made corrections as well as positive comments, the children did not seem to mind. "They acknowledged that he was a man who took their work seriously, who cared enough about it to want to improve it."

McCord has received many honors, several of them related to children's literature. The National Council of Teachers of English in 1977 named him the first recipient of its award for excellence in poetry for children, he was twice nominated for a National Book Award (for *The Star in the Pail*, 1975, and *One at a Time*), and the Boston Public Library supports an annual lecture in his name.

In addition he received eleven honorary degrees, including the first L.H.D. ever given by Harvard. In 1950 he gave the eight Lowell Lectures on Edward Lear, and in 1954 he held a Guggenheim Fellowship. He has been made a Benjamin Franklin fellow of the Royal Society of Arts and received a National Institute of Arts and Letters grant in 1961. These are samples from a very long list of awards and accomplishments. One McCord particularly cherished is the title of Grand Bostonian, awarded by the city to seven eminent residents.

On the dust jacket of McCord's *Speak Up* (1979), Marc Simont, the illustrator, depicts an old man with a pipe cocking his head with hand to ear next to a very charming mooing cow. The pipe smoker is clearly McCord. Although the title poem does not suggest the speaker is hard of hearing, as the picture does, Simont shows a poetic speaker who has the same approach to life—curious and comical—as the child speakers in McCord's poems. It is one of McCord's accomplishments that in his poems generations are unified and separated at the same time. In "Laundramat" the reader cannot be sure whether adult or child is imagining that a row of washers is "Diesel Number Three," and the person watching the bees and butterfly in "The Hammock" could be of any age. In some poems the speaker is clearly a child, "Every Time I Climb a Tree" being a famous example; and in some, like "The Fisherman," the reader hears an adult wishing as he watches a small boy fish. But the qualities which typify the poems are the same, making the unity more evident than the separation.

McCord stands out among twentieth-century poets for children—indeed among those for adults as well—in his emphasis on sounds and

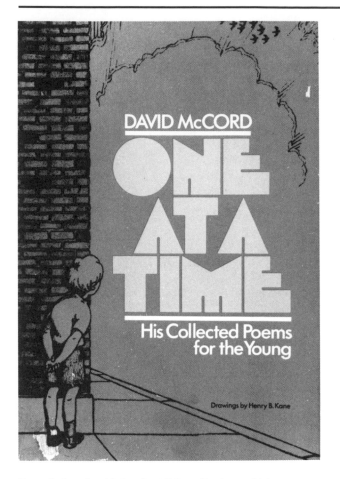

Dust jacket for McCord's 1977 collection, which contains 450 poems reprinted from five earlier volumes (Little, Brown)

sound patterns. One major result of Imagism has been that the visual aspect has received central attention in modern poetry. William Carlos Williams's "The Red Wheelbarrow" is an example: sound is built into the verse, but the primary effect is the picture of the wheelbarrow in the rain. The pendulum swing to imagery has not been as extreme in children's poems but is nonetheless there. In McCord's work, however, the love of sound emerges as the primary characteristic. It is not just that the poems have meter and rhyme (some do not), but that the author clearly enjoys his acrobatics with sounds. So in "Down by the Sea" he rhymes "thickly" with "Partickly" (particularly), and in "Pumpkins" he shows enjoyment of the title word by repeating it four times in two lines.

Not only does McCord show his pleasure in sounds through rhyme, meter, and general acrobatics, but he also writes poems *about* sound. In *Pen, Paper and Poem* (1971) McCord wrote examples of verses in various meters. These are incorpo-

rated into *One at a Time* in a section called "Write Me Another Verse." The opening poem, "The Tercet," begins:

> A tercet is a stanza of three lines
> All rhyming, like a pitchfork with three tines.
> Or like three stars if none of them outshines
> The others . . . [.]

Here the triple rhyme is demonstrated and its sound compared with two visual images. In other poems he plays with the sounds themselves: "Who Hasn't Played Gazintas?" deals with the four basic arithmetic processes but centers on the sounds related to them, as in the title, which refers to "goes into's" in division. McCord makes this frequently used relationship between sound and meaning explicit in "The Look and Sound of Words," in which the sound of words adds emotional charge to the lexical meaning:

> Words have more to them than meaning:
> Words like *equidistant, gleaning,*
> *Paradoxical* and *glisten,*
> All you have to do is *listen.*

In addition to poems about sound, the range of subjects of McCord's poetry is wide. He writes much of nature, especially birds, trees, and animals. Some poems, like "Elm Seed Blizzard," deal with nature in town, although most are set in the country. Among birds, crows are a McCord favorite. "Crows are the voice of America," he has said, and they appear often as figures of vigor and playfulness, as in the poem called "Crows." McCord worked with that theme as early as 1934, when he gave the title *The Crows* to his second book of adult verse.

Some of his poems show precise detail in nature, as in the reference in "The Newt" to the creature's "spotted veil." This exactness McCord attributed in part to a graduate student in botany at the University of Pennsylvania, whom his parents hired one summer to take him on nature walks. The scientific interest, reflected by McCord's major in physics at Harvard, shows in such poems as "Smart Mr. Doppler," about the Doppler effect. A number of McCord's poems deal with seasons and holidays. Many are spread about among the small concerns of children's lives, as the titles "What Are Pockets For?" and "Tooth Trouble" suggest.

Not all of McCord's poems focus primarily on sound. Some are visual, like "The Leaves," which describes greens and reds and yellows, as well as whispers. "This Is My Rock," one of the most frequently anthologized of his poems, evokes strongly a sense of place and of twilight; even here the repetition of "This is my rock" contributes much to the feeling of the speaker owning the rock. That McCord wrote successful visual poems should not be surprising when one learns that he was for some years a painter and had several watercolor shows.

McCord expressed surprise that after all his early years of writing light essays and verse for adults, some of which appeared in the *New Yorker* and other prestigious magazines, it was his children's verse which earned him the most literary fame. Perhaps one clue can be found in Sara Henderson Hay's review of *A Star by Day,* a collection of verse for adults published in 1950. Hay admires McCord's careful work and restraint but finds that his poems lack "warmth and fervor and passion." McCord's poems for children do have warmth; perhaps he found it easier to express feeling to a younger audience. They also have fervor for sound and nature and other matters central to children. But the children's verse does lack passion. The difference is that passion is inappropriate for a juvenile audience. Writing for children, then, McCord found an audience appreciative of his skills and insights but one which did not ask for extreme emotional intensity. He gave them craftsmanship and curiosity and humor instead, and especially respect, all of which combined to place him at the top of the field.

References:

"The Barbless Hook," *Time* (29 June 1962): 44;

David Dillon, "Perspective: David McCord," *Language Arts,* 55 (March 1978): 379-387;

Sara Henderson Hay, "Man, Poet and World," *Saturday Review of Literature,* 33 (18 November 1950): 17;

X. J. Kennedy, " 'Go and Get Your Candle Lit': An Approach to Poetry," *Horn Book,* 57 (June 1981): 273-279;

Myra Cohn Livingston, "David McCord: The Singer, the Song, and the Sung," *Horn Book,* 55 (February 1979): 24-38.

Milton Meltzer

(8 May 1915-   )

Mary Ann Heffernan
University of Tennessee

BOOKS: *A Pictorial History of the Negro in America*, by Meltzer and Langston Hughes (New York: Crown, 1956); republished as *A Pictorial History of Black Americans*, by Meltzer, Hughes, and C. Eric Lincoln (New York: Crown, 1973);

Mark Twain Himself; a Pictorial Biography (New York: Crowell, 1960; Toronto: Ambassador, 1962);

A Light in the Dark: the Life of Samuel Gridley Howe (New York: Crowell, 1964);

Tongue of Flame: the Life of Lydia Maria Child (New York: Crowell, 1965);

Time of Trial, Time of Hope: The Negro in America, 1919-1941, by Meltzer and August Meier (New York: Doubleday, 1966);

Black Magic; a Pictorial History of the Negro in American Entertainment, by Meltzer and Hughes (Englewood Cliffs, N.J.: Prentice-Hall, 1967);

Thaddeus Stevens and the Fight for Negro Rights (New York: Crowell, 1967);

Bread—and Roses: the Struggle of American Labor, 1865-1915 (New York: Knopf, 1967);

Langston Hughes: A Biography (New York: Crowell, 1968);

Brother, Can You Spare a Dime? the Great Depression, 1929-1933 (New York: Knopf, 1969);

Margaret Sanger: Pioneer of Birth Control, by Meltzer and Lawrence Lader (New York: Crowell, 1969);

Freedom Comes to Mississippi: the Story of Reconstruction (Chicago: Follett, 1970);

To Change the World; a Picture History of Reconstruction (New York: Scholastic, 1971);

Slavery, From the Rise of Western Civilization to the Renaissance (New York: Cowles, 1971);

Slavery, From the Renaissance to Today (New York: Cowles, 1972);

Hunted Like a Wolf: the Story of the Seminole War (New York: Farrar, Straus & Giroux, 1972);

The Right to Remain Silent (New York: Harcourt Brace Jovanovich, 1972);

Underground Man; a Novel (New York: Bradbury, 1972);

Milton Meltzer (photo by Catherine Noren)

Bound for the Rio Grande: the Mexican Struggle, 1845-1850 (New York: Knopf, 1974);

Remember the Days: a Short History of the Jewish American (Garden City: Zenith, 1974);

World of Our Fathers: the Jews of Eastern Europe (New York: Farrar, Straus & Giroux, 1974);

The Eye of Conscience: Photographers and Social Change, by Meltzer and Bernard Cole (Chicago: Follett, 1974);

Taking Root: Jewish Immigrants in America (New York: Farrar, Straus & Giroux, 1976);

Violins and Shovels: the WPA Arts Projects (New York: Delacorte, 1976);

Never to Forget: the Jews of the Holocaust (New York: Harper & Row, 1976);

Dorothea Lange: a Photographer's Life (New York: Farrar, Straus & Giroux, 1978);

The Human Rights Book (New York: Farrar, Straus & Giroux, 1979);

All Times, All Peoples: A World History of Slavery (New York: Harper & Row, 1980);

The Chinese Americans (New York: Crowell, 1980);

The Hispanic Americans (New York: Crowell, 1982);

214

The Truth About the Ku Klux Klan (New York: Watts, 1982);

The Jewish Americans: a History in Their Own Words, 1650-1950 (New York: Crowell, 1982);

The Terrorists (New York: Harper & Row, 1983);

A Book About Names: in which custom, tradition, law, myth, history, folklore, foolery, legend, fashion, nonsense, symbol, taboo help explain how we got our names and what they mean (New York: Crowell, 1984);

Mark Twain: A Writer's Life (New York: Watts, 1985);

Betty Friedan: a Voice for Women's Rights (New York: Viking, 1985);

Dorothea Lange: Life Through the Camera (New York: Viking, 1985);

The Jews in America; a Picture Album (Philadelphia: Jewish Publication Society of America, 1985);

Ain't Gonna Study War No More: the Story of America's Peace Seekers (New York: Harper & Row, 1985);

Poverty in America (New York: Morrow, 1986);

George Washington and the Birth of Our Nation (New York: Watts, 1986);

Winnie Mandela: The Soul of South Africa (New York: Viking, 1986);

Mary McLeod Bethune: Voice of Black Hope (New York: Viking Kestrel, 1987);

The Landscape of Memory (New York: Viking, 1987);

The American Revolutionaries: A History in Their Own Words (New York: Crowell, 1987).

OTHER: *Milestones to American Liberty: the Foundations of the Republic,* edited by Meltzer (New York: Crowell, 1961);

A Thoreau Profile, edited by Meltzer and Walter Harding (New York: Crowell, 1962);

Thoreau: People, Principles, and Politics, edited by Meltzer (New York: Hill & Wang, 1963);

In Their Own Words: A History of the American Negro, 3 volumes, edited by Meltzer (New York: Crowell, 1964-1967); revised and republished as *The Black Americans: A History in their Own Words, 1619-1983* (New York: Crowell, 1984);

Reconstruction, compiled by Meltzer (New York: Grossman, 1972);

"Where Do All The Prizes Go? The Case for Nonfiction," *Horn Book,* 52 (February 1976): 16-23;

"Beyond the Span of a Single Lifetime," in *Celebrating Children's Books: Essays on Children's Books,* edited by Betsy Hearne and Marilyn Kaye (New York: Lothrop, 1981), pp. 87-96;

Lydia Maria Child: Selected Letters, 1817-1880, edited by Meltzer and Patricia G. Holland (Amherst: University of Massachusetts Press, 1982).

As a nonfiction children's author, Milton Meltzer single-mindedly focuses upon the explication of lives devoted to the continuing struggle for human rights and social reform, effectively portraying the plights of downtrodden people oppressed by the results of acts perpetrated by man for political and economic gain.

Though best known for his histories and biographies, Meltzer has held a variety of positions within the publishing industry as both author and editor. He has been associated in editorial capacities with Science and Medicine Publishing Company, Crowell, Doubleday, and Scholastic Book Services and was the founder and editor-in-chief of the *Pediatric Herald.* He has also written for radio, television, and documentary films. Meltzer, who is married to Hilda Balinky and has two daughters, attended Columbia University from 1932 to 1936. He has received many distinguished awards throughout his career, such as the *Washington Post*-Children's Book Guild Nonfiction Award in 1981 and the Thomas Alva Edison Award for his work on American history in 1966. He has been a nominee for the National Book Award five times, and he received the Jewish Book Award for *Never to Forget: the Jews of the Holocaust* (1976).

Growing up during the depression greatly influenced Meltzer's strong commitment to the work he has chosen. His parents, Benjamin and Mary Richter Meltzer, were European immigrants who struggled to find the better life America offered. Meltzer sees an immense need for intriguing historical documentation for children because there is so little outside of the textbook genre for them to read; he feels textbook treatment of history often does little for the imagination or interest of the student.

Several main themes emerge clearly in Meltzer's works: man's inhumanity toward his fellowman; the ability of man through strength and perseverance to overcome many of the obstacles placed before him; the difficulty and yet rewards of the struggle of minority groups to gain a stronger hold on the promise of the American dream. Without overly glorifying the struggle of the oppressed, Meltzer maintains a strong standard of historical accuracy based upon a foundation of meritorious scholarship and personal commitment to his topic.

Meltzer has written and edited over fifty books, mostly for young adult readers, concerning historical events related to the fight for individual freedoms in the United States. Meltzer often bases his histories on first-person accounts of both recognizable and unknown persons. Meltzer has said that he is "especially concerned with what someone has called the 'underside' of history, that is, the hidden or hard-to-find record of what the common people have thought, felt, and done. We need to know not only what Andrew Carnegie said, but what his steelworkers at Homestead thought, not only how General Grant commanded armies, but what the black troops in the Civil War did, not only what a president's policy on poverty is, but how the people of Appalachia and the ghettos live."

An outspoken advocate of the need for the same literary regard for nonfiction as for fiction, Meltzer cites the lack of nonfiction representation of Newbery Medal winners as case in point. In his 1976 *Horn Book* article, "Where Do All The Prizes Go? The Case for Nonfiction," Meltzer insists that in writing history there is as much concern for literary merit as there is in the writing of fiction and poetry. There remains in the field of children's literature a specific, often unacknowledged, bias toward viewing fiction as more deserving of attention even though the author of a work of nonfiction is equally concerned with the artistic shape of that which he is creating. Revealing a personal style of writing is as important, Meltzer believes, for one genre as another; the writer who cares about his subject will use language, structure, and his means of expressing thoughts and feelings to the best of his abilities regardless of category.

Meltzer is a careful historian and one who understands the need to bring forth from a vast amount of information those bits of history which will both intrigue and educate the reader. His first concern is to plant seeds in an inquisitive mind by establishing a scenario from which to expand his issue, either from a group of questions or a general introduction. He presents the body of the work through short chapters constructed of a combination of various types of reference–always highlighting unique cases which clearly illuminate his focal point. His conclusions often explore the ways in which the problem at hand can be rectified, or offer an evaluation of the positive aspects of the social reformer he is portraying. Often in his conclusions Meltzer does not hesitate to involve the reader as a responsible agent for social change. Illustrations, bibliographies, indexes, and suggestions for further reading are generally included.

Meltzer explores some of the possibilities of the photographic essay in depicting specific periods in history. His first published work, *A Pictorial History of the Negro in America* (1956), coauthored with Langston Hughes, set a precedent for many works to follow. With an abbreviated text, the works are intended to allow the photography to speak for itself. Other books in this format include *Black Magic; a Pictorial History of the Negro in American Entertainment* (1967), also coauthored with Hughes; *The Jews in America; a Picture Album* (1985); and *Mark Twain Himself; a Pictorial Biography* (1960). *The Eye of Conscience: Photographers and Social Change* (1974) surveys the work of ten documentary photographers in an attempt to relate history through the personal visions of photographers who used their art to make an effective social statement.

Meltzer has devoted most of his publishing career to two minority groups in America: black Americans and Jewish Americans. *In Their Own Words: A History of the American Negro* (1964-1967), edited by Meltzer, is a three-volume chronicle of the experiences of blacks in America. Each volume contains a foreword, afterword, time line, and list of books for further reading. These books, written within a documentary format using letters, journals, court records, newspaper accounts, diaries, and other sources from people both known and unknown to the reader, are representative of a broad range of lives and experiences. Meltzer provides continuity to each book by introducing each of the people whose voice is recorded, giving each selection a specified tie to the work as a whole, as well as serving to highlight the merit of each particular selection.

Published in 1964, the first volume encompasses the years from 1619 to 1865: from the time the first slaves were brought to America to the beginnings of emancipation. The book's entries portray not only the fears, anxieties, and difficulties of slavery but also the hopes and aspirations of both free blacks in the northern states and the slaves of the South. The networks to help free the slaves and the early institutions oriented to educate blacks are also carefully delineated.

Spanning the years from 1865 to 1916, the second volume reveals the growing dissatisfaction

Dust jacket for Meltzer's 1974 survey of ten documentary photographers who used their art to make an effective social statement (Follett)

of blacks with the predicament of their situation after emancipation, as they continued to suffer inequities though they were supposedly freed from social and economic inequalities. As competition for jobs held by white workers increased and the tensions mounted between white and black factions, organizations such as the Ku Klux Klan arose. At the same time, Booker T. Washington, W. E. B. Du Bois, and other black leaders began their rise to prominence.

Volume three covers the years from 1916 to 1966, showing the struggles and strides that encompassed two world wars, the depression, the Harlem Renaissance, and the beginning of the civil rights movement. The well-known voices of Richard Wright, Marcus Garvey, Langston Hughes, W. E. B. Du Bois, and Martin Luther King, Jr., mingle with nameless sharecroppers and factory workers in selections that build in emotional intensity, and a distinguishable sense of bitterness emerges toward the limited role of the black in the twentieth century.

The Black Americans: A History in their Own Words, 1619-1983 (1984) is a one-volume compilation of the three-volume series. Revised in order to bring the study up-to-date, material by such con-

temporary figures as Maya Angelou and John E. Jacob, president of the National Urban League, is included.

Time of Trial, Time of Hope: The Negro in America, 1919-1941 (1966) is enlivened by brief accounts of major historical events and biographical sketches of well-known activists from the period between the return of the 369th Infantry to Harlem after World War I through the march-on-Washington movement of 1941. *Freedom Comes to Mississippi: the Story of Reconstruction* (1970) uses the same format to show the relationship between the short-lived gains for blacks made after the Civil War, the successes and failures of the Republican party, and the rise of the Ku Klux Klan.

Similar to his explorations of the black experience in America, Meltzer has written extensively of the plight of the Jewish immigrant. *Remember the Days: a Short History of the Jewish American* (1974) begins with the establishment of the first permanent Jewish community in New Amsterdam in 1654. From involvement in the expansion westward, through contributions made during the Civil War, and up into the mid-1970s, the history of Jewish Americans is viewed impar-

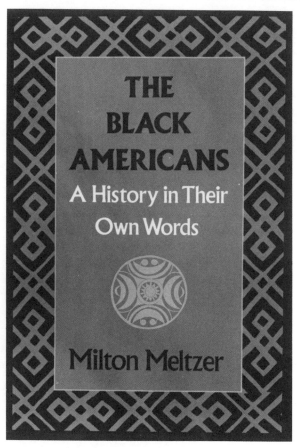

Dust jacket for Meltzer's revised and abridged compilation of his three-volume work, In Their Own Words: A History of the American Negro *(Crowell)*

tially against a rising awareness of anti-Semitism. Background material is provided in *World of Our Fathers: the Jews of Eastern Europe* (1974), a panoramic view of Jewish life in a historical perspective. Both books were nominated for a National Book Award in 1975.

Meltzer focuses on many of the realities and myths associated with assimilation during the late nineteenth and early twentieth century in *Taking Root: Jewish Immigrants in America* (1976), a companion work to *World of Our Fathers: the Jews of Eastern Europe*. The pressures the immigrant faced in order to make it in America often led to the restructuring of society in a fashion similar to that which was left behind. The emergence of the Yiddish culture and life on the Lower East Side of New York City and elsewhere is vividly and compassionately portrayed. Meltzer concludes that nostalgia for the olden days is often marred by selective memory.

The Jewish Americans: a History in Their Own Words, 1650-1950 (1982) received the Jefferson Cup Award. The structure of the book is similar to the three-volume work on the history of black Americans, drawing heavily on original sources. The themes and personal statements of assimilation and prejudice presented here are suitable to a wider rendering than specifically to the Jewish immigrant experience of coming into America.

Never to Forget: the Jews of the Holocaust (1976), Meltzer's most highly honored book, received the Jane Addams Book Award, the Association of Jewish Libraries Award, the *Boston Globe-Horn Book* award for nonfiction, and the National Jewish Book Award. It was also nominated for a National Book Award.

Focusing on the unique characteristics of Nazi Germany and the response toward and by the Jews of Germany, *Never to Forget: the Jews of the Holocaust* focuses on how the Holocaust was allowed to happen through the use of first-person accounts from survivors and by discussing the historical perspective of anti-Semitism. Meltzer is especially concerned with the treatment of the Holocaust in standard history textbooks. The unmatched brutality and horror of the death camps are a part of history that should not be forgotten or understated. In his essay entitled "Beyond the Span of a Single Lifetime" Meltzer asserts, "forgetting is inhuman. Denying the child the power of memory is inhuman. The child needs to sense that this world stretches far behind him and far ahead of him, that societies change, that people evolve during their own lives, that he himself is a blend of experience and memory. He needs to know that the past as well as the present holds meaning. He needs to listen to the tales of past human suffering and hope. The young have trouble locating themselves in anything except the here and now. But they can be helped to see over the walls of their own personalities."

The same sympathetic treatment Meltzer offers in his works of black Americans and Jewish Americans is evident in his studies of other ethnic groups. *The Chinese Americans* (1980) portrays the hardships and unfair treatment the Chinese immigrants faced upon arriving in America and the indignities suffered by each succeeding generation. Focusing on the place of this group in today's culture, Meltzer makes the reader aware that society has yet to resolve many of the damaging stereotypes of the past. Meltzer's work, which received the Carter G. Woodson Book Award sponsored by the National Council for the Social Studies, is underscored by a sense of the cruelty of both social and political acts against Chinese Americans.

Meltzer's concern about the adverse effects of racial stereotyping and discrimination is also evident in *The Hispanic Americans* (1982). Placing the blame for the plight of the economies of Puerto Rico, Cuba, and Mexico on European colonialism and American capitalism, Meltzer draws from a broad selection of first-person accounts to show clearly that Hispanic Americans have faced unrelenting problems in many facets of life since their migration to the United States began.

Discrimination is not a problem only immigrants to the United States have had to face. *Hunted Like a Wolf: the Story of the Seminole War* (1972) recounts a historical event which exemplifies far more than a battle for territorial gain. The annexation of Florida and the ensuing war were designed from grounds of bigotry, overwhelming economic considerations, and greed. Documenting much of his material from travel writer William Bartram and others, this type of conflict is Meltzer's metier. Many of the underlying reasons for the war are similar to what is presented in *Bound for the Rio Grande: the Mexican Struggle, 1845-1850* (1974), which also portrays the desperate tenacity of people fighting for what they believe is their share of the American promise.

Bringing together ideas and historical events from some of his other works, Meltzer compiled a two-volume work on the worldwide history of the "peculiar institution." *Slavery, From the Rise of Western Civilization to the Renaissance* (1971) and *Slavery, From the Renaissance to Today* (1972) show Meltzer to be a writer who searches for truths that often hide behind accepted generalizations. The patterns of economic advancement and geographical dominance emerge as these histories unfold. The two volumes also focus on the anguish of the slaves' lives and render their stories without sentimentality. Characteristic of Meltzer's work, resolutions and suggestions are included for changing the systems that allow this pattern of interaction to exist. Both books contain a broad and useful selection of illustrations including photographs, reproductions of art, documents, and maps.

Combined with the illustrations by Leonard Everett Fisher, *All Times, All Peoples: A World History of Slavery* (1980) provides a condensation of Meltzer's world history of slavery. Written for younger readers, this book is more a summary than a concise history. Meltzer uses examples from past and present and from many different

Dust jacket for Meltzer's 1980 book which portrays the hardships Chinese immigrants faced upon arriving in America and the indignities suffered by succeeding generations (Crowell)

societies showing slavery to be a concept related to specific historical occurrences. Meltzer staunchly includes a closing chapter on what can be done to prevent slavery. Fisher's powerful illustrations in black-and-white woodcuts add a deep emotional tone to this book, which received the Christopher Award in 1981 and was also nominated for a National Book Award.

Many of Meltzer's works examine specific time periods. *Bread—and Roses: the Struggle of American Labor, 1865-1915* (1967), part of the Living History Library series, portrays the wretched conditions of the American laborer caught up in the industrial revolution. The explanation of the role of the company store, strikes, and riots in the evolution of labor relations brings the story of the pioneers of the movement to the foreground in a comprehensible manner.

The Living History Library series successfully combines two approaches to writing on history–the narrative account and the documentary format. In songs, photographs, and text these wide-ranging books bring a unique liveliness to the presentation of historical information. *Brother, Can You Spare a Dime? the Great Depression, 1929-1933* (1969), another installment in the series, combines firsthand accounts from men, women, and children of various races, religions, and economic groups of how the depression personally affected them and how they endured it. This broad point of view reinforces the importance of understanding that all of history is composed of the collective lives of people. The book won the Christopher Award in 1970.

Similar in style to the Living History Library books, *Violins and Shovels: the WPA Arts Projects* (1976) presents an interesting accounting of the depression-era government program in support of the arts. Meltzer was employed in the WPA Theater Project and includes his recollections with those of other artists to present for children an aspect of the depression years that is often ignored.

Meltzer has also written several books that focus on a single issue. *The Right to Remain Silent* (1972) describes the historical origins of the Fifth Amendment dating back to the Talmud and English common law. Meltzer brings his historical perspective through the downfall of McCarthyism and up to the early 1970s, with examples that range from ancient to modern, from religious to political, and which contain a great deal of information as well as opinion. For older readers, *The Human Rights Book* (1979) combines many differing viewpoints and their respective goals in the arena of human rights. Presenting information on the violations that are evident today, the unifying feature of this work rests on the premise that the quality of individual lives depends on the ability to live with dignity as well as freedom. The underlying emotional plea for action is prevalent; documents guaranteeing human rights are reproduced in their entirety.

The history of terrorism through different time periods and countries is appropriately portrayed as a study of society, politics, and personalities in *The Terrorists* (1983). Beginning with the eleventh-century Muslim Assassins and the French Revolution in 1789, terrorism became a political tool which is flourishing under many guises in the modern world. Always questioning the justification of their actions in relation to their goals, Meltzer views terrorism as a subject better understood when placed in the historical

setting in which the actions occur.

The shroud of mystery surrounding the Ku Klux Klan is swept aside in *The Truth About the Ku Klux Klan* (1982). Meltzer is extremely objective in writing this history of a cult whose orientation is a singular belief in and devotion to the idea of white supremacy. He impresses on the reader the need to think about the meaning of this group's existence, a group against all that typifies human rights and yet one whose number of sympathizers is growing. Chilling black-and-white photographs further enforce the sinister mood of this book.

Meltzer's view of the men and women who have resisted and protested against war is presented in *Ain't Gonna Study War No More: the Story of America's Peace Seekers* (1985). From the earliest group of dissenters in the United States, the Quakers, to the conscientious objectors to the war in Vietnam, these people believe the reasons for conflict are never worth the loss of life incurred. As in all the histories written by Meltzer, his point of view is implicit throughout the work. The omnipresence of poverty and the effect on its victims are presented with a grim realism in *Poverty in America* (1986). The riveting firsthand accounts combined with case histories add relevant meaning to the statistics which alone may suggest little.

Thematically identical to his other literary works, Meltzer's biographies generally focus on a human-rights advocate whose life is an example of triumph and tremendous perseverance against prejudice and injustice. Without raising them to hero status, Meltzer offers insights into the lives of people who on many levels are little different than the average man, and beyond the scope of the biographical information itself is the reminder that the fight for human rights is as important today as during the lifetime of the individual whose life is portrayed. Meltzer's biographies treat briefly the childhood and youth of the subject and often linger on the historical and social turmoil of the time period. Most of the biographies include selected bibliographies, both on the works of the individual and information on the background of the book.

Meltzer's first biography published for young readers was *A Light in the Dark: the Life of Samuel Gridley Howe* (1964). Depicting the life of a man who committed himself to working against many different forms of slavery, the diversity of Howe's life is an excellent example of social activism. Howe fought for causes as varied as the

Title page spread for Meltzer's 1968 biography of Langston Hughes

Greek war of independence and programs for the education of the blind and the mentally disabled. Meltzer presents a picture-perfect example of the dedication of one's life for the benefit of all mankind.

Tongue of Flame: the Life of Lydia Maria Child (1965) explores the life of the brilliant suffragist who wrote one of the first antislavery books published in the United States. She also devoted her expertise in political writing to the editorship of the *National Anti-Slavery Standard* as well as to periodicals devoted to children's stories and to magazine articles concerning women's roles and homemaking. This biography shows the diversity of a life committed to the active involvement of social reformation. Child, who worked to repair social injustices of the nineteenth century, is portrayed as a woman of heroic zeal.

History has regarded Thaddeus Stevens in many lights: from magnificent to malevolent. *Thaddeus Stevens and the Fight for Negro Rights*

(1967) sketches the life of a controversial lawyer and politician during Reconstruction. He was a relentless advocate of human rights and a strong supporter of the freedom movement despite much resistance and abuse from his colleagues. Meltzer portrays not only the life of this man committed to insuring the rights of freed slaves and the poor but also recounts a historical era when controversy abounded.

One of Meltzer's books that is most successful in portraying the depth and resolve necessary to be strong in a demanding and often unfair world is *Langston Hughes: A Biography* (1968), which was a National Book Award finalist. From his childhood in Harlem to Europe, Russia, and the Spanish civil war, Hughes's life is filled with a true sense of history. His is the story of a man of great adventure and perseverance. The diversity of Hughes's life as a fighter for civil rights and as an outstanding writer is also revealed in this portrait of the creator of "Simple" and an im-

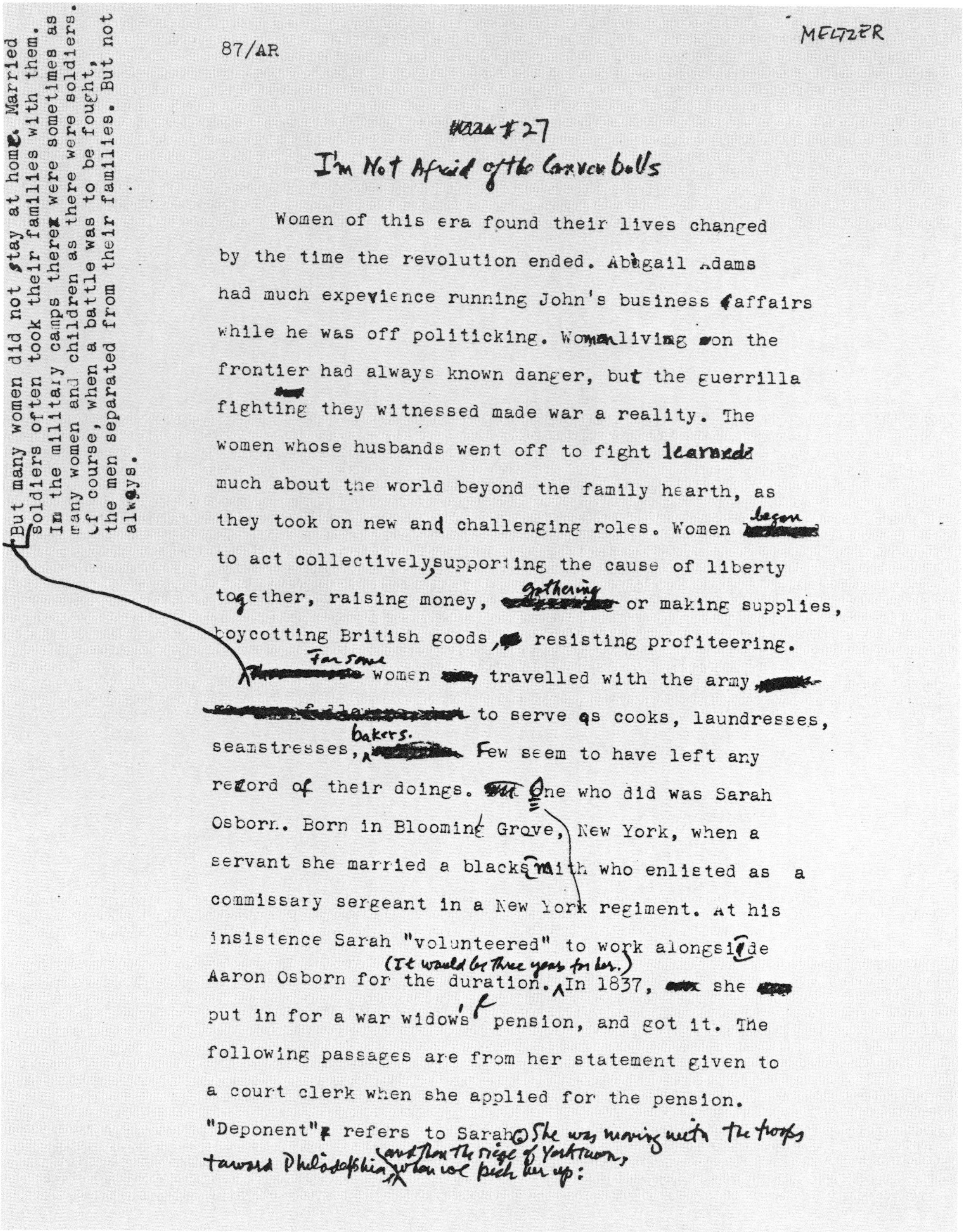

87/AR

MELTZER

####27
I'm Not Afraid of the Cannonballs

　　　Women of this era found their lives changed
by the time the revolution ended. Abigail Adams
had much experience running John's business ‌affairs
while he was off politicking. Woman living ‌on the
frontier had always known danger, but the guerrilla
fighting they witnessed made war a reality. The
women whose husbands went off to fight **learned‌**
much about the world beyond the family hearth, as
they took on new and challenging roles. Women *began*
to act collectively‌supporting the cause of liberty
together, raising money, *gathering* or making supplies,
boycotting British goods, resisting profiteering.
For some women travelled with the army
to serve as cooks, laundresses,
seamstresses, *bakers.* Few seem to have left any
record of their doings. One who did was Sarah
Osborn. Born in Blooming Grove, New York, when a
servant she married a blacksmith who enlisted as a
commissary sergeant in a New York regiment. At his
insistence Sarah "volunteered" to work alongside
Aaron Osborn for the duration. *(It would be three years for her.)* In 1837, she
put in for a war widow's pension, and got it. The
following passages are from her statement given to
a court clerk when she applied for the pension.
"Deponent" refers to Sarah. *She was moving with the troops
toward Philadelphia (and then the siege of Yorktown,) when we pick her up:*

Page from a revised typescript for Meltzer's forthcoming work on Abigail Adams (courtesy of the author)

portant member of the Harlem Renaissance.

The life of Margaret Sanger represents the ideal in the spirit of Meltzer's biographies. *Margaret Sanger: Pioneer of Birth Control* (1969) is the story of a person who devoted her life to help mankind in a way no one before her had attempted. By researching and promoting education on family planning, Sanger became a true ground breaker in the women's movement. In hindsight, what she accomplished was nothing short of incredible. Told in a straightforward manner, this biography is direct and forceful.

Meltzer has contributed four volumes to the Women of Our Time series, a selection of biographies of twentieth-century women designed for readers from ages seven to eleven. *Dorothea Lange: Life Through the Camera* (1985) is more of a depiction of the social climate of the United States during the depression and its aftermath than a true biography of Lange as an artist. Dwelling more on the subject matter of her photography and her documentary style, Meltzer does not emphasize the biographical information. Reproductions and explanations of some of the photographs of Lange's work provide, however, an interesting social commentary. More successful as a biography, *Betty Friedan: a Voice for Women's Rights* (1985) brings a greater awareness of the life of one whose commitment to an ideal was the result of a set of influences both personal and societal. Both books are sparsely illustrated and contain no bibliography. His other volumes in this series deal with Mary McLeod Bethune and Winnie Mandela.

Mark Twain: A Writer's Life (1985) was published on the occasion of the 150th anniversary of Twain's birth. Taken largely from previously published work, Meltzer has excerpted Twain's letters and speeches, selecting passages of humor and insight. Without being overly enthusiastic, Meltzer's biography is brief and well written.

Meltzer's only novel, *Underground Man,* was published in 1972. The protagonist, Joshua Bowen, is a composite figure of nameless and faceless figures which Meltzer became acquainted with over the years of his research. Born and raised in the North, Bowen moves to the South as a young man, devotes his life to the anti-slavery movement, and is eventually imprisoned for helping escaped slaves find freedom in the North. Though a work of fiction, the historical details provided in the book are as accurate as in Meltzer's other work. Bowen exemplifies much that is the promise of America and the struggle for human rights.

Meltzer does not hesitate to intersperse the history that he is presenting with his personal view. Most often found in his closing chapters, remarks such as "If each of us accepts the responsibility for the earth's survival, we can make a difference" are ubiquitous. Meltzer does not offer passive accounts of history for the sake of archival interest alone; his body of work presents the past with the intention of influencing the future.

Eve Merriam
(19 July 1916-   )

Laura M. Zaidman
University of South Carolina

BOOKS: *Family Circle*, edited, with a foreword, by Archibald MacLeish (New Haven: Yale University Press, 1946);

The Real Book about Franklin D. Roosevelt, illustrated by Bette J. Davis (Garden City: Garden City Books, 1952; London: Dobson, 1961);

Tomorrow Morning (New York: Twayne, 1953);

The Real Book about Amazing Birds, illustrated by Paul Wenck (Garden City: Garden City Books, 1955; London: Dobson, 1960);

Emma Lazarus: Woman With a Torch (New York: Citadel, 1956);

Montgomery, Alabama, Money, Mississippi, and Other Places (New York: Cameron, 1956);

The Double Bed From the Feminine Side (New York: Cameron, 1958);

The Voice of Liberty: The Story of Emma Lazarus, illustrated by Charles W. Walker (New York: Farrar, Straus & Cudahy, 1959);

Figleaf: The Business of Being in Fashion, illustrated by Burmah Burris (Philadelphia: Lippincott, 1960);

The Trouble with Love (New York: Macmillan, 1960);

A Gaggle of Geese, illustrated by Paul Galdone (New York: Knopf, 1960);

Mommies at Work, illustrated by Beni Montresor (New York: Knopf, 1961);

Basics: An I-Can-Read-Book for Grownups, illustrated by Robert Osborn (New York: Macmillan, 1962);

There Is No Rhyme for Silver, illustrated by Joseph Schindelman (New York: Atheneum, 1962);

Funny Town, illustrated by Evaline Ness (New York: Crowell-Collier, 1963);

What's in the Middle of a Riddle?, illustrated by Murray Tinkelman (New York: Collier, 1963);

After Nora Slammed the Door: American Women in the 1960's, the Unfinished Revolution (Cleveland: World, 1964);

What Can You Do With a Pocket?, illustrated by Harriet Sherman (New York: Knopf, 1964);

It Doesn't Always Have to Rhyme, illustrated by Malcolm Spooner (New York: Atheneum, 1964);

Small Fry, illustrated by Garry MacKenzie (New York: Knopf, 1965);

Don't Think About a White Bear, illustrated by Tinkelman (New York: Putnam's, 1965);

The Story of Benjamin Franklin, illustrated by Brinton Turkle (New York: Four Winds, 1965);

Do You Want to See Something?, illustrated by Abner Graboff (New York: Scholastic Books, 1965);

Miss Tibbett's Typewriter, illustrated by Rick Schreiter (New York: Knopf, 1966);

Catch a Little Rhyme, illustrated by Imero Gobbato (New York: Atheneum, 1966);

Andy All Year Round: A Picture Book of Four Seasons and Five Senses, illustrated by Margo Huff

(New York: Funk & Wagnalls, 1967);

Man and Woman: The Human Condition (Denver: Research Center on Woman, 1968);

Equality, Identity, and Complementarity (Denver: Research Center on Woman, 1968);

Independent Voices, illustrated by Arvis Stewart (New York: Atheneum, 1968);

Epaminondas, illustrated by Trina Schart Hyman (New York: Funk & Wagnalls, 1968); republished as *That Noodle-Head Epaminondas* (New York: Scholastic Books, 1972);

The Inner City Mother Goose, photographs by Lawrence Ratzkin (New York: Simon & Schuster, 1969);

The Nixon Poems, illustrated by John Gerbino (New York: Atheneum, 1970);

Finding a Poem, illustrated by Seymour Chwast (New York: Atheneum, 1970);

Growing Up Female in America: Ten Lives (Garden City: Doubleday, 1971);

Project 1-2-3, illustrated by Sherman (New York: McGraw-Hill, 1971);

I Am a Man: Ode to Martin Luther King, Jr., illustrated by Suzanne Verrier (Garden City: Doubleday, 1971);

Bam! Zam! Boom!: A Building Book, illustrated by William Lightfoot (New York: Walker, 1972);

Boys and Girls, Girls and Boys, illustrated by Sherman (New York: Holt, 1972);

Out Loud, illustrated by Sherman (New York: Atheneum, 1973);

Out of Our Father's House (New York: French, 1975);

A Husband's Notes About Her (New York: Collier, 1976);

The Club (New York: French, 1976);

Rainbow Writing (New York: Atheneum, 1976);

Ab to Zogg: A Lexicon for Science-Fiction and Fantasy Readers, illustrated by Albert Lorenz (New York: Atheneum, 1977);

Unhurry Harry, illustrated by Gail Owens (New York: Four Winds, 1978);

The Birthday Cow, illustrated by Guy Michel (New York: Knopf, 1978);

At Her Age (New York: French, 1979);

Good Night to Annie, illustrated by John Wallner (New York: Four Winds, 1980);

Dialogue for Lovers (New York: French, 1981);

A Word or Two with You: New Rhymes for Young Readers, illustrated by John Nez (New York: Atheneum, 1981);

And I Ain't Finished Yet (New York: French, 1982);

If Only I Could Tell You: Poems for Young Lovers and Dreamers, illustrated by Donna Diamond (New York: Knopf, 1983);

Jamboree: Rhymes for All Times, illustrated by Walter Gaffney-Keffel (New York: Dell, 1984);

Blackberry Ink, illustrated by Hans Wilhelm (New York: Morrow, 1985);

A Book of Wishes for You (Norwalk, Conn.: Gibson, 1985);

The Christmas Box, illustrated by David Small (New York: Morrow, 1985);

A Sky Full of Poems (New York: Dell, 1986);

The Birthday Door (New York: Morrow, 1986);

Fresh Paint: New Poems, woodcuts by David Frampton (New York: Macmillan, 1986).

OTHER: Hana Doskocilova, *Animal Tales*, translated by Merriam, illustrated by Mirko Hanak (Garden City: Doubleday, 1971);

Male and Female Under 18: Frank Comments from Young People about Their Sex Roles Today, edited by Merriam and Nancy Larrick (New York: Discus, 1973).

PERIODICAL PUBLICATION: "Some Pearls From Eve Merriam on Sharing Poetry with Children," *Learning85*, 14 (September 1985): 78-81.

Eve Merriam has written extensively for children and adults; her works include fiction, nonfiction, plays, and poetry. Her contributions to numerous poetry anthologies and many respected magazines have made her a most influential voice in educating teachers of children's literature. Recipient of the 1981 National Council of Teachers of English Award for Excellence in Poetry for Children, Merriam has been publishing poetry steadily for over forty years. This prolific writing career attests to her love of language and her dedication to sharing with children and adults her joy of reading. In "Some Pearls From Eve Merriam on Sharing Poetry with Children" she offers this advice: "Whatever you do, find ways to read poetry. Eat it, drink it, enjoy it, and share it." By inviting adults and children alike into the world of poetry, Merriam has shared the wealth of her experience with two generations. She well deserves the recognition she has received for excellence in children's poetry.

Born on 19 July 1916 in Philadelphia, Merriam grew up in a family of two older sisters and an older brother. Her parents, who owned a chain of women's dress shops, both emigrated from Russia as young children and grew up in small Pennsylvania towns. According to Merriam, the family joke about her parents' shared occupation was that the women's wear business was the only way they could afford clothing for all three girls. Her lifelong interest in fashion inspired a book-length study of fashion in America, *Figleaf: The Business of Being in Fashion* (1960). But her greatest passion is poetry.

Reading narrative and dramatic poems as a child, and light verse in particular, she was enthralled by the sound of words, by their musicality. Moreover, she recalls the thrill of being taken to Gilbert and Sullivan musicals and then chanting all the "tongue-twisting verses." No doubt she was equally entranced by the poetic quality of language in her favorite childhood classics: *Alice in Wonderland, Swiss Family Robinson*, fairy tales by Hans Christian Andersen and the Brothers Grimm, English and Irish folktales, and Greek, Roman, and Norse mythology.

Her love of poetry as a child was nourished by reading aloud poems printed in the *Philadelphia Bulletin;* for example, she recalls reciting "Gunga Din," "The Highwayman," and humorous light verse. She can still remember the sheer joy of nonsensical verse she learned as a child, such as, "I eat my peas with honey/I've done it all my life/They do taste kind of funny/It keeps them on the knife." This magical play with words led to her writing her own poems at about seven years of age. Describing a birch tree outside her bedroom window in one of her first poems, she wrote, "May my life be like the birch tree reaching upward to the sky." Typical of a child's innocent awe of nature and promises of worthy intentions, the poem was, according to Merriam, "very sanctimonious, very pure."

As an adolescent she wrote serious poems for her high school magazine and contributed light verse and political poems to the school's weekly newspaper. Merriam attributes her love for "the richness and the ambiguity of words" to "one very irascible, difficult, tendentious old Latin teacher. . . ." She also remembers one English teacher who encouraged her efforts as a writer; however, as a teenager she never planned to be a writer–she just wrote poems because she felt the need to write them, as if she could not live her life without writing them. The following fifty years prove the truth of her own feeling that "one is chosen to be a poet," for her driving ambition is clear.

Merriam received her undergraduate education at Cornell University and the University of Pennsylvania (A.B., 1937); then she did graduate work at the University of Wisconsin and Colum-

bia University. In 1939 her writing career began as a copywriter for Columbia Broadcasting System, working on radio documentaries and verse scripts. She conducted a weekly program on modern poetry for station WQXR in New York (1942-1946) and wrote a daily verse column for *PM* (1945). The following year she became feature editor of *Deb*, then fashion copy editor for *Glamour* (1947-1948). During these post-World War II years she published her first book of poetry (*Family Circle*, 1946) and started writing freelance magazine articles. She has two sons, Guy and Dee Michel. Merriam has taught courses in creative writing at City College of New York and has lectured to the public for over thirty years. She was also associated with the Bank Street College of Education's field project staff from 1958 to 1960.

Among her many awards and honors are the Yale Younger Poets Prize for *Family Circle* (1946); *Collier's* Star Fiction Award for "Make Something Happen" (1949); the William Newman Poetry Award (1957); a CBS grant to write poetic drama (1959); the Obie Award for *The Club* (1976); and most significantly, the NCTE Award (1981). This award verifies the high regard the teaching profession has for Merriam's contributions to children's poetry. Until 1977 the NCTE's annual children's book awards were given to prose works; then, the NCTE established the first award for poetry. The recipient of this award is selected by a national committee of professionals on the basis of the poet's entire canon, rather than individual poems or books of poetry. Before Merriam received this award, David McCord, Aileen Fisher, Karla Kuskin, and Myra Cohn Livingston were honored in the years 1977 through 1980 respectively. This special recognition gives Merriam added credibility as both a poet and a critic. In fact she is often quoted in scholarly journal articles about children's poetry and in textbooks used in courses on children's literature in colleges and universities. In addition she has written many articles herself; one of her best is "Some Pearls From Eve Merriam on Sharing Poetry with Children" which appeared in *Learning85*.

Persistence and hard work have been as important as inspiration in her very successful career as a poet. She won her first important award–the Yale Younger Poets Prize–after four unsuccessful annual entries. Significantly, a poet whom she idolized, Archibald MacLeish, judged her winning volume, *Family Circle*, published by

Yale University in 1946 with an introduction by MacLeish. She had slept with a copy of MacLeish's *Conquistador* under her pillow in college so no one would steal it, a testament to her great admiration of his work. Her own philosophy of poetry parallels MacLeish's "Arts Poetica"; as Merriam explains, his beginning line ("Poems should be palpable and mute, like a globed fruit") means that "one should use the fewest words possible and press the unspoken." Inspired by this master poet, Merriam evolved a similar perspective of stressing above all "the joy of the sound of language."

Sixteen years after her first book of adult poetry was published in the prestigious Yale series of Younger Poets, Merriam (now in her mid-forties) wrote her first book of children's poetry, *There Is No Rhyme for Silver* (1962), which was named a Junior Literary Guild selection—a most propitious beginning. With impressive regularity, she published book after book of children's verse: *It Doesn't Always Have to Rhyme* (1964), *Catch a Little Rhyme* (1966), *Independent Voices* (1968), *Finding a Poem* (1970)—another Junior Literary Guild selection—*I Am a Man: Ode to Martin Luther King, Jr.* (1971), *Out Loud* (1973), and *Rainbow Writing* (1976). During the 1960s and 1970s she also published sixteen other juvenile books as well as several volumes of poetry and nonfiction for adults.

In the 1980s Merriam has published several volumes of children's poetry: *A Word or Two with You: New Rhymes for Young Readers* (1981), *If Only I Could Tell You: Poems for Young Lovers and Dreamers* (1983), *Jamboree: Rhymes for All Times* (1984), *Blackberry Ink* (1985), *A Sky Full of Poems* (1986), and *Fresh Paint: New Poems* (1986).

There Is No Rhyme for Silver demonstrates Merriam's special delight in the sound of words, even words which have no rhyme. Poetry's repetition and musicality are unequaled by any other genre, she believes; consequently, these rhyming verses prove the special magic of poetry. She has discussed rhyme in critical essays on poetry, calling it "the chime that rings in time . . . like the little bell at the end of a typewriter line." This "bouncy-bouncing quality" of rhyme, however, is not essential, for even without rhyme, other poetic elements such as rhythm, assonance, alliteration, and onomatopoeia provide the reader with the special musical effects of poetry. In this collection of fifty-one poems, she invites children to leap right into the rhymes for "all seasons and all times"; in fact, her title poem, "There is no

Dust jacket for Merriam's 1966 volume of children's verse (Atheneum)

rhyme for silver," concludes with this invitation to participate in the medley of rhymes: "Rhymes to whisper, rhymes to yell,/Rhymes to chime like a swinging bell./Rhymes like a jump rope, now let's begin:/Take a turn and jump right in."

In a similar poem, "A Rhyme is a Jump Rope," Merriam shows how easy it is to play with poetry: "Perhaps we'll go sailing in the bay./We could feel the silver dots of spray./We might watch the white gulls fly away." Thus, the playful, conversational quality encourages children, indeed, to "take a turn and/Jump right in." Some poems play with foreign words, as in the delightful "Conversation" which has the Spanish, French, and Italian equivalents for "hello," "good night," and "see you soon." A child learns not only about rhythm and rhyme but also about other languages in this poem:

"Hasta luega," says Senorita Diega.
"Au revoir," says Mademoiselle Loire.
"A rividerci," says Signorina Terci.
"See you soon," says Miss Calhoun.

In addition, repetition and movement make poems successful, as this visually effective beginning in "Autumn Leaves":

Down
　down
　　down

Red
　yellow
　　brown

Merriam's conviction that exact rhyme is not absolutely necessary in a poem led to the title for her second book of poetry for children, *It Doesn't Always Have to Rhyme*. In a *Library Journal* (15 April 1964) review Ellen Rudin applauds the book as a "light, fresh spirited collection"; Merriam's poems often rhyme, "though not always tickety-tick, so what she means by her title is 'it doesn't always have to rhyme' neatly." In this book she continued to make poetry fun as well as instructional without sounding pedantic. "Inside a Poem" begins, "It doesn't always have to rhyme,/ but there's the repeat of a beat somewhere/An inner chime that makes you want to tap your feet or swerve in a curve." Thus, she assures her reader that poems open one's senses to be receptive to new experiences. The fifty-nine poems in this collection reinforce the importance of a foot-tapping rhythm—the magical beat of life. "Inside a Poem" invites the reader to "hear with your heels" and feel with "your eyes . . . what they never touched before." Another poem of the invitational mode is her often-reprinted "How to Eat a Poem," which opens with a superb metaphor for the enjoyment and nourishment poetry provides:

Don't be polite.
Bite in.
Pick it up with your fingers and lick the
　juice that may run down your chin.
It is ready and ripe now, whenever you are.

Nancy Larrick is one of many anthologists who have included "How to Eat a Poem" in their works. Another delightful metaphor is provided, appropriately enough, in "Metaphor," in which Merriam compares morning with a new sheet of paper—inspiring the would-be writer that the paper holds the same infinite possibilities as a new day brings with dawn. *It Doesn't Always Have to Rhyme* could serve as an excellent minicourse in the elements of poetry; besides "Metaphor," Merriam offers witty, informative pieces such as

"Simile: Willow and Ginkgo," "Couplet Countdown," "Quatrain," "Learning on a Limerick," "Beware of the Doggerel," "Onomatopoeia," and "A Cliché."

After *Catch a Little Rhyme*, a collection of poems in the same vein as her previous two books, Merriam wrote *Independent Voices*, which contains sketches of the lives of famous Americans in contemporary society as well as earlier periods. Her adult book *The Inner City Mother Goose* (1969) has startling modern interpretations of traditional verses. Merriam's poems from this volume were adapted into the lyrics for a musical entitled *Inner City*, which opened on Broadway on 12 December 1971. Her concern for racial equality was equally demonstrated in a later book, *I Am a Man: Ode to Martin Luther King, Jr.*, illustrated by Suzanne Verrier.

Her next book of children's poetry, *Finding a Poem*, another Junior Literary Guild selection, includes "Fantasia," a stark poem expressing the dream fantasy that someday a child will ask, "Mother, what was war?" Other poems that serve as excellent antiwar statements are "The Measure of Man" and "The Dirty Word." She goes beyond this questioning of war's inhumanity to reflect other aspects—more humorous pictures—of the milieu. Her young readers may have been blissfully unaware of the ongoing Vietnam War and the daily news reports about the war's complexities, but they knew their music, and Merriam uses this knowledge to introduce them to poetry. The gentle satire of American youth's self-centered priorities is inherent in "Umbilical," which begins:

You can take away my mother,
You can take away my sister,
but don't take away
my little transistor.

Of course, Merriam is critical of her audience's dependency on radios to provide their entertainment, but she chooses to focus on how poetry has its own music which needs no instrument beyond the voice to make it come alive.

Out Loud continues to stress the delightful ways to have fun with poetry, such as playing with shaped verse. Merriam effectively produces poems conveying rhythm and content by manipulating the positioning of words on the page. For example, in "Serpent," magical words slither and slide slowly down the poem for a total impact of visual and verbal sense. From the snakelike title to the final sibilant, the reader hears the repeated hissing and flowing consonants: the /s/ plus the /l/ of *sliding, silent, spill, sleek,* and *silk.* Even the letter *c* in ancient and sanctuary reinforces this sibilant sound. Many adolescents might not be familiar with polysyllabic words like *iridescent, sequestered, surreptitious, Narcissus, sinuous,* and *sibylline;* however, some might be inspired, as Merriam was in high school, to enrich their vocabulary by learning the etymology and meaning of these words. Even without a knowledge of each word, the reader can appreciate this memorable, multifaceted sensory experience.

As with many of Merriam's best poems, the reader learns language and cognitive development skills as well as gains pleasure through perceptions of the eye and ear. Without rhyme, other devices take precedent. Similarly, in "Windshield Wiper" the form reinforces the content as the eye moves back and forth across the page in precise rhythm, and then the last two lines ("clearing clearing veer/ clear here clear") show that the wiper comes to rest.

Another *Out Loud* poem, "Lullaby," also creates a unified impression of the senses and meaning. Unlike the menacing /s/ sound of "Serpent," the /s/ here is understood to signify quiet; in fact, the tranquil atmosphere evoked by a lullaby is created with the repetition of this sound in *wish, shuttered, fish, shore, shadows,* and *sure,* combined with the onomatopoeia of /l/ in *lullaby, lapping, slips, glide,* and *sleep, sleep.* The silence and relaxation of sleep are complete with the assurance of awaking tomorrow. *Rainbow Writing,* Merriam's next book of children's verse, contains two poems–"Grandmother Rocking" and "Say Nay"–about aging, quite a contrast to the usual focus on the carefree joys of childhood.

After *The Birthday Cow* (1978), *A Word or Two with You* (1981), and *If Only I Could Tell You* (1983), Merriam published *Jamboree: Rhymes for All Times* (1984), in which she reprinted favorites such as "How to Eat a Poem" and "A Vote for Vanilla" from *It Doesn't Always Have to Rhyme.* The latter is a typical Merriam poem celebrating exuberantly the delights of children. A fine nonsense poem in the best tradition of Edward Lear or Lewis Carroll, "A Vote for Vanilla" glorifies the simplest of the flavors. The persona roots for vanilla in cake or ice cream as well as "straight from the bean" plus "in pudding, potatoes, in fish or in stew,/In a sundae, a Monday, the whole week-long through!" No other flavor will do; "Boo, foo, eschew sarsaparilla;/More, adore, encore vanilla!" The word play ends with this silly

yet clever listing of the positive, comparative, and superlative degrees of the adjectival vanilla: "vanilla, vaniller, vanillest for me,/The flavor I favor most moderately." Another *Jamboree* poem, "Weather" celebrates the joyful expression of language and youthful playfulness in the rain. Here are the sounds–logical and nonsensical–made by the rain "freckling the windowpane." The fun of children gleefully jumping in mud puddles is also beautifully expressed.

Blackberry Ink (1985) continues with more of Merriam's humorous approach to the sheer delight of the sounds and meanings of words. In the title poem she presents a simple yet special experience children revel in–picking and eating sun-ripened berries in the summer. Still another common situation frequently remembered as special about childhood is having something new and wanting to save it. This experience is described perfectly in "Bella Had a New Umbrella." Because she did not want to ruin it, she walks in the rain without using it: "Her nose went sniff/ Her shoes went squish,/Her socks grew soggy,/ Her glasses got foggy,/Her pockets filled with water/And a little green froggy." Merriam seems to sympathize with the foolish child's priorities, though: "All she could speak was a weak *kachoo!*/ But Bella's umbrella stayed nice and new." Getting blackberry-ink tongues and rain-soaked clothes is part of childhood–experiences children can delight in and adults can reminisce about.

Fresh Paint: New Poems (1986) presents forty-five original poems that inspire the reader to take a fresh look at life's experiences–both new encounters and familiar ones seen in new ways. A first snowfall, a first airplane ride, new shoes, a new suit, and a new pencil all trigger recollections of old memories. Moreover, Merriam shares an original perspective on nature's wonders–from mushrooms to the moon–as she has done over the past two decades in her poetry. Her sharp word pictures, reinforced by David Frampton's black-and-white woodcuts, are typically vivid.

Merriam's many books of children's poetry prove her strong belief that poems are as essential to everyday lives as daily bread is to diets. She has said that poems are like magical fruit without peelings to discard; that is, they are so concentrated that there is no waste. In fact she distinguishes between poetry and prose with this analogy: "A poem is like a can of frozen juice. When you add three cans of water, you get the prose version." "How to Eat a Poem" perfectly il-

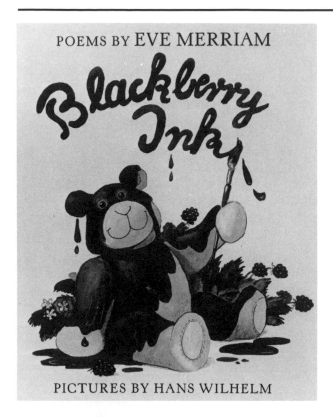

POEMS BY EVE MERRIAM

PICTURES BY HANS WILHELM

Dust jacket for Merriam's 1985 poetry volume which presents a humorous approach to the sounds and meanings of words (Morrow)

lustrates this metaphor showing her readers that poetry is needed for sustenance, to be enjoyed wholeheartedly and enthusiastically, and to be shared unselfishly with others.

After the success of *Inner City*, Merriam began to concentrate on play writing, seeing it as a logical development of her role as a poet. She has published six plays to date: *Out of Our Father's House* (1975), *The Club* (1976), *At Her Age* (1979), *Dialogue for Lovers* (1981), and *And I Ain't Finished Yet* (1982). Her habit of rewriting a good deal between rehearsals, despite the pressures of producing a play, led to her being called "the fastest pen in the East." The same may be said of her poetry writing, which is an on-going process of creating.

Merriam says she has several cycles of poetry going on at a time, several of which have been in progress for years. Craving novelty, she likes to work quickly and go from one thing to another, as evident in her description of her method of writing, *If Only I Could Tell You* (1983), love poems for teenagers: "I knew from the beginning the approximate number of poems that I was going to do. I took little notes. I didn't have time to work for quite a few months because I was involved in another project, so I got a folder, and whenever I got a notion or an idea, I'd just throw it in the folder. When my time came months later, I took out those notes. Some of them made sense, some didn't, but then I was able to write the book fairly rapidly." On the other hand, she used a more disciplined approach for *The Inner City Mother Goose*, demanding of herself a daily output of two or three poems. She attempts to polish the poems to her satisfaction, going over them repeatedly, though ultimately, she agrees with W. H. Auden that "a poem is never finished; it's just abandoned."

Included along with Merriam's poems which focus on the timeless reflections on children's feelings about themselves and the world around them—emotions that typify most of her poetry for young people—are poems about contemporary social issues, such as feminism and equality of the sexes, ecology, pacifism, and racism. Her plays and nonfiction books deal more exclusively with these concerns. Examples of her feminist writings include *The Double Bed From the Feminine Side* (1958); *After Nora Slammed the Door: American Women in the 1960's, the Unfinished Revolution* (1964); *Growing Up Female in America: Ten Lives* (1971); *Out of Our Father's House* (1975); *A Husband's Notes About Her* (1976); and *At Her Age* (1979). Depicting equality in relationships between the sexes is important for Merriam, as evidenced by poems which show both girls and boys with similar needs and the same feelings. She rewrote the folktale of Epaminondas, because she considered the language sexist, even racist; to make her point more forcefully, the book, *Epaminondas* (1968), was republished in 1972 as *That Noodle-Head Epaminondas*.

Merriam has also written picture books on the theme of equality of the sexes, such as *Mommies at Work* (1961), which portrays mothers in various nontraditional work roles as well as the traditional nurturing role at home with children, and *Boys and Girls, Girls and Boys* (1972). Another early 1970s statement about sexual equality is *Male and Female Under Eighteen: Frank Comments from Young People about Their Sex Roles Today* (1973), coedited with another much-published author and poetry anthologist, Nancy Larrick. Two other works which reflect Merriam's heightened consciousness about this subject were published in 1968 by the Research Center on Woman: *Man and Woman: The Human Condition* and *Equality, Identity, and Complementarity*.

Merriam admits that in her younger years

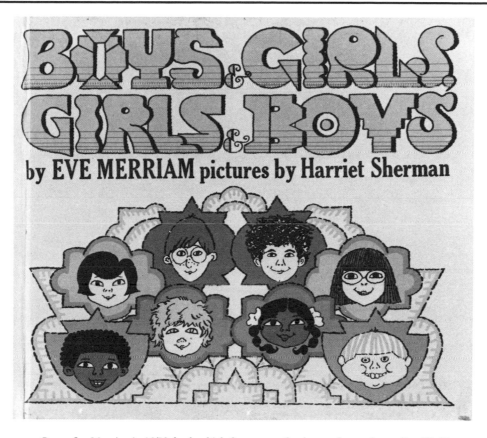

Cover for Merriam's 1972 book which focuses on the theme of sexual equality (Holt)

she feared that being stereotyped as a feminist poet would prevent her popularity. Initially, she suffered the loneliness of not having people with whom to discuss her ideas; however, the women's movement brought her the companionship of other writers sharing her concerns. "To grow up in a world where there is much more equality and much less hypocrisy between the sexes, where there is openness and frankness is good," comments Merriam, whose poetry has allowed children to explore opportunities unfettered by sexist stereotypes. She has expressed her pleasure that sexist chauvinism is no longer such a destructive force, yet believes "there is a great way to go." She is similarly optimistic about society's progress toward racial equality.

Merriam did not always feel free to express her concerns about social issues, but like other poets in the late 1960s and 1970s, she began to focus on more relevant topics. Poems about nature, animals, family, and the everyday experiences children encounter never disappeared from her children's books, yet she stretched beyond these traditional sensibilities of childhood and shifted her concerns to reflect the inner emotional conflicts and stark realities of the world fac-

ing children: anxieties, alienation, racial and social injustice, war, inhumane technology, and struggles of urban life. Hence, one notices a definite transcendence from the safe, socially acceptable poems of *Catch a Little Rhyme* to bolder statements of social and political realities in *Finding a Poem* (1970).

According to critic Judith Saltman, Merriam's work in *Finding a Poem* and *Rainbow Writing* demonstrates a "dexterous handling of metered verse, free verse, and verbal nonsense . . . allied with social satire and a fierce conscience." Research conducted by Ann Terry for a 1974 NCTE research monograph, *Children's Poetry Preferences: A National Survey of Upper Elementary Grades*, proves that children respond more favorably to contemporary, rather than traditional poems. And, according to Saltman, Merriam is considered one of the best writers of popular "sophisticated urban poetry" children enjoy. Her exuberant rhymes and her use of dialogue are not only perfect examples of the oral tradition of children's literature but also excellent illustrations of the contemporary tastes of young readers.

Merriam's development into a more socially aware poet has not changed her basic beliefs

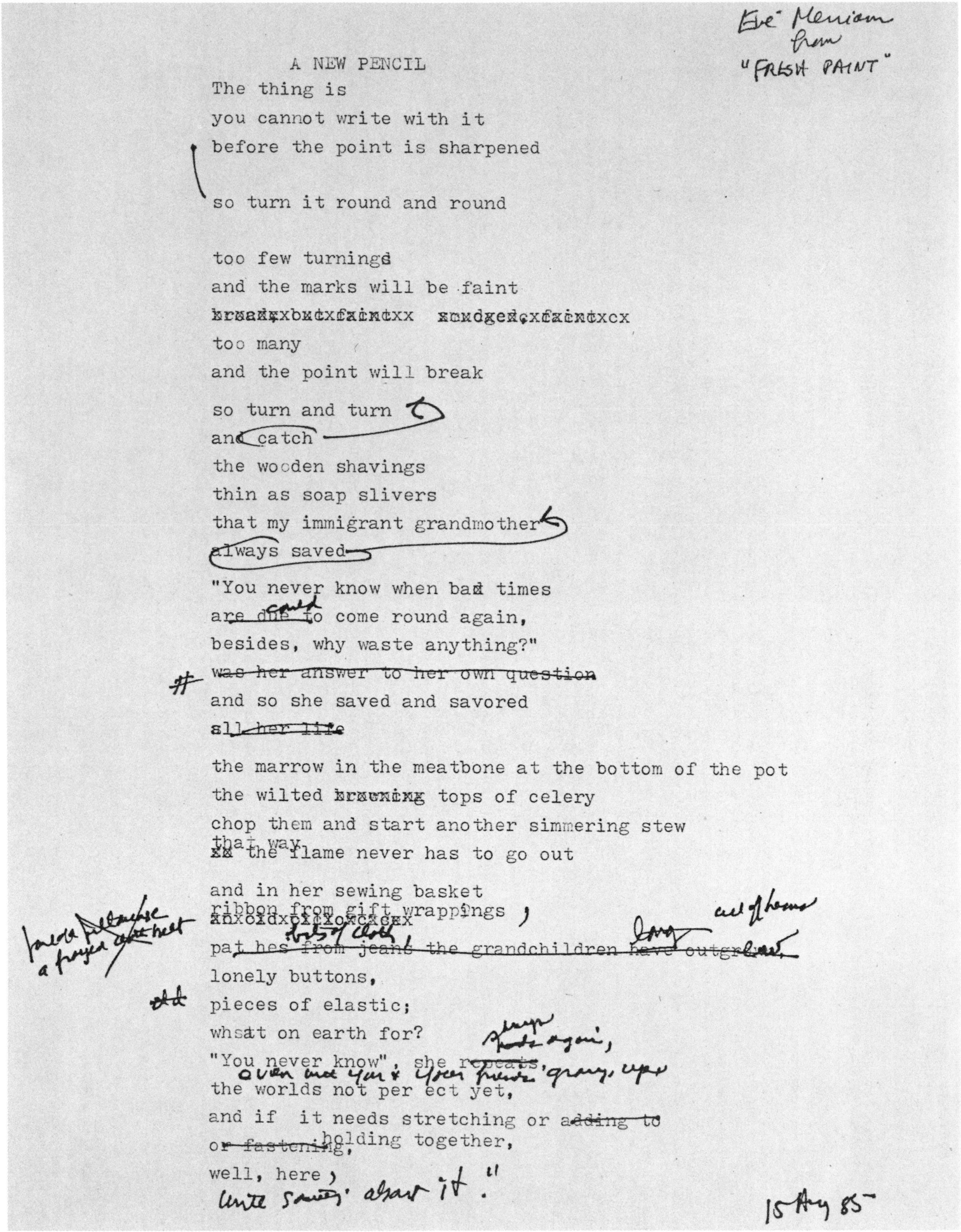

A NEW PENCIL

The thing is
you cannot write with it
before the point is sharpened

so turn it round and round

too few turnings
and the marks will be faint
~~breakxbutxfaintxx   xxxdxexxxfaintxcx~~
too many
and the point will break

so turn and turn
and catch
the wooden shavings
thin as soap slivers
that my immigrant grandmother
always saved

"You never know when bad times
are ~~due to~~ come round again,
besides, why waste anything?"
~~was her answer to her own question~~
and so she saved and savored
~~all her life~~

the marrow in the meatbone at the bottom of the pot
the wilted ~~braxxixg~~ tops of celery
chop them and start another simmering stew
that way
~~xx~~ the flame never has to go out

and in her sewing basket
ribbon from gift wrappings
~~xnxoxdxpxllxoxcxcx~~
~~patches from jeans the grandchildren here outgrew~~
lonely buttons,
pieces of elastic;
what on earth for?
"You never know", she ~~repeats~~
the worlds not perfect yet,
and if it needs stretching or ~~adding to~~
~~or fastening,~~ holding together,
well, here,

15 Aug 85

Revised typescript for a poem which appeared in Merriam's latest book, Fresh Paint: New Poems *(courtesy of the author)*

about the writing of poems. Because her poems are meant to be spoken aloud rather than to remain mute on the printed page, her imagery is alive and her diction is colloquial. While her style has often changed to reflect her subjects, her poetry exhibits a continual improvisation and experimentation with language. Because every word is significant Merriam chooses each one to achieve the greatest impact. Breaking the established rules of children's poetry which demand rigid meter and regular exact rhyme, Merriam delights in playing with the visual, aural, and intellectual effects of words. She compares the poet's awareness of punctuation and the amount of space between lines to a painter's cognizance of color and space relationships on a canvas. Even though many of her poems are abstract, and some may miss their mark, her artistry is undoubtable.

Eve Merriam's excellence in poetry has given her readers a better appreciation for a wide range of topics expressing the varieties of a child's experiences, and her insights into the way in which children should approach poetry have greatly influenced the ability of parents and teachers to help them enjoy it. By inviting two genera- tions of readers into her world of words, Eve Merriam has greatly enriched children's poetry.

References:

Patricia Bosworth, "She Ain't Finished Yet," *Working Woman* (March 1982): 136-137;

"Eve Merriam Is Named Winner of NCTE's Award for Excellence in Poetry for Children," *Language Arts*, 58 (May 1981): 590;

Lee Bennett Hopkins, "NCTE Poetry Award Winners on Nonprint Media," *Language Arts*, 59 (September 1982): 615-616;

Judith Saltman, ed., *The Riverside Anthology of Children's Literature*, 6th edition (Boston: Houghton Mifflin, 1985), p. 91;

Glenna Sloan, "Profile: Eve Merriam," *Language Arts*, 58 (November/December 1981): 957-964.

Papers:

Eve Merriam's manuscripts are located in the Kerlan Collection, University of Minnesota, Minneapolis; the de Grummond Collection, University of Southern Mississippi, Hattiesburg; and the Schlesinger Library, Radcliffe College, Cambridge.

Evaline Ness

(24 April 1911-12 August 1986)

Philip A. Sadler
Central Missouri State University

BOOKS: *Josefina February* (New York: Scribners, 1963; London: Chatto, Boyd & Oliver, 1970);

A Gift for Sula Sula (New York: Scribners, 1963);

Exactly Alike (New York: Scribners, 1964; Edinburgh: Oliver & Boyd, 1968);

Pavo and the Princess (New York: Scribners, 1964);

A Double Discovery (New York: Scribners, 1965);

Sam, Bangs, and Moonshine (New York: Holt, Rinehart & Winston, 1966; London: Bodley Head, 1967);

Long, Broad, and Quickeye, adapted and illustrated by Ness (New York: Scribners, 1969; London: Chatto, Boyd & Oliver, 1971);

The Girl and the Goatherd; or This and That and Thus and So (New York: Dutton, 1970);

Do You Have the Time, Lydia? (New York: Dutton, 1971; London: Bodley Head, 1972);

Old Mother Hubbard and Her Dog, adapted and illustrated by Ness (New York: Holt, Rinehart & Winston, 1972);

Yeck Eck (New York: Dutton, 1974);

An American Colonial Paper House to Cut Out and Color (New York: Scribners, 1975);

This Is a Paper Palace to Cut Out and Color (New York: Scribners, 1976);

Four Rooms from the Metropolitan Museum of Art to Cut Out and Color (New York: Scribners, 1977);

A Victorian Paper House to Cut Out and Color (New York: Scribners, 1978);

A Shaker Paper House to Cut Out and Color (New York: Scribners, 1979);

Marcella's Guardian Angel (New York: Holiday House, 1979);

Fierce the Lion (New York: Holiday House, 1980).

SELECTED BOOKS ILLUSTRATED: Mary J. Gibbons, *The Story of Ophelia* (New York: Doubleday, 1954);

Charlton Ogburn, *The Bridge* (Boston: Houghton Mifflin, 1957);

Elizabeth Marie Pope, *The Sherwood Ring* (Boston: Houghton Mifflin, 1958);

Elizabeth Jane Coatsworth, *Lonely Maria* (New York: Pantheon, 1960);

Evaline Ness

Maurice Osborne, *Ondine, the Story of a Bird Who Was Different* (Boston: Houghton Mifflin, 1960);

Mary Britton Miller, *Listen—the Birds: Poems* (New York: Pantheon, 1961);

Sorche Nic Leodhas, ed., *Thistle and Thyme: Tales and Legends from Scotland* (New York: Holt, Rinehart & Winston, 1962);

Helen E. Buckley, *Where Did Josie Go?* (New York: Lothrop, Lee & Shepard, 1962);

Julia Cunningham, *Macaroon* (New York: Pantheon, 1962);

Barbara Robinson, *Across from Indian Shore* (New York: Lothrop, Lee & Shepard, 1962);

Coatsworth, *The Princess and the Lion* (New York: Pantheon, 1963);

Eve Merriam, *Funny Town* (New York: Crowell-Collier, 1963);

Leodhas, *All in the Morning Early* (New York: Holt, Rinehart & Winston, 1963);

Buckley, *Some Cheese for Charles* (New York: Lothrop, Lee & Shepard, 1963);

Buckley, *Josie and the Snow* (New York: Lothrop, Lee & Shepard, 1964);

Rebecca Caudill, *A Pocketful of Cricket* (New York: Holt, Rinehart & Winston, 1964);

Cunningham, *Candle Tales* (New York: Pantheon, 1964);

Lloyd Alexander, *Coll and His White Pig* (New York: Holt, Rinehart & Winston, 1965);

Virginia Haviland, *Favorite Fairy Tales Told in Italy* (Boston: Little, Brown, 1965);

Joseph Jacobs, ed., *Tom Tit Tot: An English Folk Tale* (New York: Scribners, 1965);

Sylvia Cassedy, *Pierino and the Bell* (Garden City: Doubleday, 1966);

Alexander, *The Truthful Harp* (New York: Holt, Rinehart & Winston, 1967);

Buckley, *Josie's Buttercup* (New York: Lothrop, Lee & Shepard, 1967);

Jacobs, ed., *Mr. Miacca, an English Folk Tale* (New York: Holt, Rinehart & Winston, 1967);

Leodhas, *Kellyburn Braes* (New York: Holt, Rinehart & Winston, 1968);

Leodhas, ed., *A Scottish Songbook* (New York: Holt, Rinehart & Winston, 1969);

Lucille Clifton, *Some of the Days of Everett Anderson* (New York: Holt, Rinehart & Winston, 1970);

Buckley, *Too Many Crackers* (New York: Lothrop, Lee & Shepard, 1971);

Clifton, *Everett Anderson's Christmas Coming* (New York: Holt, Rinehart & Winston, 1971);

Maxine Kumin and Anne Sexton, *Joey and the Birthday Present* (New York: McGraw-Hill, 1971);

Algernon Black, *The Woman of the Wood: A Tale from Old Russia* (New York: Holt, Rinehart & Winston, 1973);

Clifton, *Don't You Remember?* (New York: Dutton, 1973);

Margaret Wise Brown, *The Steamroller, A Fantasy* (New York: Walker, 1974);

Kumin and Sexton, *The Wizard's Tears* (New York: McGraw-Hill, 1975);

Walter de la Mare, *The Warmint* (New York: Scribners, 1976);

Nathan Zimelman, *The Lives of My Cat Alfred* (New York: Dutton, 1976);

Kumin, *What Color is Caesar?* (New York: McGraw-Hill, 1978);

Charles Scribner, Jr., *The Devil's Bridge, A Legend* (New York: Scribners, 1978);

Steven Kroll, *The Hand-Me Down Doll* (New York: Holiday House, 1983).

OTHER: *Amelia Mixed the Mustard and Other Poems*, selected and illustrated by Ness (New York: Scribners, 1975).

PERIODICAL PUBLICATION: "Caldecott Acceptance Speech," *Horn Book* (August 1967): 435-438.

A roster of major American illustrators of books for children and young adults would include such names as Maurice Sendak, Ezra Jack Keats, Lynd Ward, Robert McCloskey, Marcia Brown, and Evaline Ness. Though each member of this impressive company of artists is unique in his or her own way, Evaline Ness belongs in the group because of her versatility, her talent and ability, and her consistency.

Ness entered the children's book field in 1954 and served a nine-year apprenticeship illustrating books by other writers. She began to receive national attention in 1964 when *All in the Morning Early* (1963), which she illustrated for Sorche Nic Leodhas, was selected as a runner-up for the Caldecott Medal. Her work warranted this recognition three years in a row before, finally, in 1967 she was awarded the medal for *Sam, Bangs, and Moonshine* (1966). In 1972 she achieved international recognition as the United States nominee for the Hans Christian Andersen award. Many of her titles have appeared on "Best Books of the Year" lists. Many of her books have been published in at least six other countries from England to Japan and continue to be widely popular and critically acclaimed.

Evaline Michelow, daughter of Albert and Myrtle Carter Michelow, was born 24 April 1911, in Union City, Ohio. Two years later the family moved to Pontiac, Michigan, where she grew up and attended high school, never dreaming of a career in art. As a child, however, as soon as she could read and write, she often copied her favorite stories on rolls of ribbon paper provided her by her older sister, a milliner. She also selected pictures from magazines to illustrate stories written by another older sister. Ness said that her first effort at drawing was an exact copy in pastels of a picture of a ship. She was very proud of that picture, but others did not think it was quite so remarkable. It was a long time later that she realized the difference between art and copying.

Ness's artistic talent remained dormant during her high-school years. Upon graduation she decided to attend Ball State Teachers College in Muncie, Indiana, to become a teacher. There she became acquainted with an illustrator who rekindled her interest in art and impressed her with stories of the money that could be made in the field of commercial illustration. Between 1933 and 1935, she studied painting and anatomy at the Art Institute of Chicago, holding jobs to pay her tuition. Quickly she learned that "anyone can master techniques; putting oneself into the work is what makes the difference." After some training, she found assignments in the fields of fashion drawing, advertising, and magazine illustration, liking the money she made but thoroughly disliking the strain of short deadlines.

In 1938 she married Eliot Ness, who was then the Public Safety Director of Cleveland. The couple moved to Washington, D.C. during World War II. There Ness enrolled at the Corcoran Gallery of Art, where she met Richard Lahey, an instructor who exerted an important influence upon her work. In her early years of study she received a first prize for painting.

In 1945 and 1946 Ness combined her interests in teaching and art by offering classes for children at the Corcoran Gallery. Then she moved to New York City where she continued teaching at the Parsons School of Design and began a three-year stint in fashion illustration at Saks Fifth Avenue. Free-lancing as an illustrator, she also produced a number of illustrations for *Seventeen, Charm, Mademoiselle,* and other magazines.

Her husband's occupation made it necessary for them to travel extensively; they spent some time in the Orient as well as in Italy. In Rome she continued her art studies at the Accademia di Belle Arti in 1951 and 1952. Notes and sketches from these travels were used often in books as seeds for stories as well as illustrations.

The Nesses divorced in 1946. In 1959 Ness married Arnold A. Bayard, an engineer who designed and manufactured heavy machinery. Bayard is now retired and lives in Philadelphia, Pennsylvania.

Ness's first effort at illustrating a book for children, *The Story of Ophelia,* by Mary Gibbons, appeared in 1954, but the book attracted little attention. Utilizing her soon-to-be distinctive style in serigraphs and woodcuts, Ness illustrated from one to four children's books each year between

Dust jacket for the first book for which Ness provided text as well as illustrations (Scribners)

1957 and 1962. For Charlton Ogburn's *The Bridge* (1957), she executed silk-screen prints, creating separate screens for each of the colors and producing the finished illustrations by hand-rubbing. These were then printed by the offset process, a printing innovation at the time. Such a process frees the artist from the rigidity of the metal type press and permits utilization of the total page area. It is possible for an artist to push the drawing beyond the margin and to move lines of type outside established boundaries, integrating text and illustration. Ness continued to experiment constantly with all types of materials, unusual and commonplace, to create patterns and textures. She also mixed media, incorporating anything that would accomplish her purpose, such as adding pen-and-ink lines to silk-screen prints or woodcuts to provide fine details.

The Bridge was followed with illustrations for Elizabeth Marie Pope's *The Sherwood Ring* (1958) in which Ness proved herself a master of stylized patterns arranged within lightly defined shapes. The illustrations are striking additions to this novel for older readers. Her silk-screen prints with additional lines for Elizabeth

Coatsworth's *Lonely Maria* (1960) reflect the golden sun in the West Indies, the setting of the book. Her serigraphs for *Ondine, the Story of a Bird Who Was Different* (1960), by Maurice Osborne, effectively highlight the story, each with an accent of one extra color. Sorche Nic Leodhas's *Thistle and Thyme: Tales and Legends from Scotland* (1962) includes unusual but delightful woodcuts with authentic Scottish settings that contribute handsomely to the book. *Thistle and Thyme* was the first in a series of profitable collaborations with this author. *Listen—the Birds: Poems*, by Mary Britton Miller (1961) gained Ness recognition on the *New York Times* Choice of Best Illustrated Books of the Year, her first such notice in the field of children's books and an omen of things to come.

Ness stated that she "struck gold" with one of the first book jackets she designed, Scott O'Dell's *Island of the Blue Dolphins* (1960), which won the Newbery Medal in 1961. Ness then received commissions to design jackets for each of the books in Lloyd Alexander's Prydain cycle. Eventually Alexander wrote *Coll and His White Pig* (1965) and *The Truthful Harp* (1967) as stories for her to illustrate.

Ness created illustrations for Helen E. Buckley's *Where Did Josie Go?* and Julia Cunningham's *Macaroon* in 1962, providing hints (in the drawings of the little girls of these two books) of the strong female protagonists of some of her own later books, *Sam, Bangs, and Moonshine, Exactly Alike* (1964) and *Fierce the Lion* (1980). The first of Buckley's Josie books also exhibits Ness's interesting use of warm oranges, pinks, and turquoise. The color in *Macaroon*, however, is more subdued and muted, a striking combination of red and brown. For Barbara Robinson's *Across from Indian Shore* (1962), Ness's illustrations are not as stylized as those for *The Sherwood Ring*, but neither are they circumscribed by frames. She also included interesting nature details that gracefully supplement the actions of the characters.

Ness received her greatest recognition for her work done between 1963 and 1967. Executed in turquoise, brown, and black, the illustrations for *All in the Morning Early* (1963) depict an increasing number of characters on each ensuing page, taxing Ness's ingenuity as a designer and artist. She solved the problem by adding colored strips down the side of each page, giving the book an added sense of unity. Text and illustrations are totally integrated in the Caldecott Honor Book.

At the suggestion of Nancy Quint, an editor at Charles Scribner's Sons, Ness wrote her first text for a children's book, *Josefina February* (1963). For this effort she utilized sketches made during a year's stay in Haiti, creating woodcuts depicting her impressions of the people and the land to illustrate the story of one of her inimitable little girls.

Josefina is unhappy because she has no money to buy a birthday present for her grandfather. Picking fruit to sell at the market, she discovers a little lost burro. Though she would like to keep the burro for herself, she searches for and finds its owner. Of course, her honesty is rewarded at the end of the story. Mr. Hippolythe, the owner, decides that he cannot care for the burro himself and asks Josefina to relieve him of his responsibility. The highly appropriate woodcuts are printed in warm orange, lavender, and brown, colors wisely chosen to reflect the West Indian island atmosphere.

Josefina February was widely acclaimed. It was included on the American Library Association's Notable Children's Book List for 1963 and was also cited by the *New York Herald Tribune* as an Honor Book. Her second book, *A Gift for Sula Sula* (1963), followed immediately. This tale of a misplaced pelican on an Aegean island reflects more of Ness's travels.

Exhibiting her newly discovered prowess as a writer, Ness continued writing stories as carefully conceived as her artwork, such as *Exactly Alike* and *Pavo and the Princess*, both published in 1964. *Exactly Alike*, illustrated in colorful woodcuts, depicts a girl named Elizabeth who has four identical smaller brothers, each with the tendency to make her miserable, though she is unable to tell them apart. The subtle differences between the boys are readily apparent in the finely detailed illustrations in four colors.

Rebecca Caudill's *A Pocketful of Cricket* (1964) was a runner-up for the Caldecott Medal in 1965. To illustrate this story of a young farm boy, Ness used black poster paint on acetate. Paint was scraped from the completed illustration to give texture and lend highlights to the composition. Accents and details were provided by pen and ink, and a large area of a single color—orange, olive green, or yellow ochre—dominates each illustration and unifies the design. Again, there is the absence of a frame for the illustration, which allows the text and illustration to flow together.

Relying on sketches, notes, and memories of

her travels in the Orient, Ness created *A Double Discovery* (1965), the story of a Japanese boy who loses his glasses while searching for a pony in a bamboo grove. Stumbling around almost unable to see, he finally captures the rather wild pony but is unable to ride her. Finally Saru, a monkey who had found Norio's glasses and used them to correct her double vision, makes friends with Norio and introduces the boy to her friend the pony. After that, Norio always makes sure his glasses are shined carefully before he shares them with Saru, which he does from time to time. The happy story is enhanced by the predominantly green woodcuts which reflect a definite Japanese feeling and style of art. *Exactly Alike* and *A Double Discovery* were both included on the *New York Times* Choice of Best Illustrated Children's Book of the Year lists.

Pink and gold accent the woodcuts by Ness in Virginia Haviland's retellings of stories in *Favorite Fairy Tales Told in Italy* (1965). Perhaps, however, the illustrations for Alexander's *Coll and His White Pig*, which also appeared in 1965, are among Ness's most colorful. In this picture book, the land of Prydain is presented in crayon and reproduced in full color. Ness produced layers of different colors and scraped away areas to reveal the desired hues. White space is incorporated into the drawings that bleed away from the backgrounds, and small decorative objects punctuate the text. The whole effect is quite charming and enhances the maké-believe story of a kidnapped pig in a mythical kingdom.

It was Joseph Jacobs's edition of *Tom Tit Tot: An English Folk Tale* (1965), however, that garnered Ness the most attention up to this point in her career. Ness's third Caldecott Honor Book, the heavy black woodcuts accented with light blue and two shades of brown beautifully dominate the pages with the text fitting into appropriate spaces. Ness experimented with the cutting of some of the words of the text into blocks for reproduction, adding an extra dimension. Old English costumes and settings are used to advantage and reflect careful research. Ness said that *Tom Tit Tot* was fun to do because the characters were so stupid that she was able to treat them humorously. The folktale is perfectly expressed in the strong and earthy illustrations.

After her three Caldecott Honor Books, Ness finally achieved top recognition in the field of American children's book illustration in 1967 for her *Sam, Bangs, and Moonshine*. As do many artists, she had created and kept a number of illustra-

tions for herself. For *Sam, Bangs, and Moonshine* she delved into this treasure-chest portfolio and found a sketch of "a ragged, displaced-person little girl who was ecstatic over a starfish." In the same portfolio were drawings of fishing boats. The little girl became Sam, the totally believable not-so-perfect little girl who lives in a world of make-believe in the midst of a realistic fishing village. She rides in a dragon-drawn chariot and makes up tales of things she wishes for: "Not even the sailors home from the sea could tell stranger stories than Sam." Her mother is a mermaid; Bangs, her cat, is a fierce lion. Sam creates her world as she wishes it to be. Her fisherman father cautions Sam about her lies because "moonshine spells trouble." The lies do almost cause tragedy when Sam sends her friend Thomas to the Blue Rock to find the baby kangaroo Sam says lives with her mother, the mermaid. Thomas goes at high tide and has to be rescued by Sam's father. Without being overly didactic, the plot permits Sam to discover the difference between real and "moonshine" and that "there's good moonshine and bad moonshine."

Designing the entire book, Ness created parts of illustrations with silk-screen techniques which were then montaged and etched with ink. Printed in two colors and black, the book has great individuality. Pictures and text flow easily and spontaneously from page to page. Flat color areas were given interesting textures achieved in various ways. A rubber roller was inked and rolled over various surfaces—crumpled aluminum foil, wood shavings, a sponge, a pile of string, or anything else that would transfer a pattern to the roller. Ness always experimented with textures and maintained a supply of interesting designs for future use. She said "anything goes" that achieves the desired effect.

In 1966 Ness illustrated *Pierino and the Bell* by Sylvia Cassedy, creating a spectacular and beautiful book influenced by her sojourn in Rome. Every detail is present in the woodcuts—the fountains, the yellow stone houses, and the pigeons, as well as the intricate decorations on the huge bell. Ness succinctly captured the real essence of Tuscany in the book.

Her illustrations for Alexander's *The Truthful Harp* (1967) are quite different in their two-color reproduction from those done earlier for Alexander's *Coll and His White Pig*. There is still the magic and the mystery of the fantasy kingdom of Prydain, however, in Ness's illustrations. *Mr. Miacca*, another Jacobs folktale, also ap-

Title-page spread for Joseph Jacobs's 1965 edition of an English folktale, illustrated by Ness (Scribners)

peared in 1967. Done in gouache, the illustrations depict London of 1750-1850, and once again Ness's careful efforts at research for costumes and backgrounds are evident. The book exudes a Dickensian feeling.

In 1968 and 1969 Ness continued her profitable collaboration with Sorche Nic Leodhas, producing woodcut illustrations for two more books, *Kellyburn Braes,* an old Scottish folksong, and *A Scottish Songbook,* which was selected for the 1969-1970 American Institute of Graphic Arts Children's Book Show, along with three of Ness's other works: *Long, Broad, and Quickeye* (1969); *Some of the Days of Everett Anderson* (1970); and *The Girl and the Goatherd; or This and That and Thus and So* (1970).

Long, Broad, and Quickeye is the Andrew Lang version of a Bohemian tale adapted by Ness and retold with lively pictures. For *Some of the Days of Everett Anderson,* by Lucille Clifton, the first collaboration for the author and the artist in this series about a small black boy, Ness created delightful yellow-and-brown line-and-wash drawings accented with textured backgrounds which have become a Ness trademark. She similarly illustrated Clifton's *Everett Anderson's Christmas Coming*

(1971) utilizing brown, lavender, and black.

The third of Ness's contributions to the AIGA show of 1969-1970 was her original story, *The Girl and the Goatherd; or, This and That and Thus and So,* about a young girl who feels that she is the ugliest girl in the world; therefore, she thinks of nothing but being beautiful. The story achieves folktale quality in its fantasy romp involving a goatherd who loves the girl for what she is and a witch and her spells. Once again Ness created beautiful three-color montages unfettered by frames. Pen-and-ink drawings are used for the subject matter. Backgrounds are textures lifted from surfaces with inking and spoon rubbings as in woodcuts. There are some woodcuts made from unplaned wood, showing the texture of the woodgrain in the final execution. Again Ness experimented with the use of type outside regular lines of the text but not in the illustrations themselves.

Continuing her busy schedule, in 1971 Ness produced the first of her collaborations with Maxine Kumin and Anne Sexton, *Joey and the Birthday Present.* She created four-color illustrations in line with textured background accents for the story of a field mouse and a little boy's pet white

Cover for Ness's Caldecott Medal-winning book
(Holt, Rinehart & Winston)

mouse. She also illustrated her own story of a little girl who never took the time to finish any project she began, *Do You Have the Time, Lydia?* (1971), utilizing another island setting. A subtly didactic story, the book is light and full of sunshine with its yellow-and-pink highlighted drawings. She used a small dowel, sharpened and dipped in ink, for the drawings on heavy rice paper. Shadings were done with pencils and lithographic crayon. Textures were again applied and pressed down on the finished drawings. The finished artwork was printed by offset. *Do You Have the Time, Lydia?* was reprinted in 1976 with the text translated into Spanish by Alma Flor Ada and entitled *¿Tienes Tiempo, Lidia?*

Ness next chose to do her version of the old nursery rhyme, *Old Mother Hubbard and Her Dog* (1972), fetchingly depicting the dog as an English sheepdog. Each double-page spread devoted to a section of the rhyme is done in full color and humorously shows the dog doing just what he is supposed to do with a smaller facing illustration of the destination of the old woman to get what the dog desires and the character she meets there.

The tongue-in-cheek interpretation of the rhyme may be Ness's most humorous book.

For Algernon D. Black's *The Woman of the Wood: A Tale from Old Russia* (1973), Ness chose a variety of techniques including ink and collage. A distinctive Russian flavor is evident in the illustrations characterized by assymetrical balance and exaggerated body forms.

The Steamroller, A Fantasy (1974), by Margaret Wise Brown, is a Christmas story done appropriately in subdued red and green. The same year, Ness published her own story *Yeck Eck*, based upon her own childhood experience of actually borrowing babies from the neighbors to bathe them, give them cookies, and put them to sleep in her doll carriage. Although Ness always had to return the babies, *Yeck Eck* is the story of how she wished it had been. Charmingly done in brown and orange, the sketches with solid color accents integrate type with illustrations. Overprinted on some of the pictures are words (without balloons as in comic books) spoken by some of the characters. This is one of Ness's most appealing books. The same device was used more sparingly in *The Wizard's Tears* by Kumin and Sexton (1975), but the book is done with beautiful and funny woodcuts colored with a preponderance of green and a smattering of red.

Ness had a special feeling for the illustrations she did for *Amelia Mixed the Mustard and Other Poems* (1975). She selected the poems about interesting girls of fact and fiction such as Jumping Joan, Pandora, Queen Nefertiti, and seventeen other girls of all ages and dispositions. Ness thoroughly enjoyed doing the humorous ombré woodcuts that reflect honesty and vitality and reveal that not all females are sweet docile creatures. The beauty and pensiveness in some of the illustrations are perfectly balanced by the whimsicality in others. The poems were selected from a broad spectrum and, with the illustrations, reflect an intense understanding of the individuality of woman.

Between 1975 and 1979 Ness changed directions and designed five volumes in a series of cut-out-and-color books: *An American Colonial Paper House to Cut Out and Color* (1975), *This Is a Paper Palace to Cut Out and Color* (1976), *Four Rooms from the Metropolitan Museum of Art to Cut Out and Color* (1977), *A Victorian Paper House to Cut Out and Color* (1978), and *A Shaker Paper House to Cut Out and Color* (1979), all published by Scribners. For these spiral-bound books she created binding boards that would become stand-up walls representing four rooms in each of the buildings depicted. She provided pages of furniture to cut out and assemble after coloring. There are fresh, original designs for walls, floors, and other decorative and functional details, all based on meticulous research. Historical notes are appended relating to materials, paints, dyes, textiles, and preferences of each period. According to their editor, Margery Cayler, the books sold well at first, but they are no longer in print due to their unique nature and the needs of libraries.

During the same period Ness also produced illustrations for Walter de la Mare's *The Warmint* (1976), Kumin's *What Color Is Caesar?* (1978), and Charles Scribner, Jr.'s retelling of *The Devil's Bridge, A Legend* (1978). All of these books were done in her varied styles and differing media. Each, however, is an important addition to Ness's work.

Marcella's Guardian Angel (1979) is Ness's original story in which a little girl's problem is that her guardian angel never stops talking. The angel is Marcella's conscience and makes her feel guilty about her rudeness and critical nature. Marcella learns the game of flip-flop, doing the opposite of the way she feels—but only every other day. Marcella's new game is shared with her friends; her friends share it with their friends; and soon Marcella has many new friends. Ness, as usual, covered her didacticism with a special charm that made her messages fun. This is a happy book with light and airy sketches done in red, muted green, and black with textured accents.

Before the publication of *Fierce: The Lion* (1980), Ness began a novel for teenagers, an unusual departure from her previous work. That novel was still in its draft stages at the time of her death, but it inspired her to do this picture story about a lion with the best act in the circus. All of the other circus animals and clowns are envious and jealous, which causes them to hate Fierce. Fierce is not accustomed to being hated; he likes to be soft, cuddly, and loved. Isobel, one of Ness's best-realized female characters, comes to his rescue by securing a job at the zoo for Fierce giving rides to children, and Isobel is always there to keep him from engaging in any "hanky panky." The children are thrilled and fall in love with Fierce—and Fierce loves them back. Once again Ness created an old-fashioned girl with high-button shoes like many of the other little girls in her earlier books. There is a special nostalgia—and beauty—in the olive green, orange, and black illustrations.

Dust jacket for Ness's last book, about a popular circus lion who is envied by the other animals
(Holiday House)

Four years passed before the publication of Ness's last published work, illustrations for Steven Kroll's *The Hand-Me-Down Doll* (1983). The beautiful picture-story included her highly respected and inimitable creations depicting a lonely doll who longed for someone to love her and give her a name. Though the story is only adequate, with a thin plot and little characterization, the illustrations are quite impressive. Zena Sutherland, in her review for the *Bulletin of the Center for Children's Books* (December 1983), states that they are "striking in details of architecture" and "costume," as well as deftly composed and "both humorous and elegant." They add life to the story, quite fittingly executed in Ness's familiar style, sketches in shades of violet-blue highlighted with fuchsia, again without frames but backed with the usual textures. Readers who have always appreciated the art of Evaline Ness can recognize her genius in this last work published before her death on 12 August 1986.

Evaline Ness worked diligently during her career as an artist and rightfully earned her place among the most outstanding illustrators of books for children. Her distinguished art deserves the acclaim and the awards she achieved, and her stories lend her career an added significance. *Sam,*

Bangs, and Moonshine, Tom Tit Tot, A Pocketful of Cricket, and her illustrations for many other books will enrich the lives of children for generations to come, and adults who know and love books for children will treasure her highly individualistic contributions to the art of children's literature.

References:

Ann Durell, "Evaline Ness," *Horn Book* (August 1967): 438-443;

Grace Allen Hogarth, "The Artist and His Editor," in *Illustrators of Children's Books, 1957-1966,* edited by Lee Kingman, Joanna Foster, and Ruth Giles Lontoft (Boston: Horn Book, 1968), pp. 37-52;

Joan Hess Michel, "Evaline Ness, the Caldecott Medalist for 1967," *American Artist* (June 1967): 32-37;

Lynd Ward, "The Book Artist: Ideas and Techniques," in *Illustrators of Children's Books, 1946-1956,* edited by Ruth Hill Viguers, Marcia Dalphin, and Bertha Mahony Miller (Boston: Horn Book, 1958), pp. 14-35;

Ernest W. Watson, "Eness, Rising Star in the Illustration Firmament," *American Artist* (January 1956): 29-33.

Papers:

Evaline Ness's manuscripts and original illustrations are in the Kerlan Collection, University of Minnesota Library, Minneapolis. Manuscript and illustrations for *Sam, Bangs, and Moonshine* are in the Detroit Public Library.

Jack Prelutsky

(8 September 1940-   )

Anita Trout

BOOKS: *A Gopher in the Garden and Other Animal Poems,* illustrated by Robert Leydenfrost (New York: Macmillan, 1967);

Lazy Blackbird and Other Verses, illustrated by Janosch (New York: Macmillan, 1969);

Three Saxon Nobles and Other Verses, illustrated by Eva Johanna Rubin (New York: Macmillan, 1969);

The Terrible Tiger, illustrated by Arnold Lobel (New York: Macmillan, 1969; London: Bodley Head, 1975);

Toucans Two and Other Poems, illustrated by Jose Aruego (New York: Macmillan, 1970); republished as *Zoo Doings and Other Poems* (London: Hamish Hamilton, 1971);

Circus, illustrated by Lobel (New York: Macmillan, 1974; London: Hamish Hamilton, 1975);

The Pack Rat's Day and Other Poems, illustrated by Margaret Bloy Graham (New York: Macmillan, 1974);

Nightmares: Poems to Trouble Your Sleep, illustrated by Lobel (New York: Greenwillow, 1976; London: A. & C. Black, 1978);

It's Halloween, illustrated by Marylin Hafner (New York: Greenwillow, 1977; Kingswood, U.K.: World's Work, 1978);

The Snopp On the Sidewalk and Other Poems, illustrated by Byron Barton (New York: Greenwillow, 1977);

The Mean Old Hyena, illustrated by Lobel (New York: Greenwillow, 1978);

The Queen of Eene, illustrated by Victoria Chess (New York: Greenwillow, 1978);

The Headless Horseman Rides Tonight: More Poems to Trouble Your Sleep, illustrated by Lobel (New York: Greenwillow, 1980);

Rainy, Rainy Saturday, illustrated by Hafner (New York: Greenwillow, 1980);

Rolling Harvey Down the Hill, illustrated by Chess (New York: Greenwillow, 1980);

It's Christmas, illustrated by Hafner (New York: Greenwillow, 1981);

The Sheriff of Rottenshot, illustrated by Chess (New York: Greenwillow, 1982);

Jack Prelutsky

Kermit's Garden of Verses, illustrated by Bruce McNally (New York: Random House, 1982);

The Baby Uggs are Hatching, illustrated by James Stevenson (New York: Greenwillow, 1982);

It's Thanksgiving, illustrated by Hafner (New York: Greenwillow, 1982);

Zoo Doings: Animal Poems, illustrated by Paul O. Zelinsky (New York: Greenwillow, 1983)—includes *A Gopher in the Garden and Other Animal Poems, Toucans Two and Other Poems,* and *The Pack Rat's Day and Other Poems;*

It's Valentine's Day, illustrated by Yossi Abolafia (New York: Greenwillow, 1983);

What I Did Last Summer, illustrated by Abolafia (New York: Greenwillow, 1984);

It's Snowing! It's Snowing!, illustrated by Jeanne Titherington (New York: Greenwillow, 1984);

The New Kid on the Block, illustrated by Stevenson (New York: Greenwillow, 1984);

My Parents Think I'm Sleeping, illustrated by Abolafia (New York: Greenwillow, 1985);

Ride a Purple Pelican, illustrated by Garth Williams (New York: Greenwillow, 1986);

Brave Little Pete of Geranium Street, illustrated by Eva Eriksson (New York: Greenwillow, 1986).

OTHER: *The Random House Book of Poetry for Children,* edited by Prelutsky, illustrated by Arnold Lobel (New York: Random House, 1983);

Read Aloud Rhymes for the Very Young, edited by Prelutsky, illustrated by Marc Brown (New York: Knopf, 1986).

TRANSLATIONS: Rudolf Neumann, *The Bad Bear,* illustrated by Eva Johanna Rubin (New York: Macmillan, 1967);

Heinrich Hoffman-Donner, *The Mountain Bounder* (New York: Macmillan, 1967);

No End of Nonsense: Humorous Verses, illustrated by Wilfred Blecher (New York: Macmillan, 1968; London: Abelard Schuman, 1970);

Barbro Lindgren, *The Wild Baby,* illustrated by Eva Eriksson (New York: Greenwillow, 1981);

Lindgren, *The Wild Baby Goes to Sea,* illustrated by Eriksson (New York: Greenwillow, 1983).

Best known for his successful mix of the frightening and the foolish, Jack Prelutsky, for the past twenty years, has been making children cringe with fear and laugh with delight. His poems often portray the macabre in such an exaggerated manner that the overall effect is a humorous one. And his nonsense verse is entertaining and fun, especially when read out loud.

Jack Prelutsky was born on 8 September 1940 in Brooklyn, New York. Nurturing his creative ability at an early age, he attended the High School of Music and Art and later went on to Hunter College, which is now part of the City University of New York. He has also studied voice at several music schools, singing with opera companies in both Massachusetts and Washington. He has lived in Cambridge, Massachusetts; Seattle, Washington; and Albuquerque, New Mexico.

His occupations, besides author, have also been diverse and eclectic. From time to time he has worked as an actor, folksinger, bookseller, taxi driver, door-to-door salesman, furniture mover, and photographer. This combination of artistic and manual pursuits is reflected in Prelutsky's interests: making both wooden toys and metal sculpture, collecting books and models of frogs, inventing word games, and bicycle riding.

Prelutsky's first book, *A Gopher in the Garden and Other Animal Poems* (1967), was published after a friend who was familiar with his work urged him to submit some of his verses to a publisher. The collection's appeal, appropriate for preschoolers and older children, lies in its internal rhyme and nonsense theme. Since the book's publication, Prelutsky has written two dozen volumes of verse, and his popularity has grown with each.

Prelutsky's poetry features animals and fantastic beasts which behave in inventive ways. He also writes of people and problems familiar to youngsters: dealing with the neighborhood bully, going to school, and being afraid of the dark. Writing in traditional poetic forms, he employs puns, alliteration, and word play in ways which have caused him to be ranked ,among the masters of contemporary verse for children.

Similar to *A Gopher in the Garden, Lazy Blackbird and Other Verses* (1969) and *Three Saxon Nobles and Other Verses* (1969) are comprised of light-hearted verse. Prelutsky's rhythmic lines and unforced rhymes attract and hold the attention of young readers.

Prelutsky's next work, *The Terrible Tiger* (1969), is meant for a preschool audience and is thus most effective when read aloud. The tiger's exaggerated ferocity is epitomized in his chant, "and anyone who comes my way / I'll surely swallow down today." As illustrated by black-and-white drawings, the tiger devours the baker, the grocer, and the farmer before having trouble with the tailor, whom he swallows complete with scissors, needle, and thread.

Another group of animal verses, *Toucans Two and Other Poems* (1970) is comprised of light, rhythmic lines which provide facts about each creature described. For example: "The ancient armadillo / is as simple as the rain / he's an armor-plated pillow / with a microscopic brain."

Prelutsky's next book, *Circus* (1974), is a collection of verses which each tell of a different circus act. Judi Barret of the *New York Times Book Review* (31 March 1974) expresses a note of disappointment: "Some of the verse leaves me wishing that it was less ordinary and its rhyme less forced." Nevertheless, Barret praised the work's overall effect, stating that "This book gives me a taste of the circus. All that's missing is the sawdust and popcorn under my feet."

Prelutsky's poem "Sheep," from *The Pack Rat's Day and Other Poems* (1974), is a good example of his early style:

Sheep are gentle, shy and meek,
They love to play at hide and seek
Their hearts are softer than their fleece,
And left alone they live in peace.

His choice of descriptive words underscores the placid nature of the sheep. Other poems in the book further illustrate Prelutsky's ability to create fresh word pictures of familiar animals. According to Ethel L. Heins in *Horn Book* (December 1974), "these new poems about animals come from a young writer who possesses a rare dexterity with words."

Prelutsky's primary fascination for children, however, seems to be his macabre delight in the darker side of fantasy and human nature. *Nightmares: Poems to Trouble Your Sleep* is aptly named. Published in 1976, this book gave full reign to Prelutsky's imaginative powers. With its companion, *The Headless Horseman Rides Tonight: More Poems to Trouble Your Sleep* (1980), it forms a catalogue of bogeymen, ghouls, and other horrific creatures. There is a shivery delight for the young reader in the gruesome detailing of crumbling bones and the implication that the reader may be the next victim. Nancy Willard in the 3 October 1976 *New York Times Book Review* recognized the appeal of the book for children when she commented, "By their standards, a good collection of monster poems should send you to bed with nightmares."

With *It's Halloween* (1977), Prelutsky began a group of books about holidays, including *It's Christmas* (1981), *It's Thanksgiving* (1982), and *It's Valentine's Day* (1983). Each of these works is illustrated by colorful, seasonal drawings, and Prelutsky portrays each occasion in an original manner. For instance, Christmas is revealed not always to be the perfect holiday when there is no snow to accompany a new sled. And the typical sentiment of Valentine's Day is replaced with "I love you more than applesauce."

In the twelve short selections of *The Snopp On the Sidewalk and Other Poems* (1977), Prelutsky introduces a loathsome band of fantastic and friendly monsters. He describes the bemused creatures in deft verse and contemporary tongue-twisting language. Another unique animal is portrayed in *The Mean Old Hyena* (1978). The hyena plays practical jokes on other characters and, as Helen Gregory of the *School Library Journal* (October 1978) states, the work is full of "well-sustained nonsense to tickle its young readers."

The Queen of Eene (1978) features primarily human characters, but their actions are no more predictable, except in their zaniness, than those of Prelutsky's improbable beasties. The fourteen poems are unrelated, forming a collection of odd rhymes. Most of the verses are double-page

Dust jackets for Prelutsky's two volumes of poetry which explore his macabre delight in the darker side of fantasy and human nature (Greenwillow)

Cover for Prelutsky's 1982 collection described by Peter Neumeyer as "an ebullient, thoroughly successful book with no pretensions other than to give lightsome fun, which it does both in picture and in verse, with never a hitch" (Greenwillow)

spreads and are accented by black-and-white illustrations. Many of the poems in this volume deal with people eating such incongruous objects as automobiles, basketballs, and soap.

A gang of mischievous boys are the stars of *Rolling Harvey Down the Hill* (1980), which depicts the types of practical jokes which boys delight in. Prelutsky comes close to the reality of childhood with these poems, for young readers will as surely cringe in sympathy with the victims as they will chortle with the pranksters.

In addition to creating original verse, Prelutsky has also translated several children's works. Among them are Rudolf Neumann's *The Bad Bear* (1967) and Heinrich Hoffman-Donner's *The Mountain Bounder* (1967), but his best-known translations are Barbro Lindgren's *The Wild Baby* (1981) and *The Wild Baby Goes to Sea* (1983). These two books tell of an uninhibited toddler named Ben who is energetic and adventurous, swinging from chandeliers and bounding down steps. In the second work, as he sails off in a wooden box, Ben is sure that any form of danger can be fun.

In *The Sheriff of Rottenshot* (1982) Prelutsky achieves humor through strong meter and word play. For example, in "The Catfish" the creature "only has one simple wish, / And that's to catch a rare mousefish." And in "The Court Jester's Last Report to the King" the jester tells his sire of the demise of his kingdom, and concludes:

Oh sire! Great sire! the tidings are dire,
A giant has trampled the school,
Your army has fled, there are bees in your bed
And your nose has come off . . . APRIL FOOL!

The Sheriff of Rottenshot was praised by critics and children alike. As Peter Neumeyer said in his *School Library Journal* review (March 1982), the work is "an ebullient, thoroughly successful book with no pretensions other than to give lightsome fun, which it does both in picture and in verse, with never a hitch."

Prelutsky's next work features the Muppet characters made famous by creator Jim Henson. *Kermit's Garden of Verses* (1982) deals with Kermit the Frog's feelings for Miss Piggy, Fozzie Bear, the Swedish Chef, and other characters. His thoughts are best summarized by the conclusion he draws about Gonzo: "Though I think he has no talent / And I know he has no taste, / Gonzo has no equal / And could never be replaced."

It's Snowing! It's Snowing! (1984) is a collection of poems in which both wit and humor are used in describing the winter landscapes. Prelutsky portrays both the beauty of the season as well as its bitter side. For instance, in the title poem he describes the air as "a silvery blur"; while, in "I Do Not Mind You, Winter Wind," he finally admits:

> But when you bowl me over
> And I land on my behind,
> Then I must tell you, Winter Wind,
> I mind . . . I really mind!

Jeanne Titherington's drawings in gray, white, and light blue complement the verses well and give the book a cool, wintery feeling.

With *The New Kid on the Block* (1984) Prelutsky continued his practice of funny, lighthearted verse. He writes of mice on tricycles, jellyfish stew, Snillies (who live in the middle of lilies), and many other odd creations. The poems in this rather lengthy collection are accented by black-and-white ink drawings.

The poems in *My Parents Think I'm Sleeping* (1985) address the traumas of having to go to sleep at night. "A spooky sort of shadow" turns out to be just a brush and comb, while in "When I'm Very Nearly Sleeping" a monster is successfully frightened off by the bedside light. The verse is highlighted by Yossi Abolafia's drawings done in blue and gold with a scattering of stars.

The seamless quality of Prelutsky's work is nowhere more apparent than in *Ride a Purple Pelican* (1986). The rhymes and cadences have the comfortable flavor of old favorites, and Garth Williams's illustrations are flamboyant or subdued, depending on the subject matter. Throughout the work Prelutsky integrates North American place names. These references are often highly visual and effective: "A white cloud floated like a swan, / high above Saskatchewan."

In addition to his work as an author, Prelutsky has edited two books of poetry. *The Random House Book of Poetry for Children* (1983) is an excellent selection of both favorite and less-familiar poems, covering a wide range of topics and moods making it a collection of great versatility. *Read Aloud Rhymes for the Very Young* (1986) is equally well chosen, covering themes that appeal to both the children and the adults who share this volume. John Ciardi, Norma Farber, Eve Merriam, and Walter de la Mare are among the more than one hundred authors represented in the work. Marc Brown's soft-colored illustrations complement the poems, and ample white space gives the book an uncluttered look.

For many children, poetry is a genre tainted by the curse of "literature," and reading it is considered drudgery. Contemporary poets such as Jack Prelutsky restore the fun and fascination in the study of the English language and its rhythmic patterns. For years he has succeeded in entertaining children with both fright and humor, and it seems certain that his audience is eager to see what Jack Prelutsky will do next.

Richard Scarry
(5 June 1919-   )

Bobbie Burch Lemontt
University of Tennessee

SELECTED BOOKS: *The Great Big Car and Truck Book* (New York: Simon & Schuster, 1951);

Rabbit and His Friends (New York: Simon & Schuster, 1953; London: Muller, 1954);

Tinker and Tanker (Garden City: Garden City Books, 1960; Feltham, U.K.: Hamlyn, 1969);

The Hickory Dickory Clock Book (Garden City: Doubleday, 1961);

My Nursery Tale Book (New York: Golden Press, 1961);

Tinker and Tanker Out West (Garden City: Doubleday, 1961; Feltham, U.K.: Hamlyn, 1969);

Tinker and Tanker and Their Spaceship (Garden City: Doubleday, 1961);

Tinker and Tanker and the Pirates (Garden City: Doubleday, 1961);

Tinker and Tanker, Knights of the Round Table (Garden City: Doubleday, 1963; Feltham, U.K.: Hamlyn, 1969);

Tinker and Tanker in Africa (Garden City: Doubleday, 1963; Feltham, U.K.: Hamlyn, 1969);

What Animals Do (New York: Golden Press, 1963);

Richard Scarry's Best Word Book Ever (New York: Golden Press, 1963; London: Hamlyn, 1964);

The Rooster Struts (New York: Golden Press, 1963); republished as *The Golden Happy Book of Animals* (New York: Golden Press, 1964);

Busy, Busy World (New York: Golden Press, 1965; London: Hamlyn, 1966);

The Bunny Book (New York: Golden Press, 1965; London: Golden Pleasure, 1966);

Storybook Dictionary (New York: Golden Press, 1966; London: Hamlyn, 1967);

Is This the House of Mistress Mouse? (New York: Golden Press, 1966);

Planes (New York: Golden Press, 1967);

Trains (New York: Golden Press, 1967);

Boats (New York: Golden Press, 1967);

Cars (New York: Golden Press, 1967);

Best Storybook Ever (New York: Golden Press, 1968; London: Hamlyn, 1970);

The Early Bird (New York: Random House, 1968; London: Collins, 1970);

What Do People Do All Day? (New York: Random House, 1968; London: Collins, 1968);

Richard Scarry

The Adventures of Tinker and Tanker, includes *Tinker and Tanker*, *Tinker and Tanker Out West*, and *Tinker and Tanker and Their Space Ship* (Garden City: Doubleday, 1968);

Richard Scarry's Teeny Tiny Tales (New York: Golden Press, 1969; Feltham, U.K.: Hamlyn, 1970);

The Great Pie Robbery (New York: Random House, 1969; London: Collins, 1969);

The Supermarket Mystery (New York: Random House, 1969; London: Collins, 1969);

Richard Scarry's Great Big Schoolhouse (New York: Random House, 1969; London: Collins, 1969);

More Adventures of Tinker and Tanker, includes *Tinker and Tanker and the Pirates*, *Tinker and*

Tanker, Knights of the Round Table, and *Tinker and Tanker in Africa* (Garden City: Doubleday, 1971);

ABC Word Book (New York: Random House, 1971; London: Collins, 1972);

Richard Scarry's Best Stories Ever (New York: Golden Press, 1971);

Richard Scarry's Fun with Words (New York: Golden Press, 1971);

Richard Scarry's Going Places (New York: Golden Press, 1971);

Richard Scarry's Great Big Air Book (New York: Random House, 1971);

Richard Scarry's Things to Know (New York: Golden Press, 1971);

Funniest Storybook Ever (New York: Random House, 1972; London: Collins, 1972);

Nicky Goes to the Doctor (New York: Golden Press, 1972; London: Hamlyn, 1972);

Richard Scarry's Great Big Mystery Book, includes *The Great Pie Robbery* and *The Supermarket Mystery* (New York: Random House, 1972);

Richard Scarry's Hop Aboard, Here We Go (New York: Golden Press, 1972);

Babykins and His Family (New York: Golden Press, 1973);

Silly Stories (New York: Golden Press, 1973);

Find Your ABC's (New York: Random House, 1973);

Richard Scarry's Please and Thank You Book (New York: Random House, 1973; London: Hamlyn, 1973);

Richard Scarry's Best Rainy Day Book Ever (New York: Random House, 1974; London: Hamlyn, 1975);

Cars and Trucks and Things That Go (New York: Golden Press, 1974; London: Collins, 1974);

Richard Scarry's Great Steamboat Mystery (New York: Random House, 1975; London: Collins, 1976);

Richard Scarry's Best Counting Book Ever (New York: Random House, 1975; London: Collins, 1976);

Richard Scarry's Animal Nursery Tales (New York: Golden Press, 1975; London: Collins, 1975);

Richard Scarry's All Day Long (New York: Golden Press, 1976);

Early Words (New York: Random House, 1976; London: Collins, 1977);

Richard Scarry's Color Book (New York: Random House, 1976; London: Collins, 1977);

Richard Scarry's Busiest People Ever (New York: Random House, 1976; London: Collins, 1977);

Richard Scarry's Collins Cubs (London: Collins, 1976);

Richard Scarry's Picture Dictionary (London: Collins, 1976);

Learn to Count (New York: Golden Press, 1976);

All Year Long (New York: Golden Press, 1976);

Richard Scarry's At Work (New York: Golden Press, 1976; London: Hamlyn, 1985);

Short and Tall (New York: Golden Press, 1976);

Richard Scarry's My House (New York: Golden Press, 1976; London: Collins, 1982);

Richard Scarry's On Vacation (New York: Golden Press, 1976);

Richard Scarry's About Animals (New York: Golden Press, 1976);

Richard Scarry's On the Farm (New York: Golden Press, 1976; London: Collins, 1979);

Richard Scarry's Lowly Worm Storybook (New York: Random House, 1977);

Richard Scarry's Best Make-It Book Ever (New York: Random House, 1977; London: Collins, 1978);

In My Town (New York: Golden Press, 1978; London: Hamlyn, 1985);

Richard Scarry's Little Bedtime Book (New York: Random House, 1978; London: Collins, 1978);

Richard Scarry's Little Counting Book (New York: Random House, 1978);

Richard Scarry's Little Word Book (New York: Random House, 1978);

Richard Scarry's Postman Pig and His Busy Neighbors (New York: Random House, 1978; London: Fontana, 1979);

Richard Scarry's Lowly Worm Sniffy Book (New York: Random House, 1978);

Richard Scarry's Mr. Fixit and Other Stories (New York: Random House, 1978; London: Collins, 1978);

Richard Scarry's Best First Book Ever (New York: Random House, 1979; London: Collins, 1980);

Richard Scarry's Mix or Match Storybook (New York: Random House, 1979; London: Collins, 1980);

Richard Scarry's Peasant Pig and the Terrible Dragon (New York: Random House, 1980; London: Collins, 1981);

Richard Scarry's Lowly Worm Word Book (New York: Random House, 1981);

Richard Scarry's Pig Will and Pig Won't: A Book of Manners (New York: Random House, 1982; London: Collins, 1984);

The Best Mistake Ever! (New York: Random House, 1984; London: Collins, 1985);

Richard Scarry's Biggest Word Book Ever! (New York: Random House, 1985);

My First Word Book (New York: Random House, 1986);

Fun with Letters (New York: Random House, 1986);

Fun with Numbers, 3 volumes (New York: Random House, 1986);

Fun with Words (New York: Random House, 1986);

Fun with Reading (New York: Random House, 1986);

Lowly Worm's Schoolbag (New York: Random House, 1987).

SELECTED BOOKS ILLUSTRATED: Kathryn Jackson, *Let's Go Fishing* (New York: Simon & Schuster, 1949);

Jackson, *Mouse's House* (New York: Simon & Schuster, 1949);

Jackson, *Duck and His Friends* (New York: Simon & Schuster, 1949);

Jackson, *Brave Cowboy Bill* (New York: Simon & Schuster, 1950);

Jackson, *The Animals' Merry Christmas* (New York: Simon & Schuster, 1950; Feltham, U.K.: Hamlyn, 1969);

Oliver O'Connor Barret, *Little Benny Wanted a Pony* (New York: Simon & Schuster, 1950);

Patricia Scarry, *Danny Beaver's Secret* (New York: Simon & Schuster, 1953);

Leah Gale, *The Animals of Farmer Jones* (New York: Simon & Schuster, 1953);

Margaret Wise Brown, *Little Indian* (New York: Simon & Schuster, 1954);

Patricia Scarry, *Pierre Bear* (New York: Golden Press, 1954);

Jane Werner, *Smokey the Bear* (New York: Simon & Schuster, 1955);

Mary Maude Reed, *My First Golden Dictionary Book* (Racine, Wis.: Western, 1957);

Patricia Scarry, *Just for Fun* (New York: Golden Press, 1960);

Jean Selligman and Levine Milton, *Tommy Visits the Doctor* (Racine, Wis.: Western, 1962);

Edward Lear, *Nonsense Alphabet* (Garden City: Doubleday, 1962);

Peggy Parish, *My Golden Book of Manners* (New York: Golden Press, 1962);

Barbara Shook Hazen, *Rudolph the Red-nosed Reindeer* (New York: Golden Press, 1964);

Jackson and others, *My Nursery Tale Book* (Racine, Wis.: Western, 1964);

Jackson and others, *The Golden Book of 365 Stories* (New York: Golden Press, 1966);

Ole Risom, *I Am a Bunny* (New York: Golden Press, 1966);

Roberta Miller, *Chipmunk's ABC* (New York: Golden Press, 1976).

OTHER: Jean de La Fontaine, *Fables,* edited, translated, and illustrated by Scarry (Garden City: Doubleday, 1963).

Young readers of a Richard Scarry book will not learn about the world in a deep or philosophical way. In contrast to the imaginative brooding in a Maurice Sendak work or the peculiar happiness of a Mercer Mayer book, Scarry's books focus on fun and information. As a creator of mass-market children's books, Scarry has achieved astronomical success, and although he has never received the prestigious Newbery or Caldecott Medals (though he did win an Edgar Allan Poe Special Award in 1976), his work draws praise from a larger critical group—the toddler and tricycle set. At this age children want to learn about the new world and to know how it works. Scarry's simplified, labeled drawings offer them a vehicle for understanding it.

Many new parents' bookshelves probably have at least one Scarry selection on them, for he has produced just about every type of book imaginable. Animal stories, humorous stories, mystery stories, picture dictionaries, alphabet books, counting books, primers, amusement, and handicraft books all have the unmistakable Scarry trademarks: fanciful round-cheeked animals and an abundance of detail. The residents of Scarryland are strictly anthropomorphized animals who completely lack the particular characteristics one would attribute to animals. If an owl flies, she takes an airplane; if a cat is undressed, he is a streaker.

Scarry defended his animals-only formula to Arthur Bell in *Publishers' Weekly* by stating that he thinks "children can identify more closely with pictures of animals than they can with pictures of another child. They see an illustration of a blond girl or a dark-haired boy, who they know is somebody other than themselves, and competition creeps in. With imagination—and children all have marvellous imagination—they can easily identify with an anteater who is a painter or a goat who is an Indian. . . ." In fact, Scarry believes so strongly in the method of creating animals based on human beings that he refused to remove the pigs from the Egyptian editions of his books (his books have not been translated into Arabic, though they have been translated into twenty-eight other languages).

If one finds little illogical fantasy in Scarry's books one does find many intensely active pictures. Spread across sturdy oversized pages are the concrete details of a crowded and comical society. Similar to a comic book in a different format, Scarry "tries to tell his stories almost entirely in pictures, with words functioning mainly to link the pictures together." His crowded scenes not only afford mental stimulation by allowing a child to discover new things not previously seen but they also offer a vision of the complexities of realistic life that is funny, interesting, and palatable. When at his best, Scarry's whimsical caricatures clearly outshine his simplistic narrative style.

A Scarry book usually depicts a utopian world where involvement, happiness, and affection prevail. His subjects include home life, behavior, occupations, numeration, language arts, and medical care, and the same cast of characters appears repeatedly. Personable, versatile, heroic, energetic characters such as Sergeant Murphy, Lowly Worm, Sam and Dudley, or Huckle Cat constantly learn how things work, are constructed, or function in a world where crazy things happen. Their madcap antics provide educational value as well as entertainment for the preschooler who finds a bourgeois society familiar. As reported by Rob Wilder in *Parents' Magazine,* Scarry believes that "children learn from a story and they grow attached to it." His strangely fetal, cherubic characters become irrepressible, congenial companions for a child by courting disaster and near calamity in many daily activities.

Richard McClure Scarry was born in Boston, Massachusetts, on 5 June 1919 to Barbara McClure and John James Scarry. His father's small chain of department stores provided the family with a comfortable income. He recalls being exposed to animal books at an early age, such as certain works by Thornton Burgess. An unenthusiastic student, Scarry took five years to get through high school, tried Harvard, and laughingly admits that no college would have him because of his poor academic record. After a short stint in the Boston Business School at his father's urging, Scarry settled into the Boston Museum School of Fine Arts from 1938 to 1941 to study drawing and painting.

From 1941 through 1946 Scarry served in the U.S. Army, claiming that his acutely myopic vision encouraged the military to draft him instead of letting him volunteer. With typical humor he says, the Army "thought I would make a good radio repair man. My exam mark was minus thir-

teen, so they decided to make me a Corporal." Scarry entered special service school and undertook a tour of duty in North Africa during World War II. As an art director for the Morale Services Section he drew maps and designed graphics for troop entertainment, information, and education, and eventually rose to the rank of captain. After leaving the army Scarry moved to New York City to pursue a career as a free-lance commercial artist. He spent many of his first years illustrating other authors' juvenile books, an activity which, as he described it to Justin Wintle and Emma Fisher in *The Pied Pipers: Interviews with the Influential Creators of Children's Literature* (1974), was often "dull, cut and dried, and without lightness."

During his free-lance period he met Patsy Murphy, from Vancouver, British Columbia, who, he says, writes kids' books, "but can't draw." After being married in 1949, the couple lived on a farm in Ridgefield, Connecticut, and collaborated on several books. In 1953 Richard McClure (Huck) Scarry II was born. Influenced by his father's profession (although not his style), Huck Scarry is also a successful author-illustrator of children's books. The family later moved to Westport, Connecticut, but working in his third-floor studio and being active in community projects could not balance the elder Scarry's passion for snow skiing. In 1968 the Scarry family moved to a chalet in Gstaad, Switzerland.

One of the hallmarks of the Scarry style is his ability to focus on variant forms of a character's activities. For example, the Tinker and Tanker series takes a rabbit and a hippopotamus out west, through Africa, up in a spaceship, and to Tootletown, where they either fight pirates, meet knights of the round table, or learn construction techniques. Although the various versions of Tinker and Tanker's adventures have been highly successful (including a coloring book), it was not until 1963 that Scarry achieved a real commercial success with the publication of *Richard Scarry's Best Word Book Ever,* which is still a bestseller.

Richard Scarry's Best Word Book Ever contains more than 1,400 defined and illustrated objects which can engage a preschooler's interest by the infectious vitality and purposefulness of the selections. The book not only labels objects and concepts for easy comprehension but also provides social comment about socialization and cultural conformity. For example, in "The New

Dust jacket for a later edition of Scarry's most popular work
(Random House)

Day" the reader can watch Little Bear's morning routine, noting that he helps with the dishes, or can follow in "Toys" simple declarative and interrogative sentences suggesting the advantages of sharing and good sportsmanship. Scarry shows that competition can be a part of friendship by saying that "When you play with toys, it is more fun if you share them with your friends. When you play games you may win and sometimes you may lose. Bear is a good sport. He is losing a game, but he might win next time."

Other stories in the volume, such as "In the City," show, by a panorama of detail, the importance of safety when crossing streets, while "Keeping Healthy" applauds a doctor and a dentist as best friends who know that a healthy smile is a happy one. Although the author tries to show in these stories that children of different backgrounds can have a good time together, often his menagerie of characters lacks the individualized distinctions to make this point clear. A variety of animal sounds for "good night" in "Last Words" may not be a forceful enough example of individuality for visual learners. *Richard Scarry's Best Word Book Ever* also well illustrates Scarry's typical signature: titles which are never given to understatement.

While animal books such as *The Rooster*

Struts (1963) pleasantly depict the habits and behavior of animals, later comic caricatures in the well-known Busy Busy World series are considerably more fun. *Busy, Busy World* (1965) is a delightful book containing thirty-three international adventures full of slapstick humor and madcap accident-prone antics. In "Sergeant Yukon of the Canadian Mounties" a trim young raccoon protects the peace in Goldtown when two bullies, wolfish Tundra Pete and grizzly Klondike Kid, terrorize the town by grabbing, splashing, and hitting. Because Mounties always get their men, the troublemakers are taken to jail where they stay until they learn "not to be bullies any more."

Scarry's definitions of meanness and bravery have an emotional transparence to them, and in stories such as "Pierre, the Paris Policeman" or "Good Luck in Rome" he seems to show that setbacks and near calamities frequently occur through no fault of one's own. In the latter story an accident-prone jewel thief literally lands in hot water after a furious chase scene (through a motorist's nightmare) past Notre Dame. The only punishment for the theft is a brief interlude when both representatives of law and disorder sit down to share a bowl of soup, with a promise that the unsuccessful thief will return to make "Robber Soup" again in the future. The story clearly implies that discipline intending rehabilitation rather than restriction is "a good idea."

In some selections Scarry's Pollyanna optimism is pushed to extreme. When Federico and Maria ask a carabiniere for directions to an important landmark in "Good Luck in Rome" their runaway car ("for some reason which can't be explained") careens around street vendors' *gelati*, bumps into plates of pasta, tumbles down a road of narrow steps, and lands squarely in the middle of the very fountain that they were looking for. Disaster is magically transformed into delight when the soggy Maria and startled Federico are told, "Most people have good luck by putting only a penny in the fountain. But look! You have put your car in! Yes, you will surely have good luck!"

Similarly, in "Couscous, The Algerian Detective," a master of disguise (so good in fact that he is indistinguishable from the other characters in the story) goes to Pepe le Gangstair's den impersonating the dancing girl Fatima. After a very brief seduction scene Algiers's criminal element is surprised and captured. In Scarryland all protagonists are very clever fellows indeed.

Stories of domestic life are often not as satisfying as Scarry's exotic adventures. For example, *Is This the House of Mistress Mouse?* (1966) is a small spiral-bound volume with a large hole in the center of the pages for inquisitive young fingers to poke through. Although this book, like *Richard Scarry's Lowly Worm Sniffy Book* (1978), invites reader participation with a scratch-and-sniff technique, both the story and the illustrations are overly cute. Basically, a child is asked to sympathize with Mr. Mouse, "who lived alone and was very lonely." A letter from Miss Mouse initiates his quest for companionship on a fuzzy seat, past a fuzzy cat, by a frumpy hen, near a fierce lion. Connubial bliss is finally achieved for the Mouses in a scene which epitomizes Scarry's desire for the ideal life in his books.

The basic values that underlie Scarry's domestic situations are extremely traditional and sometimes old-fashioned. Such simplified notions of family life may appeal to a toddler who is experiencing insecurity at his or her stage of shifting independence. However, such concepts can quickly become inane to a youngster who has outgrown them.

Some of Scarry's most successful ventures have been his picture dictionaries. One of the best is *Storybook Dictionary* (1966), which contains more than 700 entries with 1,600 variant forms and labels and includes words and concepts. Each entry tells a separate and complete story. For example, for the word "fish" three "members of the Fish Chowder Club are eating *fish* chowder and telling *fish* stories" and admonish one renegade member to "Stop floundering in the chowder, Flounder!" However, Scarry's technique of setting key words in bold type is not as effective here as in alphabet books such as *ABC Word Book* (1971) or *Find Your ABC's* (1973). In these alphabet books either a brief story for each letter of the alphabet contains the letter printed in red in the text or two detectives enlist the reader's help in finding them.

Although *Storybook Dictionary* obviously has a definite educational purpose–encouraging letter and word recognition or stimulating spelling and sentence construction–the book contains no rules and "teaches" by providing examples in attention-getting contexts. Ultimately it is *Storybook Dictionary*'s nutty and winning humor rather than its practical application that makes this book a Scarry classic. With almost urbane adult humor a cast of animal characters is introduced in bright colors and small pictures that invite repeated browsing. The fact that verb forms are often com-

plicated and phrases are seldom simple does not seem to bother Haggis the Scottie, Hepzibah the Hedgehog, or Bilgy the tiger Fishhead. However, a five-to-seven-year-old reader will probably be pleasantly baffled.

Many of the characters who appear in *Storybook Dictionary* reappear as residents of Busytown in *What Do People Do All Day?* (1968). Farmer Goat, Mayor Fox, Huckle Cat, Lowly Worm, or Sergeant Murphy are all workers, "so that there will be enough food and houses and clothing for their families." In fact in Busytown everyone is a helper, and work is of paramount importance. Society is highly productive and technological; work is equated with personal satisfaction and social tradition. In "Everyone is a Worker" all debts and credits are viewed as profits rather than losses. Farmer's wife received new earrings (eggbeaters) from the sale of the crops, and Grocer Cat purchases a new dress for Mommy Cat. Scarry's comment that Mommy Cat "earned it by taking such good care of the house" has raised more than a few feminists' eyebrows.

Many of the stories in *What Do People Do All Day?* place an emphasis on women in domestic roles. "Mother's Work is Never Done," for example, stresses a daily feminine routine of housework and child care. When Daddy returns from work outside the home, his overweight physique breaks the children's bed, and Sally and Harry sleep with Mommy while Daddy has a bed to himself. Scarry responds to feminist criticism of this work and others like it which depict stereotyped sexual role models by saying, "the criticism is valid in some instances. . . . But I still like mothers to wear aprons. If a father is washing dishes he wears an apron too."

The majority of the stories in *What Do People Do All Day?* are informative and thought provoking. Huckle's loneliness is satisfied in "Building a New House" when residential construction begins next door. Not only does he learn simplified construction techniques such as laying the foundation or framing the house but he also learns that Stitches the tailor and his abundant family are moving into it. Occupations are frequently not as important as the concepts and procedures behind them, and Scarry takes on complex subjects such as wood and how it is used; digging coal to make electricity work; building a new road; cotton and how it is used; where bread comes from; and how water is made to work for society. The author does take some artistic liberties (the pipes may not connect at exactly the right

Dust jacket for the abridged edition of Scarry's 1968 book in which he portrays a variety of animal characters in many different professions (Random House)

point), but the information has been researched and simplified so that the underlying concepts are easily understandable. Scarry is always willing to adapt the facts to make the tone and level appropriate for a young reader.

In his mystery series, *The Great Pie Robbery* (1969), *The Supermarket Mystery* (1969), and *Richard Scarry's Great Steamboat Mystery* (1975), super sleuths Sam Pig and Dudley Cat are definitely soft-boiled rather than hard-boiled detectives. They literally track down shoplifters who take pies from Ma Dog's bakery and purloin tenderloins, bananas, and bread from the grocery. The mysteries are particularly effective because Scarry follows the tried and true formula of the genre: the thieves are present (indeed underfoot) in many scenes, completely unknown to the heroes.

Richard Scarry's Great Steamboat Mystery is the most intriguing story in the series. Here Sam and Dudley are hired to protect the wedding presents at a costume party aboard Steamboat Sally. Although their method of entrapment probably would not hold up in a court of law, the stolen pearls are recovered, and the wedding party is a

merry time for all. In each of these mysteries the author does not try to control the vocabulary used in the prose, and there seems to be a particular disparity between the illustrations and the text.

Some of the best illustrations of rural or urban activity are spread across the pages of *Richard Scarry's Great Big Schoolhouse* (1969) and *Richard Scarry's Great Big Air Book* (1971). As a young reader follows the academic adventures of Huckle, the author's message is clearly that the obedient animals set good examples for their human counterparts to follow. Classroom activities and lessons about shapes, counting, or penmanship are provided under Miss Honey's tutelage. And while her almost saccharine patience with troublesome students would probably make most teachers shudder, Miss Honey is definitely Scarry's portrait of the ideal teacher because of her ability to engage her class in creative lessons. Of course, Scarry cannot resist including one of his previous books on Miss Honey's reading list.

Richard Scarry's Great Big Air Book not only explains many basic principles behind modern technology but it also demonstrates a variety of ways that air is used in modern rural and urban societies. Miss Honey points out the capability of the spring season's winds; Charlie Crow shows the techniques that made the Wright brothers famous; and World War I flying ace Rudolf Strudel performs aerobatic maneuvers. Nearly all the stories have built-in safety messages for children and some small visual non sequitur which is guaranteed to catch the eye.

The most interesting story in *Great Big Air Book* is "Air Pollution," for it is the first indication in the corpus of Scarry's work that there is trouble in paradise. Father Cat begins his walk through an urban wasteland wearing a white suit and smoking a big cigar. "Down at the waterfront, where the city garbage is being burned," he watches some fishermen catch old rubber boots. When Father Cat returns home after his quest he remarks with shocked dismay, "My new white suit! It's filthy! Why don't they do something about that dirty, polluted air?" Mother Cat points out that Father Cat has lost his moral authority by contributing to the problem by smoking a cigar. She says, "None of us should burn things any more than we have to . . . if we want to keep our air fresh and clean." Even Mother Cat is burning something in the kitchen as she admonishes her husband.

Nicky Goes to the Doctor (1972) also reminds the reader that you can be your own worst enemy. Any new parent who knows that a Band-Aid is almost as effective as kissing hurts on a young toddler's scraped knees will find the pages of this book a delight. The opening page shows over 200 Band-Aids flying out of a container strongly akin to Pandora's box. Although Nicky Bunny is only seeking medical attention for a checkup, the oversized drawings and straightforward text reassure Nicky and his readers that there is nothing to worry about. With a wonderful play on words, Scarry points out that anticipation often far exceeds the event. After his visit, Nicky's brothers and sisters all want to visit the doctor too. The children are reminded to "be patient," for Scarry is never pedantic about good behavior. In works like *Nicky Goes to the Doctor* or *Richard Scarry's Please and Thank You Book* (1973) good manners are more than the mark of a profession or the endorsement of convention. Good behavior is always defined as physical and mental respect for another person.

An effective use of the grail legend can be seen in *Richard Scarry's Peasant Pig and the Terrible Dragon* (1980). Busylande is a land of petty princes warring against one another. Society is polarized: the peasants thrash wheat and make grape juice while the royalty of the court dances before supper time. In a Tennysonian vein, under the conditions of luxury and play the will to perfection flags–for all except Princess Lily (who resembles a Hyacinth girl far more than Miss Piggy) and the very pleasant Peasant Pig. Peasant Pig wants very much to be a knight and is unwavering in his devotion to Lily. His masculine strength and earthy attention impress those around him. His whole impulse is to create harmony, order, and grape juice.

However, the territory is menaced by bandits and outlaws–the dreadful Sir Morbert and his gang (Merbert, Orgbert, Egbert, and Sherbert) –who implement foreshadowings of war by terrorizing the land in a dragon costume. They kidnap Princess Lily and put her to work making grape juice. Lowly Worm purges the land by mixing soap in the grapes, thus rendering evil powerless while purifying the soul. Peasant Pig completes the achievement of order by disrobing the dragon and wearing the costume to frighten the marauders away from their evil purposes. Faith, obedience, fidelity to duty, and loving gratitude are the means by which true wisdom is achieved in Busylande. False appearances always need to be sorted out from interior realities.

The joyful celebration of Peasant Pig's knighthood shows that devout humanity, integrity, and order are the fabric a united society is made of. Lowly Worm's final joke–jumping out of Big Hilda's beautiful new cake wearing a little dragon costume–suggests that outward signs of status are not as viable as acute perceptions of inward nobility for determining worth in man. Of all the Scarry books to date, *Peasant Pig and the Terrible Dragon* seems to have the greatest philosophical insight and literary merit.

In the thirty-six years that Richard Scarry has been working as a children's author and illustrator there have been really only minor changes in his themes and techniques. Anyone over six can easily tire of seeing the placid, clonelike faces that appear and reappear in subsequent editions and versions of the same story. In many cases the alternate version of a story is not as lively as its predecessor. Since the early 1970s he seems to have produced many books of amusement (pop-up books, scratch-and-sniff books, coloring books, cardboard poster books) and fewer works which could be classified as juvenile fiction or genuine picture books. The inexpensive prices and oversize format lend Scarry's books to home use rather than as classroom schoolbooks, and they tend to be quickly outgrown by the preschooler when he or she begins formal education.

Two of the main types of critical responses to Richard Scarry's books have focused on violence and sexism. Scarry has been faulted frequently for portraying too much violence, and accidents certainly do abound in his world. Although moments of impact are frequently left to the imagination, few pages lack some kind of collision course. Scarry defends himself by saying, some people "say I include too much violence, but it's not true violence: it's fun." Cars pile up, characters slip on banana peels, and custard pies land squarely on smiling faces. Violence here is often psychological as well as physical, and Scarry admits that "the only thing that really suffers is dignity." Scarryland has very few bad characters really. Bullies nearly always get their just rewards. In *Peasant Pig and the Terrible Dragon*, for example, Sir Morbert and his very nasty gang are sent to the castle dungeon and put to work making soap. Scarry is not very interested in portraying villains.

Scarry's female characters are by and large harried but happy housewives who keep the

Sketches for Lowly Worm's Schoolbag *(©Richard Scarry 1987)*

home fires burning. In general, they lack emotional and intellectual depth. Although Scarry is somewhat defensive about charges of sexism, his subsequent editions have yielded somewhat to the pressures of feminist ire. For example, Ms. Mouse is not only a cook and a housewife but also a painter, plumber, mechanic, bus driver, and fire fighter as well. More female characters such as Flossie the policewoman are involved in heretofore male-dominated occupations. And he has adjusted tailoring features on his male and female characters to indicate gender. One character named Tom the Telephone Worker has appeared, apparently by editorial error, wearing a pink bow. Scarry might also pay a little more attention to ethnic diversity in his work. Although his books have been translated into twenty-eight foreign languages, his appeal is directed predominantly to suburban American children rather than to those who find their playgrounds in the streets of the inner city.

Since the 1970s Lowly Worm wiggles into more and more of Scarry's pages, and he appears to be the new star. He is a very fetching character and perhaps emblematic of the Richard Scarry key to success. Scarry points out that to be a successful children's author, "You have to be able to have a rapport with children—not talk above or beneath them. . . . You have to speak to them within the framework of their learning and experience and treat them with respect."

One of the greatest compliments any author can receive from a preschool audience is to have his or her books held together with more tape than there is paper in the book itself. Tearing is an accidental toddler pastime that often suggests a book is good enough to be reread. Richard Scarry's books usually display an abundance of such mending.

Interview:

Justin Wintle and Emma Fisher, *The Pied Pipers: Interviews with the Influential Creators of Children's Literature* (New York: Paddington Press, 1974), pp. 64-76.

References:

Arthur Bell, "Richard Scarry's Best Switzerland Ever," *Publishers' Weekly* (20 October 1969): 41-42;

Rudi Chelminiski, "This is the House the Menagerie of Richard Scarry Built," *People*, 12 (15 October 1979): 105-106;

Elizabeth Fisher, "The Second Sex, Junior Division," *New York Times Book Review*, 24 May 1970, pp. 6, 44;

Selma G. Lanes, *Down the Rabbit Hole: Adventures and Misadventures in the Realm of Children's Literature* (New York: Atheneum, 1971);

Edwin McDowell, "Richard Scarry," *New York Times Book Review*, 27 April 1980, pp. 38-39;

Rob Wilder, "Richard Scarry: The Wizard of Busytown," *Parents' Magazine*, 55 (August 1980): 62-65.

Maurice Sendak
(10 June 1928-)

John Cotham
Mountain Empire Community College

BOOKS: *Kenny's Window* (New York: Harper, 1956);

Very Far Away (New York: Harper, 1957);

The Sign on Rosie's Door (New York: Harper, 1960; London: Bodley Head, 1969);

The Nutshell Library (New York: Harper & Row, 1962; London & Glasgow: Collins, 1964)–includes *Alligators All Around, Chicken Soup with Rice, One Was Johnny, Pierre*;

Where the Wild Things Are (New York: Harper & Row, 1963; London: Bodley Head, 1967);

Hector Protector And As I Went Over the Water (New York: Harper & Row, 1965);

Higglety Pigglety Pop! Or, There Must Be More to Life (New York: Harper & Row, 1967; London: Bodley Head, 1969);

In the Night Kitchen (New York: Harper & Row, 1970);

Fantasy Sketches (Philadelphia: Rosenbach Foundation, 1971);

The Magician: A Counting Book (Philadelphia: Rosenbach Foundation, 1971);

Pictures (New York: Harper & Row, 1971; London: Bodley Head, 1972);

Really Rosie, Starring the Nutshell Kids (New York: Harper & Row, 1975);

Seven Little Monsters (Zurich: Diogenes, 1975; New York: Harper & Row, 1977; London: Bodley Head, 1977);

Some Swell Pup: or Are You Sure You Want a Dog?, by Sendak and Matthew Margolis, illustrated by Sendak (New York: Farrar, Straus & Giroux, 1976);

Outside Over There (New York: Harper & Row, 1981; London: Bodley Head, 1981).

BOOKS ILLUSTRATED: M. C. Eidinoff and others, *Atomics for the Millions* (New York: McGraw-Hill, 1947);

Robert Garvey, *Good Shabbos, Everybody* (New York: United Synagogue Commission on Jewish Education, 1951);

Marcel Ayme, *The Wonderful Farm* (New York: Harper, 1951);

Maurice Sendak (photo © Candid Lang)

Ruth Krauss, *A Hole Is to Dig* (New York: Harper, 1952);

Ruth Sawyer, *Maggie Rose: Her Birthday Christmas* (New York: Harper, 1952);

Beatrice de Regnier, *The Giant Story* (New York: Harper, 1953);

Meindert DeJong, *Hurry Home, Candy* (New York: Harper, 1953);

DeJong, *Sadrach* (New York: Harper, 1953);

Krauss, *A Very Special House* (New York: Harper, 1953);

Krauss, *I'll Be You and You Be Me* (New York: Harper, 1954);

Ayme, *The Magic Pictures* (New York: Harper, 1954);

Betty MacDonald, *Mrs. Piggle-Wiggle's Farm* (Philadelphia: Lippincott, 1954);

Edward Tripp, *The Tin Fiddle* (New York: Walck, 1954);

DeJong, *The Wheel on the School* (New York: Harper, 1954);

Krauss, *Charlotte and the White Horse* (New York: Harper, 1955);

Hyman and Alice Chanover, *Happy Hanukah, Everybody* (New York: United Synagogue Commission on Jewish Education, 1955);

DeJong, *The Little Cow and the Turtle* (New York: Harper, 1955);

Gladys Baker Bond, *Seven Little Stories on Big Subjects* (New York: The Anti-Defamation League of B'nai B'rith, 1955);

de Regnier, *What Can You Do With a Shoe?* (New York: Harper, 1955);

Jean Ritchie, *The Singing Family of the Cumberlands* (New York: Giordi Music Publishing, 1955);

Jack Sendak, *The Happy Rain* (New York: Harper, 1956);

DeJong, *The House of Sixty Fathers* (New York: Harper, 1956);

Krauss, *I Want to Paint My Bathroom Blue* (New York: Harper, 1956);

Krauss, *The Birthday Party* (New York: Harper, 1957);

Jack Sendak, *Circus Girl* (New York: Harper, 1957);

Else Holmelund Minarik, *Little Bear* (New York: Harper, 1957);

DeJong, *Along Came a Dog* (New York: Harper, 1958);

Minarik, *No Fighting, No Biting!* (New York: Harper, 1958);

Krauss, *Somebody Else's Nut Tree and Other Tales from Children* (New York: Harper, 1958);

Sesyle Joslin, *What Do You Say, Dear?* (New York: Young Scott, 1958);

Minarik, *Father Bear Comes Home* (New York: Harper, 1959);

Janice May Udry, *The Moon Jumpers* (New York: Harper, 1959);

Hans Christian Andersen, *Seven Tales* (New York: Harper, 1959);

Wilhelm Hauff, *Dwarf Long-Nose*, translated by Doris Orgel (New York: Random House, 1960);

Minarik, *Little Bear's Friend* (New York: Harper, 1960);

Krauss, *Open House for Butterflies* (New York: Harper, 1960);

Udry, *Let's Be Enemies* (New York: Harper, 1961);

Minarik, *Little Bear's Visit* (New York: Harper, 1961);

Clemens Brentano, *The Tale of Gockel, Hinkel and Gackeliah*, translated by Doris Orgel (New York: Random House, 1961);

Joslin, *What Do You Do, Dear?* (New York: Young Scott, 1961);

Robert Graves, *The Big Green Book* (New York: Crowell-Collier, 1962);

Charlotte Zolotow, *Mr. Rabbit and the Lovely Present* (New York: Harper & Row, 1962);

Brentano, *Schoolmaster Whackwell's Wonderful Sons*, translated by Doris Orgel (New York: Random House, 1962);

DeJong, *The Singing Hill* (New York: Harper & Row, 1962);

Frank Stockton, *The Griffin and the Minor Canon* (New York: Holt, Rinehart & Winston, 1963);

Amos Vogel, *How Little Lori Visited Times Square* (New York: Harper & Row, 1963);

Leo Tolstoy, *Nikolenka's Childhood* (New York: Pantheon, 1963);

Doris Orgel, *Sarah's Room* (New York: Harper & Row, 1963);

Robert Keeshan, *She Loves Me, She Loves Me Not* (New York: Harper & Row, 1963);

Randall Jarrell, *The Bat-Poet* (New York: Macmillan, 1964);

Stockton, *The Bee-Man of Orn* (New York: Holt, Rinehart & Winston, 1964);

Jan Wahl, *Pleasant Fieldmouse* (New York: Harper & Row, 1964);

Jarrell, *The Animal Family* (New York: Pantheon, 1965);

Lullabies and Night Songs, edited by William Engvick, music by Alec Wilder (New York: Harper & Row, 1965);

Isaac Bashevis Singer, *Zlateh the Goat and Other Stories*, translated by Singer and Elizabeth Shub (New York: Harper & Row, 1966);

George MacDonald, *The Golden Key* (New York: Farrar, Straus & Giroux, 1967);

Minarik, *A Kiss for Little Bear* (New York: Harper & Row, 1968);

MacDonald, *The Light Princess* (New York: Farrar, Straus & Giroux, 1969);

Brothers Grimm, *The Juniper Tree and Other Tales from Grimm*, translated by Lore Segal and Randall Jarrell (New York: Farrar, Straus & Giroux, 1973);

Brothers Grimm, *King Grisley-Beard: A Tale from the Brothers Grimm*, translated by Edgar Taylor (New York: Farrar, Straus & Giroux, 1973);

Jarrell, *Fly By Night* (New York: Farrar, Straus & Giroux, 1976);

E. T. A. Hoffmann, *The Nutcracker*, translated by

Ralph Manheim (New York: Crown, 1984);

Frank Corsaro, *The Love for Three Oranges* (New York: Farrar, Straus & Giroux, 1984);

Philip Sendak, *In Grandpa's House*, translated and adapted by Seymour Barofsky (New York: Harper & Row, 1985).

TELEVISION SCRIPT: *Really Rosie, Starring the Nutshell Kids,* scenario, lyrics, and pictures by Sendak, music by Carole King, design by Jane Byers Bierhorst, CBS, 1975.

PERIODICAL PUBLICATIONS: "Caldecott Award Acceptance," *Horn Book*, 40 (August 1964): 345-351;

"Questions to an Artist Who Is also an Author; a Conversation Between Maurice Sendak and Virginia Haviland," *Library of Congress Quarterly Journal*, 28 (October 1971): 262-280;

"Laura Ingalls Wilder Acceptance Speech," *Horn Book*, 59 (August 1983): 474-477.

Maurice Sendak's career as an illustrator of children's books began in 1951 with the publication of Marcel Ayme's *The Wonderful Farm*. Since then he has illustrated over seventy books and has written and illustrated seventeen books of his own. Drawing on the great tradition of nineteenth-century book illustration, Sendak has forged a unique visual vocabulary and artistic style, at once rooted in the past yet contemporary in spirit and approach. His works, internationally acclaimed, include some of the best-loved books for children of recent years.

Beginning with the appearance in 1963 of his most famous and popular work, *Where the Wild Things Are,* both critical acclaim and controversy have heralded the publication of almost each new book. Credited by many critics and scholars as being the first artist to deal openly with the emotions of children, Sendak's honesty has troubled or frightened many who would wish to sentimentalize childhood—to shelter children from their own psychological complexity or to deny that this complexity exists.

Sendak's lasting contribution to the literature of childhood is evidenced by the critical acclaim his work has received. In addition to numerous other honors, Sendak has been presented three of the most important international awards for excellence in children's book illustration: the Caldecott Medal in 1964 for *Where the Wild Things Are,* the Hans Christian Andersen Award (1970), and the Laura Ingalls Wilder

Medal (1983) for the body of his work.

Sendak has said that if he has an unusual gift, it is not that he draws or writes better than other artists but that he has the ability to recall the emotional quality of specific moments in childhood. Given this reflection, a consideration of the nature of Sendak's childhood is especially important to an understanding of his art. Maurice Bernard Sendak was born on 10 June 1928, in Brooklyn, New York. His parents, Philip and Sarah Schindler Sendak, were both Polish immigrants who had come to New York from small Jewish villages outside Warsaw before World War I. His sister Natalie was nine and his brother Jack was five when he was born.

Undoubtedly one of the major influences which shaped his childhood was the experience of being a first-generation American. According to Sendak, the two dominant figures of his childhood were Mickey Mouse and his maternal grandfather. The image of Mickey Mouse, who was "born" the same year as Sendak, bombarded and delighted the artist throughout his childhood. His severe and bearded maternal grandfather, who had died long before Sendak's birth, was known to the artist only from a large, faded family photograph.

These images comprise a significant distillation of the two major forces at conflict during Sendak's youth. The artist has described his childhood as having been strangely concocted of disparate elements from both the Old and New Worlds. On the one hand, he was exposed to the most intoxicating and bustling of modern American cities. Juxtaposed to this experience of modern American culture were his parents' memories of life in the Old Country. Sendak has said that as a child he felt himself to be a part of both his parents' past and modern American life.

The memories of life in the Old Country shared by his parents were dramatically different. His mother described the terror of being hidden with her brothers and sisters in the basement of her father's store when Cossacks descended on their village. His father, on the other hand, came from a more affluent family and shared pleasant memories of a comfortable, middle-class village life. Both parents, however, seemed to have communicated to their children a rather dark, pessimistic view of life, which Sendak appears to have spent much of his adult life trying to overcome.

Although Sendak's family was not particularly religious and usually went to synagogue only on High Holy Days, the artist's Jewish heri-

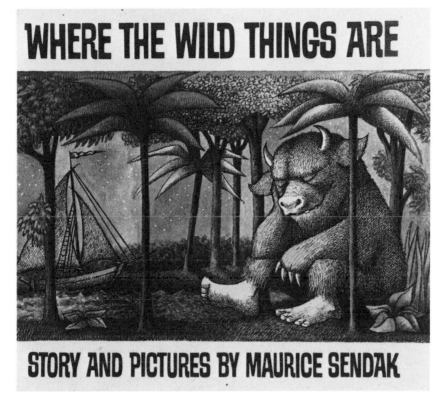

Cover for Sendak's best-known work (Harper & Row)

tage has had a perceptible impact on his work. Some early reviewers of his illustrations felt that the children portrayed looked too European. Sendak affirmed that he had indeed drawn the greenhorn immigrant children he had known in Brooklyn in his youth.

Sendak's experience of the arts as a child was limited mostly to popular culture. He had little exposure to fine art or museums, music, or literature; however, he delighted in the popular culture of the 1930s–comic books, cartoons, movies, and radio. During his childhood, Sendak would accompany his parents each Friday evening to the neighborhood movie theater. He especially enjoyed going with his older sister to Manhattan to see movies at the Roxy or Radio City Music Hall. These films of the 1930s, such as Busby Berkeley musicals and Laurel and Hardy comedies, have had a profound influence on certain of his illustrations, most notably those for *In the Night Kitchen* (1970).

Although Sendak has often described his childhood as a happy one, it would be difficult for an impartial observer to arrive at the same conclusion. His father, a dressmaker and a partner in a shop called Lucky Stitching, suffered financial hardship in the depression, but the family managed to maintain a solid, lower-middle-class standard of living. Plagued by serious illness in his early childhood, Sendak contracted a dangerous case of measles followed by double pneumonia at age two and a half and later a case of scarlet fever at age four. Frail and sickly, he remembers being terrified of death as a child. The reversal in the family fortunes increased his parents' anxiety about his health, and Sendak was an overprotected child. He has confided, "I was a miserable kid. I couldn't make friends. I couldn't skate great, I couldn't play stoopball terrific. I stayed home and drew pictures. You *know* what they all thought of me: sissy Maurice Sendak. Whenever I wanted to go out and do something, my father would say, 'You'll catch a cold.' And I did. I did whatever he told me."

Sendak's childhood was further complicated by his obesity, by his family's frequent moves, and by his complete loathing for school. Self-conscious about being overweight, he remembers fondly one childhood best friend who was even fatter than he was. During his childhood, landlords painted every few years. Rather than face this inconvenience, Sadie Sendak preferred a complete change of location if home life had to be interrupted anyway. The family moved into and out of several Brooklyn Bensonhurst neighborhoods. Of course, Sendak was happier and better adjusted in some neighborhoods than others. These frequent moves must have been especially difficult for a shy and withdrawn child. Never a particularly successful student, Sendak has spoken at great length about his hatred for school. He despised being "cloistered" with other children and being forced to compete. He was often so uncomfortable that he stammered. The artist has said that school stifles talented people and that those with talent should cultivate it in their own particular way.

Sendak developed a great love for books at an early age and decided while still very young to spend his life illustrating and making them. As young boys both Jack and Maurice Sendak made their own storybooks, combining newspaper photographs or comic strip segments with drawings they made of family members.

Perhaps because of his early illnesses and confinements in bed, Sendak developed a talent as a child for observing life. He seems to have known that he was already collecting the raw material he would use for his work. Some of his happiest childhood memories are of listening to the "beautiful, imaginative tales" invented by his father, a marvelous improvisor who would "often extend a story for several nights." Sendak feels that his father's stories were the first important source from which his work developed. Both sons seemed to have inherited their father's gift for storytelling and later were to write books for children.

Sendak's high school years during the 1940s were very anxious ones for the family. His paternal grandfather died in Poland, the news arriving the day of Sendak's bar mitzvah. Philip Sendak was unsuccessful in helping any of his brothers and sisters to escape from Poland, and they all perished in the Holocaust. Natalie's fiance, a soldier, was killed during World War II, and Jack was stationed in the Pacific. At Lafayette High School Sendak excelled in art but continued to be disinterested in other classes. He worked on the school yearbook, literary magazine, and newspaper. He also had a job with All-American Comics after school, working on background details for the "Mutt and Jeff" comic strip. During his vacations from high school, Sendak began to teach himself about illustration, and he created original drawings for a number of works including "Peter and the Wolf," "The Happy Prince," and "The Luck of Roaring Camp."

Upon graduation from high school in 1946, Sendak, not surprisingly, decided not to attend art school. He sought work as an illustrator but finally landed a full-time job in the warehouse of a Manhattan window-display company called Timely Service. He remembers this period of his life fondly and describes it as one of the happiest times in his life. He was in Manhattan meeting the kinds of people he had not met in Brooklyn–"people who felt they were really artists and considered their work for Timely Service as just a job that enabled them to paint seriously at night." Sendak moved away from home for the first time. After two years, he was promoted to a different department made up mainly of older people. Unhappy in this new environment, he left in the summer of 1948.

Sendak has characterized the bleak summer which followed as, "Out of a job, out of sorts, and out of money, and–worse–having to live at home with my parents again." He began seriously to sketch the street life of children he observed out his window. The artist borrowed from these sketches heavily for his early illustrations. He also gathered the raw material he was to use later to create Rosie, one of his best-loved characters.

During this same jobless summer, Maurice and Jack worked together to create models for six wooden mechanical toys. These toys were patterned after German eighteenth-century lever-operated toys and were designed to portray parts of corresponding nursery rhymes and fairy tales. Jack engineered the toys, Maurice painted and carved the figures and settings, and Natalie helped with the sewing. The brothers took the prototypes to the venerable Fifth Avenue toy store F.A.O. Schwarz, where the models were admired; however, the brothers were told that the toys would be too expensive to mass produce.

The trip to Schwarz proved to be important for Sendak for other reasons. Richard Nell, the window-display director, impressed with Sendak's decoration of the models, offered him a job as an assistant in the preparation of the store's window displays. For the next three years Sendak worked at Schwarz during the day and took evening classes at the Art Student's League in oil painting, life drawing, and composition. He was greatly influenced by his composition instructor, John Groth. While at Schwarz, he also used the resources of the children's book department to explore the history of children's book illustration, gaining his first exposure to both the great nineteenth-century illustrators (George Cruik-shank, Walter Crane, and Randolph Caldecott) and the new postwar European illustrators (Hans Fischer, Felix Hoffmann, and Alois Carigiet).

However, the most important thing that happened to Sendak while he worked at Schwarz was meeting Ursula Nordstrom, the distinguished children's book editor at Harper and Brothers. In 1950 Frances Chrystie, the Schwarz book buyer, arranged for Miss Nordstrom to visit the Schwarz studio one spring afternoon to see Sendak's pictures. She studied the work closely and called the next day to offer him the chance to illustrate Marcel Ayme's *The Wonderful Farm*. Sendak gratefully accepted this opportunity and became "an official person in children's books."

This rather inauspicious initial meeting proved to be the beginning of an important personal and professional relationship for both parties. Of the debt he owes to Miss Nordstrom, Sendak has said, "she treated me like a hot-house flower, watered me for ten years, and hand-picked the works that were to become my permanent backlist and bread-and-butter support." Nordstrom has said that Sendak is a genius and that "she can imagine no greater joy than that I've had working with him over the years and watching him develop."

In fact, Sendak had two commissions before his professional career as an illustrator began at Harper's. During his senior year in high school he was hired by a teacher, Hyman Ruchlis, to illustrate a physics textbook, *Atomics for the Millions* (1947). Thankful for this first opportunity, Sendak, never a science scholar, worked hard to keep the illustrations humorous but accurate. In 1950 he received a commission, based on the recommendation of children's book artist Leonard Weisgard, from the United Synagogue Commission on Jewish Education to illustrate Robert Garvey's *Good Shabbos, Everybody* (1951), a story about the Sabbath. Although awkward, the illustrations reveal Sendak's characteristic emphasis on translating, according to his biographer, Selma G. Lanes, the "emotional reality of the text."

Although Sendak's illustrations for *The Wonderful Farm* received generally favorable reviews, his first big success came with his illustrations for Ruth Krauss's *A Hole Is to Dig* (1952). This "concept book" has no plot; it consists of a group of children's definitions collected by the author. Sendak was given this assignment only after it had been turned down by the established

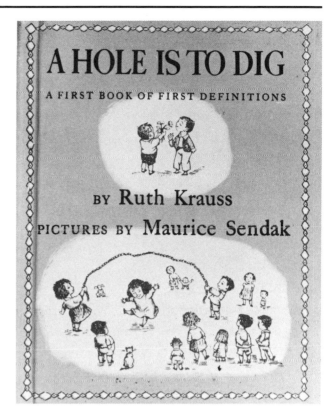

Dust jacket for Ruth Krauss's 1952 concept book, illustrated by Sendak (Harper)

children's book illustrator Nicolas Mordvinoff, who felt that it would be impossible to illustrate a book with no coherent text. Sendak was very excited about the project and collaborated closely with Krauss on the illustrations. For this book, Sendak used a small format, sepia-tinted paper, and crosshatched pen-and-ink drawings to create a mid-nineteenth-century look. The charming children vigorously depicted owe much to the artist's Brooklyn sketchbooks. The work received excellent reviews and after more than thirty years, it still sells thousands of hardcover copies a year. Encouraged by the success of *A Hole Is to Dig*, Sendak gave up his full-time job at F.A.O. Schwarz, moved into an apartment in Greenwich Village, and became a free-lance illustrator.

Sendak has called the years between 1951 and 1962 his apprenticeship. During this period he illustrated dozens of books and wrote seven of his own. Speaking of these early · works, Sendak has acknowledged his debt to other illustrators whose work he admired, explaining that he was "borrowing styles and techniques shamelessly, trying to forge them into a personal language. I was an arranger more than an innovator." Despite this apology by the artist, his early work was unusual for the period in that it was more nineteenth-century in spirit than modernist or abstract. Sendak has often cited William Blake as one of the most important influences both on his artistic style and on his growing awareness of what a deadly serious business childhood really is.

As the artist worked to master a variety of styles and techniques, some of his early illustrations were more successful than others. Particularly noteworthy are his sensitive pen-and-ink drawings for Meindert DeJong's *The House of Sixty Fathers* (1956), the childlike watercolors reminiscent of the work of Chagall for Ruth Krauss's *Charlotte and the White Horse* (1955), and the charming pen-and-ink drawings with watercolor washes used in the four "Little Bear" readers written by Else Holmelund Minarik and set by Sendak in the Victorian period. The artist has said that he considers *Little Bear* (1957), the first installment in the series, to be "a perfect book."

Sendak is not so complimentary of his illustrations for *Seven Tales* (1959) by Hans Christian Andersen, *The Moon Jumpers* (1959) by Janice May Udry, and *The Tale of Gockel, Hinkel and Gackeliah* (1961) by Clemens Brentano. Indeed much of Sendak's work during his years of apprenticeship is of interest now only because it chronicles the development of his artistic style and reveals the evolution of the themes he was to pursue in his mature work.

Sendak's first book, *Kenny's Window* (1956), tells the story of a young boy, Kenny, who awakens from a dream in which a four-legged rooster asks him seven riddling questions. Kenny must answer these questions in order to be able to live in a magic garden where he will never have to go to bed. Kenny is depicted as angry, unjust, and even cruel as he seeks to integrate his fantasies with his real life and attain control over both. In summing up this first effort Sendak has said: "The pictures are ghastly–I really wasn't up to illustrating my own texts then. And the story itself, to be honest, is nice but long-winded."

In Sendak's second book, *Very Far Away* (1957), the young protagonist Martin, angry because his mother pays more attention to his baby brother, runs away to where someone will answer all his questions. He spends the afternoon with three new friends (a bird, a horse, and a cat) and returns home only when his anger has subsided. In *Very Far Away* the theme is lighter, the conflict more direct, and the two-color artwork more humorous than in *Kenny's Window.*

In *The Sign on Rosie's Door* (1960), Sendak's third book, he drew from his Brooklyn sketchbooks to create his first fully realized character, Rosie, a young girl who lures the other children on her block into her fantasies by the force of her personality and imagination. She thus helps them to escape the boredom of a long summer afternoon. Although brash and bossy, Rosie is a likable, funny kid. Sendak's humorous three-color illustrations ably capture the mood of the story.

Sendak's next four works were published in 1962 as the four volumes of the extremely popular miniature *Nutshell Library* (1962). Over a half-million copies of the boxed set of this work have been sold since its original publication. These works, only 2 ½ by 4 inches in size, allowed Sendak to display his virtuosity not only by creating masterful, humorous illustrations in a confined space but also by rejuvenating an overworked genre. The four volumes of *The Nutshell Library* include an alphabet book, *Alligators All Around;* a seasons book, *Chicken Soup with Rice;* a forward-and-backward counting rhyme, *One Was Johnny;* and a modern cautionary tale, *Pierre.* The overall design of *The Nutshell Library* is more successful than Sendak's three previous works at integrating text, design, and illustrations.

All of these seven books written and illustrated by Sendak during his apprenticeship period share two major characteristics: an honest unsentimental presentation of the behavior of children and the use of fantasy as an integral element of the story. These early works draw on Sendak's own childhood, on his experiences in psychoanalysis, and on his research in child psychology. Of these early works Selma Lanes has said, "If there is a common failing in the stories, it is that they have a hazy quality–a tentativeness and lack of dramatic conflict–as if the author had not yet sharply defined, or come to grips head-on with, his subject matter."

At age thirty-four Sendak felt ready to try what he considers to be his first picture book. The artist has said that his years of apprenticeship ended with the publication of *Where the Wild Things Are* in 1963. The original conception of the book grew out of a thin, horizontal book dummy titled "Where the Wild Horses Are," put together by the artist in 1955. This original dummy showed the trials of a young boy searching for the Wild Horses, who ends up with a small bride on Happy Island. Sendak refined this rather pointless material into a coherent and economical text which is one of the most popular of

Dust jackets for two of the four volumes published in The Nutshell Library *(Harper & Row)*

contemporary nursery tales. The book tells the story of a young boy, Max, who misbehaves and is sent to bed without his supper by his mother, who calls him "Wild Thing." Banished to his bedroom, Max fantasizes that he travels to the island of the Wild Things and becomes their king. Later, however, homesick and hungry, Max, emerges from the fantasy to find that his mother has left supper, which is still hot, waiting for him in his bedroom.

Pressed to explain where the idea for *Where the Wild Things Are* came from, Sendak has said that his books derive more from fantasies than from ideas. Yet Sendak has pointed out repeatedly that successful fantasy "must be rooted in living fact." The exuberant illustrations for *Where the Wild Things Are* create a concrete environment for Sendak's fantasy. The artist has again used pen-and-ink drawings with watercolor washes for this work. The palette of blues, purples, and greens is reminiscent of his earlier, less successful illustrations for *The Moon Jumpers*. Sendak has used the illustrations to help to show the relationship between the real world and the fantasy world–

the bedposts grow into trees and the rug turns into grass as the fantasy begins. The artist has noticed that the film *King Kong*, which he saw as a child, may have influenced some of the illustrations. He has also said that the Wild Things are based somewhat on relatives he disliked as a child.

Sendak was surprised by the controversy this book generated. Initially, it received several negative reviews and many parents, educators, and librarians were concerned about the effect that the book might have on children. As Lanes notes, one librarian cautioned, "It is not a book to be left where a sensitive child may come upon it at twilight."

Despite this controversy, *Where the Wild Things Are* was an unprecedented success. Since its original publication, around three million copies have been sold, and the book has been published in thirteen foreign languages. The excellence of the book was recognized when Sendak was awarded the Caldecott Medal in 1964. In his acceptance speech for this award Sendak defended *Where the Wild Things Are*. He said that despite the desire to protect children from "new and painful experiences" that "from their earliest years children live on familiar terms with disrupting emotions, that fear and anxiety are an intrinsic part of their everyday lives, that they continually cope with frustration as best they can. And it is through fantasy that children achieve catharsis. It is the best means they have for taming Wild Things." He closed by stating that the "truth and passion" of his work derive from his involvement with the "awful vulnerability of children and their struggle to make themselves King of all Wild Things."

In marked contrast to the triumph of the early 1960s, the late 1960s were perhaps the most tragic period in Sendak's life. In 1967 he learned that his mother was suffering from cancer. While on a trip to England that year, Sendak suffered a major coronary attack while being interviewed on BBC-TV. Judy Taylor, his English editor, insisted that he be taken to a hospital despite the doctor's diagnosis of severe indigestion; Sendak credits her with saving his life. After spending five weeks in the Queen Elizabeth Hospital in Gateshead-upon-Tyne, he was transferred to a London nursing home to complete his recovery. He had a friend send postcards to his parents from all over Europe so that they would not find out about his heart attack.

Upon returning home, he learned that his beloved Sealyham terrier Jennie had cancer and would have to be put away. Finally, Sendak's mother died in August of 1968. Speaking of his youthful brush with death, Sendak has said that he felt a bargain had been broken in that his mission was to be cut so short. He felt that he had been granted immunity as long as he kept working to recall his childhood honestly.

Ironically, Sendak had begun working on a tribute to Jennie a year before she died. The book *Higglety Pigglety Pop! Or, There Must Be More to Life* (1967) is the artist's bid to immortalize Jennie in the World Mother Goose Theatre, the realm of children's books. He had purchased Jennie in 1954. For the next fourteen years she was to be, as Sendak put it, "the love of my life." Jennie also appeared in many of the artist's illustrations during these years.

Higglety Pigglety Pop! Or, There Must Be More to Life is a decidedly wistful and melancholy fairy tale, although there are humorous incidents—mostly related to Jennie's tremendous appetite. The book tells the story of a discontented Sealyham terrier who feels there must be more to life than having everything. She leaves home and an-

Cover for Sendak's 1967 wistful and melancholy fairy tale (Harper & Row)

swers an advertisement to be leading lady for the World Mother Goose Theatre. To gain experience, Jennie takes a job as a nursemaid to an unruly baby, saves the child from the jaws of the Downstairs Lion, and finally is accepted as the leading lady of the World Mother Goose Theatre's rendition of "Higglety Pigglety Pop!" This nonsense nursery rhyme was written in 1846 by Samuel Griswold Goodrich, an early advocate of factual work for children, who hoped that such a blatantly meaningless verse would put an end to such frivolity for good. Ironically, Sendak completely sabotaged Goodrich's original intention. At the conclusion of the book Jennie has achieved true bliss and will live happily hereafter.

The illustrations for this work are Victorian in feeling. Sendak has said that they were influenced specifically by the work of two artists of the 1860s, George Pinwell and Arthur Hughes. The meticulous realism of the pen-and-ink drawings helps give credibility to the fantasy. In fact Sendak worked from photographs of Jennie to create these intricately crosshatched illustrations. In creating illustrations for the rather opaque nursery rhyme at the close of the book, Sendak very imaginatively brought back all the characters introduced earlier in the story for a curtain call. *Higglety Pigglety Pop! Or, There Must Be More to Life*, Sendak's longest and in some ways most personal work, received very favorable reviews and has proven to be popular with college students and adults as well as with children.

Despite his personal tragedies during the 1960s, the decade was one of Sendak's most productive periods. His illustrations from these years are the work of a master in full command of his artistic medium with a clear understanding of the role of the interpretive illustrator. He has said that great illustrations must be an enlargement of the text and that the illustrator must not draw exactly what is written. Rather, he must try to find a space in the text to let the pictures do the work. He has defined the true picture book as "a visual poem." A passionate lover of music, especially the music of Mozart, Sendak has drawn inspiration for his work from listening to great music and has compared the role of the illustrator interpreting a text to that of a musical conductor interpreting a score.

In 1965 Sendak used two Mother Goose rhymes to provide a ready-made text for *Hector Protector And As I Went Over the Water,* which can be viewed as a tribute to Randolph Caldecott, who Sendak feels invented the picture-book form. In developing the illustrations for *Hector Protector* Sendak created a scenario of a rebellious little boy forced to deliver a cake to the Queen. The boy, accompanied by a lion and snake he meets along the way, terrorizes the King and Queen and is sent home to bed in disgrace. The scenario for *As I Went Over the Water* features a young sea captain whose ship is swallowed by a sea monster. The boy swims to shore, vents his anger on two blackbirds, and reclaims his ship, which the sea monster has regurgitated. The humorous illustrations are strengthened by the artist's ability to depict character and emotions so effectively. Although crosshatching is used in the drawings, broad, flat watercolor washes in clear pastel tones, reminiscent of comic-strip art of the 1930s, are the dominant element. Another comic-strip device borrowed by Sendak is the use of dialogue in balloons to further the subplots of the scenarios created to illustrate each nursery rhyme.

Sendak, who explored a variety of styles of illustration in the 1960s, views his collaborations with poet Randall Jarrell as particularly successful. His 1964 drawings for *The Bat-Poet* and his 1965 decorations for *The Animal Family* are among his finest pen-and-ink drawings; the lavish rendering of landscape is particularly noteworthy. He illustrated two works by Frank Stockton, *The Griffin and the Minor Canon* (1963) and *The Bee-Man of Orn* (1964). The illustrations for the second work are much funnier, more painterly, and

more richly detailed than the earlier work. The sophisticated use of color in the illustrations for *The Bee-Man of Orn* clearly shows the influence of two English illustrators, Randolph Caldecott and Thomas Rowlandson.

In 1965 Sendak continued this more painterly approach and pale palette in his illustrations for *Lullabies and Night Songs.* He created some of his most dramatic, powerful illustrations for Isaac Bashevis Singer's *Zlateh the Goat and Other Stories,* seven tales of Jewish folklore, which was published in 1966. Drawing from family photographs of relatives, Sendak fused detailed realism with sinister fantasy to create pen-and-ink drawings with a surreal quality, the perfect graphic complement for Singer's text.

In 1967 Sendak did the illustrations for the fifth and final "Little Bear" book. Minarik hurried to finish the book after she heard about Sendak's heart attack, and this book was the only one he illustrated during the year he took off for recovery. The draftsmanship of the illustrations for *A Kiss for Little Bear* (1968) is bolder, freer, and more richly detailed than the earlier books; however, these illustrations also have a melancholy quality, perhaps reflecting the recent tragic events in his life, not present in the earlier works. Finally, Sendak illustrated two works by George MacDonald, whom the illustrator considers to be "probably the greatest of the Victorian writers for children." *The Golden Key* appeared in 1967, and *The Light Princess* was published in 1969. The illustrations for the second work are more successful due to their consistency of style and overall authority.

In the Night Kitchen, Sendak's next major picture book, was published in 1970. Originally, he had planned to illustrate a collection of Mother Goose rhymes. However, he noticed that all his selections dealt with food and eating, and eventually he wrote his own text instead. Although the Mother Goose rhymes influenced the text, Sendak has said that this book comes from "the direct middle of me." An advertisement for Sunshine Bakers proclaiming "We Bake While You Sleep!" also inspired the text. Sendak felt his exclusion from their baking was unfair and has confessed that "this book was a sort of vendetta book to get back at them and to let them know that I was now old enough to stay up at night and know what was happening in the Night Kitchen."

This joyous, optimistic book tells the story of a young boy, Mickey, who is awakened by a noise in the night. He falls "through the dark, out of his clothes, past his parents' bedroom," and into the bustle of the Night Kitchen. He lands in batter and is nearly baked by three fat, absentminded bakers (three Oliver Hardys). Mickey escapes, makes an airplane out of bread dough, gets the cup of milk needed by the bakers, and then slides down the milk bottle back into his own bed.

The full-color illustrations for *In the Night Kitchen* can be viewed as a tribute to the artist's own childhood in New York City in the 1930s. The Busby Berkeley musicals and Mickey Mouse cartoons loved by Sendak as a child were an obvious source of inspiration. He has said that another influence was the comic-strip artwork of Winsor McCay, which Sendak had seen at an exhibition at the Metropolitan Museum. The illustrations are full of unobtrusive personal references from the artist's life. His dog Jennie's name, for example, appears on the clock Mickey floats past. The setting and mood of the story also probably owe a debt to all the hours that the sickly young Sendak spent in the kitchen with his mother. The flat, comic-book style of the drawings features bold, black outlines filled in with dark, rich colors. Perhaps Sendak's greatest graphic triumph in this book is the surreal skyline of the Night Kitchen, the New York City skyline, created with 1930s style kitchen utensils and containers.

Critical reviews of *In the Night Kitchen* almost universally praised the artwork; however, as usual, many reviewers felt compelled to warn that the book might offend some readers. Many librarians objected to the book's frontal nudity, and Sendak was infuriated by the fact that many of them painted diapers on Mickey. Although never as successful commercially as *Where the Wild Things Are*, Sendak has said that he favors *In the Night Kitchen* because it explores more fully the subconscious unreasoning world "beneath the surface of things."

Among Sendak's most masterful interpretive illustrations are the pen-and-ink drawings created between 1970 and 1973 for *The Juniper Tree and Other Tales from Grimm* (1973), a collection of twenty-seven of the Grimm brothers fairy tales. The translations of the tales, which were begun by Randall Jarrell, were completed by Lore Segal after Jarrell's death. Sendak's preparation for creating these illustrations was exhaustive. Not only did he seek out early illustrated editions of the *Household Tales*, but he also traveled extensively in Germany to get the feel of the region. After ab-

Dust jacket for Sendak's 1970 picture book about a young boy's adventures after being awakened by a noise in the night (Harper & Row)

sorbing all this background material, he decided that four of the major influences on his drawings were the illustrated editions of the *Household Tales* done by George Cruikshank, Ludwig Grimm, and Otto Ubbelohde and also the etchings of Dürer. Sendak decided to do only one illustration for each tale.

The Juniper Tree was printed in two volumes so that the type size could be invitingly large. Sendak's illustrations have a dark, brooding atmosphere well suited for the tales, none of which were bowdlerized for an audience of children. In analyzing these illustrations, Selma Lanes has written that "Sendak's pictures, almost suffocatingly claustrophobic, seem to force their way out of their small rectangular enclosures, thereby imposing their alien reality on the viewer. The close focus makes for a brutal assault on the imagination. These decidedly virile Grimm illustrations can neither be denied nor dismissed." Most of these illustrations are indeed psychologically riveting; however, the psychological synopsis of plot intended in some of the illustrations does not succeed, and the drawings appear merely flat and decorative. Sendak was disappointed that

The Juniper Tree, perhaps his masterpiece, did not receive serious criticism as art.

Most of Sendak's other work of the 1970s did not meet with tremendous success or critical acclaim. He spent two years adapting *The Sign on Rosie's Door* and *The Nutshell Library* into an animated musical television program, *Really Rosie, Starring the Nutshell Kids,* originally aired by CBS in February 1975. Sendak's scenario was set to music by Carole King. A companion book to this television special was also published under the same title.

In 1976 Sendak published *Some Swell Pup: or Are You Sure You Want a Dog?,* which he characterized as "a dog pre-training manual for children" in which a dog explains the responsibilities of owning a puppy to two exaggeratedly bratty children. The use of a dog draped in classical robes as the narrator of the book seems rather heavy-handed and incongruous for such a light, instructional subject. Most critics dismissed the book as trivial. Many reviewers objected to the literal depiction of the problems of house-training dogs.

Sendak created meticulously crosshatched, intricately detailed, masterfully surrealistic illustrations for Randall Jarrell's last book, *Fly By Night,* published in 1976. Again many critics commented on the main character's nudity. In *Seven Little Monsters* (1975), a counting book, Sendak used drawings he originally created for an animated number sequence which aired on "Sesame Street" in 1970. Originally, and sloppily, produced by his German publisher, the sixth monster is not drawn consistently throughout the book. The first American edition of the book appeared in 1977. Wounded by negative critical reviews for these books, Sendak said, "I've had the most savage reviews of my career; it must be a 'Get Sendak' year." Although one can sympathize with Sendak's hurt at negative reviews, close critical scrutiny of his work is inevitable, given the artist's reputation and acclaim, an unpleasant side effect of fame.

In 1981 Sendak published his most recent and obscure original picture book, *Outside Over There.* This book tells a story of jealousy and sibling rivalry in which a young girl named Ida bravely rescues her younger sister who has been kidnapped by goblins. To Sendak's delight this book was sold and promoted in both the children's and adult book markets. The artist credits much of the mood of the book to the music of Mozart, the paintings of Runge, and his fascination with a Grimm tale about the stealing of a baby, "The Goblins." He worked from photographs to create the beautiful paintings which illustrate the book. *Outside Over There* received mostly favorable reviews. In the 26 April 1984 issue of the *New York Times Book Review,* John Gardner said, "What Mr. Sendak offers, in short, is not an ordinary children's book done extraordinarily well but something different in kind from the ordinary children's book: a profound work of art for children."

Sendak has indicated that he views *Outside Over There* as the final volume of a trilogy including *Where the Wild Things Are* and *In the Night Kitchen.* Although he has refused to explain exactly why he considers these three seemingly unrelated picture books to be a trilogy, he has said he sees these works as a unit because "they are all variations on the same theme: how children master various feelings—anger, boredom, fear, frustration, jealousy—and manage to come to grips with the realities of their lives." He has acknowledged that the three books have gotten increasingly complex and strange. The texts have also become increasingly personal, more inaccessible, more artificially structured, more grammatically difficult, and less popular. Sendak has argued, however, that great art is rarely popular art.

In the past six years Sendak has pursued a number of theatrical projects. In 1978 he was involved with a Music Theater Lab stage production of *Really Rosie* in Washington, D.C. He designed an Off-Broadway production of an expanded version of the play in 1980. He has also designed several opera productions, including Mozart's *The Magic Flute* for the Houston Grand Opera Company in 1980 and Janacek's *The Cunning Little Vixen* for the New York Opera Company in 1981. He did the sets, costumes, and libretto for a 1980 operatic version of *Where the Wild Things Are* presented by the Brussels Opera.

In fact, two of the works most recently illustrated by Sendak, *The Nutcracker* and *The Love for Three Oranges,* both published in 1984, grew out of theatrical projects. He was approached by Kent Stowell in 1981 about designing a 1983 production of "The Nutcracker" for the Pacific Northwest Ballet in Seattle. He declined the offer at first but accepted the project after having been challenged to abandon the traditional conception of the ballet and to start afresh with E. T. A. Hoffmann. This project led to the creation of a new edition in 1984 of Hoffmann's *The Nutcracker* translated by Ralph Manheim and illustrated by Maurice Sendak. Well designed and

Poster by Sendak for the New York stage production of the play based on characters that first appeared in The Sign on Rosie's Door *and* The Nutshell Library *(© 1980 Maurice Sendak)*

זעהר גיטע אין שענע חלות אוך שבת
אוך איער חלות

PHILIP SENDAK

In Grandpa's House

⌐◦∾◦⌐

TRANSLATED AND ADAPTED BY
SEYMOUR BAROFSKY
PICTURES BY
MAURICE SENDAK
Harper & Row, Publishers
New York

Frontispiece and title page for Sendak's father's posthumously published book, illustrated by Sendak

lavishly produced, the book has incorporated Sendak's stage designs. These illustrations, which are beautifully executed in soft colors, are somehow lacking in convincing emotion. The only illustration with the psychological power one expects from Sendak is the final double-page spread–a huge picture of the nutcracker's leering face, a grotesque caricature of Sendak's own face.

The Love for Three Oranges chronicles the collaboration of Sendak as designer and Frank Corsaro as stage director of the 1982 Glyndebourne production of Prokofiev's *The Love for Three Oranges*. It records, mostly in a series of dialogues, the process through which Corsaro and Sendak arrived at design solutions for the opera's complex staging demands. Sendak's imaginative designs are again executed in watercolor paintings in soft, subtle colors reminiscent of eighteenth-century handcolored engravings. Perhaps the biggest problem with both of these books is the fact that a small picture book cannot possibly convey the impact of the costume and set designs

as they would appear on the stage. The reader longs to see these illustrations brought to life in the theater.

Sendak's most recently published illustrations appear in his father Philip's posthumously published *In Grandpa's House* (1985). This book, which is based on the stories Philip Sendak told his children when they were young, really tells two stories. The first eight pages describe Philip's childhood in Europe and America; the rest of the book is a dreamlike story set in a Polish-Jewish shtetl about a young boy, David, who is guided through a series of frightening but oddly comforting adventures by a magic bird secretly sent by his dead grandfather. At Maurice's insistence, Philip committed these stories and reminiscences to paper before his death in 1970; they were translated and adapted by Seymour Barofsky.

Sendak's illustrations for *In Grandpa's House* are similar in size, format, and mood to his illustrations for *The Juniper Tree;* however, these soft pencil drawings are more dreamlike and, perhaps, less sinister than the pen-and-ink illustrations of *The Juniper Tree*. In reviewing this book for the *New York Times Book Review*, Paul Cowan describes Philip's writing as looser, more convoluted, more didactic, and somewhat disappointing in comparison with Maurice's. However, he closes his review with the statement that, "When you read father's and son's work together, you feel privileged to watch two very special men who have transcended the abyss of geography and time to engage in an intimate, loving dialogue with one another—and with us." Given Sendak's assertion that his father's stories had an important influence on his development as an artist, this beautiful book represents a very personal, appropriate, and moving act of filial love.

Since 1972 Sendak has lived in Ridgefields, Connecticut, with three dogs. His tremendous success as an author and illustrator has given him the financial independence to be highly selective about the work he undertakes. In a recent interview with Bob Ehlert, Sendak said, "Most books I would not want to illustrate at this point. I'm illustrating a Grimm fairy tale now because it's a wonderful story.... Even my own writing I'm keeping in abeyance. I'm holding back from writing another book because I want it all, whatever it is, I want it to steep well like a good soup and then do it, or not do it. That's my wonderful choice at this point in my life."

Sendak has remained a very private person devoted to his art and reluctant to define the specific personal experiences from which it has grown. However, it is clear that the emotional veracity and power of his greatest work derive from a painstaking analysis of his own childhood. He has fused his uncompromising vision of the psychological complexity of childhood with a unique artistic style inspired by the greatest nineteenth-century illustrators. In defining the criteria that he would use to judge picture books, Sendak feels strongly that "originality of vision is paramount—someone who says something, even something commonplace, in a totally original and fresh way. For myself, the picture book is where I put down those fantasies that have been with me all my life, and where I give them a *form* that means something. I live inside the picture book; it's where I fight all my battles, and where, hopefully, I win my wars." Maurice Sendak's finest mature work admirably meets his own evaluative criteria and represents an outstanding combat record.

References:

Saul Braun, "Sendak Raises the Shade on Childhood," *New York Times Magazine*, 7 June 1970, pp. 34-35;

Randy Sue Coburn, "The Wonderful Wizard of 'Wild Things' Now Turns to Opera," *Smithsonian*, 12 (January 1982): 88-93;

Paul Cowan, "Where the Wild Things Came From," *New York Times Book Review*, 10 November 1985, p. 39;

Bob Ehlert, "Maurice Sendak," *Roanoke Times & World News*, 24 November 1985, pp. E1, E8;

Nat Hentoff, "Among the Wild Things," *New Yorker*, 41 (22 January 1966): 39-40;

John Lahr, "The Playful Art of Maurice Sendak," *New York Times Magazine*, 12 October 1980, pp. 44-49;

Selma G. Lanes, *The Art of Maurice Sendak* (New York: Abrams, 1980);

D. E. White, "Conversations with Maurice Sendak," *Horn Book*, 56 (April 1980): 145-155.

Papers:

Maurice Sendak's manuscripts are at the Museum of the Philip H. and A. S. W. Rosenbach Foundation in Philadelphia.

Uri Shulevitz
(27 February 1935-)

Sue Lile Inman
Furman University

BOOKS: *The Moon in My Room* (New York: Harper & Row, 1963);

One Monday Morning (New York: Scribners, 1967);

Rain Rain Rivers (New York: Farrar, Straus & Giroux, 1969);

Oh, What A Noise! (New York: Macmillan, 1971);

The Magician (New York: Macmillan / London: Collier-Macmillan, 1973);

Dawn (New York: Farrar, Straus & Giroux, 1974);

The Treasure (New York: Farrar, Straus & Giroux, 1978);

Writing with Pictures: How to Write and Illustrate Children's Books (New York: Watson-Guptill, 1985);

The Strange and Exciting Adventures of Jeremiah Hush as Told for the Benefit of All Persons of Good Sense and Recorded to the Best of His Limited Ability (New York: Farrar, Straus & Giroux, 1986).

BOOKS ILLUSTRATED: Charlotte Zolotow, *A Rose, A Bridge, and A Wild Black Horse* (New York: Harper & Row, 1964);

Mary Stolz, *The Mystery of the Woods* (New York: Harper & Row, 1964);

H. R. Hays and Daniel Hays, *Charley Sang a Song* (New York: Harper & Row, 1964);

Jack Sendak, *The Second Witch* (New York: Harper & Row, 1965);

Molly Cone, *Who Knows Ten?* (New York: Union of American Hebrew Congregations, 1965);

Stolz, *Maximilian's World* (New York: Harper & Row, 1966);

Sulamith Ish-Kishor, *The Carpet of So'omon* (New York: Pantheon, 1966);

Brothers Grimm, *The Twelve Dancing Princesses* (New York: Scribners, 1966);

Jean Russell Larson, *The Silkspinners* (New York: Scribners, 1967);

Dorothy Nathan, *The Month Brothers* (New York: Dutton, 1967);

Jan Wahl, *Runaway Jonah, and Other Tales* (New York: Macmillan, 1968);

John Smith, ed., *My Kind of Verse* (New York: Macmillan, 1968);

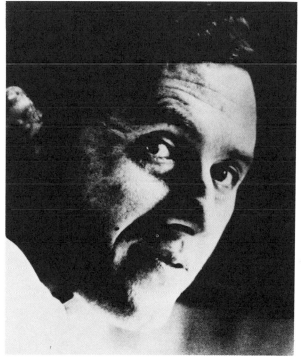

Arthur Ransome, *The Fool of the World and the Flying Ship* (New York: Farrar, Straus & Giroux, 1968);

Wahl, *The Wonderful Kite* (New York: Delacorte, 1970);

Alexander Afanasyev, *Soldier and Tsar in the Forest*, translated by Richard Lourie (New York: Farrar, Straus & Giroux, 1972);

Isaac Bashevis Singer, *The Fools of Chelm and Their History* (New York: Farrar, Straus & Giroux, 1973);

Robert Louis Stevenson, *The Touchstone* (New York: Greenwillow, 1976);

Richard Kennedy, *The Lost Kingdom of Karnica* (New York: Scribners / San Francisco: Sierra Club Books, 1979);

Singer, *The Golem* (New York: Farrar, Straus & Giroux / London: Deutsch, 1982).

OTHER: Sholem Aleichem, *Hanukah Money*, translated and adapted by Uri Shulevitz and Elizabeth Shub, illustrated by Shulevitz (New York: Greenwillow, 1978).

PERIODICAL PUBLICATIONS: "Within the Margins of a Picture Book," *Horn Book* (June 1971);
"What Is a Picture Book?," *Wilson Library Bulletin* (October 1980): 99-101.

Uri Shulevitz, the winner of the 1969 Caldecott Medal and creator of a 1980 Caldecott Honor Book, has gained international respect as an author and illustrator of children's picture books since 1963 when his first book, *The Moon in My Room,* was published. He is seen by specialists in children's literature as one of the contemporary writer-illustrators most gifted in integrating text and pictures into a complementary harmony. He feels an affinity for folk stories of the Eastern European tradition and has adapted several for the modern child from Russian and Yiddish sources. He has also illustrated books by other authors, including Charlotte Zolotow, Jean Russell Larson, Robert Louis Stevenson, and Isaac Bashevis Singer. He has a definite conception of how to write and illustrate children's books and is in demand as a teacher of workshops on the subject. That Uri Shulevitz comes to a knowledge of English after speaking Polish, Yiddish, French, Russian, and Hebrew makes his careful regard for choosing only the essential words especially sensitive and his accomplishment remarkable.

Born in Warsaw, Poland, on 27 February 1935, Uri Shulevitz experienced the German blitz when he was four. He remembers standing in line for bread when suddenly flying shrapnel and smoke confused the scene. When the smoke cleared, about a third of the people were lying on the ground, dead or wounded. A bomb fell into the stairwell of his apartment building while he was at home. He tells about having to walk down a long plank where the stairway had been, above what seemed to his four-year-old mind to be an abyss. After fleeing Poland, the Shulevitz family traveled from place to place, settling in Paris after the war.

The architecture, streets, rooftops, and chimneys of Paris captured young Shulevitz's fancy. His appreciation and knowledge of city life show in many of his illustrations in his later books, particularly his scenes of New York in *One Monday*

Morning (1967) and *Rain Rain Rivers* (1969). He was encouraged in his drawing by both his parents, Abraham and Szandla Hermanstat Shulevitz, who were also artistically talented. In 1947 Shulevitz won first prize in his grammar-school district art contest. He developed a passion for movies and for comic books and haunted the bookstalls along the Quai de la Seine. With a friend who supplied the words, he designed and drew his own comics, some of which he still has. Paris provided a feast for a young boy deprived of books during early childhood.

In 1949, with his parents and younger brother, he moved to Israel. To help with family expenses Shulevitz worked at a variety of jobs during the day and attended school at night. For two years he helped make rubber stamps, worked as a carpenter, painted houses, and issued dog licenses at Tel Aviv City Hall, where he had time to read and write at odd moments. He excelled in literature, but later, at the Teachers Institute near Tel Aviv, he deliberately decided to balance his affinity for literature and his love of fantasy with a concentration on courses in the natural sciences.

He took his first painting lessons from Ezekiel Shtreichman, a semiabstract artist to whom he later dedicated his illustrations for a 1976 edition of Robert Louis Stevenson's *The Touchstone*. He joined the Israeli Army in 1956 during the Sinai War. After basic training, Shulevitz was able to continue his interest in art by serving a youth magazine as the art director. He joined a kibbutz established by some of his friends at Ein Geddi, a verdant oasis near the Dead Sea. He recalls vividly how the thriving collective farm moved him with its lush greenness as he approached it through the desert. There he tried his hand at graphics by designing a Passover Haggadah, depicting the story of the Exodus to be read at Seder.

When he was twenty-four and had completed his military service, Shulevitz left Israel for New York, where he studied painting at the Brooklyn Museum Art School. Later he studied with Peter Hopkins, who educated him in the approach of the Renaissance masters. Students mixed their own paints, studied perspective and anatomy of humans and animals, and practiced techniques based on Rubens's quick oil sketches.

During the two years at the Brooklyn Museum Art School, he drew illustrations under strict guidelines for a Hebrew publishing company. Although rigorous and restrictive, this experience, he admits, furthered his development. However, one day while on the telephone he found himself doodling. Liking the free, spontaneous lines, he decided to develop his own approach, to work independently. He gathered his portfolio and visited publishing houses. Encouraged by editors Ursula Nordstrom and Susan Carr Hirschman, Shulevitz wrote and illustrated his first book, *The Moon in My Room*, published in 1963 by Harper and Row.

The Moon in My Room presents simple line drawings, more suggestive than fully descriptive, of a small boy's private world—his room—in which he feels that the moon and stars are his, the flower pots, whole villages. In a rather unremarkable and slim story line, Shulevitz shows the boy searching for his stuffed bear. When the two are reunited, the drawing shows the boy and bear to be the same size, as they are in the boy's mind. Suggested throughout is the belief that here in this place the boy is in full command and can dispense power where he will.

Shulevitz summarizes his method in this way: "I try to suggest and evoke, rather than state rigidly, in order to encourage the child to participate actively, filling in with his own imagination. This approach is based on the belief that my audience is intelligent and active rather than passive." His first book exemplifies this approach in the few words used, the expanse of white space on each page, and the whimsical ink drawings with touches of pink-and-green wash. Much is left implicit.

From 1964 to 1966 Shulevitz illustrated eight books written by other authors. One quality characteristic of his work shows up in these early books, each different in tone and subject. Shulevitz consciously varies the kinds of pictures he makes, depending upon the nature of the story, the milieu peculiar to each text. Working primarily in ink, he has used a Japanese reed pen for Mary Stolz's *Maximilian's World* (1966) and a Chinese brush for *The Silkspinners* (1967) by Jean Russell Larson. He has used pen-and-ink line drawings, achieving the effect of an etching by scratching with a razor blade, and quite frequently he uses ink washes with preseparated colors. His illustrations become an organic extension of each particular text, whether his or another author's.

The second book Shulevitz both wrote and illustrated, *One Monday Morning* (1967), combines

Dust jacket for Shulevitz's 1967 book, the story of a young boy alone on a rainy morning who imagines that a king, a queen, and a prince come to see him (Scribners)

realism and fantasy in a delightful story of a young boy alone on a rainy Monday morning who imagines that a king, a queen, and a prince come to see him. When he is not at home, they return on a sunny Tuesday along with a knight. Using the technique of accumulation that never fails to delight children, Shulevitz adds another character each day of the week to join the king, queen, boy, and knight: a royal guard, royal cook, royal barber, royal jester, and, on Sunday, when the little boy is finally at home, a little dog.

In startling contrast to the dreary mundane world of the bus stop, Laundromat, corner grocery store, and subway of the boy's tenement neighborhood are the brilliant colors, outlandish costumes, and exaggerated postures of the royal visitors. The last illustration in the book shows the child at his window again with the king and queen as playing cards laid out on his table. The face and costume of his stuffed toy on the window ledge are those of the royal barber. Fantasy has transformed a dull day.

This book demonstrates several qualities typical of Shulevitz's work. Having loved movies from his childhood in Paris, he often employs a cinematic method. From the opening view of a deserted city block of tenements with laundry hanging out in the rain and deserted storefronts, he focuses on the boy at the window. Each page shows change and movement with unusual angles and extensive open space. Filmmaker Tom Spain and Shulevitz made *One Monday Morning* into a film in 1971.

Respect for the childlike view is characteristic of Shulevitz and is apparent in *One Monday Morning.* The author blends the solemn dignity of the child and the royal visitors with comic proportions that suggest the naiveté of the child but with no condescension on the part of the author. The boy in the story is pleased and smiles modestly at the crowd bowing to him, but he is not surprised or ashamed of his status. To Shulevitz, the child does not acknowledge the artificial barriers the adult world often sets up.

Both his cinematic approach and his respect for the child's view are manifest in *The Fool of the World and the Flying Ship* (1968) for which he won the Caldecott Medal in 1969. Using Arthur Ransome's English text for an old Russian folktale (*Old Peter's Russian Tales,* 1916), Shulevitz designed the pictures and the layout of the words for each page. His vivid and bold illustrations, in black line and colorful ink washes, perfectly complement the text which Shulevitz calls "so full and juicy."

Like a movie camera, the artist pans the horizon with a double-page illustration, showing the Fool flying in his little ship over the farmlands heading toward the Czar's castle and away from the confinement of his peasant home, where his parents have disparaged his ever amounting to anything. From panoramic views to interior close-ups, Shulevitz moves the picture accompaniment forward, offering the reader a sense of freedom and release. As Shulevitz says, "Luckily, our Fool is foolish enough not to listen to his mother."

The Fool sets out full of song and hope, innocently trusting his fate to whatever comes. He takes pleasure in everyone he meets. His natural kindness unwittingly supplies him with the very people on board his fantastic flying ship he will need to meet the Czar's impossible demands before he can marry the Czar's daughter. Each one uses his peculiarity to aid the simple Fool. A more cynical, less childlike protagonist might mock the unlikely idiosyncrasies of the riders, but they are all fine companions for the Fool.

The book has had a remarkable effect. In an article for *Horn Book,* Shulevitz quotes a letter sent to his publisher by a librarian in Cleveland. She had been reading *The Fool of the World* to a group of black first-graders: "One little boy who hitherto had displayed a very poor memory and little progress in reading in his first-grade class stood by one desk. As he turned the pages he told the story to another staff member in each sequence, using some of the complicated words. He was so moved that he wanted to keep the book. As the youngest of three brothers, he felt akin to the young hero, and goes about calling himself the Fool of the World. The entire staff marveled at the power the book had had on both a group of children and one individual boy–who for one brief moment displayed a latent ability to comprehend, follow, and even memorize a very complicated plot on a first hearing. . . . This is one of those rare moments which I as a children's librarian and dedicated storyteller will cherish." As the artist declares, "A small miracle had taken place."

Recently, when asked in an interview if he thought the author / illustrator had a didactic role in creating children's books, he replied, "To take a kind of teacher or parental tone is something one should be very careful of. I don't want to do that. But, ultimately, when one does something one is very excited about, he does, perhaps, influence others." Certainly the reader shares the artist's sense of exhilaration over the Fool's sweeping escape from the warm prison where he was made to play the fool, to a new life of freedom, discovery, and love, despite all the obstacles.

This life-affirming attitude extends to Shulevitz's other books, giving them an infectious energy. *Rain Rain Rivers,* the third book to which Shulevitz contributed both words and pictures, was published in 1969, some years after he had first conceived the idea for it. He recalls that the inspiration for the book came through hearing rain very clearly, although, in fact, it was a clear night. At the same time he heard the rain, a series of images flashed across his mind: rain coming down the windowpanes, rain hitting the pavement, springing up like mushrooms, streams running into rivers, and finally uniting with the ocean. Shulevitz, who lived in Israel for ten years, has said, "Having to wait and wait for rain, I see water as such a precious resource, rain as something joyous."

Rain Rain Rivers, which won the International Book Exhibition Bronze Medal in 1970, con-

Dust jacket for the 1968 edition of Arthur Ransome's English translation of a Russian folktale, illustrated by Shulevitz. The book was awarded the Caldecott Medal in 1969 (Farrar, Straus & Giroux).

veys this jubilant response through its luminous illustrations, ink drawings with overlays of yellow, blue, and green washes, as a little girl sits in her attic room and listens to the rain. Tomorrow she will jump over puddles reflecting the city and the sky; she will sail her boats. Double-spread panoramas of swelling, curling ocean waves and of the ocean merging with the sky alternate with more intimate depictions of birds splashing in the street, comical frogs on lily pads, and children dancing in the mud (pictures not unlike the dancing children in Maurice Sendak's illustrations for Ruth Krauss's *A Hole Is to Dig,* 1952). At the end, Shulevitz returns the focus to the little girl who knows that her plant in the window is growing.

As important as the luminous illustrations are the words in *Rain Rain Rivers.* The choice of words and their placement possess an undeniable poetic intensity. Shulevitz uses assonance, alliteration, onomatopoeia, and occasional rhyme in a cadence that builds in power. Although he does not claim to be a poet, he nevertheless admits that he consciously chose the words for their sounds and the effect of increasing intensity. And he readily admits that he pays particular attention to line breaks and to breaks between pages when he lays out a book.

His next book, he says, he did just for fun. For *Oh, What A Noise!* (1971) Shulevitz worked with his editor at that time, Elizabeth Shub, adapting a story by William Brighty Rands for the text. The book provides a list of noises that keep the boy subjected to them from going to sleep, excuses most children would love to have. Shulevitz uses the names of his beloved cats (who have since died), Bianco and Fuzzball, on signs on the city buildings, and he puts the titles of his own books on the books in the shelf of the boy's room alongside *Mother Goose.* The flamboyant colors, outlandish figures (twenty whales seem to be stacked up and floating in the air), and the obvious rhymes may provide a moment's fun to read aloud but lack the qualities that make for picture books with staying power, qualities Shulevitz certainly displays in other books, such as *One Monday Morning, Dawn* (1974), and *The Treasure* (1978).

His fifth book, *The Magician* (1973), is a retelling of the I. L. Peretz classic Yiddish legend from the period of the Enlightenment in Eastern Europe when Jews were moving into a more secular way of life. The story recounts the visit to a peasant couple of the prophet Elijah, disguised as a tall, thin magician in ragged clothing and a top hat. The old man and woman are unsure of

Dust jacket for Shulevitz's 1973 retelling of the Yiddish legend about a peasant couple who are visited by the prophet Elijah disguised as a magician (Macmillan)

what to think of the jaunty magician who invites himself to join their empty table, quickly supplying their home with candlelight and fine furnishings, so they make a hasty visit to their rabbi for advice.

While they are away, the magician produces a sumptuous feast and disappears. Only after tasting and finding the food and wine to be real do they realize that Elijah, the guest for whom all Jews provide a cup, has visited them. Shulevitz illustrates the top half of each page with a framed three-by-four crosshatched ink drawing. The drawings possess what Zena Sutherland and May Hill Arbuthnot have called the grave yet comic quality well suited for folktales and typical of Shulevitz's rendering of other folk stories such as *The Fools of Chelm and Their History* (1973) by Isaac Bashevis Singer and *Hanukah Money* (1978) by Sholem Aleichem, which was placed on the *New York Times* Best Illustrated Children's Books of the Year list.

Shulevitz says that the original text for *The Magician* was cumbersome with detail, and he chose to make his own translation from the Yiddish after consulting one Hebrew and two En-

glish translations as references. "I applied my own approach and concept of writing. I wanted to make it as brief as possible." The precise and droll drawings and the wit and succinctness of the words make a charming read-aloud book. *The Magician* was included in the Spring Book Festival in 1973 and the Children's Book Showcase in 1974.

Dawn, which won a Christopher Award, was chosen for the Children's Book Showcase, and named an IBBY Honor Book, makes a striking contrast to *The Magician* and illustrates Shulevitz's versatility. In *Dawn* Shulevitz depicts the coming of daybreak to a mountain lake, witnessed by an old man and his grandson. The mood is hushed; the changes gradual and subtle; the words simple and spare. Using water-color washes, Shulevitz gave each painting an elliptical shape with the colors gradually changing from deep midnight blues and violets to lighter hues until the final scene is a vibrant green with bright blue and yellows. The old man and his grandson sleep curled in blankets beside the still lake; as the breeze stirs the lake, and the sky lightens bringing the surroundings into more distinct shapes, the two awake, make their fire, and soon move quietly out in their rowboat onto the lake where they witness the dawn.

Shulevitz worked on this book in Upstate New York, where he spends his summers in a converted three-story barn that rests on the side of a hill. An ancient Chinese poem by Liu Chung-yuan (773-819) that he came across several years before he began the book inspired its creation. He says, "Dawn has not changed much through the centuries, but still I wanted it to be my own experience, so one night I did not go to bed at all." He sat in his kitchen observing and took notes on all that was happening. Then, before daybreak, he drove to a nearby lake, and there he sat and took notes. He saw the one silent bat later depicted in the book. He saw how still everything was, how the lake shivered, and how the vapors rose. Then he started working on the text, "retaining only what was absolutely necessary, also retaining the basic idea of the poem that moved me so much the first time: its simplicity." Shulevitz says that he likes "the Oriental simplicity, something so simple, so everyday, and yet so miraculous, put in a way that is fresh, that normally one does not look at. 'Suddenly, everything was green.' "

The book is an exquisite rendering of dawn, appealing to all ages though sold as a

inspected the stories that follow, and approve, and endorse, and recommend them, as fit for enjoyable reading, as they represent the faithful portrait of my true self and of the events the way they happened.

(I) Jeremiah Hush Goes to Town

Being the Faithful and Detailed Account

of the Goings and Comings of Jeremiah Hush to Octapusville

and his Extraordinary Adventures There

Curiously

as told by Jeremiah Hush himself

for the Benefit of all Persons of Good Sense

and Recorded to the best of his Limited Ability

and Vouched for as to their Certainty

By Uri Shulevitz.

***

J.H.
(Proboscis Monkey)

In another solar system, on a strange planet curiously
resembling our own, there lived not too long ago, a middle aged
monkey known as Jeremiah Hush. He was a quiet and serious fellow,
young at heart and youthful in appearance. He lived alone in a
small house surrounded by trees and fields. He was content to
live by himself in an out of the way *spot* and grow vegetables
in his little garden. During the day he loved to listen to duets
of birds singing on tree branches, and at night to cricket ensem-
bles and to frog orchestras by the pond. Jeremiah Hush was a poet
at heart, although he never wrote a line of poetry.

He was a reasonably happy monkey. That is, almost happy.
He was happy when he worked in his garden, when he watched
the vegetables grow, or when he listened to the music of the
birds, crickets and frogs. But as soon as he worried, which he

Page from a draft for Shulevitz's 1986 book, The Strange and Exciting Adventures of Jeremiah Hush
(courtesy of Uri Shulevitz)

book for children between the ages of five and seven. Like *Rain Rain Rivers, Dawn* celebrates what is. Shulevitz shows that what is natural, if rendered truly, needs no embellishment, no more story line than what is provided by nature.

The Treasure (1978), which Shulevitz both wrote and illustrated, was selected as a Caldecott Honor Book in 1980 and included in the *New York Times* Best Illustrated Children's Books of the Year list. It tells the familiar story (from the Hassidic tradition, among others) of a poor man who is told in a recurring dream to go to a certain city and look for a treasure under the bridge of the royal palace. After traveling through fields, farmlands, forests, and mountains, Isaac reaches the city but must postpone his search near the royal palace because it is heavily guarded. He lingers there until he is questioned by a soldier. The captain laughingly tells him that if he believed in dreams, he himself would have searched for treasure under the stove of a man named Isaac. Isaac returns to his city and digs beneath his own stove to find the treasure. The fable's moral is inscribed later by the rich Isaac on the house of prayer he builds in gratitude: "Sometimes one must travel far to discover what is near," a precept that grows naturally from the tale.

The illustrations, each one a pleasing painting in itself, show Isaac's quest in glowing colors; the costumes of Isaac and the soldiers look eighteenth century or earlier; the castled towns with narrow streets suggest Eastern European cities. The quaint setting, remarkably uncluttered by people, carts, markets, or rubbish, suits the simple fable, and the fact that the time and place are not precise suggests the timeless quality of the teaching. The theme of a man alone traveling far to find what is valuable right at hand is a theme entirely fitting for a man who, as a child, escaped wartime Poland to wander with his family for years, who has lived in postwar Paris, the city of Tel Aviv, a kibbutz near the Dead Sea, an apartment in Greenwich Village, and a barn in upper New York.

Uri Shulevitz says he has learned that how many miles one has traveled is not as important as the discoveries one can make within himself. A persistent theme in his books for children is the power of the imagination to transport a person or to transform mundane reality, to lift the person right out of his limitations. *One Monday Morning* will continue to be a favorite because of this theme. A story without words called "Picnic," pub-

lished in the *Scribner Anthology for Young People* (1976), shows a typical Shulevitz rabbinical figure setting out on a picnic in his ship on wheels. The droll fellow must get out and push the ship up a steep hill, but before he can get back in at the top of the hill, the ship starts down and makes a journey with the fellow struggling to latch onto his craft. His fantastic ship takes him to the perfect place for a picnic. So Shulevitz shows that the action of the imagination, when it is freed, will lead the person to what he is seeking in the first place, if the person allows himself to go with what happens to him.

In 1985 Uri Shulevitz completed an extensive book for adults, a ten-year project designed to teach his craft. *Writing with Pictures: How To Write and Illustrate Children's Books* is a step-by-step introduction to writing and illustrating children's books based on his experience with books and his teaching of workshops. In it he differentiates between picture books and storybooks with illustrations and leads the reader from early conception of the story line through the stages of telling and illustrating the story to a discussion of printing basics and techniques for color reproduction.

He believes that his concentration on teaching others how to create books for children helps his own books to be "quicker, more spontaneous, of better quality." His newest book, *The Strange and Exciting Adventures of Jeremiah Hush* (1986), features animals in human garb who live on another planet remarkably similar to our own. In black-and-white drawings, Shulevitz traces the adventures of his hero Jeremiah Hush, a monkey, and his sidekick Winchester Bone, a Skye terrier, in three stories for children of all ages.

At present Shulevitz continues to teach summer workshops at Pine Lake in upper New York State and to speak to conferences on children's literature. When he is not writing, he likes to paint watercolor landscapes or work on his barn. Twice a day he practices T'ai Chi Chuan, a form of calisthenics he calls "one of the products of the Chinese genius," that exercises all parts of the body in slow circular movements while the mind focuses on the center of gravity. During the year he continues to study art with Peter Hopkins in a private workshop with some of his colleagues.

In discussing the direction his work seems to be taking him, Shulevitz says that he likes for things to come from within, that he questions continually while working on a project (most children's books take a year to complete) to what extent he has gone deeply enough. He says, "I

Shulevitz's study for The Strange and Exciting Adventures of Jeremiah Hush *(courtesy of Uri Shulevitz)*

love doing picture books. I like writing brief things." In choosing what books to undertake, he says that he is not interested in doing something just because it seems to be in vogue with children or editors; rather, he says, "I basically do what I believe in, what I like, what I truly respond to. And I think that the only allowance one has to make for children is to write as simple as possible. Otherwise, one can talk about any subject."

In his Caldecott Medal acceptance speech, Uri Shulevitz spoke of the importance of removing false, binding distinctions. In his own work Shulevitz helps to remove such distinctions between illustration and art, between imagination and reality, between adults and children, between East and West by his attitude of choosing to work

only on books he responds to, by his ability to integrate words and pictures, and by his adoption of the Chinese emphasis on space and simplicity. His books say much with few words.

References:

Marjorie Zaum K, "Uri Shulevitz," in *Newbery and Caldecott Medal Books, 1966-1975,* edited by Lee Kingman (Boston: Horn Book, 1975);

Selma G. Lanes, *Down the Rabbit Hole: Adventures and Misadventures in the Realm of Children's Literature* (New York: Atheneum, 1971);

Zena Sutherland and May Hill Arbuthnot, *Children and Books,* fifth edition (Glenview, Ill.: Scott, Foresman, 1977).

Peter Spier

(6 June 1927-   )

M. Sarah Smedman
University of North Carolina at Charlotte

BOOKS: *Of Dikes and Windmills* (Garden City: Doubleday, 1969);

Gobble, Growl, Grunt (Garden City: Doubleday, 1971; Tadsworth, U.K.: World's Work, 1972);

Crash! Bang! Boom! (Garden City: Doubleday, 1972; Tadsworth, U.K.: World's Work, 1973);

Fast-Slow, High-Low: A Book of Opposites (Garden City: Doubleday, 1972);

Tin Lizzie (Garden City: Doubleday, 1975; Tadsworth, U.K.: World's Work, 1976);

Oh, Were They Ever Happy! (Garden City: Doubleday, 1978);

Bored—Nothing to Do! (Garden City: Doubleday, 1979; Tadsworth, U.K.: World's Work, 1979);

The Legend of New Amsterdam (Garden City: Doubleday, 1979);

People (Garden City: Doubleday, 1980);

Bill's Service Station (Garden City: Doubleday, 1981);

Fire House, Hook and Ladder Company Number Twenty-Four (Garden City: Doubleday, 1981);

The Food Market (Garden City: Doubleday, 1981);

My School (Garden City: Doubleday, 1981);

The Pet Store (Garden City: Doubleday, 1981);

The Toy Shop (Garden City: Doubleday, 1981);

Rain (Garden City: Doubleday, 1982);

Peter Spier's Christmas! (Garden City: Doubleday, 1983);

Peter Spier's Little Bible Storybooks: The Creation; Noah; Jonah, retold by Peter Seymour (Garden City: Doubleday, 1983);

Peter Spier's Little Cats (Garden City: Doubleday, 1984);

Peter Spier's Little Dogs (Garden City: Doubleday, 1984);

Peter Spier's Little Ducks (Garden City: Doubleday, 1984);

Peter Spier's Little Rabbits (Garden City: Doubleday, 1984);

The Book of Jonah (Garden City: Doubleday, 1985);

Dreams (Garden City: Doubleday, 1986);

We the People (Garden City: Doubleday, 1987).

SELECTED BOOKS ILLUSTRATED: Elizabeth

Nicholds, *Thunder Hill* (Garden City: Doubleday, 1953);

Frieda Kenyon Franklin, *Last Hurdle* (New York: Crowell, 1953);

Margaret G. Otto, *Cocoa* (New York: Holt, 1953);

Joy (Conrad) Anderson, *Hippolyte, Crab King* (New York: Harcourt, Brace, 1956);

Margaret Carson Hubbard, *Boss Chombale* (New York: Crowell, 1957);

Phyllis Krasilovsky, *The Cow Who Fell in the Canal* (Garden City: Doubleday, 1957; Tadsworth, U.K.: World's Work, 1958);

Mary Mapes Dodge, *Hans Brinker; or, The Silver Skates* (New York: Scribners, 1958);

Kenneth M. Dodson, *Hector, the Stowaway Dog* (Boston: Little, Brown, 1958);

Jessica Reynolds, *Jessica's Journal* (New York: Holt, 1958);

Frances Carpenter, *Wonder Tales of Seas and Ships* (Garden City: Doubleday, 1959);

Elisabeth Fairholme and Pamela Powell, *Esmeralda Ahoy!* (Garden City: Doubleday, 1959);

Richard Watkins, *The Mystery of Willet* (New York: T. Nelson, 1959);

Ardo Flakkeberg, *The Sea Broke Through*, translated by K. E. Bendien (New York: Knopf, 1960);

Elinor Milnor Parker, ed., *100 More Story Poems* (New York: Crowell, 1960);

Lavinia Riker Davis, *Island City: Adventures in Old New York* (Garden City: Doubleday, 1961);

Dola DeJong, *The Level Land* (New York: Scribners, 1961);

George Hook Grant, *Boy Overboard!* (Boston: Little, Brown, 1961);

The Fox Went Out on a Chilly Night (Garden City: Doubleday, 1961; Tadsworth, U.K.: World's Work, 1962);

Parker, ed., *Here and There; 100 Poems about Places* (New York: Crowell, 1967);

London Bridge Is Falling Down! (Garden City: Doubleday, 1967; Tadsworth, U.K.: World's Work, 1968);

To Market! To Market! (Garden City: Doubleday, 1967; Tadsworth, U.K.: World's Work, 1968);

Hurrah, We're Outward Bound! (Garden City: Doubleday, 1968; Tadsworth, U.K.: World's Work, 1969);

The Erie Canal (Garden City: Doubleday, 1970);

The Star-Spangled Banner (Garden City: Doubleday, 1975; Tadsworth, U.K.: World's Work, 1976).

OTHER: *And So My Garden Grows*, edited and illustrated by Spier (Garden City: Doubleday, 1969; Tadsworth, U.K.: World's Work, 1969);

Jacobus Revius, *Noah's Ark*, translated and illustrated by Spier (Garden City: Doubleday, 1977); republished as *The Great Flood* (Tadsworth, U.K.: World's Work, 1978).

PERIODICAL PUBLICATION: "The Frog Belongs in the Food Market and Other Perils of an Illustrator," *Publishers Weekly*, 218 (25 July 1980): 93-94.

A celebrated contemporary illustrator and storyteller, Peter Spier hopes that he will not of-
fend anyone by admitting that when he is working, he is initially trying to please only "one person in the world, namely [himself]. The worry about what others will think comes soon enough after the work is done!" Spier's solid research, fecund imagination, piquant humor, and painstakingly accurate drawings have resulted to date in numerous picture books, three sets of toy books, and an illustrated "biography of a country" for older readers, in addition to well over a hundred books he has illustrated for other authors.

Spier's books have not failed to please adults as well as children, which ought to obviate his worry. All twenty picture books are still in print, many of them having garnered prestigious awards. In 1962 *The Fox Went Out on a Chilly Night* (1961) was a Caldecott Honor Book. In 1967 *London Bridge Is Falling Down!* won the *Boston Globe-Horn Book* prize and *To Market! To Market!* was its runner-up. In 1971 *Gobble, Growl, Grunt* received an honorable mention in the first annual Children's Science Book Award program of the New York Academy of Sciences. Three of Spier's books have received the Christopher Award, given to books embodying the highest level of human and spiritual values and enjoying wide popularity: *The Erie Canal* in 1970, *Noah's Ark* in 1977, and *People* in 1980. *People* was also nominated for an American Book Award and received the National Mass Media Award from the National Council of Christians and Jews for "outstanding contributions to better human relations and the cause of brotherhood." In 1977 *Noah's Ark* also won the Lewis Carroll Shelf Award and was cited among the *New York Times* Best Illustrated Children's Books of the Year and by the International Board on Books for Young People as the best illustrated American book for the preceding two years. In 1978 *Noah's Ark* won the coveted Caldecott Medal. Several of Spier's books have been ALA Notable Books and Junior Literary Guild selections, among them *The Fox Went Out on a Chilly Night; London Bridge Is Falling Down!; The Erie Canal; Crash! Bang! Boom!; Fast-Slow, High-Low; Gobble, Growl, Grunt; The Star-Spangled Banner;* and *Rain.*

Spier's meticulously designed picture books are characterized by energetic, almost frenetic vitality, a spontaneous freedom of movement, and a prolificacy of tiny, authentic details. The artist recalls once standing before a Brueghel painting with a poet friend who remarked: "I love a painting I can walk around in and every time I go back to it, my eyes can follow a different route to where I want to go." Spier's own work has that Brueghel-like quality, yielding fresh discoveries to each repeated reading. Spier prefers to think of himself as a skilled craftsman rather than an artist. His work is never slipshod; he works seriously and hard. In retrospect, he says, he usually sees something he might do differently were he doing the book at the present time; however, he is confident in the knowledge that at the time he did a book, he was "totally unable" to do it better.

A craftsman Spier certainly is, and to the highest degree, but if it is the artist who explores, penetrates, and interprets the human condition, then Spier is just as surely an artist. Katherine Paterson, speaking of *Noah's Ark* (1977) in her 1978 Newbery Award acceptance speech, credits the book with a quality typical of Spier's work, that of giving form to a difficult vision, "not the destruction of the world. We've had too much practice imagining that. The difficult vision which Mr. Spier has given form to is that in the midst of destruction, as well as beyond it, there is life and humor and caring along with a lot of manure shoveling." The joie de vivre of which Paterson speaks makes Spier's books fun for readers of all ages. Perhaps as much as any artist of any age, Spier has found that magic formula which produces a book *dulce et utile.*

Although Spier did not decide to make art his career until he was almost twenty, he says he "cannot remember a time when [he] did not dabble with clay, draw, or watch someone draw," for his artist father worked at home. Spier was born in Amsterdam, the Netherlands, on 6 June 1927, the first of three children of the well-known illustrator and journalist Joseph E. A. (Jo) Spier and Albertine van Raalte Spier. The family spent their winters in the city and their holidays and summers in Broek in Waterland, a small village north of Amsterdam, known in the United States as the home of Hans Brinker. After the outbreak of World War II, the family moved permanently to the country village, which Spier has described as having 1,600 farmers and 20,000 cows between which it was sometimes difficult to differentiate. From Broek the children commuted by tram to school in Amsterdam, a trip Spier describes as "varied and wonderful" in sights, sounds, and smells, which provided the children "a multitude of plausible and implausible excuses for being late," which aroused the intense envy of their schoolmates.

When Spier finished high school, he attended the Rijksacademie voor Beeldende Kunsten in Amsterdam, making study trips to Italy and France, until, in 1947, he was drafted into the Royal Netherlands Navy, becoming a lieutenant and serving at home in the Admiralty and on an aircraft carrier and cruiser for some years in the West Indies and South America. With his military service behind him, Spier went to work for *Elseviers Weekblad,* the largest Dutch weekly newspaper, and for the first year was stationed in Paris, where besides doing weekly stories and illustrations for the paper, he continued his study of art.

In 1951 Spier and his father visited the United States, driving about the country and so well liking what they saw that they decided to settle in America permanently. In 1952 Mrs. Spier and the two younger children joined them in Houston, Texas, where Elsevier Publishing Company had a branch office. After a year with Elsevier in Houston, Spier left the company to work independently. Moving to New York, he approached Doubleday, not with a portfolio, but with a couple of drawings. Doubleday had a manuscript for a book about a goat farm. When asked whether he could draw goats, Spier says, he produced one of his drawings, coincidentally that of a goat, and replied that there was nothing he would rather draw.

Thunder Hill (1953) by Elizabeth Nicholds, was the first of a long line of Spier's illustrated books for adults and children. After three or four years of illustrating for other authors, while he was also drawing for *Collier's, Saturday Evening Post,* and *Look,* Spier decided he would be happier on his own. Concluding that becoming the "master of his own destiny" would give him the economic and artistic freedom he cherishes, he decided to produce his own books, the first of which was *The Fox Went Out on a Chilly Night* (1961).

In 1958 Spier married Kathryn M. Pallister. They have two children, now grown, Thomas Pallister and Kathryn Elizabeth. The Spiers live in Shoreham, Long Island, and spend much of each summer sailing on Long Island Sound. Spier's studio is in the basement of his home. Other major interests—sailing and the building of models of old ships—find continual expression in the subjects of his books.

Spier's artistry is impeccable, issuing from a delightful and fertile imagination. His characteristic medium is line and wash watercolors. He begins by first creating accurate pencil drawings.

Cover for Spier's 1977 translation of Jacobus Revius's tale, which won the Caldecott Medal in 1978 (Doubleday)

Because many of his books have historical or defined local settings, he roams whatever locale is to become the background–London, Italian villas and gardens, New England, upper New York State, or central Wisconsin–making hundreds of sketches.

The greatest compliment he can receive, Spier remarks, comes from the person who will say, "I am from New England, and I know just where you stood when you made such and such a drawing for *The Fox Went Out on a Chilly Night*." Of course, continues Spier, that is never true because the finished drawings are always composites, but the remark indicates that he has caught the essence peculiar to a specific region–its landscapes, its roofs, the hinges of its barns. After the pencil sketches Spier does the pen-and-ink drawings and, finally, the watercolors. He has said that he works "to retain the effect of a colored pen drawing," using "only blue, red, and yellow watercolors on non-photo blues of the black key" so that "there is no black halftone in the books at all, which . . . helps the impression of crispness." His lines are spare and incredibly skilled, just enough to typify the object, to give it precision and reality. More than representational, his paintings are also expressionistic, conveying subjective emotion and the inner quality of the object as well as its outward form. The farm horses in *Tin Lizzie* (1975), for example, are workers, dependable drudges, not high-spirited, free creatures. Details are not only accurate but infinite, intricate, clever, and humorous.

Most of Spier's books have a characteristic shape and size–approximately 10 ½ by 8 inches. The artist has filled that space in a variety of ways, often incorporating the text as a visual element in the composition. The endpapers in a Spier book are always an integral part of the whole, not only of the book's aesthetic but also of its content, its theme.

Spier's books appear to fall conveniently into categories coinciding, for the most part, chronologically, for that reason offering the temptation to classify individual works as belonging, for example, to his nursery-rhyme period or his concept-book period. However, certain motifs like ships and rural landscapes, moods like a robust nostalgia for Americana, and themes like the creative enterprise and vigor of people young and old intricately interlace all his works. So, if lured by the temptation, one is faced with deciding whether *London Bridge Is Falling Down!* (1967) should be classified as a Mother Goose story (as is indicated on its title page), a folk song, history, or even a book about ships and the sea. Several of Spier's books evade categorization except on the most superficial level. Nevertheless, while carefully evading the concomitant snares, grouping specific titles does provide a serviceable method for discussing Spier's work.

Set in the farm country of the Netherlands, *The Cow Who Fell in the Canal* (1957), text by Phyllis Krasilovsky, is one of many books illustrated by Spier which depicts his penetrating knowledge and love of his native land. Alternating pen-and-ink drawings and double-page watercolors alive with humor and bustle, the book is reminiscent of the works of Randolph Caldecott. Brilliant and clear in predominately primary colors, pastoral in mode, the charm of the illustrations supports a rather tepid story, funny but with improbabilities inconsistent with first-rate fantasy.

Other books about the Netherlands illustrated by Spier include Mary Mapes Dodge's *Hans Brinker* (1958), a classic in the United States but unknown in the country of its setting, and Dola DeJong's *The Level Land* (first published in 1943 and reissued in 1961 with Spier's illustrations), a captivating, compassionate, and honest story about a lively family in Holland during World War II. Characteristic of Spier, the illustrations are pen-and-ink drawings of small figures, lines and solid shapes, usually placed at the heads of chapters. In 1969 Spier wrote and illustrated his own biography of Holland for older readers, *Of Dikes and Windmills*. To this book about the topography, geography, archaeology, architecture, and inhabitants of his native land, Spier brings the talents of the draftsman and the cartographer. Typically Spierian, the book, according to Patricia Cianciolo, is "textually interesting and scholarly and a graphic arts feat."

Spier's interest in Holland combines with his interest in his adoptive country in one of his more recent picture books, *The Legend of New Amsterdam* (1979). A somewhat disjointed text, divided in its emphasis, takes readers on a tour of New Amsterdam in 1660, to several of its 300 buildings, commercial and domestic, and introduces them to some of its 1,500 inhabitants, namely selected craftsmen and the parents and the preacher who scold the mischievous children who taunt Crazy Annie, who sees in the clouds visions of "people and stone, people and stone." The travelogue and the legend of Crazy Annie come together in the final illustration of the skyline of modern New York. A detailed map of the 1660 "City of New Amsterdam on the Island of Manhattan," with a key listing what each building was and the names of the people who lived or worked there, provides intriguing facts on decorative endpapers.

The narrator relates that the children thought teasing Annie "sidesplitting, a hilarious treat! . . . the funniest, most entertaining show in the world," but the book itself tends toward the pedantic. Although the illustrations contain marvelous touches, like a ship's model hanging from the ceiling of the church, and provide invaluable insight into the daily lives of the Dutch settlers, the text is forced; it is wanting in the subtleties, the spontaneity, and the fusion of details that have become hallmarks of Spier's work. Spier has also illustrated books about historic New York for other writers, among them Lavinia Riker Davis's *Island City: Adventures in Old New York* (1961).

Spier's love for American history and lore extends beyond that influenced by the Dutch colonists, one manifestation of which is his illustrations of songs closely connected with the American spirit. The first of these, *The Fox Went Out on a Chilly Night*, is a New England pastoral. A runner-up for the 1962 Caldecott Medal, the book was inspired by a trip through the New England countryside one summer when Spier accompanied his wife to her college reunion in Northampton, Massachusetts. Exhilarated by the atmosphere and the landscape, singing the folk song "The Fox Went Out on a Chilly Night" as they drove along, Spier was struck by the idea that the setting and the song would make a beautiful book. In this most lyrical of his works, Spier uses deeper, more intense colors, the burnished shades of fall, to recreate the New England countryside, an important character in the drama. Because of its size and remoteness, Mr. Fox can raid the farmer's barn with impunity. The night sky is never dark, but an almost phosphorescent blue, brightly lit by harvest moonshine. This book, too, alternates black and white with colored pages. The black-and-white illustrations are busy, with delicate, fluid, but forceful lines. The colored illustrations have fewer small details, which makes this book as a whole seem more spacious, less frenetic.

The first of Spier's four books in the Mother Goose Library published between 1967 and 1969, *London Bridge Is Falling Down!* illustrates eighteen verses of the folk song. This book, too, stretches the imagination and provides historical and geographical background, which

Cover for the first book Spier wrote for the Mother Goose Library series (Doubleday)

combine to give the rich flavor of eighteenth-century London life. Because the collapse of such a hive of activity will be disastrous, bewigged architects and city fathers carefully study plans for rebuilding, while "my fair Lady-O" in ruffles and hoops decorates the window.

After pages of chaotic collapse–"Wood and clay will wash away," "Iron and steel will bend and bow"–a still, blue, monochromatic double-page illustration in the middle of the book gives welcome respite to the senses before the reader re-enters the hustle of the city to visit such land-marks as the Tower of London. Each minute detail down to the shopkeepers' shingles over the stores on the bridge are authentic–all but one: M. Pallister, Maker of Scientific Instruments, is Peter Spier's father-in-law. At the close of the book, Spier provides both the music for the rhyme and a complete history of the bridge.

Like all of Spier's works, the sketches for his Mother Goose Library books were drawn on loca-tion. Because he "cannot make things come alive from photographs, travel posters, or from look-ing at *National Geographic*," because he must "be-come a part of the location [he is] to draw," Spier went with sketchbook in hand to Delaware, Mary-land, and Pennsylvania for *To Market! To Market!* (1967) "to collect the hundreds of details that go

into the book's making" and to give today's child a picture of the early-nineteenth-century town of New Castle, Delaware, and the surrounding coun-tryside. Individual pictures illustrate carefully se-lected nursery rhymes, some familiar, others not, which take the farmer through his day. Funny de-tails combine with historical ones, such as the still-existing Packet Alley, down which a farmer rides. The predominant colors for this book are, appro-priately, earth tones.

The pictures of *Hurrah, We're Outward Bound!* (1968) accompanied once more by appro-priate, though not for the most part well-known, verses, tell the story of the maiden voyage of the three-masted *Le Jeune Française*, built about 1830 in Honfleur, France, later the seat of the Impres-sionists. The almost eight-week-long voyage to New York and then back by way of Dartmouth, En-gland, is portrayed with imaginative zest as well as historical accuracy in pictures first sketched in Normandy and Devon and from historical docu-ments of old New York. *Le Jeune Française* ap-pears in every picture, at times in the fullness of its majestic splendor, in close-up of a detail of the rigging or the deck, or a mere match-stick sketch in the distance. The greens, creams, and grays in the rolling of the sea enhance this ac-count of the life of a representative nineteenth-century sailor and sailing vessel and suggest impressionism.

Italy provides the setting for the beautiful *And So My Garden Grows* (1969). The illustration preceding the title page pictures two children in a dilapidated courtyard in a Florentine suburb which is saved from utter dreariness by the green and growing plants. The postures and facial expressions of the children, caught with a few simple, skillful lines, portray their dejection. They will escape through their imaginations, indicated by the verse:

> O that I were where I would be,
> Then I would be where I am not;
> But where I am, there I must be,
> And where I would be I can not.

The imaginative journey begins as the children walk down a tunnel of trees at a villa in Fiesole, a resort town northeast of Florence. The tiny silhouetted figures, holding hands for reassurance, seem aware of the dangers and loneliness of the imagination; however, light at the end of the tunnel beckons, promising beauty and the pleasures of the imagination. One source of beauty is Spier's use of balance, discipline, and restraint, as in the picture of a water garden of a villa in Settignano, illustrating the verse, "A hedge between keeps friendships green." The period costumes, the gardeners at work in the background, the swan with her cygnet, the fountain, and the resplendent greens all provide impeccable details. Discipline and form are only one source of beauty. Contrasts between the wild and tamed, the rustic and the regal, the country and the town pervade the book. The dominant colors of the book are, as expected, greens and blues.

In the early 1970s Spier turned again to Americana, illustrating two more songs, source material he once described as "almost foolproof in popularity": *The Erie Canal* (1970) and *The Star-Spangled Banner* (1975). Spier did not consider illustrating songs an original idea, but he did believe that, with so few then around, a need for this kind of book existed. The setting for *The Erie Canal* is the 363-mile route from Albany to Buffalo in the early 1850s; the text, the words of Thomas S. Allen's "Low Bridge! Everyone Down," or "Fifteen Years on the Erie Canal."

Spier aspired to do for the Erie Canal what no previous book had done, to reproduce and so preserve the canal itself, its locks, their doors, the boats—unlike any others—and the architecture along its banks. Here, too, according to Ethel

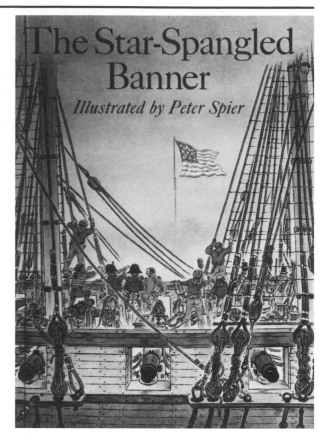

Cover for Spier's 1975 book, which illustrates the events surrounding the writing of the United States national anthem (Doubleday)

Heins in her October 1970 *Horn Book* review, Spier "records detail with the meticulous accuracy of the historian and the appreciative eye of the artist." Stills of the same bend in the waterway, in fall and winter near the beginning of the book, in spring and summer near the close, contrast seasonal activities and round out the story of life on the canal. At the end Spier provides a factual description and history of construction and operation of the Erie Canal.

The early 1970s, when preparations for the United States bicentennial celebrations were under way, afforded the timely occasion for the book on the "Star-Spangled Banner" Spier had been wanting for a long time to do. Research, he said, was a simple matter; everything he needed was beautifully preserved and easily accessible–at the Fort McHenry National Monument and Historic Shrine; at the Baltimore museum which had once been the home of Mary Young Bickersgill, the woman who had sewn the original star-spangled banner; and in local historical societies. An oversized book, *The Star-Spangled Banner* spellbinds readers in a world of blazing red glares, white rocket arcs, and dark blue nights. The book has its still interludes. Contrasting with the conflagrations of war is a peaceful pastoral scene, the flag reflecting in water ruffled only by paddling ducks, the armed soldiers mere blue and black specks on a faraway shore.

A history of the naval battle which inspired the national anthem, *The Star-Spangled Banner* is also a book about the peace and liberty, courage and determination the artist sees as inspiriting America. Spier's conception of his country as a land of free, hardworking, God-fearing people is depicted in aggregates of industrial and agricultural scenes to illustrate "Heav'n rescued land"; of small town Main Streets, elementary schools, loading docks, and legislatures in session, of historic landmarks like Bunker Hill monument, the earthworks on Marblehead, and Faneuil Hall to illustrate "The land of the free."

A factual account of the War of 1812, highlighting Francis Scott Key's part in it, a holograph of the poem in Key's hand, the music with all the verses of the song, and the receipt indicating Bickersgill was paid $405.90 "for one American ensign 40 x 32 feet of finest quality bunting" are reproduced at the end of the text. The endpapers, a series of drawings depicting with photographic accuracy the development over the years of the United States flag, conclude the product of ten months of work for Spier and a timeless piece of Americana for collectors.

In 1971 Spier took a new track and within two years produced three complex concept books for preschoolers, two of them dealing with sounds, one with opposites. The idea, he said, germinated from the publisher's suggestion that their list would be enriched by books for small children. The most striking qualities of *Gobble, Growl, Grunt* (1971) and *Crash! Bang! Boom!* (1972) are the fertility of the artist's imagination and his delight in proliferating sounds.

These books indicate that Spier's aural perception is as keen as his visual, which perceptions are given form in consummately skillful drawings, simultaneously accurate, detailed, and highly suggestive. *Gobble, Growl, Grunt* focuses on the noises made by insects, animals, and birds. While many pages detail disparate sounds and objects, some compositions are unified through a central object, such as a tree which provides the apes portrayed a common home. Less familiar animals are labeled. The cleverness of the sounds contributes a great deal to the book's humor, as does the sheer fun the animals are having.

Crash! Bang! Boom! takes sound into the human and domestic realms, where Spier gives his imagination even wider range. Although formulating the sounds for this book was just as much a problem as it was for *Gobble, Growl, Grunt*, in the March 1972 *Bulletin of the Junior Literary Guild* Spier pointed out that "it was far simpler to turn on the vacuum cleaner or the blender and then listen, than to sit for hours in front of a cage in the Bronx Zoo waiting for the dromedaries to start SPITTING and clearing their throats. . . ."

While *Gobble, Growl, Grunt* provides many extraordinary experiences, *Crash! Bang! Boom!* tickles because the keen ear which has discerned the exotic in the ordinary makes even very young readers aware that those sounds are within their own realms of experience, and they, too, have heard them. Most pages are composed of numerous discrete drawings, unified only by a common theme. Some noises, however, work together to provide an integral sound, and the drawings indicate that integration. In one of opera stars competing to rise each above the other, the sounds create dissonance; in that of the orchestra, sounds converge into a harmonious whole.

The pages of *Fast-Slow, High-Low: A Book of Opposites* (1972) are also composed of multiple frames, each making its point. Adroit selection of novel objects—for example, an elephant's trunk and a pig's nose to convey the meaning of *long* and *short*—evoke chortles indicative of pleased surprise at their aptness. Subtle pictures, for a small child with little experience, of a subway running below the surface of the water and a car on the bridge above or angels and devils to indicate *over-under* might require explanation but will add pleasurably to the knowledge of children even if the wit escapes them.

Tin Lizzie (1975) incorporates Spier's addiction to particularized settings and to American popular culture but is difficult to couple with any of his other books. Again, carefully researched and enriched by geographical and historical depths that add, seemingly effortlessly, to its spontaneity, *Tin Lizzie* is the biography of a Model T, spanning a half century from the time she first rolls off the Ford assembly line in 1909, through her active life, her retirement, and her resurrection as an antique.

A point subtly made is that when Lizzie was built, planned obsolescence was not a way of life. The difference in ethos wrought by fifty years of change is wordlessly and immediately conveyed

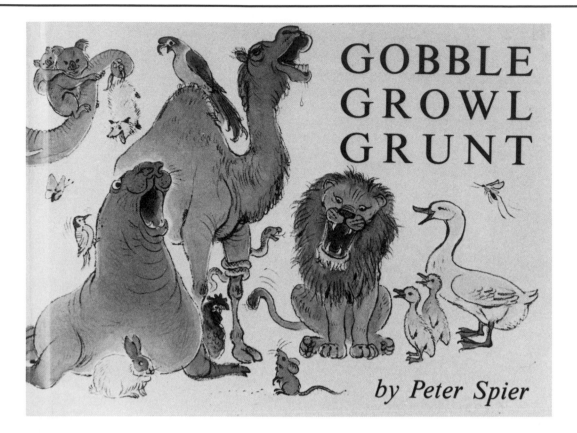

Covers for Spier's concept books which explore the nature of sound (Doubleday)

through comparison of the shocked wonder of the observers of Lizzie when she debuts in the Midwest and the nonchalance with which "that great old car" saunters down a contemporary highway, unabashed by the power and pace of compacts, semis, and tankers. The ambience of small-town nightlife radiates from the curious throng admiring Lizzie in a Wisconsin showroom window.

Characteristically varied in page design, several wordless sequences are crammed with details about conditions associated with operating the car in its earliest days, conditions that, viewed from the perspective of distance, become funny. Animation becomes pandemonium but fun as farm animals scatter in consternation at the horseless carriage. Even the water in puddles cannot get out of the way fast enough. Horses and car drink from the same fountain; horses jump bridges that car cannot. The pictures have softer, more subdued color emphases and become more tranquil as they depict Lizzie's integration into family life.

One of Spier's most charming talents is his ability to endow inanimate objects with personality and to express their interior states. Spinning along a country road in her heyday, Lizzie is content, almost smug. Working hard for her third owner, she is as steady and capable as an old dray horse. Put out to pasture, she is not only dilapidated but depressed. Her "face" is sad. She is drained of color. Refurbished, she glows with happiness. The car's mood is conveyed partly by the details which create her environment but also by her relative size, by her very posture, by the look in her headlight-eyes, and by her color. Restored, the spokes of her wheels are redder than they have ever been; her color is vivid, almost luminous. The endpapers of *Tin Lizzie*, labeled, analytical diagrams of the car's anatomy, once more reveal Spier's love for the factual. Long and close scrutiny of the prolific details rewards readers with both knowledge and pleasure.

Judging from critical acclaim, *Noah's Ark* (1977) may be a stronger contender than *Tin Lizzie* or *People* (1980) as Spier's best work. It was a story, he said in his Caldecott acceptance speech, that he had for years wanted to do. The seventeenth-century Dutch poem by Jacobus Revius was the final catalyst. Moved by its "faith" and "childlike simplicity," Spier translated it into English. He acknowledges that the idea for an Ark book was not new, yet when he studied the twenty-odd others in print, he knew there was room for one more, for one which was not a "joy-

ous sun-filled Caribbean Cruise," but which indicated "God's wrath." Spier confesses to struggling to find a balance between the romantic and the realistic during the making of the book. An honest account of Noah's story ought, thought Spier, "to depict the stench and the mess inside." Animals will be animals, and manure must be shoveled. The sheer number of details gives a sense of the congestion that occurs when so many are packed together into so small a space, not unlike living conditions of city tenement dwellers.

Katherine Paterson spoke for many of Spier's readers when she said, "those final few words, 'and he planted a vineyard,' ring with . . . joy." The ambience of the book's endpapers transmits that joy. The new covenant is indicated by the pink in the rainbow, the only place in the book that shade is used. Perhaps the most treasured award Spier received for *Noah's Ark* was his father's collection of Randolph Caldecott's works, most of them first editions, one whose every page he had as a three-year-old prodigy, "with a red crayon expertly ruined." When Jo Spier heard that his son's book had won the prestigious medal, he gave him the collection.

Eight years after *Noah's Ark*, Spier retold and illustrated another well-known Bible story, *The Book of Jonah* (1985). Translated from an archaic Dutch version, Spier's text is complete, abbreviating only Jonah's poetic prayer inside the belly of the whale. Spier's clean, clear, rhythmic prose captures both the solemnity and humor of the story and reads with a King-Jamesian sonority. Perhaps because of the amount of text, carefully integrated into page designs, *The Book of Jonah* has fewer pages crammed with small pictures; characteristically, however, most pictures are bustlingly busy in diverse ways, a notable exception being that of Jonah crossing the desert to Nineveh. Though the undulations of the sand dunes echo those of the waves, the turbulence has quieted once Jonah has acquiesced to God's command.

As perspicuously as any of Spier's books, *The Book of Jonah* makes visible the artist's knowledge of and respect for ships and the sea and its moods. The harbor at Joppa is crowded with vessels, large and small; others ride the distant horizon. Details of the ship on which Jonah books passage to Tarshish—masts, sails, rigging, deck, hold, oars—are carefully crafted. It is the sea, however, which is the tour de force, a main character as well as the major backdrop. More than in his words, the majesty, might, and magnificence of

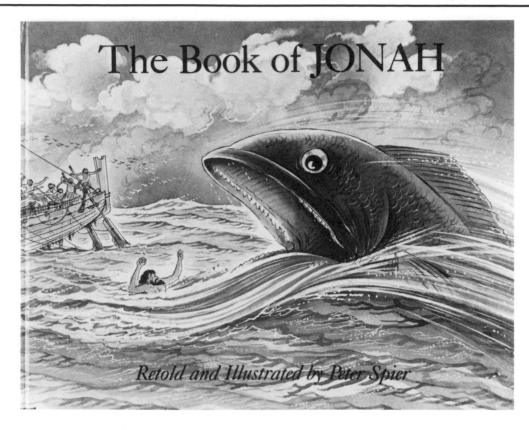

Cover for Spier's 1985 retelling of a well-known Bible story (Doubleday)

God speak eloquently from the tumultuous blend of greens, yellows, grays, blues, and violets that constitute the furious waves scourging the Tarshish-bound ship, threatening to devour it even as the whale does Jonah. The movement and color tones of the sea set the pace and moods of the story: wild and raging while the prophet is aboard ship; subsiding but still Stygian once he has been cast overboard; rich and reflective when he is in the cavernous belly of the whale.

The endpapers of *The Book of Jonah* are decorated with borders of a simple, repeated geometric design in three colors, suggestive at once of the building, the walls, even the gates of an ancient city. At the back of the book, these borders encase fascinating facts about the historical Jonah, a ship of Tarshish, the Assyrians, and the Babylonians; about Nineveh, its culture, its destruction, and its comparatively recent archaeological rediscovery; about the Bible story and its meaning. The information is accompanied by maps, diagrams, and watercolor sketches, as engrossing to older readers as the text itself. Perhaps because Jonah's story is more enigmatic than Noah's, Spier's *The Book of Jonah* is less whim-

sical and winsome than his book of Noah.

Much less weighty than the two Bible stories, *Oh, Were They Ever Happy!* (1978) and *Bored—Nothing To Do!* (1979) are the first of Spier's books about children and childhood. *Oh, Were They Ever Happy!* is a puckish, Bunyanesque tale of three children, who, to please their absent parents, tackle a long-talked-of task, painting the house. Using remnants left in a myriad of cans in the basement, they leave not so much as a windowpane uncolored. The children's gleeful satisfaction and a mounting anticipation of the end result erupt in a riot of color when the house finally emerges complete in its glorious coat of many colors. The book was inspired by a facetious reply of the artist to what may have been a desperate question from his wife: "What on earth are you going to do with all the half-full paint cans in the basement?" His answer: "They always come in handy! Someday I'll paint the house."

Bored—Nothing To Do! recounts the ingenious skill of two boys sent off with a scolding to find something to do. Utilizing anything at hand they need—wheels from the baby's carriage, sheets from the beds, slats from the fence, the TV aerial from the roof, the engine from the

Volkswagen—they build a wonderful plane that carries them serenely into the clouds, then lands them smoothly. Intoxicated by their success, they are met by worried parents with a good spanking (and a kiss) and sent to their room, where once again they sit bored, with nothing to do.

Both books reveal Spier's understanding of the child's capacity for Herculean effort, absorption in the immediate, and heedlessness of consequences. He admires children's ingenuity, intelligence, and energy, envies the directness of their approach to problems, regrets that life is not so simple as they conceive it. Humor, irony, joy, and a touch of sadness envelop the stories of these youngsters, who, like Noah, are zesty survivors. The stories are told sensitively, with an economy of phrase, commenting implicitly, often ironically, on an avalanche of visual details bursting with color.

Rain (1982) and *Peter Spier's Christmas!* (1983), both oversized wordless books, are also books about childhood, but their sphere is more particularized and their perspective broader. Events during these two special times are revealed simultaneously from the points of view of the child and of the artist, the latter an experienced, extraordinary observer of the ordinary. *Rain,* centered on a sister and brother's pleasure in a rainy day, also reveals through hundreds of details Spier's sensitivity to nature and its summer moods—to flowers and trees, insects and birds, small wild and domestic animals, and their responses to wind and rain.

Playing in a backyard, whose sandbox, tree house, pool, swings, flowers, birds, animals, and even clothes hanging on the line suggest a child's paradise provided by beneficent parents, the girl and her brother run for their rain gear when the first drops fall. With their mother's blessing, they go off to explore, reveling in water everywhere. Puddling about in streets, under gutters, in ditches, and in the park, they use their big black umbrella alternately as shelter, shield, bucket, and boat. They gaze enthralled at glistening spiderwebs and dripping pine boughs; they admire the reflective power of water—and their own reflections. They commune with dandelions, ducks, swans, and other rain lovers. Throughout the book, a contrasting commentary on the delight of the children are the little creatures who seek shelter in any available nook or corner: the cat under a car; mice under overturned garbage cans; squirrels in a tree; cardinals under a bird bath; martins under the eaves; and robins under

bridges or rabbit cages. When the wind blows the children's umbrella inside out, they race exuberantly for home, figures of flashing color in one of three double-page spreads of the darkening, burnished-pewter world of their high jinks.

At home, after baths and mugs of cocoa, both steamy, the children contentedly read, play, and have dinner. By bedtime, the rain seems to have lasted forever as they wistfully watch umbrellaed neighbors walking pets under still-tossing trees. Tomorrow, however, dawns, a new day fresh and fragrant. Sunflowers raise their bowed heads, mice crawl out of the garbage can, squirrels leap from tree to tree, and birds burst with song. Yesterday's sheets and jeans have once again been hung out to dry. The children are as sparkling as the backyard to which they return. If anything can evoke in a jaded grown-up the same childlike wonder and zest for life, it has got to be Peter Spier's sun-drenched world washed bright by an all-day rain.

As Spier has recorded the archetypal reaction to rain through accumulation of details accrued from every possible angle, so in *Peter Spier's Christmas!* he records the ritualized celebration of that holiday in white, middle-class America. An added perspective in the book is that of adults, of parents who are more than suppliers of the needs of children. Companions and caretakers still, they also have independent lives. Celebration in the book comprises well-defined familiar rituals: gargantuan preparations—shopping and cooking, card writing and mailing, selecting and trimming of a tree, decorating indoors and out; proud admiration of the hard-wrought holiday metamorphoses; Christmas Eve worship; the stillness and anticipation of the holy night; and finally on Christmas morning the presents.

In typical Spierian wry humor, the omnipresent cat, whom Santa has not forgotten, offers gentle social commentary: she nestles in the tangled tissue of her gift box, preferring the wrappings to the content. Recounted from the adult perspective, Christmas for parents also means clearing the ruins of the monumental feast, then enjoying a peaceful midnight moment before the fire.

A cyclical event, Christmas, which was but twelve days away at the beginning of the book, is, according to the Christmas Club calendar in the bank, 353 days away at the end of the book. In the final pictures of the once-more daily world, the children are smiling as happily as in the first ones, perhaps in remembrance of the Christmas just past, perhaps in anticipation of Christmas-yet-

Preliminary sketch for To Market! To Market! *(courtesy of the artist)*

to-come, and perhaps because Peter Spier is aware of and loves every bit of the fuss and flurry, the folly and fun of the festivity.

The theme of *People* (1980), a picture book for the nuclear family and the family of nations, is the wondrous variety among the peoples of the earth–their physical appearances, their homes, their languages and customs, their talents and tastes. An oversized book in bright, intense colors, overtly didactic, the book is a pictorial encyclopedia of facts shot through with vital concepts.

Influenced by the eighteenth-century social commentator and humorist William Hogarth, Spier's realism is contemporary and symbolic. Anyone who has ever been caught on a subway by a power shortage will shiver at the aptness of the artist's metaphor for how "not mighty at all" most of us are. An incident at the Bologna Children's Book Fair in 1979, where Spier displayed the dummy, demonstrated how easy it is even for a scrupulous worker to go wrong. Arab visitors, studying the forty-five styles of writing from around the globe, pointed out to the author that the five types of Arabic script he had copied from an eminent European encyclopedia were all upside down. *People* has been criticized as stereotypical in its illustrations of nonwhite, non-

Western cultures; however, those details are overpowered by the impact of the book's total vision.

Spier has considered doing books for adults but believes that, after twenty-five years, he has become so specialized and "probably knowledgeable" in juvenile publishing that he may have pigeonholed himself. He loves the freedom of producing "the whole package." Because adults buy books for children, he is gratified that children, who have the final word, have judged his books worthy of long lives. Spier does, however, move out into new directions. In the last five years he has published three sets of toy books for the mass market. The first series, the Village Books, published for an international market, had to hurdle occasional tricky obstacles in production. A French publisher, objecting to a frog appearing in a pet store, insisted, *"Mais non,* Monsieur Spier. Impossible! The frog belongs in the food market." Finally, the frog does not appear at all.

The six-by-nine-inch stand-up board books, all published in 1981, are cut in the shape of small buildings and include *Bill's Service Station; Fire House, Hook and Ladder Company Number Twenty-Four; The Food Market; My School; The Pet Store;* and *The Toy Shop.* Primarily concept books

Preliminary sketch, made in Italy, for And So My Garden Grows *(courtesy of the artist)*

to introduce the preschool reader to the places themselves and to the services provided by the people who work there, the series is of uneven quality: individual books are disjointed and the texts–where they exist–are sometimes pedestrian. Despite their weaknesses, the books are brightly attractive and have the usual careful, precise drawings and Spier's typical charm and whimsical humor. Indeed, Spier's sense of play, with, of course, his art style, provides whatever unity a book or the series has.

Published in 1983, *Peter Spier's Little Bible Storybooks* include three tiny "zig-zag" books, packaged together in a miniature library: *The Creation, Noah,* and *Jonah.* Each opens out into a thirty-inch-long panel, laminated and accordian pleated into seventeen pages. One side of each reads like a conventional picture book. Although the stories are capably retold by Peter Seymour, the pictures are the outstanding feature, and the series rightly carries Spier's name.

Many of the illustrations of *Noah* and *Jonah* are familiar to readers of *Noah's Ark* and *The Book of Jonah,* but the pictures in the miniature books do not duplicate those in the larger books. The back side of the panel is a pictorial panorama, each appropriate to its particular book. The panel for *The Creation* is divided into eight double segments, one for "In the beginning" and one for each of the days of creation; for *Noah* it is one bustling, continuous scene, depicting not only the pairs selected for boarding the Ark but those myriad from every species who had to remain behind; the panel for *Jonah* tells the prophet's story in a series of eleven paintings, the smallest covering one page, the largest two-and-a-half, and others any combination in between. Each story culminates in a layered, three-dimensional tableau inside the back cover of the book box. Although as delicate and fragile as the tiny books themselves, the workmanship is superb: the color fresh and alive; the detail, as always, astounding. Appreciative–and fortunate– owners of *Peter Spier's Little Bible Storybooks* may

well treasure them into adulthood.

The most recent of the toy books, another set of board books, is the Little Animal series, published in 1984 for toddlers. Only 3 ½ by 4 ¾ inches, these books, designed only for home libraries, will fit snugly into wee hands. *Peter Spier's Little Cats, Peter Spier's Little Dogs, Peter Spier's Little Ducks,* and *Peter Spier's Little Rabbits* are picture stories accompanied by a minimal text about curious, rambunctious baby animals who eat, romp, get into mischief, and sleep. Wide-eyed and joyous, these young ones will not only enchant children but provide them with brilliant images and accurate information about their favorite pets in their various domestic and natural habitats. Creating for the mass market appeals to the pragmatist in Spier and to the artist, who aspires to invade that market with high quality books for the small child.

Peter Spier's work, praised for his inveterate care in production and profusion of inventive detail, regardless of which of a wide variety of subjects he turns his talent, is imbued with respect for human dignity, an understanding tolerance, and a vital joyousness. In his Caldecott acceptance speech he told the story of a worker overpowered by awe and his own inarticulateness at the funeral of the president of his company. The man tried bravely to deliver his scheduled eulogy. After a couple of false starts, he swallowed hard and bellowed, "Ladies and Gentlemen . . . Hip, Hip, Hooray!" Peter Spier's audience voices that same cheer.

References:
Janet D. Chenery, "Peter Spier," *Horn Book,* 54 (August 1978): 379-381;
Patricia Cianciolo, *Illustrations in Children's Books,* second edition (Dubuque, Iowa: W. C. Brown, 1976), p. 96;
Patricia Dooley, " '. . . and he planted a vineyard.' The Art of Peter Spier," *Children's Literature Association Quarterly,* 4 (Winter 1980): 1, 30-31, 34.

William Steig

(14 November 1907-   )

Joy Anderson
University of Florida

SELECTED BOOKS: *The Rejected Lovers* (New York: Dover, 1951);

Continuous Performance (New York: Duell, Sloan & Pearce, 1963);

CDB! (New York: Windmill Books, 1968);

Roland, The Minstrel Pig (New York: Windmill Books, 1968; London: Hamish Hamilton, 1974);

Sylvester and the Magic Pebble (New York: Windmill Books, 1969; London: Abelard Schuman, 1972);

The Bad Island (New York: Windmill Books, 1969); revised and republished as *Rotten Island* (Boston: Godine, 1984);

The Bad Speller (New York: Windmill Books, 1970);

The Lonely Ones (New York: Windmill Books, 1970);

An Eye for Elephants (New York: Windmill Books, 1970);

Male / Female (New York: Farrar, Straus & Giroux, 1971);

Amos and Boris (New York: Farrar, Straus & Giroux, 1971; London: Hamish Hamilton, 1972);

Dominic (New York: Farrar, Straus & Giroux, 1972; London: Hamish Hamilton, 1973);

The Real Thief (New York: Farrar, Straus & Giroux, 1973; London: Hamish Hamilton, 1974);

Farmer Palmer's Wagon Ride (New York: Farrar, Straus & Giroux, 1974; London: Hamish Hamilton, 1975);

Abel's Island (New York: Farrar, Straus & Giroux, 1976; London: Hamish Hamilton, 1977);

The Amazing Bone (New York: Farrar, Straus & Giroux, 1976);

Caleb and Kate (New York: Farrar, Straus & Giroux, 1977);

Tiffky Doofky (New York: Farrar, Straus & Giroux, 1978);

Drawings (New York: Farrar, Straus & Giroux, 1979);

Photo by Maggie Steig

Gorky Rises (New York: Farrar, Straus & Giroux, 1980);

Doctor De Soto (New York: Farrar, Straus & Giroux, 1982);

CDC? (New York: Farrar, Straus & Giroux, 1984);

Ruminations (New York: Farrar, Straus & Giroux, 1984);

Yellow and Pink (New York: Farrar, Straus & Giroux, 1984);

Solomon and the Rusty Nail (New York: Farrar, Straus & Giroux, 1985);

Brave Irene (New York: Farrar, Straus & Giroux, 1986).

BOOKS ILLUSTRATED: Wilhelm Reich, *Listen, Little Man!* (New York: Noonday Press, 1948);

Phyllis R. Fenner, ed., *Giggle Box: Funny Stories for Boys and Girls* (New York: Knopf, 1950).

The artistic reputation of William Steig would have been remarkable even if he had never turned to writing and illustrating children's books. Indeed, he had two separate and successful careers, one beginning in 1930 at age twenty-three when his cartoons began to appear in the *New Yorker,* the second with the publication of his first major children's book in 1968, *Roland, The Minstrel Pig.* He was sixty-one, certainly past the age where he knew what modern children supposedly looked for, nor did he possess a pipeline into the specific and always shifting cultural climate, yet he has steadily produced books for the children's market which have been enthusiastically received by readers and critics.

Perhaps a life devoted to art in many forms was a natural route for William Steig, since he was born into a family where everyone participated in some form of the arts. His parents, Joseph and Laura Steig, were both painters, and his three brothers all artists, musicians, writers, or poets. Steig had his first painting lessons from his eldest brother, Irwin. Other influences that touched the mind of the young artist were *Grimms' Fairy Tales, Hansel and Gretel, Pinocchio, Tales of King Arthur,* the Katzenjammer Kids, and Charlie Chaplin movies. His vivid memories of early school days at P.S. 53, in the Bronx, inspired his "Small-Fry" drawings, first appearing in the *New Yorker.* Steig attended the National Academy of Design and later began a serious career as a cartoonist. Now the tradition in this pursuit of the imagination is carried on by his three children, Lucy, Jeremy, and Margit.

William Steig says he was first inspired to write books for children by the insightful publisher Robert Kraus of Windmill Books, who felt Steig could make a contribution in a growing field. Steig's first six books for children were all published by Windmill.

A close study of Steig's work seems to reveal that he drew his keen direction from two sources: one, a sensitivity born of an innate understanding of the quality of childhood, never underestimating or condescending to it, and two, an inner, perhaps intuitive knowledge of what makes a good book. A question can be posed as to whether the child in him knew what he liked as a result of immersion in the classics or whether a classic sense of literature exists in the tal-

ented artist living perceptively. In any case, precise and highly literate language is the element that links these qualities. Combining his almost formal incisiveness with the humorous, wry, and visionary talent of a gifted illustrator, Steig became a most unique author-illustrator. At his best, words cannot be separated from drawings. They are of a piece and mutually enhancing.

Of the several themes that thread throughout Steig's work, the importance of friends and the love and loyalty of family are foremost. But there is also romanticism present in his works, reverting to the fairy-tale tradition and employing all its elements. Steig frequently confronts outright evil: villains, not mischievous pranksters, as well as death and terror. Magic and the use of dream, not as a device, but as a means of understanding human nature, are vehicles Steig uses freely, truly a marriage of the traditional and the modern.

Perhaps it is mysticism that appears most consistently and assuredly in Steig's work; the wonder about eternity, the questions of a questing mind. One hears throughout all his books the plaintive cry of a lonely soul; not a creature without friends or love, but the plea of the individual for answers to the imponderables of the universe and mortality.

And finally, expressed best through evocative and joyful illustrations that explode into life on the page, is Steig's reverence for nature in all its forms. In presenting the sun, moon, stars, profusions of flowers, winter snows, and rain Steig makes the reader *feel* closely what is ordinarily taken for granted.

In *Roland, The Minstrel Pig* Roland, a musically talented balladeer and trustworthy individual, agrees, on the advice of his loyal friends, to seek his fame in the world. "Once Roland began thinking along these lines, he could think of nothing else. He dreamed for days of fame and wealth, and he was no longer satisfied with the life he'd been living." The romantic wandering minstrel, wearing a velvet hat with a feather plume, traveling without meeting another living soul, becomes lonely and sings a sad song. Then innocent Roland meets evil personified in the form of Sebastian the fox, who, luring him with promises of an audience with the king, plots accidents that will provide *him* with a meal: "They started out with brisk steps—Roland dreaming and the fox scheming." The King, a lion, rescues Roland from death by cooking and gives him a position of honor in the court after Roland proves himself by his talent. Roland indeed becomes the poet laureate, and the fox is given his due in the dungeon.

This tale is subconsciously satisfying because it is true to fairy-tale tradition in its archetypal form. And it is pleasing because the language is lively, the tone never condescending. The repeated use of internal rhyming provides a deep reverberation of delight. Illustrations are richly colorful and wryly humorous: the reader does not soon forget Steig's portrayal of a picnic tea party with a donkey, a goose, and a pig considering the future. Picnics and tea parties are important in all Steig's works.

Sylvester and the Magic Pebble (1969) received the Caldecott Medal in 1970, was nominated for a National Book Award in the children's category the same year, received the Lewis Carroll Shelf Award in 1978, and the Spring Book Festival Award in 1969. Steig's portrait of Sylvester Duncan, a donkey who collects unusual pebbles as a hobby and eventually discovers one that causes the rain to stop and then turns him into a rock, is his first real use of magic. The loving and forlorn family waits for Sylvester's return, which must occur with the reoccurrence of magic. And of course it does happen, at a picnic. Sylvester is transformed through a wish by Mrs. Duncan: "You can imagine the scene that followed–the embraces, the kisses, the questions, the answers, the loving looks, and the fond exclamations!" Moreover, Steig produced a whimsical fancy with charming illustrations that provided him the opportunity to show the changing seasons bursting into an extravaganza of spring flowers and the trees in all their tender beauty.

At the time Steig won the Caldecott Medal, there was some criticism of his use of pigs as police. This now seems ludicrous since Steig uses all types of animals in his stories. Pigs and donkeys seem to dominate Steig's early work. Later on, mice, geese, and dogs are prominent. Not until *Caleb and Kate* (1977) are humans introduced. It seems not to make much difference. Certainly the animal characters are used anthropomorphically; if anything, one might complain about the lack of male-female conflict until *Caleb and Kate*. While Steig families are supportive, women are wives and mothers, not doers. They usually wear aprons.

Amos and Boris (1971), which was also nominated for a National Book Award, placed on the *New York Times* Best Illustrated Children's Books of the Year list, and included in the Children's Book Council's Children's Book Showcase, marked a departure for Steig. The illustrations are low-key, muted, with only occasional bright touches of orange on a boat or from the sun, to lighten a generally silvery-gray seascape. This entire story takes place on or near the sea. And once again Steig proves himself to be a master of incongruity. Amos, a mouse, builds a boat "because he wondered about the faraway places on the other side of the water," and Boris, a whale, is on his way to the Ivory Coast of Africa to attend a whale meeting. The plot is made plausible by the authoritative ring of Steig's language. Amos, "full of wonder, full of enterprise, and full of love for life," runs into a storm and is cast adrift, to be rescued by Boris, who admires the "delicacy, the quivering daintiness, the light touch, the small voice, the gemlike radiance of the mouse."

The two become close friends and tell each other their dreams, ambitions, and hopes. Years later it is Amos's turn to rescue Boris with the help of two elephants. When the two friends part the second time they know they might never see each other again, and they cry. The story is tightly drawn, so that their tears are appropriate. Although the story is full of fast action, and even heroic, it is somehow a delicate and tender revelation of strong friendship.

Although *Dominic* (1972) won a Christopher Award in 1973 and the William Allen White Children's Book Award in 1975, was an ALA Notable Book on the *Horn Book* honor list, and was nominated for a National Book Award, it seems the least successful of all Steig's major books. He turned to the novel form for the first time, and, although the story is pleasant, it lacks the consistency of voice and strong narrative tension of his other works.

Dominic is a gregarious mutt who decides that there "wasn't enough going on in his own neighborhood to satisfy his need for adventure. He just had to get away." Steig again portrays a wandering musician as Dominic packs his piccolo for the trip. Evil presents itself immediately with the introduction of a witch-alligator looking something like little Red Riding Hood's grandmother. Dominic is thrust into one devastating adventure after another, the most terrifying of which is the attack by the Doomsday Gang, a collection of stoats, weasels, cats, and other creatures symbolically associated with trouble throughout the history of children's literature. Dominic befriends a dying pig and helps out another pig who has

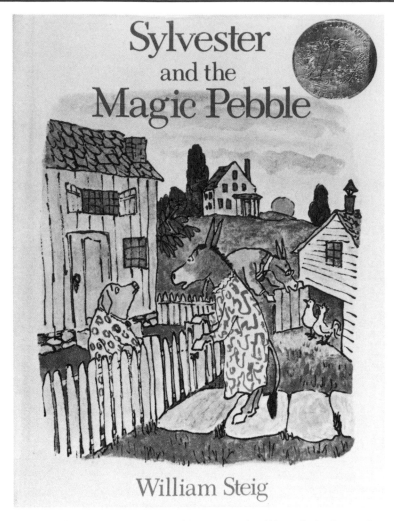

Dust jacket for Steig's 1969 story of a young donkey who collects unusual pebbles. The book won the Caldecott Medal in 1970 (Windmill Books).

been the victim of the gang's misdeeds. The ending draws openly from *The Sleeping Beauty,* with Dominic's rescue of Evelyn, "the most beautiful dog he had ever seen," a completely romantic vision.

While the illustrations in Steig's other books carry much of the weight and extend the understanding of the words, most of the meaning in *Dominic* comes through the text. The small black-and-white drawings do not elicit the same exquisite feeling of humor, wonder, and delight. However, by the time Steig wrote *Abel's Island* (1976), he had mastered the novel form. Even though the book is reminiscent of *Robinson Crusoe,* it is fresh and made somehow new with confident language that is pure Steig at his philosophical best, sure of the sophisticated humor, and comfortable in the medium he has both created and acquired.

The Real Thief (1973), an ALA Notable Book, started, according to Steig, "with the idea of a child suffering from an injustice. That's the only time I really gave myself a theme. Otherwise I just ramble around and discover for myself what will happen next. It's only when you're consciously aware of what you're doing in a book that you're in trouble."

Again Steig's cast of animal characters is lovingly portrayed. There are pigs, goats, cats, a mouse who looks like E. B. White's Stuart Little, King Basil the Bear, and the hero, Gawain the Goose. The story and atmosphere are quite different from traditional Steig; instead of universal pastoralism, the mood and tone of medieval England is all pervasive, stemming perhaps from Steig's boyhood love of *Robin Hood* and *King Arthur.* The delicate black-and-white illustrations are rich with halberds, cathedral windows,

Dust jacket for Steig's 1973 story, which began, according to the author, "with the idea of a child suffering from an injustice" (Farrar, Straus & Giroux)

bewigged judges, and palace jewels.

The story is of a highly moral nature without being moralistic. It is about lying and bravery, justice and injustice, and Steig's familiar theme, friendship. Gawain is the chief guard of the royal treasury and is dismayed to be accused of stealing the royal jewels. After Gawain suffers the ignominy of being sent into exile and the betrayal of his friends, the real thief, Derek the mouse, saves the day by recognizing the wrong he has done to himself and his friend. The story unfolds slowly, is deep and thought-provoking, with enough action and heart-wrenching drama to keep it from being a sermon.

With *Farmer Palmer's Wagon Ride* (1974), an ALA Notable Book, Steig returned to his characteristic breezy good humor, unreeling panoramas of countrysides that stir feelings of hayrides and apple cider. Pigs and donkeys are again the main characters. This uncomplicated farce is full of tongue-in-cheek whimsy and adventures the reader knows will end happily. Wordplay sparkles on the pages. "An hour before sunrise, Farmer Palmer tip-hoofed out of the house and went to the barn to wake up his hired hand,

Ebenezer." There is picture-play too; a country billboard says "Use Swan's Liniment" and shows a dog holding a bottle of liniment. When Farmer Palmer goes to town to sell his vegetables and bring back gifts for his family, he does not anticipate all the trouble that will befall him. As each episode unfolds, the ludicrous happenings achieve a cumulative humor. Farmer Palmer wonders if he will ever arrive home safely. Of course he does, and there is the loving, overjoyed fat family, who greet him with laughing, kissing, and a few tears. With this book, Steig leaves the form of fairy tale and turns to idyllic domesticity. His next three books also end with ecstatic family reunions after arduous circumstances have been survived.

Abel's Island received the Lewis Carroll Shelf Award, won William Steig his first Newbery Honor Book award in 1977, and was also placed on the *Horn Book* honor list and included in the Children's Book Showcase. Perfecting his novelistic style and illuminating the pages with enchanting line-wash black-and-white drawings, Steig created a small masterpiece.

Abel, a wealthy, privileged, dapper, and sophisticated mouse, begins his year-long odyssey by chasing after his dear wife Amanda's silk scarf during a storm. The story begins with one of Steig's ubiquitous picnics with "delicate sandwiches of pot cheese and watercress, along with hard-boiled quail eggs, onions, olives, and black caviar. They toasted each other, and everything else, with a bright champagne, which was kept cool in a bucket of ice." Steig establishes a way of life and the identity of his characters in one deft stroke. His skillful storytelling juxtaposes the elegant beginning with a soon-to-follow life of hardship, terror, near death, and learning through experience, as Abel is pushed and pummeled by a raging river to his refuge, a tree on an island. The theme is certainly this: although Abel is lost, he finds himself.

Alone on his island, Abel discovers that he is a part of the creation and has a relationship with the earth and sky and forces of nature. He draws from sources within himself that astound him. He faces loneliness for his beloved wife and family. He endures depression through the forgetfulness of a new friend, Gower the frog. He approaches death through treachery by an owl and a cat. During all this, a change occurs. Abelard (his given name) moves from being an aloof mouse to an involved one. He develops patience. In creating aesthetic forms, clay statues of

It was a brilliant day & instead of going straight home from school, Pearl dawdled.

On Parsnip Lane she looked in at the bakery & watched the bakers doing their grown-up work—taking hot loaves of pumpernickel out of the oven & dusting crullers with powdered sugar. On Cobble Road she ~~watched~~ stopped to watch the old geezers at Maltby's barn pitch their ringing horseshoes & spit tobacco juice.

Later, she sat on the ground in the ~~little~~ forest ~~woods~~ between school & home, and Spring was

Pages from the manuscript and the book dummy for The Amazing Bone *(courtesy of William Steig)*

On Cobble Road she stopped at Maltby's barn and stood gawking as the old
gaffers pitched their ringing horseshoes and spat tobacco juice.

Amanda and his friends and relatives, he finds his life work and purpose in life. And in the end, Amanda still waits: "Abel! Oh, dear Abel! It's you! It's really, really you!" After they have covered each other with kisses, Abel has the best throw-away line in modern children's literature, "I've brought you back your scarf." Steig's wry humor is the perfect blend for this charming, highly literate, compassionate, and amiable story. Who can resist a mouse who visits his absent wife in his dreams and sends her "mind-messages"?

For *The Amazing Bone* (1976), a Caldecott Honor Book, Steig chose a female protagonist for the first time, portraying a dreamy pig named Pearl, who wears a pink dress and bonnet. Her wondering spirit blends harmoniously with the impressionistic drawings; the gold, greens, lavenders, and soft growing of spring. Steig's use of color sensitizes each page of *The Amazing Bone*. The romantic quality of text and picture permeates the pages like the fragrance of flowers: "spring was so bright and beautiful, the warm air touched her so tenderly, she could almost feel herself changing into a flower. Her light dress felt like petals."

Pearl is the pig who loves everything. She never dreams harm can befall the beautiful world she lives in until amazing things happen to her. For example, she finds an "amazing bone" that speaks any language. Then, after finding such a wonderful thing, she discovers terrible evil in the form of a fox who "wore a sprig of lilac in his lapel," "carried a cane," "was grinning so the whole world could see his sharp white teeth." In the illustration for this scene, the fox nuzzles Pearl seductively, both arms around her waist. "You're exactly what I've been longing for, . . . young, plump, and tender. You will be my main course at dinner tonight. . . ." While the fox embraces Pearl, the bone screams, "Unhand her, you villain, or I'll bite your ears off!"

Here Steig uses the archetypal Red Riding Hood theme without apology, as he did in *Dominic*. The young, innocent girl is molested by a stranger who introduces her to the evil of the world, and the bone is her magic protector. However, thanks to modern fantasy, where ancient themes can be played with, the ending is happy. After suffering all kinds of verbal abuse and abject terror, the bone and Pearl philosophize,

> "I'm only just beginning to live. . . . I don't
> want it to end."
> "I know," said the bone.

Dust jacket for the book in which Steig introduced his first human characters (Farrar, Straus & Giroux)

The major difference between Steig's story and the traditional tale is that the heroine *knows* her fate. The realism of our time will not permit naiveté. But, true to fairy-tale style, there is plenty of misery and terror here—and the confrontation with the worst—death. Of course, magic saves the day. With the inventive wordplay Steig has become known for, "Adoonis ishgoolak keebokkin yibapp" turns the fox to the size of a mouse. This device is employed again in *Caleb and Kate*, establishing Steig as a master of nonsense.

The family rejoices at Pearl's miraculous escape; and miraculous it is, but it embodies the perfect reality of good fantasy—the fantasy stays alive: "The bone stayed on and became part of the family. It was given an honored place in a silver tray on the mantelpiece. Pearl always took it to bed when she retired. . . ." The book was included in the Children's Book Showcase in 1977 and received a *Boston Globe-Horn Book* honor nomination for illustration.

Steig, in *Caleb and Kate*, another National Book Award finalist, employs lovingly familiar scenes of the joyous changing countryside, delightful wordplay, a hero suddenly thwarted from ordinary pursuits by magic, and finally a joyous reunion. But there is one great difference not found in Steig's earlier books—he introduces his first human characters, and they are human in every way. "Caleb the carpenter and Kate the weaver loved each other, but not every single minute. Once in a while they'd differ about this or that and wind up in such a fierce quarrel you'd never believe they were husband and wife."

It is a quarrel that sends Caleb out into the forest. The witch Yedida comes upon him in his nap, and wheezing the words "Ammy whammy, Ibbin bammy, This is now, a bow-wow-wow," she turns him into a dog. There is a Steig dog, looking marvelously human, but still a dog. In the series of pictures that follow, Kate is seen missing her husband, traipsing through "the moon-laced forest." But all this time Caleb could not be found, though "He was behind his wife, with the shape and shadow of a dog."

After many attempts to tell Kate what happened to him, help comes in the form of robbers, whom Caleb attacks. In the ensuing frenzied action, Caleb is magically returned to his former self. He enters human life again, and there is a repeat of Amanda and Abel's reunion. "Caleb and Kate leaped into each other's arms and cleaved together for a long time." The biblical flavor of the term "cleaved" enables Steig to retain the folkloric and mythic quality of his story.

Steig is at his best in *Caleb and Kate*, combining what he has learned about prose and using all his artistic gifts: the tongue-in-cheek humor that is never beyond the child, eloquent language as well as inventive play, both in language and illustration.

Gorky Rises (1980) won the Irma Simonton Black Award in 1981 and was included in the *New York Times* Best Illustrated Children's Books of the Year list in 1980. Gorky, a frog, sets up a lab by the kitchen sink to try concocting a magic potion. He discovers that the missing ingredient is his mother's attar of roses. While he waits for the magic to take place, he heads over to Elephant Rock, "his best spot for doing nothing." Although there are reminiscent traces of Steig's familiar wordplay ("what a magic cloverous smell," Gorky sighs as he tramps through the meadow), his later incantations are sometimes forced, and even the illustrations lack the usual Steig richness and depth of humor.

Steig's metaphysics touch Gorky as, his magic potion activated, he floats alone in the sky. "Dreamily he began asking himself questions he could not answer. Did anyone know where he was? Did God, for example, know? Did his parents?" When Gorky finally manages to descend to earth he lands at Elephant Rock, which predictably becomes a real elephant. Steig provides a twist to his ubiquitous "jubilant" family reunion, however, when Gorky's father laconically says, "Well son, you must be tired after all that flying. Let's go home and get some sleep."

Doctor De Soto (1982), an animal fantasy in picture-book format, pits a mouse against a fox in an inventive "outfoxed the fox" story. Doctor De Soto, a mouse dentist, and his wife treat all types of animals, large and small, through elaborate mechanisms that permit the diminutive mouse to reach the troublesome tooth. However, a sign on the building limits the practice: "Cats and other dangerous animals not accepted for treatment." The fox connives his acceptance as a patient but loses his reward in the end—outsmarted by Dr. and Mrs. De Soto. The illustrations provide quality character identification in Steig's usual style and provide the visual drama and humor that extend the story. The book received the American Book Award in the hardcover picture-book category. *Solomon and the Rusty Nail* (1985) follows the great tradition of *Sylvester and the Magic Pebble* and *Caleb and Kate*—a tale of magical transformation from a master storyteller.

In addition to these fiction books for children, Steig wrote *CDB!* (1968), *CDC?* (1984), and *The Bad Speller* (1970), all readers, and *An Eye for Elephants* (1970), a book of verse, demonstrating his great versatility in the children's book field.

William Steig has said about his much acclaimed second profession, "You probably write for yourself as a child," and "winning is definitely fun. I never understood what was missing from my life until this began to happen. It feels darn good, like being dubbed into knighthood." From his record since the age of sixty-one, he may not have achieved the sum total of his lofty position yet. What happens after knighthood? Another career, perhaps.

Reference:

Selma G. Lanes, *Down the Rabbit Hole: Adventures and Misadventures in the Realm of Children's Literature* (New York: Atheneum, 1971).

Papers:

William Steig's papers are located in the Kerlan Collection at the University of Minnesota, Minneapolis.

Chris Van Allsburg

(18 June 1949-   )

Laura Ingram

BOOKS: *The Garden of Abdul Gasazi* (Boston: Houghton Mifflin, 1979);
Jumanji (Boston: Houghton Mifflin, 1981);
Ben's Dream (Boston: Houghton Mifflin, 1982);
The Wreck of the Zephyr (Boston: Houghton Mifflin, 1983);
The Mysteries of Harris Burdick (Boston: Houghton Mifflin, 1984);
The Polar Express (Boston: Houghton Mifflin, 1985);
The Stranger (Boston: Houghton Mifflin, 1986).

Widely recognized not only as a writer and illustrator of children's books but as a sculptor and educator as well, Chris Van Allsburg consistently takes advantage of "the opportunity to create a small world between two pieces of cardboard, where time exists yet stands still. . . ." Spurred by his obsession with "making something real that at one point is only an idea," Van Allsburg uses his talent as an artist to explore the relationship between physical reality and the world of dreams and illusion.

Chris Van Allsburg was born 18 June 1949 in Grand Rapids, Michigan, where his parents operated a dairy ("not the kind with cows," Van Allsburg clarifies, "but one that converts milk into ice cream"). He earned a bachelor of fine arts degree from the University of Michigan, where, abandoning his initial "vague idea of becoming a lawyer," he studied art to the exclusion and detriment of other subjects. He went from there to the Rhode Island School of Design, where he received a master of fine arts and remains as a teacher of illustration.

Van Allsburg's fascination with drawing and painting began in elementary school, where art classes were held twice a week. An anecdote related in his Caldecott acceptance speech demonstrates his early devotion to art: as a second grader, unwilling to miss art day, he attended school despite feeling sick at breakfast. As a result, he threw up in the boots of an unfortunate classmate, Billy Marcus, whom Van Allsburg still remembers by name. His interest in art was to

Chris Van Allsburg

waver in sixth grade, however, as Van Allsburg reached adolescence and peer pressure swayed him from pen and paper to more acceptable, traditionally masculine pursuits such as football. "Kids who draw or wear white socks and bring violins to school on Wednesdays might have cooties," he explains.

In college his interest returned to art, though this time its function in his life was, initially, a means of avoiding serious study of academic subjects. He recalls, in a story that betrays his naiveté as a freshman of college art curriculum, enrolling in an eight o'clock A.M. course listed cryptically as "Fgdrw" on his schedule. Arriving at the classroom equipped with newsprint and charcoal, he discovered "an older woman wearing a terry-cloth robe and slippers. I thought, 'What? Does she live here or something? Maybe we're early and she hasn't had time to dress.' " It was not until she took off the robe that he realized what the abbreviation "Fgdrw" stood for.

Van Allsburg's first picture book, *The Garden of Abdul Gasazi* (1979), gained him almost instantaneous recognition in the field of illustration. This tale relates the experiences of a hapless boy, Alan, whose adventures begin when Miss Hester's dog, Fritz, left in his care for the afternoon, runs through a garden gate posted with a sign warning: "ABSOLUTELY, POSITIVELY NO DOGS ALLOWED IN THIS GARDEN." After an extensive search for Fritz, illustrated in detail by Van Allsburg's graphite pencil drawings, Alan finds not the runaway dog, but Abdul Gasazi, a plump magician in Turkish garb who introduces himself as proprietor of the garden and claims to have turned Fritz into a duck. As Alan leaves the garden with the transformed Fritz under his arm, a gust of wind causes him to lose both his hat and the duck. Watching helplessly as the duck flies away, his hat in its beak, Alan returns home sadly, only to find that Fritz has arrived there before him. It is not until after convincing Alan that the magician has tricked him that Miss Hester discovers Fritz playing with Alan's lost hat.

Van Allsburg's fascination with light, shadows, and reflection, as well as his background as a sculptor, is apparent in the drawings which provide the details left untold in the text. Critics hailed *The Garden of Abdul Gasazi* as a graphic masterpiece, praising not only his technical skill but also his artistic vision. Stefan Kanfer, in his 3 December 1979 *Time* magazine article, "A Child's Portion of Good Reading," credits Van Allsburg with capturing "the incongruous logic of dreams," and Barbara Elleman, in *Booklist* (15 November 1979), recognizes his ability to "provide an underlying quality of hushed surrealism, seemingly poised at the brink of expectancy." Writing for the *New York Times Book Review* (11 November 1979), Harold C. Rice compares "the slightly ominous, surreal glow" of the illustrations with that evoked by the films of Orson Welles, while Kanfer likens them to "snapshots taken by the brain of Poe" and Paul Heines, in a February 1980 *Horn Book* review, notes that the "stippled tones of gray and the precisely outlined figures" exhibit the pointillist technique made famous by the French painter Georges Pierre Seurat.

Despite the unanimous positive reception of the visual aspects of *The Garden of Abdul Gasazi*, the accompanying story is a subject of controversy among critics. Elleman's view that "this visual enchantment is ably matched by a subtle, surprise-ending tale" is disputed by critics such as Heines, who considers the story "an ambitious libretto for a series of carefully composed, technically expert pictures" and finds the characters "singularly static" in comparison with the artwork. While conceding that the story is "nicely conceived but rather hesitantly put together," Kicki Moxon Brown in "To Amuse and Entertain" (*Times Literary Supplement*, 18 September 1981) complains that "it gives the impression of a resumé of a longer story." Likewise, Rice charges that "the text is a little stiff, even slightly condescending, and the plot seems arbitrary."

Despite these assertions that *The Garden of Abdul Gasazi* is "essentially a showcase for the illustrations," many critics, like Rice, consider the work taken as a whole as "one of the best–and most original–picture books in years." In 1979 *The Garden of Abdul Gasazi* was chosen by the *New York Times* as one of its best illustrated children's books of the year.

In 1980 the book was recipient of the *Boston Globe-Horn Book* award for illustration and the Irma Simonton Black Award and was named as a Caldecott Honor Book. In 1982 it was added to the International Board on Books Honor List for illustration. Many of the original drawings for *The Garden of Abdul Gasazi* were included among his sculptures and other drawings in Van Allsburg's one-man show in New York City's Alan Stone Gallery.

In Van Allsburg's next work, *Jumanji* (1981), the world of fantasy intrudes upon an average suburban home when Judy and Peter, two restless children left home alone, play a board game, Jumanji, "a young people's jungle adventure designed especially for the bored and restless." As in *The Garden of Abdul Gasazi*, the plunge into the realm of illusion is preceded by a warning, this time contained in the game's instructions–"VERY IMPORTANT: ONCE A GAME OF JUMANJI IS STARTED IT WILL NOT BE OVER UNTIL ONE PLAYER REACHES THE GOLDEN CITY." True to its claim, the game dispels the children's listlessness when lions materialize in the living room, monkeys appear on the kitchen table and help themselves to bananas, a volcano erupts, and a herd of rhinos rampage through the house. When Judy finally reaches the Golden City, the house is suddenly cleared of wild animals and the effects of the game have all disap-

Dust jacket for Van Allsburg's first book, about a boy who enters a bewildering garden to retrieve a troublesome dog (Houghton Mifflin)

peared. Mysteriously, no mess remains even though the children had dragged out all their toys before beginning the game.

Illustrated with black-and-white Conté crayon, *Jumanji*'s success depends heavily on visual effects. Van Allsburg's pictures, which at first glance could be mistaken for photographs, are impressive not only for their realism but for the skill with which he manipulates light and shadow to create a vaguely unsettling mood and for the odd angles which present disconcerting views of common scenes. The observant will recognize Fritz, the troublesome dog from *The Garden of Abdul Gasazi*, in the form of a wheeled pull toy among the children's playthings.

These renderings of what Denise M. Wilms, in a 15 May 1981 *Booklist* review, calls "stunning, velvet-flat black and white scenes . . . of a familiar household world gone amok," are praised by John Gardner in his 26 April 1981 *New York Times Book Review* critique of *Jumanji*, entitled "Fun and Games and Dark Imaginings," for their "beautiful simplicity of design, balance, texture and a subtle intelligence beyond the call of illustration." Mary M. Burns, reviewing for *Horn Book* (4

August 1981), admires "the masterly use of light and shadow, the interplay of design elements, and audacious changes in perspective and composition [with which] the artist conveys an impression of color without losing the dramatic contrast of black and white." Pamela D. Pollack, in a review for the May 1982 issue of *School Library Journal,* considered Van Allsburg's mastery of "eye-fooling angles, looming shadows and shifting perspectives . . . worthy of Hitchcock." What strikes Natalie Babbitt, whose cleverly titled review, "Volcano Erupts–Go Back Three Spaces," appeared in the *Washington Post*'s *Book World* (12 July 1981), are the "curious sense of silence" and the chilling quality of the light, which she describes as "cold and soft, like the light before a snowstorm." These elements, she contends, make *Jumanji* "eerie and dreamlike–even, perhaps, nightmarish," and the impression of coldness, for her, "must be assumed to be deliberate, and is in fact a feature, in a curious way, of the story itself."

Once again, the critics had mixed reactions to Van Allsburg as a writer. Most agree that the story itself is secondary to the illustrations. Gardner's criticism of *Jumanji*'s plot as having

Dust jacket for Van Allsburg's Caldecott Medal-winning book about two children who play a jungle-adventure board game during which lions, monkeys, and rhinos appear in their house (Houghton Mifflin)

"nothing much to ponder, no rare sparkle" and of Van Allsburg's efforts at prose as "though serviceable, undistinguished" is softened by his view that "the story exists as an excuse for the artwork, and [that] it serves well enough" in that capacity. Babbitt, on the other hand, asserts that children "deserve a strong story well told." In addition, she charges Van Allsburg with creating an unplayable game and finds the swiftness with which Judy reaches the Golden City implausible.

Both Gardner and Babbitt compare *Jumanji* with Dr. Seuss's *Cat in the Hat,* which shares the theme of a fantastic element which enters the world of children when no adults are present and disappears without a trace just before the return of the grown-ups. Babbitt points out that *Jumanji* conveys a sense of tension not found in Seuss's tale, which features zany cartoon characters rather than lifelike wild animals and natural disasters. According to Wilms, it is "the tone of the text [which] lightens the sense of danger in a fantasy come true."

Jumanji was chosen by the *New York Times* as

one of its best illustrated children's books of the year, was recognized as a *Boston Globe-Horn Book* honor book for illustration in 1981, and in 1982 was awarded the Caldecott Medal. In his Caldecott acceptance speech Van Allsburg revealed that "his vague disappointment in playing board games" such as Monopoly and Clue led him to create his own alternative. "Even when I owned Park Place with three hotels, I never felt truly rich," he recalls, "and not being able to interrogate Colonel Mustard personally was always a letdown." His other impetus toward the creation of *Jumanji* was his attraction to displaced objects; "pictures in newspapers of cars that have run amok and crashed into people's living rooms always get my attention. . . . It occurred to me that if an Oldsmobile in the living room looked that good, a herd of rhinoceros could have real possibilities."

Although the final drawings for *The Garden of Abdul Gasazi* and *Jumanji* only took Van Allsburg about ten days each, the technical difficulty of *Ben's Dream* (1982) required nearly six months of work. Ben, lulled by the sound of the rain, falls asleep while studying for a geography test and dreams that his house floats around a flooded world. His voyage takes him on a tour of great monuments: he passes first the Statue of Liberty, who looks as if she is waving good-bye to him, sails through the shadow of Big Ben and under the Eiffel Tower, past the Leaning Tower of Pisa, by the Parthenon and the Sphinx, where he spots his classmate Margaret, also traveling in a floating house, between the towers and domes of St. Basil's in Moscow, over China's Great Wall, and, finally, past Mount Rushmore, where all the presidents seem to be watching his progress. Here, the dream ends as George Washington says, "Wake up, Ben," and the inevitable twist–Margaret appearing at the window to tell him of *her* dream of a journey around the world in a floating house–raises the question, "Was it really a dream?" (The ubiquitous Fritz appears here as well, as a canine portrait hanging on the living-room wall of Ben's house.)

The drawings, presented on a double-page-spread format, are a radical departure from "the richly penciled, magic realism of the previous works"; instead, according to Karla Kuskin in "The Complete Illustrator," which appeared in the 25 April 1982 edition of the *New York Times Book Review*, the drawings resemble scenes "engraved from a surreal photograph." Van Allsburg once again uses skewed angles similar to those in *Jumanji*. One illustration shows the underside of the Eiffel Tower, which Kenneth Marantz described in a May 1982 *School Library Journal* review as "a striking view . . . that suggests a giant piece of a ferris wheel." He compares these drawings, so "unlike the sensuous velvet blacks he seduced us with in his first two books," to "a multitude of linear patterns, . . . with almost a total lack of solid black shapes." While some critics, such as Zena Sutherland, reviewing for the July-August 1982 issue of *Bulletin of the Center for Children's Books*, feel that the unusual perspectives from which the monuments are shown and even the subject matter itself are too advanced for the level of readership the text would suggest, Marantz maintains that "one need not know the monuments in order to sense their distinction." *Horn Book* reviewer Ethel R. Twitchell praises "dramatic angles, close-ups from above and below, and careful architectural details which . . . dazzle the eye and the imagination" in her August 1982 critique, but the *Kirkus Review* (15 April 1982)

critic contends that "they have no dramatic function."

The framework of the dream, reminiscent of *The Wizard of Oz*, Nancy Willard's *Anatole* stories, and *Little Nemo*, is charged with seeming like "a device to hang some handsome pictures on," and Sutherland claims that "the text is a vehicle for an idea rather than a story." The *Kirkus Review* critique is especially harsh, asserting that "to pretend that these essentially banal pictures have deep meanings is flimflam." Marantz disagrees, asserting that "there is a rightness to this view of our world, inviting readers to join the cruise." *Ben's Dream* was chosen as one of the best illustrated children's books of 1982 by the *New York Times*.

The Wreck of the Zephyr (1983), Van Allsburg's first children's book with full-color illustrations, is called "a tale of hubris in the classical mold" by Selma G. Lanes in her 8 April 1983 *Publishers Weekly* review. In this story-within-a-story, an old man tells the narrator the tale of a boy, the best sailor in the town, and how he was stranded during a storm on a mysterious island where boats fly above the water. The boy breaks his promise to the sailor whom he has persuaded to try to teach him to fly and sets out for home, using the islanders' magical sails on his own boat, the *Zephyr*. As he approaches his hometown, looking forward to swooping among the rooftops, ringing the *Zephyr*'s bells, and showing off his new skill, his plans for a grand entrance are thwarted by a shift in the wind which sends him crashing into the earth. The fall breaks his leg, and, predictably, no one believes his tale of a flying boat and hidden islands. "The boy never amounted to much," the old man ends his story, adding, "Most of the time he was out sailing, searching for that island and a new set of sails." *The Wreck of the Zephyr* ends as the old man limps toward the harbor, explaining, "I've got some sailing to do."

For this project, Van Allsburg worked with Rembrandt pastels, which he describes as "crayons as thick as a finger," for wide expanses of color and used pastel pencils, sharpened to a fine point, for detail. Despite the difficulty of this technique, Van Allsburg still displays a talent for manipulating light and shadow to achieve the effect of reality seen from a slightly skewed point of view. Details, such as the waft of smoke rising from behind the wreck of the sailboat and a half-full beer bottle on a tree-shadowed window ledge, add to the realism of the drawings. Standing on the dock as the fateful storm brews is

Fritz the dog. *The Wreck of the Zephyr* was hailed as "the work of a master: stunning, luminescent and conveying a sense of the mystical and magical."

Originally planned as "a novel . . . 'about an illustrator who brings in fourteen drawings to show an editor and then disappears without a trace,'" *The Mysteries of Harris Burdick* appeared in 1984. The projected novel never came to be, and instead, the collection of illustrations stands virtually alone, with no accompanying text except for the preface, which tells the anecdote of the mysterious Harris Burdick, and for each drawing, a title and a cryptic caption that only hints at the story behind the picture. Readers unfamiliar with the author's work may find the fictitious introduction entirely believable, but the style of the artwork is unmistakably Van Allsburg's, and the presence of Fritz, whose frequent and varied portrayals in Van Allsburg's work is reminiscent of Hitchcock's own fleeting appearances in each of his films, is a dead giveaway. Working once again in black and white, Van Allsburg presents fourteen unconnected scenes in a "create your own story" format designed to challenge the imagination of even the dullest observer. Some are humorous, such as a depiction of a nun in a chair levitating before two onlooking cardinals. The title, "The Seven Chairs," and the caption, "The fifth one ended up in France," raise the inevitable question "What became of the other six?" Others are downright chilling; for example, "Just Desert," captioned, "She lowered the knife and it grew even brighter," shows an aproned woman about to cut into a luminous pumpkin. In still others–like a drawing of a young girl looking sadly into her hand captioned "She knew it was time to send them back. The caterpillars softly wiggled in her hand, spelling out 'goodbye'"–humor is tempered by a sense of bittersweet melancholy. Van Allsburg's fascination with displaced objects is apparent in "Missing in Venice," which shows an ocean liner crashing into the buildings lining a Venetian canal, and in "The Third Floor Bedroom," in which a bird which is part of the wallpaper pattern lifts its head and wing from the walls as if to fly away.

Designed to challenge even those who claim to have no imagination, these pictures possess a haunting quality that hints at unseen mysteries. Though this collection appears on the children's shelves in most libraries and bookstores, Van Allsburg's teasing scenes are sophisticated enough to provoke fantasies in the adult as well

Dust jacket for Van Allsburg's 1984 book of cryptically captioned drawings which were supposedly left with a publisher by a mysterious artist (Houghton Mifflin)

as prereaders and school-aged children.

A Christmas story, *The Polar Express* (1985), was Van Allsburg's second full-color project. The tale chronicles the journey of a young boy who takes a trip one Christmas Eve to Santa's city in the North Pole on a magical train, the Polar Express. Inside the train, children, still dressed for bed, sit on red velvet seats and sing carols as white-uniformed men dispense "hot cocoa as thick and rich as melted chocolate bars" from a huge urn. Chosen a recipient of the first gift of Christmas, the gift of his choice handed out by Santa himself, the boy asks for a bell from Santa's sleigh. On the trip home, he discovers that the bell has disappeared from his bathrobe pocket, but the next morning, after all the presents have been opened, a small box containing the bell and a cryptic note signed Mr. C. remains beneath the tree. When the boy rings the bell, he and his sister think its sound is the most beautiful they have ever heard, but their parents hear nothing and think the bell is broken. This fable, reminiscent of William Blake's *Songs of Innocence*, reaffirms Van Allsburg's contention that the fantastic *is* possible for those who believe.

These drawings, with fuzzy backgrounds suggestive, as those in *The Garden of Abdul Gasazi*, of pointillism and sharply defined objects in the fore-

Dust jacket for Van Allsburg's second Caldecott Medal winner, a Christmas story which chronicles a young boy's journey to the North Pole on a magical train (Houghton Mifflin)

ground, differ from those in Van Allsburg's first color-picture book in that they explore the effects of indoor lighting and what a critic for *Newsweek* described as "the sumptuous pastel effects [of] train lights seen through falling snow." Van Allsburg's growing sophistication in the manipulation of texture is apparent here as well: the fur of the wolves seems to bristle, Santa's whip looks as if it is about to snap off the page at any moment, and, in the last panel, picturing the bell, the metal looks cold and shiny in contrast to the velvety leather thong attached to the bell and the deep rich tones of the wood table on which it rests. Fritz, this time a hand puppet on the boy's bedpost, makes his appearance in the first drawing, adding a touch of humor to this serious, though cheerful story which the *Newsweek* reviewer considers "one of Van Allsburg's most treasurable visions." *The Polar Express* was the Caldecott Medal winner for 1986.

The Stranger (1986), Van Allsburg's most recent publication to date, begins on a distressing note one autumn day as Mr. Bailey, a farmer, runs into a man with his truck. At the farmer's home, where the stranger has been brought to re-

cuperate, the Baileys discover that he is mute and without memory, though apparently unhurt. He becomes a part of the family, working in the fields with Mr. Bailey and becoming the close friend of Katy, the Baileys' young daughter. In the few weeks of the visitor's stay, the weather seems odd, as if it has become summer again, though when he finally leaves his new friends, with tears in his eyes, it is suddenly winter outside, just as it should be. Every year after the stranger's departure, winter is a week late on the Bailey farm, and on the windows is written in frost, "See you next fall!"

Ann Rice, writing about *The Stranger* for the *New York Times Book Review*, asserts that the stranger is "Jack Frost, or the spirit of winter" and even entitles her review "Jack Frost's Amnesia." Hints in the story, besides the stranger's effect on the weather, support this view: the mercury stuck at the bottom of the thermometer when the doctor takes the man's temperature, the stranger's fascination with steam, the cold draft Mrs. Bailey feels when he blows on his soup, his success in approaching wild rabbits who run from others, and his distress at the sight of a

Illustration from Van Allsburg's 1986 book, The Stranger *(copyright © 1986 by Chris Van Allsburg; reprinted by permission of Houghton Mifflin Company).*

flock of geese flying south.

Rice notes that this story is "deeper and more intriguing . . . than his earlier tales" and attributes some of its charm to the fact that "everyday human life is presented as wondrous. It seduces and satisfies the supernatural visitor." However, it is the "warmth and intimacy of the illustrations. . . , almost without precedent in the artist's other books, which are more cerebral and more remote" that provides a new facet to Van Allsburg's work. The expression on the stranger's bland, innocent face is transformed, in turn, from one of awe and amazement to delight and, finally, recognition. Details, like Mrs. Bailey's grin of crazed glee as she plays the piano and the stranger's untied shoelaces flapping as he and Katy dance, add a manic quality to an otherwise sentimental scene, and, in another drawing, the outstretched hand holding a broken thermometer and the expressions on the faces of two cats as they watch an almost magical-looking bird poised on the edge of a birdbath transform an ordinary front yard into a surreal landscape. Fritz, hidden in the bottom corner, is almost indistinguishable from the field full of sheep surrounding him.

Despite frequent criticism that Van Allsburg uses children's fiction as a vehicle for his artwork, the body of his work, separately and taken as a whole, "successfully explores" what Mary M. Burns calls "the semi-magical country of the mind in which reality and illusion exist as conjoined yet distinct entities." In his review of *Jumanji,* critic Marantz asks, "Are we to speculate . . . about the nature of reality?" Van Allsburg's answer, apparently, is an emphatic "yes."

Afterword: Children's Book Illustration in the Twentieth Century

Anne Devereaux Jordan

The illustrator of children's books is a visual storyteller. He adds dimension to the writer's words, guiding the child through worlds of fable and fantasy or through instructional lessons. His job is to use his imagination and skill to choose the style, colors, and subjects necessary to blend art and text so completely that the reader comes to remember the illustrations as an integral part of the story. So *Alice's Adventures in Wonderland* (1865) immediately brings to mind John Tenniel along with Lewis Carroll, and Wilbur, in *Charlotte's Web* (1952), may be said to belong as much to Garth Williams as to E. B. White.

Previous to the nineteenth century, this harmony between art and words was virtually unknown due to the limitations of the printing process which restricted the techniques available to the artist. During the nineteenth century new developments occurred in metal engraving—machine lithography was introduced reducing printing costs, and the first steps were taken in color printing. Nineteenth-century artists were much more limited in their use of color than in present day. Generally, illustrations in color could not appear on a text page. They had to be printed separately on heavier, coated stock and were usually "tipped-in" by hand or wrapped around one or more signatures when the book was being prepared for binding. Even so, publishers were happy to trade the production difficulties for the appeal and attraction color illustrations added to their books.

In England these innovations were capitalized upon by Edmund Evans, a printer who saw that children's books could be beautiful in both design and color and need not be the cheap, drab little books printed to that time. He encouraged three artists in particular to join him in creating children's books—Walter Crane (1845-1915), Kate Greenaway (1846-1901), and Randolph Caldecott (1846-1886); together, these four set a tenor for children's book illustration that lasted well into the twentieth century.

Each of these three illustrators had his own highly personal and recognizable style yet, as James Steele Smith notes, each also shared in the dominant trend of nineteenth-century book illustration, "a sort of romantic naturalism—recognizable representation of things and events combined with a love of elegant elaboration, rhythmic gracefulness and delicacy, and melodramatic contrast." Kate Greenaway's demure, romanticized children in old-fashioned dress are immediately recognizable. Her drawings are quiet and delicate with a restrained use of color. Walter Crane's illustrations are both imaginative and decorative, and reflect, as do Greenaway's, the sentimentalism characteristic of romantic naturalism. Randolph Caldecott's art is bouyant with humor, goodwill, and melodrama, yet also contains a certain elegance that was typical of illustration at that time.

Greenaway, Crane, and Caldecott were soon joined by other illustrators. Arthur Rackham (1867-1939) began creating his dark and twisted woodlands peopled by gnomes and delicate heroines. Leslie Brooke (1862-1940) started charming children with the whimsy of his *Johnny Crow* books (1903, 1907, 1935). British illustrators poured forth bright, attractive, and entertaining books that children were eager to read and look at.

Children's book illustration in the United States was progressing at a slower pace. This was due in part to the popularity of books from France and England. American artists were lost in the deluge of books illustrated by British artists such as Crane and Greenaway, and French artists such as Maurice Boutet de Monvel (1850-1913). American illustrations were frequently disparaged as primitive or cartoonlike, and American artists too often felt that to illustrate a children's book was of no significance. The influential event which drew artists into the field of children's illustration in the United States was the publication and subsequent popularity of *St. Nicholas, A Magazine for Boys and Girls,* edited by Mary Mapes Dodge.

When *St. Nicholas* began publication in 1873, Mrs. Dodge outlined her editorial policy which included the goal, "To inspire them [young people] with a fine appreciation of pictorial art." Just as she sought genius in her authors, so she looked for the best from her illustrators, securing many distinguished artists who led others into the field. One stands out for utilizing the best of romantic naturalism from England and for influencing other illustrators of children's books: Howard Pyle (1853-1911), who has been called the father of modern American illustrators.

In 1873 Howard Pyle sent a verse entitled "The Magic Pill" to *St. Nicholas,* accompanied by a number of black-and-white sketches. Mrs. Dodge was taken by both the verse and the sketches, and Pyle became a regular contributor to the magazine. At first his writings consisted of short, illustrated fables, but his interest in folk literature soon led him to the retelling of fairy tales and thence to medieval legend. From short pieces in *St. Nicholas* and other magazines for young people he went on to write and illustrate his own books. His *Merry Adventures of Robin Hood* appeared in 1883, followed by *Otto of the Silver Hand* (1888), *King Arthur and His Knights* (1903), and many others. It is debatable whether Pyle is to be praised more for his writing or his illustrations. Düreresque and romantic, his illustrations capture the mood and mystery of each story yet are carefully accurate as to period clothing and weaponry. He had a flair for delineating character with line and shading and for bringing the action on a page to life. By the example of his own work and through his teaching, Howard Pyle gave an impetus to book and magazine illustration in America and set a standard for quality while establishing a close relationship between text and art.

One disciple of Pyle was his pupil, N. C. Wyeth (1882-1945), who, like Pyle, combined realism with romanticism but who went a step further, indulging in a richness of color and a use of blue-and-purple shadow, giving his illustrations depth and elegance. He created a realistic world in his art, yet one filled with a melodramatic sense of good versus evil. His *Robinson Crusoe* (1920) and *Treasure Island* (1911) have become classics in art and still bring to life Crusoe's Friday and Jim Hawkins's island for thousands of children.

Another of Pyle's pupils was Jessie Wilcox Smith (1863-1935). She captures a sense of romantic splendor in her work, as does Pyle, and, like her mentor, creates strong, memorable figures. But her work is quieter, more subdued in mood and color than either that of Pyle or Wyeth. Her soft, shadowed colors are completely feminine, her figures idealized, as in her illustrations for *Little Women* (1934). Smith, Wyeth, and Pyle's art remains a vital part of children's books today through the reprinting of the various classics they illustrated; their artwork does not dim with the passing years, its quality is still evident.

These three and others brought the illustrated book to maturity through their work. However, when we think of children's books today we tend to think in terms of the picture book rather than the illustrated book in which only certain scenes and actions are chosen by the artist for illumination. The picture book as we recognize it today, in which pictures and text are integrated and move, one with the other, at the same pace, did not emerge until the 1920s despite some fine, earlier examples such as British author-illustrator Beatrix Potter's *The Tale of Peter Rabbit* (1901).

The 1920s saw an increased interest on the part of the educational establishment in reading for children. As a result there was a growing demand for books suitable for beginning readers. This paralleled improvements in printing techniques which freed the artist and allowed him the opportunity for experimentation in medium and in page design. As Diana Klemin observes in *The Art of Art for Children's Books,* "Offset printing gradually superseded letterpress, the artist was no longer confined even by the mechanical limitations of a letterpress type page. He could 'bleed' his illustrations by drawing or printing to the extreme edges of the book page, and he could place type as freely as he did the drawings outside the traditional text areas." The artist could arrange his page so as to best complement both text and art and had available to him, because of improved reproduction methods, a wider range of mediums—line, pencil or wash drawings, woodcuts, lithograph, watercolor, either in tempera or gouache; even collages of different mediums emerged later, as in the work of Lio Lionni and Ezra Jack Keats.

Henry C. Pitz, in his *Illustrating Children's Books,* divides the reproductive methods now available to the artist into two categories: Direct processes which are largely done by hand; and Indirect processes done by mechanical means. The Direct includes: (1) *Relief or raised printing—*

woodcut, wood engraving, linoleum cut, and relief etching; (2) *Intaglio or below-surface printing*–etching, drypoint, copper or steel engraving, aquatint, and mezzotint; (3) *Surface or planographic printing*–lithographic, stencil, or silk screen. Indirect or mechanical reproduction consists of: (1) *Relief or letter press printing*–line plate, half-tone, and electro-plates made from them; (2) *Intaglio or below-surface printing*–photogravure; and (3) *Surface or below-surface printing*–lithography, offset, and collotype. Because of its low cost, the indirect method of offset printing is used almost exclusively today.

Similarly the application of color falls into direct and indirect categories. A "color separation," in which the individual colors on a page are broken down for printing can be done either by hand or by mechanical means. In separating by hand the base drawing is on one board and the color is applied on separate and successive overlays. Mechanical separation, far more common now due to advances in technology, is done photographically using a series of filters and the individual negatives are then used to produce the four plates which print the process colors of yellow, magenta, cyan blue, and black.

This variety in reproduction methods opened up entire new areas for the artist interested in book illustration. Although color reproduction is still a costly factor in illustration, the methods and mediums available to the artist are virtually limitless today. Starting in the 1920s, this led to an influx of artists into the field of children's book illustration who previously might have shunned it as too limited. It also led to the development of the diversity of styles seen today in the field.

This variety of styles makes for difficulty in classification; perhaps they are best categorized under three general groupings: representationalists, in the tradition of Greenaway, Crane, and Pyle; abstract expressionists–who blend realism and abstraction to express poetic and personal feelings while representing the text; and instructional, the rendering of people, objects, and animals for the purposes of instruction in nonfiction children's books.

The number of artists who fall within the category of representational outnumber those in either of the other two categories both because the designation itself is so broad, and because, in children's books, most people agree that the child expects to see things represented realistically because he has not yet developed the ability

to grasp total abstraction in art. But in addition to putting the right number of fingers on a hand, or the correct color of shoes on a character, the artist also creates a sense of mood and dimension, expanding and opening up the story for the child, so the child can participate in the tale and feel what both the author and the artist feel.

Whether softening harshness or pointing up the comic, the representational artist still portrays reality. The representational artist is a realistic visual storyteller whether his subjects are animals, as in the striking work of Conrad Buff; people, as in the sweet, romantic scenes of Marguerite de Angeli; or objects, as in the bright, bold illustrations of Virginia Burton.

One important artist who accurately portrayed both animals and people with sympathetic humor was Kurt Wiese (1887-1974). Born in Germany, Wiese had traveled throughout the world before settling in the United States. His experience as a traveler provided him with the background to portray distant peoples and places, as in his *Liang and Lo* (1930) and in his illustrations for Kipling's *Jungle Book* (1932). Today, however, he is best known perhaps for his illustrations of *The Story About Ping* (1933) by Marjorie Flack, who was herself an illustrator in the representational mode. As Barbara Bader points out, "This was one of the first instances in picturebooks proper of a story being written by one person to be pictured by another. . . . Marjorie Flack didn't know China, Kurt Wiese did, that was the genesis; the ramifications were many." The collaboration between Wiese and Flack demonstrated that a writer of picture books need not also play the role of artist nor the artist provide material to illustrate as was common before the publication of *Ping*.

The Story About Ping is a memorable book in its own right, however. It is filled with humor and vitality in both text and pictures. Wiese's lithographs are rich with colors that capture the feel of the Orient and the gay innocence of the little duck, Ping. The pictures are bled to the upper page edges and, as Ping discovers he has been left behind by his boat, Wiese utilizes a two-page spread to capture the feel of distance and the vastness of the river. Wiese puts his knowledge of the Orient to good use while conveying mood, enhancing reality, and bringing the story to life for the reader.

The 1930s abounded with artists such as Wiese, who were able to utilize the technology suddenly available to create striking and memorable picture books. Wanda Gag's (1893-1946) *Millions of Cats* (1928) began what was called "The Golden Thirties" of picture books. *Millions of Cats,* with its folktale flavor and cosy, homespun black-and-white pictures, became an instant success with children and set a standard for integration of art, text, and format to be followed by artists then entering the field of children's book illustration. The hand-lettered text is surrounded by black-and-white lithographs just as the very old man and woman are surrounded by cats: "Cats here, cats there, Cats and kittens everywhere . . . ."

The 1930s saw the emergence of artists whose works still seem vivid and fresh, and whose styles, although portraying life faithfully, are highly individualistic and recognizable. Edward Ardizzone (1900-) is both a master storyteller and illustrator who, like Virginia Burton, thoroughly understands the world of the child. His well-known *Little Tim and the Brave Sea Captain* (1936) was first published with no text at all, and so expressive are the illustrations that the story communicates itself dramatically without the need for words. Ardizzoni uses line drawings to which he adds a soft wash. He captures a broad range of emotions and personalities and does not hesitate to experiment with format, often borrowing from the balloon inserts of the comics for dialogue. His goal is always to delight children with both story and pictures.

Marguerite de Angeli (1889-) and Tasha Tudor (1915-) illustrate in the tradition of Howard Pyle and the romantic naturalists. They are gently expressive, at times almost sentimental. Their compositions have a graceful flow to them, and the characters they depict are idealized and lovely. The use of pastel colors and subtle shading, combined with a careful selection of detail, lends a sense of warmth and the romantic to their art.

While de Angeli and Tudor were "gentling down" reality, other artists of the 1930s were poking fun at it. James Daugherty (1889-1974), Robert Lawson (1891-1957), and Robert McCloskey (1914-) took animals and people as their subjects and pointed out how warmly humorous life can be. Daugherty's *Andy and the Lion* (1938), his first attempt at doing a picturebook although he had done art for illustrated books, borders on caricature. Much of his art is expressive of the American spirit, as he conceived it.

Robert Lawson's art ranges from gentle humor in books such as Munroe Leaf's *The Story of Ferdinand* (1936) and his own *Rabbit Hill* (1944) to satiric portrayals of life and history in books such as Richard and Florence Atwater's *Mr. Popper's Penguins* (1938) and Lawson's *Ben and Me* (1939). Robert McCloskey's comical ducks and the people who "make way" for them in *Make Way for Ducklings* (1941) are also portrayed satirically. Each of these artists has an eye for detail that enhances his humor.

While these artists were portraying a humor that is essentially American, others were focusing their attention on foreign lands. Maud (1890-1971) and Miska Petersham's (1888-1960) fictional works are filled with the colors and designs of their native Hungary. *Miki* (1929), written for their son, is full of Miska's memories of his childhood in Hungary. May Massee, then head of Doubleday's juvenile division, dubbed *Miki* "the first of the international picturebooks," because it shows a boy's life in America and in Hungary.

Similar books soon followed. Feodor Rojankovsky (1891-1970) mixed tales and rhymes which are typically American with artwork recalling his native Russia. The line drawings of Ludwig Bemelmans (1898-1962), with color overlaid, are quick and facile, possessing a quality of fun and exuberance, and capturing the scenes and wit of France in all of his books, but most charmingly in *Madeline* (1939). Through his *Madeline* books, Bemelmans acquaints children with the landmarks of Paris as well as entertaining them with Madeline's uproarious trials and tribulations.

Norwegian-born Ingri (1905-) and Edgar Parin d'Aulaire (1898-) capture the hugeness and permanence of the Norse myths, even when dealing with typically American subjects such as *Pocahontas* (1946) or *Abraham Lincoln* (1939). Using stone lithography, which gives unusual strength and solidity to their pictures, they mix folk art and modernist art, using unusual combinations of perspective and light to achieve the almost primitive effect of children's art. Their first books, *Ola* (1932), *Ola and Blakken* (1933), and *Children of the Northlights* (1935), according to Barbara Bader, "made the d'Aulaires' reputation as Norwegian emissaries to the United States."

In recognition of this wave of illustrative talent, publisher Frederic Melcher founded the Randolph Caldecott Award awarded annually by the American Library Association to the artist of the most distinguished American picture book for children published during the preceding year.

The Caldecott Medal was first awarded in 1938.

The "Golden Thirties" of picture books were ended by World War II with its restrictions that were imposed to conserve materials needed for the war effort. The paper then available for bookmaking was of an inferior quality and could not reflect the vibrancy of original artwork, and even so, paper was in very short supply. Moreover, the number of books published was reduced, limiting the opportunities for children's book illustrators.

After World War II there was an increased interest in the diverse methods of educating children. The war had expanded people's horizons and the postwar baby boom, accompanied by a new prosperity in middle-class America, led to a personal interest in education by more Americans than ever before. As a result, adults turned a more critical eye on children's books. Books no longer had to appeal only to the child or the child-within-the-adult; they also had to conform to the most exacting principles of adult art.

Leonard Weisgard (1916-), as Barbara Bader points out, used "a simplified, formalized and more expressive symbol of the things represented . . . employing 'broad generalizations of form and non-imitative use of color' . . . ." He first introduced Cubist planes into children's books in Margaret Wise Brown's *The Noisy Book* (1939). *The Noisy Book* is the story of the noises a little dog, Muffin, hears when her eyes are bandaged because of an injury. *The Noisy Book* is bright with solid, unshadowed colors which capture the essence of the text without great detail. Weisgard adapted the techniques of adult art strikingly and effectively for children.

The most pervasive influence on children's books of the postwar period may have been Henri Matisse, who, in 1947, after a lifetime of painting, produced an adult book, *Jazz*, in which he combined his handwritten text with collage and influenced a whole school of children's book illustrators who, after his example, used new shape-line-color-texture patterns to express a feeling and tell a story. The majority of these artists emerged during the second "Golden Age" of picture books, the late 1950s and the 1960s. Paul Rand (1914-) was among the first who utilized collage techniques to create visually interesting books for children. His first book, co-authored with his wife, Ann Rand (*I Know A Lot of Things*, 1956) fell short of the mark though, showing in its coyness a lack of awareness about how a child thinks or acts. Their second book, *Sparkle and Spin* (1957), however, demonstrates Paul Rand's eye for graphic design. In the illustrations Rand analyzes figures and landscapes, breaking them down into their essential shapes and unifying them by the use of bright, vivid colors. The collage technique he employed emphasizes the shapes of people and objects in the pictures, giving them a boldness and strength.

Lio Lionni (1910-) entered the field of children's book illustration in 1959. His career as an artist had been distinguished, but he had not given any thought to children's books until he began telling stories to his grandchildren. According to the jacket copy for *Little Blue and Little Yellow* (1959), Lionni "believes that abstract figures can not only communicate but be highly suggestive to a child's creative sense." Using only colored paper pasted on a plain background, Lionni created a charming story for children. While *Little Blue and Little Yellow* is totally abstract, in his later books Lionni tells the stories more representationally, more closely uniting text and art. *The Biggest House in the World* (1968) is perhaps Lionni's most harmonious book. In this story, a small snail tells his father he would like to have "the biggest house in the world," and the father responds with the tale of a little snail whose shell grew and grew, with unexpected results. Lionni used preprinted paper to construct the bright and complex collages that illustrate the story. He is typical of the abstract expressionists in that, in each book, he experiments with new mediums and techniques, creating new textures suited to particular stories.

Ezra Jack Keats (1916-1983) uses oils and collage to create books which are both simple and sophisticated. His 1902 book, *The Snowy Day*, received the Caldecott Medal, and *Goggles!* (1969) was a Caldecott Honor Book. Keats employs textured and patterned materials, cutting with a simplicity of line and broadness of form. In his early books he used only collage, capturing the essense of shapes just as a small child might view things. As his main character, Peter, grows older, Keats supplements his collages with oils to lend more dimension to the scenes in his books. His heavy use of black line and swirling colors reflects the sense of turbulence Peter feels.

While those artists using collage techniques come to our attention partially because of their boldness in color, form, and texture, other abstract expressionists are equally worthy of note. Abstract expressionism allows for a free rein of the imagination, and Remy Charlip (1929-) is one artist who makes full use of this freedom. His illustrations for *Four Fur Feet* (1961) by Margaret Wise Brown is a masterpiece of design and play. In it he creates the abstraction of four fur feet walking around the world; the child must follow them by turning the book around. His illustrations make full use of the book as tool and the child's delight in participation.

To some extent abstract expressionism has become commonplace in children's book illustrations today, although the various techniques used continue to be striking. However, because of the prevalent feeling that the child needs a representation of reality and because children's books involve description and narration, the majority of books being published for children today are representational in their art.

At the same time that abstract expressionism was gaining wide use, representational artists were seeing new developments within their realm. An offshoot of comic book art, a subgenre of illustrative art, was emerging: the cartoon type of art seen in two major innovators, Walt Disney and Dr. Seuss (Theodor Seuss Geisel, 1904-). Over the years both the artwork of Disney and that of Dr. Seuss have settled into formula. The Walt Disney books and movies, James Steele Smith writes "are actually very canny compromises; they offer children many unusual, invented creatures like Cinderella's mouse horses, the fearsome witch, and the Disney squirrels, but in a world of quite conventional representation of conventional objects and experiences, all against a background of decorative abstractions...." Seuss's world, as is seen in *Horton Hatches the Egg* (1940), for example, or his very popular *The Cat in the Hat* (1957), is more fantastic and irrational than Disney's. Violent colors tend to dominate Seuss's drawings which are a frenzy of activity and movement. The art produced by the Walt Disney Studios and that of Dr. Seuss are completely predictable, and over the years there has been little change in either. This is not to say they lack appeal for children; children delight in the pastiche of a Disney book or movie, and in the ridiculous, mad antics of the Cat in the Hat. But the art of Disney and Seuss is the doggerel of children's book illustration.

At the opposite end of the scale, the "fine art" of representationalism was also influenced by the comic book. This is particularly true of one post-World War II artist without mention of whom any discussion of contemporary children's book illustration would be incomplete: Maurice Sendak (1928-).

"The good illustrator," Edward Ardizzone wrote in a 1958 *Motif* article, "does more than just make a pictorial comment on the written word. He produces a visual counterpoint which adds a third dimension to the book, making more vivid and understandable the author's intention." Perhaps more than any other contemporary artist, Maurice Sendak consistently achieves this counterpoint in both the books he has illustrated and in those for which he is both author and artist. Though Marcel Ayme's *The Wonderful Farm* (1951) was the first children's book Sendak illustrated, he first came to the attention of the children's book world with his whimsical one-color pictures for Ruth Krauss's *A Hole is to Dig* (1952). Following *A Hole is to Dig*, Sendak did line drawings for Meindert DeJong's *Shadrach* (1953), *Hurry Home, Candy* (1953), *The Wheel on the School* (1954), *The Little Cow and the Turtle* (1955), and *The House of Sixty Fathers* (1956). For Ruth Krauss's *Charlotte and the White Horse* (1955), Sendak began to work in color. Using an impressionistic technique, and line and color reminiscent of William Blake, Sendak gives a sense of the ethereal to this delicate story.

Charlotte and the White Horse is but one example of how Sendak, perhaps more than any other illustrator, adapts technique to subject matter, integrating text and art. Krauss's story calls for the fragile luminescence seen in Sendak's softened, glowing colors and gentle lines. In Janice May Udry's *The Moon Jumpers* (1959), Sendak employs pointillism and manipulates light and shadow to capture the moon's haunting qualities. With *The Griffin and the Minor Canon* (1963) by Frank R. Stockton, Sendak turns to caricature to interpret character and atmosphere for full comic effect.

By his concern for design and format, Sendak achieves a harmony between text and pictures. He is as excited by the *mise en pages* as he is with story interpretation. This is best seen in his own *Where The Wild Things Are* (1963) for which he received the Caldecott Medal in 1964. In this interpretation of a child's dream, Sendak arranges the text and pictures carefully, slowly drawing the reader into the child's world, "where the wild things are," and then safely bringing both the child and reader back to reality. By Sendak's own count, the story contains 384 words, and he arranges sentences, even punctuation, for the fullest effect:

The night Max wore his wolf suit and

made mischief of one kind

and another

his mother called him "Wild thing!"

and Max said "I'LL EAT YOU UP!"
so he was sent to bed without eating anything.

As Max becomes more and more involved in his
dream, the illustrations take up more and more
space in proportion to the text until the middle
of the book, which is also the middle of the
dream. There, an absence of text shows that Max
and the reader are wholly involved in the dream.
As the dream moves to its conclusion, this process is reversed, text returns, until, on the final
page, even Max is removed, and the text stands
without illustration, allowing the reader to return
to the reality of the world. Sendak combines the luminescence of color seen in *The Moon Jumpers*
and the cartoonlike caricature of figures seen in
The Griffin and the Minor Canon to create illustrations in *Where the Wild Things Are* that are both
stunning and comical.

While Sendak is perhaps the best-known artist in contemporary children's book illustration,
other artists show the same regard for the book
as a unity of text and art. Uri Shulevitz's (1935-)
Dawn (1974), the story of a boy and his grandfather awakening in early morning by a lake, combines abstract forms with an impressionistic use
of color to produce a strong, richly emotional
and pictorially beautiful book. On the other
hand, *The Fool of the World and the Flying Ship*
(1968) by Arthur Ransome, for which Shulevitz received the 1969 Caldecott Medal, is brilliant with
color and captures the style of the Russian background of the book.

Garth Williams (1912-) shares with Sendak
a superb gift of characterization and an ability to
sense what will delight the reader. He has a
warm, unaffected way of drawing pictures and
bringing characters to life. His almost human animals with their amazing facial expressions are in-
separable from their stories. One cannot imagine
E. B. White's *Stuart Little* (1945) or *Charlotte's Web*
without Williams's line drawings, and his cozy illustrations for Laura Ingalls Wilder's *Little House*
(1953) books, which Williams spent ten years making, bring the Ingalls family and the hardships of
the frontier to life for the reader.

Barbara Cooney (1917-) uses color to its

best effect to interpret mood and expand the
text. In her first color book, Lee Kingman's *Peter's Long Walk* (1953), she employs muted hues to
portray the New England countryside and a
child's long journey. Cooney's illustrations for *A
White Heron* (1963), by Sarah Orne Jewett, captures with beauty and intensity of detail the quiet
setting of Maine.

Today there are many notable artists–Steven
Kellogg, James Marshall, Trina Schart Hyman,
William Steig, Richard Scarry among them–who
deserve attention and whose work is immediately
recognizable. Yet one group of artists, illustrators
of informational and instructional books, are
often overlooked because their primary purpose
is to convey information, and art is secondary.
The artist is restricted to the text, but his job is
to try to achieve the same harmony of text and pictures that the fictional book illustrator strives for.

Although almost all the illustrators previously mentioned have illustrated informational
books at one time or another, there are a number of artists who have made this area their spe-
cialty. Dorothy Waugh, who started in the 1930s,
has produced a number of informational books
of high quality. Her *Warm Earth* (1943), for example, explains how the earth's nourishing elements
are formed. Her shaded pencil drawings of the
earth and of various fruits and flowers are mar-
vels of textures and pattern. She demonstrates
how effectively the informational illustrator can
use the freedom to select and emphasize detail,
to interpret and compose.

During the 1940s and 1950s, artists of informational books experimented with style and technique just as fictional illustrators did. The 1950s
saw the publication of the stylized, childlike illustrations of Leonard Kessler (1921-) in such
books as his *What's in a Line?* (1951) and John
Lewellen's *Tommy Learns to Fly* (1956). Detail and
humor characterize Kessler's illustrations which
combine wit with realism to effectively communicate information.

Just as the late 1950s and 1960s proved the
second Golden Age for picture books, so was it a
Golden Age for informational books; the experimentation of style and technique seen in the
work of fictional illustrators also appeared in informational illustrations. Helen Borton's (1930-)
illustrations for *The Moon Seems to Change* (1960)
by Franklyn M. Branley was one of many books
published during that time that demonstrated
the idea that informational books did not have to
be strictly realistic to teach or inform. Using ab-

ors, Borton's illustrations, as Barbara Bader points out, serve "less to clarify than to conjure up, to present images of glaring heat and deepest cold, of size and distance and want of life."

Books! (1962) by John Alcorn (1935-) also employs elements of abstraction. He uses printers' symbols and type as part of his illustrations. In *The Art of Art for Children's Books* Diana Klemin notes "Alcorn's startling color combinations of pink, yellow, and black in various shapes and forms, [make] the flat surfaces have that tempting quality of a cutout book."

Realistic art was not abandoned in the 1960s; rather it was enhanced by this new freedom to experiment. Anthony Ravielli (1916-) combines expert draftsmanship with an interest in format, arranging type on the page to create unity of text and art. Color combined with an impressionistic style makes the art of Joseph Low (1911-) outstanding and memorable. Artists were suddenly free to interpret their subjects rather than merely "showing" them, resulting in informational books that are truly beautiful.

Superior visual storytelling, whether of a fictional or nonfictional nature, has always been the goal of the children's book illustrator. But it can have its dangers. The goal of the illustrator is to achieve a unity of text and pictures. Sometimes, however, superior illustrations can hide literary merit or obscure inferior verbal storytelling. In evaluating the art of a children's book one must consider not only the aesthetics of technique, style, use of color, design and format, as one does in adult illustration, but also how well that art functions in relation to the text. The superior children's book is one that visually and verbally creates a memorable moment in the life of a child. Children's book illustration is a challenging task, but it offers unusual rewards in the effects it may have on its audience.

References:

May Hill Arbuthnot and Zena Sutherland, *Children and Books,* fourth edition (Glenview, Ill.: Scott, Foresman, 1972);

Barbara Bader, *American Picturebooks from Noah's Ark to the Beast Within* (New York: Macmillan/ London: Collier-Macmillan, 1976);

Patricia Cianciolo, *Illustrations in Children's Books* (Dubuque, Iowa: Brown, 1970);

Jean Poindexter Colby, *Writing, Illustrating and Editing Children's Books* (New York: Hastings, 1967);

Lee Kingman, Joanna Foster, and Ruth Giles Lontoft, *Illustrators of Children's Books, 1957-1966* (Boston: Horn Book, 1968);

Kingman, Grace Allen Hogarth, and Harriet Quimby, *Illustrators of Children's Books, 1967-1976* (Boston: Horn Book, 1978);

Diana Klemin, *The Art of Art for Children's Books* (New York: Potter, 1966);

Klemin, *The Illustrated Book, Its Art and Craft* (New York: Potter, 1970);

Cornelia Meigs and others, *A Critical History of Children's Literature* (New York: Macmillan, 1953);

Henry C. Pitz, *Illustrating Children's Books* (New York: Watson-Guptill, 1963);

James Steele Smith, *A Critical Approach to Children's Literature* (New York: McGraw-Hill, 1967).

Appendix

Children's Book Awards and Prizes

Children's Book Awards and Prizes

Before 1950 there were few book awards that a writer or an illustrator of a children's book could receive to indicate that he or she had created a significant work. Since 1950, and especially during the last twenty-five years, the number of these awards has increased dramatically. Currently, the scope of children's book awards and prizes established by state, national, and international professional organizations offers ample opportunity to underscore significant publishing for children by genre and type.

The following list provides the terms and recipients of the major awards that are given to authors or illustrators of books for children. For a complete list of children's book awards and prizes, the reader should consult Dolores Blythe Jones's *Children's Literature Awards and Winners: A Directory of Prizes, Authors, Illustrators* (Detroit: Gale Research, 1983), its supplement (1984), as well as the Children's Book Council's *Children's Books: Awards and Prizes* (New York: Children's Book Council, 1986). Both reference sources provide award terms and a list of award recipients. For an annual update of children's book award recipients, the reader should consult periodicals such as *Publishers Weekly*, *Horn Book*, and *Top of the News*.

HANS CHRISTIAN ANDERSEN AWARD

This international children's book award was established in 1956 by the International Board on Books for Young People (IBBY). A medal is awarded in the spring every two years to a living author and, since 1966, to a living illustrator who has made an important and lasting contribution to books for children. Each national section of IBBY nominates one author and one illustrator, and a committee of five, each from a different country, makes the final choice.

1956 Eleanor Farjeon (Great Britain)

1958 Astrid Lindgren (Sweden)

1960 Erich Kästner (Germany)

1962 Meindert DeJong (U.S.A.)

1964 René Guillot (France)

1966 Author: Tove Jansson (Finland)
Illustrator: Alois Carigiet (Switzerland)

1968 Authors: James Krüss (Germany); Jose Maria Sanchez-Silva (Spain)
Illustrator: Jiri Trnka (Czechoslovakia)

1970 Author: Gianni Rodari (Italy)
Illustrator: Maurice Sendak (U.S.A.)

1972 Author: Scott O'Dell (U.S.A.)
Illustrator: Ib Spang Olsen (Denmark)

1974 Author: Maria Gripe (Sweden)
Illustrator: Farshid Mesghali (Iran)

1976 Author: Cecil Bodker (Denmark)
Illustrator: Tatjana Mawrina (U.S.S.R.)

1978 Author: Paula Fox (U.S.A.)
Illustrator: Otto S. Svend (Denmark)

1980 Author: Bohumil Riha (Czechoslovakia)
Illustrator: Suekichi Akaba (Japan)

1982 Author: Lygia Gojunga Nunes (Brazil)
Illustrator: Zbigniew Rychlicki (Poland)

1984 Author: Christine Nostlinger (Austria)
Illustrator: Mitsumasa Anno (Japan)

1986 Author: Patricia Wrightson (Australia)
Illustrator: Robert Ingehen (Australia)

INTERNATIONAL BOARD ON BOOKS FOR YOUNG PEOPLE (IBBY) HONOR LIST

Biennially since 1956 the IBBY Honor List is announced at the time that the Hans Christian Andersen medal recipients are announced. Since 1974 each national section of IBBY has selected two books, one for text and one for illustration, published in a two-year period before the year of the award. Important considerations for honor list titles are that the books be representative of the best in children's literature from each country and that the books are recommended as suitable for publication throughout the world which supports the IBBY objective of encouraging world understanding through children's literature. In 1978 a third category was added for translator with at least one example of his or her work noted in the honor list.

A committee of the Association for Library Service to Children of the American Library Association selects the United States books. The list below includes United States honor list titles only.

1956 Jean Lee Latham for *Carry On, Mr. Bowditch* (Houghton Mifflin)
Katherine Shippen for *Men, Microscopes and Living Things* (Viking)
Marie Hall Ets for *Play With Me* (Viking)

1958 Meindert DeJong for *The House of Sixty Fathers* (Harper)

1960 Meindert DeJong for *Along Came a Dog* (Harper)
Elizabeth George Speare for *The Witch of Blackbird Pond* (Houghton Mifflin)

1962 Scott O'Dell for *Island of the Blue Dolphins* (Houghton Mifflin)

1964 Elizabeth George Speare for *The Bronze Bow* (Houghton Mifflin)

1966 Maurice Sendak for *Where the Wild Things Are* (Harper & Row)

1968 Aileen Fisher for *Valley of the Smallest* (Crowell)

1970 Irene Hunt for *Up a Road Slowly* (Follett)

1972 E. B. White for *Trumpet of the Swan* (Harper & Row)

1974 Author: Zilptha Keatley Snyder for *The Headless Cupid* (Atheneum)
Illustrator: Blair Lent for *The Funny Little Woman*, retold by Arlene Mosel (Dutton)

1976 Author: Virginia Hamilton for *M. C. Higgins, The Great* (Macmillan)

Illustrator: Uri Shulevitz for *Dawn* (Farrar, Straus & Giroux)

1978 Author: Natalie Babbit for *Tuck Everlasting* (Farrar, Straus & Giroux)
Illustrator: Margot Zemach for *Hush Little Baby* (Dutton)
Translator: Sheila La Farge for *Glassblower's Children*, by Maria Gripe (Delacorte/Lawrence)

1980 Author: Beverly Cleary for *Ramona and Her Father* (Morrow)
Illustrator: Peter Spier for his *Noah's Ark* (Doubleday)
Translator: Richard & Clara Winston for *The Magic Stone*, by Leonie Kooiker (Morrow)

1982 Author: Lois Lowry for *Autumn Street* (Houghton Mifflin)
Illustrator: Chris Van Allsburg for his *The Garden of Abdul Gasazi* (Houghton Mifflin)
Translator: Elizabeth Shub for her translations of books by Isaac Bashevis Singer, especially *Zlateh the Goat and Other Stories* (Harper & Row)

1984 Author: Joan Phipson for *The Watcher in the Garden* (Atheneum)
Illustrator: Pamela Allen for *Who Sank the Boat* (Putnam's)
Translator: No award.

1986 Author: Paula Fox for *One-Eyed Cat* (Bradbury)
Illustrator: Leo and Diane Dillon for *The People Could Fly: American Black Folktales* by Virginia Hamilton (Knopf)
Translator: Edward Fenton for translations of the works of Alki Zei, including *Wildcat Under Glass* (Holt)

BOSTON GLOBE-HORN BOOK AWARDS

Established in 1967 by the *Boston Globe* and *Horn Book*, these two awards, one for outstanding text and one for outstanding illustrations, were given through 1975. Beginning in 1976, three categories were established: outstanding fiction or poetry, outstanding nonfiction, and outstanding illustration. A $200 cash award is given to each recipient of the award. The awards are announced in the fall.

1967 Text: *The Little Fishes* by Erik Christian Haugaard (Houghton Mifflin)
Illustration: *London Bridge Is Falling Down* by Peter Spier (Doubleday)

1968 Text: *The Spring Rider* by John Lawson (Crowell)
Illustration: *Tikki Tikki Tembo* by Arlene Mosel, illustrated by Blair Lent (Holt, Rinehart & Winston)

1969 Text: *A Wizard of Earthsea* by Ursula K. Le Guin (Houghton Mifflin)
Illustration: *The Adventures of Paddy Pork* by John S. Goodall (Harcourt, Brace & World)

1970 Text: *The Intruder* by John Rowe Townsend (Lippincott)
Illustration: *Hi, Cat!* by Ezra Jack Keats (Macmillan)

1971 Text: *A Room Made of Windows* by Eleanor Cameron (Atlantic/Little, Brown)
Illustration: *If I Built a Village* by Kazue Mizumura (Crowell)

1972 Text: *Tristan and Iseult* by Rosemary Sutcliff (Dutton)
Illustration: *Mr. Gumpy's Outing* by John Burningham (Holt, Rinehart & Winston)

1973 Text: *The Dark Is Rising* by Susan Cooper (Atheneum)
Illustration: *King Stork* by Trina Schart Hyman (Little, Brown)

1974 Text: *M. C. Higgins: The Great* by Virginia Hamilton (Macmillan)
Illustration: *Jambo Means Hello* by Muriel Feelings, illustrated by Tom Feelings (Dial)

1975 Text: *Transport 7-41* by T. Degens (Viking)
Illustration: *Anno's Alphabet* by Mitsumasa Anno (Crowell)

1976 Fiction: *Unleaving* by Jill Paton Walsh (Farrar, Straus & Giroux)
Nonfiction: *Voyaging to Cathay: Americans in the China Trade* by Alfred Tamarin and Shirley Glubok (Viking)
Illustration: *Thirteen* by Remy Charlip and Jerry Joyner (Parents' Magazine Press)

1977 Fiction: *Child of the Owl* by Laurence Yep (Harper & Row)
Nonfiction: *Chance, Luck and Destiny* by Peter Dickinson (Atlantic/Little, Brown)
Illustration: *Granfa' Grig Had a Pig and Other Rhymes* by Wallace Tripp (Little, Brown)

1978 Fiction: *The Westing Game* by Ellen Raskin (Dutton)
Nonfiction: *Mischling, Second Degree: My Childhood in Nazi Germany* by Ilse Koehn (Greenwillow)
Illustration: *Anno's Journey* by Mitsumasa Anno (Philomel)

1979 Fiction: *Humbug Mountain* by Sid Fleischman (Atlantic/Little, Brown)
Nonfiction: *The Road from Home: The Story of an Armenian Girl* by David Kherdian (Greenwillow)
Illustration: *The Snowman* by Raymond Briggs (Random House)

1980 Fiction: *Conrad's War* by Andrew Davies (Crown)
Nonfiction: *Building: The Fight Against Gravity* by Mario Salvadori (Atheneum)
Illustration: *The Garden of Abdul Gasazi* by Chris Van Allsburg (Houghton Mifflin)

1981 Fiction: *The Leaving* by Lynn Hall (Scribners)
Nonfiction: *The Weaver's Gift* by Kathryn Lasky (Warne)
Illustration: *Outside Over There* by Maurice Sendak (Harper & Row)

1982 Fiction: *Playing Beatie Bow* by Ruth Park (Atheneum)
Nonfiction: *Upon the Head of the Goat: A Childhood in Hungary, 1939-1944* by Aranka Siegal (Farrar, Straus & Giroux)
Illustration: *A Visit to William Blake's Inn: Poems for Innocent and Experienced Travelers* by Nancy Willard, illustrated by Alice and Martin Provensen (Harcourt Brace Jovanovich)

1983 Fiction: *Sweet Whispers, Brother Rush* by Virginia Hamilton (Philomel)
Nonfiction: *Behind Barbed Wire: The Imprisonment of Japanese Americans During World War II* by Daniel S. Davis (Dutton)
Illustration: *A Chair for My Mother* by Vera B. Williams (Greenwillow)

1984 Fiction: *A Little Fear* by Patricia Wrightson (Atheneum)
Nonfiction: *The Double Life of Pocahontas* by Jean Fritz (Putnam's)
Illustration: *Jonah and the Great Fish* retold and illustrated by Warwick Hutton (Atheneum)

1985 Fiction: *The Moves Make the Man* by Bruce Brooks (Harper & Row)
Nonfiction: *Commodore Perry in the Land of the Shogun* by Rhoda Blumberg (Lothrop, Lee & Shepard)
Illustration: *Mama Don't Allow* by Thacher Hurd (Harper & Row)

1986 Fiction: *In Summer Light* by Zibby O'Neal (Viking Kestrel)
Illustration: *The Paper Crane* by Molly Bang (Greenwillow)
Nonfiction: *Auks, Rocks and the Odd Dinosaur: Inside Stories from the Smithsonian's Museum of Natural History* by Peggy Thompson (Crowell)

RANDOLPH CALDECOTT MEDAL

Awarded by the Association for Library Service to Children of the American Library Association since 1938, the medal is given for illustration of the most distinguished picture book for children published in the United States during the preceding year. Honor books may be selected. The award is limited to residents or citizens of the United States. The award is announced in January.

1938 *Animals of the Bible. A Picture Book* (Stokes)
Illustrator: Dorothy P. Lathrop
Compiler: Helen Dean Fish

Honor Books
Four and Twenty Blackbirds: Nursery Rhymes of Yesterday Recalled for Children of Today (Lippincott)
Illustrator: Robert Lawson
Compiler: Helen Dean Fish

Seven Simeons: A Russian Tale (Viking)
Author and Illustrator: Boris Artzybasheff

1939 *Mei Li* (Doubleday, Doran)
Author and Illustrator: Thomas Handforth

Honor Books
Andy and the Lion (Viking)
Author and Illustrator: James Daugherty

Barkis (Harper)
Author and Illustrator: Clare Turlay Newberry

The Forest Pool (Longmans, Green)
Author and Illustrator: Laura Adams Armer

Snow White and the Seven Dwarfs (Coward-McCann)
Translator and Illustrator: Wanda Gág

Wee Gillis (Viking)
Illustrator: Robert Lawson
Author: Munro Leaf

1940 *Abraham Lincoln* (Doubleday, Doran)
Authors and Illustrators: Edgar Parin and Ingri d'Aulaire

Honor Books
The Ageless Story With Its Antiphons (Dodd, Mead)
Author and Illustrator: Lauren Ford

Cock-a-Doodle Doo (Macmillan)
Authors and Illustrators: Elmer and Berta Hader

Madeline (Simon & Schuster)
Author and Illustrator: Ludwig Bemelmans

1941 *They Were Strong and Good* (Viking)
Author and Illustrator: Robert Lawson

Honor Books
April's Kittens (Harper)
Author and Illustrator: Clare Turlay Newberry

Nothing At All (Coward-McCann)
Author and Illustrator: Wanda Gág

Paddle-to-the-sea (Houghton Mifflin)
Author and Illustrator: Holling Clancy Holling

1942 *Make Way for Ducklings* (Viking)
Author and Illustrator: Robert McCloskey

Honor Books
An American ABC (Viking)
Authors and Illustrators: Maud and Miska Petersham

In My Mother's House (Viking)
Illustrator: Ann Nolan Clark
Author: Velino Herrera

1943 *The Little House* (Houghton Mifflin)
Author and Illustrator: Virginia Lee Burton

Honor Books
Dash and Dart (Viking)
Authors and Illustrators: Conrad and Mary Buff

Marshmallow (Harper)
Author and Illustrator: Clare Turlay Newberry

1944 *Many Moons* (Harcourt, Brace)
Illustrator: Louis Slobodkin
Author: James Thurber

Honor Books
A Child's Good Night Book (Scott)
Illustrator: Jean Charlot
Author: Margaret Wise Brown

Good Luck Horse (Whittlesey House)
Illustrator: Plato Chan
Author: Chih-Yi Chan

Mighty Hunter (Macmillan)
Authors and Illustrators: Elmer and Berta Hader

Pierre Pigeon (Houghton Mifflin)
Illustrator: Arnold Edwin Bare
Author: Lee Kingman

Small Rain: Verses from the Bible (Viking)
Illustrator: Elizabeth Orton Jones
Author: Jessie Horton Jones

1945 *Prayer for a Child* (Macmillan)
Illustrator: Elizabeth Orton Jones
Author: Rachel Field

Honor Books
The Christmas Anna Angel (Viking)
Illustrator: Kate Seredy
Author: Ruth Sawyer

In the Forest (Viking)
Author and Illustrator: Marie Hall Ets

Mother Goose (Oxford)
Compiler and Illustrator: Tasha Tudor

Yonie Wondernose (Doubleday, Doran)
Author and Illustrator: Marguerite de Angeli

1946 *The Rooster Crows* (Macmillan)
Authors and Illustrators: Maud and Miska Petersham

Honor Books
Little Lost Lamb (Doubleday, Doran)
Illustrator: Leonard Weisgard
Author: Golden MacDonald

My Mother is the Most Beautiful Woman in the World (Lothrop, Lee & Shepard)
Illustrator: Ruth C. Gannett
Author: Becky Reyher

Sing Mother Goose (Dutton)
Illustrator: Marjorie Torrey
Music by Opal Wheeler

You Can Write Chinese (Viking)
Author and Illustrator: Kurt Wiese

1947 *The Little Island* (Doubleday, Doran)
Illustrator: Leonard Weisgard
Author: Golden MacDonald

Honor Books
Boats on the River (Viking)
Illustrator: Jay Hyde Barnum
Author: Marjorie Flack

Pedro, the Angel of Olvera Street (Scribners)
Author and Illustrator: Leo Politi

Rain Drop Splash (Lothrop, Lee & Shepard)
Illustrator: Leonard Weisgard
Author: Alvin R. Tresselt

Sing in Praise: A Collection of Best Loved Hymns (Dutton)
Illustrator: Marjorie Torrey
Author: Opal Wheeler

Timothy Turtle (Welch)

Illustrator: Tony Palazzo
Author: Al Graham

1948 *White Snow, Bright Snow* (Lothrop, Lee & Shepard)
Illustrator: Roger Duvoisin
Author: Alvin Tresselt

Honor Books
Bambino the Clown (Viking)
Author and Illustrator: Georges Schreiber

McElligot's Pool (Random House)
Author and Illustrator: Dr. Seuss

Roger and the Fox (Doubleday)
Illustrator: Hildegard Woodward
Author: Lavinia R. Davis

Song of Robin Hood (Houghton Mifflin)
Illustrator: Virginia Lee Burton
Editor: Anne B. Malcolmson

Stone Soup (Scribners)
Author and Illustrator: Marcia Brown

1949 *The Big Snow* (Macmillan)
Authors and Illustrators: Elmer and Berta Hader

Honor Books
All around the Town (Lippincott)
Illustrator: Helen Stone
Author: Phyllis McGinley

Blueberries for Sal (Viking)
Author and Illustrator: Robert McCloskey

Fish in the Air (Viking)
Author and Illustrator: Kurt Weise

Juanita (Scribners)
Author and Illustrator: Leo Politi

1950 *Song of the Swallows* (Scribners)
Author and Illustrator: Leo Politi

Honor Books
America's Ethan Allen (Houghton Mifflin)
Illustrator: Lynd Ward
Author: Stewart Holbrook

Bartholomew and the Oobleck (Random House)
Author and Illustrator: Dr. Seuss

The Happy Day (Harper)
Illustrator: Marc Simont
Author: Ruth Krauss

Henry-Fisherman (Scribners)
Author and Illustrator: Marcia Brown

The Wild Birthday Cake (Doubleday)
Illustrator: Hildegard Woodward
Author: Lavinia R. Davis

1951 *The Egg Tree* (Scribners)
Author and Illustrator: Katherine Milhous

Honor Books
Dick Whittington and His Cat (Scribners)
Author and Illustrator: Marcia Brown

If I Ran the Zoo (Random House)
Author and Illustrator: Dr. Seuss

The Most Wonderful Doll in the World (Lippincott)
Illustrator: Helen Stone
Author: Phyllis McGinley

T-Bone, the Baby Sitter (Harper)
Author and Illustrator: Clare Turlay Newberry

The Two Reds (Harcourt, Brace)
Illustrator: Nicolas Mordvinoff
Author: William Lipkind

1952 *Finders Keepers* (Harcourt, Brace)
Illustrator: Nicolas Mordvinoff
Authors: William Lipkind and Nicolas Mordvinoff

Honor Books
All Falling Down (Harper)
Illustrator: Margaret Bloy Graham
Author: Gene Zion

Bear Party (Viking)
Author and Illustrator: William Pène Du Bois

Feather Mountain (Houghton Mifflin)
Author and Illustrator: Elizabeth Olds

Mr. T. W. Anthony Woo: the Story of a Cat and a Dog and a Mouse (Viking)

Author and Illustrator: Marie Hall Ets

Skipper John's Cook (Scribners)
Author and Illustrator: Marcia Brown

1953 *The Biggest Bear* (Houghton Mifflin)
Author and Illustrator: Lynd Ward

Honor Books
Ape in a Cape: An Alphabet of Odd Animals (Harcourt, Brace)
Author and Illustrator: Fritz Eichenberg

Five Little Monkeys (Houghton Mifflin)
Author and Illustrator: Juliet Kepes

One Morning in Maine (Viking)
Author and Illustrator: Robert McCloskey

Puss in Boots (Scribners)
Illustrator: Marcia Brown
Author: Charles Perrault

The Storm Book (Harper)
Illustrator: Margaret Bloy Graham
Author: Charlotte Zolotow

1954 *Madeline's Rescue* (Viking)
Author and Illustrator: Ludwig Bemelmans

Honor Books
Green Eyes (Capitol)
Author and Illustrator: Abe Birnbaum

Journey Cake, Ho! (Viking)
Illustrator: Robert McCloskey
Author: Ruth Sawyer

The Steadfast Tin Soldier (Scribners)
Illustrator: Marcia Brown
Author: Hans Christian Andersen

A Very Special House (Harper)
Illustrator: Maurice Sendak
Author: Ruth Krauss

When Will the World Be Mine? The Story of a Snowshoe Rabbit (Scott)
Illustrator: Jean Charlot
Author: Miriam Schlein

1955 *Cinderella; or, the Little Glass Slipper* (Scribners)
Illustrator: Marcia Brown
Author: Charles Perrault

Honor Books
Marguerite de Angeli's Book of Nursery and Mother Goose Rhymes (Doubleday)
Compiler and Illustrator: Marguerite de Angeli

The Thanksgiving Story (Scribners)
Illustrator: Helen Sewell
Author: Alice Dalgliesh

Wheel on the Chimney (Lippincott)
Illustrator: Tibor Gergely
Author: Margaret Wise Brown

1956 *Frog Went A-Courtin'* (Harcourt, Brace)
Illustrator: Feodor Rojankovsky
Author: John Langstaff

Honor Books
Crow Boy (Viking)
Author and Illustrator: Taro Yashima

Play With Me (Viking)
Author and Illustrator: Marie Hall Ets

1957 *A Tree is Nice* (Harper)
Illustrator: Marc Simont
Author: Janice May Udry

Honor Books
Anatole (Whittlesey House)
Illustrator: Paul Galdone
Author: Eve Titus

Gillespie and the Guards (Viking)
Illustrator: James Daugherty
Author: Benjamin Elkin

Lion (Viking)
Author and Illustrator: William Pène Du Bois

Mr. Penny's Race Horse (Viking)
Author and Illustrator: Marie Hall Ets

One is One (Oxford University Press)
Author and Illustrator: Tasha Tudor

1958 *Time of Wonder* (Viking)
Author and Illustrator: Robert McCloskey

Honor Books
Anatole and the Cat (Whittlesey House)

Illustrator: Paul Galdone
Author: Eve Titus

Fly High, Fly Low (Viking)
Author and Illustrator: Don Freeman

1959 *Chanticleer and the Fox* (Crowell)
Author and Illustrator: Barbara Cooney

Honor Books
The House That Jack Built: A Picture Book in Two Languages (Harcourt, Brace)
Author and Illustrator: Antonio Frasconi

Umbrella (Viking)
Author and Illustrator: Taro Yashima

What Do You Say, Dear? (Scott)
Illustrator: Maurice Sendak
Author: Sesyle Joslin

1960 *Nine Days to Christmas* (Viking)
Illustrator: Marie Hall Ets
Authors: Aurora Labastida and Marie Hall Ets

Honor Books
Houses from the Sea (Scribners)
Illustrator: Adrienne Adams
Author: Alice E. Goudey

The Moon Jumpers (Harper)
Illustrator: Maurice Sendak
Author: Janice May Udry

1961 *Baboushka and the Three Kings* (Parnassus)
Illustrator: Nicolas Sidjakov
Author: Ruth Robbins

Honor Book
Inch by Inch (Obolensky)
Author and Illustrator: Leo Lionni

1962 *Once a Mouse . . .* (Scribners)
Author and Illustrator: Marcia Brown

Honor Books
The Fox Went Out on a Chilly Night (Doubleday)
Author and Illustrator: Peter Spier

Little Bear's Visit (Harper & Row)
Illustrator: Maurice Sendak
Author: Else Holmelund Minarik

The Day We Saw the Sun Come Up (Scribners)
Illustrator: Adrienne Adams
Author: Alice E. Goudey

1963 *The Snowy Day* (Viking)
Author and Illustrator: Ezra Jack Keats

Honor Books
The Sun Is a Golden Earring (Holt, Rinehart & Winston)
Illustrator: Bernarda Bryson
Author: Natalia M. Belting

Mr. Rabbit and the Lovely Present (Harper & Row)
Illustrator: Maurice Sendak
Author: Charlotte Zolotow

1964 *Where the Wild Things Are* (Harper & Row)
Author and Illustrator: Maurice Sendak

Honor Books
Swimmy (Pantheon)
Author and Illustrator: Leo Lionni

All in the Morning Early (Holt, Rinehart & Winston)
Illustrator: Evaline Ness
Author: Sorche Nic Leodhas

Mother Goose and Nursery Rhymes (Atheneum)
Illustrator: Philip Reed

1965 *May I Bring a Friend?* (Atheneum)
Illustrator: Beni Montresor
Author: Beatrice Schenk de Regniers

Honor Books
Rain Makes Applesauce (Holiday House)
Illustrator: Marvin Bileck
Author: Julian Scheer

The Wave (Houghton Mifflin)
Illustrator: Blair Lent
Author: Margaret Hodges

A Pocketful of Cricket (Holt, Rinehart & Winston)
Illustrator: Evaline Ness
Author: Rebecca Caudill

1966 *Always Room for One More* (Holt, Rinehart & Winston)

Illustrator: Nonny Hogrogian
Author: Sorche Nic Leodhas

Honor Books
Hide and Seek Fog (Lothrop, Lee & Shepard)
Illustrator: Roger Duvoisin
Author: Alvin Tresselt

Just Me (Viking)
Author and Illustrator: Marie Hall Ets

Tom Tit Tot (Scribners)
Author and Illustrator: Evaline Ness

1967 *Sam, Bangs & Moonshine* (Holt, Rinehart & Winston)
Author and Illustrator: Evaline Ness

Honor Book
One Wide River to Cross (Prentice-Hall)
Illustrator: Ed Emberley
Author: Barbara Emberley

1968 *Drummer Hoff* (Prentice-Hall)
Illustrator: Ed Emberley
Author: Barbara Emberley

Honor Books
Frederick (Pantheon)
Author and Illustrator: Leo Lionni

Seashore Story (Viking)
Author and Illustrator: Taro Yashima

The Emperor and the Kite (World)
Illustrator: Ed Young
Author: Jane Yolen

1969 *The Fool of the World and the Flying Ship* (Farrar, Straus & Giroux)
Illustrator: Uri Shulevitz
Author: Arthur Ransome

Honor Book
Why the Sun and the Moon Live in the Sky (Houghton Mifflin)
Illustrator: Blair Lent
Author: Elphinstone Dayrell

1970 *Sylvester and the Magic Pebble* (Windmill)
Author and Illustrator: William Steig

Honor Books
Goggles! (Macmillan)

Author and Illustrator: Ezra Jack Keats

Alexander and the Wind-Up Mouse (Pantheon)
Author and Illustrator: Leo Lionni

Pop Corn & Ma Goodness (Viking)
Illustrator: Robert Andrew Parker
Author: Edna Mitchell Preston

Thy Friend, Obadiah (Viking)
Author and Illustrator: Brinton Turkle

The Judge (Farrar, Straus & Giroux)
Illustrator: Margot Zemach
Author: Harve Zemach

1971 *A Story—A Story* (Atheneum)
Author and Illustrator: Gail E. Haley

Honor Books
The Angry Moon (Atlantic/Little, Brown)
Illustrator: Blair Lent
Author: William Sleator

Frog and Toad Are Friends (Harper & Row)
Author and Illustrator: Arnold Lobel

In the Night Kitchen (Harper & Row)
Author and Illustrator: Maurice Sendak

1972 *One Fine Day* (Macmillan)
Author and Illustrator: Nonny Hogrogian

Honor Books
If All the Seas Were One Sea (Macmillan)
Author and Illustrator: Janina Domanska

Moja Means One: Swahili Counting Back (Dial)
Illustrator: Tom Feelings
Author: Muriel Feelings

Hildilid's Night (Macmillan)
Illustrator: Arnold Lobel
Author: Cheli Duran Ryan

1973 *The Funny Little Woman* (Dutton)
Illustrator: Blair Lent
Adaptor: Arlene Mosel

Honor Books
Anansi the Spider (Holt, Rinehart & Winston)
Adaptor and Illustrator: Gerald McDermott

Hosie's Alphabet (Viking)

Illustrator: Leonard Baskin
Authors: Hosea, Tobias, and Lisa Baskin

Snow-White and the Seven Dwarfs (Farrar, Straus & Giroux)
Illustrator: Nancy Ekholm Burkert
Translator: Randall Jarrell

When Clay Sings (Scribners)
Illustrator: Tom Bahti
Author: Byrd Baylor

1974 *Duffy and the Devil* (Farrar, Straus & Giroux)
Illustrator: Margot Zemach
Author: Harve Zemach

Honor Books
Three Jovial Huntsmen (Bradbury)
Author and Illustrator: Susan Jeffers

Cathedral: The Story of Its Construction (Houghton Mifflin)
Author and Illustrator: David Macaulay

1975 *Arrow to the Sun* (Viking)
Adaptor and Illustrator: Gerald McDermott

Honor Book
Jambo Means Hello (Dial)
Illustrator: Tom Feelings
Author: Muriel Feelings

1976 *Why Mosquitoes Buzz in People's Ears* (Dial)
Illustrators: Leo and Diane Dillon
Adaptor: Verna Aardenia

Honor Books
The Desert Is Theirs (Scribners)
Illustrator: Peter Parnall
Author: Byrd Baylor

Strega Nona (Prentice Hall)
Adaptor and Illustrator: Tomie dePaola

1977 *Ashanti to Zulu: African Traditions* (Dial)
Illustrators: Leo and Diane Dillon
Author: Margaret Musgrove

Honor Books
The Amazing Bone (Farrar, Straus & Giroux)
Author and Illustrator: William Steig

The Contest (Greenwillow)
Adaptor and Illustrator: Nonny Hogrogian

Fish for Supper (Dial)
Author and Illustrator: M. B. Goffstein

The Golem (Lippincott)
Author and Illustrator: Beverly Brodsky McDermott

Hawk, I'm Your Brother (Scribners)
Illustrator: Peter Parnall
Author: Byrd Baylor

1978 *Noah's Ark* (Doubleday)
Author and Illustrator: Peter Spier

Honor Books
Castle (Houghton Mifflin)
Author and Illustrator: David Macaulay

It Could Always Be Worse (Farrar, Straus & Giroux)
Adaptor and Illustrator: Margot Zemach

1979 *The Girl Who Loved Wild Horses* (Bradbury)
Author and Illustrator: Paul Goble

Honor Books
Freight Train (Greenwillow)
Author and Illustrator: Donald Crews

The Way to Start a Day (Scribners)
Illustrator: Peter Parnall
Author: Byrd Baylor

1980 *Ox-Cart Man* (Viking)
Illustrator: Barbara Cooney
Author: Donald Hall

Honor Books
Ben's Trumpet (Greenwillow)
Author and Illustrator: Rachel Isadora

The Garden of Abdul Gasazi (Houghton Mifflin)
Author and Illustrator: Chris Van Allsburg

1981 *Fables* (Harper & Row)
Author and Illustrator: Arnold Lobel

Honor Books
The Grey Lady and the Strawberry Snatcher (Four Winds)
Author and Illustrator: Molly Bang

Truck (Greenwillow)
Author and Illustrator: Donald Crews

Mice Twice (Atheneum)
Author and Illustrator: Joseph Low

The Bremen-Town Musicians (Doubleday)
Adaptor and Illustrator: Ilse Plume

1982 *Jumanji* (Houghton Mifflin)
Author and Illustrator: Chris Van Allsburg

Honor Books
Where the Buffaloes Begin (Warne)
Illustrator: Stephen Gammell
Author: Olaf Baker

On Market Street (Greenwillow)
Illustrator: Anita Lobel
Author: Arnold Lobel

Outside Over There (Harper & Row)
Author and Illustrator: Maurice Sendak

A Visit to William Blake's Inn (Harcourt Brace Jovanovich)
Illustrators: Alice and Martin Provensen
Author: Nancy Willard

1983 *Shadow* (Scribners)
Translator and Illustrator: Marcia Brown
Author: Blaise Cendrars

Honor Books
When I Was Young in the Mountains (Dutton)
Illustrator: Diane Goode
Author: Cynthia Rylant

A Chair for My Mother (Greenwillow)
Author and Illustrator: Vera B. Williams

1984 *The Glorious Flight: Across the Channel with Louis Blériot* (Viking)
Authors and Illustrators: Alice and Martin Provensen

Honor Books
Ten, Nine, Eight (Greenwillow)
Author and Illustrator: Molly Bang

Little Red Riding Hood (Holiday House)
Adaptor and Illustrator: Trina Schart Hyman

1985 *St. George and the Dragon* (Little, Brown)
Illustrator: Trina Schart Hyman
Adaptor: Margaret Hodges

Honor Books
Hansel and Gretel (Dodd)
Illustrator: Paul O. Zelinsky
Adaptor: Rika Lesser

Have You Seen My Duckling? (Greenwillow)
Author and Illustrator: Nancy Tafuri

The Story of Jumping Mouse (Lothrop, Lee & Shepard)
Author and Illustrator: John Steptoe

1986 *The Polar Express* (Houghton Mifflin)
Author and Illustrator: Chris Van Allsburg

Honor Books
The Relatives Came (Bradbury)
Illustrator: Stephen Gammell
Author: Cynthia Rylant

King Bidgood's in the Bathtub (Harcourt Brace Jovanovich)
Illustrator: Don Wood
Author: Audrey Wood

1987 *Hey, Al* (Farrar, Straus & Giroux)
Illustrator: Richard Egielski
Author: Arthur Yorinks

Honor Books
The Village of Round and Square Houses (Little, Brown)
Author and illustrator: Ann Grifalconi

Alphabatics (Bradbury)
Author and illustrator: Suse MacDonald

Rumpelstiltskin (Dalton)
Adaptor and illustrator: Paul O. Zelinsky

LEWIS CARROLL SHELF AWARDS

Given annually since 1958 by the University of Wisconsin School of Education, the award is made from books nominated by publishers from their lists that they consider worthy to sit on a shelf with *Alice in Wonderland*. The final selections, which may vary in number each year, are selected by a committee of librarians, teachers, parents, and writers. A Gold Cheshire Cat Seal is awarded to each book selected. The award was discontinued in 1980.

1958 *The Blue Cat of Castle Town* by Catherine Cate Coblentz (Longmans, Green, 1949)

Caps for Sale: A Tale of a Peddlar, Some Monkeys and Their Monkey Business by Esphyr Slobodkina (Scott, 1947)

Horton Hatches the Egg by Dr. Seuss (Random House, 1940)

The Little Bookroom: Eleanor Farjeon's Short Stories for Children Chosen by Herself by Eleanor Farjeon (Oxford University Press, 1955; Walck, 1956)

The Little Engine That Could by Watty Piper (Platt & Munk, 1930)

Little House in the Big Woods by Laura Ingalls Wilder (Harper, 1953)

Millions of Cats by Wanda Gág (Coward-McCann, 1928)

Mr. Popper's Penguins by Richard and Florence Atwater (Little, Brown, 1938)

Ol' Paul, the Mighty Logger by Glen Rounds (Holiday House, 1936)

Pecos Bill, the Greatest Cowboy of All Time by James Cloyd Bowman (Whitman, 1937)

Prayer for a Child by Rachel Field (Macmillan, 1944)

The Story of Doctor Dolittle by Hugh Lofting (Lippincott, 1920, 1948)

The Tale of Peter Rabbit by Beatrix Potter (Warne, 1903)

The Three Hundred and Ninety-Seventh White Elephant by Rene Guillot (Phillips, 1957)

The Wind in the Willows by Kenneth Grahame (Scribners, 1908)

The World of Pooh by A. A. Milne (Dutton, 1957)

1959 *Caddie Woodlawn* by Carol Ryrie Brink (Macmillan, 1935)

Charlotte's Web by E. B. White (Harper, 1952)

The Courage of Sarah Noble by Alice Dalgliesh (Scribners, 1954)

The Five Chinese Brothers by Claire H. Bishop (Coward-McCann, 1938)

LiLun, Lad of Courage by Carolyn Treffinger (Abingdon-Cokesbury, 1947)

The Little House by Virginia Lee Burton (Houghton Mifflin, 1942)

The "Minnow" Leads to Treasure by A. Philippa Pearce (World, 1958)

The Secret Garden by Frances Hodgson Burnett (Lippincott, 1911, 1938)

Snipp, Snapp, Snurr and the Red Shoes by Maj Lindman (Whitman, 1936)

The Story of Babar, the Little Elephant by Jean de Brunhoff (Random House, 1933)

The Boy Cody by Leon Wilson (Watts, 1950)

Tirra Lirra: Rhymes Old and New by Laura E. Richards (Little, Brown, 1902)

The White Stag by Kate Seredy (Viking, 1937)

1960 *Blind Colt* by Glen Rounds (Holiday House, 1941)

The Borrowers by Mary Norton (Harcourt, Brace, 1953)

Curious George Takes a Job by H. A. Rey (Houghton Mifflin, 1947)

Johnny Crow's Garden: A Picture Book by L. Leslie Brooke (Warne, 1903)

The Jungle Book by Rudyard Kipling (Doubleday, 1893, 1952)

Lavender's Blue by Kathleen Lines (Watts, 1954)

The Matchlock Gun by Walter D. Edmonds (Dodd, Mead, 1941)

Onion John by Joseph Q. Krumgold (Crowell, 1959)

Young Fu of the Upper Yangtze by Elizabeth Foreman Lewis (Winston, 1932)

1961 *And to Think That I Saw it on Mulberry Street* by Dr. Seuss (Vanguard, 1937)

Ben and Me by Robert Lawson (Little, Brown, 1939)

Blue Willow by Doris Gates (Viking, 1940)

The Door in the Wall: Story of Medieval London by Marguerite de Angeli (Doubleday, 1949)

Grishka and the Bear by Rene Guillot (Criterion, 1959)

Hitty, Her First Hundred Years by Rachel Field (Macmillan, 1929)

Island of the Blue Dolphins by Scott O'Dell (Houghton Mifflin, 1960)

The Moffats by Eleanor Estes (Harcourt, Brace, 1941)

Misty of Chincoteague by Marguerite Henry (Rand McNally, 1947)

A Roundabout Turn by Robert H. Charles (Warne, 1930)

When I Was a Boy by Erich Kastner (Watts, 1961)

1962 *The Adventures of Huckleberry Finn* by Samuel Clemens (Grosset, 1884, 1948)

The Dark Frigate by Charles Boardman Hawes (Atlantic, 1923; Little, Brown, 1934)

Daughter of the Mountains by Louise S. Rankin (Viking, 1948)

Inch by Inch by Leo Lionni (Obolensky, 1960)

The Lion, the Witch and the Wardrobe by C. S. Lewis (Macmillan, 1950)

Paddle-to-the-Sea by Holling Clancy Holling (Houghton Mifflin, 1941)

Padre Porko: The Gentlemanly Pig by Robert Davis (Holiday House, 1948)

A Penny a Day by Walter de la Mare (Knopf, 1925, 1960)

The Tailor of Gloucester by Beatrix Potter (Warne, 1903)

Thistle and Thyme: Tales and Legends from Scotland by Sorche Nic Leodhas (Holt, Rinehart & Winston, 1962)

Thumbelina by Hans Christian Andersen (Scribners, 1961)

Winter Danger by William O. Steele (Harcourt, Brace, 1954)

The World of Christopher Robin by A. A. Milne (Dutton, 1958)

1963 *Annuzza: A Girl of Romania* by Hertha Seuberlich (Rand McNally, 1962)

The Art of Ancient Egypt by Shirley Glubok (Atheneum, 1962)

The Cricket in Times Square by George Selden (Farrar, Straus & Cudahy, 1960)

Dwarf Long-nose by Wilhelm Hauff (Random House, 1960)

The Griffin and the Minor Canon by Frank R. Stockton (Holt, Rinehart & Winston, 1963)

Invincible Louisa: The Story of the Author of "Little Women" by Cornelia Meigs (Little, Brown, 1933, 1961)

The Man Who was Don Quixote: The Story of Miguel Cervantes by Rafaello Busoni (Prentice-Hall, 1958)

Moccasin Trail by Eloise J. McGraw (Coward-McCann, 1952)

Rabbit Hill by Robert Lawson (Viking, 1944, 1962)

The Reluctant Dragon by Kenneth Grahame (Holiday House, 1938, 1953)

The Superlative Horse by Jean Merrill (Scott, 1961)

Tom's Midnight Garden by A. Philippa Pearce (Oxford University Press, 1958; Lippincott, 1959)

Uncle Remus: His Songs and Sayings by Joel Chandler Harris (Hawthorn, 1880, 1921)

The Water Babies by Charles Kingsley (Watts, 1863, 1961)

The Wheel on the School by Meindert DeJong (Harper, 1954)

The Yearling by Marjorie Kinnan Rawlings (Scribners, 1939, 1961)

1964 *A Little Princess: Being the Whole Story of Sara Crewe Now Told for the First Time* by Frances Hodgson Burnett (Scribners, 1938)

Old Wind and Liu Li-San by Aline Glasgow (Harvey, 1962)

Rascal: A Memoir of a Better Era by Sterling North (Dutton, 1963)

Rifles for Watie by Harold Keith (Crowell, 1957)

Roller Skates by Ruth Sawyer (Viking, 1936)

Roosevelt Grady by Louisa R. Shotwell (World, 1963)

Where the Wild Things Are by Maurice Sendak (Harper & Row, 1963)

1965 *Bond of the Fire* by Anthony Fon Eisen (World, 1965)

The Cock, the Mouse and the Little Red Hen by Felicite LeFevre (Macrae, 1947)

Joel and the Wild Goose by Helga Sandburg (Dial, 1963)

My Side of the Mountain by Jean Craighead

George (Dutton, 1959)

The Nightingale by Hans Christian Andersen (Harper & Row, 1965)

The Pushcart War by Jean Merrill (Scott, 1964)

The Return of the Twelves by Pauline Clarke (Coward-McCann, 1963)

Smoky, the Cowhorse by Will James (Scribners, 1926)

The Story about Ping by Marjorie Flack (Viking, 1933)

The Wolves of Willoughby Chase by Joan Aiken (Doubleday, 1963)

A Wrinkle in Time by Madeleine L'Engle (Farrar, Strauss, 1962)

1966 *Across Five Aprils* by Irene Hunt (Follett, 1964)

Banner in the Sky: the Story of a Boy and a Mountain by James Ramsey Ullman (Lippincott, 1954)

A Child's Garden of Verses by Robert Louis Stevenson (Watts, 1966)

An Edge of the Forest by Agnes Smith (Viking, 1959)

Jed: The Story of a Yankee Soldier and a Southern Boy by Peter Burchard (Coward-McCann, 1960)

Once a Mouse by Marcia Brown (Scribners, 1961)

Papa Pellerin's Daughter by Maria Gripe (Day, 1966)

1967 *More Just So Stories* (phonodisc) by Rudyard Kipling (Caedmon 1205)

Tom Sawyer (phonodisc) by Samuel Clemens (Caedmon 1088)

1968 *The Ark* by Margot Benary-Isbert (Harcourt, Brace, 1953)

Drummer Hoff adapted by Barbara Emberley (Prentice-Hall, 1967)

Earthfasts by William Mayne (Dutton, 1966)

The Emperor and the Kite by Jane Yolen (Collins-World, 1967)

The Fiddler of High Lonesome by Brinton Turkle (Viking, 1968)

From the Mixed-up Files of Mrs. Basil E. Frankweiler by E. L. Konigsburg (Atheneum, 1967)

The Hunter I Might Have Been by George Mendoza (Astor-Honor, 1968)

My Father's Dragon by Ruth Stiles Gannett (Random House, 1948)

No Room: An Old Story Retold by Rose Dobbs (McKay, 1944)

Reflections on a Gift of Watermelon Pickle and Other Modern Verse by Edward Lueders (Lothrop, Lee & Shepard, 1966)

The Wizard of Oz by L. Frank Baum (Reilly & Lee, 1956)

1969 *The Children of Green Knowe* by L. M. Boston (Faber, 1954; Harcourt, Brace, 1955)

Constance: A Story of Early Plymouth by Patricia Clapp (Lothrop, Lee & Shepard, 1968)

Edge of Two Worlds by Weyman Jones (Dial, 1968)

Little Toot by Hardie Gramatky (Putnam's, 1939)

Little Women by Louisa May Alcott (Little, Brown, 1868, 1968)

McBroom Tells the Truth by Sid Fleischman (Norton, 1966)

Seventeenth Summer by Maureen Daly (Dodd, Mead, 1942, 1962)

The Story of Comock the Eskimo as Told to Robert Flaherty (Simon & Schuster, 1968)

The Storyteller's Pack by Frank R. Stockton (Scribners, 1968)

Usha the Mouse Maiden written by Mehlli Gobhai (Hawthorn, 1969)

Wild Horses of the Red Desert by Glen Rounds (Holiday House, 1969)

1970 *The Animal Family* by Randall Jarrell (Pantheon, 1965)

The Cay by Theodore Taylor (Doubleday, 1969)

The Egypt Game by Zilpha Keatley Snyder (Atheneum, 1967)

The Enormous Egg by Oliver Butterworth (Little, Brown, 1956)

Gautama Buddha, in Life and Legend by Betty Kelen (Lothrop, Lee & Shepard, 1967)

Gone-away Lake by Elizabeth Enright (Harcourt, Brace, 1957)

A Herd of Deer by Ellis Dillon (Funk & Wagnall, 1969)

Honk the Moose by Phil Stong (Dodd, Mead, 1935)

The Midnight Fox by Betsy Byars (Viking, 1968)

Old Ben by Jesse Stuart (McGraw-Hill, 1970)

Otto of the Silver Hand by Howard Pyle (Scribners, 1954)

Sounder by William H. Armstrong (Harper & Row, 1969)

The Summer I was Lost by Phillip Viereck (Day, 1965)

To Be a Slave by Julius Lester (Dial, 1968)

The Tomten by Astrid Lindgren (Coward-McCann, 1961)

The Weirdstone of Brisingamen and a Tale of

Alderly by Alan Garner (Walck, 1969)

1971 *Boy Alone* by Reginald Ottley (Harcourt, Brace & World, 1966)

Down, Down the Mountain by Ellis Credle (Nelson, 1934, 1961)

The Endless Steppe: Growing Up in Siberia by Esther Hautzig (Crowell, 1968)

Farmer Hoo and the Baboons by Ida Chittum (Delacorte, 1971)

The Incredible Journey: A Tale of Three Animals by Sheila Burnford (Little, Brown, 1961)

Journey Outside by Mary Q. Steele (Viking, 1969)

Lift Every Voice and Sing: Words and Music by J. Rosamund and James Weldon Johnson (Hawthorn, 1970)

The Nonsense Book compiled by Duncan Emrich (Four Winds, 1970)

The Soul Brothers and Sister Lou by Kristin Hunter (Scribners, 1968)

Undine by Friedrich de la Motte Fouque (Simon & Schuster, 1957, 1971)

The Velveteen Rabbit: Or How Toys Become Real by Margery Williams (Doubleday, 1958)

The Witch's Brat by Rosemary Sutcliff (Walck, 1970)

1972 *The Art and Industry of Sandcastles* by Jan Adkins (Walker, 1971)

Bear Circus by William Pène du Bois (Viking, 1971)

Ceremony of Innocence by James Forman (Hawthorn, 1970)

The Diary of Nina Kosterina by Nina Kosterina (Crown, 1968)

Dorp Dead by Julia Cunningham (Pantheon, 1965)

The Duchess Bakes a Cake by Virginia Kahl (Scribners, 1955)

Emmet Otter's Jug-Band Christmas by Russell Hoban (Parents Magazine Press, 1971)

The Forgotten Door by Alexander Key (Westminster, 1965)

The Hawkstone by Jay A. Williams (Walck, 1971)

The Little Old Woman Who Used Her Head by Hope Newell (Nelson, 1935, 1966)

Long Journey Home: Stories from Black History by Julius Lester (Dial, 1972)

Mrs. Frisby and the Rats of Nimh by Robert C. O'Brien (Atheneum, 1971)

The Planet of Junior Brown by Virginia Hamilton (Macmillan, 1971)

Simon Boom Gives a Wedding by Yuri Suhl (Four Winds, 1972)

1973 *Anansi the Spider: A Tale From the Ashanti* by Gerald McDermott (Holt, Rinehart & Winston, 1972)

Cockleburr Quarters by Charlotte Baker (Prentice-Hall, 1972)

Four Women in a Violent Time by Deborah Crawford (Crown, 1970)

The Girl Who Loved the Wind by Jane Yolen (Crowell, 1972)

Jack Tar by Jean Russell Larson (Macrae, 1970)

The Knee-high Man and Other Tales by Julius Lester (Dial, 1972)

Little Tim and the Brave Sea Captain by Edward Ardizzone (Walck, 1955)

North to Freedom by Anne S. Holm (Harcourt, Brace & World, 1965)

Pippi Longstocking by Astrid Lindgren (Viking, 1950)

The Runaway's Diary by Marilyn Harris (Four Winds, 1971)

The Silver Pony by Lynd Ward (Houghton Mifflin, 1973)

Snow White and the Seven Dwarfs by Jacob and Wilhelm Grimm (Farrar, Straus & Giroux, 1972)

The Stolen Pony by Glen Rounds (Holiday House, 1948, 1969)

1974 No Awards

1975 *Dust of the Earth* by Bill and Vera Cleaver (Lippincott, 1975)

A Hero Ain't Nothin' but a Sandwich by Alice Childress (Coward, McCann & Geoghegan, 1973)

The Pig-tale by Lewis Carroll (Little, Brown, 1889, 1975)

1976 *The Day the Circus Came to Lone Tree* by Glen Rounds (Holiday House, 1973)

Don't take Teddy by Babbis Friis-Baastad (Scribners, 1967)

Duffy and the Devil by Harve Zemach (Farrar, Straus & Giroux, 1973)

M. C. Higgins, the Great by Virginia Hamilton (Macmillan, 1974)

Saturday, the Twelfth of October by Norma Fox Mazer (Delacorte, 1975)

1977 *Abel's Island* by William Steig (Farrar, Straus & Giroux, 1976)

Sailing to Cythera and Other Anatole Stories by Nancy Willard (Harcourt Brace Jovanovich, 1974)

Slake's Limbo by Felice Holman (Scribners, 1974)

1978 *Bridge to Terabithia* by Katherine Paterson (Crowell, 1977)

Come to the Edge by Julia Cunningham (Pantheon, 1977)

Dear Bill, Remember Me? and Other Stories by Norma Fox Mazer (Delacorte, 1976)

Manya's Story by Bettyanne Gray (Lerner, 1978)

Mischling, Second Degree: My Childhood in Nazi Germany by Ilse Koehn (Greenwillow, 1977)

Mr. Yowder and the Giant Bull Snake by Glen Rounds (Holiday House, 1978)

Noah's Ark by Peter Spier (Doubleday, 1977)

The No-Return Trail by Sonia Levitin (Harcourt Brace Jovanovich, 1978)

Stevie by John Steptoe (Harper & Row, 1969)

Sylvester and the Magic Pebble by William Steig (Windmill/Simon & Schuster, 1969)

Tuck Everlasting by Natalie Babbitt (Farrar, Straus & Giroux, 1975)

Who's in Rabbit's House?: a Masai tale by Verna Aardema (Dial, 1977)

1979 *The Chocolate War* by Robert Cormier (Pantheon, 1974; Dell, 1975)

Dragonwings by Laurence Yep (Harper & Row, 1975)

The Island of the Grass King: The Further Adventures of Anatole by Nancy Willard (Harcourt Brace Jovanovich, 1979)

Lyle, Lyle, Crocodile by Bernard Waber (Houghton Mifflin, 1965)

The Road from Home: The Story of an Armenian Girl by David Kherdian (Greenwillow, 1979)

The Snowman by Raymond Briggs (Random House, 1978)

The Wizard of Earthsea by Ursula K. LeGuin (Parnassus, 1968)

INTERNATIONAL READING ASSOCIATION CHILDREN'S BOOK AWARD

Sponsored by the Institute for Reading Research, the award, first given in 1975, is administered by the International Reading Association. The award is given annually for a book, published in the preceding year, written by an author "who shows unusual promise in the children's book field." Beginning in 1987 two categories are noted: young adult and primary. Books originating in any country are eligible. The award is announced in the spring of each year and each recipient receives a cash award of $1000.

1975 *Transport 7-41-R* by T. Degens (Viking)

1976 *Dragonwings* by Laurence Yep (Harper & Row)

1977 *A String in the Harp* by Nancy Bond (Atheneum)

1978 *A Summer to Die* by Lois Lowry (Houghton Mifflin)

1979 *Reserved for Mark Anthony Crowder* by Alison Smith (Dutton)

1980 *Words by Heart* by Ouida Sebestyen (Atlantic/Little, Brown)

1981 *My Own Private Sky* by Delores Beckman (Dutton)

1982 *Good Night, Mr. Tom* by Michelle Magorian (Harper & Row)

1983 *The Darkangel* by Meredith Ann Pierce (Atlantic/Little, Brown)

1984 *Ratha's Creature* by Clare Bell (Atheneum)

1985 *Badger on the Barge* by Janni Howker (Greenwillow)

1986 *Prairie Songs* by Pam Conrad (Harper & Row)

1987 Young Adult: *After the Dancing Days* by Margaret I. Rostkowski (Harper & Row)
Primary: *The Line up Book* by Marisabina Russo (Greenwillow)

CORETTA SCOTT KING AWARD

Established in 1970 by the Social Responsibilities Roundtable of the American Library Association, the award is "designed to commemorate and foster the life, works and dreams of the late Dr. Martin Luther King, Jr. and to honor Mrs. Coretta Scott King for her courage and determination to work for peace and world brotherhood." The award is given annually to an author, and, since 1979, to an illustrator for an outstanding contribution designed to promote a better understanding and appreciation of the culture and contribution of all peoples to life in America. The award is announced in January.

1970 Author: Lillie Patterson for *Martin Luther King, Jr. Man of Peace* (Garrard)

1971 Author: Charlemae Rollins for *Black Troubador: Langston Hughes* (Rand McNally)

1972 Author: Elton C. Fax for *17 Black Artists* (Dodd, Mead)

1973 Author: Jackie Robinson as told to Alfred Duckett for *I Never Had It Made* (Putnam's)

1974 Author: Sharon Bell Mathis for *Ray Charles* (Crowell)

1975 Author: Dorothy Robinson for *The Legend of Africania* (Johnson)

1976 Author: Pearl Bailey for *Duey's Tale* (Harcourt Brace Jovanovich)

1977 Author: James Haskins for *The Story of Stevie Wonder* (Lothrop, Lee & Shepard)

1978 Author: Eloise Greenfield for *Africa Dream* (Day/Crowell)

1979 Author: Ossie Davis for *Escape to Freedom* (Viking)
Illustrator: Tom Feelings for *Something On My Mind* by Nikki Grimes (Dial)

1980 Author: Walter Dean Myers for *The Young Landlords* (Viking)
Illustrator: Carole Bayard for *Cornrows* by Camille Yarbrough (Coward, McCann & Geoghegan)

1981 Author: Sidney Poitier for *This Life* (Knopf)
Illustrator: Ashley Bryan for his *Beat the Story-Drum, Pum-Pum* (Atheneum)

1982 Author: Mildred D. Taylor for *Let the Circle Be Unbroken* (Dial)
Illustrator: John Steptoe for *Mother Crocodile* by Birago Diop, translated and adapted by Rosa Guy (Delacorte)

1983 Author: Virginia Hamilton for *Sweet Whispers, Brother Rush* (Philomel)
Illustrator: Peter Magubane for his *Black Child* (Knopf)

1984 Author: Lucille Clifton for *Everett Anderson's Goodbye* (Holt, Rinehart & Winston)
Illustrator: Pat Cummings for *My Mama Needs Me* by Mildred P. Walter (Lothrop, Lee & Shepard)

1985 Author: Walter Dean Myers for *Motown and Didi* (Viking)
Illustrator: None

1986 Author: Virginia Hamilton for *The People Could Fly: American Black Folktales* (Knopf)
Illustrator: Jerry Pinkney for *Patchwork Quilt* by Valerie Flournoy (Dial)

1987 Author: Mildred Pitts Walter for *Justin and the Best Biscuits in the World* (Lothrop, Lee & Shepard)
Illustrator: Jerry Pinckney for *Half a Moon and One Whole Star* by Crescent Dragonwagon (Macmillan)

NATIONAL BOOK AWARD/ AMERICAN BOOK AWARD

The National Book Award program was established in 1950 and operated through 1979 when it was replaced by the American Book Award. From 1969 until 1979 a children's book prize was incorporated in the award system. The $1000 cash award, contributed by the Children's Book Council and administered by the National Book Committee, was presented annually to a juvenile book judged by a panel of experts to be the most distinguished written by an American citizen and published in the United States during the preceding year.

1969 *Journey from Peppermint Street* by Meindert DeJong (Harper & Row)

1970 *A Day of Pleasure: Stories of a Boy Growing Up in Warsaw* by Isaac Bashevis Singer (Farrar, Straus & Giroux)

1971 *The Marvelous Misadventures of Sebastian* by Lloyd Alexander (Dutton)

1972 *The Slightly Irregular Fire Engine* by Donald Barthelme (Farrar, Straus & Giroux)

1973 *The Farthest Shore* by Ursula K. Le Guin (Atheneum)

1974 *The Court of the Stone Children* by Eleanor Cameron (Dutton)

1975 *M. C. Higgins, the Great* by Virginia Hamilton (Macmillan)

1976 *Bert Breen's Barn* by Walter D. Edmonds (Little, Brown)

1977 *The Master Puppeteer* by Katherine Paterson (Crowell)

1978 *The View from the Oak* by Judith and Herbert Kohl (Sierra Club/Scribners)

1979 *The Great Gilly Hopkins* by Katherine Paterson (Crowell)

This award was discontinued in 1979 and replaced by the American Book Award.

AMERICAN BOOK AWARD

1980 Hardcover: *A Gathering of Days: A New England Girl's Journal, 1830-32* by Joan W. Blos (Scribners)
Paperback: *A Swiftly Tilting Planet* by Madeleine L'Engle (Dell)

1981 Fiction:
Hardcover: *The Night Swimmers* by Betsy Byars (Delacorte)
Paperback: *Ramona and Her Mother* by Beverly Cleary (Dell)
Nonfiction: *Oh, Boy! Babies!* by Alison Cragin Herzig and Jane Lawrence Mali (Little, Brown)

1982 Fiction:
Hardcover: *Westmark* by Lloyd Alexander (Dutton)
Paperback: *Words by Heart* by Ouida Sebestyen (Bantam)
Nonfiction: *A Penguin Year* by Susan Bonners (Delacorte)
Picture Books:
Hardcover: *Outside Over There* by Maurice Sendak (Harper & Row)
Paperback: *Noah's Ark* by Peter Spier (Zephyr Books/Doubleday)

1983 Fiction:
Hardcover: *Homesick: My Own Story* by Jean Fritz (Putnam's)
Paperback: *A Place Apart* by Paula Fox (Signet/NAL); *Marked by Fire* by Joyce Carol Thomas (Avon Flare)
Nonfiction: *Chimney Sweeps* by James Cross Giblin (Crowell)
Picture Books:
Hardcover: *Miss Rumphius* by Barbara Cooney (Viking) *Doctor De Soto* by William Steig (Farrar)
Paperback: *A House Is a House for Me* by Mary Ann Hoberman (Viking)

The children's book section of the American Book Award was discontinued after the 1983 award.

JOHN NEWBERY MEDAL

Established in 1922, the Newbery Medal is given by the Association for Library Service to Children of the American Library Association to the author of the most distinguished contribution to American literature for children published during the preceding year. Honor books may be selected. The award is limited to residents or citizens of the United States. The award is announced in January.

1922 *The Story of Mankind* by Hendrik Willem Van Loon (Boni & Liveright)

Honor Books
Cedric the Forester by Bernard G. Marshall (Appleton)

The Golden Fleece and the Heroes Who Lived Before Achilles by Padraic Colum (Macmillan)

The Great Quest: A Romance of 1826 by Charles Boardman Hawes (Little, Brown)

The Old Tobacco Shop: A True Account of What Befell a Little Boy in Search of Adventure by William Bowen (Macmillan)

Windy Hill by Cornelia Meigs (Macmillan)

1923 *The Voyages of Doctor Dolittle* by Hugh Lofting (Stokes)

1924 *The Dark Frigate* by Charles Boardman Hawes (Atlantic Monthly Press)

1925 *Tales from Silver Lands* by Charles J. Finger (Macmillan)

Honor Books
Dream Coach by Dillwyn and Anne Parrish (Macmillan)

Nicholas: A Manhattan Christmas Story by Anne Carroll Moore (Putnam's)

1926 *Shen of the Sea: A Book for Children* by Arthur Bowie Chrisman (Dutton)

Honor Book
The Voyagers: Being Legends and Romances of Atlantic Discovery by Padraic Colum (Macmillan)

1927 *Smoky, the Cowhorse* by Will James (Scribners)

1928 *Gay-neck: The Story of a Pigeon* by Dham Gopal Mukerji (Dutton)

Honor Books
Downright Dencey by Caroline Dale Snedeker (Doubleday)

The Wonder-Smith and His Son: A Tale from the Golden Childhood of the World by Ella Young (Longmans, Green)

1929 *Trumpeter of Krakow* by Eric P. Kelly (Macmillan)

Honor Books
The Boy Who Was by Grace T. Hallock (Dutton)

Clearing Weather by Cornelia Meigs (Little, Brown)

Millions of Cats by Wanda Gág (Coward-McCann)

The Pigtail of Ah Lee Ben Loo with Seventeen Other Laughable Tales and 200 Comic Silhouettes by John Bennett (Longmans)

The Runaway Papoose by Grace P. Moon (Doubleday)

Tod, of the Fens by Elinor Whitney (Macmillan)

1930 *Hitty, Her First Hundred Years* by Rachel Field (Macmillan)

Honor Books
A Daughter of the Seine: The Life of Madame Roland by Jeanette Eaton (Harper)

Jumping-off Place by Marian Hurd McNeely (Longmans, Green)

Little Blacknose: The Story of a Pioneer by Hildegarde Swift (Harcourt, Brace)

Pran of Albania by Elizabeth C. Miller (Doubleday, Doran)

Tangle-Coated Horse and Other Tales: Episodes from the Fionn Saga by Ella Young (Longmans, Green)

Vaino, A boy of New Finland by Julia Davis (Dutton)

1931 *The Cat Who Went to Heaven* by Elizabeth Coatsworth (Macmillan)

Honor Books
The Dark Star of Itza by Alida Malkus (Harcourt, Brace)

Floating Island by Anne Parrish (Harper)

Garram the Hunter: A Boy of the Hill Tribes by Herbert Best (Doubleday, Doran)

Meggy MacIntosh by Elizabeth Janet Gray (Doubleday, Doran)

Mountains Are Free by Julia Davis Adams (Dutton)

Ood-Le Yn Uk the Wanderer by Alice Lide and Margaret Johansen (Little, Brown)

Queer Person by Ralph Hubbard (Doubleday, Doran)

Spice and the Devil's Cave by Agnes D. Hewes (Knopf)

1932 *Waterless Mountain* by Laura Adams Armer (Longmans, Green)

Honor Books
Boy of the South Seas by Eunice Tietjens (Coward-McCann)

Calico Bush by Rachel Field (Macmillan)

The Fairy Circus by Dorothy P. Lathrop (Macmillan)

Jane's Island by Marjorie Hill Allee (Houghton Mifflin)

Out of the Flame by Eloise Lownsbery (Longmans, Green)

Truce of the Wolf and Other Tales of Old Italy by Mary Gould Davis (Harcourt, Brace)

1933 *Young Fu of the Upper Yangtze* by Elizabeth Foreman Lewis (Winston)

Honor Books
Children of the Soil: a Story of Scandinavia by Nora Burglon (Doubleday, Doran)

The Railroad to Freedom: a Story of the Civil War by Hildegarde Swift (Harcourt, Brace)

Swift Rivers by Cornelia Meigs (Little, Brown)

1934 *Invincible Louisa: the Story of the Author of "Little Women"* by Cornelia Meigs (Little, Brown)

Honor Books
ABC Bunny by Wanda Gág (Coward-McCann)

Apprentices of Florence by Anne Kyle (Houghton Mifflin)

Big Tree of Bunlahy: Stories of My Own Countryside by Padraic Colum (Macmillan)

Forgotten Daughter by Caroline Dale Snedeker (Doubleday, Doran)

Glory of the Seas by Agnes Hewes (Knopf)

New Land by Sarah L. Schmidt (McBride)

Swords of Steel: the Story of a Gettysburg Boy by Elsie Singmaster (Houghton Mifflin)

Winged Girl of Knossos by Erick Berry (Appleton)

1935 *Dobry* by Monica Shannon (Viking)

Honor Books

Davy Crockett by Constance Rourke (Harcourt, Brace)

A Day on Skates: the Story of a Dutch Picnic by Hilda Van Stockum (Harper)

The Pageant of Chinese History by Elizabeth Seeger (Longmans, Green)

1936 *Caddie Woodlawn* by Carol Ryrie Brink (Macmillan)

Honor Books

All Sail Set: a Romance of the "Flying Cloud" by Armstrong Sperry (Winston)

The Good Master by Kate Seredy (Viking)

Honk the Moose by Phil Stong (Dodd, Mead)

Young Walter Scott by Elizabeth Janet Gray (Viking)

1937 *Roller Skates* by Ruth Sawyer (Viking)

Honor Books

Audubon by Constance M. Rourke (Harcourt, Brace)

The Codfish Musket by Agnes D. Hewes (Doubleday, Doran)

The Golden Basket by Ludwig Bemelmans (Viking)

Phebe Fairchild: Her Book by Lois Lenski (Lippincott)

Whistler's Van by Idwal Jones (Viking)

Winterbound by Margery Bianco (Viking)

1938 *The White Stag* by Kate Seredy (Viking)

Honor Books

Bright Island by Mabel L. Robinson (Random House)

On the Banks of Plum Creek by Laura Ingalls Wilder (Harper)

Pecos Bill: the Greatest Cowboy of All Time by James Cloyd Bowman (Whitman)

1939 *Thimble Summer* by Elizabeth Enright (Farrar & Rinehart)

Honor Books

Leader by Destiny: George Washington, Man and Patriot by Jeanette Eaton (Harcourt, Brace)

Mr. Popper's Penguins by Richard and Florence Atwater (Little, Brown)

Nino by Valenti Angelo (Viking)

Penn by Elizabeth Janet Gray (Viking)

1940 *Daniel Boone* by James H. Daugherty (Viking)

Honor Books

Boy with a Pack by Stephen W. Meader (Harcourt, Brace)

By the Shores of Silver Lake by Laura Ingalls Wilder (Harper)

Runners of the Mountain Tops: the Life of Louis Agassiz by Mabel L. Robinson (Random House)

The Singing Tree by Kate Seredy (Viking)

1941 *Call It Courage* by Armstrong Sperry (Macmillan)

Honor Books

Blue Willow by Doris Gates (Viking)

The Long Winter by Laura Ingalls Wilder (Harper)

Nansen by Anna Gertrude Hall (Viking)

Young Mac of Fort Vancouver by Mary Jane Carr (Crowell)

1942 *The Matchlock Gun* by Walter D. Edmonds (Dodd, Mead)

Honor Books
Down Ryton Water by Eva Roe Gaggin (Viking)

George Washington's World by Genevieve Foster (Scribners)

Indian Captive: the Story of Mary Jemison by Lois Lenski (Stokes)

Little Town on the Prairie by Laura Ingalls Wilder (Harper)

1943 *Adam of the Road* by Elizabeth Janet Gray (Viking)

Honor Books
Have You Seen Tom Thumb? by Mabel Leigh Hunt (Stokes)

The Middle Moffat by Eleanor Estes (Harcourt, Brace)

1944 *Johnny Tremain* by Esther Forbes (Houghton Mifflin)

Honor Books
Fog Magic by Julia L. Sauer (Viking)

Mountain Born by Elizabeth Yates (Coward-McCann)

Rufus M. by Eleanor Estes (Harcourt, Brace)

These Happy Golden Years by Laura Ingalls Wilder (Harper)

1945 *Rabbit Hill* by Robert Lawson (Viking)

Honor Books
Abraham Lincoln's World by Genevieve Foster (Scribners)

The Hundred Dresses by Eleanor Estes (Harcourt, Brace)

Long Journey: the Life of Roger Williams by Jeanette Eaton (Harcourt, Brace)

The Silver Pencil by Alice Dalgliesh (Scribners)

1946 *Strawberry Girl* by Lois Lenski (Lippincott)

Honor Books
Bhimsa, the Dancing Bear by Christine Weston (Scribners)

Justin Morgan Had A Horse by Marguerite Henry (Wilcox & Follett)

The Moved-Outers by Florence Crannell Means (Houghton Mifflin)

New Found World by Katherine B. Shippen (Viking)

1947 *Miss Hickory* by Carolyn Sherwin Bailey (Viking)

Honor Books
The Avion My Uncle Flew by Cyrus Fisher (Appleton-Century)

Big Tree by Conrad and Mary Buff (Viking)

The Heavenly Tenants by William Maxwell (Harper)

The Hidden Treasure of Glaston by Eleanore Myers Jewett (Viking)

The Wonderful Year by Nancy Barnes (Messner)

1948 *The Twenty-One Balloons* by William Pène Du Bois (Viking)

Honor Books
Cow-Tail Switch and Other West African Stories by George Herzog and Harold Courlander (Holt)

Li Lun, Lad of Courage by Carolyn Treffinger (Abingdon-Cokesbury)

Misty of Chincoteague by Marguerite Henry (Rand McNally)

Pancakes-Paris by Claire Huchet Bishop (Viking)

The Quaint and Curious Quest of Johnny Longfoot, the Shoe King's Son by Catherine Besterman (Bobbs-Merrill)

1949 *King of the Wind* by Marguerite Henry (Rand McNally)

Honor Books
Daughter of the Mountains by Louise S. Rankin (Viking)

My Father's Dragon by Ruth Stiles Gannett (Random House)

Seabird by Holling Clancy Holling (Houghton Mifflin)

Story of the Negro by Arna W. Bontemps (Knopf)

1950 *The Door in the Wall: Story of Medieval London* by Marguerite de Angeli (Doubleday)

Honor Books
The Blue Cat of Castle Town by Catherine C. Coblentz (Longmans, Green)

George Washington: An Initial Biography by Genevieve Foster (Scribners)

Kildee House by Rutherford Montgomery (Doubleday)

Song of the Pines: a Story of Norwegian Lumbering in Wisconsin by Walter and Marion Havighurst (Winston)

Tree of Freedom by Rebecca Caudill (Viking)

1951 *Amos Fortune, Free Man* by Elizabeth Yates (Aladdin)

Honor Books
Abraham Lincoln, Friend of the People by Clara I. Judson (Wilcox & Follett)

Better Known as Johnny Appleseed by Mabel Leigh Hunt (Lippincott)

Gandhi, Fighter Without a Sword by Jeanette Eaton (Morrow)

The Story of Appleby Capple by Anne Parrish (Harper)

1952 *Ginger Pye* by Eleanor Estes (Harcourt, Brace)

Honor Books
Americans Before Columbus by Elizabeth Chesley Baity (Viking)

The Apple and the Arrow by Conrad and Mary Buff (Houghton Mifflin)

The Defender by Nicholas Kalashnikoff (Scribners)

The Light at Tern Rock by Julia L. Sauer (Viking)

Minn of the Mississippi by Holling Clancy Holling (Houghton Mifflin)

1953 *Secret of the Andes* by Ann Nolan Clark (Viking)

Honor Books
The Bears on Hemlock Mountain by Alice Dalgliesh (Scribners)

Birthdays of Freedom: America's Heritage from the Ancient World by Genevieve Foster (Scribners)

Charlotte's Web by E. B. White (Harper)

Moccasin Trail by Eloise J. McGraw (Coward-McCann)

Red Sails to Capri by Ann Weil (Viking)

1954 *And Now Miguel* by Joseph Krumgold (Crowell)

Honor Books
All Alone by Claire Huchet Bishop (Viking)

Hurry Home, Candy by Meindert DeJong (Harper)

Magic Maize by Conrad and Mary Buff (Houghton Mifflin)

Shadrach by Meindert DeJong (Harper)

Theodore Roosevelt, Fighting Patriot by Clara I. Judson (Follett)

1955 *The Wheel on the School* by Meindert DeJong (Harper)

Honor Books
Banner in the Sky by James Ramsey Ullman (Lippincott)

The Courage of Sarah Noble by Alice Dalgliesh (Scribners)

1956 *Carry On, Mr. Bowditch* by Jean Lee Latham (Houghton Mifflin)

Honor Books
The Golden Name Day by Jennie D. Lindquist (Harper)

Men, Microscopes and Living Things by Katherine B. Shippen (Viking)

The Secret River by Marjorie Kinnan Rawlings (Scribners)

1957 *Miracles on Maple Hill* by Virginia Sorensen (Harcourt)

Honor Books
The Black Fox of Lorne by Marguerite de Angeli (Doubleday)

The Corn Grows Ripe by Dorothy Rhoads (Viking)

The House of Sixty Fathers by Meindert DeJong (Harper)

Mr. Justice Holmes by Clara I. Judson (Follett)

Old Yeller by Fred Gipson (Harper)

1958 *Rifles for Watie* by Harold Keith (Crowell)

Honor Books
Gone-Away Lake by Elizabeth Enright (Harcourt, Brace)

The Great Wheel by Robert Lawson (Viking)

The Horsecatcher by Mari Sandoz (Westminster)

Tom Paine, Freedom's Apostle by Leo Gurko (Crowell)

1959 *The Witch of Blackbird Pond* by Elizabeth George Speare (Houghton Mifflin)

Honor Books
Along Came a Dog by Meindert DeJong (Harper)

Chrucaro: Wild Pony of the Pampa by Francis Kalnay (Harcourt, Brace)

The Family Under the Bridge by Natalie Savage Carlson (Harper)

1960 *Onion John* by Joseph Krumgold (Crowell)

Honor Books
America is Born: A History for Peter by Gerald W. Johnson (Morrow)

The Gammage Cup by Carol Kendall (Harcourt, Brace)

My Side of the Mountain by Jean Craighead George (Dutton)

1961 *Island of the Blue Dolphins* by Scott O'Dell (Houghton Mifflin)

Honor Books
America Moves Forward by Gerald W. Johnson (Morrow)

Old Ramon by Jack Schaefer (Houghton Mifflin)

The Cricket in Times Square by George Selden (Farrar, Straus & Cudahy)

1962 *The Bronze Bow* by Elizabeth George Speare (Houghton Mifflin)

Honor Books
Frontier Living by Edwin Tunis (World)

The Golden Goblet by Eloise McGraw (Coward, McCann & Geoghegan)

Belling the Tiger by Mary Stolz (Harper & Row)

1963 *A Wrinkle in Time* by Madeleine L'Engle (Farrar, Straus & Giroux)

Honor Books
Thistle and Thyme by Sorche Nic Leodhas (Holt, Rinehart & Winston)

Men of Athens by Olivia Coolidge (Houghton Mifflin)

1964 *It's Like This, Cat* by Emily Cheney Neville (Harper & Row)

Honor Books
Rascal by Sterling North (Dutton)

The Loner by Esther Wier (McKay)

1965 *Shadow of a Bull* by Maia Wojciechowska (Atheneum)

Honor Book
Across Five Aprils by Irene Hunt (Follett)

1966 *I, Juan de Pareja* by Elizabeth Borten de Trevino (Farrar, Straus & Giroux)

Honor Books
The Black Cauldron by Lloyd Alexander (Holt, Rinehart & Winston)

The Animal Family by Randall Jarrell (Pantheon)

The Noonday Friends by Mary Stolz (Harper & Row)

1967 *Up a Road Slowly* by Irene Hunt (Follett)

Honor Books
The King's Fifth by Scott O'Dell (Houghton Mifflin)

Zlateh the Goat and Other Stories by Isaac Bashevis Singer (Harper & Row)

The Jazz Man by Mary H. Weik (Atheneum)

1968 *From the Mixed-Up Files of Mrs. Basil E. Frankweiler* by E. L. Konigsburg (Atheneum)

Honor Books
Jennifer, Hecate, Macbeth, William McKinley, and Me, Elizabeth by E. L. Konigsburg (Atheneum)

The Black Pearl by Scott O'Dell (Houghton Mifflin)

The Fearsome Inn by Isaac Bashevis Singer (Scribners)

The Egypt Game by Zilpha Keatley Snyder (Atheneum)

1969 *The High King* by Lloyd Alexander (Holt, Rinehart & Winston)

Honor Books
To Be a Slave by Julius Lester (Dial)

When Shlemiel Went to Warsaw and Other Stories by Isaac Bashevis Singer (Farrar, Straus & Giroux)

1970 *Sounder* by William H. Armstrong (Harper & Row)

Honor Books
Our Eddie by Sulamith Ish-Kishor (Pantheon)

The Many Ways of Seeing: An Introduction to the Pleasures of Art by Janet Gaylord Moore (World)

Journey Outside by Mary Q. Steele (Viking)

1971 *Summer of the Swans* by Betsy Byars (Viking)

Honor Books
Kneeknock Rise by Natalie Babbitt (Farrar, Straus & Giroux)

Enchantress from the Stars by Sylvia Louise Engdahl (Atheneum)

Sing Down the Moon by Scott O'Dell (Houghton Mifflin)

1972 *Mrs. Frisby and the Rats of NIMH* by Robert C. O'Brien (Atheneum)

Honor Books
Incident at Hawk's Hill by Allan W. Eckert (Little, Brown)

The Planet of Junior Brown by Virginia Hamilton (Macmillan)

The Tombs of Atuan by Ursula K. Le Guin (Atheneum)

Annie and the Old One by Miska Miles (Atlantic/Little, Brown)

The Headless Cupid by Zilpha Keatley Snyder (Atheneum)

1973 *Julie of the Wolves* by Jean George (Harper & Row)

Honor Books
Frog and Toad Together by Arnold Lobel (Harper & Row)

The Upstairs Room by Johanna Reiss (Crowell)

The Witches of Worm by Zilpha Keatley Snyder (Atheneum)

1974 *The Slave Dancer* by Paula Fox (Bradbury)

Honor Book
The Dark Is Rising by Susan Cooper (Atheneum)

1975 *M. C. Higgins, the Great* by Virginia Hamilton (Macmillan)

Honor Books
Figgs & Phantoms by Ellen Raskin (Dutton)

My Brother Sam Is Dead by James Lincoln Collier & Christopher Collier (Four Winds)

The Perilous Gard by Elizabeth Marie Pope (Houghton Mifflin)

Philip Hall Likes Me, I Reckon Maybe by Bette Greene (Dial)

1976 *The Grey King* by Susan Cooper (Atheneum)

Honor Books
The Hundred Penny Box by Sharon Bell Mathis (Viking)

Dragonwings by Laurence Yep (Harper & Row)

1977 *Roll of Thunder, Hear My Cry* by Mildred D. Taylor (Dial)

Honor Books
Abel's Island by William Steig (Farrar, Straus & Giroux)

A String in the Harp by Nancy Bond (Atheneum)

1978 *Bridge to Terabithia* by Katherine Paterson (Crowell)

Honor Books
Anpao: An American Indian Odyssey by Jamake Highwater (Lippincott)

Ramona and Her Father by Beverly Cleary (Morrow)

1979 *The Westing Game* by Ellen Raskin (Dutton)

Honor Book
The Great Gilly Hopkins by Katherine Paterson (Crowell)

1980 *A Gathering of Days: A New England Girl's Journal, 1830-32* by Joan Blos (Scribners)

Honor Book
The Road from Home: The Story of an American Girl by David Kherdian (Greenwillow)

1981 *Jacob Have I Loved* by Katherine Paterson (Crowell)

Honor Books
The Fledgling by Jane Langton (Harper & Row)

A Ring of Endless Light by Madeleine L'Engle (Farrar, Straus & Giroux)

1982 *A Visit to William Blake's Inn: Poems for Innocent and Experienced Travelers* by Nancy Willard (Harcourt Brace Jovanovich)

Honor Books
Ramona Quimby, Age 8 by Beverly Cleary (Morrow)

Upon the Head of a Goat by Aranka Siegal (Farrar, Straus & Giroux)

1983 *Dicey's Song* by Cynthia Voigt (Atheneum)

Honor Books
The Blue Sword by Robin McKinley (Greenwillow)

Dr. De Soto by William Steig (Farrar, Straus & Giroux)

Graven Images by Paul Fleischman (Harper & Row)

Homesick: My Own Story by Jean Fritz (Putnam's)

Sweet Whispers, Brother Rush by Virginia Hamilton (Philomel)

1984 *Dear Mr. Henshaw* by Beverly Cleary (Morrow)

Honor Books
The Sign of the Beaver by Elizabeth George Speare (Houghton Mifflin)

A Solitary Blue by Cynthia Voigt (Atheneum)

Sugaring Time by Kathryn Lasky (Macmillan)

The Wish Giver by Bill Brittain (Harper & Row)

1985 *The Hero and the Crown* by Robin McKinley (Greenwillow)

Honor Books
Like Jake and Me by Mavis Jukes (Knopf)

The Moves Make the Man by Bruce Brooks (Harper & Row)

One-Eyed Cat by Paula Fox (Bradbury)

1986 *Sarah, Plain and Tall* by Patricia MacLachlan (Harper & Row)

Honor Books
Commodore Perry in the Land of the Shogun by Rhoda Blumberg (Lothrop, Lee & Shepard)

Dogsong by Gary Paulsen (Bradbury)

1987 *The Whipping Boy* by Sid Fleischman (Greenwillow)

Honor Books
On My Honor by Marion Dene Bauer (Clarion)

Volcano: The Eruption and Healing of Mt. St. Helens by Patricia Lauker (Bradbury)

A Eine White Dust by Cynthia Ryeant (Bradbury)

SCOTT O'DELL AWARD FOR HISTORICAL FICTION

Established in 1981 by Scott O'Dell and administered by the Advisory Committee of the *Bulletin of the Center for Children's Books*, the award is for a work of historical fiction of unusual literary merit that is written by a citizen of the United States and set in the New World. The award is given to a book published in the United States during the preceding year of the award. In some years, no award may be given.

1984 *The Sign of the Beaver* by Elizabeth George Speare (Houghton Mifflin)

1985 *The Fighting Ground* by Avi [Wortis] (Harper & Row)

1986 *Sarah, Plain and Tall* by Patricia MacLachlan (Harper & Row)

1987 *Streams to the River, River to the Sea: A Novel of Sacajawea* by Scott O'Dell (Houghton Mifflin)

PHOENIX AWARD

Established in 1985 by the Children's Literature Association, the award is given for a book first published twenty years earlier which did not win a major award but which has passed the test of time and is deemed of high literary quality.

1985 *The Mark of the Horse Lord* by Rosemary Sutcliff (Walck, 1965)

1986 *Queenie Peavy* by Robert Burch (Viking, 1966)

THE LAURA INGALLS WILDER AWARD

Established in 1954, the award has been presented every five years from 1960 until 1980. Since 1980 the award has been given every three years. It is administered by the Association for Library Service to Children of the American Library Association. The award recognizes an author or illustrator whose books, published in the United States, have, over a period of years, made a substantial contribution to literature for children. The medal recipient is announced in January of the year of the award.

1954 Laura Ingalls Wilder

1960 Clara Ingram Judson

1965 Ruth Sawyer

1970 E. B. White

1975 Beverly Cleary

1980 Theodor Geisel (Dr. Seuss)

1983 Maurice Sendak

1986 Jean Fritz

NATIONAL COUNCIL OF TEACHERS OF ENGLISH ACHIEVEMENT AWARD FOR POETRY FOR CHILDREN

First given in 1977, this award is presented to a living American poet for his or her contribution to children's poetry. The award, sponsored by the National Council of Teachers of English, was originally annual but is now given every three years.

1977 David McCord

1978 Aileen Fisher

1979 Karla Kushkin

1980 Myra Cohn Livingston

1981 Eve Merriam

1982 John Ciardi

1985 Lilian Moore

THE NEW YORK TIMES CHOICE OF BEST ILLUSTRATED CHILDREN'S BOOKS OF THE YEAR

First awarded in 1952, *The New York Times's* Choice of Best Illustrated Children's Book of the year was established to honor the highest quality illustrations in children's books. The number of books chosen varies from year to year, but is approximately ten. The children's books special supplement to the *New York Times Book Review* in mid November announces the winners.

1952 *The Animal Farm* (Simon & Schuster)
Authors and Illustrators: Alice and Martin Provensen

Beasts and Nonsense (Viking)
Author and Illustrator: Marie Hall Ets

The Dogcatcher's Dog (Holt)
Author and Illustrator: Andre Dugo

Five Little Monkeys (Houghton Mifflin)
Author and Illustrator: Juliet Kepes

The Happy Place (Little, Brown)
Author and Illustrator: Ludwig Bemelmans

A Hole Is to Dig (Harper)
Author: Ruth Krauss
Illustrator: Maurice Sendak

The Magic Currant Bun (Lippincott)
Author: John Symonds
Illustrator: Andre Francois

1953 *Fast Is Not a Ladybug: A Book About Fast and Slow Things* (Scott)
Author: Miriam Schlein
Illustrator: Leonard Kessler

Florinda and the Wild Bird (Walck)
Author: Selina Chonz
Illustrator: Alois Carigiet
Translators: Anne and Ian Serraillier

The Golden Bible for Children: The New Testament (Golden)
Illustrators: Alice and Martin Provensen
Editor: Elsa Jane Werner

Green Eyes (Capitol)
Author and Illustrator: Abe Birnbaum

A Hero by Mistake (Scott)
Author: Anita Brenner
Illustrator: Jean Charlot

Lucky Blacky (Watts)
Author: Eunice Lackey
Illustrator: Winifred Greene

Madeline's Rescue (Viking)
Author and Illustrator: Ludwig Bemelmans

Mother Goose Riddle Rhymes (Harcourt, Brace)
Authors: Ruth and Joseph Low
Illustrator: Joseph Low

Pitschi: The Kitten Who Always Wanted to Be Something Else (Harcourt, Brace)
Author and Illustrator: Hans Fischer

Who Gave Us . . . Peacocks? Planes? and Ferris Wheels? (Pantheon)
Author and Illustrator: Madeleine Gekiere

1954 *Andy Says . . . Bonjour!* (Vanguard)
Author: Pat Diska
Illustrator: Chris Jenkyns

The Animal Frolic (Putnam's)
Adaptor: Velma Varner
Illustrator: Toba Sojo

Circus Ruckus (Harcourt, Brace)
Author: William Lipkind
Illustrator: Nicolas Mordvinoff

The Happy Lion (McGraw-Hill)
Author: Louise Fatio
Illustrator: Roger Duvoisin

Heavy Is a Hippopotamus (Scott)
Author: Miriam Schlein
Illustrator: Leonard Kessler

I'll Be You and You Be Me (Harper)
Author: Ruth Krauss
Illustrator: Maurice Sendak

Jenny's Birthday Book (Harper)
Author and Illustrator: Esther Averill

A Kiss Is Round: Verses (Lothrop, Lee & Shepard)
Author: Blossom Budney
Illustrator: Vladimir Bobri

The Sun Looks Down (Abelard-Schuman)
Author: Miriam Schlein
Illustrator: Abner Graboff

The Wet World (Lippincott)
Author: Norma Simon
Illustrator: Jane Miller

1955 *Beasts from a Brush (Imaginative Animal Drawings), with Brief Verses* (Pantheon)
Author and Illustrator: Juliet Kepes

Chaga (Harcourt, Brace)
Author: William Lipkind
Illustrator: Nicolas Mordvinoff

The Happy Lion in Africa (McGraw-Hill)
Author: Louise Fatio
Illustrator: Roger Duvoisin

A Little House of Your Own (Harcourt, Brace)
Author: Beatrice Schenk de Regniers
Illustrator: Irene Hunt

Parsley (Harper & Row)
Author and Illustrator: Ludwig Bemelmans

Rumpelstiltskin (Rand McNally)
Authors: Jacob and Wilhelm Grimm
Illustrator: Jan B. Balet
Adaptor: Patricia Jones

See and Say: A Picture Book in Four Languages (Harcourt, Brace)
Author and Illustrator: Antonio Frasconi

Switch on the Night (Pantheon)
Author: Ray Bradbury
Illustrator: Madeleine Gekiere

The Three Kings of Saba (Lippincott)
Author: Alf Evers
Illustrator: Helen Sewell

Uncle Ben's Whale (Dodd, Mead)
Author: Walter D. Edmonds
Illustrator: William Gropper

1956 *Babar's Fair Will Be Opened Next Sunday . . .* (Random House)
Author and Illustrator: Laurent de Brunhoff
Translator: Merle Haas

Crocodile Tears (Universe)
Author and Illustrator: Andre Francois

I Know a Lot of Things (Harcourt, Brace)
Authors: Ann and Paul Rand
Illustrator: Paul Rand

I Want to Paint My Bathroom Blue (Harper)
Author: Ruth Krauss
Illustrator: Maurice Sendak

I Will Tell You of a Town (Houghton Mifflin)
Author: Alastair Reid
Illustrator: Walter Lorraine

Jonah the Fisherman (Pantheon)
Author and Illustrator: Reiner Zimnik
Translators: Richard and Clara Winston

Little Big-Feather (Abelard-Schuman)
Author: Joseph Longstreth
Illustrator: Helen Borten

The Little Elephant (Harper)
Author and Illustrator: Ylla

Really Spring (Harper)
Author: Gene Zion
Illustrator: Margaret Bloy Graham

Was It a Good Trade? (Harcourt, Brace)
Author: Beatrice Schenk de Regniers
Illustrator: Irene Haas

1957 *Big Red Bus* (Doubleday)
Author: Ethel Kessler
Illustrator: Leonard Kessler

The Birthday Party (Harper)
Author: Ruth Krauss
Illustrator: Maurice Sendak

Curious George Gets a Medal (Houghton Mifflin)
Author and Illustrator: H. A. Rey

Dear Garbage Man (Harper)
Author: Gene Zion
Illustrator: Margaret Bloy Graham

The Fisherman and His Wife (Pantheon)
Authors: Jacob and Wilhelm Grimm
Illustrator: Madeleine Gekiere

The Friendly Beasts (Parnassus)
Author: Laura Baker
Illustrator: Nicholas Sidjakov

The Red Balloon (Doubleday)
Author: Albert Lamorisse
Illustrated with photographs by Lamorisse

Sparkle and Spin: A Book about Words (Harcourt, Brace)
Authors: Ann and Paul Rand
Illustrator: Paul Rand

This Is the Story of Faint George Who Wanted to Be a Knight (Houghton Mifflin)
Author and Illustrator: Robert E. Barry

The Unhappy Hippopotamus (Vanguard)
Author: Nancy Moore
Illustrator: Edward Leight

1958 *All Aboard: Poems* (Pantheon)
Author: Mary Britton Miller
Illustrator: Bill Sokol

Chouchou (Scribners)
Author and Illustrator: Francoise

The Daddy Days (Abelard-Schuman)
Author: Norma Simon
Illustrator: Abner Graboff

A Friend Is Someone Who Likes You (Harcourt, Brace)
Author and Illustrator: Joan Walsh Anglund

The Golden Book of Animals (Simon & Schuster)
Author: Anne Terry White
Illustrator: W. Suschitzy

The House that Jack Built: A Picture Book in Two Languages (Harcourt, Brace)
Author and Illustrator: Antonio Frasconi

How to Hide a Hippopotamus (Dodd, Mead)
Author and Illustrator: Volney Croswell

The Magic Feather Duster (Harcourt, Brace)
Author: William Lipkind
Illustrator: Nicolas Mordvinoff

Roland (Harcourt, Brace)
Author: Nelly Stephane
Illustrator: Andre Francois

What Do You Say, Dear? (Scott)
Author: Sesyle Joslin
Illustrator: Maurice Sendak

1959 *Animal Babies* (Harper)
Author: Arthur Gregor
Illustrators: Arthur Gregor and Ylla

Father Bear Comes Home (Harper)
Author: Else Holmelund Minarik
Illustrator: Maurice Sendak

The First Noel: The Birth of Christ from the Gospel According to St. Luke (Golden)
Illustrators: Alice and Martin Provensen

Full of Wonder (World)
Author and Illustrator: Ann Kirn

The Girl in the White Hat (McGraw-Hill)
Author and Illustrator: Walter Thies Cummings

Kasimir's Journey (Lippincott)
Author: Monroe Stearns
Illustrator: Marlene Reidel

Little Blue and Little Yellow (Obolensky)
Author and Illustrator: Leo Lionni

Pablo Paints a Picture (Little, Brown)
Author: Warren Miller
Illustrator: Edward Sorel

The Reason for the Pelican (Lippincott)
Author: John Ciardi
Illustrator: Madeleine Gekiere

This Is London (Macmillan)
Author and Illustrator: Miroslav Sasek

1960 *The Adventures of Ulysses* (Criterion)
Author: Jacques Lemarchand
Illustrator: Andre Francois
Translator: E. M. Hatt

Baboushka and the Three Kings (Parnassus)
Author: Ruth Robbins
Illustrator: Nicolas Sidjakov

Bruno Munari's ABC (World)
Author and Illustrator: Bruno Munari

Inch by Inch (Obolensky)
Author and Illustrator: Leo Lionni

Open House for Butterflies (Harper)
Author: Ruth Krauss
Illustrator: Maurice Sendak

Scrappy the Pup (Lippincott)
Author: John Ciardi
Illustrator: Jane Miller

The Shadow Book (Harcourt, Brace)
Authors: Beatrice Schenk de Regniers and Isabel Gordon
Illustrator: Isabel Gordon

This Is New York (Macmillan)
Author and Illustrator: Miroslav Sasek

Twenty-six Ways to Be Somebody (Pantheon)
Author and Illustrator: Devorah Boxer

Two Little Birds and Three (Houghton Mifflin)
Author and Illustrator: Juliet Kepes

1961 *The Big Book of Animal Stories* (Watts)
Editor: Margaret Green
Illustrator: Janusz Grabianski

Dear Rat (Houghton Mifflin)
Author: Julia Cunningham
Illustrator: Walter Lorraine

The Happy Hunter (Lothrop, Lee & Shepard)
Author and Illustrator: Roger Duvoisin

Listen - the Birds (Pantheon)
Author: Mary Britton Miller
Illustrator: Evaline Ness

My Time of Year (Walck)
Author: Katharine Dow
Illustrator: Walter Erhard

Once a Mouse (Scribners)
Author and Illustrator: Marcia Brown

Sandpipers (Crowell)
Author: Edith Thacher Hurd
Illustrator: Lucienne Bloch

The Snow and the Sun: A South American Folk Rhyme in Two Languages (Harcourt, Brace & World)
Author and Illustrator: Antonio Frasconi

Umbrellas, Hats and Wheels (Harcourt, Brace & World)
Authors: Jerome Snyder and Ann Rand
Illustrator: Jerome Snyder

The Wing on a Flea: A Book About Shapes (Little, Brown)
Author and Illustrator: Ed Emberley

1962 *Books!* (Simon & Schuster)
Author: Murray McCain
Illustrator: John Alcorn

The Emperor and the Drummer Boy (Pantheon)
Author: Ruth Robbins
Illustrator: Nicolas Sidjakov

Gennarino (Lippincott)
Author and Illustrator: Nicola Simbart

The Island of Fish in the Trees (World)
Author: Eva-Lis? Wuorio
Illustrator: Edward Ardizzone

Kay-Kay Comes Home (Obolensky)
Author: Nicholas Samstag
Illustrator: Ben Shahn

Little Owl (Atheneum)
Authors: Hanne Axmann and Reiner Zimnick
Illustrator: Hanne Axmann

The Princesses: Sixteen Stories abut Princesses (Harper & Row)
Editor: Sally P. Johnson
Illustrator: Beni Montresor

The Singing Hill (Harper & Row)
Author: Meindert DeJong
Illustrator: Maurice Sendak

The Tale of a Wood (Knopf)
Author and Illustrator: Henry B. Kane

The Three Robbers (Atheneum)
Author and Illustrator: Tomi Ungerer

1963 *The Great Picture Robbery* (Atheneum)
Author: Leon Harris
Illustrator: Joseph Schindelman

Gwendolyn and the Weathercock (Golden)
Author: Nancy Sherman
Illustrator: Edward Sorel

A Holiday for Mister Muster (Harper & Row)
Author and Illustrator: Arnold Lobel

Hurly Burly and the Knights (Platt & Munk)
Author: Milton Rugoff
Illustrator: Emanuele Luzzati

John J. Plenty and Fiddler Dan (Lippincott)
Author: John Ciardi
Illustrator: Madeleine Gekiere

Karen's Curiosity (Golden)
Authors and Illustrators: Alice and Martin Provensen

Once upon a Totem (Atheneum)
Author: Christie Harris
Illustrator: John Frazer Mills

Plunkety Plunk (Farrar, Straus)
Author and Illustrator: Peter J. Lippman

Swimmy (Pantheon)
Author and Illustrator: Leo Lionni

Where the Wild Things Are (Harper & Row)
Author and Illustrator: Maurice Sendak

1964 *The Bat-poet* (Macmillan)
Author: Randall Jarrell
Illustrator: Maurice Sendak

Casey at the Bat (Watts)
Author: Ernest L. Thayer
Illustrator: Leonard Everett Fisher

The Charge of the Light Brigade (Golden)
Author: Alfred Tennyson
Illustrators: Alice and Martin Provensen

Exactly Alike (Scribners)
Author and Illustrator: Evaline Ness

The Giraffe of King Charles X (McGraw-Hill)
Author and Illustrator: Miche Wynants

The Happy Owls (Atheneum)
Author and Illustrator: Celestino Piatti

I'll Show You Cats (Harper & Row)
Author: Crosby Newell Bonsall
Illustrator: Ylla

The Life of a Queen (Braziller)
Author and Illustrator: Colette Portal
Translator: Marcia Nardi

Rain Makes Applesauce (Holiday House)
Author: Julian Scheer
Illustrator: Marvin Bileck

The Wave (Houghton Mifflin)
Author: Margaret Hodges
Illustrator: Blair Lent

1965 *Alberic the Wise and Other Journeys* (Pantheon)
Author: Norton Juster
Illustrator: Domenico Gnoli

The Animal Family (Pantheon)
Author: Randall Jarrell
Illustrator: Maurice Sendak

A Double Discovery (Scribners)
Author and Illustrator: Evaline Ness

Hide and Seek Fog (Lothrop, Lee & Shepard)
Author: Alvin Tresselt
Illustrator: Roger Duvoisin

Kangaroo & Kangaroo (Doubleday)
Author: Kathy Braun
Illustrator: Jim McMullan

Please Share That Peanut! A Preposterous Pageant in Fourteen Acts (Harcourt, Brace & World)
Authors: Sesyle Joslin and Simms Taback
Illustrator: Simms Taback

Punch and Judy: A Play for Puppets (Little, Brown)
Illustrator: Ed Emberley

Sven's Bridge (Harper & Row)
Author and Illustrator: Anita Lobel

1966 *Ananse the Spider: Tales from an Ashanti Village* (Pantheon)
Author: Peggy Appiah
Illustrator: Peggy Wilson

A Boy Went out to Gather Pears (Harcourt, Brace & World)
Author and Illustrator: Felix Hoffmann

Celestino Piatti's Animal ABC (Atheneum)
Author and Illustrator: Celestino Piatti

The Jazz Man (Atheneum)
Author: Mary Hays Weik
Illustrator: Ann Grifalconi

The Magic Flute (Putnam's)
Author: Stephen Spender
Illustrator: Beni Montresor

The Monster Den: Or, Look What Happened at My House - and to It (Lippincott)
Author: John Ciardi
Illustrator: Edward Gorey

Nothing Ever Happens on My Block (Atheneum)
Author and Illustrator: Ellen Raskin

Shaw's Fortune: The Picture Story of a Colonial Plantation (World)
Author and Illustrator: Edwin Tunis

Wonderful Time (Lippincott)
Author: Phyllis McGinley
Illustrator: John Alcorn

Zlateh the Goat and Other Stories (Harper & Row)
Author: Isaac Bashevis Singer
Illustrator: Maurice Sendak

1967 *Animals of Many Lands* (Hill & Wang)
Editor: Hanns Reich
Illustrated with photographs

Brian Wildsmith's Birds (Watts)
Author and Illustrator: Brian Wildsmith

A Dog's Book of Bugs (Atheneum)
Author: Elizabeth Griffen
Illustrator: Peter Parnall

Fables of Aesop (Dover)
Author: Sir Roger L'Estrange
Illustrator: Alexander Calder

Frederick (Pantheon)
Author and Illustrator: Leo Lionni

The Honeybees (Knopf)
Author: Franklin Russell
Illustrator: Colette Portal

Hubert, the Caterpillar Who Thought He Was a Mustache (Quist)
Authors: Susan Richards and Wendy Stang
Illustrator: Robert L. Anderson

Knee-deep in Thunder (Atheneum)
Author: Sheila Moon
Illustrator: Peter Parnall

Seashore Story (Viking)
Author and Illustrator: Taro Yashima

1968 *Harriet and the Promised Land* (Windmill/Simon & Schuster)
Author and Illustrator: Jacob Lawrence

A Kiss for Little Bear (Harper & Row)
Author: Else Holmelund Minarik
Illustrator: Maurice Sendak

Malachi Mudge (McGraw-Hill)
Author: Edward Cecil
Illustrator: Peter Parnall

Mister Corbett's Ghost (Pantheon)
Author: Leon Garfield
Illustrator: Alan Cober

The Real Tin Flower: Poems about the World at Nine (Crowell/Collier)
Author: Aliki Barnstone
Illustrator: Paul Giovanopoulos

The Secret Journey of Hugo the Brat (Quist)
Author: Francois Ruy-Vidal
Illustrator: Nicole Claveloux

Spectacles (Atheneum)
Author and Illustrator: Ellen Raskin

Story Number 1 (Quist)
Author: Eugene Ionesco
Illustrator: Etienne Delessert

Talking without Words (Viking)
Author and Illustrator: Marie Hall Ets

The Very Obliging Flowers (Grove)
Author: Claude Roy
Illustrator: Alain LeFoll
Translator: Gerald Bertin

1969 *Arm in Arm* (Parents Magazine Press)
Author and Illustrator: Remy Charlip

Bang Bang You're Dead (Harper & Row)
Authors: Louise Fitzhugh and Sandra Scoppettone
Illustrator: Louise Fitzhugh

Birds (Walker)
Author and Illustrator: Juliet Kepes

The Circus in the Mist (World)
Author and Illustrator: Bruno Munari

The Dong with a Luminous Nose (Scott)
Author: Edward Lear
Illustrator: Edward Gorey

Free as a Frog (Addison-Wesley)
Author: Elizabeth J. Hodges
Illustrator: Paul Giovanopoulo

The Light Princess (Farrar, Straus & Giroux)
Author: George MacDonald
Illustrator: Maurice Sendak

Sara's Granny and the Groodle (Doubleday)
Author: Joan Gill
Illustrator: Seymour Chwast

What Is It For? (Simon & Schuster)
Author and Illustrator: Henry Humphrey

Winter's Eve (Holt, Rinehart & Winston)
Author: Natalia M. Belting
Illustrator: Alan E. Cober

1970 *Alala* (Quist)
Author: Guy Monreal
Illustrator: Nicole Claveloux

Finding a Poem (Atheneum)
Author: Eve Merriam
Illustrator: Seymour Chwast

The Gnu and the Guru Go Behind the Beyond
(Houghton Mifflin)
Author: Peggy Clifford
Illustrator: Eric von Schmidt

Help, Help, the Globolinks! (McGraw-Hill)
Author: Gian-Carlo Menotti
Illustrator: Milton Glaser
Adaptor: Leigh Dean

In the Night Kitchen (Harper & Row)
Author and Illustrator: Maurice Sendak

Lift Every Voice and Sing: Words and Music
(Hawthorn)
Authors: J. Rosamund and James Weldon
Johnson
Illustrator: Mozelle Thompson

Matilda Who Told Lies and Was Burned to Death
(Dial)
Author: Hilaire Belloc
Illustrator: Steven Kellogg

Timothy's Horse (Pantheon)
Author: Vladimir Mayakovsky
Illustrator: Flavio Constantini
Adaptor: Guy Daniels

Topsy Turvies: Pictures to Stretch the Imagination
(Walker/Weatherhill)
Author and Illustrator: Mitsumasa Anno

You are Ri-di-cu-lous (Pantheon)
Author and Illustrator: Andre Francois

1971 *Amos and Boris* (Farrar, Straus & Giroux)
Author and Illustrator: William Steig

Bear Circus (Viking)
Author and Illustrator: William Pène du Bois

The Beast of Monsieur Racine (Farrar, Straus
& Giroux)
Author and Illustrator: Tomi Ungerer

Changes, Changes (Macmillan)
Author and Illustrator: Pat Hutchins

Look Again! (Macmillan)
Author and Illustrator: Tana Hoban

Look What I Can Do (Scribners)
Author and Illustrator: Jose Aruego

The Magic Tears (Harper & Row)
Author: Jack Sendak
Illustrator: Mitchell Miller

Mr. Gumpy's Outing (Holt, Rinehart & Winston)
Author and Illustrator: John Burningham

One Dancing Drum (Phillips)
Authors: Gail Kredenser and Stanley Mack
Illustrator: Stanley Mack

The Shrinking of Treehorn (Holiday House)
Author: Florence Parry Heide
Illustrator: Edward Gorey

1972 *Behind the Wheel* (Holt, Rinehart & Winston)
Author and Illustrator: Edward Koren

Count and See (Macmillan)
Author and Illustrator: Tana Hoban

George and Martha (Houghton Mifflin)
Author and Illustrator: James Marshall

Hosie's Alphabet (Viking)
Authors: Hosea, Tobias, and Lisa Baskin
Illustrator: Leonard Baskin

Just So Stories (Doubleday)
Author: Rudyard Kipling
Illustrator: Etienne Delessert

A Little Schubert (Harper & Row)
Author and Illustrator: M. B. Goffstein

Miss Jaster's Garden (Golden)
Author and Illustrator: N. M. Bodecker

Mouse Cafe (Lothrop, Lee & Shepard)
Author and Illustrator: Patricia Coombs

Simon Boom Gives a Wedding (Four Winds)
Author: Yuri Suhl
Illustrator: Margot Zemach

Where's Al? (Seabury)
Author and Illustrator: Byron Barton

1973 *Cathedral: The Story of Its Construction* (Houghton Mifflin)
Author and Illustrator: David Macaulay

The Emperor's New Clothes: A Fairy Tale (Addison-Wesley)
Author: Hans Christian Andersen
Illustrator: Monica Laimgruber

Hector Penguin (McGraw-Hill)
Author: Louise Fatio
Illustrator: Roger Duvoisin

The Juniper Tree and Other Tales from Grimm (Farrar, Straus & Giroux)
Illustrator: Maurice Sendak
Translators: Lore Segal and Randall Jarrell

King Grisly-Beard: A Tale from the Brothers Grimm (Farrar, Straus & Giroux)
Illustrator: Maurice Sendak
Translator: Edgar Taylor

The Number 24 (Quist)
Author and Illustrator: Guy Billout

A Prairie Boy's Winter (Houghton Mifflin)
Author and Illustrator: William Kurelek

The Silver Pony (Houghton Mifflin)
Author and Illustrator: Lynd Ward

Tim's Last Voyage (Walck)
Author and Illustrator: Edward Ardizzone

1974 *The Girl Who Cried Flowers* (Crowell)
Author: Jane Yolen
Illustrator: David Palladini

A Home (Putnam's)
Author: Lennart Rudstrom
Illustrator: Carl Larsson

Lumberjack (Houghton Mifflin)
Author and Illustrator: William Kurelek

The Man Who Took the Indoors Out (Harper & Row)
Author and Illustrator: Arnold Lobel

Miss Suzy's Birthday (Parents Magazine Press)
Author: Miriam Young
Illustrator: Arnold Lobel

A Storybook (Watts)
Editor and Illustrator: Tomi Ungerer

There Was an Old Woman (Parents Magazine Press)
Editor and Illustrator: Steven Kellogg

1975 *Anno's Alphabet: An Adventure in Imagination* (Crowell)
Author and Illustrator: Mitsumasa Anno

A Book of A-maze-ments (Quist)
Author: Jean Seisser

Mr. Michael Mouse Unfolds his Tale (Merrimack)
Author and Illustrator: Walter Crane

The Pig-tale (Little, Brown)
Author: Lewis Carroll
Illustrator: Leonard B. Lubin

There's a Sound in the Sea: A Child's Eye View of the Whale (Scrimshaw)
Compiler: Tamar Griggs
Illustrated with paintings by school children

Thirteen (Parents Magazine Press)
Authors and Illustrators: Jerry Joyner and Remy Charlip

The Tutti-Frutti Case: Starring the Four Doctors of Goodge (Prentice-Hall)
Author: Harry Allard
Illustrator: James Marshall

1976 *As Right as Right Can Be* (Dial)
Author: Anne Rose
Illustrator: Arnold Lobel

Ashanti to Zulu: African Traditions (Dial)
Author: Margaret Musgrove
Illustrators: Leo and Diane Dillon

The Bear and the Fly (Crown)
Author and Illustrator: Paula Winter

Everyone Knows What a Dragon Looks Like (Four Winds)
Author: Jay Williams
Illustrator: Mercer Mayer

Fly by Night (Farrar, Straus & Giroux)
Author: Randall Jarrell
Illustrator: Maurice Sendak

Little though I Be (McGraw-Hill)
Author and Illustrator: Joseph Low

Merry Ever After: The Story of Two Medieval Weddings (Viking)
Author and Illustrator: Joe Lasker

The Mother Goose Book (Random House)
Authors and Illustrators: Alice and Martin Provensen

A Near Thing for Captain Najork (Atheneum)
Author: Russell Hoban
Illustrator: Quentin Blake

1977 *The Church Mice Adrift* (Atheneum)
Author: Lore Segal
Illustrator: Graham Oakley

Come Away from the Water, Shirley (Crowell)
Author and Illustrator: John Burningham

It Could Always Be Worse: A Yiddish Folk Tale (Farrar, Straus & Giroux)
Adaptor and Illustrator: Margot Zemach

Jack and the Wonder Beans (Putnam's)
Author: James Still
Illustrator: Margot Tomes

Merry, Merry FIBruary (Parents' Magazine Press)
Author: Doris Orgel
Illustrator: Arnold Lobel

My Village, Sturbridge (Farrar, Straus & Giroux)
Author: Gary Bowen
Illustrators: Gary Bowen and Randy Miller

Noah's Ark (Doubleday)
Author and Illustrator: Peter Spier

The Surprise Picnic (Atheneum)
Author and Illustrator: John S. Goodall

When the Wind Blew (Harper & Row)
Author: Margaret Wise Brown
Illustrator: Geoffrey Hayes

1978 *Cloudy with a Chance of Meatballs* (Atheneum)
Author: Judi Barrett
Illustrator: Ron Barrett

The Forbidden Forest (Harper & Row)
Author and Illustrator: William Pène du Bois

The Great Song Book (Doubleday)
Editor: Timothy John
Illustrator: Tomi Ungerer
Music Editor: Peter Hankey

Hanukah Money (Greenwillow)
Author: Sholem Aleichem
Adaptor and Illustrator: Uri Shulevitz

The Legend of Scarface: A Blackfoot Indian Tale (Doubleday)
Author: Robert San Souci
Illustrator: Daniel San Souci

This Little Pig-a-Wig and Other Rhymes about Pigs (Atheneum)
Author: Lenore Blegvad
Illustrator: Erik Blegvad

The Nutcrackers and the Sugar-Tongs (Atlantic/Little, Brown)
Author: Edward Lear
Illustrator: Marcia Sewall

Odette: A Bird in Paris (Prentice-Hall)
Author: Kay Fender
Illustrator: Phillipe Dumas

A Peaceable Kingdom: The Shaker Abecedarius (Viking)
Illustrators: Alice and Martin Provensen

There Once Was a Woman Who Married a Man (Addison)
Author: Norma Farber
Illustrator: Lydia Dabcovich

1979 *By Camel or by Car: A Look at Transportation* (Prentice-Hall)
Author and Illustrator: Guy Billout

The Garden of Abdul Gasazi (Houghton Mifflin)
Author and Illustrator: Chris Van Allsburg

Happy Birthday, Oliver! (Random House)
Author and Illustrator: Pierre Le-Tan

King Krakus and the Dragon (Greenwillow)
Author and Illustrator: Janina Domanska

The Long Dive (Atheneum/Jonathan)
Authors and Illustrators: Catriona and Ray Smith

Natural History (Farrar, Straus & Giroux)
Author and Illustrator: M. B. Goffstein

Ox-Cart Man (Viking)
Author: Donald Hall
Illustrator: Barbara Cooney

The Tale of Fancy Nancy: A Spanish Folk Tale (Chatto & Windus)
Adaptor: Marion Koenig
Illustrator: Klaus Ensikat

Tilly's House (Atheneum)
Author and Illustrator: Faith Jacques

The Treasure (Farrar, Straus & Giroux)
Author and Illustrator: Uri Shulevitz

1980 *An Artist* (Harper & Row)
Author and Illustrator: M. B. Goffstein

A Child's Christmas in Wales (Godine)
Author: Dylan Thomas
Illustrator: Edward Ardizzone

Gorky Rises (Farrar, Straus & Giroux)
Author and Illustrator: William Steig

The Headless Horseman Rides Tonight: More Poems to Trouble Your Sleep (Greenwillow)
Author: Jack Prelutsky
Illustrator: Arnold Lobel

Howard (Greenwillow)
Author and Illustrator: James Stevenson

The Lucky Yak (Parnassus/Houghton Mifflin)
Author: Annetta Lawson
Illustrator: Allen Say

Mr. Miller the Dog (Atheneum)
Author and Illustrator: Helme Heine

Stone and Steel: A Look at Engineering (Prentice-Hall)
Author and Illustrator: Guy Billout

Unbuilding (Houghton Mifflin)
Author and Illustrator: David Macaulay

The Wonderful Travels and Adventures of Baron Munchhausen (Chatto & Windus)
Author: Peter Nicki
Illustrator: Binette Schroeder
Translator: Elizabeth Buchanan Taylor

1981 *My Mom Travels a Lot* (Warne)
Author: Caroline Feller Bauer
Illustrator: Nancy Winslow Parker

On Market Street (Greenwillow)
Author: Arnold Lobel
Illustrator: Anita Lobel

The Story of Old Mrs. Brubeck: And How She Looked for Trouble and Where She Found Him (Pantheon)
Author: Lore Segal
Illustrator: Marcia Sewall

The Crane Wife (Morrow)
Adaptor: Sumiko Yagawa
Illustrator: Suekichi Akaba

Flight: A Panorama of Aviation (Pantheon)
Author: Melvin B. Zisfein
Illustrator: Robert Andrew Parker

The Maid and the Mouse and the Odd-Shaped House: A Story in Rhyme (Dodd, Mead)
Adaptor and Illustrator: Paul O. Zelinsky

Jumanji (Houghton Mifflin)
Author and Illustrator: Chris Van Allsburg

Outside Over There (Harper & Row)
Author and Illustrator: Maurice Sendak

The Nose Tree (Atheneum)
Adaptor and Illustrator: Warwick Hutton

Where the Buffaloes Begin (Warne)
Author: Olaf Baker
Illustrator: Stephen Gammell

1982 *Anno's Britain* (Putnam's)
Author and Illustrator: Mitsumasa Anno

Squid & Spider (Prentice-Hall)
Author and Illustrator: Guy Billout

The Tiny Visitor (Pantheon)
Author and Illustrator: Oscar de Mejo

The Strange Disappearance of Howard Cranebill (Morrow)
Author and Illustrator: Henrik Drescher

Paddy Goes Traveling (Atheneum)
Author and Illustrator: John S. Goodall

My Uncle (Atheneum)
Author and Illustrator: Jenny Thorne

Ben's Dream (Houghton Mifflin)
Author and Illustrator: Chris Van Allsburg

Smile, Ernest and Celestine (Greenwillow)
Author and Illustrator: Gabrielle Vincent

The Gift of the Magi (Picture Book Studio)
Author: O. Henry
Illustrators: Lizbeth Zwerger and Michael Neugebauer

Rainbows Are Made: Poems by Carl Sandburg (Harcourt Brace Jovanovich)
Editor: Lee Bennett Hopkins
Illustrator: Fritz Eichenberg

1983 *Round Trip* (Greenwillow)
Author and Illustrator: Ann Jonas

Twelve Cats for Christmas (Pelham/Merrimack)
Author and Illustrator: Martin Leman

Little Red Cap (Morrow)
Authors: Brothers Grimm
Illustrator: Lisbeth Zwerger

Leonard Baskin's Miniature Natural History: First Series (Pantheon)
Author and Illustrator: Leonard Baskin

The Wreck of the Zephyr (Houghton Mifflin)
Author and Illustrator: Chris Van Allsburg

Simon's Book (Lothrop, Lee & Shepard)
Author and Illustrator: Henrik Drescher

Tools (Four Winds)
Author and Illustrator: Ken Robbins

The Favershams (Farrar, Straus & Giroux)
Author and Illustrator: Roy Gerrard

Up a Tree (Harper & Row)
Illustrator: Ed Young

1984 *Saint George and the Dragon* (Little, Brown)
Author: Margaret Hodges
Illustrator: Trina Schart Hyman

Sir Cedric (Farrar, Straus & Giroux)
Author and Illustrator: Roy Gerrard

Nutcracker (Crown)
Author: E. T. A. Hoffman
Illustrator: Maurice Sendak

Animal Alphabet (Dial)
Author and Illustrator: Bert Kitchen

The Mysteries of Harris Burdick (Houghton Mifflin)
Author and Illustrator: Chris Van Allsburg

If There Were Dreams to Sell (Lothrop, Lee & Shepard)
Author: Barbara Lalicki
Illustrator: Margot Tomes

Where the River Begins (Dial)
Author and Illustrator: Thomas Locker

The Napping House (Harcourt Brace Jovanovich)
Author: Audrey Wood
Illustrator: Don Wood

Babushka (Holiday House)
Author and Illustrator: Charles Mikolaycak

Jonah and the Great Fish (Atheneum)
Author and Illustrator: Warwick Hutton

1985 *The Nightingale* (Harcourt Brace Jovanovich)
Author: Hans Christian Andersen
Illustrator: Demi

Hazel's Amazing Mother (Dial)
Author and Illustrator: Rosemary Wells

Gorilla (Knopf)
Author and Illustrator: Anthony Browne

The Story of Mrs. Lovewright and Purrless the Cat (Knopf)
Author: Lore Segal
Illustrator: Paul O. Zelinsky

Granpa (Crown)
Author and Illustrator: John Burningham

The Relatives Came (Bradbury)
Author: Cynthia Rylant
Illustrator: Stephen Gammell

The Polar Express (Houghton Mifflin)
Author and Illustrator: Chris Van Allsburg

The People Could Fly: American Black Folktales (Knopf)
Author: Virginia Hamilton
Illustrators: Leo and Diane Dillon

The Inside-Outside Book of New York City (Dodd, Mead)
Author and Illustrator: Roxie Munroe

The Legend of Rosepetal (Picture Book Studio)
Author: Clemens Brentano
Illustrator: Lisbeth Zwerger

1986 *The Stranger* (Houghton Mifflin)
Author and Illustrator: Chris Van Allsburg

The Ugly Duckling (Knopf)
Author: Hans Christian Andersen
Illustrator: Robert Van Nutt

Flying (Greenwillow)
Author and Illustrator: Donald Crews

The Owl Scatterer (Atlantic)
Author: Howard Norman
Illustrator: Michael McCurdy

Rembrandt Takes a Walk (Potter)
Author: Mark Strand
Illustrator: Red Grooms

Cherries and Cherry Pits (Greenwillow)
Author and Illustrator: Vera B. Williams

Molly's New Washing Machine (Harper & Row)
Author: Laura Geringer
Illustrator: Petra Mathers

Brave Irene (Farrar, Straus & Giroux)
Author and Illustrator: William Steig

One Morning (Picture Book Studio)
Author: Canna Funakoshi
Illustrator: Yohji Izawa

Pigs from A to Z (Houghton Mifflin)
Author and Illustrator: Arthur Geisert

Checklist of Further Readings

This bibliography includes studies that deal with twentieth-century American children's literature, especially poetry, picture books, and nonfiction. Important general studies and critical works that have become standards in the study of children's literature have been included when these works address the focus of this volume.

Although major journals in the field of children's literature have been omitted from the list, they are valuable sources of information on many of the writers covered in this volume. Among the best known and most useful periodicals are: Children's Literature Association *Quarterly; Children's Literature,* the annual journal of the Children's Literature Division of the Modern Language Association; *Children's Literature in Education; Horn Book Magazine; Phaedrus: An International Journal of Children's Literature Research;* and *The Lion and the Unicorn.* Articles from these and related periodicals may be identified in general and subject periodical indexes under headings related to children's literature.

Of interest to students of twentieth-century American children's literature are: *Children's Literature Abstracts,* No. 1- , May 1973- (Birmingham, England: International Federation of Library Associations, Sub-section on Library Work with Children); Virginia Haviland's *Children's Literature: A Guide to Reference Sources* (Washington, D.C.: Library of Congress, 1966) and its supplements; Suzanne Rahn's *Children's Literature: An Annotated Bibliography of the History and Criticism* (New York: Garland, 1981); W. Bernard Lukenbill's *A Working Bibliography of American Doctoral Dissertations in Children's and Adolescents' Literature, 1930-1971* (Occasional Paper, No. 103. Urbana: University of Illinois, Graduate School of Library Science, 1972); Dianne Monson and Bette J. Peltola's *Research in Children's Literature* (Newark, Delaware: International Reading Association, 1976), and *Something About the Author,* edited by Anne Commire (Detroit: Gale Research, 1971-).

SURVEYS AND CRITICAL STUDIES

Bator, Robert, ed. *Signposts to Criticism of Children's Literature.* Chicago: American Library Association, 1983.

Butler, Francelia, and Richard Rotert, eds. *Reflections on Literature for Children.* Hamden, Conn.: Shoe String/Library Professional Publications, 1984.

Carpenter, Humphrey, and Mari Prichard. *The Oxford Companion to Children's Literature.* New York: Oxford University Press, 1984.

Egoff, Sheila A. *Thursday's Child: Trends and Patterns in Contemporary Children's Literature.* Chicago: American Library Association, 1981.

Egoff, G. T. Stubbs, and L. F. Ashley, eds. *Only Connect: Readings on Children's Literature.* 2nd ed. New York: Oxford University Press, 1980.

Fenwick, Sara Innis. *A Critical Approach to Children's Literature.* Chicago: University of Chicago Press, 1967.

Field, Elinor Whitney, ed. *Horn Book Reflections: On Children's Books and Reading: Selected from Eighteen Years of the Horn Book Magazine, 1948-1966.* Boston: Horn Book, 1969.

Fox, Geoff, and others, eds. *Writers, Critics and Children: Articles from Children's Literature in Education.* New

York: Agathon Press, 1976.

Haviland, Virginia, ed. *Children and Literature: Views and Reviews.* Glenview, Ill.: Scott, Foresman, 1973.

Haviland, ed. *The Openhearted Audience: Ten Authors Talk About Writing for Children.* Washington, D.C.: Library of Congress, 1980.

Hearne, Betsy, and Marilyn Kay, eds. *Celebrating Children's Books: Essays on Children's Literature in Honor of Zena Sutherland.* New York: Lothrop, Lee & Shepard, 1981.

Heins, Paul, ed. *Crosscurrents of Criticism: Horn Book Essays: 1968-1977.* Boston: Horn Book, 1977.

Huck, Charlotte, and others. *Children's Literature in the Elementary School.* 4th ed. New York: Holt, Rinehart & Winston, 1987.

Lanes, Selma G. *Down the Rabbit Hole: Adventures and Misadventures in the Realm of Children's Literature.* New York: Atheneum, 1971.

Lukens, Rebecca J. *A Critical Handbook of Children's Literature.* 3rd ed. Glenview, Ill.: Scott, Foresman, 1986.

Lystad, Mary. *From Dr. Mather to Dr. Seuss: 200 Years of American Books for Children.* Boston: G. K. Hall, 1980.

May, Jill P., ed. *Children and Their Literature: A Readings Book.* West Lafayette, Ind.: ChLA Publications, 1983.

Meigs, Cornelia L., et al. *A Critical History of Children's Literature: A Survey of Children's Books in English.* Rev. ed. New York: Macmillan, 1969.

Peterson, Linda, and Marilyn Solt, comps. *Newbery and Caldecott Medal and Honor Books: An Annotated Bibliography.* New York: G. K. Hall, 1982.

Smith, Lillian. *The Unreluctant Years: A Critical Approach to Children's Literature.* Chicago: American Library Association, 1953.

Sutherland, Zena. *Children and Books.* 7th ed. Glenview, Ill.: Scott, Foresman, 1986.

Sutherland, ed. *The Arbuthnot Lectures: 1970-1979.* Chicago: American Library Association, 1980.

Townsend, John Rowe. *Written for Children: An Outline of English Children's Literature.* Philadelphia: Lippincott, 1983.

POETRY

Behn, Harry. *Chrysalis: Concerning Children and Poetry.* New York: Harcourt, Brace & World, 1968.

Hall, Donald, ed. *The Oxford Book of Children's Verse in America.* New York: Oxford University Press, 1985.

Hughes, Ted. *Poetry Is.* Garden City: Doubleday, 1970.

Livingston, Myra Cohn. *The Child as Poet: Myth or Reality?* Boston: Horn Book, 1984.

Olexer, Marycile E. *Poetry Anthologies for Children and Young People.* Chicago: American Library Association, 1985.

Opie, Iona and Peter, eds. *The Oxford Book of Children's Verse.* New York: Oxford University Press, 1980.

PICTURE BOOKS

Bader, Barbara. *American Picturebooks from Noah's Ark to The Beast Within.* New York: Macmillan, 1976.

Brown, Marcia. *Lotus Seeds: Children, Pictures, and Books.* New York: Scribners, 1986.

Canaday, John. *What Is Art? An Introduction to Painting, Sculpture and Architecture.* New York: Knopf, 1981.

Cianciolo, Patricia. *Illustrations in Children's Books.* 2nd ed. Dubuque, Iowa: W. C. Brown, 1976.

Cianciolo, ed. *Picture Books for Children.* Chicago: American Library Association, 1973.

Darling, Harold, and Peter Neumeyer, eds. *Image & Maker: An Annual Dedicated to the Consideration of Book Illustration.* La Jolla, Cal.: Green Tiger Press/Star & Elephant, 1984.

Hurlimann, Bettina. *Picture Book World.* Translated and edited by Brian Alderson. New York: World, 1969.

Kingman, Lee, ed. *The Illustrator's Notebook.* Boston: Horn Book, 1978.

Kingman, ed. *Newbery and Caldecott Medal Books: 1956-1965.* Boston: Horn Book, 1965.

Kingman, ed. *Newbery and Caldecott Medal Books: 1966-1975.* Boston: Horn Book, 1975.

Kingman, ed. *Newbery and Caldecott Medal Books: 1976-1985.* Boston: Horn Book, 1986.

Kingman, Joanna Foster, and Ruth Giles Lontoft, comps. *Illustrators of Children's Books, 1957-1966.* Boston: Horn Book, 1968.

Kingman, Foster, and Lontoft, comps. *Illustrators of Children's Books, 1967-1976.* Boston: Horn Book, 1978.

Klemin, Diana. *The Art of Art for Children's Books: A Contemporary Survey.* New York: Potter, 1966.

Klemin. *The Illustrated Book: Its Art and Craft.* New York: Potter, 1970.

Lacy, Lyn Ellen. *Art and Design in Children's Picture Books: An Analysis of Caldecott Award Winning Books.* Chicago: American Library Association, 1986.

MacCann, Donnarae, and Olga Richard. *The Child's First Books: A Critical Study of Pictures and Text.* New York: H. W. Wilson, 1973.

Schwarcz, Joseph H. *Ways of the Illustrator: Visual Communication in Children's Literature.* Chicago: American Library Association, 1982.

Shulevitz, Uri. *Writing with Pictures: How to Write and Illustrate Children's Books.* New York: Watson-Guptill, 1985.

NONFICTION

Altick, Richard D. *Lives and Letters: A History of Literary Biography in England and America.* New York: Knopf, 1965.

Bowen, Catherine Drinker. *Biography: The Craft and the Calling.* New York: Little, 1968.

Carr, Jo, ed. *Beyond Fact: Nonfiction for Children and Young People.* Chicago: American Library Association, 1982.

Fisher, Margery. *Matters of Fact: Aspects of Non-fiction for Children.* New York: Crowell, 1972.

INTERVIEWS AND PROFILES

Cott, Jonathan. *Pipers at the Gates of Dawn: The Wisdom of Children's Literature.* New York: Random House, 1983.

Hopkins, Lee Bennett. *Books Are by People: Interviews with 104 Authors and Illustrators of Books for Young Children.* New York: Citation Press, 1969.

Hopkins. *More Books by More People.* New York: Citation Press, 1974.

Wintle, Justin, and Emma Fisher. *The Pied Piper: Interviews with the Influential Creators of Children's Literature.* New York: Paddington Press, 1974.

RESEARCH COLLECTIONS

Field, Carolyn W., ed. *Special Collections in Children's Literature.* Chicago: American Library Association, 1982.

Fraser, James, comp. *Children's Authors and Illustrators: A Guide to Manuscript Collections in United States Research Libraries.* New York: K. G. Saur, 1980.

Hoyle, Karen Nelson, and staff, comps. *The Kerlan Collection Manuscripts and Illustrations for Children's Books: A Checklist.* Minneapolis: Kerlan Collection, University of Minnesota Libraries, 1985.

Contributors

Janice Alberghene..*Bowling Green State University*
Joy Anderson ....*University of Florida*
Norma Bagnall ....*Missouri Western State College*
O. Mell Busbin ....*Appalachian State University*
John Cotham .... *Mountain Empire Community College*
Hugh Crago ....*Wagga Wagga, Australia*
Nellvena Duncan Eutsler ....*Kinston, North Carolina*
Susan Garness ....*University of Minnesota*
Jacqueline Gmuca ....*University of North Carolina at Charlotte*
Priscilla N. Grundy..*North Central College*
Mary Ann Heffernan ....*University of Tennessee*
Laura Ingram...*Columbia, South Carolina*
Sue Lile Inman ....*Furman University*
Anne Devereaux Jordan .... *University of Hartford*
Hugh T. Keenan .... *Georgia State University*
Myra Kibler...*Belmont College*
Bobbie Burch Lemontt .... *University of Tennessee*
Millicent Lenz.....................................*State University of New York at Albany*
Lesley S. Potts .... *University of Tennessee*
P. Gila Reinstein...*Port Jefferson, New York*
Hazel Rochman...*Booklist Magazine*
Philip A. Sadler...*Central Missouri State University*
Richard Seiter ....*Central Michigan University*
Anne Sherrill ....*East Tennessee State University*
M. Sarah Smedman ....*University of North Carolina at Charlotte*
Agnes D. Stahlschmidt...*Tucson, Arizona*
Jon C. Stott .... *University of Alberta*
Douglas Street ....*Bryan, Texas*
Anita Trout.. *Aiken, South Carolina*
Laura M. Zaidman ....*University of South Carolina*

371

Cumulative Index

Dictionary of Literary Biography, Volumes 1-61
Dictionary of Literary Biography Yearbook, 1980-1986
Dictionary of Literary Biography Documentary Series, Volumes 1-4

Cumulative Index

DLB before number: *Dictionary of Literary Biography,* Volumes 1-61
Y before number: *Dictionary of Literary Biography Yearbook, 1980-1986*
DS before number: *Dictionary of Literary Biography Documentary Series,* Volumes 1-4

Cumulative Index

C

E

F

G

I

Cumulative Index

J

Cumulative Index

L

O

P

Q

R

S

U

Y

Z